Statistics for Social and Behavioral Sciences

Advisors:

S.E. Fienberg
W.J. van der Linden

For other titles published in this series, go to
http://www.springer.com/series/3463

Alina A. von Davier
Editor

Statistical Models for Test Equating, Scaling, and Linking

With a foreword by Paul W. Holland

Springer

Editor
Dr. Alina A. von Davier
Educational Testing Service
Rosedale Road
08541 Princeton New Jersey
USA
avondavier@ets.org

ISBN 978-1-4614-2710-0 ISBN 978-0-387-98138-3 (eBook)
DOI 10.1007/978-0-387-98138-3
Springer New York Heidelberg Dordrecht London

Printed on acid-free paper

Springer is part of Springer Science+Business Media (www.springer.com)

To my late grandparents, Constanţa and Zaharia Culache.

—A.v.D.

Foreword

More than 27 years ago, Don Rubin and I edited a book titled *Test Equating* (Holland & Rubin, 1982). At that time there was very little literature other than journal articles and technical reports to guide researchers towards the interesting problems in this small but very practical branch of educational measurement. Now, Alina von Davier is editing a new book with this same aim, to expose researchers to the most recent ideas and topics in test equating.

In our day, there was an extreme paucity of material on equating. Of course, there was Angoff's famous 1971 chapter in *Educational Measurement* that was the single most read piece on equating (so much so that ETS reprinted it as a separate volume in 1984), and there was Lord's 1950 technical exegesis of what linear equating was all about with standard errors and careful analysis, as well as the test equating chapter in his 1980 book on IRT where he gives his (in)famous theorem that test equating is either impossible or unnecessary. But that was about it. I have heard through the grapevine that during that time ETS's president even went so far as to suggest that equating research was no longer a subject that ETS ought to support—fortunately, he was persuaded otherwise.

When Don Rubin and I were editing our book, people learned about test equating by doing it, with no help from their graduate education at any of the best psychometric training centers, anywhere, just the small literature mentioned above. That day is fortunately gone. There is now a fabulous textbook (Kolen & Brennan, 2004) now in its second edition. Test equating is often a part of the graduate-school curriculum in quantitative methods in education. Of course, I must mention my 2004 book with Alina von Davier and Dorothy Thayer, *The Kernel Method of Test Equating*, because it is an attempt to unify many aspects of test equating into a single coherent system.

In the late 1990s, test equating became interesting even to the U.S. Congress, which asked the National Academy of Science if all elementary school tests of, for example, mathematics, could be "equated" somehow, and thereby remove the need for President Clinton's proposal for a single National Voluntary Test. The National Academy panel of experts said no (Feuer, Holland, Green, Bertenthal, & Hemphill,

1999). The (Republican) congressional response was to ask the question again, and, in return, was asked, What part of "*No*" don't you understand? (Koretz, Barron, Mitchell, & Stecher, 1999).

There has always been a small body of literature on test equating in the educational measurement journals (after all, the equating of test forms under various conditions of data collection is what many of the people in the field of educational measurement actually do, so it is not surprising that they write about what they have figured out in order to help others who need to equate tests in similar circumstances). Yet, since the 1980s, this literature has exploded. The above mentioned textbook (Kolen & Brennan, 2004) grew out of this enormous growth in the technical literature on equating.

Alina von Davier, in this remarkable volume, is pulling together the most recent and advanced parts of this literature to set the stage for further exciting and innovative work on test equating. The topics are important, and the contributors are some of the best in the field. I expect this volume to move the theory and practice of test equating forward on many fronts.

St. Petersburg, FL
May 16, 2009

Paul W. Holland

Preface

This edited volume provides an overview from a statistical theory viewpoint of recent research directions in the field of equating, linking, and scaling.

The idea for this volume emerged in December 2007 while I was planning my own research studies and other research projects funded under the Equating and Applied Psychometrics research initiative, which I have lead for the past four years at Educational Testing Service (ETS). At the same time this planning took place, I was also overseeing the research in support of the international testing programs in my center at ETS. I realized that equating and linking were becoming more visible due to the increase in number and variety of standardized assessments in the United States and around the world. I also came to see that the research on equating and linking had changed, moving from applications of existing psychometric equating models to development of new and more theoretical equating models. In particular, research in the field has soared since the publishing of two test equating books in 2004, the second edition of *Test Equating, Scaling, and Linking: Methods and Practices* (Kolen & Brennan, 2004) and *The Kernel Method of Test Equating* (von Davier, Holland, & Thayer, 2004b). Much of the new work has focused on statistical aspects of the equating process, and several examples of this sort of work are represented in this volume.

In addition to covering statistical methods, most of the existing books on equating also focus on the practice of equating, the implications of test development and test use for equating practice and policies, and the daily equating challenges that need to be solved. In some sense, the scope of this book is narrower than of other existing books: to view the equating and linking process as a statistical estimation task. The goal of this volume is to propose new equating models, to take theoretical statistical tools and apply them to the practice of equating in novel and useful ways, and to tie explicitly the assumptions made by each of the equating models to observable (or at least inferable) data conditions.

The intended audience for this volume is rather broad: researchers and graduate students in statistics, psychometrics, and educational measurement who are looking for useful research topics. Among the volume's goals are to push the work on equating, linking, and scaling in new directions and to invite the readership to consider the research questions raised here and further the work.

In order to bring newly hired psychometricians in testing organizations quickly up to speed on equating details, it is best to provide a controlled framework consisting of a wide range of formal decision aids, ranging from visual displays and charts to indices and flags. Many of these tools are direct applications of statistical methodologies. Given this, another purpose of this book is to bring about the development of quality control, statistical process control, and decision tools to assist throughout the equating process, often done in an extremely fast-paced operational environment.

How this volume is organized. The volume covers recently developed models for equating, linking, and scaling and new approaches to testing hypotheses, assumptions, and model fit. The book starts with a chapter that presents a statistical perspective on the test equating process. The book is then divided into three parts. The first part focuses on data collection designs and assumptions made in the measurement process in standardized testing to avoid the confounding of test form differences with ability differences. The second part of the book focuses on new measurement and equating models. The third part of this volume presents research methodologies in support of the evaluation of equating results. The structure of the book is described in more detail in the *Overview* section.

This book provides a snapshot in time. The list of models and approaches presented here is neither exhaustive nor definitive. It is hoped that readers will find inspiration from the chapters of this book and will approach the field of linking and equating with curiosity and interest in continuing the presently underway research and in making improvements to operational practice. Not everything presented here is ready to be applied in the practical and complex world of standardized educational assessments. However, my hope is that the models presented here give a perspective on the abundance of possibilities and create a fertile framework for future research ideas and practical implementations.

Acknowledgments. The book was funded by ETS in the framework of the Equating and Applied Psychometrics research initiative. I am indebted to ETS and to many ETS researchers and psychometricians for their assistance and encouragement in the production of this book: Ida Lawrence, who established and continues to support the Equating and Applied Psychometrics research initiative; John Mazzeo and Dianne Henderson-Montero for their managerial support and feedback; Dan Eignor, Shelby Haberman, and Jim Carlson for their careful reviews of all ETS manuscripts and many of the other chapters not written by ETS staff; and Kim Fryer for editorial support and assistance in the production of the book. I am thankful to Paul Holland, from whom I learned everything I know about equating. Last but not least, I am thankful to my family—especially to my husband, son, and father—for their unconditional love and support.

Princeton, NJ
April 15, 2010

Alina A. von Davier

Overview

In the introductory chapter of this book, "A Statistical Perspective on Equating Test Scores," which sets the stage for the reminder of the volume, I describe the equating process as a feature of complex statistical models used for measuring abilities in standardized assessments. I also propose a framework for organizing all existing observed-score equating methods.

The remaining chapters in the book are organized in three parts. The first part, *Research Questions and Data Collection Designs*, includes studies that focus on the appropriate data collection designs for equating, linking, and scaling, and the challenges and assumptions associated with each of the designs and the methods. There are six chapters in Part I.

The Dorans, Moses, and Eignor chapter, "Equating Test Scores: Toward Best Practices," emphasizes the practical aspects of the equating process, the need for a solid data collection design for equating, and the challenges involved by applying specific equating procedures. The chapter by Kolen, Tong, and Brennan, "Scoring and Scaling Educational Tests," provides a detailed overview of scaling procedures, covering the current thinking on scaling approaches, from the scoring unit employed to the policy issues that surround score uses. The chapter by Carlson, "Statistical Models for Vertical Linking," transitions into a specific design and research question challenge: How to link vertically the results of several testing instruments that were constructed to intentionally differ in difficulty and that were taken by groups of examinees who differ in ability. Carlson presents an overview of the models in practical use for vertical linking. The chapter by McArdle and Grimm, "An Empirical Example of Change Analysis by Linking Longitudinal Item Response Data From Multiple Tests," presents an even more challenging research question: How can one develop a longitudinal scale over a very long period of time and with sparse data. McArdle and Grimm illustrate the use of linking techniques and their challenges in a different context than educational assessments: In the area of research on life-span and on the dynamics of aging. The Holland and Strawderman chapter, "How to Average Equating Functions, If You Must," addresses the question of how to stabilize the results of the equating process if results from more than one equating are available. If you build an equating plan, or as it is called, a braiding plan, can you average the resulting distinct equating conversions from the different strands of the braiding plan? Is the result still an equating function? The authors describe a procedure that might be considered for averaging equating conversions. The chapter by Livingston and Kim, "New Approaches to Equating With Small Samples," addresses a very practical problem: If you know that the test forms to be equated differ in difficulty and the samples are too small to reliably conduct any classical equating procedures, what can you do? The authors discuss several models for equating with small samples.

Part II of this volume, *Measurement and Equating Models*, includes eight chapters that propose new models for test equating and linking. Most of the material presented in this part of the book describes new equating and linking models that clearly fit within the traditional frameworks of observed-score equating and of IRT linking and equating, as discussed in the introductory chapter.

Four of the eight chapters describe new methods for transforming the discrete test score distributions into continuous distributions in order to achieve equipercentile equating: The chapter by Haberman, "Using Exponential Families for Equating," describes the use of exponential families for continuizing test score distributions; the chapter by Wang, "An Alternative Continuization Method: The Continuized Log-Linear Method," describes the application of log-linear models to continuize the test score distributions; and the chapter by Lee and von Davier, "Equating Through Alternative Kernels," discusses how various continuous variables with distributions (normal, logistic, and uniform) can be used as kernels to continuize test score distributions. The chapter by Karabatsos and Walker, "A Bayesian Nonparametric Model for Test Equating," provides a Bayesian equating model for the continuized distribution of test scores, by means of a mixture of beta distributions. Under Bayes theorem, the prior distributions for the test score distributions are combined with the data to achieve (continuous) posterior distributions and the classical equipercentile equating function that uses these posterior distributions can then be applied.

The chapter by Chen, Livingston, and Holland, "Generalized Equating Functions for NEAT Designs," describes new hybrid models within the kernel equating framework. One of the most interesting hybrid models proposed is a nonlinear version of Levine linear equating. Most of these equating models can be integrated into the observed-score equating framework described in the introduction, including the hybrid models. The van der Linden chapter, "Local Observed-Score Equating," beautifully describes the need for developing an equating model that is derived from Lord's equity requirement. I had a difficult time deciding whether this chapter fit best in Part I or Part II. The chapter shows that the local observed-score equating method also fits well under an observed-score equating framework described in the introduction, although this chapter also provides a nice transition to the chapters that investigate IRT-based methods.

The other two chapters in this second part of the book focus on IRT parameter linking. The chapter by von Davier and von Davier, "A General Model for IRT

Scale Linking and Scale Transformations," presents a framework for the currently used IRT parameter-linking methods: Fixed-item-parameters, concurrent calibration, mean-mean, mean-sigma (Kolen & Brennan, 2004), and the Stocking and Lord (1983) and Haebara (1980) methods are considered. This framework can potentially include more complex types of linking, such as those that account for a growth factor. The chapter by Xu, Douglas, and Lee, "Linking With Nonparametric IRT Models," discusses how to link ability scales from separate calibrations of two different test forms of the same assessment, when the calibration is accomplished by fitting nonparametric IRT models to the data. The linking of the item characteristic curves of the common items is attained on an interim scale—uniform or normal—by minimizing a loss-function. It is interesting to note the similarities between the loss-function used by Xu et al., the traditional Stocking and Lord (1983) and Haebara (1980) scale-linking methods, and the restriction function used by von Davier and von Davier. Conceptually, they are all very similar.

Part III of this book, *Evaluation*, includes chapters on procedures that can be used to evaluate the equating, linking, and scaling results by employing new accuracy measures, by investigating the robustness of the results when the assumptions are met to varying degrees, by testing hypotheses about the equating models, and by monitoring the stability of the results over time. This part includes five chapters.

The chapter by Ogasawara, "Applications of Asymptotic Expansion in Item Response Theory Linking," presents the formulas for the asymptotic standard error of the IRT scale transformation coefficients from the moment methods: The mean-mean, mean-sigma, and the mean-geometric mean scale linking methods are considered (see also Kolen & Brennan, 2004, for a description of the methods). The chapter by Sinharay, Holland, and von Davier, "Evaluating the Missing Data Assumptions of the Chain and Poststratification Equating Methods," presents a detailed investigation of the untestable assumptions behind two popular nonlinear equating methods used with a nonequivalent groups design. The chapter describes a manipulated data set, or *pseudo-data set*, that allows testing of the untestable assumptions. The chapter by Glas and Béguin, "Robustness of IRT Observed-Score Equating," investigates the robustness of the IRT true score equating methods and applies the Wald statistic to test hypotheses. More precisely, the Wald test is used to evaluate the null hypothesis that the expected score distributions on which the equating procedure is based are constant over subsamples against the alternative that they are not. The chapter by Rijmen, Qu, and von Davier, "Hypothesis Testing of Equating Differences in the Kernel Equating Framework," applies the formula of the standard error of equating difference developed by von Davier, Holland, and Thayer (2004b) to the full vector of equated raw-scores and constructs a test for testing linear hypotheses about the equating results. The chapter by Li, Li, and von Davier, "Applying Time-Series Analysis to Detect Scale Drift," proposes the use of time-series methods for monitoring the stability of reported scores over a long sequence of administrations. This study is related to traditional scale drift studies (Kolen & Brennan, 2004; Morrison & Fitzpatrick, 1992; Petersen, Cook, & Stocking, 1983) in the sense that the time series analysis investigated can potentially detect any unusual pattern in the reported scores, including the pattern resulting from a potential scale drift.

I expect that this collection of chapters will be of interest to a broader audience than practitioners of equating. The field of test equating, linking, and scaling is rich in opportunities for psychologists, mathematicians, and statisticians to work on important applications.

Contents

Contributors

Anton Béguin Cito, Nieuwe Oeverstraat 50, P.O. Box 1034, 6801 MG, Amhem, Netherlands, Anton.Beguin@cito.nl

Robert L. Brennan University of Iowa, 210D Lindquist Center, Iowa City, IA 52242, USA, robert-brennan@uiowa.edu

James E. Carlson Educational Testing Service, Rosedale Rd, Princeton, NJ 08541, USA, jcarlson@ets.org

Haiwen H. Chen Educational Testing Service, Rosedale Rd, Princeton, NJ 08541, USA, hchen@ets.org

Neil J. Dorans Educational Testing Service, Rosedale Rd, Princeton, NJ 08541, USA, ndorans@ets.org

Jeff A. Douglas 101 Illini Hall, 725 S. Wright St, Champaign, IL 61820, USA, jeffdoug@uiuc.edu

Daniel R. Eignor Educational Testing Service, Rosedale Rd, Princeton, NJ 08541, USA, deignor@ets.org

C.A.W. Glas University of Twente, P.O. Box 217, 7500 AE Enschede, Netherlands, C.A.W.Glas@gw.utwente.nl

Kevin J. Grimm University of California, 1 Shields Ave, Davis, CA 95616, USA, kjgrimm@ucdavis.edu

Shelby J. Haberman Educational Testing Service, Rosedale Rd, Princeton, NJ 08541, USA, shaberman@ets.org

Paul W. Holland Paul Holland Consulting Corporation, 200 4th Ave South, Apt 100, St Petersburg, FL 33701, USA, pholland@ets.org

George Karabatsos College of Education, 1040 W. Harrison St. (MC 147), Chicago, IL 60607-7133, USA, georgek@uic.edu

Sooyeon Kim Educational Testing Service, Rosedale Rd, Princeton, NJ 08541, USA, skim@ets.org

Michael J. Kolen 224 B1 Lindquist Center, The University of Iowa, Iowa City, IA 52242, USA, michael-kolen@uiowa.edu

Yi-Hsuan Lee Educational Testing Service, Rosedale Rd, Princeton, NJ 08541, USA, ylee@ets.org

Young-Sun Lee Teachers College, Columbia University, 525 W.120th St, New York, NY 10027, USA, yslee@tc.columbia.edu

Deping Li Educational Testing Service, Rosedale Rd, Princeton, NJ 08541, USA, dli@ets.org

Shuhong Li Educational Testing Service, Rosedale Rd, Princeton, NJ 08541, USA, sli@ets.org

Samuel A. Livingston Educational Testing Service, Rosedale Rd, Princeton, NJ 08541, USA, slivingston@ets.org

John J. McArdle University of Southern California, Dept. of Psychology, SGM 501, 3620 South McClintock Ave, Los Angeles, CA 90089, USA, jmcardle@usc.edu

Tim P. Moses Educational Testing Service, Rosedale Rd, Princeton, NJ 08541, USA, tmoses@ets.org

Haruhiko Ogasawara Otaru University of Commerce, 3-5-21 Midori, Otaru 047-8501, Japan, hogasa@res.otaru-uc.ac.jp

Yanxuan Qu Educational Testing Service, Rosedale Rd, Princeton, NJ 08541, USA, yqu@ets.org

Frank Rijmen Educational Testing Service, Rosedale Rd, Princeton, NJ 08541, USA, frijmen@ets.org

Sandip Sinharay Educational Testing Service, Rosedale Rd, Princeton, NJ 08541, USA, ssinharay@ets.org

William E. Strawderman Department of Statistics, Rutgers University, 110 Frelinghuysen Rd, Room 561, Hill Center Building for the Mathematical Sciences, Busch Campus, Piscataway, NJN08854, USA, straw@stat.rutgers.edu

Ye Tong Pearson, 2510 North Dodge Street, Iowa City, IA 52245, USA, ye.tong@pearson.com

Wim J. van der Linden CTB/McGraw-Hill, 20 Ryan Ranch Rd, Monterey, CA 93940, USA, wim_vanderlinden@ctb.com

Alina A. von Davier Educational Testing Service, Rosedale Rd, Princeton, NJ 08541, USA, avondavier@ets.org

Matthias von Davier Educational Testing Service, Rosedale Rd, Princeton, NJ 08541, USA, mvondavier@ets.org

Stephen G. Walker Institute of Mathematics, Statistics and Actuarial Science, University of Kent, Canterbury, Kent, CT2 7NZ, UK, S.G.Walker@kent.ac.uk

Tianyou Wang University of Iowa, 210B Lindquist Center, Iowa City, IA 52242, USA, tianyouwang@yahoo.com

Xueli Xu Educational Testing Service, Rosedale Rd, Princeton, NJ 08541, USA, xxu@ets.org

Chapter 1
A Statistical Perspective on Equating Test Scores

Alina A. von Davier

> "The fact that statistical methods of inference play so slight a role... reflect[s] the lack of influence modern statistical methods has so far had on current methods for test equating."
>
> Rubin (1982, p. 53)

> "The equating problem reduces to one of modeling and statistical theory."
>
> Morris (1982, p. 170)

1.1 Introduction

The comparability of scores across different test forms of a standardized assessment has been a major focus of educational measurement and the testing industry for the past 90 years (see Holland, 2007, for a history of linking). This chapter focuses on the statistical methods available for equating test forms from standardized educational assessments that report scores at the individual level (see also Dorans, Moses, & Eignor, Chapter 2 of this volume). The overview here is given in terms of frameworks[1] that emphasize the statistical perspective with respect to the equating methodologies that have been developed by testing practitioners since the 1920s. The position taken in this paper is that the purpose of the psychometricians' work is to accurately and fairly measure and compare educational skills using multiple test forms from an educational assessment. Therefore, from this measurement perspective, equating of test forms is only one necessary step in the measurement process. Equating is only necessary because a standardized educational assessment uses

[1]*Conceptual frameworks* (theoretical frameworks) are a type of intermediate theory that have the potential to connect to all aspects of inquiry (e.g., problem definition, purpose, literature review, methodology, data collection and analysis). Conceptual frameworks act like maps that give coherence to empirical inquiry ("Conceptual Framework," n.d.).

A.A. von Davier
Educational Testing Service, Rosedale Rd, Princeton, NJ 08541, USA
e-mail: avondavier@ets.org

A.A. von Davier (ed.), *Statistical Models for Test Equating, Scaling, and Linking*,
Statistics for Social and Behavioral Sciences,
DOI 10.1007/978-0-387-98138-3_1,

numerous test forms that tend to differ in difficulty although they are built to the same specifications ("nominally parallel test forms," Lord & Novick, 1968, p. 180). Hence, equating can be viewed as the process of controlling statistically for the confounding variable "test form" in the measurement process. If the test development process were perfect, then equating would not be necessary. See also Lord's (1980) theorem 13.3.1 in Chapter 13. The term *linking* has slightly different meanings in the field of educational measurement, and it is used here as (a) a general term for denoting a relationship between test forms (at the total score level, at the item parameter level, etc.); (b) as a weaker form of equating; and (c) as a synonym to the process of placing item response theory (IRT) item parameter estimates on the same scale, which sometimes is also called IRT *calibration*. In this chapter I refer to *equating* as a strong form of linking and as a subclass of linking methods (Holland & Dorans, 2006). Test equating can be carried out both using observed-score equating (OSE) and IRT methods, but the word *equating* is most often associated with the raw scores of a test. See Holland and Dorans, Kolen and Brennan (2004), Dorans et al. (Chapter 2 of this volume), and Yen and Fitzpatrick (2006) for an extensive view of categories of linking methods.

The process of measuring and comparing competencies in an educational assessment is described here in ways that integrate various existing approaches. A discussion of equating as a part of the measurement process is given first. Then I introduce the idea of applying a testlet or a bifactor model to measure skills and equate scores. This type of model would capture the test-form effect as a latent variable with a distribution. This variable, the test-form effect, can be (a) monitored over time to inform on the stability of equating, (b) used as feedback for the test developers to improve upon the degree of parallelism of test forms, and (c) used for monitoring the form effect on subgroups. Next, an equating framework for the OSE methods is introduced. I discuss how the search for a theory of OSE led to the development of a framework that provides a map that gives coherence to empirical inquiry. A framework for IRT parameter linking is given by M. von Davier and von Davier (Chapter 14 of this volume), and a practical perspective on equating methods is given by Dorans et al. in Chapter 2. The last section of this chapter and the *Overview* outline the rest of the volume. The chapters are grouped according to the steps of a measurement process that are described in the next section.

1.2 The Measurement Model, the Unit of Measurement, and Equating

Parallels between a generic statistical modeling process and an educational measurement process that includes the equating of test forms are presented in this section. Subsequently, a link between the equating methodologies and the unit of measurement is discussed.

1.2.1 Statistical Modeling and Assumptions

The measurement process in standardized testing, which includes test form equating, follows the same steps as a typical statistical modeling process. Statistical models are ideal and simplistic representations of a (complex) reality that aid in the description and understanding of a specific process or that explain or predict future outcomes. Statistical modeling is accomplished by first identifying the main variables and their interactions that explain the particular process. Using a simple model to describe a complex reality requires making many assumptions that allow the reality to be simplified. The usual steps in any statistical modeling process are as follows:

1. Statistical modeling starts with a research question and with a set of data.
2. One of the challenges of statistical modeling is the danger of confounding: The inferences one makes about one variable based on a model might be confounded by interactions with other variables that exist in the data and that have not been explicitly modeled. The confounding trap can be addressed by elegant and elaborate sampling procedures, data collection designs, and explicit modeling of the variables.
3. A statistical model is proposed and fitted to the data, and the model parameters are estimated.
4. Assumptions are made about the data generating process. If the model fits the data to an acceptable degree,[2] then inferences are made based on the model.
5. The results are evaluated with respect to (sampling) error and bias. Given that all statistical models are approximations of reality and that they almost never fit the data, statisticians have developed indices that attempt to quantify the degree to which the results are accurate. The bias introduced by the modeling approach is investigated.

The same sequence of events describes the process of measurement in standardized testing (see also Braun & Holland, 1982). The steps in the measurement process are as follows:

1. The measurement process starts with two or more test forms built to the same specifications (nominally parallel test forms), with the research question being how to measure and compare the skills of the test takers regardless of which form they took.
2. The challenge in measuring the skills of test takers, who take different forms of a test, is how to avoid the confounding of differences in form difficulty with the differences in the ability of the test takers. In order to disentangle the test forms differences and ability differences, data are collected in specific ways and assumptions about the data generating process are explicitly incorporated.

[2] "All models are wrong but some are useful" (Box & Draper, 1987, p. 74).

See von Davier, Holland, and Thayer (2004b, Chapter 2) and Dorans et al. (Chapter 2 of this volume) for details on data collection designs.

3. The next step is modeling the data generating process. Data from educational tests are in most cases noisy and models have been proposed to fit them (log-linear models, spline functions, IRT models). These models rely on assumptions. The measurement models that include equating also have underlying assumptions. For example, in OSE, the model-estimated test-score distributions are linked using an equipercentile function. The equipercentile function is a mathematical function composition that requires that the data be continuous, and the test scores usually are not. Hence, the data need to be continuized. Continuization involves an approximation approach commonly employed in probability theory and statistical theory. IRT models make different assumptions from OSE. For example, the estimated item or ability parameters are linked using a linear transformation assuming the IRT model fits the data well for each test form. Or, the method called *IRT true-score equating* assumes that the relationship between the true-scores holds also for the observed-scores.
4. Hence, assumptions are made about the data generating process. If the model fits the data to an acceptable degree, then inferences are made based on the model.
5. Since the parameters of the equating models are sample estimates, the equating results are subject to sample variability. At the end of the equating procedure (after several steps of making assumptions), one will quantify the degree of error cumulated in the process. This is obtained through the use of statistical indices: standard errors of parameters, standard errors of equating (SEE), standard errors of equating differences (SEED), as well as other statistical indices such as the likelihood ratio statistics, Freeman-Tukey residuals, and the Akaike criterion (Bishop, Fienberg, & Holland, 1975; Bozdogan, 1987). In addition, the potential bias in the equating results should be evaluated according to different criteria, such as the historical information available, stability of results over time, consistency checks when multiple equating methods are available, changes in demographics, population invariance, and scale drift. One might employ quality assurance methods or statistical process control methods to monitor the stability of the reported scores over time—such as cumulative sum charts and time series analyses (See Li, Li, & von Davier, Chapter 20 of this volume).

The parallel between a generic statistical process and the educational measurement process is illustrated in Figure 1.1. As already mentioned, no model fits the data perfectly; moreover, many models are very complex and rely on assumptions that are not easily tested. Therefore, a discussion of the merits of different models requires investigation of the assumptions that underlie the models and, more importantly, analysis of the consequences of failure to meet these assumptions.

In very simple data collection equating designs, such as the equivalent-groups design and the single-group design, the OSE methods assume very little. As Braun and Holland (1982) noted, the OSE methods are

> ... completely atheoretical in the sense that they are totally free of any conception (or misconception) of the subject matter of the two tests X and Y ... . We are only

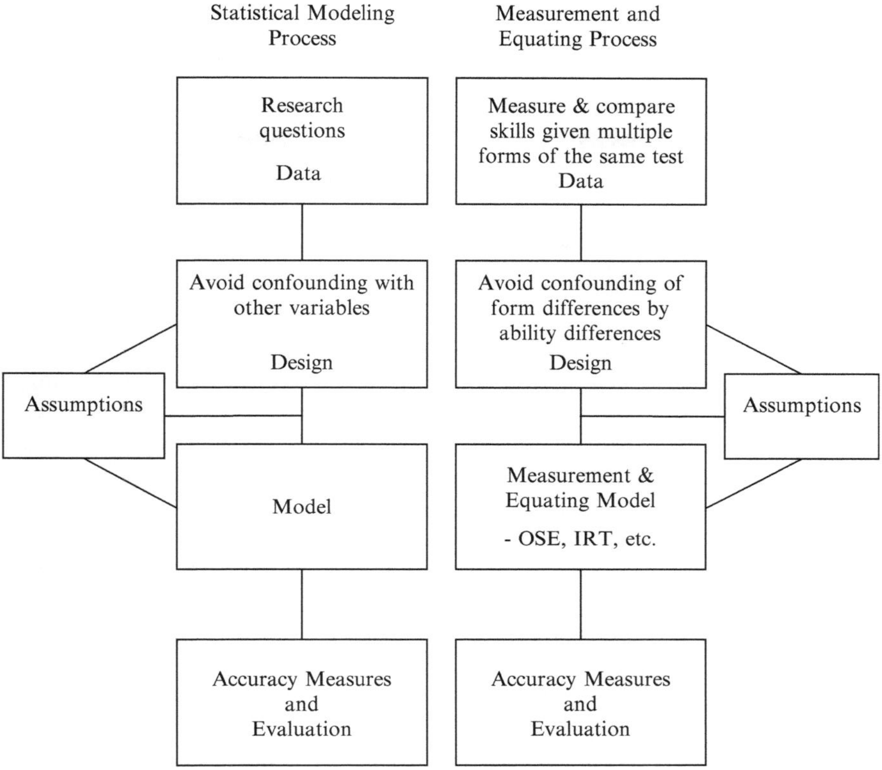

Fig. 1.1 The parallel between a generic statistical process and the educational measurement process. IRT = item response theory; OSE = observed-score equating

> preventing from equating a verbal test to a mathematical test by common sense. This is an inherent problem with observed-score equating. (p. 16)

On the other hand, with the more complex nonequivalent groups with an anchor test (NEAT) design all OSE methods make more assumptions, some of them untestable (see Sinharay, Holland, & von Davier, Chapter 17 of this volume; also, Braun & Holland, 1982). Due to these untestable assumptions, some OSE models are difficult to evaluate with the data at hand. The IRT model assumptions are equally demanding and difficult to evaluate.

The question with both sets of equating models (OSE and IRT) is whether the model errors necessarily invalidate the procedures or whether the errors are sufficiently limited in their consequences so that the equating approaches are acceptable. This analysis can be difficult to carry out both with IRT and OSE methods when employing complex designs. IRT does provide more possibilities in complex linking situations that are sometimes not feasible with OSE (such as in survey assessments, where the data are collected following a matrix design—where not all test takers take all items). However, a matrix design and a complex IRT model also involve an increased level of difficulty with respect to verification of assumptions and an increased reliance on strong assumptions that are needed to compensate for missing data. The selection of an equating method mainly matters when the need for equating is strongest (that is, when the forms differ in difficulty) and all methods produce similar results when the forms and populations are identical.

1.2.2 Equating and Measurement

The purpose of this section is to identify the unit of measurement in a measurement process that includes equating of test forms. Then I identify what is to be linked when the equating of scores is desired, when OSE and IRT methods are employed. It is assumed that an appropriate data collection design is available for equating (see Holland & Dorans, 2006). An interesting discussion of similar questions has been given in Braun and Holland (1982), and Morris (1982).

As Lord and Novick (1968) pointed out, any measurement "begins with a procedure for identifying elements of the real world with the elements or constructs of an abstract logical system (a model)" (p. 16). Lord and Novick continued,

> To specify this measurement we must do three things: First we must identify the object being measured, the person, or the experimental unit. Then we must identify the property or behavior being directly measured.... Finally, we must identify the numerical assignment rule by which we assign a number to this property of the unit being measured. (p. 16)

Educational testing programs apply a measurement tool (the test form) to test takers assumed to be randomly sampled from a population. The assessments measure a specific skill that can be "the examinee's responses to the items" (Lord & Novick, 1968, p. 16), a latent skill, or a merely unobserved skill. "Theoretical constructs are often related to the behavioral domain through observable variables by considering the latter as measures or indicants of the former" (Lord & Novick, 1968, p. 19). The idea that a measurement is something true ("the property or behavior" that the instrument is supposed to measure) plus an error of measurement is an old concept developed initially in astronomy and other physical sciences (see Lord & Novick, 1968, p. 31; see Holland, 2007, for a history of testing and psychometrics). The measurement takes place indirectly through a number of carefully developed items that comprise the test form given to a sample of test takers (the random variable with a distribution). The measurement data can be in the form of arrays of direct responses, such as arrays of 0s and 1s representing correct or incorrect responses to multiple-choice items, or in some cases, further aggregated (through adding the number of correct responses) to total scores and distributions. Kolen, Tong, and Brennan (Chapter 3 of this volume) called the unit of measurement "raw score:" "Raw scores can be as simple as a sum of the item scores or be so complicated that they depend on the entire pattern of item responses." Regardless of how the scores are obtained, they are the realizations of the random variable—the testing instrument and form.

In a standardized educational assessment many test forms are built to the same specifications, and each of these test forms is a testing instrument. These nominally parallel test forms (Lord & Novick, 1968, p. 180) usually differ in difficulty, and therefore, the measurement challenge is how to disentangle the unintended differences in difficulty among the test forms from the ability of the test takers. In other words, the role of equating is to insure an accurate measurement of an underlying skill for a test taker, regardless of what test form has been taken by this test taker (see Figure 1.1). The method chosen to equate test forms depends on the model used for measurement.

In assessments where the OSE methods are employed, the item information is aggregated across the test takers, and the test-score distribution is used as the basis for equating the test forms. Test forms are random variables with distributions, and the scores are realizations of these random variables. In (equipercentile) OSE, the cumulative distributions of the random variables test forms are mapped onto each other such that the percentiles on one will match the percentiles on the other. As indicated earlier by quoting Braun and Holland (1982), OSE does not explicitly require a meaning of the score used (i.e., total observed score, number-correct score, weighted number-correct score, formula-score). In conclusion, for the OSE methods, the unit of measurement is the total test score (regardless of how it was obtained), and the equating is accomplished through matching the two test-score distributions (either in terms of percentiles or in terms of their means and standard deviations).

In assessments where IRT-based methods are used for equating, the analysis starts with data as arrays of 0s and 1s representing correct or incorrect responses to multiple-choice items for each person.[3] Then the measurement of the underlying skill is obtained through modeling the interaction between the features of the items and of the persons who take those items. The IRT-based methods rely on a model for the probability of a correct response to a particular item by a particular person. Assuming the model fits the data, the adjustment for differences between the two test forms is accomplished through linking the item (or ability) parameters. In a subsequent step, this linking might be applied to raw test scores, and therefore, achieve equating of scores, or it might be directly applied to scale scores (Yen, 1986). Hence, for IRT-based methods, the unit of measurement is the probability that a person answers an item correctly (item by person's skill) and the adjustment for form differences is done through a linear transformation of the item parameters or of the parameters of the distribution of the underlying skill.

The appeal of the IRT models lies within the psychometric theory: IRT models are mathematical models of a test to infer the ability of a test taker and to classify the test takers according to their ability. Linking the item parameters to adjust for form differences is inherent to the IRT model. In contrast, as Braun and Holland (1982) pointed out, the OSE methods are atheoretical.

---

[3]There are models for accomplishing the same things with tests using polytomously scored items.

The measurement and equating models that use a total test score as a unit of measurement and match the percentiles of test-score distributions, and models that use the item–person interaction as a unit of measurement and link item or person parameters, do have similarities; sometimes they overlap or build on each other. This volume offers an account of several methods of this sort (see the following chapters: Karabatsos & Walker, Chapter 11; Chen, Livingston, & Holland, Chapter 12; van der Linden, Chapter 13; Glas & Béguin, Chapter 18).

In my opinion, the value of thinking of equating as a part of a complex measurement process lies in the multitude of possibilities that become available to the researcher. These possibilities may include applying existing models from (or developing new models in) other areas of psychology, econometrics, statistics, or even from other parts of psychometrics. That is, borrowing or developing new measurement models in a very different framework than educational measurement that could also achieve equating becomes easier to conceptualize in a broader framework. In the next section I give an example of such a cross-contamination of ideas.

1.3 Measurement of Skills and Equating of Test Scores Using a Testlet Model

At least three models have been developed to account for the effects of specific groups of items or testlets that might be included in an assessment. These item bundles may refer to the same passage, or the same test material, and the responses to the items from the testlets might not be independent given the ability, and therefore, the assumption of unidimensionality of the IRT model might be violated. One way to account for the testlet effect is to incorporate specific dimensions in addition to the general underlying dimension of the IRT model. Three such models are the bifactor model (Gibbons & Hedeker, 1992), the second-order factor model (Rijmen, 2009b), and the testlet model (Bradlow, Wainer, & Wang, 1999). The last two models were shown to be formally equivalent in Rijmen, and therefore, I will briefly discuss only the bifactor and second-order model here.

In the bifactor model (Gibbons & Hedeker, 1992), each item measures a general dimension and one of K specific dimensions. Typically, all dimensions are assumed to be independent. Here I will use a less general restriction: These dimensions are assumed to be independent given the general dimension. Figure 1.2 shows a bifactor model with the conditional independence restriction using a directed acyclic graph for four sets of items y_1 to y_4, the general ability θ_g, and the specific testlets' effects, θ_1 to θ_4.

A second-order model also includes separate testlet effects. Figure 1.3 illustrates a second-order model with the same conditional independence restriction. In a second-order model, each testlet has a separate dimension. As in the bifacor model, the specific testlet effects are assumed to be conditionally independent,

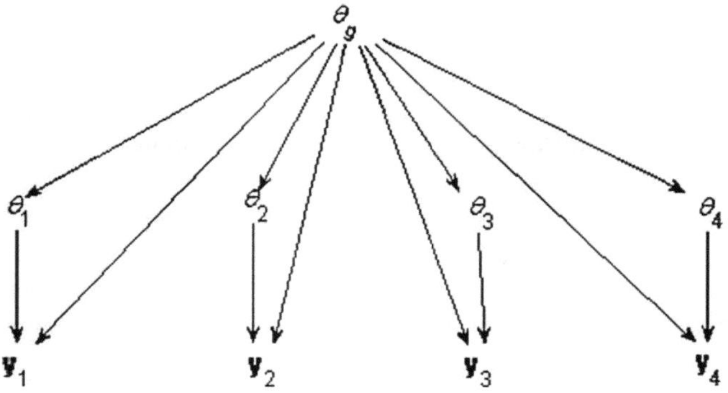

Fig. 1.2 Directed acyclic graph of the bifactor model. From *Three Multidimensional Models for Testlet Based Tests*, by F. Rijmen, 2009b, Princeton, NJ: ETS, p. 2. Copyright 2009 ETS. Reprinted with permission

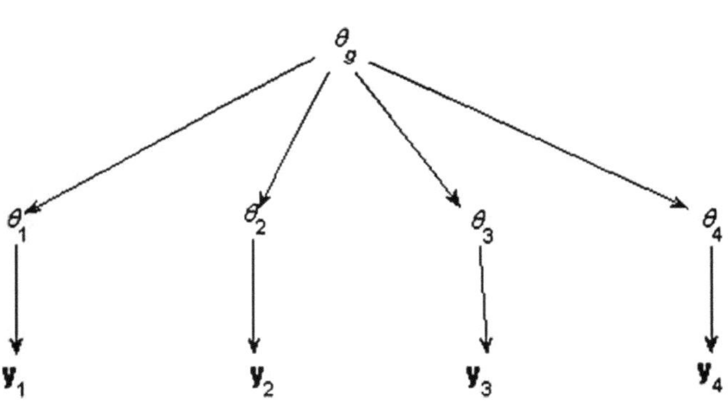

Fig. 1.3 Directed acyclic graph of the second-order model. From *Three Multidimensional Models for Testlet Based Tests*, by F. Rijmen, 2009b, Princeton, NJ: ETS, p. 5. Copyright 2009 ETS. Reprinted with permission

given the general ability. In this model the general ability is indirectly measured by the items, through the specific testlet factors. In Figure 1.3 this is represented through the absence of directed edges between the general ability θ_g and the specific testlets' effects, θ_1 to θ_4.

Now assume that each of the y_1 to y_4 actually denote a test form in Figures 1.2 and 1.3. Assume that these test forms are nominally equivalent forms that need to be equated. Assume for simplicity reasons that each of the four forms represented in Figures 1.2 and 1.3 does not include any testlets. Under these assumptions, each of the three models, the bifactor, the second-order, or the testlet model, can be applied as the measurement model for a single-group data collection design, where the same test takers took all four test forms. Other data collection designs can be eventually considered (see Rijmen, 2009a, where the model was applied to a matrix design from the Progress in International Reading Literacy Study). This assumption is made here only to simplify the parallels between the concurrent unidimensional IRT calibration and linking, and equating of scores on one side, and the concurrent calibration with a testlet model, and equating of scores on the other side. Once the concurrent calibration of items has been achieved, and the items, test forms, and ability parameters have been estimated using one of the testlet models mentioned here, then equating of scores can be achieved through the general ability θg using the method called IRT true-score equating, or using the method called IRT OSE, or using the local equating method (van der Linden, Chapter 13 of this volume).

Obviously, the length of the test forms, the sample size, the specifics of the data collection design, the degree of correlation between the various dimensions, each can be a challenge for fitting successfully a complex model such as any of the testlet models mentioned above. This will be the topic of future research.

In my opinion, the advantage of using a testlet or test-form model for linking and equating lies in the estimate of the test-form effect. As a practitioner, I can see the advantages of monitoring the distribution of the test-form effect over time to support reporting stable equating results and of providing meaningful feedback to the test developers. This feature might be of particular interest for assessments with an almost continuous administration mode. For assessments with numerous administrations one could apply the statistical process control charts to several variables (the means of the general-ability and the form-effect dimensions estimates over time together with a standard deviation band). If differential test-form functioning is of concern, then these specific test-form variables can be monitored for the subgroups of interest. The testlet model applied to test forms also can be extended to incorporate testlets inside each form, as in a hierarchical model.

Another example of a cross-contamination of ideas is presented in Rock (1982). In his paper, "Equating Using Confirmatory Factor Analysis," Rock showed how to use maximum-likelihood factor analysis procedures to estimate the equating parameters, under the assumption that the components of the vector of the test scores have a multivariate normal distribution.

Next, a mathematical framework that includes all OSE methods is described. The OSE framework follows the measurement model described in Figure 1.1 and follows the description of the OSE methods as equating approaches that match the test score distributions.

1.4 An OSE Framework

In this section, a framework for the OSE methods is introduced. The advantages of a single framework that includes all OSE methods are (a) a formal level of cohesiveness, (b) a modular structure that leads to one software package for all methods, and (c) the facilitation of development and comparison of new equating models. This framework is referred as the *OSE framework*. This framework follows the line of argument from the previous two sections.

Identifying a framework that connects the methods used in observed-score equating practice is part of the continuous search for a theory of equating (see also Holland & Hoskens, 2003; von Davier, in press). This equating framework together with Dorans and Holland's five requirements of an equating procedure (Dorans & Holland, 2000), is the closest to a theory that is available for observed-score equating.

The OSE framework outlined here consists of the five steps in the OSE process as described in von Davier et al. (2004a) for the kernel equating and includes an explicit description of the relationship between the observed-score equipercentile and linear equating functions. Moreover, the framework described here shows conceptual similarities with the mathematical framework introduced in Braun and Holland (1982). Next, the notation and the OSE framework are presented.

In the following exposition, it is assumed that an appropriate data collection design is available for measuring skills on a standardized educational assessment, where equating of test scores is needed. The two nominally parallel test forms to be equated are assumed to be well constructed and equally reliable. As in Figure 1.1, the research question is how to measure accurately and fairly the educational skills of the test takers who took these two nominally parallel test forms. The two test forms to be equated are denoted here by X and Y; the same notation is also used for the test scores as random variables with distributions. Score distributions are usually discrete, so to describe them, both their possible values and the associated probabilities of these possible values are given. The possible values for the random variables X and Y are denoted by x_j (with $j = 1, \ldots, J$) and y_k (with $k = 1, \ldots, K$), respectively. As mentioned earlier, for the OSE methods, the unit of measurement is the test score, and the equating is accomplished by matching the two test score distributions (either in terms of percentiles or in terms of their means and standard deviations). In the simple case of total-number-correct scoring, the possible values for X are consecutive integers, such as $x_1 = 0$, $x_2 = 1$, etc. In other cases, the possible values can be negative or have fractional parts—as it is the case of unrounded formula scores or ability estimates from models that use IRT. We assume in the following that the unit of measurement is the total number correct score.

Most OSE functions (in particular the nonlinear ones) depend on the score probability distributions on a target population, called T here. The vectors of the score probabilities are denoted by $\mathbf{r}$ and $\mathbf{s}$ on T:

$$\mathbf{r} = (r_1, \ldots, r_J), \text{ and } \mathbf{s} = (s_1, \ldots, s_K). \tag{1.1}$$

and each r_j and s_k are defined by

$$r_j = P\{X = x_j | T\} \text{ and } s_k = P\{Y = y_k | T\}. \tag{1.2}$$

The score probabilities for X are associated with the X raw scores, $\{x_j\}$, and those for Y are associated with the Y raw scores, $\{y_k\}$. The steps of the OSE framework describe the equating process and are covered in detail in the following subsections.

1.4.1 Step 1: Presmoothing

It is customary to presmooth the data to remove some of the sampling noise if the samples are below 20,000. The score probabilities are either estimated through various procedures such as fitting log-linear models to the observed-score test probabilities or by estimating them using the sample frequencies if the samples are large; either way, they are subsequently collected as part of a row vector, $\hat{\mathbf{u}}$. A description of log-linear model presmoothing is not given here because (a) it is richly documented in the literature (Holland & Thayer, 1987, 1989, 2000; Moses & Holland, 2008); (b) it is an equating step that is already widely followed and understood by practitioners of equating; and (c) in theory (and consistent with the goals of this paper), it can be achieved using other methods and models that easily can be made to match the OSE framework.

1.4.2 Step 2: Estimating the Score Probabilities

The estimated marginal score probabilities $\hat{\mathbf{r}}$ and $\hat{\mathbf{s}}$ are actually computed (explicitly or not) using the design function (DF) described below. The estimated equating function can be written to express the influence of the data collection design as

$$\hat{e}_y(x) = e_y[x; \mathrm{DF}(\hat{\mathbf{u}})]. \tag{1.3}$$

Equivalently, it can be written as

$$\hat{e}_y(x) = e_y(x; \hat{\mathbf{r}}, \hat{\mathbf{s}}), \tag{1.4}$$

where $\mathbf{u}$ is generic notation for the data vector that reflects the way the data are collected and $\hat{\mathbf{u}}$ denotes its estimate.

For example, if the data are collected from an equivalent-groups design, then the data are in the form of two univariate distributions; in this case the design function is the identity function and $\mathbf{u} = (\mathbf{r}, \mathbf{s})$. If the data are collected following a single-group design, where the same group of test takers takes both test forms X and Y, then $\mathbf{u}$ is the vector whose components are the joint probabilities from the bivariate distribution. In this case, the design function is a linear function that computes the marginal probabilities $\mathbf{r}$ and $\mathbf{s}$ from this bivariate distribution. The design function becomes more complex as the various equating methods for the NEAT design become more complex, but the results of its application to vector $\mathbf{u}$ are always the score probability vectors, $\mathbf{r}$ and $\mathbf{s}$ on T.

1.4.3 Step 3: Continuization

There are different ways to continuize the discrete score distributions. In the case of kernel equating (Gaussian, uniform, logistic), the kernel functions are the added continuous random variables to the original discrete variable. I am describing the kernel method of continuization because it also includes the linear interpolation. The traditional equipercentile equating function uses a piecewise linear function as the new continuous distribution. This also can be expressed as in Equations 1.5 and 1.6, with V being a uniform kernel (see Holland & Thayer, 1989, and Lee & von Davier, Chapter 10 of this volume).

Consider $X(h_X)$ as a continuous transformation of X such that

$$X(h_X) = a_X(X + h_X V) + (1 - a_X)\mu_{XT}, \tag{1.5}$$

where

$$a_X^2 = \frac{\sigma_{XT}^2}{\sigma_{XT}^2 + \sigma_V^2 h_X^2} \tag{1.6}$$

and h_X is the bandwidth controlling the degree of smoothness. In Equation 1.5, V is a continuous (kernel) distribution with variance σ_V^2 and mean 0. The mean and the variance of X on T are denoted by μ_{XT} and σ_{XT}^2, respectively. The role of a_X in Equation 1.5 is to insure that the first two moments of the transformed random variable $X(h_X)$ are the same as the first two moments of the original discrete variable X. When h_X is large, the distribution of $X(h_X)$ approximates the distribution of V; when h_X is small, $X(h_X)$ approximates X, but as a continuous function. In von Davier et al. (2004a), V follows a standard normal distribution (that is, a Gaussian kernel, with mean 0 and variance 1), which is why the terms *Gaussian kernel equating* and *kernel equating* are sometime used interchangeably. However, Lee and von Davier (2008; also see Chapter 10 of this volume) discussed the use of alternative kernels for equating, and in their approach V is a generic continuous distribution. The Y distribution is continuized in a similar way.

One important property of the OSE framework that was developed for kernel equating functions (Gaussian or other kernels) is that by manipulating the bandwidths for the new distributions one can obtain a family of equating functions that includes linear equating (when the bandwidths are large) and equipercentile equating (when the bandwidths are small) as special cases. The choice of bandwidth balances the closeness of the continuous distribution to the data and the smoothness of the new continuous function. The continuized function $X(h_X)$ can be evaluated or diagnosed by comparing its moments to the moments of the discrete score distribution, in this case, of X. Other OSE methods employ different strategies to continuize the distributions (see Haberman, Chapter 8 of this volume; Wang, Chapter 9 of this volume).

1.4.4 Step 4: Computing the Equating Function

Once the discrete distribution functions have been transformed into continuous cumulative distribution functions (CDFs), the observed-score equipercentile equating function that equates X to Y is computed as

$$\hat{e}_y(x) = e_y[x; \mathrm{DF}(\hat{\mathbf{u}})] = G_{Tc}{}^{-1}[F_{Tc}(x; \hat{\mathbf{r}}); \hat{\mathbf{s}}], \tag{1.7}$$

where G_{Tc} is the continuized cumulative distribution function of Y on the target population T and F_{Tc} is the continuized cumulative distribution function of X on T. The equating function e_Y in Equation 1.7 can have different formulas (linear or nonlinear, for example). In a NEAT design, it can take the form of chained equating, poststratification equating, Levine equating, and so on.

1.4.5 Step 5: Evaluating the Equating Results and Computing Accuracy Measures

The equating function can be evaluated by comparing the moments of the equated scores distribution $\hat{e}_y(x)$ to the moments of the targeted discrete-score distribution, in this case, of Y. See von Davier et al. (2004b, Chapter 4) for a diagnostic measure, called the percent relative error, that compares the moments of the distributions of the equated scores to the moments of the reference distribution. Other commonly used diagnostic measures involve accuracy measures (see below) and historical information available about the equating results from previous administrations of forms of the assessment. One might employ quality assurance methods or statistical process control methods to monitor the stability of the reported scores over time—such as cumulative sum charts, time series analyses, and so on (see Li et al., Chapter 20 of this volume).

The standard error of equating (SEE) and the standard error of equating difference (SEED) are described next. von Davier et al. (2004b) applied the *delta method* (Kendall & Stuart, 1977; Rao, 1973) to obtain both the SEE and the SEED. The delta method was applied to the function from Equation 1.7 that depends on the parameter vectors **r** and **s** on T. According to the delta method, the analytical expression of the asymptotic variance of the equating function is given by

$$\mathrm{Var}[\hat{e}_y(x)] = \mathrm{Var}\{e_y[x; \mathrm{DF}(\hat{\mathbf{u}})]\} \sim \mathbf{J}_{e_y}\mathbf{J}_{DF}\hat{\Sigma}\mathbf{J}_{DF}^{t}\mathbf{J}_{e_y}^{t}, \tag{1.8}$$

where $\hat{\Sigma}$ is the estimated asymptotic variance of the vectors **r** and **s** after presmoothing; $\mathbf{J}_{e_y}$ is the Jacobian vector of e_y, that is, the vector of the first derivatives of e_y $(x;$ **r, s**$)$ with respect to each component of **r** and **s**; and $\mathbf{J}_{\mathrm{DF}}$ is the Jacobian matrix of DF, that is, the matrix of the first derivatives of the design function with respect to each component of vector **u**.

The asymptotic SEE for $e_y(x)$ is the square root of the asymptotic variance in Equation 1.8, and it depends on three factors that correspond to the data collection and manipulation steps carried out so far: (a) presmoothing (using a log-linear model, for example) through estimating the **r** and **s** and their estimated covariance matrix $\hat{\Sigma}$; (b) the data collection design through the $\mathbf{J}_{\mathrm{DF}}$, and (c) the combination of continuization and the mathematical form of the equating function from Step 4 (computing the equating function) in the OSE framework.

Moreover, the formula given in Equation 1.8 makes obvious the modular character of the OSE framework (and implicitly, of the software package developed for the OSE framework): If one chooses a different log-linear model, then the only thing that will change in the formula given in Equation 1.8 is $\hat{\Sigma}$. If one changes the data collection design, the only thing that will change in the formula given in Equation 1.8 is $\mathbf{J}_{\mathrm{DF}}$. Finally, if one changes the equating method (linear or nonlinear, chained versus frequency estimation, etc.), the only piece that will change in Equation 1.8 is $\mathbf{J}_{e_y}$.

Hence, the formula of the estimated asymptotic variance of the equating function from Equation 1.8, that is,

$$\text{OSE framework} \sim \mathbf{J}_{e_y}\mathbf{J}_{\mathrm{DF}}\hat{\Sigma}\mathbf{J}_{\mathrm{DF}}^t\mathbf{J}_{e_y}^t, \tag{1.9}$$

could be seen simplistically as the formal representation of the OSE framework.

In addition to the five steps in the equating process described above that are synthesized in Equation 1.9, the OSE framework includes an explicit description of the relationship between the observed-score equipercentile and linear equating functions, which is described below.

1.4.6 The Relation Between Linear and Equipercentile Equating Functions

von Davier et al. (2004a, b) argued that all OSE functions from X to Y on T can be regarded as equipercentile equating functions that have the form shown in Equations 1.7 and 1.10:

$$\mathrm{Equi}_{XY\,T}(x) = G_{Tc}^{-1}[F_{Tc}(x)], \tag{1.10}$$

where $F_{Tc}(x)$ and $G_{Tc}(y)$ are continuous forms of the CDFs of X and Y on T, and $y = G_{Tc}^{-1}(p)$ is the inverse function of $p = G_{Tc}(y)$. Different assumptions about $F_{Tc}(x)$ and $G_{Tc}(y)$ lead to different versions of $\mathrm{Equi}_{XY\,T}(x)$, and, therefore, to different OSE functions (e.g., chained equating, frequency estimation, etc.).

Let μ_{XT}, μ_{YT}, σ_{XT}, and σ_{YT} denote the means and standard deviations of X and Y on T that are computed from $F_{Tc}(x)$ and $G_{Tc}(y)$, as in $\mu_{XT} = \int x dF_{Tc}(x)$, and so on.

In general, any linear equating function is formed from the first two moments of X and Y on T as

$$\mathrm{Lin}_{XY\,T}(x) = \mu_{YT} + (\sigma_{YT}/\sigma_{XT})(x - \mu_{XT}). \tag{1.11}$$

The linear equating function in Equation 1.11 that uses the first two moments computed from $F_{Tc}(x)$ and $G_{Tc}(y)$ will be said to be compatible with $\mathrm{Equi}_{XY\,T}(x)$ in Equation 1.10. The compatible version of $\mathrm{Lin}_{XY\,T}(x)$ appears in the theorem below (see von Davier et al. 2004a, for the proof of the theorem). The theorem connects the equipercentile function, $\mathrm{Equi}_{XY\,T}(x)$, in Equation 1.10 to its compatible linear equating function, $\mathrm{Lin}_{XY\,T}(x)$, in Equation 1.11.

Theorem. *For any population, T, if $F_{Tc}(x)$ and $G_{Tc}(y)$ are continuous CDFs, and F_0 and G_0 are the standardized CDFs that determine the shapes of $F_{Tc}(x)$ and $G_{Tc}(y)$, that is, both F_0 and G_0 have mean 0 and variance 1 and*

$$F_{Tc}(x) = F_0\left(\frac{x - \mu_{XT}}{\sigma_{XT}}\right) \text{ and } G_{Tc}(y) = G_0\left(\frac{y - \mu_{YT}}{\sigma_{YT}}\right), \tag{1.12}$$

then

$$\mathrm{Equi}_{XY\,T}(x) = G_{Tc}^{-1}[F_{Tc}(x)] = \mathrm{Lin}_{XY\,T}(x) + R(x), \tag{1.13}$$

$$\text{where the remainder term, } R(x), \text{ is equal to } \sigma_{YT}\, r\left(\frac{x - \mu_{XT}}{\sigma_{XT}}\right), \tag{1.14}$$

and $r(z)$ is the function

$$r(z) = G_0^{-1}[F_0(z)] - z. \tag{1.15}$$

When $F_{Tc}(x)$ and $G_{Tc}(y)$ have the same shape, it follows that $r(z) = 0$ in Equation 1.15 for all z, so that the remainder in Equation 1.13 satisfies $R(x) = 0$, and thus $\mathrm{Equi}_{XY\,T}(x) = \mathrm{Lin}_{XY\,T}(x)$.

It is important to recognize that, for the various methods used in the NEAT design, it is not always true that the means and standard deviations of X and Y used to compute $\mathrm{Lin}_{XY\,T}(x)$ are the same as those from $F_{Tc}(x)$ and $G_{Tc}(y)$ that are used in Equation 1.8 to form $\mathrm{Equi}_{XY\,T}(x)$. The compatibility of a linear and equipercentile equating function depends on both the equating method employed and how the continuization process for obtaining $F_{Tc}(x)$ and $G_{Tc}(y)$ is carried out. The compatibility of linear and nonlinear equating functions does hold for the kernel equating methods but does not hold for all classes of equating methods, as discussed in von Davier, Fournier-Zajack, and Holland (2007). For example, the traditional method of continuization by linear interpolation (Kolen & Brennan, 2004) does not reproduce the variance of the underlying discrete distribution. The piecewise linear continuous CDF that the linear interpolation method produces is only guaranteed to reproduce the mean of the discrete distribution that underlies it. The variance of the continuized CDF is larger than that of the underlying discrete distribution by 1/12 (Holland & Thayer, 1989). Moreover, the four moments of X and Y on T that are implicitly used by the chained linear or the Tucker linear method are not necessarily the same, nor are they the same as those of the continuized CDFs of frequency estimation or the chained equipercentile methods.

In conclusion, the OSE framework includes the five steps of the equating practice formally described in Equation 1.9 and incorporates both the linear and nonlinear equating functions together with a description of their relationship. The theorem above, which shows that the linear and equipercentile equating methods are related, emphasizes the generalizability of the framework. It was shown that the OSE framework is a statistical modeling framework as described in Figure 1.1, where the unit of measurement is the test score and the equating of scores is accomplished via distribution matching.

1.5 Discussion and Outline of the Book

This chapter reviews the existing measurement and equating models for (one-dimensional) tests that measure the same construct. The intention is to have the reader conceptually anchor the new models and approaches presented in the following chapters of the volume into the frameworks outlined in this introduction.

The measurement model presented in Figure 1.1 is the basis for the structure of this volume. In order to reflect the steps in the measurement model as described in Figure 1.1, the book has three parts: (a) *Research Questions and Data Collection Designs*, (b) *Measurement and Equating Models*, and (c) *Evaluation*. The chapters have been grouped to reflect the match between the research methodologies of their focus and each of the steps in the measurement process. The classification of the chapters in these three parts is, of course, approximate; each of the components of the measurement process is addressed in every paper.

Author Note: Many thanks go to my colleagues Paul Holland, Jim Carlson, Shelby Haberman, Dan Eignor, Dianne Henderson-Montero, and Kim Fryer for their detailed reviews and comments on the material that led to this chapter. Any opinions expressed in this chapter are those of the author and not necessarily of Educational Testing Service.

Part I
Research Questions and Data Collection Designs

Chapter 2
Equating Test Scores: Toward Best Practices

Neil J. Dorans, Tim P. Moses, and Daniel R. Eignor

Score equating is essential for any testing program that continually produces new editions of a test and for which the expectation is that scores from these editions have the same meaning over time. Different editions may be built to a common blueprint and designed to measure the same constructs, but they almost invariably differ somewhat in their psychometric properties. If one edition is more difficult than another, examinees would be expected to receive lower scores on the harder form. Score equating seeks to eliminate the effects on scores of these unintended differences in test form difficulty. Score equating is necessary to be fair to examinees and to provide score users with scores that mean the same thing across different editions or forms of the test.

In high-stakes testing programs, in particular, it is extremely important that test equating be done carefully and accurately. The reported scores, even though they represent the endpoint of a large test production, administration, and scoring enterprise, are the most visible part of a testing program. An error in the equating function or score conversion can affect the scores for all examinees, which is both a fairness and a validity concern. The credibility of a testing organization hinges on activities associated with producing, equating, and reporting scores because the reported score is so visible.

This chapter addresses the practical implications of score equating. Section 2.1 introduces test score equating as a special case of the more general class of procedures called score linking procedures. Section 2.2 is concerned with the material that is available before data are collected for equating, the tests, the anchor tests, the old form or reference form raw to scale scaling function, and the number of reference forms available. Section 2.3 lists most common data collection designs that are used in the equating of test scores. In Section 2.4, we list some common observed-score equating functions. Section 2.5 describes common data-processing

N.J. Dorans (✉), T.P. Moses, and D.R. Eignor
Educational Testing Service, Rosedale Rd, Princeton, New Jersey 08541, USA
e-mail: ndorans@ets.org

A.A. von Davier (ed.), *Statistical Models for Test Equating, Scaling, and Linking*, Statistics for Social and Behavioral Sciences,
DOI 10.1007/978-0-387-98138-3_2,

practices that occur prior to computations of equating functions. In Section 2.6, attention is given to how to evaluate an equating function and postequating activities.

2.1 Linking and Equating: Foundational Aspects

Score linking is used to describe the transformation from a score on one test to a score on another test; score equating is a special type of score linking. Much has been written on score equating and linking. The most complete coverage of the entire field of score equating and score linking, in general, is provided by Kolen and Brennan (2004). Other works include: von Davier, Holland, and Thayer (2004b); Feuer, Holland, Green, Bertenthal, and Hemphill (1999); Koretz, Bertenthal, and Green (1999); Livingston (2004); Holland and Dorans (2006); Flanagan (1951); Angoff (1971); Petersen, Kolen, and Hoover (1989); and several chapters in Dorans, Pommerich, and Holland (2007; see Cook, 2007; Holland, 2007; Kolen, 2007; Petersen, 2007; von Davier, 2007). With all this background material available to the reader, we can be brief and incisive in our treatment of the salient issues, first distinguishing different types of linking and then using these distinctions when describing equating issues in Sections 2.2–2.6.

2.1.1 Classes of Score Linking Methods: Definition of Terms

A *link* between scores on two tests is a transformation from a score on one test to a score on another test. The different types of links have been divided into three basic categories called *predicting*, *scale aligning* and *equating* (Holland & Dorans, 2006). It is essential to understand the differences between these categories because they are often confused in practice. Understanding the distinctions among these categories can prevent violations of professional practice.

2.1.1.1 Predicting

Predicting, the oldest form of score linking, has been confused with equating from the earliest days of psychometrics. The confusion still occurs; Ebretson and Reise (2000) wrote, "In linear equating, for example, scores on one test form are regressed on the other test form" (p. 21). The goal of predicting is to minimize errors of prediction of a score on the dependent or criterion variable from information on other predictor variables. This goal guarantees an asymmetry between what is being predicted and what is used to make the prediction. This asymmetry prevents prediction from meeting one of the fundamental prerequisites of equating, the goal of which is to produce scores that can be used interchangeably.

2.1.1.2 Scale Aligning

The goal of scale aligning is to transform the scores from two different tests onto a common scale. Scaling procedures are about 100 years old. Scale aligning is the second category in the Holland and Dorans (2006) framework. It has many subcategories, including activities such as battery scaling (Kolen, 2004), anchor scaling (Holland & Dorans, 2006), vertical scaling (Harris, 2007; Kolen & Brennan, 2004; Patz & Yao, 2007; Yen, 2007), calibration (Holland & Dorans, 2006), and concordance (Pommerich & Dorans, 2004). Scale aligning and score equating are often confused because the statistical procedures used for scale alignment also can be used to equate tests.

2.1.1.3 Equating

Equating is the strongest form of linking between the scores on two tests. Equating may be viewed as a form of scale aligning in which very strong requirements are placed on the tests being linked. The goal of equating is to produce a linkage between scores on two test forms such that the scores from each test form can be used as if they had come from the same test. Strong requirements must be put on the blueprints for the two tests and on the method used for linking scores in order to establish an effective equating. Among other things, the two tests must measure the same construct at almost the same level of difficulty and with the same degree of reliability. Some practices that can help ensure the achievement of equating requirements are described in Section 2.2.

2.1.1.4 What Constitutes an Equating?

The goal of equating is what distinguishes it from other forms of linking. The goal of score equating is to allow the scores from both tests to be used interchangeably. Experience has shown that the scores and tests that produce the scores must satisfy very strong requirements to achieve this demanding goal of interchangeability. There are five requirements that are widely viewed as necessary for a linking to be an equating (Holland & Dorans, 2006):

1. *The equal-construct requirement*: The two tests should both be measures of the same construct (latent trait, skill, ability).
2. *The equal-reliability requirement*: The two tests should have the same level of reliability.
3. *The symmetry requirement*: The equating transformation for mapping the scores of test Y to those of test X should be the *inverse* of the equating transformation for mapping the scores of X to those of Y.
4. *The equity requirement*: It should be a matter of indifference to an examinee as to which of two tests the examinee actually takes.

5. *The population-invariance requirement*: The equating function used to link the scores of X and Y should be the same regardless of the choice of population or subpopulation from which it is derived.

Both formal and informal statements of subsets of these five requirements appear in a variety of earlier sources (Angoff, 1971; Kolen & Brennan, 2004; Lord, 1950, 1980; Petersen et al., 1989). Dorans and Holland (2000) explicitly discussed these five requirements and indicated various ways in which the five "can be criticized as being vague, irrelevant, impractical, trivial or hopelessly stringent" (p. 283).

2.2 Test Specifications and Score Linking Plans

2.2.1 Test Specifications

Based on the equity condition (Requirement 4 in Section 2.1.2.1), Lord (1980) stated that equating was either unnecessary (because it pertains to test forms intended to be parallel) or impossible (because strictly parallel test forms are not likely to be constructed in practice). Even so, equatings are conducted to ensure fair assessment. Although not much can be done about the impossible aspect, best practices can be used to try to make equating as unnecessary as possible. Poor-quality tests cannot be equated properly for several reasons. For one, they may not measure the same construct. Proper test development increases the likelihood that equating will be unnecessary. Well-defined test specifications are a necessary first step. Test editions need to be constructed to the same blueprint. Under proper assembly rules, old and new forms are equally reliable measures of the same construct that are built to the same set of well-specified content and statistical specifications.

Untried or new test questions need to be pretested, and pretested under conditions that reflect actual test administration conditions. When the test forms include unpretested questions or questions pretested in small samples, there is greater likelihood that test forms will not be identical and that equating adjustments will be necessary. Plans for test development should be based on the availability of high-quality pretested material. Continuous testing often can undermine the quality of tests and test scores by draining pools of pretested items quicker than these items can be replenished.

2.2.2 Anchor Test

Often an anchor test plays a crucial role in the equating process. It is generally considered good practice to construct the anchor test according to the test specifications, so that it is a miniversion of the two tests being equated. That means it should have the same difficulty level and contain the same content as the tests to be equated. In the case where the anchor is internal to the test, context effects become a possible issue. To minimize these effects, internal anchor (or common) items are often placed in the same location within each test.

2.2.3 Score Linking Plans

The raw-to-raw equating is not an end, but the means to an end, namely an appropriate score conversion function. This critical point is sometimes given short shrift in discussions of equating that focus on methods. A multistep process is used to put scores from a new test onto an existing score-reporting scale. Before the new test form is administered, there exists a conversion, $s(y)$, for an old test form that takes raw scores, y, on the old test form Y onto the score-reporting scale. This old-form scaling function, $s(y)$, is independent of the new form. Once data are collected on the new form, data from the new form and the old form are used to compute a raw-to-raw equating function, $e(x)$, that links raw scores x on a new test X to those of an old test form Y.

The final step in the process is to produce a function that converts the equated X raw scores to the score-reporting scale by composing the equating function, $y = e(x)$ with $s(y)$. This puts the raw scores of X onto the reporting scale, $ss(e(x))$. The existing score scale for a test limits the quality of the new-form scaling that can be achieved via the equating of a new form. Equatings can produce poor new-form scalings if the old-form scaling is problematic. Even tests as widely used as the SAT® could have undesirable new-form scalings that were affected by poor alignment of the score scale with the intended uses of the test score. In the case of the SAT, poor score scale alignment in which the average Math score was 50 points higher than the average Verbal score led to widespread misinterpretations about a person's relative verbal and mathematical ability and was rectified by recentering of the SAT scores (Dorans, 2002). Many score scales suffer from poor construction, whereas others discard useful information because of the way the meaning of the scale has changed over time. In other words, the value that best equating practices have for reported scores is sometimes constrained by factors that lie outside the domain of equating.

Testing programs that use best practices have well-designed score equating plans and well-aligned score scales that increase the likelihood that scores on different forms can be used interchangeably. Links to multiple old forms are preferable to a link to a single old form. The SAT plan is an example of a sound linking plan that works well, as demonstrated by Haberman, Guo, Liu, and Dorans (2008). Some testing programs link in a haphazard way as if some magical method of score equating might play the role of *deus ex machina* to set scores straight. Data collection planning, developing linking plans, and maintaining score scales are crucial best practices.

2.3 Data Collection Designs Used in Test Score Equating

To obtain the clearest estimates of test-form difficulty differences, all score equating methods must control for differential ability of the examinee groups employed in the linking process. Data collection procedures should be guided by a concern for obtaining equivalent groups, either directly or indirectly. Often, two different tests that are not strictly parallel are given to two different groups of examinees of unequal ability. Assuming that the samples are large enough to ignore sampling error, differences in the distributions of the resulting scores can be due to one or both of two factors: the relative *difficulty* of the two tests and the relative *ability* of the two groups of examinees on these tests. Differences in difficulty are what test score equating is supposed to take care of; difference in ability of the groups is a confounding factor that needs to be eliminated before the equating process can take place.

In practice, there are two distinct approaches for addressing the separation of test difficulty and group ability differences. The first approach is to use a common population of examinees, so there are no ability differences. The other approach is to use an anchor measure of the construct being assessed by X and Y. When the same examinees take both tests, we achieve direct control over differential examinee ability. In practice, it is more common to use two equivalent samples of examinees from a common population instead of identical examinees. The second approach assumes that performance on a set of common items or an anchor measure can quantify the ability differences between two distinct, but not necessarily equivalent, samples of examinees. The use of an anchor measure can lead to more flexible data collection designs than the use of common examinees. However, the use of anchor measures requires users to make various assumptions that are not needed when the examinees taking the tests are either the same or from equivalent samples. When there are ability differences, the various statistical adjustments for ability differences often produce different results.

In all of our descriptions, we will identify one or more populations of examinees and one or more samples from these populations. We will assume that all samples are random samples, even though in practice this may be only an approximation. More extended discussions of data collection designs are given in Angoff (1971), Petersen et al. (1989), von Davier et al. (2004b), Kolen and Brennan (2004), and Holland and Dorans (2006).

The *single-group design* is the simplest data collection design. In the single-group design, all examinees in a single sample of examinees from population P take both tests. The single-group design can provide accurate equating results with relatively small sample sizes.

In most equating situations, it is impossible to arrange for enough testing time for every examinee to take more than one test. The simplest solution is to have two separate samples take each form of the test. In the *equivalent-groups design*, two equivalent samples are taken from a common population P; one is tested with test form X and the other with test form Y. The equivalent-groups design is often used for equating. Sometimes test booklets are assigned randomly to groups, which is why this design is sometimes called the *random-groups design* (Kolen & Brennan, 2004). A more common situation is to construct the two samples by "spiraling" the test booklets for the two tests. The booklets are alternated in the packaging process so that when the tests are distributed to examinees they are alternated, first form X, then form Y, and then form X again, and so on. Well-executed, spiraled samples are often more "equivalent" (i.e., less different) than random samples because they are approximately *stratified* random samples. The equivalent-groups design is fairly convenient to administer. It does not require that the two tests have any items in common, but this design can be used even when they do have items in common. When samples sizes are large and forms can be reused without security problems, the equivalent-groups design is usually regarded as a good choice because it avoids the issue of possible order effects that can arise in the single-group design where each examinee takes *both* tests.

In order to allow for the possibility of order effects in the single-group design, the sample is sometimes randomly divided in half; in each half-sized subsample the two tests are taken in different orders—form X first and then form Y, or vice versa. The result is the *counterbalanced data collection design.* The counterbalanced design contains both the single-group and equivalent-groups designs. Usually, the counterbalanced design requires a special study for collecting the data.

In *anchor test designs* there are two populations P and Q, with a sample of examinees from P taking test X, and a sample from Q taking test Y. In addition, both samples take an anchor test, A. We follow the terminology of von Davier et al. (2004b) and call this the *nonequivalent groups with anchor test* (NEAT) design. Kolen and Brennan (2004) and others referred to this as the *common-item nonequivalent groups design* or simply the *common item* or the *anchor test* design.

The role of the anchor test is to quantify the differences in ability between samples from P and Q that affect their performance on the two tests to be equated, X and Y. The best kind of an anchor for equating is a test that measures the same construct that X and Y measure. The anchor A is usually a shorter and less reliable test than the tests to be equated.[1]

Formally, the NEAT design contains two single-group designs. The anchor test design is more flexible than the equivalent-groups design because it allows the two samples taking X and Y to be different, or nonequivalent. It is also more efficient than the single-group design because it does not require examinees to take both X and Y.

Although the use of anchor tests may appear to be a minor variation of the previous data collection designs, the use of common items involves new assumptions that are

[1]There are exceptions to this general case. For example, sometimes a multiple-choice anchor test is used to link two versions of an all constructed response test. Here the anchor score is more reliable than the scores to be equated. Although the characteristics of anchor tests are usually not specifically described in the requirements of equating or in summaries of these requirements, in practice linkings that utilize anchors that measure different constructs than the tests to be equated are considered unlikely to meet the requirements of equating.

not necessary in the use of single-group, equivalent-groups, and counterbalanced designs, where common examinees are used; see Sections 2.1–2.3 of Holland and Dorans (2006). Some type of assumption, however, is required in the NEAT design to make up for the fact that X is never observed for examinees in Q and Y is never observed for examinees in P. For this reason, there are several distinct methods of scaling and equating tests using the NEAT design. Each of these methods corresponds to making different untestable assumptions about the missing data.

One way to think about the difference between the NEAT design and the single-group, equivalent-groups, and counterbalanced designs is as the difference between observational studies versus experimental designs (Rosenbaum, 1995). The single-group design is like a repeated measures design with a single group and two treatments, the equivalent-groups design is like a randomized comparison with two treatment groups, and the counterbalanced design is like a repeated measures design with a single group and counterbalanced order of treatments. In contrast, the NEAT design is like an observational study with two nonrandomized study groups that are possibly subject to varying amounts of self-selection.

2.3.1 Discussion of Data Collection Designs

Data collection is one of the most important aspects of best practices in equating. Each of the data collection designs mentioned in this section has advantages and disadvantages that make it more or less useful for different situations. For equating, the single-group design requires the smallest sample sizes, and the equivalent-groups design requires the largest sample sizes to achieve the same level of accuracy, as measured by the standard error of equating (see Lord, 1950; Holland & Dorans, 2006). The anchor test (i.e., NEAT) designs require sample sizes somewhere in between those of the single- and equivalent-groups designs, although the sample size requirements depend on how strongly correlated the anchor test is with the two tests to be equated and how similar the two populations are. Higher correlations and smaller differences in proficiency between populations require smaller sample sizes than lower correlations and larger differences in proficiency between populations.

We would argue that the ideal design, in theory and in terms of best practice, is a large-sample, equivalent-groups design with an external anchor test. If the anchor test is administered last, only the anchor test can be affected by possible order effects. A comparison of the distributions of the anchor test in the two (equivalent) samples then allows differential order effects to be identified. If they are substantial, the anchor test can be ignored, leaving a simple equivalent-groups design, where no order effects are possible. If the anchor test is internal to the two tests, then context or order (e.g., item location effects) may arise and need to be dealt with.

An important potential drawback of the equivalent-groups design for score equating is that the test form that has been previously equated has to be given at least twice—once when it was originally equated and then again as the old form in the equating of a new form. In some testing programs, it may be problematic for reasons of test security to reuse operational forms. This leads to consideration of special administrations for purposes of equating. However, if special nonoperational test administrations are arranged to collect equating data using the equivalent-groups design, then the issue of examinee motivation arises, as discussed in Holland and Dorans (2006).

The single-group design requires a smaller sample size to achieve the same level of statistical accuracy as that obtained by an equivalent-groups design with a larger sample, but it brings with it issues of order effects and requires twice as much time to administer both tests. A particular problem with the single-group design is that there is no way to assess for order effects. The counterbalanced design, on the other hand, allows order effects to be estimated. However, if they are large and different for the two tests, then there may be no option but to ignore the data from the tests given second and treat the result as an equivalent-groups design. Because of the greatly reduced sample size, the resulting equivalent-groups design may produce equating results that are less accurate than desired. von Davier et al. (2004b) proposed making a formal statistical decision for the counterbalanced design to assess the order effects.

The anchor test design is the most complex design to execute well, especially if differences in ability between the old- and new-form equating samples are large. Whether an equating test is an external anchor or an internal anchor also has an impact, as do the number of anchor tests and the type of score linking plan employed.

2.3.2 Considerations for External Anchor Tests

It is often advised that the anchor test should be a miniversion of the two tests being equated (Angoff, 1971). Making the anchor test a miniversion of the whole test is sometimes in conflict with the need to disguise an external anchor test to make it look like one of the scored sections of the test. For example, to be a miniversion of the test, the anchor test might need to include a variety of item types, whereas, to mirror a specific section of the test, the anchor test might need to include only a limited number of item types. The phrase *external anchor* usually refers to items that are administered in a separately timed section and that do not count towards the examinee's score. One major advantage of external anchors is that they may serve multiple purposes, for example, equating, pretesting, and tryout of new item types. This is accomplished by spiraling versions of the test with different content in this "variable" section. This process also can be used to improve test security by limiting the exposure of the anchor test to a relatively small proportion of the total group tested.

For best practices, it is important to disguise the external anchor test so that it appears to be just another section of the test. One reason for this is that some examinees may identify the anchor test and, knowing that it does not count towards their final score, skip it or use the time to work on sections that count towards their score (even though they are instructed not to do this). Although this type of behavior may appear to benefit these examinees, because of the way that the anchor test is used in equating, such behavior actually may result in lowering the scores of all examinees if enough of them do it. This counterintuitive result can be explained as follows. The anchor test is used to compare the performance of the current group of examinees on the anchor test to that of a previous group. If a substantial number of the current examinees underperform on the anchor test, this will make them appear less able than they really are. As a consequence, the new test will appear to be somewhat easier than it really is relative to the old test. In score equating, a raw score on an easier test is converted to a lower scaled score than that for the same raw score on a harder test. Therefore, the scores reported on the new test will be lower than they would have been had all examinees performed up to their abilities on the anchor test. As indicated in Section 2.5.1, it is best practice to exclude from the equating analysis any examinees whose anchor test performance is inconsistent with their total test performance.

2.3.3 Considerations for Internal Anchor Tests

Items in an internal anchor test are part of the assessment and count towards each examinee's score. Internal anchor items are usually spread throughout the test. Some external anchors (i.e., items that are left out of or are external to the total score) are administered internally and consequently face some of the issues associated with internal anchors. For the observed-score equating methods described in Section 2.4, where the score on the anchor test plays an important role, it is desirable for the anchor test to be a miniversion of the two tests. This may be more feasible for internal anchor tests than for external anchor tests.

Because the items in an internal anchor test count towards the score, examinees are unlikely to skip them. On the other hand, once anchor test items have been used in the test administration of the old form, the items may become susceptible to security breaches and become known by examinees taking the new form to be equated. For anchor items to be effective, they must maintain their statistical properties across the old and new forms. The primary problems with internal anchor tests are context effects, along with the just-mentioned security breaches. Context effects can occur when common items are administered in different locations (e.g., common Item 10 in one form is Item 20 in the other form) or under different testing conditions (i.e., paper and pencil versus computer delivered), or when they are adjacent to different kinds of items in the two tests. These effects are well documented (Brennan, 1992; Harris & Gao, 2003; Leary & Dorans, 1985). Security breaches are an unfortunate reality for many testing programs, and due diligence is required to prevent them or to recognize them when they occur.

2.3.4 Strengthening the Anchor Test

When there are only small differences in ability between the two samples of examinees used in an anchor test design, all linear equating methods tend to give similar results, as do all nonlinear equating methods. Linear and nonlinear equating methods are discussed in Section 2.4. To the extent that an anchor test design (Section 2.3.4) is almost an equivalent-groups design (Section 2.3.2) with an anchor test, the need for the anchor test is minimized and the quality of equating increases.

When the two samples are very different in ability, the use of the anchor test information becomes critical, because it is the only means for distinguishing differences in ability between the two groups of examinees from differences in difficulty between the two tests that are being equated. The most important properties of the anchor test are its stability over occasions when it is used (mentioned above) and its correlation with the scores on the two tests being equated. The correlation should be as high as possible. Long internal and external anchors are generally better for equating than short ones, as longer anchors are usually more reliable and more highly correlated with the tests.

In many settings, there is only one old form. Some tests are equated to two old forms, sometimes routinely, sometimes in response to a possible equating problem with one of the old forms. The SAT links each new form back to four old forms through four different anchor tests (Haberman et al., 2008). This design reduces the influence of any one old form on the determination of the new-form raw-to-scale conversion. It is desirable to have links to multiple old forms, especially in cases where a large ability difference is anticipated between the groups involved in one of the links.

2.4 Procedures for Equating Scores

Many procedures have been developed over the years for equating tests. Holland and Dorans (2006) considered three factors when attempting to develop a taxonomy of equating methods: (a) common-population versus common-item data collection designs, (b) observed-score versus true-score procedures, and (c) linear versus nonlinear methods.

Because equating is an empirical procedure, it requires a data collection design and a procedure for transforming scores on one test form to scores on another. Linear methods produce a linear function for mapping the scores from X to Y, whereas nonlinear methods allow the transformation to be curved. Observed-score procedures directly transform (or equate) the observed scores on X to those on Y. True-score methods are designed to transform the *true scores* on X to the true scores of Y. True score methods employ a statistical model with an examinee's true score defined as their expected observed test score based on the chosen statistical model. The psychometric models used to date are those of classical test theory and item response theory. Holland and Hoskens (2003) showed how these two psychometric models may be viewed as aspects of the same model.

In this section, we will limit our discussion to observed-score equating methods that use the data collection designs described in Section 2.3. Our focus is on observed-score equating because true scores are unobserved and consequently primarily of theoretical interest only. Consult Holland and Dorans (2006) for more complete treatments of observed-score and true-score procedures.

2.4.1 Observed-Score Procedures for Equating Scores in a Common Population

Three data collection designs in Section 2.3 make use of a common population of examinees: the single-group, the equivalent-groups, and the counterbalanced designs. They all involve a single population P, which is also the target population, T.

We will use a definition of observed-score equating that applies to either linear or nonlinear procedures, depending on whether additional assumptions are satisfied. This allows us to consider both linear and nonlinear observed-score equating methods from a single point of view.

Some notation will be used throughout the rest of this chapter. The *cumulative distribution function* (CDF) of the scores of examinees in the target population, T, on test X is denoted by $F_{\mathrm{T}}(x)$, and it is defined as the proportion of examinees in T who score at or below x on test X. More formally, $F_{\mathrm{T}}(x) = P\{X \leq x \mid T\}$, where $P\{. \mid T\}$ denotes the population proportion or probability in T. Similarly, $G_{\mathrm{T}}(y) = P\{Y \leq y \mid T\}$, is the CDF of Y over T. CDFs increase from 0 up to 1 as x (or y) moves from left to right along the horizontal axis in a two-way plot of test score by proportion of examinees. In this notation, x and y may be any real values, not necessarily just the possible scores on the two tests. For distributions of observed scores such as number right or rounded formula scores, the CDFs are step functions that have points of increase only at each possible score (Kolen & Brennan, 2004). In Section 2.4.3 we address the issue of the discreteness of score distributions in detail.

2.4.1.1 The Equipercentile Equating Function

The equipercentile definition of *comparable* scores is that x (a score on test form X) and y (a score on test form Y) are comparable in T if $F_{\mathrm{T}}(x) = G_{\mathrm{T}}(y)$. This means that x and y have the same percentile in the target population, T. When the two CDFs are continuous and strictly increasing, the equation $F_{\mathrm{T}}(x) = G_{\mathrm{T}}(y)$ can always be satisfied and can be solved for y in terms of x. Solving for y leads to the *equipercentile function*, $\mathrm{Equi}_{\mathrm{YT}}(x)$, that links x to y on T, defined by

$$y = \mathrm{Equi}_{\mathrm{YT}}(x) = G_{\mathrm{T}}^{-1}(F_{\mathrm{T}}(x)). \tag{2.1}$$

In Equation 2.1, $y = G_T^{-1}(p)$ denotes the inverse function of $p = G_T(y)$. Note that with discrete data, this relationship does not hold because for most x scores there is no y score for which the two cumulative distributions, one for x and one for y are exactly equal. Hence, with most applications, steps are taken to make the data appear continuous, and different steps can yield different answers.

Note that the target population T is explicit in the definition of $\text{Equi}_{YT}(x)$ (Dorans & Holland, 2000; Holland & Dorans, 2006; von Davier et al., 2004b). In general, there is nothing to prevent $\text{Equi}_{YT}(x)$ from varying with the choice of T, thereby violating Requirement 5, the subpopulation-invariance requirement, of Section 2.1.2.1. The equipercentile function is used for equating and other kinds of linking. For equating, we expect the influence of T to be small or negligible, and we call the scores *equivalent*. In other kinds of linking, T can have a substantial effect, and we call the scores *comparable in T*.

2.4.1.2 The Linear Equating Function

If Equation 2.1 is satisfied, then $\text{Equi}_{YT}(x)$ will transform the distribution of X on T so that it is the same as the distribution of Y on T.

It is sometimes appropriate to assume that the two CDFs, $F_T(x)$ and $G_T(y)$, have the same shape and only differ in their means and standard deviations. To formalize the idea of a common shape, suppose that $F_T(x)$ and $G_T(y)$ both have the form,

$$F_T(x) = K[(x - \mu_{XT})/\sigma_{XT}] \text{ and } G_T(y) = K[(y - \mu_{YT})/\sigma_{YT}], \tag{2.2}$$

where K is a CDF with mean zero and standard deviation 1.

When Equation 2.2 holds, $F_T(x)$ and $G_T(y)$ both have the shape determined by K. In this case, it can be shown that the equipercentile function is the *linear function*, $\text{Lin}_{YT}(x)$, defined as

$$\text{Lin}_{YT}(x) = \mu_{YT} + (\sigma_{YT}/\sigma_{XT})(x - \mu_{XT}). \tag{2.3}$$

The linear function also may be derived as the transformation that gives the X scores the same mean and standard deviation as the Y scores on T. Both of the linear and equipercentile functions satisfy the symmetry requirement (Requirement 3) of Section 2.1.2.1. This means that $\text{Lin}_{XT}(y) = \text{Lin}_{YT}^{-1}(x)$, and $\text{Equi}_{XT}(y) = \text{Equi}_{YT}^{-1}(x)$, i.e., equating Y to X is the inverse of the function for equating X to Y. In general, the function $\text{Equi}_{YT}(x)$ curves around the function $\text{Lin}_{YT}(x)$.

The linear function requires estimates of the means and standard deviations of X and Y scores over the target population, T. It is easy to obtain these estimates for the single-group and equivalent-groups designs described in Section 2.3 (see Angoff, 1971, or Kolen & Brennan, 2004). It is less straightforward to obtain estimates for the counterbalanced design, as noted by Holland and Dorans (2006).

2.4.2 Procedures for Equating Scores on Complete Tests When Using Common Items

The anchor test design is widely used for equating scores because its use of common items to control for differential examinee ability gives it greater operational flexibility than the approaches using common examinees. Examinees need only take one test, and the samples need not be from a common population. However, this flexibility comes with a price. First of all, the target population is less clear-cut for the NEAT design (see Section 2.3.4)—there are two populations, P and Q, and either could serve as the target population. In addition, the use of the NEAT design requires additional assumptions to allow for the missing data—X is never observed in Q and Y is never observed in P. We use the term *complete test* to indicate that everyone in P sees all items on X and that that everyone in Q sees all items on Y. Our use of the term *missing data* is restricted to data that are missing by design. The assumptions needed to make allowances for the missing data are not easily tested with the observed data, and they are often unstated. We will discuss two distinct sets of assumptions that may be used to justify the observed-score procedures that are commonly used with the NEAT design.

Braun and Holland (1982) proposed that the target population for the NEAT design, or what they called the *synthetic population*, be created by weighting P and Q. They denoted the synthetic population by $T = wP + (1 - w)Q$, by which they meant that distributions (or moments) of X or Y over T are obtained by first computing them over P and Q, separately, and then averaging them with w and $(1 - w)$ to get the distribution over T. There is considerable evidence that the choice of w has a relatively minor influence on equating results; for example, see von Davier et al. (2004b). This insensitivity to w is an example of the population-invariance requirement of Section 2.1.2.1. The definition of the synthetic population forces the user to confront the need to create distributions (or moments) for X on Q and Y in P, where there are no data. In order to do this, assumptions must be made about the missing data.

Equating methods used with the NEAT design can be classified into two major types, according to the way they use the information from the anchor. The first type of missing-data assumption commonly employed is of the *poststratification equating* (PSE) type; the second is of the *chain equating* (CE) type. Each of these types of assumptions asserts that an important distributional property that connects scores on X or Y to scores on the anchor test A is the same for any $T = wP + (1 - w)Q$, in other words, is population invariant. Our emphasis here is on the role of such assumptions for observed-score equating because that is where they are the most completely understood at this time.

The PSE types of assumptions all have the form that the conditional distribution of X given A (or of Y given A) is the same for any synthetic population, $T = wP + (1 - w)Q$. In this approach, we estimate, for each score on the anchor test, the distribution of scores on the new form and on the old form in T. We then use these estimates for equating purposes as if they had actually been observed in T. The PSE type of equating assumes that the relationship that generalizes from each equating sample to the target population is a conditional relationship. In terms of the missing data in the NEAT design, this means that conditional on the anchor test score, A, the distribution of X in Q (where it is missing) is the same as in P (where it is not missing). In the special case of an equivalent-groups design with anchor test, $P = Q$ and the PSE assumptions hold exactly. When P and Q are different, the PSE assumptions are not necessarily valid, but there are no data to contradict them.

The CE assumptions all have the form that a linking function from X to A (or from Y to A) is the same for any synthetic population, $T = wP + (1 - w)Q$. In this approach, we link the scores on the new form to scores on the anchor and then link the scores on the anchor to the scores on the old form. The "chain" formed by these two links connects the scores on the new form to those on the old form. The CE type of equating approach assumes that the linking relationship that generalizes from each equating sample to the target population is an equating relationship. It is less clear for the CE assumptions than for the PSE assumptions what is implied about the missing data in the NEAT design (Kolen & Brennan, 2004, p. 146).

In the special case of an equivalent-groups design with anchor test, $P = Q$ and the CE assumptions hold exactly. In this special situation, the corresponding methods based on either the PSE or the CE assumptions will produce identical results. When P and Q are different, the PSE assumptions and CE assumptions can result in equating functions that are different, and there are no data to allow us to contradict or help us choose between either set of assumptions.

In addition to the PSE and CE types of procedures, classical test theory may be used to derive an additional *linear observed-score* procedure for the NEAT design—the Levine observed-score equating function, $\mathrm{Lev}_{YT}(x)$ (Kolen & Brennan, 2004). $\mathrm{Lev}_{YT}(x)$ may be derived from two population-invariance assumptions that are different from those that we have considered so far and that are based on classical test theory.

2.5 Data Processing Practices

Prior to equating, several steps should be taken to improve the quality of the data. These best practices of data processing deal with sample selection, item screening, and continuizing and smoothing score distributions.

2.5.1 Sample Selection

Tests are designed with a target population in mind (defined as T throughout Section 2.4). For example, admissions tests are used to gather standardized information about candidates who plan to enter a college or university. The SAT excludes individuals who are not juniors or seniors in high school from its equating samples because they are not considered members of the target population (Liang, Dorans, & Sinharay,

2009). Consequently, junior high school students, for whom the test was not developed but who take the test, are not included in the equating sample. In addition, it is common practice to exclude individuals who may have taken the anchor test (whether internal or external) at an earlier administration. This is done to remove any potential influence of these individuals on the equating results. Examinees who perform well below chance expectation on the test are sometimes excluded, though many of these examinees already might have been excluded if they were not part of the target group. There is an issue as to whether nonnative speakers of the language in which the test is administered should also be excluded. One study by Liang et al. (2009) suggested this may not be an issue as long as the proportion of nonnative speakers does not change markedly across administrations.

Statistical outlier analysis can be used to identify those examinees whose anchor test performance is substantially different from their performance on the operational test, namely the scores are so different that both scores cannot be plausible indicators of the examinee's ability. Removing these examinees from the equating sample prevents their unlikely performance from having an undue effect on the resulting equating function.

2.5.2 Checking That Anchor Items Act Like Common Items

For both internal anchor (anchor items count towards the total score) and external anchor (items do not count towards the score) tests, the statistical properties of the common items should be evaluated to make sure they have not differentially changed from the one test administration to the other. Differential item functioning methods may be used to compare the performance of the common items with the two test administrations treated as the reference and focal groups, and the total score on the common items as the matching criterion (see Holland & Wainer, 1993, especially Chapter 3). Simple plots of item difficulty values and other statistics also may be used to detect changes in items. Internal common items are susceptible to context effects because they may be embedded within different sets of items in the two tests. Changes in widely held knowledge also may lead to changes in performance on anchor test items. For example, a hard question about a new law on a certification exam may become very easy once the law becomes part of the standard training curriculum. There are many examples of this type of "rapid aging" of test questions.

2.5.3 The Need to Continuize the Discrete Distributions of Scores

The equipercentile function defined in Section 2.5.2 can depend on how $F_T(x)$ and $G_T(y)$ are made continuous or *continuized.* Test scores are typically integers, such as number-right scores or rounded formula-scores. Because of this, the inverse function, required in Equation 2.1 of Section 2.4.1.1, is not well defined—for many values of p, there is no score, y, for which $p = G_T(y)$. This is not due to the *finiteness of real samples*, but rather to the *discreteness of real test scores*. To get around this, three methods of continuization of $F_T(x)$ and $G_T(y)$ are in current use. Holland and Dorans (2006) treated two of these methods, the linear interpolation and kernel smoothing methods, in detail. The linear equating function defined in Equation 2.3 of Section 2.4.1.2 is a third continuization method.

The first two approaches to continuization have two primary differences. First, the use of linear interpolation results in an equipercentile function that is piecewise linear and continuous. Such functions may have "kinks" that practitioners feel need to be smoothed out by a further smoothing, often called postsmoothing (Fairbank, 1987; Kolen & Brennan, 2004). In contrast, kernel smoothing results in equipercentile functions that are completely smooth (i.e., differentiable everywhere) and that do not need further postsmoothing. Second, the equipercentile functions obtained by linear interpolation always map the highest score on test form X into the highest score on test form Y and the same for the lowest scores (unlike kernel smoothing and the linear equating function). While it is sometimes desirable, in some cases the highest score on an easier test should not be mapped onto the highest score of a harder test. For more discussion of this point, see Petersen et al. (1989), Kolen and Brennan (2004), and von Davier et al. (2004b).

2.5.4 Smoothing

Irregularities in the score distributions can produce irregularities in the equipercentile equating function that do not generalize to other groups of test takers. Consequently, it is generally considered advisable to smooth the raw-score frequencies, the CDFs, or the equipercentile equating function itself (Holland & Thayer, 1987, 2000; Kolen & Jarjoura, 1987; Kolen & Brennan, 2004; von Davier et al., 2004b). The purpose of this step is to eliminate some of the sampling variability present in the raw-score frequencies, in order to produce smoother CDFs for computation of the equipercentile function.

When presmoothing data, it is important to achieve a balance between a good representation of the original data and smoothness. Smoothness reduces sampling variability, whereas a good representation of the data reduces the possibility of bias. For example, if a log-linear model is used, it needs to preserve the most important features of the data, such as means, variances and skewnesses, and any other special features. The more parameters employed in the smoothing, the better the model will represent the original data, but the less smooth the fitted model becomes.

2.6 Evaluating an Equating Function

Quality and similarity of tests to be equated, choice of data collection design, characteristics of anchor test in relation to the total tests, sample sizes and examinee characteristics, screening items, and tests for outliers and choice of analyses all involve best practices that contribute to a successful equating. First, we summarize best practices. Then we discuss challenges to the production of a quality equating and close by discussing directions for additional research.

2.6.1 Best Practices

The amount of data collected (sample size) has a substantial effect on the usefulness of the resulting equating. Because it is desirable for the statistical uncertainty associated with test equating to be much smaller than the other sources of variation in test results, it is important that the results of test equating be based on samples that are large enough to insure this.

Ideally, the data should come from a large representative sample of motivated examinees that is divided in half either randomly or randomly within strata to achieve equivalent groups. Each half is administered either the new form or the old form of a test. If timing is generous and examinees are up to the task of taking both tests, a counterbalanced design could be employed in which each half of the sample is broken into halves again and then both the new and old forms are administered to examinees in a counterbalanced order.

When an anchor test is used, the items are evaluated via differential item functioning procedures to see if they are performing in the same way in both the old- and new-form samples. The anchor test needs to be highly correlated with the total tests. All items on both tests are evaluated to see if they are performing as expected.

It is valuable to equate with several different models, including both linear and equipercentile models. In the equivalent-groups case, the equipercentile method can be compared to the linear method using the standard error of equating, which describes sampling error, and the difference that matters, an effect size that can be used to assess whether differences in equating functions have practical significance or is an artifact of rounding. Holland and Dorans (2006) described the difference that matters, the standard error of equating, and the standard error of equating difference. If the departures from linearity are less than the difference that matters and less than what would be expected due to sampling error, the linear model is often chosen on the grounds of parsimony because it was not sufficiently falsified by the data. Otherwise, the more general, less falsifiable, equipercentile model is selected. Rijmen, Qu, and von Davier (Chapter 19, this volume) provide another approach to choosing among linking functions.

In the anchor test case, it is particularly important to employ multiple models, as each model rests on different sets of assumptions. The search for a single best model that could be employed universally would be unwise data analysis (Tukey, 1963).

An equating should be checked for its reasonableness. How do we determine reasonableness? We compare the raw-to-scale conversion for the new form to those that have been obtained in the past. Is the new form conversion an outlier? Is it consistent with other difficulty information that may be available for that form and other forms that have been administered in the past? Is the performance of the group taking the new form consistent with the performance of other groups that are expected to be similar to it? For example, in testing programs with large volumes and relatively stable populations, it is reasonable to expect that the new-form sample will have a similar scale score distribution to that obtained at the same time the year before. If the test is used to certify mastery, then the pass rates should be relatively stable from year to year, though not necessarily across administrations within a year.

2.6.2 Challenges to Producing High-Quality Equatings

Large, representative, motivated samples that result from a random assignment of test forms to examinees are not always attainable. Reliability is not always as high as desired. Anchor tests may not be very reliable, especially internal anchors with few items. Anchors, especially external anchors, are not always highly related to the tests being equated. Tests are not always appropriate for the group that takes them. These issues often arise when best design and data collection practices are not followed.

2.6.2.1 Data Collection Design Issues

Some threats to sound equating are related to the choice of data collection design. The NEAT design is often used because of the greater flexibility it provides. Statistical procedures are needed to adjust for ability differences between groups when the NEAT design is used. Assumptions need to be made in order to make these adjustments. The assumptions may be flawed.

2.6.2.2 Psychometric Properties of the Tests and Anchors

Characteristics of the test to be equated affect the quality of equating. Pretesting of untried items prior to their operational use produces higher quality exams. The absence of pretesting may result in tests with fewer scorable items than planned. The resulting shorter, less reliable tests are harder to equate because a greater portion of score variability is noise and the resultant equating functions are less stable. More importantly, tests made up of unpretested items can turn out to be different in content and difficulty from the tests to which they are to be equated; these factors increase the difficulty of equating.

The role of the anchor test is to provide a common score that can be used to adjust for group ability differences before adjusting for test difficulty differences via equating. Scores from short anchor tests tend to have inadequate reliabilities and consequently less than desirable correlations with the test scores. Low correlations also may result when the content of the anchor test differs from the test. Context effects can affect the comparability of anchor items. Anchors that are too hard or too easy for the target population produce skewed score distributions that are not helpful for equating.

To disguise the anchor items in a NEAT design, the items are often embedded within sections of scored operational items. Internal anchors or common items may not be located in the same item positions within the old and new forms, making them more susceptible to context effects that may diminish their utility as measures of ability. In addition, the common items may be few in number, making the anchor test relatively unreliable and less useful for identifying differences in ability between the samples.

2.6.2.3 Samples

Unrepresentative or unmotivated samples undermine equating. Special care should be taken to ensure that only members of the population of interest are included in the samples. If possible, the sample should be representative of the population as well.

With the NEAT design, the old- and new-form samples may perform very differently on the anchor test. Large ability differences on the anchor test tend to yield situations where equating is unsatisfactory unless the anchor is highly related to both tests to be equated. In this setting, different equating methods tend to give different answers unless the anchor test is strongly related to both the old and new tests. This divergence of results is indicative of a poor data collection design.

Equating cannot be done effectively in small samples. The smaller the sample size, the more restricted is the class of stable equating methods. Smoothing score distributions works in moderately sized samples but does not help much with very small samples, especially when it is not clear how representative the sample is of the intended population. In these situations, one option may be to make strong assumptions about the equating function (Livingston & Kim, Chapter 7, this volume). For example, it may be necessary to assume the identity is a reasonable approximation to the equating function or that the identity shifted by a constant that is estimated by the data provides a reasonable approximation.

The best practices solution to the small sample size problem may be to report raw scores and state that they cannot be compared across test forms. If the sample size suggested by consideration of standard errors is not achieved, raw scores could be reported with the caveat that they are not comparable to other scores, but that they could be made comparable when adequate data become available. This would protect testing organizations from challenges resulting from the use of either biased linking functions or unstable equating functions. To do otherwise might be problematic over the long term.

2.6.2.4 Lack of Population Invariance

One of the most basic requirements of score equating is that equating functions, to the extent possible, should be subpopulation invariant.[2] The "same construct" and "equal reliability" requirements are prerequisites for subpopulation invariance. One way to demonstrate that two tests are not equatable is to show that the equating functions used to link their scores are not invariant across different subpopulations of examinees. Lack of invariance in a linking function indicates that the differential difficulty of the two tests is not consistent across different groups. Note that subpopulation invariance is a matter of degree. In the situations where equating is usually performed, subpopulation invariance implies that the dependence of the equating function on the subpopulation used to compute it is small enough to be ignored.

Score equity assessment focuses on whether or not test scores on different forms that are expected to be used interchangeably are in fact interchangeable across different subpopulations (Dorans & Liu, 2009). The subpopulation invariance of linking functions is used across important subgroups (e.g., gender groups) to assess the degree of score exchangeability. Score equity assessment focuses on invariance at the reported score level. It is a basic quality control tool that can be used to assess whether a test construction process is under control, as can checks on the consistency of raw-to-scale conversions across forms (Haberman et al., 2008).

2.6.3 Additional Directions for Future Research

There is a need for comprehensive empirical investigations of equating conditions as well as additional theoretical work that can further inform the best practices described in this chapter. The various challenges discussed in previous portions of this section should be explored via systematic investigations of the appropriateness of different equating procedures in a variety of realistic settings. These empirical investigations have their progenitors, such as the comprehensive studies conducted by Marco, Petersen, and Stewart (1983a) as well as other studies cited in Kolen and Brennan (2004). Recent work by Sinharay and Holland (2010) is indicative of the kind of work that can be done to better understand the robustness of various procedures to violation of their assumptions (See also Sinharay, Holland, & von Davier, Chapter 17, this volume.)

Foremost among factors that need to be studied are the effects on equating results of the magnitude of ability differences between P and Q as measured by the anchor items and of the shape of the score distributions. In addition, it would be

[2]Note that these subpopulations should not be defined on the basis of the tests to be equated or the anchor test, because the assumptions made by equating methods are sensitive to direct selection on the test or anchor, as demonstrated by Wright and Dorans (1993).

worthwhile to manipulate difficulty differences between X, Y and A as well as the reliability of the total score and the anchor score, expanding on investigations such as Moses and Kim (2007). Correlations of the anchor score with total score and sample size should also be manipulated and studied. Ideally, real data would be used as the starting point for these studies.

Another area that needs attention is the consistency of equating results over long periods of time, a point made by Brennan (2007) and studied recently on the SAT® by Haberman et al. (2008). These researchers examined the consistency of SAT Math and SAT Verbal equatings between 1995 and 2005 and found them to be very stable. This type of work is especially important in settings where tests are administered on an almost continuous basis (Li, Li, & von Davier, Chapter 20, this volume). In these settings, substantial score drift may occur such that scores may not be comparable across periods as short as one year. The quest to test continuously may subvert one of the basic goals of fair assessment.

Several new methods for equating as well as some new definitions have been and will be introduced. These methods should be stress tested and adapted before they are adopted for use. Procedures that make strong assumptions about the data may give answers that are theoretically pleasing but are difficult to apply in practice and even more difficult to justify to test users. Holland (1994) noted that tests are both measurements and contests. They are contests in the sense that examinees expect to be treated fairly—equal scores for comparable performance. Equating, as discussed by Dorans (2008), can be thought of as a means of ensuring fair contests: An emphasis needs to be placed on fair and equitable treatment of examinees that is commensurate with their actual performance on the test they took. The use of best practices in equating is essential to achieving this goal.

The focus of this chapter has been on best practices for score equating. Score equating is only one aspect of the score reporting process. Other components of the score reporting process affect the final raw-to-scale conversions. Because these components are not as amenable to mathematical treatment as score equating methods, they have not received as much treatment as they should. The best score equating practices can be undermined by a weakness elsewhere in the process, such as poorly defined test specifications or the use of a flawed old-form scaling function. A few of these non-score-equating components have been mentioned in this report, but the treatment has not been as complete as it should be.

Author Note: Any opinions expressed in this chapter are those of the authors and not necessarily of Educational Testing Service.

Chapter 3
Scoring and Scaling Educational Tests

Michael J. Kolen, Ye Tong, and Robert L. Brennan

The numbers that are associated with examinee performance on educational or psychological tests are defined through the process of *scaling*. This process produces a *score scale*, and the scores that are reported to examinees are referred to as *scale scores*. Kolen (2006) referred to the term *primary score scale*, which is the focus of this chapter, as the scale that is used to underlie psychometric properties for tests.

A key component in the process of developing a score scale is the *raw score* for an examinee on a test, which is a function of the *item scores* for that examinee. Raw scores can be as simple as a sum of the item scores or be so complicated that they depend on the entire pattern of item responses.

Raw scores are transformed to scale scores to facilitate the meaning of scores for test users. For example, raw scores might be transformed to scale scores so that they have predefined distributional properties for a particular group of examinees, referred to as a *norm group*. Normative information might be incorporated by constructing scale scores to be approximately normally distributed with a mean of 50 and a standard deviation of 10 for a national population of examinees. In addition, procedures can be used for incorporating content and score precision information into score scales.

The purpose of this chapter is to describe methods for developing score scales for educational and psychological tests. Different types of raw scores are considered along with models for transforming raw scores to scale scores. Both traditional and item response theory (IRT) methods are considered. The focus of this chapter is

M.J. Kolen (✉)
University of Iowa, 224 B1 Lindquist Center, Iowa City, IA 52242, USA
e-mail: michael-kolen@uiowa.edu

Y. Tong
Pearson, 2510 North Dodge Street, Iowa City, IA 52245, USA
e-mail: ye.tong@pearson.com

R.L. Brennan
University of Iowa, 210D Lindquist Center, Iowa City, IA 52242, USA
e-mail: robert-brennan@uiowa.edu

A.A. von Davier (ed.), *Statistical Models for Test Equating, Scaling, and Linking*, Statistics for Social and Behavioral Sciences,
DOI 10.1007/978-0-387-98138-3_3,

on fixed tests, rather than on computer-adaptive tests (Drasgow, Luecht, & Bennett, 2006), although many of the issues considered apply to both.

3.1 Unit and Item Scores

Kolen (2006) distinguished unit scores from item scores. A *unit score* is the score on the smallest unit on which a score is found, which is referred to as a *scoreable* unit. An item score is a score over all scoreable units for an item.

For multiple-choice test questions that are scored right-wrong, unit scores and item scores often are the same. Such scores are either incorrect (0) or correct (1). Unit and item scores are often distinguishable when judges score the item responses. As an example, consider an essay item that is scored 1 (*low*) through 5 (*high*) by each of two judges, with the item score being the sum of scores over the two judges. In this situation, there is a unit score for Judge 1 (range 1 to 5), a unit score for Judge 2 (range 1 to 5), and an item score over the two judges (range 2 to 10).

Or, consider a situation in which a block of five questions is associated with a reading passage. If a test developer is using IRT and is concerned that there might be conditional dependencies among responses to questions associated with a reading passage, the developer might treat the questions associated with passage as a single item, with scores on this item being the number of questions associated with the passage that the examinee answers correctly. In this case, each question would have a unit score of 0 or 1, and the item score would range from 0 to 5. According to Kolen (2006), "The characteristic that most readily distinguishes unit scores from item scores is... whereas there may be operational dependencies among unit scores, item scores are considered operationally independent" (p. 157).

Let V_i be a random variable indicating score on item i and v_i be a particular score. For a dichotomously scored item, $v_i = 0$ when an examinee incorrectly answers the item and $v_i = 1$ when an examinee correctly answers the item.

Consider the essay item described earlier. For this item, $V_i = 2, 3, \ldots, 10$ represent the possible scores for this item. In this chapter, it is assumed that when polytomously scored items are used, they are ordered response item scores represented by consecutive integers. Higher item scores represent more proficient performance on the item.

Item types exist where responses are not necessarily ordered, such as nominal response scoring. Such item types are not considered in this chapter.

3.2 Traditional Raw Scores

Let X refer to the raw score on a test. The *summed score*, X, is defined as

$$X = \sum_{i=1}^{n} V_i, \tag{3.1}$$

where n is the number of items on the test. Equation 3.1 is often used as a raw score when all of the items on a test are of the same format.

The *weighted summed score*, X_w,

$$X_w = \sum_{i=1}^{n} w_i V_i, \tag{3.2}$$

uses weights, w_i, to weight the item score for each item. Various procedures for choosing weights include choosing weights that maximize score reliability and choosing weights so that each item contributes a desired amount to the raw score.

3.3 Traditional Scale Scores

Raw scores such as those in Equations 3.1 and 3.2 have limitations as primary score scales for tests. *Alternate* test *forms* are test forms that are built to a common set of content and statistical specifications. With alternate test forms, the raw scores typically do not have a consistent meaning across forms. For this reason, scores other than raw scores are used as primary score scales, whenever alternate forms of a test exist. The primary score scale typically is developed with an initial form of the test, and test equating methods (Holland & Dorans, 2006; Kolen & Brennan, 2004) are used to link raw scores on new forms to the score scale.

The raw score is transformed to a scale score. For summed scores, the scale score, S_X, is a function of the summed score, X, such that $S_X = S_X(X)$. This transformation often is provided in tabular form. For weighted summed scores, the scale score, S_{wX}, is a function of the weighted summed score, X_w, such that $S_{wX} = S_{wX}(X_w)$. For weighted summed scores, there are often many possible scale scores, so a continuous function may be used. In either case, scale scores are typically rounded to integers for score reporting purposes.

Linear or nonlinear transformations of raw scores are used to produce scale scores that can be meaningfully interpreted. Normative, score precision, and content information can be incorporated. Transformations that can be used to incorporate each of these types of meaning are considered next.

3.3.1 Incorporating Normative Information

Incorporating normative information begins with the administration of the test to a norm group. Statistical characteristics of the scale score distribution are set relative to this norm group. The scale scores are meaningful to the extent that the norm group is central to score interpretation.

For example, a third-grade reading test might be administered to a national norm group intended to be representative of third graders in the nation. The mean and standard deviation of scale scores on the test might be set to particular values for this norm group. By knowing the mean and standard deviation of scale scores, test users would be able to quickly ascertain, for example, whether a particular student's score was above the mean. This information would be relevant to the extent that scores for the norm group are central to score interpretation. Kolen (2006, pp. 163–164) provided equations for linearly transforming raw scores to scale scores with a particular mean and standard deviation.

Nonlinear transformations also are used to develop score scales. Normalized scores involve one such transformation. To normalize scores, percentile ranks of raw scores are found and then transformed using an inverse normal transformation. These normalized scores are then transformed to have a desired mean and standard deviation. Normalized scale scores can be used to quickly ascertain the percentile rank of a particular student's score using facts about the normal distribution. For example, with normalized scores, a score that is one standard deviation above the mean has a percentile rank of approximately 84. Kolen (2006, pp. 164–165) provided a detailed description of the process of score normalization.

Scale scores typically are reported to examinees as integer scores. For example, McCall (1939) suggested using T scores, which are scale scores that are normalized with an approximate mean of 50 and standard deviation of 10, with the scores rounded to integers. Intelligence test scores typically are normalized scores with a mean of 100 and a standard deviation of 15 or 16 in a national norm group (Angoff, 1971/1984, p. 525–526), with the scores rounded to integers.

3.3.2 Incorporating Score Precision Information

According to Flanagan (1951), scale score units should "be of an order of magnitude most appropriate to express their accuracy of measurement" (p. 246). Flanagan indicated that the use of too few score points fails to "preserve all of the information contained in raw scores" (p. 247). However, the use of too many scale score points might lead test users to attach significance to scale score differences that are predominantly due to measurement error.

Based on these considerations, rules of thumb have been developed to help choose the number of distinct score points to use for a scale. For example, the scale for the Iowa Tests of Educational Development (ITED, 1958) was constructed so that an approximate 50% confidence interval for true scores could be found by adding 1 scale score point to and subtracting 1 scale score point from an examinee's scale score. Similarly, Truman L. Kelley (W. H. Angoff, personal communication, February 17, 1987) suggested constructing scale scores so that an approximate 68% confidence interval could be constructed by adding 3 scale score points to and subtracting 3 scale score points from each examinee's scale score.

Kolen and Brennan (2004, pp. 346–347) showed that by making suitable assumptions, the approximate range of scale scores that produces the desired score scale property is

$$6\frac{h}{z_\gamma\sqrt{1-\rho_{XX'}}}, \tag{3.3}$$

where h is the width of the desired confidence interval (1 for the ITED rule, 3 for the Kelley rule), z_γ is the unit-normal score associated with the confidence coefficient γ ($z_\gamma \approx .6745$ for the ITED rule and $z_\gamma \approx 1$ for the Kelley rule), and $\rho_{XX'}$ is test reliability.The result from Equation 3.3 is rounded to an integer. As an example, assume that test reliability is .91. Then for the ITED rule, Equation 3.3 indicates that 30 distinct scale score points should be used, and Kelley's rule indicates that 60 distinct score points should be used.

Noting that conditional measurement error variability is typically unequal along the score scale, Kolen (1988) suggested using a variance stabilizing transformation to equalize error variability. Kolen (1988) argued that when scores are transformed in this way, a single standard error of measurement could be used when reporting measurement error variability. He used the following arcsine transformation suggested by Freeman and Tukey (1950):

$$g(X) = .5\left\{ \sin^{-1}\left[\left(\frac{X}{n+1}\right)\right]^{\frac{1}{2}} + \sin^{-1}\left[\left(\frac{X+1}{n+1}\right)\right]^{\frac{1}{2}} \right\}. \tag{3.4}$$

Scores transformed using Equation 3.4 are then transformed to have a desired mean and standard deviation and to have a reasonable number of distinct integer score points. Kolen, Hanson, and Brennan (1992) found that this transformation adequately stabilized error variance for tests with dichotomously scored items. Ban and Lee (2007) found a similar property for tests with polytomously scored items.

3.3.3 Incorporating Content Information

Ebel (1962) stated, "To be meaningful any test scores must be related to test content as well as to the scores of other examinees" (p. 18). Recently, focus has been on providing content meaningful scale scores.

One such procedure, *item mapping*, was reviewed by Zwick, Senturk, Wang, and Loomis (2001). In item mapping, test items are associated with various scale score points. For dichotomously scored items, the probability of correct response on each item is regressed on scale score. The *response probability* (RP) level is defined as the probability (expressed as a percentage) of correct response on a test-item given scale score that is associated with mastery, proficiency, or some other category as defined by the test developer. The same RP level is used for all dichotomously scored items on the test. Using regressions of item score on scale score, an item is said to map at the scale score associated with an RP of correctly answering the item. RP values typically range from .5 to .8. Additional criteria are often used when choosing items to report on an item map, such as item discrimination and test developer judgment. Modifications of the procedures are used with polytomously scored items.The outcome of an item mapping procedure is a map illustrating which items correspond to each of an ordered set of scale scores.

Another way to incorporate content information is to use *scale anchoring*. The first step in scale anchoring is to develop an item map. Then, a set of scale score points is chosen, such as a selected set of percentiles. Subject-matter experts review the items that map near each of the selected points and develop general statements that represent the skills of the examinees scoring at each point. See Allen, Carlson, and Zelenak (1999) for an example of scale anchoring with the National Assessment of Educational Progress and ACT (2001) for an example of scale anchoring as used with the ACT Standards for Transition.

Standard setting procedures, as recently reviewed by Hambleton and Pitoniak (2006), begin with a statement about what competent examinees know and are able to do. Structured judgmental processes are used to find the scale score point that differentiates candidates who are minimally competent from those who are less than minimally competent. In achievement testing situations, various achievement levels are often stated, such as basic, proficient, and advanced. Judgmental standard-setting techniques are used to find the scale score points that differentiate between adjacent levels.

3.3.4 Using Equating to Maintain Score Scales

Equating methods (Holland & Dorans, 2006; Kolen & Brennan, 2004) are used to maintain scale scores as new forms are developed. For equating to be possible, the new forms must be developed to the same content and statistical specifications as the form used for scale construction. With traditional scaling and equating methodology, a major goal is to transform raw scores to scale scores on new test forms so that the distribution of scale scores is the same in a population of examinees.

3.4 IRT Proficiency Estimates

Traditional methods focus on scores that are observed rather than on true scores or IRT proficiencies. Procedures for using psychometric methods to help evaluate scale scores with traditional methods exist and are described in a later section of this chapter. First, scale scores based on IRT (Thissen & Wainer, 2001) are considered.

The development of IRT scaling methods depends on the use of an IRT model. In this section, IRT models are considered in which examinee proficiency, θ, is assumed to be unidimensional. A *local independence assumption* also is required, in which, conditional on proficiency, examinee responses are assumed to be independent. The focus of the IRT methods in this section is on polytomously scored items. Note, however, that dichotomously scored items can be viewed as polytomously scored items with two response categories (wrong and right).

A curve is fit for each possible response to an item that relates probability of that response given proficiency that is symbolized as $P(V_i = v_i|\theta)$ and is referred to as the *category response function*. IRT models considered here have the responses ordered a priori, where responses associated with higher scores are indicative of greater proficiency. Popular models for tests containing dichotomously scored items are the Rasch, two-parameter logistic, and three-parameter logistic models. Popular models for tests containing polytomously scored items are the graded-response model, partial-credit model, and generalized partial-credit model. Nonparametric models also exist. See Yen and Fitzpatrick (2006) and van der Linden and Hambleton (1997) for reviews of many of these models.

In IRT, the category response functions are estimated for each item. Then, proficiency is estimated for each examinee. In this chapter, initial focus is on IRT proficiency estimation. Later, the focus is on the transformed (often linearly, but sometimes nonlinearly) proficiencies typically used when developing scale scores. For this reason, IRT proficiency estimates can be thought of as raw scores that are subsequently transformed to scale scores.

Estimates of IRT proficiency can be based on summed scores (Equation 3.1), weighted summed scores (Equation 3.2), or on *complicated scoring functions* that can be symbolized as

$$X_c = f(V_1, V_2, \ldots, V_n), \tag{3.5}$$

where f is the function used to convert item scores to total score. Some models, such as the Rasch model, consider only summed scores. With other models, the psychometrician can choose which scoring function to use. Procedures for estimating IRT proficiency are described next.

3.4.1 IRT Maximum Likelihood Scoring

IRT maximum likelihood scoring requires the use of a complicated scoring function for many IRT models. Under the assumption of local independence, θ is found that maximizes the likelihood equation,

$$L = \prod_{i=1}^{n} p(V_i = v_i|\theta), \tag{3.6}$$

and it is symbolized as $\hat{\theta}_{MLE}$.

3.4.2 IRT With Summed Scores Using the Test Characteristic Function

In IRT it is possible to estimate proficiency as a function of summed scores or weighted summed scores. Assume that item i is scored in m_i ordered categories, where the categories are indexed $k = 1, 2, \ldots, m_i$. Defining W_{ik} as the score associated with item i and category k, the *item response function* for item i is defined as

$$\tau_i(\theta) = \sum_{k=1}^{m_i} W_{ik} \cdot P(V_i = k|\theta), \tag{3.7}$$

which represents the expected score on item i for an examinee of proficiency θ. For IRT models with ordered responses, it is assumed that $\tau_i(\theta)$ is monotonic increasing.

The *test characteristic function* is defined as the sum, over test items, of the item response functions such that

$$\tau(\theta) = \sum_{i=1}^{n} \tau_i(\theta), \tag{3.8}$$

which represents the true score for an examinee of proficiency θ. This function is also monotonic increasing.

A weighted test characteristic function also can be defined as

$$\tau_w(\theta) = \sum_{i=1}^{n} w_i \tau_i(\theta), \tag{3.9}$$

where the w_i are positive-valued weights that are applied to each of the items when forming a total score.

An estimate of proficiency, based on a summed score for an examinee, can be found by substituting the summed score for $\tau(\theta)$ in Equation 3.8 and then solving for θ using numerical methods. Similarly, proficiency can be estimated for weighted sum scores. The resulting estimate using Equation 3.8 is referred to as $\hat{\theta}_{TCF}$ and is monotonically related to the summed score. The resulting estimate using Equation 3.9 is referred to as $\hat{\theta}_{wTCF}$ and is monotonically related to the weighted summed score.

3.4.3 IRT Bayesian Scoring With Complicated Scoring Functions

IRT Bayesian estimates of proficiency can make use of a complicated scoring function. In addition, they require specification of the distribution of proficiency in the population, $g(\theta)$. The Bayesian modal estimator is the θ that maximizes

$$L \cdot g(\theta) = \prod_{i=1}^{n} P(V_i = v_i|\theta) \cdot g(\theta) \tag{3.10}$$

and is symbolized as $\hat{\theta}_{BME}$. The Bayesian expected a posteriori (EAP) estimator is the mean of the posterior distribution and is calculated as

$$\begin{aligned}\hat{\theta}_{EAP} &= E(\theta|V_1 = v_1, V_2 = v_2, \ldots, V_n = v_n) \\ &= \frac{\int_\theta \theta \prod_{i=1}^{n} P(V_i = v_i|\theta) g(\theta) d\theta}{\int_\theta \prod_{i=1}^{n} P(V_i = v_i|\theta) g(\theta) d\theta} .\end{aligned} \tag{3.11}$$

3.4.4 Bayesian Scoring Using Summed Scores

A Bayesian EAP estimate of proficiency based on the summed score is

$$\begin{aligned}\hat{\theta}_{sEAP} &= E(\theta|X) \\ &= \frac{\int_\theta \theta \cdot P(X = x|\theta) \cdot g(\theta) d\theta}{\int_\theta P(X = x|\theta) \cdot g(\theta) d\theta} .\end{aligned} \tag{3.12}$$

The term $P(X = x|\theta)$ represents the probability of earning a particular summed score given proficiency and can be calculated from item parameter estimates using a recursive algorithm provided by Thissen, Pommerich, Billeaud, and Williams (1995) and illustrated by Kolen and Brennan (2004, pp. 219-221), which is a generalization of a recursive algorithm developed by Lord and Wingersky (1984).

Concerned that the estimate in Equation 3.12 treats score points on different item types as being equal, Rosa, Swygert, Nelson, and Thissen (2001) presented an alternative Bayesian EAP estimator. For this alternative, define X_1 as the summed score on the first item type and X_2 as summed score on the second item type. The EAP is the expected proficiency given scores on each item type and is

$$\begin{aligned}\hat{\theta}_{s2EAP} &= E(\theta|X_1, X_2) \\ &= \frac{\int_\theta \theta \cdot P(X_1 = x_1|\theta) \cdot P(X_2 = x_2|\theta) \cdot g(\theta) d\theta}{\int_\theta P(X_1 = x_1|\theta) \cdot P(X_2 = x_2|\theta) \cdot g(\theta) d\theta} ,\end{aligned} \tag{3.13}$$

where $P(X_1 = x_1|\theta)$ and $P(X_2 = x_2|\theta)$ are calculated using the recursive algorithm provided by Thissen et al. (1995). Note that this estimate is, in general, different for examinees with different combinations of scores on the two item types. Rosa et al. (2001) presented results for this method in a two-dimensional scoring table, with summed scores on one item type represented by the rows and summed scores on the other item type represented by the columns. Rosa et al. indicated that this method can be generalized to tests with more than two item types. Thissen, Nelson, and Swygert (2001) provided an approximate method in which the EAP is estimated separately for each item type and then a weighted average is formed. Bayesian EAP estimates have yet to be developed based on the weighted summed scores defined in Equation 3.2.

3.4.5 Statistical Properties of Estimates of IRT Proficiency

The maximum likelihood estimator $\hat{\theta}_{MLE}$ and test characteristic function estimators $\hat{\theta}_{TCF}$ and $\hat{\theta}_{wTCF}$ do not depend on the distribution of proficiency in the population, $g(\theta)$. All of the Bayesian estimators depend on $g(\theta)$.

$\hat{\theta}_{MLE}$, $\hat{\theta}_{TCF}$, and $\hat{\theta}_{wTCF}$ do not exist (are infinite) for examinees whose item score is the lowest possible score on all of the items. In addition, these estimators do not exist for examinees whose item score is the highest possible score on all of the items. Other extreme response patterns exist for which $\hat{\theta}_{MLE}$ does not exist. Also, for models with a lower asymptote item parameter, like the three-parameter logistic model, $\hat{\theta}_{TCF}$ does not exist for summed scores that are below the sum, over items, of the lower asymptote parameters. A similar issue is of concern for $\hat{\theta}_{wTCF}$. In practice, ad hoc rules are used to assign proficiency estimates for these response patterns or summed scores. The Bayesian estimators typically exist in these situations, which is a benefit of these estimators.

The maximum likelihood estimator of proficiency, $\hat{\theta}_{MLE}$, is consistent (Lord, 1980, p. 59), meaning that it converges to θ as the number of items becomes large. Thus,

$$E(\hat{\theta}_{MLE}|\theta) \approx \theta. \tag{3.14}$$

Note also that $E(X|\theta) = \tau(\theta) = \sum_{i=1}^{n} \tau_i(\theta)$, which means that the summed score X is an unbiased estimate of true summed score τ. This suggests that $E(\hat{\theta}_{TCF}|\theta)$ is close to θ.

The Bayesian estimators are shrinkage estimators intended to be biased when a test is less than perfectly reliable. So for most values of θ,

$$E(\hat{\theta}_{EAP}|\theta) \neq \theta. \tag{3.15}$$

Defining μ_θ as the mean of the distribution of proficiency,

$$\begin{aligned}&\text{If } \theta < \mu_\theta, \text{ then } E(\hat{\theta}_{EAP}|\theta) > \theta\\ &\text{If } \theta > \mu_\theta, \text{ then } E(\hat{\theta}_{EAP}|\theta) < \theta.\end{aligned} \tag{3.16}$$

Similar relationships hold for the other Bayesian estimators.

Test information is a central concept in IRT when considering conditional error variability in estimating IRT proficiency. Conditional error variance in estimating proficiency in IRT using maximum likelihood is equal to 1 divided by test information. Expressions for conditional error variances of the maximum likelihood estimators, $\text{var}(\hat{\theta}_{MLE}|\theta)$, and for the test characteristic function estimators, $\text{var}(\hat{\theta}_{TCF}|\theta)$ and $\text{var}(\hat{\theta}_{wTCF}|\theta)$, for dichotomous models have been provided by Lord (1980) and for polytomous models by Muraki (1993), Samejima (1969), and Yen and Fitzpatrick (2006). Note that the square root of the conditional error variance is the *conditional standard error of measurement* for estimating IRT proficiency.

An expression for the conditional error variance for Bayesian EAP estimators was provided by Thissen and Orlando (2001) and is as follows for $\hat{\theta}_{EAP}$:

$$\begin{aligned}&\text{var}(\hat{\theta}_{EAP}|V_1 = v_1, V_2 = v_2, \ldots, V_n = v_n)\\ &= \frac{\int_\theta (\hat{\theta}_{EAP} - \theta)^2 \prod_{i=1}^{n} P(V_i = v_i|\theta)g(\theta)d\theta}{\int_\theta \prod_{i=1}^{n} P(V_i = v_i|\theta)g(\theta)d\theta}.\end{aligned} \tag{3.17}$$

Similar expressions can be used for $\hat{\theta}_{sEAP}$.

Note that the Bayesian conditional variances are conditional on examinee response patterns, which is typical for Bayesian estimators, rather than on θ, as is the case with the maximum likelihood and test characteristic function estimators. This observation highlights a crucial difference in the meaning of conditional error variances for Bayesian and maximum likelihood estimates of proficiency.

The following relationship is expected to hold:

$$\text{var}(\hat{\theta}_{TCF}|\theta) \geq \text{var}(\hat{\theta}_{MLE}|\theta) \geq \text{var}(\hat{\theta}_{EAP}|\theta). \tag{3.18}$$

Note that $\text{var}(\hat{\theta}_{TCF}|\theta) \geq \text{var}(\hat{\theta}_{MLE}|\theta)$ because $\hat{\theta}_{TCF}$ is based on summed scores, which leads to a loss of information as compared to $\hat{\theta}_{MLE}$. Also, $\text{var}(\hat{\theta}_{MLE}|\theta) \geq \text{var}(\hat{\theta}_{EAP}|\theta)$, because Bayesian estimators are shrinkage estimators that generally have smaller error variances than maximum likelihood estimators. However, the Bayesian estimators are biased, which could cause the conditional mean-squared error for $\hat{\theta}_{EAP}$, defined as $MSE(\hat{\theta}_{EAP}|\theta) = E[(\hat{\theta}_{EAP} - \theta)|\theta]^2$, to be greater than the mean-squared error for $\hat{\theta}_{MLE}$. Note that conditional mean-squared error takes into account both error variance and bias. In addition it is expected that

$$\mathrm{var}(\hat{\theta}_{EAP}|\theta) \geq \mathrm{var}(\hat{\theta}_{sEAP}|\theta), \tag{3.19}$$

because there is less error involved with pattern scores than summed scores, resulting in less shrinkage with $\hat{\theta}_{EAP}$ than with $\hat{\theta}_{sEAP}$.

The relationships between conditional variances have implications for the marginal variances. In particular, the following relationship is expected to hold if the distribution of θ is well specified:

$$\mathrm{var}(\hat{\theta}_{TCF}) \geq \mathrm{var}(\hat{\theta}_{MLE}) \geq \mathrm{var}(\hat{\theta}_{EAP}) \geq (\hat{\theta}_{sEAP}). \tag{3.20}$$

As illustrated in the next section, the inequalities can have practical implications.

3.4.6 Example: Effects of Different Marginal Distributions on Percentage Proficient

Suppose there are four performance levels (Levels I through IV) for a state assessment program. Based on a standard setting study, cut scores on the θ scale are -0.8 for Level I-II, 0.2 for Level II-III and 1.3 for Level III-IV. As illustrated in this section, the choice of proficiency estimator can have a substantial effect on the percentage of students classified at each of the performance levels.

In this hypothetical example, the scaling data for Grade 7 of the Vocabulary test of the Iowa Tests of Basic Skills were used. The test contains 41 multiple-choice items. For more information on the dataset used, see Tong and Kolen (2007). For each student in the dataset ($N = 1{,}199$), $\hat{\theta}_{MLE}$, $\hat{\theta}_{EAP}$, $\hat{\theta}_{sEAP}$, and $\hat{\theta}_{TCF}$ were computed based on the same set of item parameter estimates. Table 3.1 shows the mean and standard deviation (*SD*) of the proficiency estimates for all the students included in the example. Figure 3.1 shows the cumulative frequency distribution of the proficiency estimates for these students. The variabilities of these estimators are ordered, as expected based on Equation 3.20, as

$$SD(\hat{\theta}_{sEAP}) < SD(\hat{\theta}_{EAP}) < SD(\hat{\theta}_{MLE}) < SD(\hat{\theta}_{TCF}).$$

Table 3.1 Example: Effects of IRT Proficiency Estimator on Percent in Proficiency Level

Proficiency estimator	*M*	*SD*	Percentage proficiency by level			
			I	II	III	IV
$\hat{\theta}_{MLE}$	0.012	1.143	20.77	35.95	32.53	10.76
$\hat{\theta}_{EAP}$	−0.002	0.949	19.27	38.70	33.86	8.17
$\hat{\theta}_{sEAP}$	0.000	0.933	19.43	36.53	37.20	6.84
$\hat{\theta}_{TCF}$	−0.003	1.164	22.02	33.94	33.53	10.51

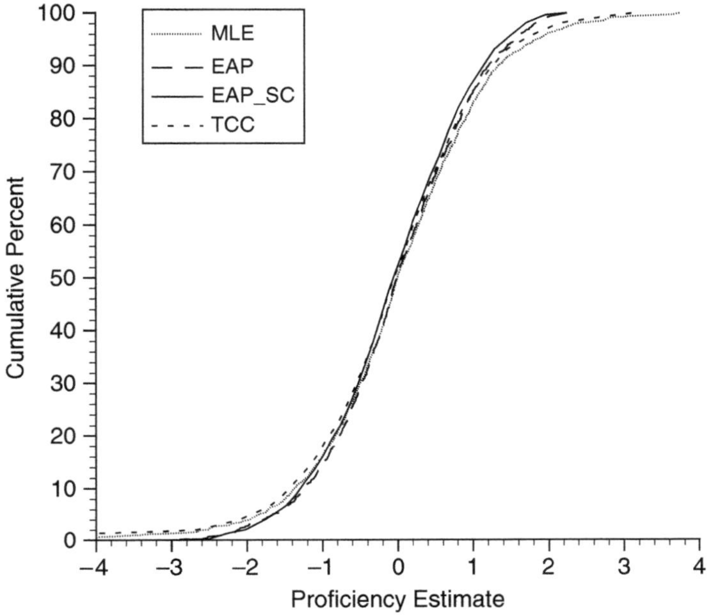

Fig 3.1 Cumulative distributions for various proficiency estimators

From Figure 3.1, the cumulative distributions for $\hat{\theta}_{EAP}$ and $\hat{\theta}_{sEAP}$ are similar to one other and the cumulative distributions for $\hat{\theta}_{TCF}$ and $\hat{\theta}_{MLE}$ are similar to one other.

Using the θ cut scores from standard setting, students were classified into each of the four performance levels using the four proficiency estimates. The percentage in each level for each of the estimators is reported in Table 3.1. As can be observed, $\hat{\theta}_{MLE}$ and $\hat{\theta}_{TCF}$ tend to produce larger percentages of students in Levels I and IV, consistent with the observation that these estimators have relatively larger variability. Of the 1,199 students in the data, 31 students (about 13%) had different performance-level classifications using different proficiency estimators. The differences were within one performance level. These results illustrate that, in practice, the choice of IRT proficiency estimator can affect the proficiency level reported for a student.

3.5 IRT Scale Scores

IRT scale scores often are developed by linearly transforming IRT proficiencies and then rounding to integers. When a linear transformation is used, the estimators and their statistical properties can be found directly based on the linear transformation. Sometimes IRT scale scores are transformed nonlinearly to scale scores. Lord (1980, pp. 84–88) argued that a nonlinear transformation of θ could be preferable to θ.

Define h as a continuous monotonically increasing function of proficiency, such that

$$\theta^* = h(\theta). \tag{3.21}$$

Lord (1980, pp. 187–188) showed that the maximum likelihood estimator for a nonlinear transformed proficiency could be found by applying the nonlinear transformation to the maximum likelihood estimator parameter estimate. That is, he showed that

$$\hat{\theta}^*_{MLE} = h(\hat{\theta}_{MLE}). \tag{3.22}$$

Estimates based on the test characteristic function are found by a similar substitution. Lord (1980, pp. 187–188) also showed that Bayesian estimators do not possess this property. Thus, for example,

$$\hat{\theta}^*_{EAP} \neq h(\hat{\theta}_{EAP}). \tag{3.23}$$

To find $\hat{\theta}^*_{EAP}$ would require computing the estimate using Equation 3.11 after substituting θ^* for each occurrence of θ.

One nonlinear transformation that is often used is the *domain score* (Bock, Thissen, & Zimowski, 1997; Pommerich, Nicewander, & Hanson, 1999), which is calculated as follows:

$$\theta^*_{domain} = \frac{1}{n_{domain}} \sum_{i=1}^{n_{domain}} \tau_i(\theta), \tag{3.24}$$

where $\tau_i(\theta)$ is defined in Equation 3.7, and the summation is over all n_{domain} items in the domain, where the domain is a large number of items intended to reflect the content that is being assessed. Substituting $\hat{\theta}_{MLE}$ for θ in Equation 3.24 produces the maximum likelihood estimator of θ^*_{domain}. However, substituting $\hat{\theta}_{EAP}$ for θ in Equation 3.24 does *not* produce a Bayesian EAP estimator of θ^*_{domain}.

3.6 Multidimensional IRT Raw Scores for Mixed Format Tests

In applying IRT with mixed item types, an initial decision that is made is whether or not a single dimension can be used to describe performance. Rodriguez (2003) reviewed the construct equivalence of multiple-choice and constructed-response items. He concluded that these item types typically measure different constructs, although in certain circumstances the constructs are very similar. Wainer and Thissen (1993) argued that the constructs often are similar enough that the mixed item types can be reasonably analyzed with a unidimensional model. If a test developer decides that a multidimensional model is required, it is sometimes possible to analyze each item type using a unidimensional model. IRT proficiency can be estimated separately for each item type, and then a weighted composite of the two proficiencies computed as an overall estimate of proficiency. This sort of procedure was used, for example, with the National Assessment of Educational Progress Science Assessment (Allen et al., 1999).

3.7 Psychometric Properties of Scale Scores

Psychometric properties of scale scores include (a) the expected (true) scale score, (b) the conditional error variance of scale scores, and (c) the reliability of scale scores for an examinee population. In addition, when alternate forms of a test exist, psychometric properties of interest include (a) the extent to which expected scale scores are the same on the alternate forms, often referred to as *first-order equity*; (b) the extent to which the conditional error variance of scale scores is the same on the alternate forms, often referred to as *second-order equity*; and (c) the extent to which reliability of scale scores is the same on alternate forms.

Assuming that scale scores are a function of summed scores of a test consisting of dichotomously scored items, Kolen et al. (1992) developed procedures for assessing these psychometric properties using a strong true-score model. For the same situation, Kolen, Zeng, and Hanson (1996) developed procedures for assessing these psychometric properties using an IRT model. Wang, Kolen, and Harris (2000) extended the IRT procedures to summed scores for polytomous IRT models.

The Wang et al. (2000) approach is used to express the psychometric properties as follows. Recall that $S_X(X)$ represents the transformation of summed scores to scale scores. The expected (true) scale score given θ is expressed as

$$\tau_{S_X} = \sum_{j=\min X}^{\max X} S_X(j) \cdot P(X = j|\theta), \tag{3.25}$$

where $P(X = j|\theta)$ is calculated using a recursive algorithm (Thissen et al., 1995), and min X and max X are the minimum and maximum summed score. Conditional error variance of scale scores is expressed as

$$\text{var}(S_X|\theta) = \sum_{j=\min X}^{\max X} [S_X(j) - \tau_{S_X}]^2 \cdot P(X = j|\theta). \tag{3.26}$$

Reliability of scale scores is expressed as

$$\rho(S_X, S_{X'}) = 1 - \frac{\int\limits_{\theta} \text{var}(S_X|\theta) g(\theta) d\theta}{\sigma^2_{S_X}}, \tag{3.27}$$

where $\sigma^2_{S_X}$ is the variance of scale scores in the population. Using examples from operational testing programs, this framework has been used to study the relationship between θ and true scale score, the pattern of conditional standard errors of measurement, the extent to which the arcsine transformation stabilizes error variance, first-order equity across alternate forms, second-order equity across alternate forms, reliability of scale scores, and the effects of rounding on reliability for different scales (Ban & Lee, 2007; Kolen et al., 1992, 1996; Tong & Kolen, 2005; Wang et al., 2000). These procedures have yet to be extended to weighted summed scores or to more complex scoring functions.

When the IRT proficiency scale is nonlinearly transformed as in Equation 3.21, based on Lord (1980, p. 85) the conditional error variance of $\hat{\theta}^*_{MLE}$ is approximated as

$$\mathrm{var}\left(\hat{\theta}^*_{MLE}|\theta\right) \approx \left(\frac{d\theta^*}{d\theta}\right)^2 \mathrm{var}\left(\hat{\theta}_{MLE}|\theta\right), \tag{3.28}$$

where $\left(\frac{d\theta^*}{d\theta}\right)^2$ is the squared first derivative of the transformation of θ to θ^*. A similar relationship holds for $\hat{\theta}^*_{TCC}$ and $\hat{\theta}^*_{wTCC}$. Note that this conditional error variance does not take rounding into account. To find the conditional error variance for Bayesian estimators for transformed variables, in Equation 3.17 θ is replaced by θ^* and $\hat{\theta}_{EAP}$ is replaced by $\hat{\theta}^*_{EAP}$. For these procedures, the transformation of θ to θ^* must be monotonic increasing and continuous. When the transformation to scale scores is not continuous, such as when scale scores are rounded to integers, these procedures at best can provide an approximation to conditional error variance. In such cases, simulation procedures can be used to estimate bias and conditional error variance of scale scores.

3.8 Concluding Comments

Currently a variety of raw scores is used with educational tests that include summed scores, weighted summed scores, and various IRT proficiency estimates. We have demonstrated that the choice of raw score has practical implications for the psychometric properties of scores, including conditional measurement error, reliability, and score distributions. Raw scores are transformed to scale scores to enhance score interpretations. The transformations can be chosen so as to incorporate normative, content, and score precision properties.

Chapter 4
Statistical Models for Vertical Linking

James E. Carlson

4.1 Introduction

Vertical linking, sometimes referred to as vertical scaling or cross-grade scaling, comprises a variety of techniques used to develop and maintain vertical scales that are developmental in nature, encompassing two or more grades in schools. Separate tests designed to measure achievement on the same dimension at each grade level are linked through various procedures to enable the measurement of growth across the levels. Formal equating, having the goal of interchangeability of scores on different test forms, is not possible for vertical linking because interchangeability is not feasible in this context: The appropriate content of the tests for the different grade levels necessarily differ because the curricula differ. In addition, the difficulty levels of tests at two adjacent grade levels are typically different, so the tests cannot be parallel as required for a formal equating. Most of the designs used to accomplish vertical linking do, however, involve some content that is appropriate for adjacent grade levels.

Several of the statistical procedures discussed in other chapters of this work, for example item response theory (IRT), can be applied to the problem of vertical linking. Although non-IRT approaches such as equipercentile methods can be used, most vertical linking is done in large-scale assessment programs that use IRT scaling, so those methods will be the focus of this chapter.

Although grade-level tests are used in discussions here, note that several test publishers have developed vertical scales comprising levels each of which may be administered at several grade levels. The designs for vertical linking discussed in this chapter all use cross-sectional data. That is, the data are assumed to be collected during a given time period using independent samples from the different grade levels. An alternative that has not, to my knowledge, been used is a longitudinal

J.E. Carlson
Educational Testing Service, Rosedale Rd, Princeton, New Jersey 08541, USA
e-mail: jcarlson@ets.org

A.A. von Davier (ed.), *Statistical Models for Test Equating, Scaling, and Linking*, Statistics for Social and Behavioral Sciences,
DOI 10.1007/978-0-387-98138-3_4,

design in which data are collected in successive years from the same cohort of students. For example, the same student cohort is tested at the third grade in one year and the fourth grade in the following year. With such a design, the samples will not be independent and data will not be available on all students for both years, due to students' transferring schools or being held at the same grade level. Such characteristics of longitudinal samples must be taken into consideration when using those designs.

4.2 Designs for Vertical Linking

Holland and Dorans (2006, pp. 197-201), Kolen (2006, pp. 173–174), and Kolen and Brennan, 2004, pp. 372–418) described several common-item and equivalent-groups designs that may be used for collecting the data necessary to develop a vertical scale. There are alternatives to those discussed in these sources. One example of the common-item design and one of the equivalent-groups design will be used as illustrations.

In both designs, a linking procedure typically involves starting by linking scales in two adjacent grades (e.g., the second- to the first-grade level), continues by linking scales in the next grade (e.g., third grade to second), and proceeds similarly until scales in all grades in the assessment are linked to form the vertical scale. The linking can begin at any grade level, for example starting with a middle grade and linking upward and downward from there. Another design discussed by Kolen and Brennan (2004), the scaling test design, involves administering one test form (the scaling test) to all grades. The results of that administration are used to set the vertical scale. The scales of test forms at each grade level are subsequently linked to that vertical scale. In my opinion, this design is not appropriate for most educational assessments because it involves testing most students with a number of items that are too difficult or too easy for them, hence yielding no information for those students. An additional issue involves testing students on content that they have not had the opportunity to learn. Although this is partially an ethical issue, the lack of information yielded by the data is also a technical issue that is mentioned where relevant to each design.

4.2.1 Common-Item Designs

In a common-item design, a group of students at each grade level is selected to be administered blocks of items. Some blocks comprising the common items (referred to as anchor blocks) are administered at adjacent grade levels. One form of this design is illustrated in Table 4.1. In this design students at each grade level are administered some blocks of items unique to their grade level and some

Table 4.1 A Common-Item Design With On-Grade and Anchor Item Blocks

Student grade	On-grade item block	Anchor (linking) item block					
		G3-4	G4-5	G5-6	G6-7	G7-8	G8-9
3	G3	X	–	–	–	–	
4	G4	X	X				
5	G5		X	X			
6	G6			X	X		
7	G7				X	X	
8	G8					X	X
9	G9						X

anchor-item blocks shared with adjacent grade levels. The latter provide the vehicle for linking.

For example, third-grade students take a block (G3) of third-grade items and a linking block (G3-4) of items appropriate for Grades 3 and 4. The fourth-grade students take a block (G4) of fourth-grade items and two linking blocks: one of items appropriate for Grades 3 and 4, and the other of items appropriate for Grades 4 and 5 (G4-5). Using scores on the linking block (G3-4) from students from Grades 3 and 4, scales from G3 and G4 can be linked. Saying the G3-4 block is appropriate for Grades 3 and 4 means that students at both grade levels have had the opportunity to learn the content being tested.

4.2.2 Equivalent-Groups Design

In the equivalent-groups design, randomly equivalent groups of students at the same grade level are administered different blocks of items, and most of the blocks are administered to groups at adjacent grade levels. One example of this design is illustrated in Table 4.2. In this design one sample of students at each grade level takes a test form including a block of items in common with the adjacent grade below, one sample takes item blocks only for that grade, and the third sample takes a block of items in common with the adjacent grade above. For the lowest and highest grades in the design they can, of course, only share item blocks with one adjacent grade. For example, the shaded portion of Table 4.2 shows that there are three randomly equivalent samples at the fourth grade. Sample 4a takes a block (3B) of third-grade items and a block (4A) of fourth-grade items, Sample 4b takes two blocks (4A, 4B) of fourth-grade items, and Sample 4c takes a block (4B) of fourth-grade items and a block (5A) of fifth-grade items. Two blocks within each grade are used for illustrative purposes; different assessments will use different numbers of blocks depending on issues such as content coverage and the need for different forms because of security issues. One important aspect of the content coverage issue for vertical scaling designs is that administering items at a grade level above that of the students would not be appropriate if the students have not

Table 4.2 Equivalent Groups Design with Common Blocks of Items at Adjacent Grades

Student grade	Student samples	Item blocks by grade													
		G3		G4		G5		G6		G7		G8		G9	
		3A	3B	4A	4B	5A	5B	6A	6B	7A	7B	8A	8B	9A	9B
3	3a	X	X												
	3b		X	X											
4	4a		X	X											
	4b			X	X										
	4c				X	X									
5	5a				X	X									
	5b					X	X								
	5c						X	X							
6	6a						X	X							
	6b							X	X						
	6c								X	X					
7	7a								X	X					
	7b									X	X				
	7c										X	X			
8	8a										X	X			
	8b											X	X		
	8c												X	X	
9	9a												X	X	
	9b													X	X

Note. Student samples randomly equivalent within grade.

been exposed to the relevant content in the item blocks. To do so would not yield any useful information for scaling or for scoring. Hence, for example, Block 4A in Table 4.2 must contain content appropriate for both third- and fourth-grade students. In order to cover all fourth-grade content in the assessment, however, typically additional blocks at that grade level must cover content not appropriate for administration to students in Grades 3 or 5.

Note that Kolen and Brennan (2004) illustrated a simpler equivalent-groups design that has common items only with the grade below, so the lowest grade shares no blocks with an adjacent grade. One problem with their design is that all item blocks except one each for the lowest and highest grades must be comprised of content appropriate for two grade levels. That is, the design does not allow for items with content appropriate for a single grade level. As discussed above, adequately covering all the important curricular content at each grade level likely requires including blocks of items testing content that is only appropriate for one of the grades in the assessment. Other variations on this design are also possible.

4.3 IRT Models for Vertical Linking

Methods based on IRT models discussed in other chapters of this work are most commonly used in vertical linking (see also Holland & Dorans, 2006; Kolen, 2006; Patz & Yao, 2007; Thissen & Steinberg, 1986; Yen & Fitzpatrick, 2006). Although those sources provide discussion of many models, this chapter focuses on the models most commonly used in operational educational assessment programs. Either the common-item or the equivalent-groups design may be used to gather the data, as described below.

Most of the IRT models commonly used in assessments using vertical scaling are special cases of a model that can be written in one general form. Define

$$\begin{aligned} f_{jk} &= Da_j(\theta - b_{jk}) \\ (k &= 0,\ 1,\ 2,\ \ldots,\ m_j - 1) \\ b_{j0} &= 0.0 \end{aligned} \tag{4.1}$$

where D is a scaling factor of 1.7 (Haley, as cited in Lord & Novick, 1968, p. 399; specified so that the logistic and normal ogive models differ by less than .01 for all θ values), a_j is the discrimination parameter for item j, θ is the proficiency variable, and b_{jk} is a location parameter for the kth-level of item j having m_j score levels numbered from zero to m_j–1. Then, the general form of the logistic model (an alternative is a similar normal model; see Lord & Novick, 1968) for item j is

$$\begin{aligned} P_{jk}(\theta) &= c_j + \frac{(1-c_j)e^{\sum_{t=0}^{k} f_{jt}}}{\sum_{s=0}^{m_j-1} e^{\sum_{t=0}^{s} f_{jt}}} = c_j + \frac{(1-c_j)e^{f_{j0}}\, e^{f_{j1}} \ldots e^{f_{jk}}}{e^{f_{j0}} + e^{f_{j0}}e^{f_{j1}} + \ldots + e^{f_{j0}}e^{f_{j1}} \ldots e^{f_{jm_j-1}}} \\ &= c_j + \frac{(1-c_j)\prod_{t=0}^{k} e^{f_{jt}}}{\sum_{s=0}^{m_j-1}\prod_{t=0}^{s} e^{f_{jt}}} \end{aligned} \tag{4.2}$$

where c_j is the lower asymptote parameter. Note that for all two-parameter models c_j is zero, including two equivalent models that were independently developed at about the same time: Yen's (as cited in Yen & Fitzpatrick, 2006) two-parameter partial-credit model and Muraki's (1992) generalized partial-credit model.[1] Yen's model defines the expression in Equation 4.1 as

$$\begin{aligned} f_{jk} &= k\alpha_j\theta - \sum_{t=0}^{m_j-1} \gamma_{jt} \\ (k &= 1,\ 2,\ 3,\ \ldots,\ m_j - 1) \\ \gamma_{j0} &= 0.0, \end{aligned}$$

[1]Yen developed her model in 1991 (published in a technical report in 1992, as cited in Yen & Fitzpatrick, 2006).

whereas Muraki defines it as

$$f_{jk} = a_j(\theta - b_j + d_{jk})$$
$$d_{j0} = 0.0,$$

The three parameterizations of the model are related as follows:

$$\alpha_j = a_j$$
$$\gamma_{jk} = a_j b_{jk}$$
$$b_j = \frac{1}{m_j - 1} \sum_{k=1}^{m_j-1} b_{jk}$$
$$d_{jk} = b_j - b_{jk} \quad (k = 1, 2, 3, ..., m_j - 1),$$

Note also that for a dichotomously scored item m_j is 2 and Equation 4.2 reduces to one of the logistic models: one-parameter logistic (1PL), 2PL, and 3PL. With *a*, *b*, and *c* all present it is the 3PL; with *c* set to zero it is the 2PL; and if *a* is set to 1.0 (*a* actually can be any constant value across all items) and *c* to 0.0, it is the 1PL.

Most, if not all, of the IRT models discussed by Thissen and Steinberg (1986) and Yen and Fitzpatrick (2006, pp. 113-118), and in other chapters of this book, can be used to fit an IRT model to the data used in vertical scaling. A competitor to the two-parameteror generalized partial-credit model is Samejima's (1969) graded-response model, which is used for vertical scaling purposes in a number of educational assessment programs. Again, the graded-response model can be expressed in either normal ogive or logistic form, and the latter can be expressed as

$$P_{jk}(\theta) = \left[1 + e^{-f_{jk}}\right]^{-1} - \left[1 + e^{-f_{j,k+1}}\right]^{-1},$$

where f_{jk} and $f_{j,k+1}$ are as defined in Equation 4.1.

4.3.1 The Common-Item Design

As mentioned above, in the common-item design linking is carried out through an anchor block of items administered at adjacent grade levels under the assumption that the parameters of the items are common to the two levels. Also as mentioned above, the content covered in the anchor block of items must be appropriate for students at both grade levels to avoid testing some students with items that yield no information, due to lack of opportunity to learn in their grade-level curriculum. Fitting the IRT model to the data is usually referred to as a calibration of the items and results in estimates of parameters for each item. The item parameter estimates for the anchor block of items in two adjacent grade levels are then used to perform the linking. When underlying assumptions are satisfied and the tests of two adjacent grade levels are separately calibrated, as described by Kolen (2006, p. 176), the parameters of the anchor items at the two levels are linearly related and therefore can be placed on the same scale via a linear transformation. The item parameters and proficiency variable are transformed via

$$\begin{aligned} \theta^* &= K_2 + K_1\theta \\ b^* &= K_2 + K_1 b \\ a^* &= \frac{a}{K_1}, \end{aligned}$$

where the quantities with the asterisks represent the transformed quantities and the constants, K_1 and K_2 are determined by the specific linear transformation method employed. Methods of doing this include mean-mean, mean-sigma, and the Stocking-Lord and Haebara test characteristic-curve (TCC) methods (see Yen & Fitzpatrick, 2006, pp. 134-135; Kolen & Brennan, 2004, pp. 387-388).

An alternative to the linear transformation methods is concurrent calibration, in which data from several grades are calibrated together. This method assumes that the anchor items have the same parameters in each grade to which they are administered.

To link all grades via linear transformation methods, the process begins by defining one grade level as the base level and proceeding to link the other grades in a chain of transformations. For example, to link Grades 3–9, the Grade 3 calibration results could be used to define the base scale. Using the anchor items common to Grades 3 and 4, the linear transformation method would be used to transform the anchor items' calibration results in the fourth grade to the third-grade scale. Nonanchor items on the fourth-grade test would undergo the same transformation to place them on the scale. A similar procedure would be used to place the fifth-grade results on the scale, using the anchor items common to Grades 4 and 5. This procedure would be continued until the scale encompassed all seven grade levels.

4.3.1.1 Mean-Mean and Mean-Sigma Methods

As mentioned by Kolen and Brennan (2004), the mean-mean and mean-sigma methods use the means, or means and standard deviations, respectively, of the location parameter estimates for the anchor items to define the linear transformations. The transformation constants are defined as

$$\begin{aligned} K_2 &= \frac{s_t}{s_u} \\ K_1 &= M_t - K_2 M_u, \end{aligned}$$

where N_t and s_t represent the mean and standard deviation of the target location parameters and M_u and s_u represent the mean and standard deviation of the untransformed location parameter estimates. For the mean-mean method, K_2 is set to 1.0 and K_1 is simply the difference between the target mean and the untransformed mean of the location parameters.[2]

As mentioned by Kolen and Brennan (2004, p. 168) and Yen and Fitzpatrick (2006, pp. 134-145) these simple linear transformations of parameter estimates can be problematic in that different combinations of these IRT parameter estimates can result in very similar item response functions (IRFs, discussed below). The TCC methods avoid this problem by using the IRFs and TCCs rather than the individual parameter estimates. Yen and Fitzpatrick also mentioned that the TCC methods have the advantage of "using weights for the minimization based on a distribution of abilities, so that more weight is given in parts of the scale where there are more examinees" and minimize "differences in expected scores rather than observed scores or parameters" (p. 135). I prefer the TCC methods for another reason mentioned by Yen and Fitzpatrick. In many assessments, the TCC is the basis for estimates of examinees' scores using estimation methods presented by Yen (1984; see also Yen & Fitzpatrick, 2006, p. 137). Hence, matching the TCCs for the anchor items on two forms of a test provides a criterion that is directly related to commonly used scoring procedures. To apply the TCC methods, separately calibrate the data within samples of the two datasets whose scales are to be linked. The TCC in one group serves as the target for the transformation, and the other is to be transformed to match as closely as possible that target TCC. The untransformed and transformed TCCs in the latter group are usually referred to as the *provisional* and *transformed curves*.

4.3.1.2 The Stocking-Lord TCC Method

The TCC method of Stocking and Lord (1983) is probably the most widely used method for vertical linking through anchor items. One formulation of the criterion for the Stocking-Lord method is minimization of the sum over examinees of squared differences between the target and transformed TCCs at given values of the latent variable (proficiency) in the IRT model. Using $\hat{P}_{jki}(\theta_i)$ to represent the target-group estimated probability (calculated using estimates of the item parameters) for the *kth* level of item j for a specific value of proficiency, θ_i, and $\hat{P}^*_{jki}(\theta_i)$ the probability estimate of the other group after the transformation (hence

[2]Note that Kolen and Brennan (2004) used parameters ($\boldsymbol{\mu}$ and $\boldsymbol{\sigma}$ for means and standard deviations, respectively), whereas I use statistics. Because actual linking procedures are carried out using sample data, I use statistical notation consistent with this practice. The transformation constants can, of course, be considered to be estimates of parameters defined using the population means and standard deviations.

incorporating the two transformation constants, K_1 and K_2), the Stocking-Lord method finds the transformation constants that minimize the expression

$$\sum_{i \in Q} w_i \left[\sum_{j=1}^{J} \sum_{k=1}^{m_j - 1} k\hat{P}_{jki}(\theta_i) - \sum_{j=1}^{J} \sum_{k=1}^{m_j - 1} k\hat{P}^*_{jki}(\theta_i) \right]^2, \tag{4.3}$$

where Q represents a set of values of the proficiency variable θ, J represents the number of anchor items, and the w_i are weights.

The set Q can be defined in a number of ways. It may include the values on the θ scale where the estimates have been found for the entire sample of examinees, or it may be a set of values on the scale at equal intervals between two extremes of the scale. The weights in the latter case would represent the densities of the distribution of proficiencies at the points on the scale. These densities can be determined from an assumed distribution (e.g., the normal) or from the distribution of sample estimates. Kolen and Brennan (2004) listed five ways of defining the points in Q. Note that the two terms within brackets in Equation 4.3 represent sums of values of the IRF for the jth item, before and after transformation. For example, the target IRF for item j is

$$IRF_{ji} = \sum_{k=1}^{m_j - 1} k\hat{P}_{jki}(\theta_i),$$

and the sum of the IRFs at θ_i is

$$\widehat{\zeta_i} = \sum_{j=1}^{J} \sum_{k=1}^{m_j - 1} k\hat{P}_{jki}(\theta_i),$$

where $\widehat{\zeta_i}$ represents the value of the sample TCC at θ_i which can be considered to be an estimate of the population value, ζ_i. Minimizing Equation 4.3 involves finding the K_1 and K_2 that minimize the weighted sum of squared differences between the target and transformed TCCs. Note that for a dichotomously scored item the IRF is simply the item characteristic curve.

4.3.1.3 The Haebara TCC Method

A method developed by Haebara (as cited in Kolen & Brennan, 2004) is an alternative to the Stocking-Lord method. This method defines the sum of squared differences between the IRFs of the common items across values on the scale and determines the values of K_1 and K_2 that minimize the sum of this quantity over examinees. The expression for the quantity minimized in this procedure is

$$\sum_{i \in Q} w_i \sum_{j=1}^{J} \left[\sum_{k=1}^{m_j - 1} \hat{P}_{jki}(\theta_i) - \sum_{k=1}^{m_j - 1} \hat{P}^*_{jki}(\theta_i) \right]^2.$$

Hence, the Haebara method finds the transformation constants that minimize the weighted sum (over items and proficiency values, θ_i) of squared differences between the two sets of IRFs, whereas the Stocking Lord method minimizes the weighted sum (over proficiency values) of squared differences between the two TCCs.

4.3.1.4 Concurrent Calibration

An alternative to the transformation methods described above is a concurrent calibration. This method, as described by Kolen (2006, pp. 176–177), entails using a multiple-group calibration program, enabling the development of a scale that allows for the expected differences in score distributions across grades on the vertical scale. All items at all grade levels are placed on the same vertical scale without the need for further transformations. The groups are the grade levels, and the common-item blocks across grades are critical to the scaling. Without those linking blocks, the results of the calibration analysis would be identical to separate calibration analyses at each grade level

4.3.2 The Equivalent-Groups Design

Developing a vertical scale using this design, as mentioned above, involves selecting randomly equivalent samples of examinees at each grade level. Separate calibration analyses are first conducted for each group of examinees at a specified grade level (hence separate analyses within each grade level for each of the equivalent groups). Referring to Table 4.2, the two randomly equivalent third-grade samples would be separately calibrated, yielding two independent sets of estimates of the item parameters in item Block 3B, and at the same time Blocks 3A and 4A would be calibrated on the same scale. The independent estimates for Block 3B could be averaged to provide the best estimates of those item parameters. The resulting means, however, may yield biased estimates. An alternative is concurrent calibration within grades. On the other hand, independent calibration followed by examination of differences in Block 3B IRFs of the two samples would be useful for studying model fit or sample equivalency issues. Similarly, the three independent equivalent samples at the fourth grade would be separately calibrated, yielding estimates of fourth-grade Blocks 4A and 4B as well as of Blocks 3B and 5A, all on the same scale. Then, the mean-mean, mean-sigma, Stocking-Lord, or Haebara method would be used to place the third- and fourth-grade items on the same scale. Similar analyses in a chain of linking analyses across the grade levels would result in the vertical scale across the seven grades. This part of the methodology is hence similar to that described above for the nonequivalent-groups designs. Alternatively, concurrent calibration procedures could be used to place all item parameters across all grade levels on the same vertical scale.

An alternative to the equivalent-groups design discussed above involves administering tests for two grade levels in randomly equivalent samples in the higher of the two grade levels. I will illustrate using Grades 3, 4, and 5 as an example. The first step is to administer Grade 3 item blocks to one fourth-grade sample and Grade 4 item blocks to a randomly equivalent fourth-grade sample. Then, use the mean-sigma procedure to align the estimates of proficiency (θ) to place the Grades 3 and 4 item parameter estimates on the same scale. In the second step, repeat this with Grades 4 and 5 item blocks administered to two randomly equivalent Grade 5 student samples. Finally, link the Grade 3–4 and Grade 4–5 scales using the Grade 4 items as an anchor set in a TCC method.

4.4 Model Fit Procedures

Model fit procedures can be used when conducting a vertical linking by both the common-item and equivalent-groups designs. A number of model fit procedures are available for assessing the calibration results of IRT scaling in general. Here I focus only on the methods used during vertical linking.

One of the most common procedures is to compare plots of the anchor item IRFs of each item for the two groups (equivalent-groups design, as mentioned above) or for the two forms (common-item design). In practice this procedure is usually limited to examination of the plots. Conceivably, however, IRT methods sometimes used to compare IRFs in the context of differential item functioning analyses could be used in the vertical scaling context. Although individual item parameter estimates could be compared, as mentioned above different sets of estimates can result in highly similar IRFs, and the similarity of the latter is most important in using this method to examine model fit.

Another methodology that is often used with designs involving anchor item sets is comparison of the three TCCs involved. To illustrate, consider that a scale has been established within the third grade in the common-item design of Table 4.1 and we are linking the fourth-grade scale to it. The three TCCs are of (a) the Grade 3 target data, (b) the untransformed Grade 4 data, and (c) the transformed Grade 4 data. In this example, the criterion of importance is that the transformed Grade 4 TCC be as identical as possible to the target Grade 3 TCC. Comparison of the untransformed with the transformed Grade 4 data simply provides information about how the transformation affected the TCC.

Another important aspect of the vertical scale development that should be examined is the progression of the scaling results across grade levels. One way of examining this is to plot the TCCs of each grade level as separate curves in a single plot. If the vertical scaling has been successful, the plot should show curves that do not cross, with an orderly progression of location of the curves across grades (lowest grade located lowest on the scale and each higher grade located somewhat higher than the next lower grade). The distances between these curves need not be the same, because there is usually no basis for assuming that grade itself (i.e., Grade 3, Grade 4) is an interval scale.

In a typical testing program, different test forms are used within each grade in each assessment year. The new forms are usually equated within each grade level to the old forms. As the vertical scale is used across calendar years, the model-fit methodology results should be compared from year to year. Such comparison may reveal problems developing with the scale or the scaling procedures. Some items, for example, may show changes in the IRFs across years due to item parameter drift. If the exact same set of items is used year to year, drift can be detected through examination of the TCCs. If alternate forms are used each year, differences in the TCCs could reflect selection of differentially difficult items, but this normally would be taken care of through the within-grade year-to-year equating. Changes in the patterns of the TCCs across grades from year to year may be an indication of scale drift. If such things are observed, investigation through discussion with content experts and school officials should be undertaken to determine any curricular or population changes. In the event that these cross-year comparisons bring into question the validity of the scale, the scale may need to be reset by redoing the vertical linking with more recent data than used to develop the original scale.

4.5 Discussion

In this chapter I have described the most commonly used designs and methodology for developing vertical scales. Because the most common application is in large-scale educational assessment programs, the focus has been on methods used in such programs, primarily those using IRT models. There are many variations on the methodology discussed and alternative methodology not discussed in this chapter, so the reader is encouraged to refer to references cited herein as well as sources cited in those references. Additionally, I would like to point out that new research and development in this area is currently produced with some frequency, so those individuals wishing to keep current on the topics of this chapter should read the latest journals and conference programs in which psychometric methods are reported.

Author Note: Any opinions expressed in this chapter are those of the authors and not necessarily of Educational Testing Service.

Chapter 5
An Empirical Example of Change Analysis by Linking Longitudinal Item Response Data From Multiple Tests

John J. McArdle and Kevin J. Grimm

Linking, *equating*, and *calibrating* refer to a series of statistical methods for comparing scores from tests (scales, measures, etc.) that do not contain the same exact set of measurements but presume to measure the same underlying construct. Lord (1955a,1955b) provided one of the first examples of this kind where one test (x) was administered to 1,200 people, while two other tests (y_1 & y_2) were each only administered to a different half of the group. The resulting data and analysis were reprinted in Cudeck (2000), who showed that the assumption of a single factor model for all three tests (x, y_1, y_2) made it possible to identify a maximum likelihood estimator of the correlation among the two variables that were never measured on the same persons (y_1 & y_2). In contemporary terms the common score (x) served as an anchor for the correlation of the other two scores, and this simple design is one version of what is termed a *nonequivalent anchor test* (von Davier, Holland, & Thayer, 2004b).

There has been a great deal of work on similar incomplete data problems at the level of items. The introduction of item response methods led to improved linking techniques (e.g., common-item equating, common-person equating) as item response models have built-in linking mechanisms for incomplete data (Embretson, 1996). Most of the recent work on this topic has been summarized in Dorans, Pommerich, and Holland (2007), and Dorans (2007) provided a good readable overview of linking scores. Dorans examined the general assumptions of different data collection designs and gave explicit definitions of equating, calibrating, and linking. Dorans also provided a compelling example of the importance of adequate linking using multiple health outcome instruments, and how an individual's health

J.J. McArdle (✉)
Dept. of Psychology, University of Southern California, SGM 501 3620 South McClintock Ave, Los Angeles, CA 90089, USA
e-mail: jmcardle@usc.edu

K.J. Grimm
University of California, 1 Shields Ave, Davis, CA 95616, USA
e-mail: kjgrimm@ucdavis.edu

A.A. von Davier (ed.), *Statistical Models for Test Equating, Scaling, and Linking*, Statistics for Social and Behavioral Sciences,
DOI 10.1007/978-0-387-98138-3_5,

may be misunderstood if alternative tests presumed to measure the same construct fail to do so.

The research we present here has far fewer consequences because it is not intended for high-stakes decision making. Instead, we attempt to use the new approaches in item linking to deal with a perplexing problem in lifespan research—we ask, "How can we get a reasonable measure of the same construct when the tests themselves are changing over age and time?" The approach we present here is intended to be useful for research into the dynamics of aging but is not intended as a placement device or as an improved marker of health.

5.1 Challenges in Lifespan Developmental Research

Examining change over extended periods of time or during critical developmental periods where the expression of the construct changes is a complex undertaking. Often the measurement of the construct must change to adequately capture the construct. In these situations changes in measurement and changes in the construct are difficult to separate. One empirical example comes from the Intergenerational Studies (IGS) of Human Development, a collection of three studies initiated at the University of California-Berkeley in 1928. A main interest of the IGS was to examine the growth and change of cognitive abilities during infancy, childhood, adolescence, and adulthood. In the IGS, cognitive abilities have been measured with a variety of tests across the 70 years of the study, including the California First-Year Mental Scale (Bayley, 1933), California Preschool Mental Scale (Jaffa, 1934), Stanford-Binet (Terman, 1916), Stanford-Binet Form L and Form M (Terman & Merrill, 1937), Wechsler-Bellevue Intelligence Scale (Wechsler, 1946), Wechsler Adult Intelligence Scale (WAIS; Wechsler, 1955), and the Wechsler Adult Intelligence Scale-Revised (WAIS-R; Wechsler, 1981). These measures were chosen because they were the best available age-appropriate tests.

Changes in cognitive abilities could be measured for each developmental period. For example, Figure 5.1 is a series of longitudinal plots for specific developmental periods where the same cognitive test was administered. Plots A and B in Figure 5.1 are of the California First-Year Mental Scale and California Preschool Mental Scale for participants in the Berkeley Growth Study and Berkeley Guidance-Control Study, respectively. These two plots cover a similar developmental period (i.e., birth through age 5) using different cognitive tests but generally show a pattern of rapid increase. Plot C in Figure 5.1 shows mental age from the series of Stanford-Binet tests (i.e., 1916, Form L, Form M), mostly collected from ages 6–17. Plot D in Figure 5.1 shows Block Design scores from the Wechsler-Bellevue Intelligence Scale measured from ages 16–27 years and shows a period of slight growth and stability. Plot E in Figure 5.1 shows Block Design scores from the WAIS, which was administered once; therefore individual change patterns cannot be captured. Finally, Plot F in Figure 5.1 shows Block Design scores from the WAIS-R and shows stability in the change pattern and large between-person differences therein. It is important to note that the Block Design scores from the Wechsler tests are

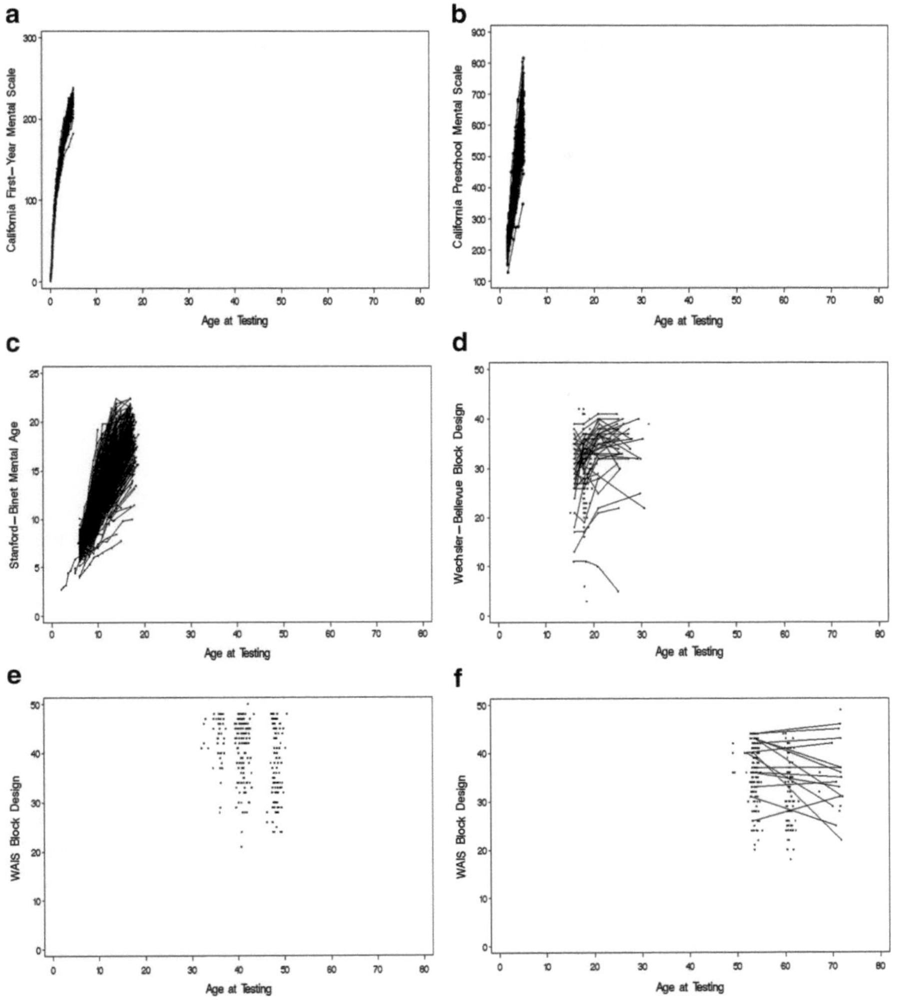

Fig. 5.1 Longitudinal plot of (**a**) First-Year Mental Scale total score, (**b**) Preschool Mental Scale total score, (**c**) Stanford-Binet mental age, (**d**) Wechsler-Bellevue Block Design, (**e**) Wechsler Adult Intelligence Scale (WAIS) Block Design, and (**f**) WAIS-Revised (WAIS-R) Block Design

not on a common scale; however, some items are identical across edition of the Wechsler. Additionally, the tests described above may be measuring different constructs at the total score level, even though they are all intelligence tests.

An alternative view regarding the developmental process is that it is continuously evolving. Thus, by selecting items from different tests that measure a common construct and scaling them with an appropriate model, a *lifespan* trajectory of specific cognitive abilities may be represented. Scaling items, in essence, would equate items from different tests, recognizing their differences in level of difficulty and relationship with the underlying construct. In order to link the tests, there must be sufficient item overlap within and between test forms. Item overlap occurs because different tests were administered at the same occasion and because different tests contain the same items.

In this chapter we describe an example of using item response linking procedures with scarce longitudinal item-level data collected over a 70-year period to help understand and evaluate theories of cognitive growth and decline. Data for this project come from the IGS and the Bradway-McArdle Longitudinal Study (BMLS). We realize that IGS and BMLS data are weak in terms of equating but recognize their longitudinal strength. Building on the data's strength, we link items measuring nonverbal intelligence and model within-person changes in the lifespan development of nonverbal intelligence and the between-person differences therein.

5.2 Longitudinal Item-Level Data

Longitudinal studies provide an added dimension (e.g., time/age) to consider when linking item-level data. Measurement invariance is tremendously important in longitudinal studies as researchers are most interested in studying change; however, measurement invariance is often overlooked or assumed because the same test is often administered in longitudinal studies. In many instances in longitudinal studies it is not reasonable to administer the same test (see Edwards & Wirth, 2009; McArdle, Grimm, Hamagami, Bowles, & Meredith, 2009). Potential reasons include age appropriateness, improved and revised tests become available, and prior poor experiences. For example, the Child-Behavior Checklist (Achenbach & Rescorla, 2001), an informant-based behavior rating scale, is an often-used measure of behavior problems in children and has two age-appropriate forms. One form is appropriate for children between the ages of 1½ and 5 years, whereas the second form is appropriate for children between 6 and 18 years old. The two forms share the same dimensions of behavior problems (e.g., internalizing and externalizing) and share several items, but they do have items specific to each age-appropriate form. Also, there are items that both forms share but are expected to relate to the underlying dimensions in different ways (e.g., a question about crying is part of the internalizing dimension in the 6–18 form but not part of the internalizing or externalizing dimensions in the 1½–5 form).

5.3 Method

We start with descriptions of the samples and measures, an overview of the item response and longitudinal models, and results from fitting these models to the longitudinal data. Table 5.1 contains information regarding the cognitive tests that were administered at each age for each sample.

Table 5.1 Summary of Measurement Occasions for Each Sample

Age	Berkeley Growth	Guidance-Control	Oakland Growth	Bradway-McArdle Longitudinal
2–5 ½	–	–	–	SB-L, SB-M (139)
6	1916 SB (60)	1916 SB (205)	–	–
7	1916 SB (47), SB-L (8)	1916 SB (204)	–	–
8	SB-L (51)	SB-L (187)	–	–
9	SB-L (53)	SB-L (94), SB-M (98)	–	–
10	SB-M (53)	SB-L (102), SB-M (88)	–	–
11	SB-L (48)	SB-L (77)	–	–
12	SB-M (50)	SB-L (90), SB-M (43)	1916 SB (192)	–
13–14	SB-L (42)	SB-L (82), SB-M (97)	–	SB-L (111)
15	–	SB-M (51)	–	–
16	WB-I (48)	–	–	–
17	SB-M (44)	–	SB-M (147)	–
18	WB-I (41)	WB-I (157)	–	–
21	WB-I (37)	–	–	–
25	WB-I (25)	–	–	–
29	–	–	–	WAIS, SB-L (110)
36	WAIS (54)	–	–	–
40	–	WAIS (156)	–	WAIS, SB-LM (48)
50	–	–	WAIS (103)	–
53	WAIS-R (41)	WAIS-R (118)	–	WAIS (53)
60	–	–	WAIS-R (78)	–
63	–	–	–	WAIS (48)
72	WAIS-R (31)	–	–	–

Note: Sample sizes are contained within parentheses next to the test name; more than one sample size within a single testing age denotes different participants. 1916 SB = 1916 edition of the Stanford-Binet, SB-L = Revised Stanford-Binet Form L, SB-M = Revised Stanford-Binet Form M, SB-LM = Revised Stanford-Binet Form LM, WB = Wechsler-Bellevue Intelligence Scale, WAIS = Wechsler Adult Intelligence Scale, WAIS-R = Wechsler Adult Intelligence Scale-Revised

5.3.1 Berkeley Growth Study

The Berkeley Growth Study was initiated by Nancy Bayley in 1928. Sixty-one infants were enrolled between September 15, 1928, and May 15, 1929, to trace early mental, motor, and physical development during the first years of life. An additional 13 infants were enrolled in the Berkeley Growth Study within 3 years of the start of the study, bringing the final sample size to 74.

Data collection in the Berkeley Growth Study began within 4 days of an infant's birth as anthropometric, neurological, and physiological measurements were made in the hospital by pediatricians. Participating infants were assessed at the Institute of Human Development at the University of California-Berkeley every month from 1–15 months of age, every 3 months from 18–36 months of age, and then annually from 4–18 years of age. In adulthood the participants were measured at 21, 25, 30, 36, 52, and 72 years of age. The Berkeley Growth Study was the most measurement-intensive IGS study.

5.3.2 Berkeley Guidance-Control Study

The Berkeley Guidance-Control Study began in early 1928 under the leadership of Jean Macfarlane. The 248 original participants in the Berkeley Guidance-Control Study were drawn from a survey of every third birth in Berkeley from January 1, 1928, through June 30, 1929. The initial nature of the Berkeley Guidance-Control Study was a 6-year project with goals of (a) documenting the frequency and occurrence of behavior and personality problems in a cross-sectional sample of young children during the preschool years, (b) identifying the biological and environmental factors associated with the presence or absence of such behavioral problems, and (c) estimating the effects of guidance activities with the parents of these children.

Monthly home visits began when infants were 3 months old and continued through 18 months of age. When the infants were 21 months of age, half of the sample ($n = 124$) was assigned to the guidance condition, and the remaining half of the sample ($n = 124$) was assigned to the control condition. Parents of the infants in the guidance condition engaged in intensive discussions with public health nurses and other project staff. An initial, intensive assessment of the infants and their parents was conducted at 21 months. Thereafter, infants and parents were interviewed and tested every 6 months from the child's age of 2–4 years and then annually from 5–18 years of age. In adulthood, the Berkeley Guidance-Control Study participants were assessed at ages 30, 40, and 52.

5.3.3 Oakland Growth Study

The Oakland Growth Study began in 1931 under the guidance of Harold Jones, Mary Jones, and Herbert Stolz. A total of 212 students attending five elementary schools in Oakland, California, were enrolled into the study. The goal of the Oakland Growth Study was to study normal adolescence, particularly physical and physiological maturation and peer relationships. Initial measurements were taken in 1932 when the participants ranged in age from 10–12 years. Participants in the Oakland Growth Study were assessed semiannually during the six years of junior and senior high school. In adulthood, the participants were assessed at ages 38, 48, and 60.

5.3.4 Bradway-McArdle Longitudinal Study

The Bradway-McArdle Longitudinal Study began in 1931 when 139 children aged 2½ to 5 years were tested as part of the standardization of the Revised Stanford-Binet (Terman & Merrill, 1937). The sample was tested by Katherine Bradway

(Bradway, 1944, 1945a. 1945b) with the Revised Stanford-Binet in 1941. The sample was tested in 1957, 1969, 1984, and 1992. McArdle, Hamagami, Meredith, and Bradway (2000) coordinated the last three waves of data collection. It is important to note that this sample took Forms L and M of the Stanford-Binet in the same occasion in 1931; Form L of the Stanford-Binet and the WAIS in 1957; Form LM of the Stanford-Binet and the WAIS in 1969, and the WAIS and additional WAIS-R items in 1992.

5.3.5 Measures of Nonverbal Intelligence

The cognitive measures administered in these studies and examined here include the 1916 Stanford-Binet (Terman, 1916), Revised Stanford-Binet (Form L, Form M, & Form LM; Terman & Merrill, 1937, 1960), Wechsler-Bellevue Intelligence Scale (Wechsler, 1946), WAIS (Wechsler, 1955), and the WAIS-R (Wechsler, 1981). From these scales, nonverbal intelligence items were selected. For the Stanford-Binet tests, item selection was based on a categorization conducted by Bradway (1945). A list of nonverbal items selected from the Stanford-Binet tests is presented in Table 5.2. The first column of Table 5.2 contains a running total of the number of items that measure nonverbal intelligence from the Stanford-Binet tests. As seen, 65 items from the Stanford-Binet measure nonverbal intelligence. The second column contains the name of the item, and the third through sixth columns contain the Stanford-Binet item number if the item appeared on the edition of the test. These columns were left blank if the item did not appear on the edition. Items on the Stanford-Binet tests are grouped by age appropriateness (as opposed to construct), and item numbers reflect this. For example, II-1 means this item is the first item from the age 2 items. Table 5.2 shows the level (or lack thereof) of item overlap across editions of the Stanford-Binet. Each edition of the Stanford-Binet contains items that are unique and shared with other editions.

For the Wechsler tests, items from Picture Completion, Picture Arrangement, Block Design, and Object Assembly were chosen to represent nonverbal intelligence. A list of the nonverbal items from the Wechsler tests is presented in Table 5.3. As in Table 5.2, the first column is a running total of the number of items selected from the Wechsler series of tests. As seen, 68 distinct items were selected. Column 2 contains the subscale from which the item comes from, and columns 3–5 indicate the item number from each edition of the Wechsler intelligence scales. Columns were left blank if the edition did not contain the item allowing for the examination of item overlap across Wechsler editions. It is important to note that, in several cases, the scoring of items had to be modified to be considered equivalent because of different time bonuses. In the Wechsler series of intelligence tests, the scoring system from the WAIS was adopted for the Wechsler-Bellevue and WAIS-R where appropriate. Several items were similar on the surface and in name but were slightly different in presentation or scoring.

Table 5.2 Nonverbal Items From the Stanford-Binet Intelligence Scales and Their Overlap Across Test Forms

Item number	Item	1916 Stanford-Binet	Stanford-Binet Form L	Stanford-Binet Form M	Stanford-Binet Form LM
01	Delayed Response	–	–	II-1	II-2
02	Form Board (1)	–	II-1	II-4	II-1
03	Block Tower	–	II-4	–	II-4
04	Motor Coordination (1)	–	–	IIH-2	–
05	Form Board - Rotated (1)	–	IIH-6	–	–
06	Stringing Beads (2)	–	–	IIH-A	–
07	Vertical Line	–	–	III-4	III-6
08	Stringing Beads (4)	–	III-1	–	III-1
09	Block Bridge	–	III-3	III-1	III-3
10	Circle (1)	–	III-5	–	III-5
11	Form Board - Rotated (2)	–	III-A	III-A	IIH-A
12	Patience: Pict (1)	–	–	IIIH-2	IIIH-2
13	Animal Pict. (4)	–	–	IIIH-3	IIIH-3
14	Sorting Buttons	–	–	IIIH-5	IIIH-5
15	Matching Obj. (3)	–	–	IIIH-A	–
16	Cross	–	IIIH-A	–	–
17	Stringing Beads (7)	–	–	IV-2	–
18	Compar. Lines	IV-1	–	–	–
19	Discrimination of Forms (3)	IV-2	–	–	–
20	Pict. Comp. (Man)	–	IV-3	–	–
21	Discrimination of Forms (8)	–	IV-5	–	IV-5
22	Animal Pict. (6)	–	–	IV-A	–
23	Animal Pict. (7)	–	–	IVH-1	–
24	Pict. Compl. (Bird)	–	–	IVH-4	–
25	Pict. Compar. (3)	–	IVH-3	–	–
26	Patience: Pict. (2)	V-5	–	IVH-A	–
27	Pictorial Sim. & Dif II (9)	–	–	V-3	V-5
28	Patience Rec. (2)	–	–	V-4	V-6
29	Pict. Compl. (Man)	–	V-1	–	V-1
30	Folding Triangle	–	V-2	–	V-2
31	Square (1)	IV-4	V-4	–	V-4
32	Mut. Pict. (3)	VI-2	–	V-6	–
33	Mut. Pict. (4)	–	–	–	VI-3
34	Knot	VII-4	V-A	V-A	V-A
35	Bead Chain I	–	VI-2	VI-2	–
36	Mut. Pict. (4)	–	VI-3	–	–
37	Pict. Compar. (5)	–	VI-5	–	–
38	Pict. Absurd. I (3)	VII-2	VII-1	–	–
39	Pict. Absurd. I (4)	–	–	–	VII-1
40	Diamond (2)	–	VII-3	–	–
41	Diamond (1)	VII-6	–	–	VII-3
42	Pict. Absurd. I (2)	–	–	VII-3	–
43	Ball & field	VIII-1	–	–	–
44	Paper Cutting I (1)	–	IX-1	–	IX-1
45	Pict. Absurd. II	–	X-2	–	–
46	Absurditites (4)	X-2	-	-	-
47	Pict. Absurd. II	–	–	XII-5	XII-3
48	Plan of Search	–	XIII-1	XIII-1	XIII-1

(*continued*)

Table 5.2 (continued)

Item number	Item	1916 Stanford-Binet	Stanford-Binet Form L	Stanford-Binet Form M	Stanford-Binet Form LM
49	Paper Cutting I (2)	–	XIII-3	–	XIII-A
50	Reasoning	–	–	XIV-1	XIV-3
51	Induction	XIV-2	XIV-2	–	XIV-2
52	Pict. Absurd. III	–	XIV-3	XIV-2	–
53	Ingenuity (1)	–	XIV-4	XIV-5	XIV-4
54	Codes (1.5)	–	AA-2	AA-4	–
55	Ingenuity (2)	–	AA-6	AA-2	AA-2
56	Directions I (4)	–	–	AA-6	AA-6
57	Paper Cutting	–	–	AA-8	AA-A
58	Boxes (3)	AA-4	SAI-2	–	–
59	Enclosed Box (4)	–	–	–	SAI-2
60	Ingenuity (3)	–	–	SAII-2	SAII-4
61	Codes II (1)	–	–	SAII-5	SAII-A
62	Code	AA-6	–	–	–
63	Paper Cutting II	SA-2	SAIII-4	–	–
64	Reasoning	–	SAIII-5	–	SAIII-5
65	Ingenuity	SA-6	–	–	–

Note: Item numbers represent the age level and item number; for example, II-1 is the first item at the age 2 level. IIH = age 2½ items; AA = Average Adult level; SAI = Superior Adult I; SAII = Superior Adult II; SAIII = Superior Adult III; -A = represents alternative item

These items were treated as distinct instead of requiring assumptions regarding their equivalence. This data collation leads to 3,566 people-occasions measured on 130 items.

5.4 Models

5.4.1 Measurement Models

We focus on a strong measurement model to account for the within-time relationships among the nonverbal intelligence items. We begin with a longitudinal one-parameter logistic (1PL) or Rasch model (Rasch, 1960). A longitudinal 1PL model can be written as

$$\ln\left(\frac{P(X_i[t]=1)_n}{1-P(X_i[t]=1)_n}\right)=\theta[t]_n-\beta_i \tag{5.1}$$

where $\theta[t]_n$ is person n's ability at time t, β_i is item i's difficulty parameter, and $P(X_i[t]=1)_n$ is the probability that person n answered item i correctly at time t given the person's ability and item's difficulty. The longitudinal 1PL model was

Table 5.3 Nonverbal Items From the Wechsler Intelligence Scales and Their Overlap Across Test Forms

Subscale & item number	Item	Wechsler-Bellevue	Wechsler Adult Intelligence Scale	Wechsler Adult Intelligence Scale-Revised
01	Picture Completion	–	1	1
02	Picture Completion	8	–	–
03	Picture Completion	–	–	2
04	Picture Completion	–	–	3
05	Picture Completion	4	5	4
06	Picture Completion	–	4	–
07	Picture Completion	–	–	5
08	Picture Completion	10	6	6
09	Picture Completion	–	7	7
10	Picture Completion	–	–	8
11	Picture Completion	–	9	–
12	Picture Completion	–	–	9
13	Picture Completion	–	12	–
14	Picture Completion	–	–	10
15	Picture Completion	11	16	–
16	Picture Completion	–	–	11
17	Picture Completion	5	15	–
18	Picture Completion	–	–	12
19	Picture Completion	–	8	13
20	Picture Completion	15	18	14
21	Picture Completion	–	–	15
22	Picture Completion	–	–	16
23	Picture Completion	–	–	17
24	Picture Completion	–	19	18
25	Picture Completion	14	21	19
26	Picture Completion	–	20	20
27	Picture Completion	6	2	–
28	Picture Completion	1	3	–
29	Picture Completion	13	10	–
30	Picture Completion	–	11	–
31	Picture Completion	–	13	–
32	Picture Completion	7	14	–
33	Picture Completion	–	17	–
34	Picture Completion	2	–	–
35	Picture Completion	3	–	–
36	Picture Completion	9	–	–
37	Picture Completion	12	–	–
38	Block Design	–	1 (Time = 60)	1 (Time = 60)
39	Block Design	–	2 (Time = 60)	2 (Time = 60)
40	Block Design	1 (Time = 75)	3 (Time = 60)	
41	Block Design	2 (Time = 75)	4 (Time = 60)	3 (Time = 60)
42	Block Design	3 (Time = 75)	5 (Time = 60)	4 (Time = 60)
43	Block Design	4 (Time = 75)	6 (Time = 60)	5 (Time = 60)
44	Block Design	5 (Time = 150)	7 (Time = 120)	6 (Time = 120)
45	Block Design	6 (Time = 150)	8 (Time = 120)	7 (Time = 120)
46	Block Design	–	9 (Time = 120)	8 (Time = 120)
47	Block Design	–	10 (Time = 120)	9 (Time = 120)
48	Block Design	7 (Time = 196)	–	–
49	Picture Arrangement	–	1 (Time = 60)	–
50	Picture Arrangement	1 (Time = 60)	2 (Time = 60)	1 (Time = 60)
51	Picture Arrangement	2 (Time = 60)	3 (Time = 60)	–
52	Picture Arrangement	–	4 (Time = 60)	4 (Time = 60)
53	Picture Arrangement	–	5 (Time = 60)	–

(*continued*)

Table 5.3 (continued)

Subscale & item number	Item	Wechsler-Bellevue	Wechsler Adult Intelligence Scale	Wechsler Adult Intelligence Scale-Revised
54	Picture Arrangement	4 (Time = 120)	6 (Time = 60)	2 (Time = 60)
55	Picture Arrangement	6 (Time = 120)	7 (Time = 120)	–
56	Picture Arrangement	5 (Time = 120)	8 (Time = 120)	10 (Time = 120)
57	Picture Arrangement	-	–	3 (Time = 60)
58	Picture Arrangement	–	–	6 (Time = 90)
59	Picture Arrangement	–	–	7 (Time = 90)
60	Picture Arrangement	–	–	9 (Time = 120)
61	Picture Arrangement	3 (Time = 60)	–	–
62	Picture Arrangement	–	–	5 (Time = 90)
63	Picture Arrangement	–	–	8 (Time = 90)
64	Object Assembly	1 (Time = 120)	1 (Time = 120)	1 (Time = 120)
65	Object Assembly	–	2 (Time = 120)	2 (Time = 120)
66	Object Assembly	2 (Time = 180)	–	–
67	Object Assembly	3 (Time = 180)	3 (Time = 180)	3 (Time = 180)
68	Object Assembly	–	4 (Time = 180)	4 (Time = 180)

then extended to accommodate multicategory (polytomous) response formats because several items from the Wechsler tests have partial credit scoring. This model can be written as

$$\ln\left(\frac{P(X_i[t] = x)_n}{1 - P(X_i[t] = x)_n}\right) = \theta[t]_n - \delta_{ij} \tag{5.2}$$

where $P(X_i[t] = x)_n$ is the probability the response of person n to item i is in category x, given the response is either in category x or $x - 1$, and δ_{ij} is the step-difficulty for step j of item i. This measurement model is a straightforward longitudinal extension of Masters's partial-credit model (Masters, 1982). In both equations, we note that person ability is time dependent and item difficulty (or step difficulty) does not depend on time. It is also important to note that we are going to estimate $\theta[t]_n$ for each person at each measurement occasion.

5.4.2 *Longitudinal Models*

To model lifespan changes in nonverbal ability, we use growth curves with an interest in exponential change patterns, as exponential patterns have been found to adequately fit lifespan changes in a variety of cognitive abilities (see McArdle, Ferrer-Caja, Hamagami, & Woodcock, 2002; McArdle et al., 2009). The basic growth curve for the ability estimates can be written as

$$\begin{aligned}
\theta[t]_n &= g_{0n} + g_{1n}(A[t]) + e[t]_n \\
g_{0n} &= \mu_0 + d_{0n} \\
g_{1n} &= \mu_1 + d_{1n}
\end{aligned} \tag{5.3}$$

where g_{0n} is the intercept for person n, g_{1n} is the slope for person n, A is a vector of basis functions, and $e[t]_n$ is the time-dependent (Level 1) residual term. The Level 1 intercept and slope are decomposed into a sample-level (Level 2) means (μ_0 and μ_1) and individual deviations (d_{0n} and d_{1n}) from the sample-level means. Individual deviations are assumed to be multivariate normally distributed with a mean of 0, variances (σ_0^2 and σ_1^2), and a covariance (σ_{01}). The time-dependent residuals are assumed to be normally distributed with a mean of 0 and a single variance (σ_e^2). We fit the growth curves with the following basis functions: level only ($A[t]=0$), linear ($A[t]=t$), exponential ($A[t] = (1 - e^{-\pi_g \cdot t})$), and dual exponential ($A[t] = (e^{-\pi_d \cdot t} - e^{-\pi_g \cdot t})$). The dual exponential was of specific interest because the model captures growth and decline as π_d is the decline rate and π_g is the growth rate. With this model, we can test whether the decline rate is significantly different from zero ($\pi_d \neq 0$). The decline rate is an important parameter in the lifespan development of cognitive abilities because a significant decline rate indicates ability declines as adults age.

5.4.3 Analysis Plan

There are several alternative ways to analyze these kinds of data using these types of models (see McArdle et al., 2009). For clarity here, we only present a two-phase approach for analyzing the longitudinal item-level data. In the first phase the measurement model (Equation 5.2) is fit to the longitudinal item-level data, without capitalizing on the repeated measures nature of the data. The benefit of this first analysis is that it provides a linking equation for conversion of the observed score pattern of any test (items administered) at any occasion. In any case where a person has responded to a series of items, theoretical ability scores ($\theta[t]_n$) from the overall measurement model are estimated and treated as observed longitudinal data in the second phase. The explicit assumption of invariance of the construct over time is similar to those made for scales using metric factorial invariance (see McArdle, 1994, 2007). However, we recognize that the lack of common overlapping items within occasions makes it difficult to reject this strict invariance hypothesis, so our original substantive choice of item content is critical.

In the second phase the linked scores (ability estimates) from Step 1 are treated as observed data for each person at each time and the within-person changes in the ability estimates are modeled using growth curves (Equation 5.3). On the other hand, the combined model (Equations 5.2 and 5.3) can be estimated, and this approach is often seen as optimal, as it produces easy-to-use parameter estimates and allows the modeling of nonverbal ability as a latent entity instead of an observed (estimated) entity.

Although we do not want to treat this two-phase approach as optimal, it certainly is practical. This two-phase approach is not optimal from a statistical point of view—the nonverbal ability scores have to be estimated using the prior model assumptions, and these assumptions are likely to have some faults. However, as we demonstrate here, this two-phase approach is simple, is computationally efficient, and allows exploration of longitudinal patterns in the ability estimates from the first step (as in McArdle et al., 2009). It is possible to create a joint estimation of the scores within the longitudinal growth models (as in McArdle et al., 2009), and these and more complex programming scripts can be downloaded from http://psychology.ucdavis.edu/labs/Grimm/personal/downloads.html.

5.5 Results

5.5.1 Step 1: Nonverbal Ability Estimates

A total of 65 items from the Stanford-Binet were deemed to measure nonverbal intelligence, 68 items (37 Picture Completion, 11 Block Design, 15 Picture Arrangement, and 5 Object Assembly) from the Wechsler intelligence tests, and a total of 3,566 person-occasions. The partial-credit model was fit to these data; ability estimates were calculated for 3,184 (nonextreme) person-occasions, and item difficulties were calculated for 123 (nonextreme) items. By fitting the partial-credit model to the item-level data in this way, we assumed the item parameters did not vary across time. That is, item difficulty and discrimination were the same for a given item regardless of age, year, and occasion.

Fit of the partial credit model was evaluated in terms of the item fit. Commonly used item fit indices are termed INFIT, OUTFIT, and point biserial correlation. INFIT and OUTFIT consider the amount of noise when the ability level of the participant is close to and far from the item difficulty, respectively. There is an expected amount of noise for each item and person, based on the probabilistic nature of the model. When the amount of noise is as expected, INFIT and OUTFIT statistics will be 1.0. If a person or item is acting too predictably, the person/item is considered muted and the INFIT and OUTFIT will show this by being considerably less than one, while noisy people/items will have values greater than one. Generally acceptable limits on INFIT and OUTFIT statistics are 0.8 – 1.2 with 0.6 – 1.4 being liberal boundaries. It's important to note that the OUTFIT statistic may be unreliable for extreme cases (easiest and hardest). The point biserial correlation is another indication of item fit as it is the correlation between the participant's probability of correctly answering the item and participant's score on the test, basically determining whether people with higher overall scores tend to correctly answer the item. The fit of the nonverbal items to the partial credit model was generally good as only five items showed misfit based on liberal boundaries of INFIT. Based on OUTFIT, 29 items showed misfit with most items showing less noise than expected, which may be a function of repeated testing. Point biserial correlations were positive for 114 items; negative point biserial correlations were found for nine items. Items with negative biserial correlations tended to have few responses.

Person reliability was generally high (.92); however, it might have been overestimated because the repeated measures nature of the data was not accounted for in

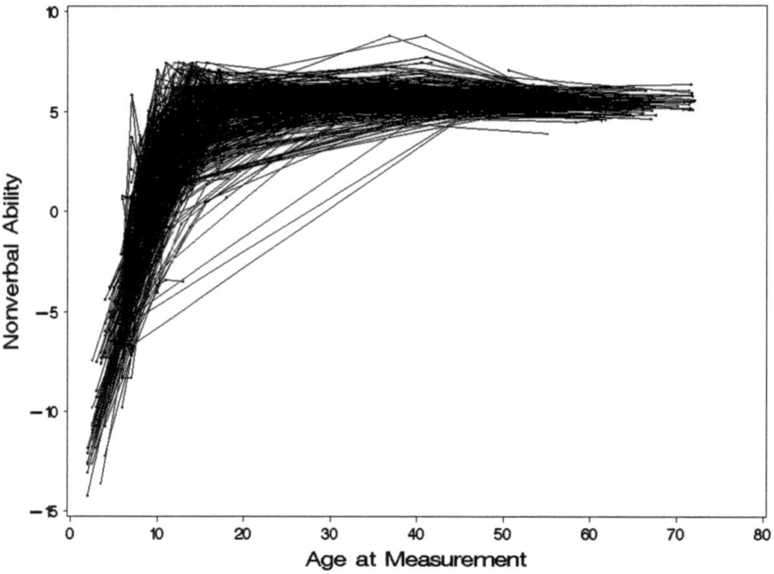

Fig. 5.2 Longitudinal plot of nonverbal ability estimates

this model. Estimates of nonverbal ability were calculated for each person at each occasion using the partial-credit model. The ability estimates were a simple function of the items administered at each occasion and the participant's responses to those items, ignoring age at measurement. The scaling of the ability estimates was such that the average item difficulty was 0 (i.e., $\Sigma\beta\iota = 0$), and between- and within-person differences were scaled in a logit metric reflecting linear probability changes.

After calculating nonverbal ability estimates for each person at each occasion, they were plotted against the persons' age at testing in the lifespan trajectory plot displayed in Figure 5.2. The lifespan trajectories of nonverbal ability are represented for each person, and the ability estimates have, under the partial-credit model, the same interpretation at ages ranging from 2–72. From Figure 5.2, it is easy to see that the trajectories of nonverbal ability rose rapidly through childhood, decelerated during adolescence, flattened out during adulthood, and potentially show a slow but terminal decline into older adulthood. Most importantly, there appear to be sizable individual differences in both the level of nonverbal ability and between-person differences in those changes across the lifespan.

5.5.2 *Step 2: Growth Modeling of Nonverbal Ability*

Several growth models (i.e., level only, linear, single exponential, dual exponential) were fit to the ability estimates from the partial-credit model. The level-only model provided baseline fit statistics for comparison purposes to determine whether there

Table 5.4 Parameter Estimates From the Dual Exponential Growth Model Fit to the Nonverbal Ability Estimates

Parameter	Parameter estimate	Standard error
Fixed effects		
Intercept (η_0)	5.46	.045
Slope (η_1)	0.71	.098
Growth rate (π_g)	0.20	.006
Decline rate (π_d)	0.09	.011
Random effects		
Intercept (σ_0^2)	0.57	.063
Slope (σ_1^2)	0.01	.002
Intercept-slope covariance (ρ_{01})	−0.02	.007
Residual (σ_e^2)	1.09	.033

were systematic changes in nonverbal ability span. The linear and quadratic models did not converge, indicating they were not appropriate for these data. The single and dual exponential models fit better than the level-only model, and the dual exponential model fit significantly better than the single exponential model (Δ-*2LL* = 81, Δ*parms* = 1), indicating that nonverbal ability declined during older adulthood.

Parameter estimates from the dual exponential model are contained in Table 5.4. The average rate of change was positive (η_1 = .71), and there was significant variation in the average rate of change (${\sigma_1}^2$ = .10). The mean intercept, centered at 20 years, was 5.46, and there was significant variation in nonverbal ability at this age (${\sigma_0}^2$ = .57). There was a negative covariance (σ_{01} = -.02; ρ_{01} = -.31) between the intercept and rate of change such that participants with more nonverbal ability at age 20 tended to have slower rates of change. The expected mean (and between-person deviations) of the age-based latent curve of nonverbal ability is displayed in Figure 5.3. Figure 5.3 shows the sharp increases during childhood before changes in nonverbal ability decelerated, peaked around 30 years of age, and slowly declined through older adulthood. It also becomes apparent that even though the decline rate was significantly different from zero, there was only a small amount of decline in nonverbal ability for participants in these studies.

5.6 Discussion

Analyzing item-level data in longitudinal studies could become the norm in applied longitudinal research because of its many practical benefits, including the possibility of using longitudinal data where the scales have changed (see McArdle et al., 2009). Of course, there are also many limitations to analyzing item-level data, some of which researchers and publishers may need to overcome. That is, it would be possible to create "translation tables" from larger scale cross-sectional studies using common items and apply these to our inevitably smaller longitudinal studies.

The benefits of using item-level data in longitudinal studies include the potential reduction practice effects by administering different tests at different occasions, checks and tests of item drift and differential item functioning across time

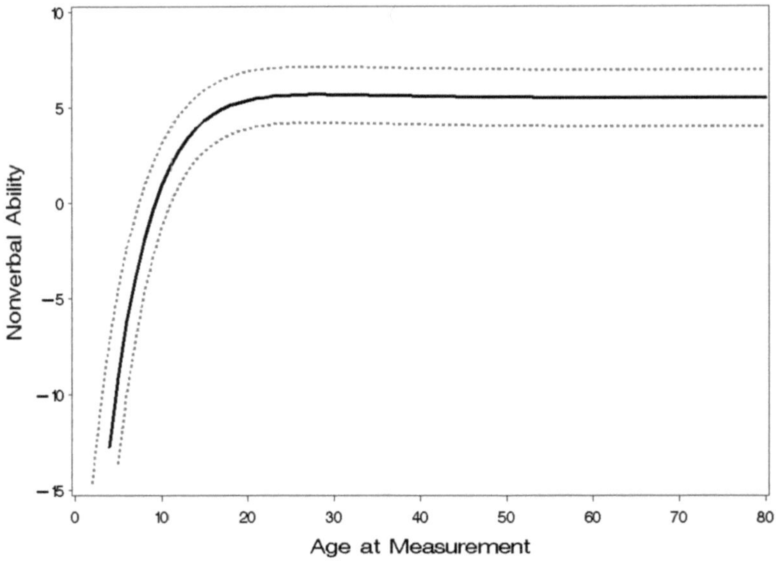

Fig. 5.3 Predicted trajectory for nonverbal ability based on the dual exponential growth model

and age, more precise estimates of ability compared to simple sum scores, and information regarding the relative magnitudes of measurement error within and across time. One way to reduce practice effects is to administer a new test (and therefore items) at each successive occasion. This would reduce item-specific retest effects, which may be contributing to the lack of significant decline in nonverbal ability reported here. Next, tests of measurement equivalence or the invariance of item discrimination and difficulty (and thresholds) parameters can be examined across time or age to make sure the measurement properties are stable. Items may become more difficult or may not relate to the underlying construct in the same way across time.

There are many ways to consider the utility of factorial invariance in longitudinal studies (McArdle, 2007). In one approach to this problem, Horn and McArdle (1992) and McArdle and Cattell (1994) treated factorial invariance as a desirable property—so desirable that the search was extended (over groups) to allow resulting invariant functions, which are highly complex representations of the original data. In contrast, in the approach suggested by Horn, McArdle, and Mason (1983) and Edwards and Wirth (2009), the lack of measurement invariance is not necessarily a bad result, and it largely becomes problematic if measurement invariance is assumed and not tested. Unfortunately, this is exactly the problem of the typical longitudinal study with completely changing measurements, where it becomes difficult to provide formal tests of hypotheses. What is needed in new longitudinal studies is more appreciation of the utility of overlapping items from one time to the next, because as of now there is no formal way to go back in time to add such useful items (F. M. Lord, personal communication, June 1977).

In this context, longitudinal analysis of item-level data helps our precision in two ways. First, our estimates of ability are more precise since we are only focusing on the items that each participant answered and their response pattern, as opposed to making assumptions regarding the correctness and incorrectness of items that were not administered to the participant based on starting and stopping rules common to intelligence tests. Second, using item-level data allows for estimating the standard error of measurement for each individual response pattern at each occasion. This information can be used to weight data in the estimation of statistical models to provide more precise estimates of important model parameters.

Drawbacks of using item-level data in longitudinal research stem from sample size restrictions and availability of user-friendly software for combining item response models with higher order statistical models to examine applied research questions. Item response models often have many parameters to estimate, which are poorly estimated with small and nonrepresentative samples—the types of samples that are often found in psychological and longitudinal research. One way to overcome this problem is for researchers and test makers to publish item parameters. In this situation, item parameters can be fixed to known values and the benefits of item response models are carried forward to the examination of the applied research question, without having to estimate item parameters with a small and potentially biased sample.

This research is intended to raise new questions about the optimal use of item responses in longitudinal data. For example, it is clear that dropping some items at later occasions is a reasonable technique, especially if the item does not have high discriminatory power. It is also clear that dropping items is reasonable when there is a large mismatch between item difficulty and person ability, and we see this in the administration of commonly used cognitive assessments with their built-in starting and stopping rules. However, it is not yet clear how much statistical power will be lost in the longitudinal assessments if items are dropped, even though they had been presented at earlier occasions. Careful study of the existing item-level longitudinal data can be useful in the determination of what is most reasonable for future studies. But we hope it is also obvious that the goal of this study is to improve the scales used in lifespan dynamics research. This research does not deal with the more difficult situation faced by high-stakes testing, and this longitudinal item-linking approach will certainly need to be improved before these critical issues can be considered.

5.7 Concluding Remarks

Longitudinal data are not ideal for equating tests because of item-level practice effects, item drift, and changes in ability level. Ideally, equating multiple tests would be conducted with large and appropriately aged samples measured at appropriate time periods. However, given the nature of the IGS and BMLS data, this was not possible. As mentioned, the data described here were weak for linking multiple tests forms. Sample sizes were small at any given occasion, especially when multiple test forms were administered (e.g., $n = 110$ for the BMLS when the WAIS and Stanford-Binet Form L were administered). Additionally, only age-appropriate items were administered at any measurement occasion. Thus, equating at a given occasion would have led to highly unstable item parameters. Instead, we utilized the longitudinal strength of the data and fit an item response model to all of available data leading to more stable estimates of item parameters that are on the same scale. Finally, we leaned heavily on a very simple item response model with strong assumptions (e.g., longitudinal measurement invariance, equal discrimination) that were untestable given our limited data. To the extent that model assumptions are not met by our data, our results are misleading.

Chapter 6
How to Average Equating Functions, If You Must

Paul W. Holland and William E. Strawderman

6.1 Introduction and Notation

An interest in *averaging* two or more equating functions can arise in various settings. As the motivation for the *angle bisector* method described later in this paper, Angoff (1971) mentioned situations with multiple estimates of the same linear equating function for which averaging the different estimates may be appropriate. In the nonequivalent groups with anchor test (NEAT) equating design, several possible linear and nonlinear equating methods are available. These are based on different assumptions about the missing data in that design (von Davier, Holland, & Thayer, 2004b). It might be useful to average the results of some of the options for a final *compromise* method. Other recent proposals include averaging an estimated equating function with the *identity transformation* to achieve more stability in small samples (Kim, von Davier, & Haberman, 2008) as well as creating *hybrid* equating functions that are averages of linear and equipercentile equating functions, putting more weight on one than on the other (von Davier, Fournier-Zajac, & Holland, 2006). In his discussion of the angle bisector, Angoff implicitly weighted the two linear functions equally. The idea of *weighting* the two functions differently is a natural and potentially useful added flexibility to the averaging process that we use throughout our discussion.

We denote by $e_1(x)$ and $e_2(x)$ two different equating functions for linking scores on test X to scores on test Y. We will assume that $e_1(x)$ and $e_2(x)$ are *strictly increasing* continuous functions of x over the entire real line. The use of the entire real line is appropriate for both *linear* equating functions and for the method of

P.W. Holland (✉)
Paul Holland Consulting Corporation, 200 4th Ave South, Apt 100, St Petersburg, FL 33701, USA
e-mail: pholland@ets.org

W.E. Strawderman
Department of Statistics, Rutgers University, 110 Frelinghuysen Rd., Room 561 Hill Center Building for the Mathematical Sciences, Busch Campus, Piscataway, NJ N08854, USA
e-mail: straw@stat.rutgers.edu

A.A. von Davier (ed.), *Statistical Models for Test Equating, Scaling, and Linking*, Statistics for Social and Behavioral Sciences,
DOI 10.1007/978-0-387-98138-3_6,

kernel equating (von Davier et al., 2004b). Our main discussion concerns averages of equating functions that are defined for *all real x*.

Suppose it is desired to *average* $e_1(x)$ and $e_2(x)$ in some way, putting weight w on $e_1(x)$ and $1 - w$ on $e_2(x)$. In order to have a general notation for this, we will let $\oplus$ denote an *operator* that forms a weighted average of two such functions, e_1 and e_2, and puts weight w on e_1 and $1 - w$ on e_2. At this point we do not define exactly what $\oplus$ is and let it stand for any method of averaging. Our notation for any such weighted average of e_1 and e_2 is

$$we_1 \oplus (1 - w)e_2 \tag{6.1}$$

to denote the resulting equating *function*. We denote its *value* at some X-score, x, by

$$we_1 \oplus (1 - w)e_2(x). \tag{6.2}$$

If there are three such functions, e_1, e_2, e_3, then their *weighted average function* is denoted as

$$w_1e_1 \oplus w_2e_2 \oplus w_3e_3, \tag{6.3}$$

where the weights, w_i, sum to 1.

6.2 Some Desirable Properties of Averages of Equating Functions

Using our notation we can describe various properties that the operator, $\oplus$, should be expected to possess. The first five appear to be obvious requirements for any type of averaging process.

6.2.1 Property 1

Property 1: The order of averaging does not matter, so that

$$we_1 \oplus (1 - w)e_2 = (1 - w)e_2 \oplus we_1. \tag{6.4}$$

6.2.2 Property 2

Property 2: The weighted average should lie between the two functions being averaged, so that

$$\text{if } e_1(x) \leq e_2(x), \text{then } e_1(x) \leq we_1 \oplus (1 - w)e_2(x) \leq e_2(x). \tag{6.5}$$

Property 2 also implies the following natural property:

6.2.3 *Property 3*

Property 3: If the two equating functions are equal at a score, x, the weighted average has that same common value at x, so that

$$\text{if } e_1(x) = e_2(x), \text{then } we_1 \oplus (1 - w)e_2(x) = e_1(x). \tag{6.6}$$

6.2.4 *Property 4*

It also seems reasonable for the average of two equating functions (that are always strictly increasing and continuous) to have both of these conditions as well. Thus, our next condition is Property 4: For any w, $we_1 \oplus (1 - w)e_2(x)$ is a continuous and strictly increasing function of x.

6.2.5 *Property 5*

When it is desired to average three equating functions, as in Equation 6.3, it also seems natural to require the averaging process to get the same result as first averaging of a pair of the functions and then averaging that average with the remaining function, that is, Property 5: If w_1, w_2, w_3 are positive and sum to 1.0, then

$$w_1e_1 \oplus w_2e_2 \oplus w_3e_3 = w_1e_1 \oplus (1 - w_1)[\frac{w_2}{1 - w_1}e_2 \oplus \frac{w_3}{1 - w_1}e_3]. \tag{6.7}$$

Again, without dwelling on notational issues in Equation 6.7, the order of the pair-wise averaging should not matter, either.

6.2.6 *Property 6*

There are other, less obvious assumptions that one might expect of an averaging operator for equating functions. One of them is Property 6: If e_1 and e_2 are *linear* functions then so is $we_1 \oplus (1 - w)e_2$, for any w. We think that Property 6 is a reasonable restriction to add to the list, because one justification for the linear equating function is its simplicity. An averaging process that changed linear functions to a nonlinear one seems to us to add a complication where there was none before.

6.2.7 Property 7

In addition to Properties 1–6 for $\oplus$, there is one very special property that has long been regarded as important for any equating function—the property of *symmetry*. This means that linking X to Y via the function $y = e(x)$ is assumed to imply that the link from Y to X is given by the *inverse function*, $x = e^{-1}(y)$, as noted by Dorans and Holland (2000). The traditional interpretation of the symmetry condition when applied to averaging equating functions is that averaging the inverse functions, e_1^{-1} and e_2^{-1}, results in the *inverse* function of the *average* of e_1 and e_2.

Using our notation for $\oplus$, the *condition of symmetry* may be expressed as Property 7:

$$\text{For any } w,\ (w e_1 \oplus (1-w)e_2)^{-1} = we_1^{-1} \oplus (1-w)e_2^{-1}. \tag{6.8}$$

From Equation 6.8 we can see that the symmetry property requires that the averaging operator, $\oplus$, be formally *distributive* relative to the *inverse operator*.

6.3 The Point-Wise Weighted Average

The simplest type of weighted average that comes to mind is the simple *point-wise weighted average* of e_1 and e_2. It is defined as

$$m(x) = we_1(x) + (1-w)e_2(x), \tag{6.9}$$

where w is a fixed value, such as $w = 1/2$.

Geometrically, m is found by averaging the values of e_1 and e_2 along the vertical line located at x. For its heuristic value, our notation in Equations 6.1 and 6.2 was chosen to mimic Equation 6.9 as much as possible. In general, $m(x)$ in Equation 6.9 will satisfy Properties 1–6, for any choice of w. However, $m(x)$ will not always satisfy the symmetry property, Property 7. That is, if the inverses, $e_1^{-1}(y)$ and $e_2^{-1}(y)$, are averaged to obtain

$$m^*(y) = we_1^{-1}(y) + (1-w)e_2^{-1}(y), \tag{6.10}$$

then only in special circumstances will $m^*(y)$ be the inverse of $m(x)$ in Equation 6.9.

This is easiest to see when e_1 and e_2 are *linear*. For example, suppose e_1 and e_2 have the form

$$e_1(x) = a_1 + b_1x, \text{ and } e_2(x) = \; = a_2 + b_2x. \tag{6.11}$$

The point-wise weighted average of Equation 6.11 becomes

$$m(x) = \bar{a} + \bar{b}x, \tag{6.12}$$

where

$$\bar{b} = w\,b_1 + (1 - w)\,b_2 \text{ and } \bar{a} = w\,a_1 + (1 - w)a_2. \tag{6.13}$$

However, the inverse functions for e_1 and e_2 are also linear with slopes $1/b_1$ and $1/b_2$, respectively. Thus, the point-wise average of the inverse functions, $m^*(x)$, has a slope that is the average of the reciprocals of the b_is:

$$b^* = w(1/b_1) + (1 - w)(1/b_2). \tag{6.14}$$

The inverse function of $m^*(x)$ is also linear and has slope $1/b^*$, where b^* is given in Equation 6.14. Thus, the slope of the inverse of $m^*(x)$ is the *harmonic* mean of b_1 and b_2. So, in order for the slope of the inverse of $m^*(x)$ to be the point-wise weighted average of the slopes of e_1 and e_2, the mean and the harmonic means of b_1 and b_2 must be equal. It is well known that this is only true if b_1 and b_2 are equal, in which case the equating functions are parallel. It is also easy to show that the intercepts do not add any new conditions. Thus we have Result 1 below.

6.3.1 Result 1

Result 1: The point-wise weighted average in Equation 6.9 satisfies the symmetry property for two linear equating functions if and only if the slopes, b_1 and b_2, are equal.

When $e_1(x)$ and $e_2(x)$ are non-linear they may still be *parallel* with a constant difference between them, that is

$$e_1(x) = e_2(x) + c \text{ for all } x. \tag{6.15}$$

When Equation 6.15 holds, it is easy to establish Result 2.

6.3.2 Result 2

Result 2: If $e_1(x)$ and $e_2(x)$ are nonlinear but parallel so that Equation 6.15 holds, then the point-wise weighted average also will satisfy the symmetry property, Property 7. In this case, the point-wise average is simply a constant added (or subtracted) to either e_1 or e_2, for example,

$$m(x) = e_2(x) + wc = e_1(x) - (1 - w)c. \tag{6.16}$$

Thus, although the point-wise weighted average does not always satisfy the symmetry property, it does satisfy it if $e_1(x)$ and $e_2(x)$ are parallel curves or lines.

6.4 The Angle Bisector Method of Averaging Two Linear Functions

Angoff (1971) made passing reference to the *angle bisector* method of averaging two linear equating functions. In discussions with Angoff, Holland was informed that this method was explicitly proposed as a way of preserving the symmetry property, Property 7. Figure 6.1 illustrates the angle bisector, denoted by e_{AB}.

While the geometry of the angle bisector is easy to understand, for computations a formula is more useful. Holland and Strawderman (1989) give such a formula. We state their result next, and outline its proof in Section 6.5.

6.4.1 *Result 3: Computation of the Unweighted Angle Bisector*

Result 3: If $e_1(x)$ and $e_2(x)$ are two linear equating functions as in Equation 6.9 that intersect at a point, then the linear function that bisects the angle between them is the point-wise weighted average

$$e_{AB} = We_1 + (1 - W)e_2, \tag{6.17}$$

with W given by

$$W = \frac{(1 + b_1^2)^{-1/2}}{(1 + b_1^2)^{-1/2} + (1 + b_2^2)^{-1/2}}. \tag{6.18}$$

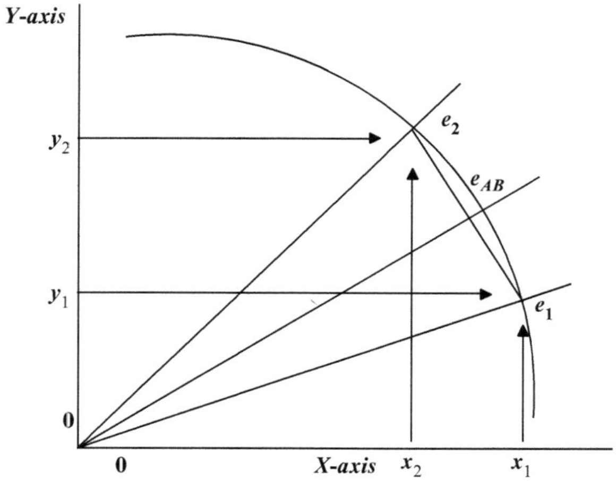

Fig. 6.1 The angle bisector is also the chord bisector

Note that in Result 3, if the two slopes are the same then $W = ½$ and the formula for the angle bisector reduces to the equally weighted point-wise average of the two parallel lines. It may be shown directly that the angle bisector given by Equations 6.17 and 6.18 satisfies the symmetry property, Property 7, for any two linear equating functions. Thus, in order for the point-wise weighted average Equation 6.9 to satisfy Property 7 for any pair of linear equating functions, it is necessary for the weight, w, to depend on the functions being averaged. It cannot be the same value for all pairs of functions.

6.5 Some Generalizations of the Angle Bisector Method

One way to understand the angle bisector for two linear functions is to imagine a circle of radius 1 centered at the point of intersection of the two lines. For simplicity, and without loss of generality, assume that the intersection point is at the origin, $(x, y) = (0, 0)$. This is also illustrated in Figure 6.1.

The linear function, e_i, intersects the circle at the point $(x_i, y_i) = (x_i, b_i x_i)$, and because the circle has radius 1 we have

$$\begin{aligned} (x_i)^2 + (b_i x_i)^2 &= 1, \text{ or} \\ x_i &= (1 + (b_i)^2)^{-1/2}. \end{aligned} \tag{6.19}$$

Thus, the linear function, e_i, intersects the circle at the point

$$(x_i, y_i) = ((1 + (b_i)^2)^{-1/2},\ b_i(1 + (b_i)^2)^{-1/2}). \tag{6.20}$$

The line that bisects the *angle* between e_1 and e_2 also bisects the *chord* that connects the intersection points, (x_1, y_1) and (x_2, y_2) given in Equation 6.20. The point of bisection of the chord is $((x_1 + x_2)/2, (y_1 + y_2)/2)$. From this it follows that the line through the origin that goes through the point of bisection of the chord has the slope,

$$b = \frac{y_1 + y_2}{x_1 + x_2} = Wb_1 + (1 - W)b_2, \tag{6.21}$$

where W is given by Equation 6.18. This shows that the angle bisector is the point-wise weighted average given in Result 3.

One way to generalize the angle bisector to include weights, as in Equation 6.1, is to divide the chord between (x_1, y_1) and (x_2, y_2) given in Equation 6.20 *proportionally* to w and $1 - w$ instead of *bisecting* it. If we do this, the point on the chord that is w of the way *from* (x_2, y_2) *to* (x_1, y_1) is $(wx_1 + (1-w)x_2, wy_1 + (1-w)y_2)$. It follows that the line through the origin that goes through this w-point on the chord has the slope

$$b = \frac{wy_1 + (1 - w)y_2}{wx_1 + (1 - w)x_2} = Wb_1 + (1 - W)b_2, \tag{6.22}$$

where W is now given by

$$W = \frac{w(1+b_1^2)^{-1/2}}{w(1+b_1^2)^{-1/2} + (1-w)(1+b_2^2)^{-1/2}}. \tag{6.23}$$

Hence, a weighted generalization of the angle bisector of two linear equating functions is given by Equation 6.17, with W specified by Equation 6.23.

This generalization of the angle bisector will divide the *angle* between e_1 and e_2 proportionally to w and $1-w$ only when $w = ½$. Otherwise, this generalization only approximately divides the angle proportionately. In addition, direct calculations show that this generalization of the angle bisector will satisfy all of the properties, Properties 1–7.

However, the angle bisector may be generalized in other ways as well. For example, instead of a circle centered at the point of intersection, suppose we place an L_p-circle there instead. An L_p-circle is defined by Equation 6.24:

$$|x|^p + |y|^p = 1, \tag{6.24}$$

where $p > 0$. Examples of L_p-circles for various choices of $p = 1$ and 3 are given in Figures 6.2 and 6.3.

If we now use the chord that connects the intersection points of the two lines with a given L_p-circle, as we did above for the ordinary circle, we find the following

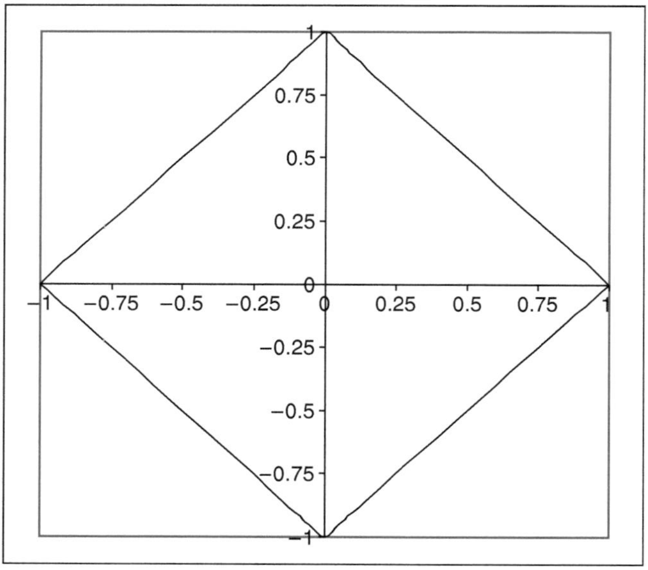

Fig. 6.2 Plot of the unit L_p-circle, $p = 1$

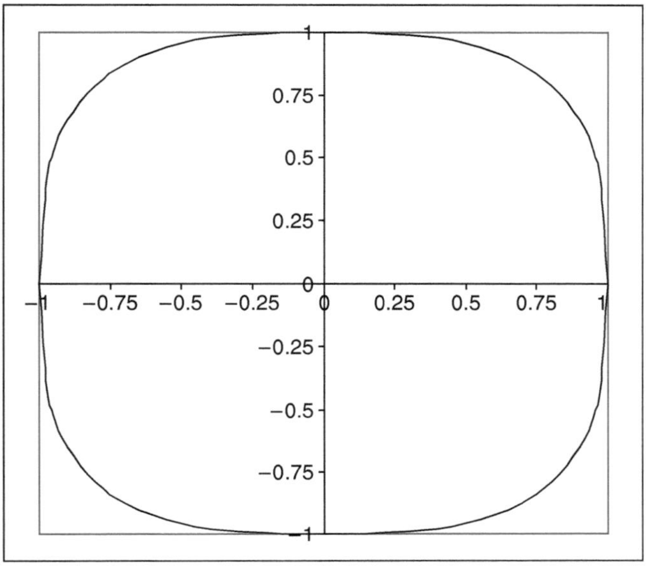

Fig. 6.3 Plot of the unit L_p-circle, $p = 3$

generalization of the angle bisector. We form the point-wise weighted average in Equation 6.17, but we use as W the following weight:

$$W = \frac{w(1 + b_1^p)^{-1/p}}{w(1 + b_1^p)^{-1/p} + (1 - w)(1 + b_2^p)^{-1/p}}, \tag{6.25}$$

for some $p > 0$, and $0 < w < 1$. It is a simple exercise to show that the use of W from Equation 6.25 as the weight in Equation 6.17 also will satisfy Properties 1–7 for any choice of $p > 0$, and $0 < w < 1$. We will find the case of $p = 1$ of special interest later. In that case W has the form

$$W = \frac{w(1 + b_1)^{-1}}{w(1 + b_1)^{-1} + (1 - w)(1 + b_2)^{-1}}. \tag{6.26}$$

Thus, the system of weighted averages (Equation 6.17) with weights that depend on the two slopes, as in Equation 6.25, produces a variety of ways to average linear equating functions that all satisfy Properties 1–7. Thus, the angle bisector is seen to be only one of an infinite family of possibilities. It is worth mentioning here that when $w = ½$, all of these averages of two linear equating functions using Equation 6.25 have the property of putting *more* weight on the line with the *smaller* slope. As a simple example, if $b_1 = 1$ and $b_2 = 2$, then for w = ½, Equation 6.26 gives the value $W = 0.6$ for the case of $p = 1$.

An apparent limitation of all of these circle methods of averaging two linear functions is that they do not immediately generalize to the case of three or more such functions. When there are three functions, they do not necessarily meet at a point; there could be three intersection points. In such a case, the idea of using an L_p-circle centered at the "point of intersection" makes little sense. However, the condition Property 5 gives us a way out of this narrow consideration. Applying it to the point-wise weighted average results obtained so far, it is tedious but straightforward to show that the *multiple function generalization* of Equation 6.17 coupled with Equation 6.25 is given by Result 4.

6.5.1 Result 4

Result 4: If $\{w_i\}$ are positive and sum to 1.0 and if $\{e_i\}$ are linear equating functions, then Property 5 requires that the pair-wise averages based on Equations 6.17 and 6.25 lead to

$$w_1e_1 \oplus w_2e_2 \oplus w_3e_3 \oplus \ldots = \sum_i W_ie_i \tag{6.27}$$

where

$$W_i \frac{w_i(1+b_i^p)^{-1/p}}{\sum_j w_j(1+b_j^p)^{-1/p}}. \tag{6.28}$$

Result 4 gives a solution to the problem of averaging several different linear equating functions that is easily applied in practice, once choices for p and w are made.

Holland and Strawderman (1989) introduced the idea of the *symmetric weighted average* (swave) of two equating functions that satisfies conditions of Properties 1–7 for any pair of linear or nonlinear equating functions. In the next two sections we develop a generalization of the symmetric average.

6.6 The Geometry of Inverse Functions and Related Matters

To begin, it is useful to illustrate the geometry of a strictly increasing continuous function, $y = e(x)$, and its inverse, $x = e^{-1}(y)$. First, fix a value of x in the domain of $e(\cdot)$, and let $y = e(x)$. Then the four points, (x, y), (x, x), (y, y) and (y, x), form the four corners of a square in the (x, y) plane, where the length of each side is $|x - y|$. The two points, (x, x) and (y, y), both lie on the 45-degree line; the other two points lie on opposite sides of the 45-degree line on a line that is at right angles, or orthogonal, to it. In addition, (x, y) and (y, x) are equidistant from the 45-degree line. However, by definition of the inverse function, when $y = e(x)$, it is also the case that $x = e^{-1}(y)$. Hence, the four points mentioned above can be re-expressed as $(x, e(x))$, (x, x), $(e(x), e(x))$, and $(y, e^{-1}(y))$, respectively.

The points $(x, e(x))$ and $(y, e^{-1}(y))$ are equidistant from the 45-degree line and on opposite sides of it. Furthermore, the line connecting them is orthogonal to the 45-degree line and is bisected by it. These simple facts are important for the rest of this discussion. For example, from them we immediately can conclude that the graphs of $e(\cdot)$ and $e^{-1}(\cdot)$ are reflections of each other about the 45-degree line in the (x, y) plane. This observation is the basis for the swave defined in Section 6.7.

Another simple fact that we will make repeated use of is that a strictly increasing continuous function of x, $e(x)$, crosses any line that is orthogonal to the 45-degree line in exactly one place. This is illustrated in Figure 6.4 for the graphs of two functions. In order to have a shorthand term for lines that are orthogonal to the 45-degree line, we will call them the *orthogonal lines* when this is unambiguous.

We recall the elementary fact that the equation for what we are calling an orthogonal line is

$$y = -x + c, \text{or } y + x = c, \text{for some constant, } c. \tag{6.29}$$

Thus, we have the relationship

$$e(x_1) + x_1 = c = y + x \tag{6.30}$$

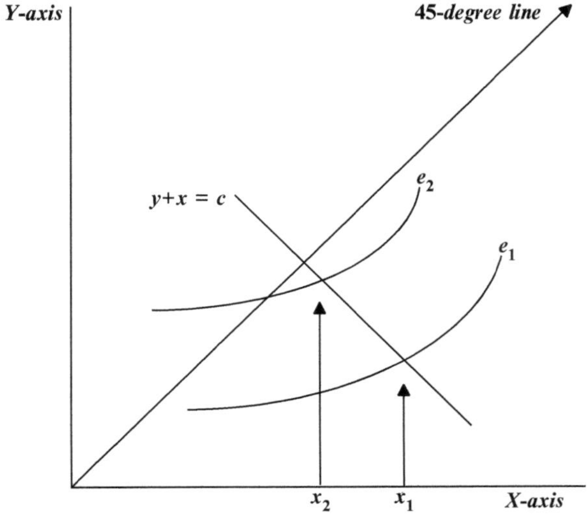

Fig. 6.4 An illustration of the intersections of $e_1(x)$ and $e_2(x)$ with an orthogonal line

for any other point, (x, y), that is on the orthogonal line. Equation 6.30 plays an important role in the definition of the *swave* in Section 6.7. Finally, we note that if e is a strictly increasing continuous function, then its inverse, e^{-1}, is one as well.

6.7 The Swave: The Symmetric *w*-Average of Two Equating Functions

With this preparation, we are ready to define the symmetric w-average or swave of two linear or nonlinear equating functions, $e_1(x)$ and $e_2(x)$. Note that from the above discussion, any orthogonal line, of the form given by Equation 6.29, will intersect $e_1(x)$ at a point, x_1, and $e_2(x)$ at another point, x_2. This is also illustrated in Figure 6.4.

The idea is that the value of the swave, $e_w(\cdot)$, is given by the point on the orthogonal line that corresponds to the weighted average of the two points, $(x_1, e_1(x_1))$ and $(x_2, e_2(x_2))$:

$$(\bar{x}, e_w(\bar{x})) = \mathrm{w}(x_1, e_1(x_1)) + (1 - \mathrm{w})(x_2, e_2(x_2)). \tag{6.31}$$

This is illustrated in Figure 6.5.

The point, $((\bar{x}, e_w(\bar{x})))$, is the weighted average of the two points, $(x_1, e_1(x_1))$ and $(x_2, e_2(x_2))$. Thus,

$$\bar{x} = wx_1 + (1 - w)x_2, \tag{6.32}$$

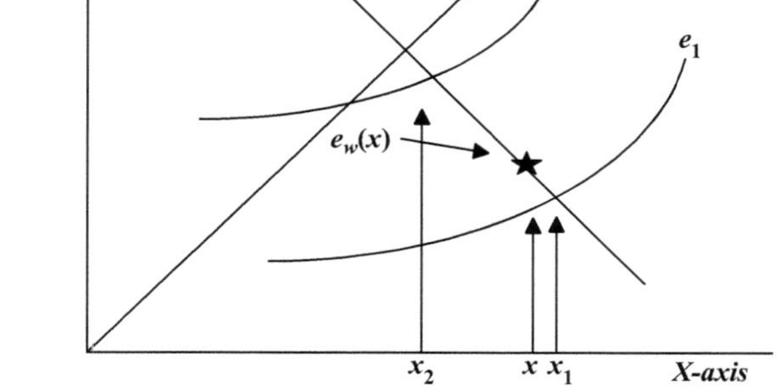

Fig. 6.5 An illustration of the swave of $e_1(x)$ and $e_2(x)$ at $x = w\,x_1 + (1 - w\,)\,x_2$ for a w greater than ½

and

$$e_w(\bar{x}) = we_1(x_1) + (1 - w)e_2(x_2). \tag{6.33}$$

In Equation 6.31, $\bar{x}$ is given by Equation 6.32. In order to define $e_w(x)$ for *an arbitrary* point, x, we start with x and define $x_1 = x - (1 - w)t$ and $x_2 = x + wt$ for some, as yet unknown, positive or negative value, t. Note that from the definitions of x_1 and x_2, their weighted average, $wx_1 + (1 - w)x_2$, equals x, so the given x can play the role $\bar{x}$ of Equation 6.32.

Next, we find a value of t such that $(x_1, e_1(x_1))$ and $(x_2, e_2(x_2))$ lie on the same orthogonal line, as in Figure 6.5. From Equation 6.30, this condition on t requires that Equation 6.34 is satisfied:

$$e_1(x_1) + x_1 = e_2(x_2) + x_2. \tag{6.34}$$

Equation 6.34 may be expressed in terms of x and t as

$$e_1(x - (1 - w)t) + x - (1 - w)t = e_2(x + wt) + x + wt.$$

or

$$t = e_1(x - (1 - w)t) - e_2(x + wt). \tag{6.35}$$

Equation 6.35 plays an important role in what follows.

In general, for each value of x, Equation 6.35 is a nonlinear equation in t. As we show in the Appendix, for any choice of x and w and for any strictly increasing continuous equating functions, e_1 and e_2, Equation 6.35 always has a *unique* solution for t. The solution of Equation 6.35 for t implicitly defines t as a function of x, which we denote by $t(x)$. Once $t(x)$ is in hand, the value of the swave at x, $e_w(x)$, is computed from the expression,

$$e_w(x) = we_1(x - (1 - w)t(x)) + (1 - w)e_2(x + wt(x)). \tag{6.36}$$

The definition of e_w in Equation 6.36 is an example of the operator $\oplus$ in Equation 6.1. In Equation 6.36, there is a clear sense in which the weight w is applied to e_1 and $1 - w$ is applied to e_2. We show later that the swave differs from the point-wise weighted average in Equation 6.9, except when the two equating functions are parallel, as discussed above. Moreover, the definition of the swave is a *process* that requires the whole functions, e_1 and e_2, rather than just their evaluation at the selected x-value. In the Appendix we show that the solution for t in Equations 6.35 and 6.36 is unique.

In the Appendix we show that the swave satisfies conditions in Properties 2 and 4. We discuss below the application of the swave to linear equating functions and show that it satisfies Property 6. That the swave satisfies Property 7, the symmetry property, is given in Result 5, next.

6.7.1 Result 5

Result 5: The swave, $e_w(x)$, defined by Equations 6.35 and 6.36, satisfies the symmetry property, Property 7.

Proof. Suppose we start with the inverse functions, e_1^{-1} and e_2^{-1}, and form their swave, denoted $e*_w(y)$, for a given y-value. Then Equations 6.35 and 6.36 imply that for any choice of y there is a value $t*$ that satisfies

$$t^* = e_1^{-1}(y - (1 - w)t^*) - e_2^{-1}(x + wt^*) \tag{6.37}$$

and

$$e^*{}_w(y) = we_1^{-1}(y - (1 - w)t^*) + (1 - w)e_2^{-1}(y + wt^*). \tag{6.38}$$

Now let

$$y_1 = y - (1 - w)t^*, \text{and}\, y_2 = y + wt^*.$$

Also, define x, x_1, and x_2 by

$$x = e^*{}_w(y), x_1 = e_1^{-1}(y_1), \text{ and}\, x_2 = e_2^{-1}(y_2). \tag{6.39}$$

Hence, by definition of the inverse,

$$y_1 = e_1(x_1), y_2 = e_2(x_2), \text{and}\, y = e^{*-1}_w(x). \tag{6.40}$$

From the definition of the swave, the following three points are all on the same orthogonal line:

$$(y, e^*{}_w(y)), (y_1, e_1^{-1}(y_1)), \text{and}\, (y_2, e_2^{-1}(y_2)).$$

However, using the relationships in Equations 6.38 and 6.39, these three points are the same as the following three points, which are also on that orthogonal line:

$$\left(e^*{}_w{}^{-1}(x), x\right), (e_1(x_1), x_1), \text{ and}\, (e_2(x_2), x_2).$$

Furthermore, the following three points are on that same orthogonal line:

$$\left(x, e^*{}_w{}^{-1}(x)\right), (x_1, e_1(x_1)), \text{and}\, (x_2, e_2(x_1)).$$

Yet, from Equation 6.38 it follows that

$$x = wx_1 + (1 - w)x_2, \tag{6.41}$$

so we let $t = x_2 - x_1$, and therefore, $x_1 = x - (1 - w)t$, and $x_2 = x + wt$.

Furthermore, from the definitions of y_1 and y_2, we have

$$y = wy_1 + (1 - w)y_2$$

and therefore

$$y = we_1(x_1) + (1 - w)e_2(x_2),$$

so that

$$y = e^{*-1}_{w}(x) = we_1(x - (1 - w)t) + (1 - w)e_2(x + wt). \tag{6.42}$$

Thus, the inverse function, $e{*_w}^{-1}$, satisfies Equation 6.36 for the swave. The only question remaining is whether the value of t in Equation 6.42 satisfies Equation 6.35.

However, the points $(x_1, e_1(x_1))$ and $(x_2, e_2(x_2))$ are on the same orthogonal line. Therefore, they satisfy Equation 6.34, from which Equation 6.35 for t follows.

This shows that the inverse function, $e{*_w}^{-1}$, satisfies the condition of the symmetric w-average, e_w, so that from the uniqueness of the solution to Equation 6.35 we have $e{*_w}^{-1} = e_w$, which proves Result 5. From the definitions of y_1, y_2, x_1, and x_2 in the proof of Result 5, it is easy to see that the t^* that solves Equation 6.37 for the inverse functions and the t that solves Equation 6.35 for the original functions are related by $t^* = x_1 - x_2 = -t$, so that t and t^* have the same *magnitude* but the opposite *sign*.

6.8 The Swave of Two Linear Equating Functions

In this section we examine the form of the swave in the linear case. The equation for t, Equation 6.35, now becomes linear in t and can be solved explicitly. So assume that

$$e_1(x) = a_1 + b_1x, \text{and}\, e_2(x) = a_2 + b_2x. \tag{6.43}$$

Then, Equation 6.35 is

$$t = a_1 + b_1(x - (1 - w)t) - a_2 - b_2(x + wt).$$

Hence,

$$t(1 + (1 - w)b_1 + wb_2) = (a_1 - a_2) + (b_1 - b_2)x$$

so that

$$t(x) = \frac{(a_1 - a_2) + (b_1 - b_2)x}{1 + (1 - w)b_1 + wb_2}. \tag{6.44}$$

Substituting the value of $t(x)$ from Equation 6.44 into the equation for $e_w(x)$ in Equation 6.36 results in

$$e_w(x) = \bar{a} + \bar{b}x - w(1-w)(b_1 - b_2)\frac{a_1 - a_2 + (b_1 - b_2)x}{1 + (1-w)b_1 + wb_2}, \tag{6.45}$$

where $\bar{a} = wa_1 + (1-w)a_2$ and $\bar{b} = wb_1 + (1-w)b_2$ denote the weighted averages of the intercepts and slopes of e_1 and e_2, respectively.

From Equation 6.45 we immediately see that, in the linear case, the swave, $e_w(x)$, is identical to the point-wise weighted average in Equation 6.9 if and only if the two slopes, b_1 and b_2, are identical, and the two linear functions are parallel. Simplifying Equation 6.45 further we obtain

$$e_w(x) = We_1(x) + (1-W)e_2(x), \tag{6.46}$$

where

$$W = \frac{w(1+b_1)^{-1}}{w(1+b_1)^{-1} + (1-w)(1+b_2)^{-1}}. \tag{6.47}$$

Thus, in the linear case, the swave is exactly the point-wise weighted average that arises for an L_p-circle with $p = 1$, in other words, Equation 6.26, discussed in Section 6.5. From Result 5, we know that the swave always satisfies the symmetry condition, Property 7, but this is also easily shown directly. We see that, in the linear case, the swave also satisfies Property 6.

Chapter 6 Appendix

6.A.1 Computing the Swave for Two Equating Functions

The key to computing e_w is Equation 6.35. This equation for $t(x)$ is nonlinear in general, so computing $t(x)$ requires numerical methods. A derivative-free approach that is useful in this situation is *Brent's method.* To use this method to solve Equation 6.35 for t we first define $g(t)$ as follows:

$$g(t) = t - e_1(x - (1-w)t) + e_2(x + wt). \tag{6.A.1}$$

If t_0 solves Equation 6.35, then t_0 is a zero of $g(t)$ in Equation 6.A.1. Brent's method is a way of finding the zeros of functions. It requires that two values of t are known, one for which $g(t)$ is positive and one for which $g(t)$ is negative. Theorem 1 summarizes several useful facts about $g(t)$ and provides the two needed values of t for use in Brent's method.

Theorem 1. *If e_1 and e_2 are strictly increasing continuous functions, then $g(t)$ defined in Equation 6.A.1 is a strictly increasing continuous function that has a unique zero at t_0. Furthermore, t_0 is positive if and only if $e_1(x) - e_2(x)$ is positive. Consequently, if $e_1(x) - e_2(x)$ is positive, then $g(0)$ is negative and $g(e_1(x) - e_2(x))$ is positive; furthermore, if $e_1(x) - e_2(x)$ is negative, then $g(0)$ is positive and $g(e_1(x) - e_2(x))$ is negative.*

Proof. The functions t, $-e_1(x - (1 - w)\, t)$, and $e_2(x + w\, t)$ are all strictly increasing continuous functions of t so that their sum, $g(t)$, is also a strictly increasing continuous function of t. Hence, if $g(t)$ has a zero at t_0, this is its only zero. In order to show that $g(t)$ does have a zero at some t_0 it suffices to show that, for large enough t, $g(t) > 0$ and, for small enough t, $g(t) < 0$. But if $t > 0$, it follows from the strictly increasing (in t) nature of $-e_1(x - (1 - w)\, t)$ and of $e_2(x + w\, t)$ that

$$g(t) > t - [e_1(x) - e_2(x)]. \tag{6.A.2}$$

The right side of Equation 6.A.2 is greater than 0 if t is larger than $e_1(x) - e_2(x)$. Similarly, if $t < 0$, it also follows that

$$g(t) < t - [e_1(x) - e_2(x)]. \tag{6.A.3}$$

The right side of Equation 6.A.3 is less than 0 if t is less than $e_1(x) - e_2(x)$. Hence, these two inequalities show that $g(t)$ always has a single zero at a value we denote by t_0.

Now, suppose that $t_0 > 0$. Then $g(t_0) = 0$ by definition so that

$$0 < t_0 = e_1(x - (1 - w)\, t_0) - e_2(x + w\, t_0) \tag{6.A.4}$$

But by the strict monotonicity of e_1 and e_2, we have

$$e_1(x - (1 - w)\, t_0) < e_1(x), \text{and} - e_2(x + w\, t_0) < - e_2(x)$$

so that

$$e_1(x - (1 - w)\, t_0) - e_2(x + wt_0) < e_1(x) - e_2(x). \tag{6.A.5}$$

Combining Equations 6.A.4 and 6.A.5 shows that if $t_0 > 0$, then $e_1(x) - e_2(x) > 0$.

A similar argument shows that if $t_0 < 0$, then $e_1(x) - e_2(x) < 0$. Hence t_0 is positive if and only if $e_1(x) - e_2(x)$ is positive. Note that we can always compute $e_1(x) - e_2(x)$ because it is assumed that these functions are given to us. Thus, from the relative sizes of $e_1(x)$ and $e_2(x)$ we can determine the sign of the zero, t_0.

Because $g(t)$ is strictly increasing we have the following additional result. If $e_1(x) - e_2(x)$ is positive, then t_0 is also positive and therefore $g(0)$ is negative. Also, if $e_1(x) - e_2(x)$ is negative, then t_0 is also negative and therefore $g(0)$ is positive.

Now suppose again that $e_1(x) - e_2(x)$ is positive so that t_0 is also positive. However, from Equation 6.19, for any positive t, $g(t) > t - [e_1(x) - e_2(x)]$, so let $t = t_0$. Hence,

$$0 = g(t_0) > t_0 - [e_1(x) - e_2(x)], \tag{6.A.6}$$

so that

$$0 < t_0 < e_1(x) - e_2(x). \tag{6.A.7}$$

Hence, $g(e_1(x) - e_2(x))$ is positive as well. Thus, whenever $e_1(x) - e_2(x)$ is positive, then $g(0)$ is negative and $g(e_1(x) - e_2(x))$ is positive. When $e_1(x) - e_2(x)$ is negative, a similar argument shows that

$$e_1(x) - e_2(x) < t_0 < 0. \tag{6.A.8}$$

Hence $g(e_1(x) - e_2(x))$ is negative. This finishes the proof of Theorem 1.

6.A.2 Properties of the Swave

Theorem 2. *The swave, $e_w(x)$, satisfies Property 2 and lies strictly between $e_1(x)$ and $e_2(x)$, for all x.*

Proof. Consider the case when $e_1(x) > e_2(x)$ (the reverse case is proved in a similar way). We wish to show that $e_1(x) > e_w(x) > e_2(x)$. Because $e_1(x) > e_2(x)$, from Theorem 1 it follows that $t(x) > 0$ as well. From the strictly increasing natures of e_1 and e_2, it follows that

$$e_1(x_1) < e_1(x), \text{and } e_2(x_2) > e_2(x).$$

We wish to show that $e_1(x) > e_w(x) > e_2(x)$, so consider first the upper bound. By definition,

$$e_w(x) = we_1(x_1) + (1 - w)e_2(x_2) < we_1(x) + (1 - w)e_2(x_2).$$

However,

$$0 < t(x) = e_1(x_1) - e_2(x_2), \text{so that } e_2(x_2) < e_1(x_1) < e_1(x).$$

Combining these results give us

$$e_w(x) < we_1(\mathrm{x}) + (1 - w)e_1(x) = e_1(x),$$

the result we wanted to prove. The lower bound is found in an analogous manner.

Theorem 3. *The swave is strictly increasing if* e_1 *and* e_2 *are.*

Facts: $e(x)$ monotone implies $c(x) = x + e(x)$ is strictly monotone (since it is a sum of a monotone and a strictly monotone function). Also, $c(x^*) > c(x)$ implies $x^* > x$ and $e(x^*) > e(x)$.

Let $c_i(x) = x + e_i(x)$, $i = 1, 2$. Also let $e_w(x) = we_1(x_1) + (1 - w)e_2(x_2)$, where $x = wx_1 + (1 - w)x_2$ and $c_1(x_1) = c_2(x_2)$, i.e., $x_1 + e_1(x_1) = x_2 + e_2(x_2)$ so that $(x_i, e_i(x_i))$ are on same orthogonal line.

Assume $e_i(x)$ are both monotone increasing. Now suppose $x^* > x$ where $x = wx_1 + (1 - w)x_2$ and $x^* = wx_1{}^* + (1 - w)x_2{}^*$ and suppose further that $c_1(x_1) = c_2(x_2)$ and that $c_1(x_1{}^*) = c_2(x_2{}^*)$. Then, $(x_i, e_i(x_i))$ are both on the same orthogonal line and $(x_i{}^*, e_i(x_i{}^*))$ are too (but possibly a different line). We want to conclude that $x_1{}^* > x_1$ and $x_2{}^* > x_2$. This will allow us to conclude that $e_i(x_i{}^*) > e_i(x_i)$ and hence that $e_w(x^*) > e_w(x)$, thereby proving the monotonicity of e_w.

Proof. Assume to the contrary that $x_1{}^* \leq x_1$. Then $c_2(x_2{}^*) = c_1(x_1{}^*) \leq c_1(x_1) = c_2(x_2)$, so that $x_2{}^* \leq x_2$. This in turn implies that $x^* = wx_1{}^* + (1 - w)x_2{}^* \leq wx_1 + (1 - w)x_2 = x$, or $x^* \leq x$, contradicting the assumption that $x^* > x$. A similar argument shows that $x_2{}^* > x_2$. Hence, $e_i(x_i{}^*) > e_i(x_i)$ and $e_w(x^*) > e_w(x)$, thereby proving the monotonicity of e_w.

Chapter 7
New Approaches to Equating With Small Samples

Samuel A. Livingston and Sooyeon Kim

7.1 Overview

The purpose of this chapter is to introduce the reader to some recent innovations intended to solve the problem of equating test scores on the basis of data from small numbers of test takers. We begin with a brief description of the problem and of the techniques that psychometricians now use in attempting to deal with it. We then describe three new approaches to the problem, each dealing with a different stage of the equating process: (1) data collection, (2) estimating the equating relationship from the data collected, and (3) using collateral information to improve the estimate. We begin with Stage 2, describing a new method of estimating the equating transformation from small-sample data. We also describe the type of research studies we are using to evaluate the effectiveness of this new method. Then we move to Stage 3, describing some procedures for using collateral information from other equatings to improve the accuracy of an equating based on small-sample data. Finally, we turn to Stage 1, describing a new data collection plan in which the new form is introduced in a series of stages rather than all at once.

7.2 The Problem

Equating test scores is a statistical procedure, and its results, like those of most other statistical procedures, are subject to sampling variability. The smaller the samples of test takers from which the equating is computed, the more the equating results are likely to deviate from what they would be in a different pair of samples—or in the population that the samples represent. For tests equated through randomly

S.A. Livingston (✉) and S. Kim
Educational Testing Service, Rosedale Rd, Princeton, New Jersey 08541, USA
e-mail: slivingston@ets.org

A.A. von Davier (ed.), *Statistical Models for Test Equating, Scaling, and Linking*, Statistics for Social and Behavioral Sciences,
DOI 10.1007/978-0-387-98138-3_7,

equivalent groups, with no anchor, the important number is the total number of test takers available for the equating administration—possibly 200, 100, or even fewer. For tests equated through common items, the problem becomes particularly acute when very few test takers take the new test form at its first administration—possibly 30, 20, or even fewer. As the psychometricians responsible for the equating of the scores, we need to find a raw-to-scale score conversion that will make the scores of the test takers who take the new form comparable to the scores of test takers who took other forms of the test. We cannot make the problem go away by simply claiming that the test takers whose scores we can observe in time for the equating are the entire target population for the equating of those two test forms. In many cases, a test form taken at first by only a few test takers will be administered later to many others. We can accumulate data over two or more administrations of the new form and re-equate the scores, but the scores of the first group of test takers will already have been reported.

Even if the new form will not be administered again, the problem remains. The important principle is that an individual test taker's reported score should not depend heavily (ideally, not at all) on the particular group of test takers whose data are used to equate the scores on the form that the test taker happened to take.[1] We need to determine an equating relationship that will generalize to other groups that may differ in ability. What we really want is a good estimate of the equipercentile equating relationship in the population of potential test takers—not simply an equating of means and standard deviations on the two forms, but an equating of the full score distributions.

7.3 Current Practice

One way to improve the accuracy of equipercentile equating in small samples of test takers is to presmooth the score distributions (see Livingston, 1993). However, if the samples of test takers are quite small, this technique may not reduce the sampling variability in the equating to an acceptable level.

Another procedure that has been recommended is to establish a minimum sample size for equating. If the available samples meet the sample size requirement, equate the scores; if samples of the specified size are not available, assume the new form and reference form to be of equal difficulty throughout the score range (see Kolen & Brennan, 1995, p. 272; Kolen & Brennan, 2004, pp. 289-290). We believe there are better ways to deal with the problem.

Possibly the most common approach to estimating a relationship in a population on the basis of small-sample data is to use a strong model. Strong models require

[1]This principle is the basis for the requirement of *population invariance* (see, e.g., Dorans, Moses, & Eignor, Chapter 2 of this volume). In the case of equating with small samples, a greater problem is that the samples of test takers may not adequately represent any population.

only a small number of parameters to be estimated from the data, in effect substituting assumptions for data. In test score equating, the strong model most commonly used is the linear equating model. Its basic assumption is that in the target population, the distributions of scores on the new form (to be equated) and on the reference form (to which it is being equated) differ only in their means and standard deviations. An even stronger model is that of *mean equating*, a linear equating model that assumes that the score distributions on the new form and reference form in the target population differ only in their means (see Kolen & Brennan, 1995, pp. 29-30; Kolen & Brennan, 2004, pp. 30-31). Both of these models constrain the equating relationship to be linear. However, when test forms differ in difficulty, the equating relationship between them typically is not linear. If the difficulty difference is substantial, the relationship is not even approximately linear. A harder form and an easier form, administered to the same group of test takers, will tend to produce differently skewed distributions. The stronger test takers' scores will tend to vary more on the harder form than on the easier form; the weaker test takers' scores will tend to vary more on the easier form than on the harder form. Consequently, the slope of the equating transformation will not be the same for the weaker test takers as for the stronger test takers. A linear transformation, with its constant slope, cannot adequately model the equating relationship.

7.4 Circle-Arc Equating

Circle-arc equating is a strong model that does *not* assume the equating relationship to be linear. It is based on an idea from Divgi (1987). Divgi's idea was to constrain the equating curve to pass through two prespecified end points and an empirically determined middle point. Although the circle-arc model is different from Divgi's, it also constrains the equating curve to pass through two prespecified end points and an empirically determined middle point. In circle-arc equating, the lower end point corresponds to the lowest meaningful score on each form. On a multiple-choice test scored by counting the number of correct answers, the lowest meaningful score would typically be the chance score—the expected score for a test taker who responds at random (e.g., without reading the questions). The upper end point corresponds to the maximum possible score on each form. The middle point is determined by equating at a single point in the middle of the score distribution.

7.4.1 The Circle-Arc Method

The circle-arc equating method requires only one point on the equating curve to be estimated from the small-sample data. The first step of the method is to determine that point. The user of the method can choose the x-value at which to make the estimate, and that x-value need not be a score that actually can be obtained on the test. The part of the score scale where the equated scores can be estimated most accurately, particularly in small samples, is the middle of the distribution. If the equating is a direct equating (e.g., an equivalent-groups equating), the middle point can be determined by equating the mean score on the new form directly to the mean score on the reference form. If the equating is through an anchor score (e.g., a common-item equating), the middle point can be determined by equating at the mean score of the smaller group of test takers. Typically, the smaller group will be the group taking the new form.

If the middle point happens to lie on the line connecting the end points, that line is the estimated equating curve. If not, the next step is to use the end points and the middle point to determine the equating curve. There are two versions of circle-arc equating, and they differ in the way they fit a curve to these three points. We call one version *symmetric circle-arc equating* and the other *simplified circle-arc equating*. Symmetric circle-arc equating is actually simpler conceptually, but its formulas are a bit cumbersome. Simplified circle-arc equating uses a slightly more complicated model in order to simplify the formulas. In the research studies we have done (which we describe later in this chapter), the two versions of the circle-arc method have produced about equally accurate results. The formulas for both versions appear in the Appendix to this chapter. Both versions are described in Livingston and Kim (2008); only the simplified version is included in Livingston and Kim (2009), but the formulas for the symmetric version are given in Livingston and Kim (2010).

Both methods are applications of the geometrical fact that if three points do not lie on a straight line, they uniquely determine a circle. Symmetric circle-arc equating fits a circle arc directly to the three data points. Simplified circle-arc equating transforms the three data points by decomposing the equating function into a linear component and a curvilinear component (an idea borrowed from von Davier, Holland, & Thayer, 2004b, pp. 11–13). The linear component is the line connecting the two end points. The curvilinear component is the vertical deviation of the equating curve from that line. It is estimated by fitting a circle arc to the three transformed data points.

Figure 7.1 illustrates the simplified circle-arc procedure. The horizontal axis represents the score on the new form, that is, the test form to be equated. The vertical axis represents the corresponding score on the reference form. The two prespecified end points and the empirically determined middle point are indicated by the three small circles. The line connecting the two end points is the linear component of the estimated equating curve. The three data points are transformed by subtracting the y-value of that line, which we call $L(x)$. The three transformed points are indicated by the squares at the bottom of Figure 7.1. Both end points are transformed onto the horizontal axis. The middle point is transformed to a point above or below the horizontal axis—above it if the new form is harder than the reference form, and below it if the new form is easier than the reference form. In the example illustrated by Figure 7.1, the new form is harder than the reference form. Consequently, the original middle point is above the line $L(x)$, and the transformed middle point is above the horizontal axis.

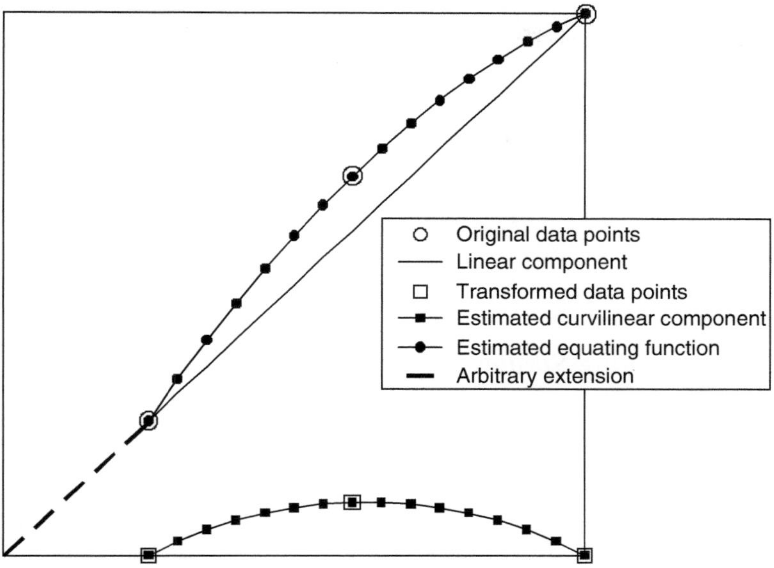

Fig. 7.1 Illustration of the simplified circle-arc equating method

The three transformed data points uniquely determine an arc of a circle. The arc connecting the three transformed data points is shown at the bottom of Figure 7.1. This arc serves as an estimate of the curvilinear component of the equating function. For each possible raw score on the new form, there is a corresponding point on the arc. The next step is to add the linear component back in, by adding the height of the line $L(x)$ to the height of the arc. The three original data points are retransformed back to their original positions, and the full arc is transformed into an estimate of the equipercentile equating function, shown in the upper portion of the figure. The last step is to extend the equating transformation below the lower end point, by connecting that point linearly to the point corresponding to the minimum possible score on each form. This line is arbitrary—hardly a problem, since the lower end point of the curve corresponds to the lowest meaningful score on each form.

Purists may object that simplified circle-arc equating is not truly an equating method, because it is not symmetric in its treatment of the new form and reference form. Indeed, it is not symmetric, but we are not suggesting either circle-arc method as a way to define the equating relationship in the population. We are suggesting them as tools for estimating the equipercentile equating relationship in the population. The equipercentile equating relationship is symmetric, but the best available procedure for estimating it from small-sample data may not be symmetric.

Because the end points of the estimated equating curve are constrained, the estimate produced by either circle-arc method has a sampling variance of zero at the end points. The conditional standard error of equating (CSEE) at those points is zero. At the middle point, the CSEE depends on the equating method used to determine the y value for that point. The CSEE at that point can be estimated by whatever procedure is appropriate for that method. At any other point, the CSEE can be approximated by a simple proportion; the CSEE values at any two points are approximately proportional to their deviations from the line connecting the two end points. If (x_2, y_2) is the middle point, for which an estimate of the CSEE is available, and (x_j, y_j) is the point for which the CSEE is to be estimated, then

$$\frac{CSEE(y_j)}{CSEE(y_2)} \doteq \left(\frac{y_j - L(x_j)}{y_2 - L(x_2)} \right) \tag{7.1}$$

7.4.2 Resampling Studies

We have been conducting resampling studies to evaluate the accuracy of equating in small samples by several methods, including the two circle-arc methods. We have investigated both common-item equating and random-groups equating, using somewhat larger sample sizes in the random-groups design. The basic procedure for a random-groups design is as follows (Livingston & Kim, 2010):

Choose an existing test form of approximately 100 or more items, a form that has been administered to several thousand test takers. Consider those test takers as the target population for equating. Divide the test form into two nonoverlapping subforms, parallel in content but unequal in difficulty. Designate one subform as the new form and the other as the reference form for equating. Compute the direct equipercentile equating of the new form to the reference form in the full target population; this equating is the criterion equating for the resampling study. To evaluate the small-sample equating methods, for a given sample size, perform several hundred replications of this procedure:

1. Draw a pair of nonoverlapping samples of test takers, sampling from the full population.
2. Compute the distribution of scores on the new form in one sample of test takers and on the reference form in the other sample.
3. Use those score distributions to equate the new form to the reference form, by all the small-sample methods to be compared.
4. At each new-form raw-score level, record the difference between the results of each small-sample equating method and the criterion equating.

Summarize the results for each small-sample equating method, summarizing over the several hundred replications by computing, for each raw score on the new form, the root-mean-square deviation (RMSD) of the sample equatings from the population equating.

We repeated this procedure with six operational test forms, each from a different test. To average the results over the six test forms, we expressed the RMSD values in terms of the standard deviation of the scores on the reference form in the full population. We then conditioned on percentiles of the distribution of scores on the new form in the population and took the root mean square, over the six test forms, of the RMSD values at those percentiles. The result is a set of curves, one for each small-sample equating method. Figure 7.2 shows the resulting curves for the two circle-arc methods, for three other equating methods, and for the identity, with samples of 200 test takers for each form (a small sample size for random-groups equating). In the middle of the distribution, all the equating methods performed about equally well. At the low end of the distribution, the two circle-arc methods and mean equating were more accurate than linear or equipercentile equating. At the high end of the distribution, the two circle-arc methods were much more accurate than the other methods at estimating the equipercentile equating in the population.

The resampling procedure for common-item equating (Kim & Livingston, 2010) was a bit more complicated. Again, we used data from test forms taken by several thousand examinees, but in this case we selected forms that had been given on two separate occasions to populations that differed somewhat in ability. As in the random-groups studies, we used the items in the full test form as an item pool to construct subforms to be equated, but in this case the subforms included a set of items in common, for use as an anchor in the small-sample equatings. The criterion equating was the direct equipercentile equating of the two subforms in the combined population of test takers taking the full test form. In the resampling studies, instead of selecting both new-form and reference-form samples from the same population of test takers, we designated the test takers from one testing occasion as the new-form population and those from the other testing occasion as the reference-form population. The sample sizes we investigated were smaller than those in the random-groups studies. We also specified the reference-form sample to

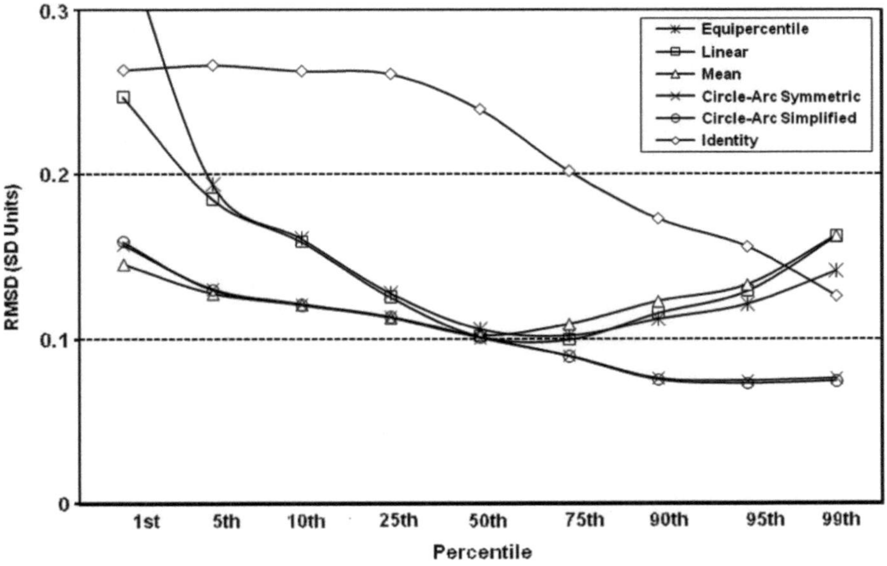

Fig. 7.2 Example of resampling study results

be 3 times as large as the new-form sample, to reflect the usual small-sample common-item equating situation, in which reference-form data are accumulated over two or more testing occasions. The results of the common-item equating studies in small samples (50 or smaller for the new form, 150 or smaller for the reference form) were generally similar to those of the random-groups studies, with one difference: At the low end of the score distribution, mean equating was clearly the most accurate method, even more accurate than the circle-arc methods (which were the most accurate in the upper portion of the score distribution).

7.5 Equating With Collateral Information

When we psychometricians equate test scores on the basis of data from very small groups of test takers, we are trying to estimate the equating relationship we would find if we had data from very large groups of test takers. One way to improve an estimation process, especially when the data come from a small sample, is to incorporate collateral information (see, e.g., Efron & Morris, 1977). Collateral information for equating test scores is often available from equatings of other forms of the test we want to equate and of other tests.

7.5.1 Empirical Bayes Estimation

The idea of using collateral information suggests an empirical Bayes approach. The basic premise is that the current, small-sample equating can be regarded as a single observation randomly sampled from a large domain of possible equatings, each with its own new form, reference form, and samples of test takers. For a given pair of test forms, there is a "true" equating function: the function that would result from averaging over all the equatings of that particular pair of test forms with different samples of test takers. All the equatings in the domain are assumed to provide information that may be relevant for estimating this true equating function. Therefore, how broadly to define the domain is an important question. (We discuss it briefly under Section 7.5.2, Problems and Limitations, below.)

Developing a Bayesian estimate for an equating function turns out to be a complex problem. A practical way to simplify the problem is to estimate the equating transformation *one point at a time*. For each possible raw score on the new form, there is a single equated score on the reference form to be estimated. Estimating a single equated score is a much more manageable task than estimating the equating transformation all at once.[2]

[2]For an alternative approach based on modeling the discrete bivariate distribution of scores on the two forms to be equated, see Karabatsos and Walker (Chapter 11 of this volume).

For a given raw score x on the new form, the empirical Bayes estimate of the corresponding equated score y on the reference form is a weighted average of a "current" estimate and a "prior" estimate, which we will call $y_{current}$ and y_{prior}. The current estimate is the equated score implied by the small-sample equating. The prior estimate is the average of the equating results in all the equatings used as collateral information, with the addition of the current equating. The current equating is included in the prior estimate because the prior estimate is intended to represent a domain of possible equatings, and the current equating is a member of the domain.

The Bayesian formula for combining the current and prior estimates is

$$\ddot{y}_{EB} = \frac{\frac{1}{\mathrm{var}(y_{current})}y_{current} + \frac{1}{\mathrm{var}(y_{prior})}y_{prior}}{\frac{1}{\mathrm{var}(y_{current})} + \frac{1}{\mathrm{var}(y_{prior})}} = \frac{[\mathrm{var}(y_{prior})]y_{current} + [\mathrm{var}(y_{current})]y_{prior}}{\mathrm{var}(y_{prior}) + \mathrm{var}(y_{current})} \tag{7.2}$$

The smaller the samples of test takers in the current equating, the more unstable the results are likely to be, resulting in a larger variance for $y_{current}$ and a smaller weight for it in the empirical Bayes estimate. On the other hand, the fewer equatings that contribute to the prior estimate and the more those equatings differ, the larger the variance of y_{prior} and the smaller the weight for it in the empirical Bayes estimate.[3]

7.5.2 *Problems and Limitations*

One feature of the real world of testing that complicates this Bayesian procedure is that test forms differ in length. Even alternate forms of the same test sometimes differ in length, because of the exclusion of one or more items from the scoring. One solution to this "apples and oranges" problem is to convert the scores on all the forms, in the current equating and in all the prior equatings, to percentages. This tactic creates a common metric and makes it possible to use interpolation to determine corresponding scores on forms that do not have exactly the same number of items.

Another difficulty in implementing this approach is that the empirical Bayes formula requires, at each new-form raw-score value, an estimate of the sampling variance of the current equating (i.e., the square of the CSEE). An estimate computed from the small-sample data in the current equating is likely to be

[3]We thank Charles Lewis for his help in working out the details of this procedure. A paper by Livingston and Lewis (2009) contains a more complete description and explanation of the procedure.

inaccurate. We have been investigating the possibility of using data from many equatings to develop estimates of this variance, as a function of sample size, test length, and approximate test difficulty.

Yet another difficulty in implementing this approach is that of deciding what equatings to include as collateral information. Should the collateral information include equatings of other tests? If so, how different from the test to be equated can another test be and still provide useful information? This question is an empirical question, and the answers may differ for different kinds of tests. We have been doing some research (consisting of resampling studies), and the results indicate that the most important factor is, not surprisingly, the way in which new forms of the test differ in difficulty from the forms to which they are equated (Kim, Livingston, & Lewis, 2008, 2009).

To see what can go wrong, consider a situation in which the new form to be equated is easier than the reference form, but in all the prior equatings used as collateral information, the new form was harder than the reference form. In this case, the collateral information will pull the equated score toward a value that is typical for the domain but wrong for the current equating. The same problem will occur if the new form to be equated is much harder or much easier than the reference form but in all the prior equatings the new form and reference form were very similar in difficulty.

7.5.3 A Simpler Approach to Using Collateral Information

The empirical Bayes procedure described above is highly sensitive to the choice of equatings used as collateral information. In addition, the calculations involved are laborious. However, there is another procedure, based on similar reasoning, that does not depend as heavily on the choice of collateral information and is also simpler to use operationally.

Consider the prior estimate of the equated score at each score level. The Bayesian procedure described above uses the mean of a group of equatings. Its results depend heavily on the choice of those equatings. Now suppose the domain of equatings that provide collateral information includes two equatings for each pair of test forms—equating form X to form Y and equating form Y to form X. In that case, averaging over all the equatings in the domain will yield a result very close to the identity ($Y = X$). Instead of using the mean of a specified set of equatings, we can simply use the identity as the prior estimate toward which the small-sample equating results will be pulled.

Using the identity is not a new idea. Some writers have advocated using the identity as the equating function whenever the size of the samples available falls below a specified threshold—one that depends on the extent to which test forms are expected to differ in difficulty (Kolen & Brennan, 1995, p. 272; Kolen & Brennan, 2004, pp. 289-290; Skaggs, 2005, p. 309). We think there is a better way to take sample size into account. Instead of making an "either–or" decision, compute a weighted average of the small-sample equating and the identity. For a given raw-score x, if $y_{obs}(x)$ represents the equated score observed in the small-sample equating, the adjustment is simply

$$y_{adj}(x) = w[y_{obs}(x)] + (1 - w)x\,, \tag{7.3}$$

where w is a number between 0 and 1.

The practical question for implementing this procedure is how to choose a value for w. Kim, von Davier, and Haberman (2008) investigated this method with the value of w fixed at 0.5, but ideally, the value of w should vary with the size of the samples; the larger the samples, the greater the weight for the observed equating. The Bayesian formula of Equation 7.2 offers a solution, for a user who can estimate the sampling variance of the small-sample equating and the variance of the equated scores in the domain. Both of these quantities will vary from one score level to another and not necessarily in proportion with each other. Therefore, with this approach, the value of w in Equation 7.3 would vary from one score level to another.

The variance of the small-sample equating—$\mathrm{var}(y_{current})$ in Equation 7.2—at a given new-form raw-score level—$\mathrm{var}(y_{current})$ in Equation 7.2— is simply the square of the CSEE. There are formulas for estimating this quantity for various equating methods, but the resulting estimates may be highly inaccurate if they are based on data from very small samples of test takers. A possible solution to this problem would be to conduct a series of resampling studies to estimate the CSEE empirically for samples of various sizes.

The variance of the equated scores in the domain of equatings, for a given new-form raw score—$\mathrm{var}(y_{prior})$ in Equation 7.2—can be estimated empirically from prior equatings. The key question is which prior equatings to include in the estimate. We prefer to define the domain of equatings broadly. Limiting the domain to the forms of a single test often narrows the field of prior equatings down to a small sample that may not be representative of a domain that includes the equatings of all future forms of the test. The greatest danger is that the previous forms of a single test may have been much more alike in difficulty than the future forms will be (for an example, see Kim, Livingston, & Lewis, 2008). Limiting the domain of prior equatings to forms of that single test would yield too low a value for $\mathrm{var}(y_{prior})$. The resulting adjustment formula would place too much weight on the identity and too little on the observed equating.

7.6 Introducing the New Form by Stages

Another, very different approach to the small-sample equating problem is to change the way in which new forms of the test are introduced. A new technique, developed by Grant (see Puhan, Moses, Grant, & McHale, 2009) and now being used operationally, is to introduce the new form in stages, rather than all at once. This technique requires that the test be structured in *testlets*, small-scale tests that each represent the full test

Table 7.1 *Plan for Introducing a New Form by Stages*

Form A	Form B	Form C	Form D	Form E	Form F	Form G
Testlet 1	Testlet 7*	Testlet 7	Testlet 7	Testlet 7	Testlet 7	Testlet 7
Testlet 2	Testlet 2	Testlet 8*	Testlet 8	Testlet 8	Testlet 8	Testlet 8
Testlet 3	Testlet 3	Testlet 3	Testlet 9*	Testlet 9	Testlet 9	Testlet 9
Testlet 4	Testlet 4	Testlet 4	Testlet 4	Testlet 10*	Testlet 10	Testlet 10
Testlet 5	Testlet 5	Testlet 5	Testlet 5	Testlet 5	Testlet 11*	Testlet 11
Testlet 6*	Testlet 6	Testlet 6	Testlet 6	Testlet 6	Testlet 6	Testlet 12*

*Not included in computing the test takers' scores.

in content and format. It also requires that the test form given at each administration include one testlet that is not included in computing the test takers' scores.

As an example, consider a test consisting of five testlets that are included in computing the test takers' scores and one additional testlet that is not included in the scores. Table 7.1 shows a plan that might be followed for assembling the first seven forms of this test. The asterisks indicate the testlets that are not included in computing the test takers' scores—one such testlet in each form. With each new form, one of the scored testlets in the previous form is replaced. It is replaced in the printed new form by a new testlet, which is not scored. It is replaced in the scoring of the new form by the testlet that was new (and therefore was not scored) in the previous form.

Each new test form is equated to the previous form in the group of test takers who took the previous form. Form B is equated to Form A in the group of test takers who took Form A, Form C is equated to Form B in the group of test takers who took Form B, and so on. This single-group equating is extremely powerful, because any difference in ability between the sample of test takers and the population is the same for the new form as for the reference form; the equating sample for both forms consists of the same individuals. In addition, the forms to be equated are highly similar, since they have four fifths of their items in common. This overlap of forms limits the extent to which the equating in the sample can deviate from the equating in the population. Because of these two features, this data collection plan is called the single-group, nearly equivalent test (SiGNET) design.

An additional advantage of the SiGNET design is that each new form is equated on the basis of data collected in the administration of the previous form. Therefore, each new form can be equated before it is administered. If a form is administered two or more times before the next form is introduced, the data from those administrations can be combined to provide a larger sample for equating the next form.

Notice in Table 7.1 that Form F is the first form that does not include any of the scored items in Form A. However, Form E has only one fifth of its items in common with Form A, about the same as would be expected if Form E were to be equated to Form A through common items. How does the accuracy of equating Form E to Form A through the chain of single-group equatings in the SiGNET design compare with the accuracy of equating Form E to Form A in a single common-item equating? A resampling study by Puhan, Moses, Grant, and McHale (2009) provides an answer. That study compared the RMSD of equating through a chain of four single-group equatings in a SiGNET design with the accuracy of a single common-item equating. When all the equating samples in both designs included 50 test takers, the RMSD of the SiGNET equating was about two thirds that of the conventional common-item equating.

7.7 Combining the Approaches

It is certainly possible to combine two or more of the new approaches described above. The circle-arc method, the procedures for using collateral information, and the SiGNET design address different aspects of the equating process. The SiGNET design answers the question, "How should I collect the data for equating?" The circle-arc method answers the question, "How should I use those data to estimate the equating function?" The procedures for incorporating collateral information answer the question, "How should I adjust the estimate to decrease its reliance on the data when the samples are small?"

The possibility of combining these approaches multiplies the number of options available for equating scores on test forms taken by small numbers of test takers. The larger number of possibilities complicates the task of evaluating these procedures. It is useful to know how effective each procedure is when used alone, but it is also useful to know how effective the various combinations of procedures are. To what extent do they supplement each other? To what extent are they redundant? Does the SiGNET design make the use of collateral information unnecessary, or even counterproductive? Would the SiGNET design be even more effective if the single-group equatings were done by the circle-arc method? And, of course, the answers to these questions are likely to depend heavily on the sample size. There are enough research questions here to keep several psychometricians and graduate students busy for a while.

Chapter 7 Appendix

7.A.1 Formulas for Circle-Arc Equating

In the symmetric circle-arc method, the estimated equating curve is an arc of a circle. Let (x_1, y_1) represent the lower end point of the equating curve, let (x_2, y_2) represent the empirically determined middle point, and let (x_3, y_3) represent the upper end point. Let r represent the radius of the circle, and label the coordinates of its center (x_c, y_c).

The equation of the circle is $(X - x_c)^2 + (Y - y_c)^2 = r^2$ or, equivalently, $|Y - y_c| = \sqrt{r^2 - (X - x_c)^2}$. If the new form is harder than the reference form, the middle point will lie above the line connecting the lower and upper points, so that the center of the circle will be below the arc. For all points (X, Y) on the arc, $Y > y_c$, so that $|Y - y_c| = Y - y_c$, and the formula for the arc will be

$$Y = y_c + \sqrt{r^2 - (X - x_c)^2}. \tag{7.A.1}$$

If the new form is easier than the reference form, the middle point will lie below the line connecting the lower and upper end points, so that the center of the circle will be above the arc. For all points (X, Y) on the arc, $Y<y_c$, so that $|Y - y_c| = y_c - Y$, and the formula for the arc will be

$$Y = y_c - \sqrt{r^2 - (X - x_c)^2}. \tag{7.A.2}$$

A simple decision rule is to use Equation 7.A.1 if $y_2>y_c$ and Equation 7.A.2 if $y_2<y_c$.

The formulas for x_c and y_c in the symmetric circle-arc method are a bit cumbersome:

$$x_c = \frac{(x_1^2 + y_1^2)(y_3 - y_2) + (x_2^2 + y_2^2)(y_1 - y_3) + (x_3^2 + y_3^2)(y_2 - y_1)}{2[x_1(y_3 - y_2) + x_2(y_1 - y_3) + x_3(y_2 - y_1)]} \tag{7.A.3}$$

and

$$y_c = \frac{(x_1^2 + y_1^2)(x_3 - x_2) + (x_2^2 + y_2^2)(x_1 - x_3) + (x_3^2 + y_3^2)(x_2 - x_1)}{2[y_1(x_3 - x_2) + y_2(x_1 - x_3) + y_3(x_2 - x_1)]}, \tag{7.A.4}$$

but the formula for r^2 is simply

$$r^2 = (x_1 - x_c)^2 + (y_1 - y_c)^2. \tag{7.A.5}$$

In the simplified circle-arc method, the transformed points to be connected by a circle arc are $(x_1, 0)$, (x_2, y_2^*), and $(x_3, 0)$, where

$$y_2^* = y_2 - \left(\frac{y_3 - y_1}{x_3 - x_1}\right)(x_2 - x_1). \tag{7.A.6}$$

The transformation of the data points results in a much simpler set of formulas for the coordinates of the center of the circle:

$$x_c = \frac{x_1 + x_3}{2}, \tag{7.A.7}$$

$$y_c = \frac{(x_1^2)(x_3 - x_2) - (x_2^2 + (y_2^*)^2)(x_3 - x_1) + (x_3^2)(x_2 - x_1)}{2[y_2^*(x_1 - x_3)]}, \tag{7.A.8}$$

and a slightly simpler formula for r^2:

$$r^2 = (x_1 - x_c)^2 + y_c^2. \tag{7.A.9}$$

Author Note: Any opinions expressed in this chapter are those of the author and not necessarily of Educational Testing Service.

Part II
Measurement and Equating Models

Chapter 8
Using Exponential Families for Equating

Shelby J. Haberman

8.1 Introduction

In common equipercentile equating methods such as the percentile-rank method or kernel equating (von Davier, Holland, & Thayer, 2004b), sample distributions of test scores are approximated by continuous distributions with positive density functions on intervals that include all possible scores. The use of continuous distributions with positive densities facilitates the equating process, for such distributions have continuous and strictly increasing distribution functions on intervals of interest, so conversion functions can be constructed based on the principles of equipercentile equating. When the density functions are also continuous, as is the case in kernel equating, the further gain is achieved that the conversion functions are differentiable. This gain permits derivation of normal approximations for the distribution of the conversion function, so estimated asymptotic standard deviations (EASDs) can be derived.

An obvious challenge with any approach to equipercentile equating is the accuracy of an approximation of a discrete distribution by a continuous distribution. The percentile-rank approach, even with log-linear smoothing, provides an approximating continuous distribution with the same expectation as the original sample distribution but with a different variance. The kernel method provides an approximating continuous distribution with the same mean and variance as the original sample distribution, but higher order moments do not normally coincide.

With continuous exponential families, continuous distributions with positive and continuous density functions are obtained with a selected collection of moments that are consistent with the corresponding sample moments for the test scores. For example, one can specify that the first four moments of a distribution from a continuous exponential family are equal to the first four moments from a sample distribution.

S.J. Haberman
Educational Testing Service, Rosedale Rd. Princeton, New Jersey 08541, USA
e-mail: shaberman@ets.org

A.A. von Davier (ed.), *Statistical Models for Test Equating, Scaling, and Linking*, Statistics for Social and Behavioral Sciences,
DOI 10.1007/978-0-387-98138-3_8,

For simplicity, two equating designs are considered, a design for randomly equivalent groups and a design for single groups. In each design, Forms 1 and 2 are compared. Raw scores on Form 1 are real numbers from c_1 to d_1, and raw scores on Form 2 are real numbers from c_2 to d_2. For j equal 1 or 2, let X_j be a random variable that represents the score on form j of a randomly selected population member, so that X_j has values from c_j to $d_j > c_j$. It is not necessary for the X_j to have integer values or to be discrete, but many typical applications do involve raw scores that are integers. To avoid cases of no interest, it is assumed that X_j has a positive variance $\sigma^2(X_j)$ for each form j.

The designs under study differ in terms of data collection. In the design for randomly equivalent groups, two independent random samples are drawn. For j equal 1 or 2, sample j has size n_j. The observations X_{ij}, $1 \le i \le n_j$, are independent and identically distributed with the same distribution as X_j. In the design for a single group, one sample of size $n_1 = n_2 = n$ is drawn with observations $\mathbf{X}_i = (X_{i1}, X_{i2})$ with the same distribution as $\mathbf{X} = (X_1, X_2)$.

For either sampling approach, many of the basic elements of equating are the same. For any real random variable Y, let $F(Y)$ denote the distribution function of Y, so that $F(x, Y)$, x real, is the probability that $Y \le x$. Let the quantile function $Q(Y)$ be defined for p in (0,1) so that $Q(p,Y)$ is the smallest x such that $F(x, Y) \ge p$. The functions $F(X_j)$ and $Q(X_j)$ are nondecreasing; however, they are not continuous in typical equating problems in which the raw scores are integers or fractions and thus are not readily employed in equating. In addition, even if $F(X_j)$ and $Q(X_j)$ are continuous, the sample functions $\bar{F}(X_j)$ and $\bar{Q}(X_j)$ are not. Here $\bar{F}(x, X_j)$ is the fraction of $X_{ij} \le x$, $1 \le i \le n_j$, and $\bar{Q}(p, X_j)$, $0 < p < 1$, is the smallest x such that $\bar{F}(x, X_j) \ge p$.

Instead of $F(X_j)$ and $Q(X_j)$, j equal 1 or 2, equipercentile equating uses continuous random variables A_j such that each A_j has a positive density $f(A_j)$ on an open interval B_j that includes $[c_j, d_j]$, and the distribution function $F(A_j)$ of A_j approximates the distribution function $F(X_j)$. For x in B_j, the density of A_j has value $f(x, A_j)$. Because the distribution function $F(A_j)$ is continuous and strictly increasing, the quantile function $Q(A_j)$ of A_j satisfies $F(Q(p, A_j), A_j) = p$ for p in (0,1), so that $Q(A_j)$ is the strictly increasing continuous inverse of the restriction of $F(A_j)$ to B_j. The equating function $e(A_1, A_2)$ for conversion of a score on Form 1 to a score on Form 2 is the composite function $Q(F(A_1), A_2)$, so that, for x in B_1, $e(A_1, A_2)$ has value $e(x, A_1, A_2) = Q(F(x, A_1), A_2)$ in B_2. Clearly, $e(A_1, A_2)$ is strictly increasing and continuous. The conversion function $e(A_2, A_1) = Q(F(A_2), A_1)$ from Form 2 to Form 1 may be defined so that $e(A_2, A_1)$ is a function from B_2 to B_1. The functions $e(A_1, A_2)$ and $e(A_2, A_1)$ are inverses of each other, so that $e(e(x, A_1, A_2), A_2, A_1) = x$ for x in B_1 and $e(e(x, A_2, A_1), A_1, A_2) = x$ for x in B_2. If $f(A_j)$ is continuous on B_j for each form j, then application of standard results from calculus show that the restriction of the distribution function $F(A_j)$ to B_j is continuously differentiable with derivative $f(x, A_j)$ at x in B_j, the quantile function $Q(A_j)$ is continuously differentiable on (0,1) with derivative $1/f(Q(p, A_j), A_j)$ at p in (0,1), the conversion function $e(A_1; A_2)$ is continuously differentiable with derivative $e'(x, A_1, A_2) = f(x, A_1)/f(e(x, A_1, A_2)A_2)$ at x in B_1, and the conversion function

$e(A_2, A_1)$ is continuously differentiable with derivative $e'(x, A_2, A_1) = f(x, A_2)/f(e, (x, A_1, A_2)A_2)$ at x in B_2.

In Section 8.2, continuous exponential families are considered for equivalent groups, and in Section 8.3, continuous exponential families are considered for single groups. The treatment of continuous exponential families in equating is closely related to Wang (2008, this volume); however, the discussion in this chapter differs from Wang in terms of numerical methods, model evaluation, and the generality of models for single groups.

8.2 Continuous Exponential Families for Randomly Equivalent Groups

To define a general continuous exponential family, consider a bounded real interval C with at least two points. Let K be a positive integer, and let $\mathbf{u}$ be a bounded K-dimensional integrable function on C. In most applications in this chapter, given C and K, $\mathbf{u}$ is $\mathbf{v}(K,C)$, where $\mathbf{v}(K,C)$ has coordinates $v_k(C), 1 \leq k \leq K$; $v_k(C), k \geq 0$, is a polynomial of degree k on C with values $v_k(x, C)$ for x in C; and, for a uniformly distributed random variable U_C on the interval C, the $v_k(C)$ satisfy the orthogonality constraints

$$E(v_i(U_C, C)v_k(U_C, C)) = \begin{cases} 1, & i = k, \\ 0, & i \neq k, \end{cases}$$

for integers i and k, $1 \leq i \leq k \leq K$. Computation of the $v_k(C)$ is discussed in the Appendix. The convention is used in the definition of $v_k(x, C)$ that the coefficient of x^k is positive.

The definition of a continuous exponential family is simplified by use of standard vector inner products. For K-dimensional vectors $\mathbf{y}$ and $\mathbf{z}$ with respective coordinates y_k and z_k, $1 \leq k \leq K$, let $\mathbf{y}'\mathbf{z}$ be $\sum_{k=1}^{K} y_k z_k$. To any K-dimensional vector $\mathbf{y}$ corresponds a random variable $Y(\mathbf{y}, \mathbf{u})$ with values in C with a density function $f(Y(\mathbf{y}, \mathbf{u}))$ equal to

$$g(\mathbf{y}, \mathbf{u}) = \gamma(\mathbf{y}, \mathbf{u})\exp(\mathbf{y}'\mathbf{u}), \tag{8.1}$$

where

$$1/\gamma(\mathbf{y}, \mathbf{u}) = \int_C \exp(\mathbf{y}'\mathbf{u})$$

(Gilula & Haberman, 2000) and $g(\mathbf{y}, \mathbf{u})$ has value $g(z, \mathbf{y}, \mathbf{u})$ at z in C. The family of distributions with densities $g(\mathbf{y}, \mathbf{u})$ for K-dimensional vectors $\mathbf{y}$ is the continuous exponential family of distributions defined by $\mathbf{u}$. A fundamental characteristic of these distributions is that they have positive density functions on C. These density functions are continuous if $\mathbf{u}$ is continuous. In all cases, if 0_K denotes the K-dimensional vector with all coordinates 0, then $Y(0_K, \mathbf{u})$ has the same uniform distribution on C as does U_c. If $\mathbf{u} = \mathbf{v}_2(C)$ and $y_2 < 0$, then $Y(\mathbf{y}, \mathbf{u})$ is distributed as a normal random variable X, conditional on X being in C. To ensure that all distributions in the continuous exponential family are distinct, it is assumed that the covariance matrix of $\mathbf{u}(U_C)$ is positive definite. Under this condition, the covariance matrix $\mathbf{V}(\mathbf{y}, \mathbf{u})$ of $\mathbf{u}(Y(\mathbf{y}, \mathbf{u}))$ is positive definite for each $\mathbf{y}$. As a consequence of the fundamental theorem of algebra, this condition on the covariance matrix of $\mathbf{u}(U_C)$ holds in the polynomial case of $\mathbf{u} = \mathbf{v}(K, C)$.

For continuous exponential families, distribution functions are easily constructed and are strictly increasing and continuous on C. Let the indicator function $\chi_C(x)$ be the real function on C such that $\chi_C(x)$ has value $\chi_C(z, x) = 1$ for $z \leq x$ and value $\chi_C(z, x) = 0$ for $z > x$. Then the restriction of the distribution function $F(Y(\mathbf{y}, \mathbf{u}))$ of $Y(\mathbf{y}, \mathbf{u})$ to C is $G(\mathbf{y}, \mathbf{u})$, where, for x in C, $G(\mathbf{y}, \mathbf{u})$ has value

$$G(x, \mathbf{y}, \mathbf{u}) = \int_C \chi_C(x) g(\mathbf{y}, \mathbf{u}).$$

As in Gilula and Haberman (2000), the distribution of a random variable Z with values in C may be approximated by a distribution in the continuous exponential family of distributions generated by $\mathbf{u}$. The quality of the approximation provided by the distribution with density $g(\mathbf{y}, \mathbf{u})$ is assessed by the expected log penalty

$$H(Z, \mathbf{y}, \mathbf{u}) = -E(\log\, g(Z, \mathbf{y}, \mathbf{u})) = -\log\, \gamma(\mathbf{y}, \mathbf{u}) + \mathbf{y}'E(\mathbf{u}(Z)). \tag{8.2}$$

The smaller the value of $H(Z, \mathbf{y}, \mathbf{u})$, the better is the approximation.

Several rationales can be considered for use of the expected logarithmic penalty $H(Z, \mathbf{y}, \mathbf{u})$, according to Gilula and Haberman (2000). Consider a probabilistic prediction of Z by use of a positive density function h on C. If $Z = z$, then let a log penalty of $-\log\, h(z)$ be assigned. If $-\log f(Z)$ has a finite expectation, then the expected log penalty is $H(h) = E(-\log\, h(Z))$. If Z is continuous and has positive density f and if the expectation of $-\log f(Z)$ is finite, then $I(Z) = H(f) \leq H(h)$, so that the optimal probability prediction is obtained with the actual density of Z. In addition, $H(h) = I(Z)$ only if f is a density function of Z. This feature in which the penalty is determined by the value of the density at the observed value of Z and the expected penalty is minimized by selection of the density f of Z is only encountered if the penalty from use of the density function h is of the form $a - b\, \log\, h(z)$ for $Z = z$ for some real constants a and $b > 0$.

This rationale is not applicable if Z is discrete. In general, if Z is discrete, then the smallest possible expected log penalty $E(-\log\, h(Z))$ is $-\infty$, for, given any real $c > 0$, h may be defined so that $h(Z) = c$ with probability 1 and the expected log penalty is $-\log\, c$. The constant c may be arbitrarily large, so the expected log penalty may be arbitrarily small. Nonetheless, the criterion $E(-\log\, h(Z))$ cannot be made arbitrarily small if adequate constraints are imposed on h. In this section, the requirement that the density function used for prediction of Z is $g(\mathbf{y}, \mathbf{u})$ from Equation 8.1 suffices to ensure existence of a finite infimum $I(Z, \mathbf{u})$ of the expected log penalty $H(Z, \mathbf{y}, \mathbf{u})$ from Equation 8.2 over all $\mathbf{y}$.

Provided that $\text{Cov}(\mathbf{u}(Z))$ is positive definite, a unique K-dimensional vector $\boldsymbol{\theta}(Z, \mathbf{u})$ with coordinates $\boldsymbol{\theta}_k(Z, \mathbf{u})$, $1 \leq k \leq K$, exists such that $H(Z, \boldsymbol{\theta}(Z, \mathbf{u}))$ is equal to the infimum $I(Z, \mathbf{u})$ of $H(Z, \mathbf{y}, \mathbf{u})$ for K-dimensional vectors $\mathbf{y}$. Let $Y_*(Z, \mathbf{u}) = Y(\boldsymbol{\theta}(Z, \mathbf{u}), \mathbf{u})$. Then $\boldsymbol{\theta}(Z, \mathbf{u})$ is the unique solution of the equation

$$E(\mathbf{u}(Y_*(Z, \mathbf{u}))) = E(\mathbf{u}(Z)).$$

The left-hand side of the equation is readily expressed in terms of an integral. If

$$\boldsymbol{\mu}(\mathbf{y}, \mathbf{u}) = \int_C \mathbf{u} g(\mathbf{y}, \mathbf{u}),$$

then

$$E(\mathbf{u}(Y(\mathbf{y}, \mathbf{u}))) = \boldsymbol{\mu}(\mathbf{y}, \mathbf{u}).$$

Thus,

$$\boldsymbol{\mu}(\boldsymbol{\theta}(Z, \mathbf{u}), \mathbf{u}) = E(\mathbf{u}(Z)).$$

In the polynomial case of $\mathbf{u} = \mathbf{v}(K, C)$, the fundamental theorem of calculus implies that $\text{Cov}(\mathbf{u}(Z))$ is positive definite, unless a finite set C_0 with no more than K points exists such that $P(Z \in C_0) = 1$. In addition, the moment constraints $E([Y_*(Z, \mathbf{v}(K, C))]^k) = E(Z^k)$ hold for $1 \leq k \leq K$.

The value of $\boldsymbol{\theta}(Z, \mathbf{u})$ may be found by the Newton-Raphson algorithm. Let

$$\mathbf{V}(\mathbf{y}, \mathbf{u}) = \int_C [\mathbf{u} - \boldsymbol{\mu}(\mathbf{y}, \mathbf{u})][\mathbf{u} - \boldsymbol{\mu}(\mathbf{y}, \mathbf{u})]' g(\mathbf{y}, \mathbf{u})].$$

Given an initial approximation $\boldsymbol{\theta}_0$, the algorithm at step $t \geq 0$ yields a new approximation

$$\boldsymbol{\theta}_{t+1} = \boldsymbol{\theta}_t + [\mathbf{V}(\boldsymbol{\theta}_t, \mathbf{u})]^{-1} [E(\mathbf{u}(Z)) - \boldsymbol{\mu}(\boldsymbol{\theta}_t, \mathbf{u})] \quad (8.3)$$

of $\boldsymbol{\theta}(Z, \mathbf{u})$. Normally, $\boldsymbol{\theta}_t$ converges to $\boldsymbol{\theta}(Z, \mathbf{u})$ as t increases. The selection of $\boldsymbol{\theta}_0 = \mathbf{0}_K$ is normally acceptable. When $\mathbf{u}$ is infinitely differentiable with bounded derivatives of all orders on C, use of Gauss-Legendre integration facilitates numerical work (Abramowitz & Stegun, 1965, p. 887).

8.2.1 Estimation of Parameters

Estimation of $\boldsymbol{\theta}(Z, \mathbf{u})$ is straightforward. Let U_n be a uniformly distributed random variable on the integers 1 to n. For any n-dimensional vector $\mathbf{z}$ of real numbers, let

$c(\mathbf{z})$ be the real random variable such that $c(\mathbf{z})$ has value z_i if $U_n = i$, $1 \leq i \leq n$. Thus $E(\mathbf{u}(c(\mathbf{z})))$ is the sample average $n^{-1}\sum_{i=1}^{n} \mathbf{u}(z_i)$. Let Z_i, $1 \leq i \leq n$, be independent and identically distributed random variables with common distribution Z, and let $\mathbf{Z}$ be the n-dimensional vector with coordinates Z_i, $1 \leq i \leq n$. Then $\boldsymbol{\theta}(Z,\mathbf{u})$ has estimate $\boldsymbol{\theta}(c(\mathbf{Z}),\mathbf{u}))$ whenever the sample covariance matrix of the $\mathbf{u}(Z_i)$, $1 \leq i \leq n$, is positive definite. The estimate $\boldsymbol{\theta}(c(\mathbf{Z}),\mathbf{u})$ converges to $\boldsymbol{\theta}(Z,\mathbf{u})$ with probability 1 as n approaches ∞. If $\mathbf{V}_*(Z,\mathbf{u})$ is $\mathbf{V}(\boldsymbol{\theta}(Z,\mathbf{u}),\mathbf{u})$, then $n^{1/2}[\boldsymbol{\theta}(c(\mathbf{Z}),\mathbf{u}) - \boldsymbol{\theta}(Z,\mathbf{u})]$ converges in distribution to a multivariate normal random variable with zero mean and with covariance matrix

$$\Sigma(Z,\mathbf{u}) = [\mathbf{V}_*(Z,\mathbf{u})]^{-1}\mathrm{Cov}(\mathbf{u}(Z))[\mathbf{V}_*(Z,\mathbf{u})]^{-1}. \tag{8.4}$$

The estimate $\Sigma(c(\mathbf{Z}),\mathbf{u})$ converges to $\Sigma(Z,\mathbf{u})$ with probability 1 as the sample size n increases. For any K-dimensional vector $\mathbf{d}$ that is not equal to 0_K, approximate confidence intervals for $\mathbf{d}'\boldsymbol{\theta}(Z,\mathbf{u})$ may be based on the observation that

$$\frac{\mathbf{d}'\boldsymbol{\theta}(c(\mathbf{Z}),\mathbf{u}) - \mathbf{d}'\boldsymbol{\theta}(Z,\mathbf{u})}{[\mathbf{d}'\Sigma(c(\mathbf{Z}),\mathbf{u})\mathbf{d}/n]^{1/2}}$$

converges in distribution to a standard normal random variable. The denominator $[\mathbf{d}'\Sigma(c(\mathbf{Z}),\mathbf{u})\mathbf{d}/n]^{1/2}$ may be termed the EASD of $\mathbf{d}'\boldsymbol{\theta}(c(\mathbf{Z}),\mathbf{u})$.

The estimate $I(c(\mathbf{Z}),\mathbf{u})$ converges to $I(Z,\mathbf{u})$ with probability 1, and $n^{1/2}[I(c(\mathbf{Z}),\mathbf{u}) - I(Z,\mathbf{u})]$ converges in distribution to a normal random variable with mean 0 and variance $\sigma^2(I,Z,\mathbf{u})$ equal to the variance of $\boldsymbol{\theta}(Z,\mathbf{u})/\mathrm{Cov}(\mathbf{u}(Z))/\boldsymbol{\theta}(Z,\mathbf{u})$ of $\log g(Z,\boldsymbol{\theta}(Z,\mathbf{u}),\mathbf{u})$. As the sample size n increases, $\sigma^2(I,c(\mathbf{Z}),\mathbf{u})$ converges to $\sigma^2(I,Z,\mathbf{u})$ with probability 1, so that the EASD of $I(c(\mathbf{Z}),\mathbf{u})$ is $[\sigma^2(I,c(\mathbf{Z}),\mathbf{u})/n]^{1/2}$.

The estimated distribution function $F_*(x,c(\mathbf{Z}),\mathbf{u}) = F(x,Y_*(c(\mathbf{Z}),\mathbf{u}),\mathbf{u})$ converges with probability 1 to $F_*(x,Z,\mathbf{u}) = F(x,Y_*(Z,\mathbf{u}))$ for each x in C, and the estimated quantile function $Q_*(p,c(\mathbf{Z}),\mathbf{u}) = Q(p,Y_*(c(\mathbf{Z}),\mathbf{u}))$ converges with probability 1 to $Q_*(p,Z,\mathbf{u}) = Q(p,Y_*(Z,\mathbf{u}))$ for $0 < p < 1$. The scaled difference $n^{1/2}[F_*(x,c(\mathbf{Z}),\mathbf{u}) - F_*(x,Z,\mathbf{u})]$ converges in distribution to a normal random variable with mean 0 and variance

$$\sigma^2(F_*,x,Z,\mathbf{u}) = [\mathbf{T}_*(x,Z,\mathbf{u})]'\Sigma(Z,\mathbf{u})[\mathbf{T}_*(x,Z,\mathbf{u})],$$

where

$$\mathbf{T}_*(x,Z,\mathbf{u}) = \mathbf{T}(x,\boldsymbol{\theta}(Z,\mathbf{u}),\mathbf{u})$$

and

$$\mathbf{T}(x,\mathbf{y},\mathbf{u}) = \int_C \chi_C(x)[\mathbf{u} - \mu(\mathbf{y},\mathbf{u})]g(\mathbf{y},\mathbf{u}).$$

The estimate $\sigma^2(F_*, x, c(\mathbf{Z}), \mathbf{u})$ converges with probability 1 to $\sigma^2(F_*, x, Z, \mathbf{u})$. Let $g_*(Z, \mathbf{u}) = g(\boldsymbol{\theta}(Z, \mathbf{u}), \mathbf{u})$ have value $g_*(x, Z, \mathbf{u})$ at x in C. If $\mathbf{u}$ is continuous at $Q_*(p, Z, \mathbf{u})$, then $n^{1/2}[Q_*(p, c(\mathbf{Z}), \mathbf{u}) - Q_*(p, Z, \mathbf{u})]$ converges in distribution to a normal random variable with mean 0 and variance

$$\sigma^2(Q_*, p, Z, \mathbf{u}) = \frac{\sigma^2(F_*, Q_*(p, Z, \mathbf{u}), Z, \mathbf{u})}{[g_*(Q_*(p, Z, \mathbf{u}), Z, \mathbf{u})]^2}.$$

The estimate $\sigma^2(Q_*, p, c(\mathbf{Z}), \mathbf{u})$ converges with probability 1 to $\sigma^2(Q_*, p, Z, \mathbf{u})$ as n increases. Note that if $\mathbf{u}$ is $\mathbf{v}(K, C)$, then the continuity requirement always holds.

8.2.2 Equating Functions for Continuous Exponential Families

In the equating application, for j equals 1 or 2, let K_j be a positive integer, and let $\mathbf{u}_j$ be a bounded, K_j-dimensional, integrable function on B_j. Let $\mathrm{Cov}(\mathbf{u}_j(X_j))$ be positive definite. Then one may consider the conversion function

$$e_*(X_1, \mathbf{u}_1, X_2, \mathbf{u}_2) = e(Y_*(X_1, \mathbf{u}_1), Y_*(X_2, \mathbf{u}_2))$$

for conversion from Form 1 to Form 2 and the conversion function

$$e_*(X_2, \mathbf{u}_2, X_1, \mathbf{u}_1) = e(Y_*(X_2, \mathbf{u}_2), Y_*(X_1, \mathbf{u}_1))$$

for conversion from Form 2 to Form 1. For x in B_1, let $e_*(X_1, \mathbf{u}_1, X_2, \mathbf{u}_2)$ have value $e_*(x, X_1, \mathbf{u}_1, X_2, \mathbf{u}_2)$. For x in B_2, let $e_*(X_2, \mathbf{u}_2, X_1, \mathbf{u}_1)$ have value $e_*(x, X_2, \mathbf{u}_2, X_1, \mathbf{u}_1)$.

Given the available random sample data X_{ij}, $1 \le i \le n_j$, $1 \le j \le 2$, estimation of the conversion functions is straightforward. Let $\mathbf{X}_j$ be the n_j-dimensional vector with coordinates X_{ij}, $1 \le i \le n_j$. Then $e_*(x, c(\mathbf{X}_1), \mathbf{u}_1, c(\mathbf{X}_2), \mathbf{u}_2)$ converges with probability 1 to $e_*(x, X_1, \mathbf{u}_1, X_2, \mathbf{u}_2)$ for x in B_1, and $e_*(x, c(\mathbf{X}_2), \mathbf{u}_2, c(\mathbf{X}_1), \mathbf{u}_1)$ converges with probability 1 to $e_*(x, X_2, \mathbf{u}_2, X_1, \mathbf{u}_1)$ for x in B_2 as n_1 and n_2 approach ∞. If $\mathbf{u}$ is continuous at $e_*(x, X_1, \mathbf{u}_1, X_2, \mathbf{u}_2)$ for an x in B_1, then

$$\frac{e_*(x, c(\mathbf{X}_1), \mathbf{u}_1, c(\mathbf{X}_2), X_2, \mathbf{u}_2) - e_*(x, X_1, \mathbf{u}_1, X_2, \mathbf{u}_2)}{\sigma(e_*, x, X_1, \mathbf{u}_1, X_2, \mathbf{u}_2, n_1, n_2)}$$

converges in distribution to a standard normal random variable as n_1 and n_2 become large, as in Equation 8.4, where

$$\sigma^2(e_*, x, X_1, \mathbf{u}_1, X_2, \mathbf{u}_2, n_1, n_2) = \frac{\sigma^2(F_*, x, X_1, \mathbf{u}_1)}{n_1[g(e_*(x, X_1, \mathbf{u}_1, X_2, \mathbf{u}_2)]^2} + \frac{\sigma^2(Q_*, F_*(x, X_1, \mathbf{u}_1), X_2, \mathbf{u}_2)}{n_2}. \tag{8.5}$$

In addition, the ratio

$$\frac{\sigma^2(e_*, x, c(\mathbf{X}_1), \mathbf{u}_1, c(\mathbf{X}_2), \mathbf{u}_2, n_1, n_2)}{\sigma^2(e_*, x, X_1, \mathbf{u}_1, X_2, \mathbf{u}_2, n_1, n_2)} \tag{8.6}$$

converges to 1 with probability 1, so that the EASD of $e_*(x, c(\mathbf{X}_1), \mathbf{u}_1, c(\mathbf{X}_2), \mathbf{u}_2)$ is $\sigma(e_*, x, c(\mathbf{X}_1), \mathbf{u}_1, c(\mathbf{X}_2), \mathbf{u}_2, n_1, n_2)$. Similar results apply to conversion from Form 2 to Form 1. Note that continuity requirements always hold in the polynomial case with $\mathbf{u}_j = \mathbf{v}(K_j, B_j)$.

8.2.3 Example

Table 7.1 of von Davier et al. (2004b) provided two distributions of test scores that are integers from $c_j = 0$ to $d_j = 20$. To illustrate results, the intervals $B_j = (-0.5, 20.5)$ are employed. Results in terms of estimated expected log penalties are summarized in Table 8.1. These tables suggest that gains over the quadratic case ($K_j = 2$) are very modest for both X_1 and X_2.

Equating results are provided in Table 8.2 for conversions from Form 1 to Form 2. Given Table 8.1, the quadratic model is considered for both X_1 and X_2, so that $K_1 = K_2 = 2$. Two comparisons are provided with familiar equating procedures. In the case of kernel equating, comparable quadratic log-linear models were used. The bandwidths employed by Version 2.1 of the LOGLIN/KE program (Chen, Yan, Han, & von Davier, 2006) were employed. The percentile-rank computations correspond to the use of the tangent rule of integration in Wang (2008) for the quadratic continuous exponential families. In terms of continuous exponential families, the percentile-rank results also can be produced if $\mathbf{v}(x, 2, B_j)$ is replaced by the rounded approximation $\mathbf{v}(\mathrm{rnd}(x), 2, B_j)$, where $\mathrm{rnd}(x)$ is the nearest integer to x. The convention to adopt for the definition of $\mathrm{rnd}(x)$ for values such as $x = 1.5$ has no material effect on the analysis; however, the discontinuity of $\mathrm{rnd}(x)$ for such values does imply that asymptotic normality approximations are not entirely satisfactory. As a consequence, they are not provided. In this example, the three conversions are very similar for all possible values of X_1. For the two methods for which EASDs are available, results are rather similar. The results for the continuous exponential family are relatively best at the extremes of the distribution.

Table 8.1 Estimated Expected Log Penalties for Variables X_1 and X_2 for Polynomial Models

Variable	Degree	Estimate	EASD
X_1	2	2.747	0.015
X_1	3	2.747	0.015
X_1	4	2.745	0.015
X_2	2	2.773	0.014
X_2	3	2.772	0.014
X_2	4	2.771	0.014

Note: EASD = estimated asymptotic standard deviation.

Table 8.2 Comparison of Conversions From Form 1 to Form 2

Value	Continuous exponential		Kernel		Percentile-rank estimate
	Estimate	EASD	Estimate	EASD	
0	0.091	0.110	−0.061	0.194	0.095
1	1.215	0.209	1.234	0.235	1.179
2	2.304	0.239	2.343	0.253	2.255
3	3.377	0.240	3.413	0.253	3.325
4	4.442	0.230	4.473	0.242	4.392
5	5.504	0.214	5.529	0.225	5.458
6	6.564	0.198	6.582	0.207	6.522
7	7.621	0.182	7.634	0.189	7.585
8	8.677	0.169	8.685	0.174	8.647
9	9.732	0.159	9.734	0.162	9.706
10	10.784	0.155	10.781	0.155	10.761
11	11.834	0.155	11.825	0.153	11.823
12	12.880	0.160	12.865	0.156	12.859
13	13.919	0.168	13.900	0.163	13.898
14	14.950	0.177	14.925	0.172	14.928
15	15.966	0.184	15.936	0.179	15.947
16	16.959	0.187	16.925	0.182	16.949
17	17.912	0.179	17.879	0.178	17.927
18	18.802	0.156	18.799	0.164	18.871
19	19.592	0.109	19.723	0.145	19.760
20	20.240	0.040	20.818	0.119	20.380

Note: EASD = estimated asymptotic standard deviation.

8.3 Continuous Exponential Families for a Single Group

In the case of a single group, the joint distribution of $\mathbf{X} = (X_1, X_2)$ is approximated by use of a bivariate continuous exponential family. The definition of a bivariate continuous exponential family is similar to that for a univariate continuous exponential family. However, in bivariate exponential families, a nonempty, bounded, convex open set C of the plane is used such that each value of $\mathbf{X}$ is in a closed subset D of C.

As in the univariate case, let K be a positive integer, and let $\mathbf{u}$ be a bounded K-dimensional integrable function on C. In many cases, $\mathbf{u}$ is defined by use of bivariate polynomials. To any K-dimensional vector $\mathbf{y}$ corresponds a two-dimensional random variable $\mathbf{Y}(\mathbf{y},\mathbf{u}) = (Y_1(\mathbf{y},\mathbf{u}), Y_2(\mathbf{y},\mathbf{u}))$ with values in C with a density function f $\mathbf{Y}$(**y**,**u**)) equal to

$$g(\mathbf{y},\mathbf{u}) = \gamma(\mathbf{y},\mathbf{u})\ \exp(\mathbf{y}'\mathbf{u}),$$

where from Equation 8.1

$$1/\gamma(\mathbf{y},\mathbf{u}) = \int_C \exp(\mathbf{y}'\mathbf{u})$$

and $g(\mathbf{y},\mathbf{u})$ has value $g(\mathbf{z},\mathbf{y},\mathbf{u})$ at $\mathbf{z}$ in C. As in the univariate case, the family of distributions with densities $g(\mathbf{y},\mathbf{u})$ for K-dimensional vectors $\mathbf{y}$ is the continuous exponential family of distributions defined by $\mathbf{u}$. These density functions are always positive on C, and they are continuous if $\mathbf{u}$ is continuous. If $\mathbf{U}_C$ is a random vector with a uniform distribution on C, then problems of parameter identification may be avoided by the requirement that $\mathbf{u}(\mathbf{U}_C)$ have a positive-definite covariance matrix. As in the univariate case, $\mathbf{Y}(0_K,\mathbf{u})$ has the same distribution as $\mathbf{U}_C$.

In equating applications, marginal distributions are important. For j equal 1 or 2, let C_j be the open set that consists of real x such that $x = x_j$ for some (x_1,x_2) in C. For x in C_j, let $\chi_{jC}(x)$ be the set of (x_1,x_2) in C_1 with $x_j \le x$. Then the restriction $G_j(\mathbf{y},\mathbf{u})$ of the distribution function $F(Y_j(\mathbf{y},\mathbf{u}))$ to C_j has value

$$G_j(x,\mathbf{y},\mathbf{u}) = \int_C \chi_{jC}(x)g(\mathbf{y},\mathbf{u})$$

at x in C_j. The function $G_j(\mathbf{y},\mathbf{u})$ is continuous and strictly increasing on C_j, and $Y_j(\mathbf{y},\mathbf{u})$ has density function $g_j(x,\mathbf{y},\mathbf{u})$. For z_1 in C_1,

$$g_1(z_1,\mathbf{y},\mathbf{u}) = \int_{C_2(z_1)} g(\mathbf{z},\mathbf{y},\mathbf{u})dz_2,$$

where $C_2(z_1) = \{z_2 \in C_2 : (z_1,z_2) \in C_2\}$. Similarly,

$$g_2(z_2,\mathbf{y},\mathbf{u}) = \int_{C_1(z_2)} g(\mathbf{z},\mathbf{y},\mathbf{u})dz_1,$$

where $C_1(z_2) = \{z_1 \in C_1 : (z_1,z_2) \in C_1\}$. The function $G_j(\mathbf{y},\mathbf{u})$ is continuously differentiable if $\mathbf{u}$ is continuous.

As in the univariate case, the distribution of the random vector $\mathbf{X}$ with values in C may be approximated by a distribution in the continuous exponential family of distributions generated by $\mathbf{u}$. The quality of the approximation provided by the distribution with density $g(\mathbf{y},\mathbf{u})$ is assessed by the expected log penalty from Equation 8.2

$$H(\mathbf{X},\mathbf{y},\mathbf{u}) = -E(\log\, g(\mathbf{X},\mathbf{y},\mathbf{u})) = -\log\, \gamma(\mathbf{y},\mathbf{u}) + \mathbf{y}'E(\mathbf{u}(\mathbf{Z})).$$

The smaller the value of $H(\mathbf{X},\mathbf{y},\mathbf{u})$, the better is the approximation.

Provided that $\mathrm{Cov}(\mathbf{u}(\mathbf{X}))$ is positive definite, a unique K-dimensional vector $\boldsymbol{\theta}(\mathbf{X},\mathbf{u})$ with coordinates $\boldsymbol{\theta}_k(\mathbf{X},\mathbf{u})$, $1 \le k \le K$, exists such that $H(\mathbf{X},\boldsymbol{\theta}(\mathbf{X},\mathbf{u}))$ is equal to the infimum $I(\mathbf{X},\mathbf{u})$ of $H(\mathbf{X},\mathbf{y},\mathbf{u})$ for K-dimensional vectors $\mathbf{y}$. Let $\mathbf{Y}_*(\mathbf{X},\mathbf{u}) = (Y_{*1}(\mathbf{X},\mathbf{u}),Y_{*2}(\mathbf{X},\mathbf{u})) = \mathbf{Y}(\boldsymbol{\theta}(\mathbf{X},\mathbf{u}),\mathbf{u}))$. Then $\boldsymbol{\theta}(\mathbf{X},\mathbf{u})$ is the unique solution of the equation

$$E(\mathbf{u}(\mathbf{Y}_*(\mathbf{X},\mathbf{u}))) = E(\mathbf{u}(\mathbf{X})).$$

If

$$\boldsymbol{\mu}(\mathbf{y},\mathbf{u}) = \int_C \mathbf{u}g(\mathbf{y},\mathbf{u}),$$

then

$$E(\mathbf{u}(\mathbf{Y}(\mathbf{y},\mathbf{u}))) = \boldsymbol{\mu}(\mathbf{y},\mathbf{u}),$$

and

$$\boldsymbol{\mu}(\boldsymbol{\theta}(\mathbf{X},\mathbf{u}),\mathbf{u}) = E(\mathbf{u}(\mathbf{X})).$$

The value of $\boldsymbol{\theta}(\mathbf{X},\mathbf{u})$ may be found by the Newton-Raphson algorithm. Note that the positive-definite covariance matrix of $\mathbf{Y}(\mathbf{y},\mathbf{u})$ is

$$\mathbf{V}(\mathbf{y},\mathbf{u}) = \int_C [\mathbf{u} - \boldsymbol{\mu}(\mathbf{y},\mathbf{u})][\mathbf{u} - \boldsymbol{\mu}(\mathbf{y},\mathbf{u})]'g(\mathbf{y},\mathbf{u}).$$

Given an initial approximation $\boldsymbol{\theta}_0$, the algorithm at step $t \geq 0$ yields a new approximation

$$\boldsymbol{\theta}_{t+1} = \boldsymbol{\theta}_t + [\mathbf{V}(\boldsymbol{\theta}_t,\mathbf{u})]^{-1}[E(\mathbf{u}(\mathbf{X})) - \boldsymbol{\mu}(\boldsymbol{\theta}_t,\mathbf{u})]$$

of $\boldsymbol{\theta}(\mathbf{X},\mathbf{u})$ as in Equation 8.3. Normally, $\boldsymbol{\theta}_t$ converges to $\boldsymbol{\theta}(\mathbf{X},\mathbf{u})$ as t increases. As in the univariate case, the selection of $\boldsymbol{\theta}_0 = 0_K$ is normally acceptable.

8.3.1 Estimation of Parameters

Estimation of $\boldsymbol{\theta}(\mathbf{X},\mathbf{u})$ is quite similar to the corresponding estimation in the univariate case. For any n-by-2 real matrix $\mathbf{z}$ with elements z_{ij}, $1 \leq i \leq n$, $1 \leq j \leq 2$, let $\mathbf{c}(\mathbf{z})$ be the two-dimensional random variable such that $\mathbf{c}(\mathbf{z})$ has value (z_{i1}, z_{i2}) if $U_n = i$, $1 \leq i \leq n$. Let $\mathbf{Z}$ be the n-by-2 matrix with elements X_{ij}, $1 \leq i \leq n$, $1 \leq j \leq 2$. Then $\boldsymbol{\theta}(\mathbf{X},\mathbf{u})$ has estimate $\boldsymbol{\theta}(\mathbf{c}(\mathbf{Z}),\mathbf{u})$ whenever the sample covariance matrix of the $\mathbf{u}(\mathbf{X}_i)$, $1 \leq i \leq n$, is positive definite. The estimate $\boldsymbol{\theta}(c(\mathbf{Z}),\mathbf{u})$ converges to $\boldsymbol{\theta}(\mathbf{X},\mathbf{u})$ with probability 1 as n approaches ∞. If $\mathbf{V}_*(\mathbf{X},\mathbf{u})$ is $\mathbf{V}(\boldsymbol{\theta}(\mathbf{X},\mathbf{u}),\mathbf{u})$, then $n^{1/2}[\boldsymbol{\theta}(c(\mathbf{Z}),\mathbf{u}) - \boldsymbol{\theta}(\mathbf{X},\mathbf{u})]$ converges in distribution to a multivariate normal random variable with zero mean and with covariance matrix

$$\Sigma(\mathbf{X},\mathbf{u}) = [\mathbf{V}_*(\mathbf{X},\mathbf{u})]^{-1}\mathrm{Cov}(\mathbf{u}(\mathbf{X}))[\mathbf{V}_*(\mathbf{X},\mathbf{u})]^{-1},$$

as in Equation 8.4.

The estimate $\Sigma(\mathbf{c}(\mathbf{Z}),\mathbf{u})$ converges to $\Sigma(\mathbf{X},\mathbf{u})$ with probability 1 as the sample size n increases. For any K-dimensional vector $\mathbf{d}$ that is not equal to 0_K, approximate confidence intervals for $\mathbf{d}'\boldsymbol{\theta}(\mathbf{X},\mathbf{u})$ may be based on the observation that

$$\frac{\mathbf{d}'\boldsymbol{\theta}(\mathbf{c}(\mathbf{Z}),\mathbf{u})\mathbf{d} - \mathbf{d}'\boldsymbol{\theta}(\mathbf{X},\mathbf{u})}{[\mathbf{d}'\Sigma(c(\mathbf{Z}),\mathbf{u})\mathbf{d}/n]^{1/2}}$$

converges in distribution to a standard normal random variable. The denominator $[\mathbf{d}'\Sigma(c(\mathbf{Z}),\mathbf{u})\mathbf{d}/n]^{1/2}$ may be termed the EASD of $\mathbf{d}'\boldsymbol{\theta}(\mathbf{c}(\mathbf{Z}),\mathbf{u})$.

The estimate $I(\mathbf{c}(\mathbf{Z}),\mathbf{u})$ converges to $I(\mathbf{X},\mathbf{u})$ with probability 1, and $n^{1/2}[I(\mathbf{c}(\mathbf{Z}),\mathbf{u}) - I(\mathbf{X},\mathbf{u})]$ converges in distribution to a normal random variable with mean 0 and variance $\sigma^2(I,\mathbf{X},\mathbf{u})$ equal to the variance of $\log g(\mathbf{X},\boldsymbol{\theta}(\mathbf{X},\mathbf{u}),\mathbf{u})$. This variance is $[\boldsymbol{\theta}(\mathbf{X},\mathbf{u})]'\ \mathrm{COV}(\mathbf{u}(\mathbf{X}))\ \boldsymbol{\theta}(\mathbf{X},\mathbf{u})$. As the sample size n increases, $\sigma^2(I,\mathbf{c}(\mathbf{Z}),\mathbf{u})$ converges to $\sigma^2(I,\mathbf{X},\mathbf{u})$ with probability 1, so that the EASD of $I(\mathbf{c}(\mathbf{Z}),\mathbf{u})$ is $[\sigma^2(I,\mathbf{c}(\mathbf{Z}),\mathbf{u})/n]^{1/2}$.

For x in C_j and j equal 1 or 2, $F_{j*}(x,\mathbf{c}(\mathbf{Z}),\mathbf{u}) = F(x,Y_{j*}(\mathbf{c}(\mathbf{Z}),\mathbf{u}),\mathbf{u})$ converges to $F_{j*}(x,\mathbf{X},\mathbf{u})$ with probability 1 for each x in C. Thus, the estimated quantile function $Q_{*j}(p,\mathbf{c}(\mathbf{Z}),\mathbf{u}) = Q(p,Y_{*j}(\mathbf{c}(\mathbf{Z}),\mathbf{u}))$ converges with probability 1 to $Q_{*j}(p,\mathbf{X},\mathbf{u})$ for $0 < p < 1$. The scaled difference $n^{1/2}[F_{*j}(x,\mathbf{c}(\mathbf{Z}),\mathbf{u}) - F_{*j}(x,\mathbf{X},\mathbf{u})]$ converges in distribution to a normal random variable with mean 0 and variance

$$\sigma^2(F_{*j},x,\mathbf{X},\mathbf{u}) = [\mathbf{T}_{*j}(x,\mathbf{X},\mathbf{u})]'\Sigma(\mathbf{X},\mathbf{u})[\mathbf{T}_{*j}(x,\mathbf{X},\mathbf{u})],$$

where

$$\mathbf{T}_{*j}(x,Z,\mathbf{u}) = \mathbf{T}_j(x,\boldsymbol{\theta}(\mathbf{X},\mathbf{u}),\mathbf{u})$$

and

$$\mathbf{T}_j(x,\mathbf{y},\mathbf{u}) = \int_C \chi_{jC}(x)[\mathbf{u} - \mu(\mathbf{y},\mathbf{u})]g(\mathbf{y},\mathbf{u}).$$

The estimate $\sigma^2(F_*,x,\mathbf{c}(\mathbf{Z}),\mathbf{u})$ converges with probability 1 to $\sigma^2(F_*,x,\mathbf{X},\mathbf{u})$. Let $g_{*j}(\mathbf{X},\mathbf{u}) = g(\boldsymbol{\theta}(\mathbf{X},\mathbf{u}),\mathbf{u})$ have value $g_{*j}(x,\mathbf{X},\mathbf{u})$ at x in C_j. If $\mathbf{u}$ is continuous, then $n^{1/2}[Q_{*j}(p,\mathbf{c}(\mathbf{Z}),\mathbf{u}) - Q_{*j}(p,\mathbf{X},\mathbf{u})]$ converges in distribution to a normal random variable with mean 0 and variance

$$\sigma^2(Q_{*j},p,\mathbf{X},\mathbf{u}) = \frac{\sigma^2(F_{*j},Q_{*j}(p,\mathbf{X},\mathbf{u}),\mathbf{X},\mathbf{u})}{[g_{*j}(Q_{*j}(p,\mathbf{X},\mathbf{u}),\mathbf{X},\mathbf{u})]^2}.$$

The estimate $\sigma^2(Q_{*j},p,\mathbf{c}(\mathbf{Z}),\mathbf{u})$ converges with probability 1 to $\sigma^2(Q_*,p,\mathbf{X},\mathbf{u})$ as n increases.

8.3.1.1 Conversion Functions

The conversion function $e_{*1}(\mathbf{X},\mathbf{u}) = e(Y_{*1}(\mathbf{X},\mathbf{u}), Y_{*2}(\mathbf{X},\mathbf{u}))$ may be used for conversion from Form 1 to Form 2. The conversion function $e_{*2}(\mathbf{X},\mathbf{u}) = e(Y_{*2}(\mathbf{X},\mathbf{u}), Y_{*1}(\mathbf{X},\mathbf{u}))$ may be used for conversion from Form 2 to Form 1. For x in C_j, let $e_{*j}(\mathbf{X},\mathbf{u})$ have value $e_{*j}(x,\mathbf{X},\mathbf{u})$. Then $e_{*j}(x,\mathbf{c}(\mathbf{Z}),\mathbf{u})$ converges with probability 1 to $e_{*j}(x,\mathbf{Z},\mathbf{u})$. If $\mathbf{u}$ is continuous and $h = 3 - j$, so that $h = 1$ if $j = 2$ and $h = 2$ if $j = 1$, then $n^{1/2}[e_{*j}(x,c(\mathbf{Z}),\mathbf{u}) - e_{*j}(x,\mathbf{X},\mathbf{u})]$ converges in distribution to a normal random variable with mean 0 and variance

$$\sigma^2(e_{*j},x,\mathbf{X},\mathbf{u}) = [\mathbf{T}_{dj}(x,\mathbf{X},\mathbf{u})]'\Sigma(\mathbf{X},\mathbf{u})\mathbf{T}_{dj}(x,\mathbf{X},\mathbf{u}),$$

as in Equation 8.4 and 8.5, where

$$\mathbf{T}_{dj}(x,\mathbf{X},\mathbf{u}) = \mathbf{T}_{*j}(x,\mathbf{X},\mathbf{u}) - \mathbf{T}_{*h}(e_{*j}(x,\mathbf{X},\mathbf{u}),\mathbf{X},\mathbf{u}).$$

The estimate $\sigma^2(e_{*j},x,\mathbf{c}(\mathbf{Z}),\mathbf{u})$ converges with probability 1 to $\sigma^2(e_{*j},x,\mathbf{X},\mathbf{u})$.

8.3.1.2 Polynomials

In the simplest case, C is the Cartesian product $B_1 \times B_2$, so that C consists of all pairs (x_1,x_2) such that each x_j is in B_j. One common case has $K_j \geq 2$ and $\mathbf{u} = \mathbf{v}(K_1,K_2,B_1,B_2)$, where, for $\mathbf{x} = (x_1,x_2)$ in C, coordinate k of $\mathbf{v}(K_1,K_2,B_1,B_2)$ has value $v_k(\mathbf{x},K_1,K_2,B_1,B_2) = v_k(x_1,K_1,B_1)$ for $1 \leq k \leq K_1$, coordinate $K_1 + k$ has value $v_k(x_2,K_2,B_2)$ for $1 \leq k \leq K_2$, and coordinate $k = K_1 + K_2 + 1$ is $v_1(x_1,K_1,B_1)v_2(x_2,K_1,B_2)$. For this definition of $\mathbf{u}$, $\mathbf{u}$ is continuous, so that all normal approximations apply. For the marginal variable $Y_{*j}(\mathbf{X},\mathbf{u})$, the first K_j moments are the same as the corresponding moments of X_j. In addition, the covariance of $Y_{*1}(\mathbf{X},\mathbf{u})$ and $Y_{*2}(\mathbf{X},\mathbf{u})$ is the same as the covariance of X_1 and X_2. If $K_1 = K_2 = 2$ and if $\boldsymbol{\theta}_2(\mathbf{X},\mathbf{u})$ and $\boldsymbol{\theta}_4(\mathbf{X},\mathbf{u})$ are negative, then $\mathbf{X}$ is distributed as the conditional distribution of a bivariate normal vector given that the vector is in C. Other choices are possible. For example, Wang (2008) considered a case with $K = K_1K_2$, $C = B_1 \times B_2$, and with each coordinate of $\mathbf{u}(\mathbf{x})$ a product $v(x_1,k_1,B_1)$ $v(x_2,k_2,B_2)$ for k_j from 1 to K_j. If $\mathbf{u}$ is the vector with the first $K_1 + K_2$ coordinates of $\mathbf{v}(K_1,K_2,B_1,B_2)$, then it is readily seen that $e_{*j}(x,\mathbf{X},\mathbf{u})$ is the same as the conversion function $e_*(x,X_j,\mathbf{v}(K_j,B_j),X_h,\mathbf{v}(K_h,B_h))$ from the case of equivalent groups, although the use of single groups typically leads to a different normal approximation for $e_{*j}(x,\mathbf{c}(\mathbf{Z}),\mathbf{u})$ than the normal approximation for $e_*(x,c(\mathbf{X}_j),\mathbf{v}(K_j,B_j),c(\mathbf{X}_h),\mathbf{v}(K_h,B_h))$.

8.3.2 *Example*

Table 8.2 of von Davier et al. (2004b) provided an example of a single-group design with $c_j = 0$ and $d_j = 20$ for $1 \leq j \leq 2$. To illustrate results, let

$B_1 = B_2 = (-0.5, 20.5)$, $C = B_1 \times B_2$, and $\mathbf{u} = \mathbf{v}(K, K, B_1, B_2)$, $2 \leq K \leq 4$. Results in terms of estimated expected log penalties are summarized in Table 8.3. These results suggest that gains beyond the quadratic case are quite small, although the quartic case differs from the cubic case more than the cubic case differs from the quadratic case.

Not surprisingly, the three choices of K lead to rather similar conversion functions. Consider Table 8.4 for the case of conversion of Form 1 to Form 2. A bit more variability in results exists for very high or very low values, although estimated asymptotic standard deviations are more variable than are estimated conversions. Note that results are also similar to those for kernel equating (von Davier et al., 2004b, Ch. 8) shown in Table 8.5. These results employ a log-linear model for the joint distribution of the scores, which is comparable to the model defined by $K = 3$ for a continuous exponential family. The log-linear fit preserves the initial three marginal moments for each score distribution as well as the covariance of the two scores. As a consequence, the marginal distributions produced by the kernel method have the same means and variances as do the corresponding distributions of X_{i1} and

Table 8.3 Estimated Expected Log Penalties

K	Estimate	EASD
2	4.969	0.022
3	4.968	0.022
4	4.960	0.022

Note: EASD = estimated asymptotic standard deviation.

Table 8.4 Comparison of Conversions From Form 1 to Form 2

Value	$K = 2$		$K = 3$		$K = 4$	
	Estimate	EASD	Estimate	EASD	Estimate	EASD
0	0.111	0.077	−0.040	0.113	0.404	0.262
1	1.168	0.128	0.927	0.204	1.404	0.264
2	2.144	0.135	1.917	0.208	2.269	0.221
3	3.091	0.130	2.910	0.182	3.121	0.176
4	4.028	0.120	3.899	0.151	3.987	0.140
5	4.959	0.108	4.881	0.122	4.874	0.117
6	5.889	0.097	5.854	0.101	5.785	0.105
7	6.819	0.086	6.819	0.087	6.721	0.100
8	7.748	0.076	7.775	0.080	7.679	0.095
9	8.677	0.069	8.722	0.078	8.653	0.090
10	9.606	0.065	9.661	0.078	9.634	0.086
11	10.536	0.064	10.591	0.077	10.611	0.085
12	11.465	0.066	11.512	0.077	11.574	0.088
13	12.394	0.073	12.425	0.077	12.514	0.092
14	13.324	0.081	13.331	0.081	13.427	0.094
15	14.256	0.091	14.231	0.090	14.310	0.096
16	15.193	0.102	15.128	0.105	15.166	0.101
17	16.141	0.113	16.033	0.126	16.003	0.116
18	17.119	0.121	16.967	0.149	16.838	0.142
19	18.173	0.123	17.985	0.167	17.716	0.174
20	19.495	0.094	19.304	0.150	18.842	0.198

Note: EASD = estimated asymptotic standard deviation.

Table 8.5 Conversions From Form 1 to Form 2 by Kernel Equating

Value	Estimate	EASD
0	−0.002	0.162
1	0.999	0.221
2	1.981	0.221
3	2.956	0.193
4	3.926	0.159
5	4.890	0.128
6	5.850	0.104
7	6.805	0.089
8	7.756	0.080
9	8.702	0.078
10	9.643	0.077
11	10.580	0.077
12	11.512	0.077
13	12.439	0.078
14	13.362	0.083
15	14.283	0.095
16	15.206	0.115
17	16.140	0.140
18	17.105	0.167
19	18.155	0.185
20	19.411	0.158

Note: EASD = estimated asymptotic standard deviation.

X_{i2}. However, the kernel methods yields the distribution of a continuous random variable for the first form with a skewness coefficient that is 0.987 times the original skewness coefficient for X_{i1} and a distribution of a continuous random variable for the second form with a skewness coefficient that is 0.983 times the original skewness coefficient for X_{i2}.

8.4 Conclusions

Equating via continuous exponential families can be regarded as a viable competitor to kernel equating and to the percentile-rank approach. Continuous exponential families lead to simpler procedures and more thorough moment agreement, for fewer steps are involved in equating by continuous exponential families, due to elimination of kernel smoothing. In addition, equating by continuous exponential families does not require selection of bandwidths.

One example does not produce an operational method, and kernel equating is rapidly approaching operational use, so it is important to consider some required steps. Although equivalent-groups designs and single-group designs are used in testing programs, a large fraction of equating designs are more complex. Nonetheless, these designs typically can be explored by repeated application of single-group or equivalent-groups designs. For example, the single-group design provides the basis for more complex linking designs with anchor tests (von Davier et al., 2004b,

Ch. 9). No reason exists to expect that continuous exponential families cannot be applied to any standard equating situation to which kernel equating has been applied.

It is certainly appropriate to consider a variety of applications to data, and some work on quality of large-sample approximations is appropriate when smaller sample sizes are contemplated. Although this gain is not apparent in the examples studied, a possible gain from continuous exponential families is that application to assessments with unevenly spaced scores or very large numbers of possible scores is completely straightforward. Thus, direct conversion from a raw score on one form to an unrounded scale score on a second form involves no difficulties. In addition, in tests with formula scoring, no need exists to round raw scores to integers during equating.

Chapter 8 Appendix

8.A.1 Computation of Orthogonal Polynomials

Computation of the orthogonal polynomials $v_k(C)$, $k \geq 0$, is rather straightforward given standard properties of Legendre polynomials (Abramowitz & Stegun, 1965, Ch. 8, 22). The Legendre polynomial of degree 0 is $P_0(x) = 1$; the Legendre polynomial of degree 1 is $P_1(x) = x$; and the Legendre polynomial $P_{k+1}(x)$ of degree $k + 1$, $k \geq 1$, is determined by the recurrence relationship

$$P_{k+1}(x) = (k+1)^{-1}[(2k+1)xP_k(x) - kP_{k-1}(x)], \quad (8.A.1)$$

so that $P_2(x) = (3x^2 - 1)/2$. For nonnegative integers i and k, the integral $\int_{-1}^{1} P_i P_k$ is 0 for $i \neq k$ and $1/(2k+1)$ for $i = k$. Use of elementary rules of integration shows that one may let

$$v_k(x, C) = (2k+1)^{1/2} P_k([2x - \inf(C) - \sup(C)]/[\sup(C) - \inf(C)]).$$

Author Note: Any opinions expressed in this chapter are those of the author and not necessarily of Educational Testing Service.

Chapter 9
An Alternative Continuization Method: The Continuized Log-Linear Method

Tianyou Wang

9.1 Introduction

von Davier, Holland and Thayer (2004b, pp. 45–47) described a five-step, test-equating framework: (a) presmoothing, (b) estimating score probabilities, (c) continuization, (d) equating, and (e) calculating the standard error of equating. In this framework, the presmoothing step is usually done with log-linear smoothing. Step 2 is to transform smoothed distribution into two marginal distributions for the target population (sometimes called synthetic population). In their framework, Step 3 is done with an adjusted Gaussian kernel procedure.

The advantage of the von Davier et al. (2004b) framework is that it modularizes the equating process so that different designs and methods only affect certain steps. For instance, different data collection designs will result in different design functions in Step 2. For a random-groups design, Step 2 is usually omitted in the traditional description of the equating process, but in this framework an identity design function is used. Likewise, different equating methods only affect Step 4.

The main difference between this framework and previous equating procedures is that it has a continuization step, so that the equating step is based on two continuous distributions rather than two discrete distributions. Denote the random variables for the test scores for test X as *X* and for test Y as *Y*, and the target population cumulative distributions of *X* and *Y* as *F(X)* and *G(Y)*, respectively. Then the equipercentile equating function $\hat{e}_Y(x)$ is given by Equation 9.1:

$$\hat{e}_Y(X) = G^{-1}(F(X)), \tag{9.1}$$

The traditional, percentile rank-based, equating procedure also can be viewed as a uniform-kernel continuization procedure under this framework. However,

T. Wang
The University of Iowa, 210B Lindquist Center, Iowa City, IA 52242, USA
e-mail: tianyouwang@yahoo.com

A.A. von Davier (ed.), *Statistical Models for Test Equating, Scaling, and Linking*, Statistics for Social and Behavioral Sciences,
DOI 10.1007/978-0-387-98138-3_9, © Springer Science+Business Media, LLC 2011

uniform kernel produces piecewise linear culumlative distributions, which may not be the ideal procedure. Wang (2008) proposed an alternative continuization method that directly takes the log-linear function in the presmoothing step and transforms it into a continuous distribution. This method is called the continuized log-linear (CLL) method and is described for different data collection designs in the next two sections.

9.2 The CLL Method for the Equivalent-Groups Design

For the equivalent-groups design, the design function is the identity function. The distributions obtained from Step 2 are the same as those from Step 1. For this design, an alternative continuization procedure that utilizes the polynomial log-linear function obtained in the log-linear smoothing step is presented here, the CLL distribution. The probability density function (PDF) is expressed as

$$f(x) = \frac{1}{D} exp(\mathbf{b}^T \boldsymbol{\beta}), \tag{9.2}$$

where $\mathbf{b}^T = (1, x, x^2, \ldots, x^M)$ is a vector of polynomial terms of test X score x, $\boldsymbol{\beta} = (\beta_0, \beta_1, \beta_2, \ldots, \beta_M)^T$ is the vector of parameters, and M is the order (or degree) of the polynomial. Holland and Thayer (1987, 2000) gave detailed descriptions about model parameter estimation and how to select the polynomial degree M. D is a normalizing constant that ensures that $f(x)$ is a PDF.

It is easy to show that all the moments of the CLL distribution are approximately equal to those of the smoothed discrete distribution by the following relationship between *i-th* noncentral moments of the CLL distribution and the smoothed discrete distribution:

$$\frac{\int_l^u x^i exp(\mathbf{b}^\mathbf{T} \boldsymbol{\beta}) dx}{\int_l^u exp(\mathbf{b}^\mathbf{T} \boldsymbol{\beta}) dx} \approx \frac{1}{N} \sum_{x=0}^{J} x^i exp(\mathbf{b}^\mathbf{T} \boldsymbol{\beta}), \tag{9.3}$$

where J is the number of test items, and l and u are the lower and upper limit of integration. In this case, they are set to be -0.5 and $J + 0.5$, respectively, so that the probabilities of the end points of the discrete distribution are allowed to spread out in both directions. N is the sample size. This approximation holds because the right side of the equation is actually an expression for numerical integration of the left side with equally spaced quadrature points. The numerator and denominator of the left side can be separately expressed as

$$\int_l^u x^i exp(\mathbf{b}^\mathbf{T} \boldsymbol{\beta}) dx \approx \sum_{x=0}^{J} x^i exp(\mathbf{b}^\mathbf{T} \boldsymbol{\beta}),$$

and

$$D = \int_{l}^{u} exp(\mathbf{b}^{\mathrm{T}}\boldsymbol{\beta})dx \approx \sum_{x=0}^{J} exp(\beta_0 + \beta_1 x + \cdots + \beta_M x^M) = N. \qquad (9.4)$$

This means that the normalizing constant is approximately equal to the sample size, which is known prior to equating. This result significantly simplifies the computation. The above expressions are very similar to the trapezoidal rule (see Thisted, 1988, p. 264; note that the subinterval length equals 1). The range of the continuous distribution is set from -0.5 to $J + 0.5$ so that in the quadrature the function is evaluated at the midpoints of the subintervals rather than at the end points, as in the regular trapezoidal rule. This range is consistent with the range of the percentile-rank method in conventional equipercentile equating (Kolen & Brennan, 2004, pp. 39–46). Because of the smoothness of the log-linear function, the approximation can be quite close when the number of quadrature points (i.e., the score points J) gets large.

The proposed CLL continuization seems to have several advantages over kernel continuization. First, CLL continuization is simpler and more direct. Second, it is smoother and is guaranteed to be without the small bumpiness in the kernel continuization. Third, it preserves all the moments of the discrete distribution to the precision of equally spaced numerical integration with $J + 1$ quadrature points. The next section illustrates these points with two data sets, one from von Davier et al. (2004b) and the other from Kolen and Brennan (2004).

9.3 The CLL Method for Other Designs

The CLL approach for the equivalent-groups design can be extended to other designs, such as the single-group design, the single-group counterbalanced design, and the nonequivalent groups with anchor test (NEAT) design. Typically, these designs require a bivariate log-linear smoothing procedure in Step 1 of the test equating framework described earlier in this paper. With the Gaussian kernel continuization method, Step 2 is the step that applies the design functions, and Step 3 is the continuization step. With the CLL continuization method, because the continuization step must directly utilize the log-linear function from Step 1, continuization must be carried out immediately after Step 1. So, the design function must be applied after the continuization step and must be applied on continuous distribution functions rather than on discrete distributions, as in the kernel method. Another difference in the design function is that with the kernel method, the design functions are applied to discrete distributions and are thus in matrix form (see von Davier et al., 2004b, Ch. 2 for a detailed description). However, with the CLL method, the design function is a conceptual term that encapsulates the procedures (usually expressed as a set of equations) that transform the continuized distributions into two marginal distributions for X and Y in the target population. The following subsections describe the procedures for various equating designs. For the equivalent-groups design described in the precious section, the design function is an identity function, which means that no such procedure is needed.

9.3.1 For the Single-Group, Counterbalanced Design

For the single-group design, both test X and test Y are administered to the same group of examinees. For the counterbalenced design, the whole group takes both test X and test Y; however, approximately half of the group takes test X first and then test Y, whereas the other half takes test Y first and then test X. The first half group will be labeled as Group 1 and the second half as Group 2. The single-group design can be viewed as a special case of the counterbalanced design where there is only Group 1.

The log-linear functions are taken directly from Step 1 (treating them as continuous functions) and normalized to be PDFs. For Group 1, the PDF can be expressed as Equation 9.5:

$$f_1(x,y) = \frac{1}{D_1} exp(\mathbf{b}^T \boldsymbol{\beta}), \tag{9.5}$$

where $\mathbf{b}^T = (1, x, x^2, \ldots, x^{M_X}, y, y^2, \ldots, y^{M_Y}, xy, x^2y, xy^2, \ldots, x^{C_X}y^{C_Y})$ is a vector of polynomial terms of x and y, $\beta = (\beta_{00}, \beta_{01}, \beta_{02}, \ldots, \beta_{0M_X}, \beta_{10}, \beta_{20}, \ldots, \beta_{M_Y0}, \beta_{11}, \beta_{12}, \beta_{21}, \ldots, \beta_{C_XC_Y})^T$ is a vector of parameters, M_X and M_Y are the orders of marginal polynomial terms for X and Y, C_X and C_Y are the orders of the cross-product terms for X and Y, and D_1 is a normalizing constant that ensures that $f_1(x, y)$ is a PDF. Again, it can be shown that the normalizing constant approximates the sample size.

The joint PDF of Group 2, $f_2(x, y)$, can be found in a similar fashion. Given the weights of X and Y for Group 1, w_X and w_Y, the combined marginal distributions of X and Y can be expressed as follows:

$$f(x) = w_X \int_{l_Y}^{u_Y} f_1(x,y)dy + (1 - w_X) \int_{l_Y}^{u_Y} f_2(x,y)dy, \tag{9.6}$$

$$f(y) = w_y \int_{l_X}^{u_X} f_1(x,y)dx + (1 - w_y) \int_{l_X}^{u_X} f_2(x,y)dx. \tag{9.7}$$

Numerical integration is used in carrying out the necessary integrations. The rest of the equating procedure is the same as for the equivalent-groups design.

9.3.2 For the NEAT Design

For the NEAT design, Group 1 from Population 1 takes test X plus the anchor set V, and Group 2 from Population 2 takes test Y plus the anchor set V. The continuous bivariate PDFs $f_1(x,v)$ for X and V, $f_2(y,v)$ for Y and V can be obtained in a similar fashion as described in the previous section for the counterbalanced design. The NEAT design has essentially two equating methods: the frequency estimation (also called poststratification) and the chained equipercentile equating method. The frequency estimation method is based on the assumption that the conditional distributions of test scores conditioning on an anchor test score remain invariant across populations, which can be expressed as follows:

$$f_2(x|v) = f_1(x|v) = f_1(x,v)/f_1(v), \tag{9.8}$$

$$f_1(y|v) = f_2(y|v) = f_2(y,v)/f_2(v), \tag{9.9}$$

The marginal distributions can be found by the following expressions:

$$f_1(x) = \int_{l_V}^{u_V} f_1(x,v)dv, \tag{9.10}$$

$$f_2(y) = \int_{l_V}^{u_V} f_2(y,v)dv, \tag{9.11}$$

$$f_1(v) = \int_{l_X}^{u_X} f_1(x,v)dx, \tag{9.12}$$

$$f_2(v) = \int_{l_Y}^{u_Y} f_2(y,v)dy, \tag{9.13}$$

With this assumption and given the weight of Population 1 in the target population, w_1, the marginal distributions of X and Y for the target population are

$$f_T(x) = w_1 f_1(x) + (1 - w_1)\int_{l_V}^{u_V} f_1(x|v)f_2(v)dv, \tag{9.14}$$

$$f_T(y) = w_1 \int_{l_V}^{u_V} f_2(y|v)f_1(v)dv + (1 - w_1)f_2(y), \tag{9.15}$$

The rest of the equating procedure is the same as in the equivalent-groups design.

The chained equipercentile equating method first equates X to V using $f_1(x)$ and $f_1(v)$, and then equates the V equivalent X scores to Y using $f_2(v)$ and $f_2(y)$. Given all the continuous marginal distributions in Equations 9.10–9.13, Equation 9.1 must be applied twice to accomplish the chain equipercentile equating procedure.

9.4 Standard Error of Equating for CLL under the Equivalent-Groups Design

von Davier et al. (2004b) derived this general expression for the asymptotic standard error of equating (SEE):

$$SEE_Y(x) = \left\|\hat{J}_{eY}\hat{J}_{DF}C\right\|. \tag{9.16}$$

This expression is decomposed into three parts, each relating to a different stage of the equating process. $\hat{J}_{eY}$ is related to continuization (Step 3) and equating (Step 4). $\hat{J}_{DF}$ is related to the estimation of score probabilities (Step 2). C is related to presmoothing (Step 1). Because the CLL method uses the log-linear function directly in the continuization step, the cumulative distribution functions of test X and test Y depend on the the estimated parameter vectors $\hat{\boldsymbol{\beta}}_X$ and $\hat{\boldsymbol{\beta}}_Y$ of the log-linear models rather than on the estimated score probabilities $\hat{r}$ and $\hat{s}$ in von Davier et al. (2004b). Let F denote the cumulative distribution functions of X and G denote the cumulative distribution functions of Y. The equating function from X to Y can be expressed as

$$e_Y(x) = e_Y(x; \boldsymbol{\beta}_\mathbf{X}, \boldsymbol{\beta}_\mathbf{Y}) = G^{-1}(F(x; \boldsymbol{\beta}_\mathbf{X}); \boldsymbol{\beta}_\mathbf{Y}), \tag{9.17}$$

where

$$F(x; \beta_X) = \frac{\int_l^x exp(\mathbf{b}_\mathbf{X}^T \boldsymbol{\beta}_\mathbf{X})dt}{\int_l^u exp(\mathbf{b}_\mathbf{X}^T \boldsymbol{\beta}_\mathbf{X})dt}, \tag{9.18}$$

and

$$G(y; \beta_Y) = \frac{\int_l^y exp(\mathbf{b}_\mathbf{Y}^T \boldsymbol{\beta}_\mathbf{Y})dt}{\int_l^u exp(\mathbf{b}_\mathbf{Y}^T \boldsymbol{\beta}_\mathbf{Y})dt}. \tag{9.19}$$

Using the δ-method and following a similar approach as in Holland, King, and Thayer (1989), the square of the SEE can be expressed as

$$\boldsymbol{\sigma}_Y^2(x) = (\boldsymbol{\partial} e_Y)^T \Sigma (\boldsymbol{\partial} e_Y) \tag{9.20}$$

where

$$\Sigma = \begin{bmatrix} \Sigma_{\hat{\beta}_X} & \Sigma_{\hat{\beta}_X \hat{\beta}_Y} \\ \Sigma_{\hat{\beta}_X \hat{\beta}_Y} & \Sigma_{\hat{\beta}_Y} \end{bmatrix}, \tag{9.21}$$

and

$$(\partial e_Y) = \begin{bmatrix} \dfrac{\partial e_Y}{\partial \boldsymbol{\beta}_X} \\ \dfrac{\partial e_Y}{\partial \boldsymbol{\beta}_Y} \end{bmatrix}. \tag{9.22}$$

The elements of Σ are further obtained by the following equations:

$$\mathbf{\Sigma}_{\hat{\beta}_X} = (B_X^T \mathbf{\Sigma}_{mX} B_X)^{-1}, \tag{9.23}$$

where B_X is the design matrix for X in the log-linear model (see Holland & Thayer, 1987) and

$$\mathbf{\Sigma}_{mX} = N(D_{p_X} - p_X p_X^T), \tag{9.24}$$

where p_X is the vector of probabilities in the multinomial categories for Form X and D_{p_X} is a diagonal matrix made from p_X. $\Sigma_{\hat{\beta}_Y}$ can be obtained in a similar fashion. Because X and Y are two independent groups, it follows that the model parameter estimates for the two groups are also independent, which is expressed as

$$\mathbf{\Sigma}_{\hat{\beta}_X \hat{\beta}_Y} = \mathbf{0}. \tag{9.25}$$

The elements of (∂e_Y) can be obtained from Equations 9.26 and 9.27:

$$\frac{\partial e_Y}{\partial \boldsymbol{\beta}_{Xi}} = \frac{1}{\frac{\partial G(y;\boldsymbol{\beta}_Y)}{\partial y}} \Big|_{y=e_Y(x)} \frac{\partial F(x;\boldsymbol{\beta}_X)}{\partial \boldsymbol{\beta}_{Xi}} \tag{9.26}$$

$$\frac{\partial e_Y}{\partial \boldsymbol{\beta}_{Yi}} = -\frac{1}{\frac{\partial G(y;\boldsymbol{\beta}_Y)}{\partial y}} \Big|_{y=e_Y(x)} \frac{\partial G(y;\boldsymbol{\beta}_Y)}{\partial \boldsymbol{\beta}_{Yi}} \Big|_{y=e_Y(x)}. \tag{9.27}$$

Given Equations 9.18 and 9.19, the derivatives in Equations 9.26 and 9.27 can be derived straightforwardly. Their expressions can be quite messy and thus are omitted here.

The general expression of SEE in Equation 9.20 applies to all designs. However, for designs other than the equivalent-groups design, calculating expression in Equation 9.22 could be quite complicated, depending on the specific design and equating method, and is beyond the scope of this chapter.

9.5 Illustration With Real Test Data

9.5.1 Comparison of the Continuization Procedures

Because the CLL method performs the continuization step before applying the design function, and the kernel method applies the design function before the continuization step, the two continuization procedures only can be compared directly under the equivalent-groups design where the design function is the

Table 9.1 The Moments and Differences in Moments for the 20-Item Data Set (With Kernel Moments Computed Based on Formula)

Test X	Raw dist.	Log-linear	Kernel			CLL
			0.33	0.622	1.0	
Moments						
Mean	10.8183	10.8183	10.8183	10.8183	10.8183	10.8283
SD	3.8059	3.8059	3.8059	3.8059	3.8059	3.7909
Skewness	0.0026	−0.0649	−0.0641	−0.0623	−0.0587	−0.0502
Kurtosis	2.5322	2.6990	2.6588	2.5604	2.3616	2.6723
Difference in moments with the log-linear discrete distribution						
Mean	-	-	0.0000	0.0000	0.0000	0.0100
SD	-	-	0.0000	0.0000	0.0000	−0.0150
Skewness	-	-	0.0007	0.0025	0.0062	0.0147
Kurtosis	-	-	−0.0401	−0.1386	−0.3373	−0.0267

Note. CLL = continuzed log-linear

identity function and thus can be skipped. This section compares the CLL and kernel continuization methods using two real data sets in terms of the smoothness of the continuous distribution and preservation of moments.

The first data set is taken from von Davier et al. (2004b, Table 9.1) and is a 20-item test data set. Only test form X data are used here. First, the log-linear model is fitted with degree 2 to the raw frequency data. Then the kernel continuization is implemented with three different bandwidth parameter values: $h = 0.33$, $h = 0.622$, and $h = 1.0$. The h value of 0.622 represents the optimal h that minimizes the combined penalty function for this data set. The other two h values are somewhat arbitrary, but with one somewhat smaller than the optimal value and the other somewhat larger than the optimal value.

The CLL distribution is plotted against the kernel distribution in Figure 9.1. The upper part shows that the kernel distributions are very close to the CLL distribution. In fact, the three lines almost coincide with each other, except with $h = 1$ making the kernel distribution depart slightly from the CLL distribution, especially at the ends of the score scale. As discussed previously, this departure reflects a distortion of the shape of the discrete distribution.

The lower part of Figure 9.1 plots the differences between the kernel distributions and the CLL distribution. It can be seen that with h =.622 the kernel distribution still has some bumps,although they are too small to be seen in the upper part of Figure 9.1.(Note that the vertical scales for the upper and lower part of Figure 9.1 are very different.)

The moments for different continuizations for this data set are in Table 9.1. Note that log-linear smoothing with degree 2 maintains the first two moments of the raw score distribution. The moments for the kernel distributions were computed based on the theoretical results in von Davier et al. (2004b), namely, that the first two moments of kernel distribution are the same as the log-linear discrete distribution, but the skewness and kurtosis differ by a factor of $(a_X)^3$ and $(a_X)^4$, respectively. The moments for CLL were empirically computed using numerical integration. For the

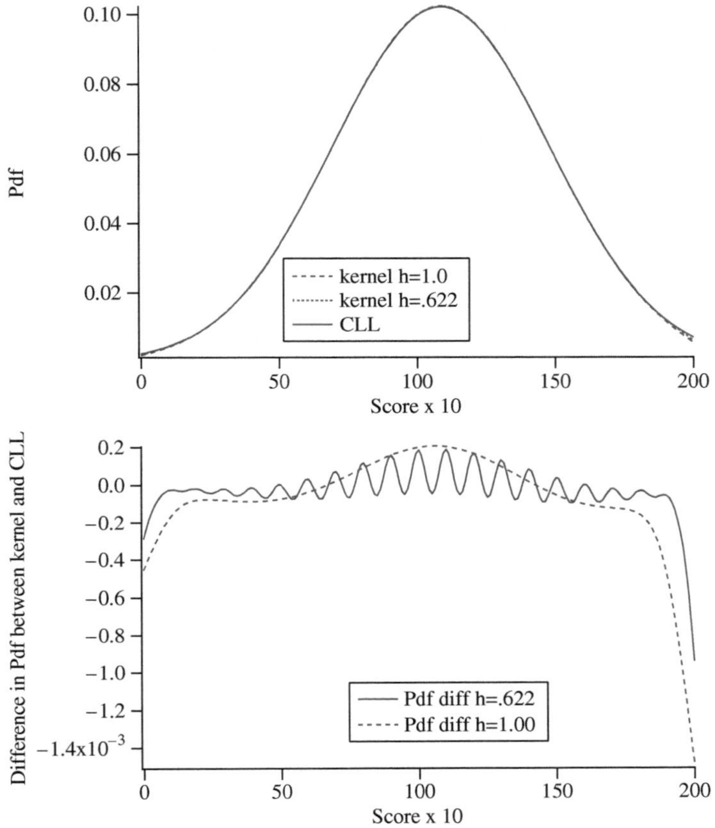

Fig. 9.1 Comparisons of kernel continuization and continuzed log-linear (CLL) for the 20-item data set. Pdf = probability density function

kernel method, the case of $h = .33$ can be ignored, since it produced unacceptably large bumps. All CLL moments approximate those of the log-linear distribution reasonably well, whereas the kernel methods have bigger differences in kurtosis. The kernel continuization did not distort the skewness of the distribution, even when a large h was specified, because the skewness of the discrete distribution was very small.

The same analyses were repeated for the 40-item ACT mathematics data in Kolen and Brennan (2004). A log-linear model with a degree of 6 was fitted to the raw frequency. The same kernel and CLL procedures were applied as for the first illustrative example. Three h parameter values were used for this data set: 0.33, 0.597, and 1.0. The value 0.597 represents the optimal h that minimizes the combined penalty function. (It turns out that in both data sets, the second penalty function PEN_2 does not have any effect on the combined penalty because there is no

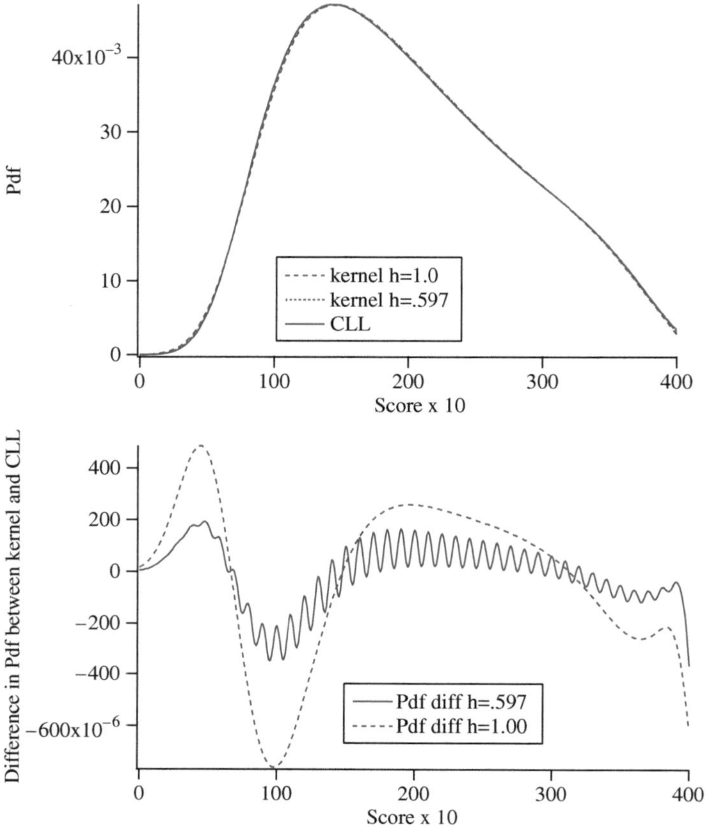

Fig. 9.2 Comparisons of kernel continuization and continuzed log-linear (CLL) for the 40-item data set. Pdf = probability density function

U-shaped distribution around any score point.) Results are plotted in Figure 9.2. These plots show similar patterns of comparisons to those for the 20-item data set in the first example.

The moments of various distributions for this data set are in Table 9.2. The CLL moments are slightly closer to the discrete distribution moments than the kernel moments, although both methods produce very close moments. The CLL method preserves moments better in this case because the number of score points is larger and the approximation in Equation 9.3 is more accurate when the number of score points is larger.

Overall, these two illustrations confirm that the CLL continuization method has certain advantages over the kernel method with respect to simplicity, a smoother continuous distribution, and preserving moments better when the number of score points is relative large and the discrete distributions are highly skewed.

Table 9.2 The Moments and Differences in Moments for the 40-Item Data Set (With Kernel Moments Computed Based on Formula)

Test X	Raw dist.	Log-linear	Kernel			CLL
			0.33	0.622	1.0	
Moments						
Mean	19.8524	19.8524	19.8524	19.8524	19.8524	19.8512
SD	8.2116	8.2116	8.2116	8.2116	8.2116	8.2105
Skewness	0.3753	0.3753	0.3744	0.3722	0.3671	0.3751
Kurtosis	2.3024	2.3024	2.2950	2.2783	2.2356	2.3023
Difference in moments with the log-linear discrete distribution						
Mean	-	-	0.0000	0.0000	0.0000	−0.0012
SD	-	-	0.0000	0.0000	0.0000	−0.0012
Skewness	-	-	−0.0009	−0.0031	−0.0082	−0.0001
Kurtosis	-	-	−0.0074	−0.0241	−0.0668	−0.0001

Note. CLL = continuzed log-linear

9.5.2 *Comparisons of Equating Functions*

The 40-item test data sets are also used to compare the equating functions under the equivalent-groups design based on three methods: (a) the traditional equipercentile equating method based on percentile ranks, (b) the kernel method, and (c) the CLL method. The optimal h parameters were used to compute the kernel continuous distributions. The traditional equipercentile method is also applied to the unsmoothed raw frequency data as a baseline for comparison. The results for the 40-item data set are in Table 9.3. The equating functions and their differences are plotted in Figure 9.3. The results showed that the equating functions based on these three methods were quite similar. Except at the end points of the score scale, the differences were within 0.1.

Another set of real test data with a pairs of test forms was taken from Kolen and Brennan (2004, p. 147) to compare the CLL method with the kernel method under the NEAT design. The test had 36 items with a 12-item internal anchor test. The sample size was 1,655 for the X group and 1,638 for the Y group. A bivariate log-linear smoothing procedure was used for the smoothing step. The frequency estimation method was used for computing the equating function. The frequency estimation method under the NEAT design requires a rather complicated design function. Three continuization and equating methods are computed and compared: (a) the traditional equipercentile equating method based on percentile ranks, (b) the kernel method, and (c) the CLL method. The results are in Table 9.4. The equating functions and their differences are plotted in Figure 9.4. The results showed that the CLL method produces equating results similar to the kernel method but slightly different from the traditional log-linear equipercentile method.

9.5.3 *Comparison of SEE Estimates*

The SEEs for the CLL method were computed for the 20-item data set using Equation 9.25 and are contained in Table 9.5. The SEEs for the kernel method were also computed and are presented in Table 9.5, which shows that the SEEs for the two methods were very similar.

9.6 Summary

Wang (2008) proposed an alternative continuization method for the test equating framework constructed by von Davier et al. (2004b). With this new continuization method, there are two major differences between the proposed CLL method and the kernel method: (a) The proposed CLL method directly uses the function from the

Table 9.3 The Equating Functions for the 40-Item Data Set Under an Equivalent-Groups Design

Score	Raw equating	Log-linear	kernel (.597)	CLL equating
0	0.0000	−0.4384	−0.7031	−0.4199
1	0.9796	0.1239	0.0537	0.1406
2	1.6462	0.9293	0.9143	0.9664
3	2.2856	1.8264	1.8069	1.8473
4	2.8932	2.7410	2.7072	2.7369
5	3.6205	3.6573	3.6082	3.6300
6	4.4997	4.5710	4.5112	4.5266
7	5.5148	5.4725	5.4191	5.4291
8	6.3124	6.3577	6.3355	6.3411
9	7.2242	7.2731	7.2648	7.2668
10	8.1607	8.2143	8.2119	8.2111
11	9.1827	9.1819	9.1819	9.1792
12	10.1859	10.1790	10.1798	10.1762
13	11.2513	11.2092	11.2101	11.2067
14	12.3896	12.2750	12.2761	12.2734
15	13.3929	13.3764	13.3784	13.3770
16	14.5240	14.5111	14.5147	14.5146
17	15.7169	15.6784	15.6790	15.6801
18	16.8234	16.8638	16.8623	16.8647
19	18.0092	18.0566	18.0541	18.0580
20	19.1647	19.2469	19.2449	19.2497
21	20.3676	20.4262	20.4263	20.4312
22	21.4556	21.5911	21.5916	21.5961
23	22.6871	22.7368	22.7365	22.7404
24	23.9157	23.8595	23.8588	23.8623
25	25.0292	24.9594	24.9586	24.9616
26	26.1612	26.0374	26.0369	26.0394
27	27.2633	27.0954	27.0955	27.0973
28	28.1801	28.1357	28.1364	28.1375
29	29.1424	29.1606	29.1621	29.1625
30	30.1305	30.1729	30.1750	30.1746
31	31.1297	31.1749	31.1777	31.1765
32	32.1357	32.1691	32.1726	32.1705
33	33.0781	33.1576	33.1618	33.1588
34	34.0172	34.1424	34.1470	34.1434
35	35.1016	35.1250	35.1300	35.1257
36	36.2426	36.1064	36.1118	36.1068
37	37.1248	37.0873	37.0929	37.0873
38	38.1321	38.0676	38.0729	38.0670
39	39.0807	39.0462	39.0514	39.0448
40	39.9006	40.0202	40.0256	40.0177

Note. CLL = continuzed log-linear.

log-linear smoothing step and makes it into a PDF, and (b) the continuization step occurs before the design function is applied. The illustration with real test data shows that with a relatively long test length, the CLL method produces smoother continuous score distributions and preserves the moments better than the kernel method. The equating results from the CLL method are quite similar to the kernel

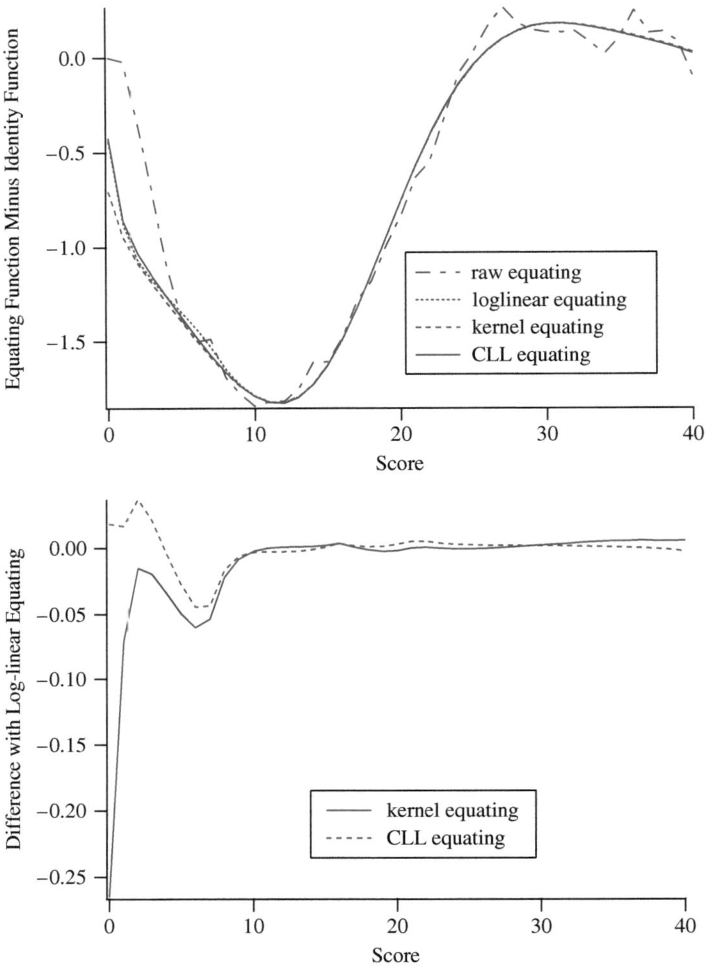

Fig. 9.3 Comparisons of equating functions for the 40-item data set under an equivalent-groups design. CLL = continuzed log-linear

method results under both the equivalent-groups design and the NEAT design. The similarity of the equating results make it difficult to make any recommendation about which method is the best choice under real testing situations. The comparisons are not comprehensive and lack objective criteria to evaluate the equating errors. A more thorough simulation study is needed to compare the kernel and CLL methods in order to make some practical recommendations.

A few differences between the CLL method and the kernel method merit discussion. First, because the CLL method requires that the continuization step occur before the design function is applied, the design function is applied to

Table 9.4 The Frequency-Estimation Equating Functions for the 36-Item Data Set Under a NEAT Design

Score	Log-linear frequency estimation	Kernel frequency estimation	CLL frequency estimation
0	−0.0129	0.0313	0.0059
1	1.0242	1.0827	1.0723
2	2.0988	2.1552	2.1357
3	3.1986	3.2375	3.2256
4	4.3091	4.3239	4.3132
5	5.4200	5.4122	5.4031
6	6.5194	6.5007	6.4929
7	7.5971	7.5880	7.5828
8	8.6759	8.6729	8.6688
9	9.7542	9.7546	9.7515
10	10.8305	10.8322	10.8303
11	11.9035	11.9053	11.9048
12	12.9721	12.9733	12.9738
13	14.0353	14.0357	14.0370
14	15.0924	15.0923	15.0941
15	16.1426	16.1423	16.1447
16	17.1854	17.1854	17.1881
17	18.2200	18.2209	18.2238
18	19.2460	19.2483	19.2513
19	20.2627	20.2668	20.2698
20	21.2694	21.2756	21.2783
21	22.2653	22.2740	22.2770
22	23.2495	23.2612	23.2636
23	24.2209	24.2362	24.2386
24	25.1784	25.1982	25.2004
25	26.1207	26.1464	26.1480
26	27.0466	27.0804	27.0813
27	27.9550	27.9997	27.9998
28	28.8454	28.9046	28.9050
29	29.7179	29.7964	29.7949
30	30.5739	30.6769	30.6760
31	31.4295	31.5496	31.5461
32	32.2939	32.4192	32.4163
33	33.1700	33.2920	33.2908
34	34.0732	34.1764	34.1807
35	35.0130	35.0836	35.1035
36	35.9983	36.0326	36.0800

Note. CLL = continuzed log-linear method; NEAT = nonequivalent groups with anchor test.

continuous distributions. This makes the expression of the design function easier to describe and program than with the kernel method. For example, for the frequency estimation method under the NEAT design, the kernel method applies a complicated set of matrix and vector operations in order to estimate the marginal distributions for the target population. For the CLL method, the design function is expressed nicely in Equations 9.8–9.15.

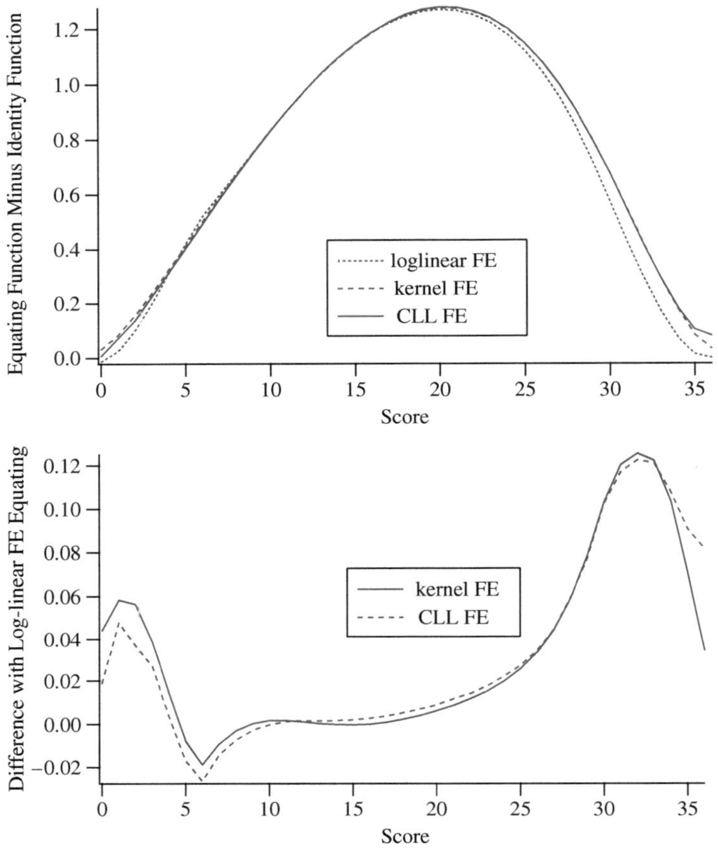

Fig. 9.4 Comparisons of equating functions for the 36-item data set under a nonequivalent groups with anchor test (NEAT) design. CLL = continuzed log-linear; FE = frequency estimation

Seond, the kernel method appears to have closed mathematical form in the continuization and equating steps, whereas the CLL method requires numerical integration. A closer look shows that computing the normal cumulative distribution functions in the kernel method also requires numerical integration or some approximation algorithm. Therefore, computationally speaking, both methods require some kind of numerical method for computation, although the CLL method requires more frequent use of numerical integration.

Finally, the kernel method requires a bandwidth parameter h for the Gaussian kernel. Having this parameter presents advantages and disadvantages. The advantage is that users can manipulate this parameter to achieve some goal. For example, when h is set very large, the kernel method becomes a linear equating method. The disadvantage is that it is rather arbitrary. Although von Davier et. al (2004b) proposed a penalty function to compute the optimal bandwidth, this penalty

Table 9.5 The Standard Errors of Equating (SEEs) for the 20-Item Data Set

Score	Kernel SEE	CLL SEE
0	0.2200	0.2100
1	0.2895	0.2933
2	0.2875	0.2904
3	0.2664	0.2682
4	0.2410	0.2418
5	0.2170	0.2169
6	0.1967	0.1963
7	0.1812	0.1808
8	0.1708	0.1705
9	0.1646	0.1646
10	0.1619	0.1622
11	0.1621	0.1627
12	0.1653	0.1661
13	0.1721	0.1731
14	0.1827	0.1839
15	0.1951	0.1969
16	0.2038	0.2064
17	0.1990	0.2028
18	0.1700	0.1747
19	0.1186	0.1170
20	0.0703	0.0396

function itself is also arbitrary in some sense. The CLL method, on the other hand, does not have such a parameter and thus saves a step in the computation.

The software used to computed the procedures described in this paper is available from the author upon request (tianyouwang@yahoo.com).

Chapter 10
Equating Through Alternative Kernels

Yi-Hsuan Lee and Alina A. von Davier

10.1 Introduction

The need for test equating arises when two or more test forms measure the same construct and can yield different scores for the same examinee. The most common example involves multiple forms of a test within a testing program, as opposed to a single testing instrument. In a testing program, different test forms that are similar in content and format typically contain completely different test items. Consequently, the tests can vary in difficulty depending on the degree of control available in the test development process.

The goal of test equating is to allow the scores on different forms of the same test to be used and interpreted interchangeably. Test equating requires some type of control for differential examinee ability in the assessment of, and adjustment for, differential test difficulty; the differences in abilities are controlled by employing an appropriate data collection design.

Many observed-score equating methods are based on the equipercentile equating function, which requires that the initial, discrete score distribution functions have been continuized. Several important observed-score equating methods may be viewed as differing only in the way the continuization is achieved. The classical equipercentile equating method (i.e., the percentile-rank method) uses linear interpolation to make the discrete distribution piecewise linear and therefore continuous. The kernel equating (von Davier, Holland, & Thayer, 2004b) method uses Gaussian kernel (GK) smoothing to approximate the discrete histogram by a continuous density function.

A five-step process of kernel equating was introduced in von Davier et al. (2004b) for manipulation of raw data from any type of data collection design, either for common examinees (e.g., the equivalent-groups, single-group, and counterbalanced

Y.-H. Lee (✉) and A.A. von Davier
Educational Testing Service, Rosedale Rd, Princeton, New Jersey 08541, USA
e-mail: ylee@ets.org

A.A. von Davier (ed.), *Statistical Models for Test Equating, Scaling, and Linking*, Statistics for Social and Behavioral Sciences,
DOI 10.1007/978-0-387-98138-3_10,

designs) or for common items (e.g., the nonequivalent groups with anchor test, or NEAT, design). The five steps are (a) presmoothing of the initial, discrete score distributions using log-linear models (Holland & Thayer, 2000); (b) estimation of the marginal discrete score distributions by applying the design function, which is a mapping reflecting the data-collection design; (c) continuization of the marginal, discrete score distributions; (d) computation and diagnosis of the equating functions; and (e) evaluation of statistical accuracy in terms of standard error of equating (SEE) and standard error of equating difference (SEED). Description of the five-step process can be found in the introductory chapter of this volume.

Kernel smoothing is a means of nonparametric smoothing. It continuizes a discrete random variable X by adding to it a continuous and independent random variable V with a positive constant h_X controlling the degree of smoothness. Let $X(h_X)$ denote the continuous approximation of X. Then

$$X(h_X) = X + h_X V. \tag{10.1}$$

The h_X is the so-called *bandwidth* and is free to select to achieve certain practical purpose. Kernel function refers to the density function of V. When kernel smoothing was first introduced to test equating by Holland and Thayer (1989), V was assumed to be a standard normal random variable. As a continuation, the conceptual framework of kernel equating was further established and introduced in von Davier et al. (2004b) with concentration on GK.

Equation 10.1 can be regarded as the central idea of kernel smoothing. In principle, it is feasible to substitute any continuous random variable for the one following a standard normal distribution. The choice of bandwidth h_X is often believed to be more crucial than the choice of kernel function in kernel regression (Wasserman, 2006); however, knowledge of ordinary kernel smoothing is not necessarily applicable in kernel equating without further justification. One example is the selection of bandwidth. In most applications of observed-score equating, the test scores X of each test are discrete variables. The selection of h_X involves a compromise between two features. First, the distribution function of $X(h_X)$ has to be relatively smooth. Second, $X(h_X)$ should be a close approximation of X at each possible score. The common expectation that the constant h_X approaches 0 as the sample size becomes large should not hold in kernel equating.

A by-product of smoothing is that $X(h_X)$ will carry not only the characteristics of X but also the characteristics of V. Thus, there is cause of concern about the impact of the characteristics of V on each step of the equating process after continuization. To illustrate, two alternative kernel functions, the logistic kernel (LK) and the (continuous) uniform kernel (UK), will be employed along with the GK. In item-response theory, a logistic function is acknowledged to closely approximate the classical normal-ogive curve with mathematical convenience. It has a simple expression for the cumulative distribution function (CDF), avoiding the integration involved in the CDF of a normal distribution and resolves many theoretical and numerical problems in conjunction with the computation of CDF. The same convenience also advantages the process of kernel equating when deriving formulas for SEE and SEED. When V follows a uniform distribution, Equation 10.1 leads to the product of linear interpolation. The inclusion of UK in the framework allows direct comparisons through SEE and SEED between equating results from kernel equating with a specific kernel function and those from the percentile-rank method.

LK shares much common ground with GK with respect to distributional characteristics, with the exception of heavier tails and sharper peak. UK has a finite range and can be viewed as a no-tail distribution. These characteristics can be quantified by moments or cumulants of various orders, and it appears natural to evaluate the continuous approximations of LK, UK, and GK through these measures to see how the distributional properties are inherited.

Some notations are needed before we proceed. Two tests are to be equated, test form X and test form Y, and a target population, T, on which this is to be done. Assume that T is fixed throughout this chapter. Let X be the score on test X and Y be the score on test Y, where X and Y are random variables. The possible scores of X and Y are x_i, $1 \leq i \leq I$, and y_j, $1 \leq j \leq J$, respectively. The corresponding score probabilities are $\mathbf{r} = \{r_i\}_{1 \leq i \leq I}$ and $\mathbf{s} = \{s_j\}_{1 \leq j \leq J}$ with $r_i = P(X = x_i)$ and $s_j = P(Y = y_j)$. In the case of concern, assume x_i, $1 \leq i \leq I$, to be consecutive integers; similarly for y_j, $1 \leq j \leq J$. The CDFs for X and Y are $F(x) = \mathrm{P}(X \leq x)$ and $G(y) = \mathrm{P}(Y \leq y)$. If $F(x)$ and $G(y)$ were continuous and strictly increasing, the equipercentile equating function for the conversion from test X to test Y would be defined as $e_Y(x) = G^{-1}(F(x))$, and the conversion from test Y to test X would be defined similarly as $e_X(y) = F^{-1}(G(y))$. In practice, $F(x)$ and $G(y)$ are made continuous before applying the equipercentile equating functions. Let $F_{h_X}(x; \mathbf{r})$ and $f_{h_X}(x; \mathbf{r})$ be the CDF and probability density function (PDF) of $X(h_X)$. Similarly, let $Y(h_Y)$ denote the continuous approximation of Y with bandwidth h_Y, and let $G_{h_Y}(y; \mathbf{s})$ and $g_{h_Y}(y; \mathbf{s})$ be its CDF and PDF, respectively.

The LK and UK considered in this study are presented in Section 10.2, including details about the quantities needed in the equating process. Section 10.3 focuses on the step of continuization using LK and UK. Most of the results are applicable to generic kernel functions. In Section 10.4, LK, UK, and GK are applied to the equivalent-groups data given in Chapter 7 of von Davier et al. (2004b). Results are concluded in Section 10.5. The computation of SEE and SEED involves the first derivatives of $F_{h_X}(x; \mathbf{r})$ and $G_{h_Y}(y; \mathbf{s})$ with respect to $\mathbf{r}$ and $\mathbf{s}$, respectively. In the Appendix, the formulas for the derivatives are generalizations to LK and UK.

10.2 Alternative Kernels

The name of logistic or uniform distribution can refer to a family of distributions with variation in the parameters for location and scale or for boundaries. Moments and cumulants are functions of these parameters, but standardized measures such as skewness and kurtosis are invariant in this respect. The main concern is how choices of V can affect the equating process. One relevant issue regards the impact of employing two distributions that diverge only in the scales. To investigate this issue, two distributions were chosen from each family of distributions under consideration.

10.2.1 Logistic Kernel (LK)

Suppose V is a logistic random variable. Its PDF has the form

$$k(v) = \frac{\exp(-v/s)}{s(1+\exp(-v/s))^2},$$

and its CDF is given by

$$K(v) = \frac{1}{1+\exp(-v/s)},$$

where s is the scale parameter. V has mean 0 and variance $\sigma_V^2 = \pi^2 s^2/3$. Varying the scale parameter would expand or shrink the distribution. If s=1, the distribution is called the *standard logistic*, whose variance is $\pi^2/3$. The distribution can be rescaled to have mean 0 and identity variance by setting $s = \sqrt{3}/\pi$, which is called the *rescaled logistic* herein. In the rest of the chapter, *SLK* stands for the cases where standard logistic is used as the kernel function, and *RLK* stands for those with rescaled logistic kernel function.

The heavier tails and sharper peak of a logistic distribution lead to larger cumulants of even orders than do those of a normal distribution. When V follows a standard logistic distribution, for $|t|<1$, the moment-generating function of V is given by

$$\begin{aligned} M_V(t) = \mathrm{E}(\exp(tV)) &= \int_{-\infty}^{\infty} \exp(tv) \cdot \frac{\exp(-v)}{(1+\exp(-v))^2} dv \\ &= \int_0^1 \xi^{-t}(1-\xi)^t d\xi \\ &= B(1-t, 1+t) \\ &= \Gamma(1-t)\Gamma(1+t), \end{aligned}$$

where $\xi = (1+\exp(v))^{-1}$, $B(\cdot,\cdot)$ is the beta function, and $\Gamma(\cdot)$ is the gamma function (Balakrishnan, 1992). The cumulant-generating function of V is

$$\log M_V(t) = \log \Gamma(1-t) + \log \Gamma(1+t). \quad (10.2)$$

Let $\Gamma^{(n)}(\cdot)$ be the nth derivative of $\Gamma(\cdot)$ for any positive integer n. The cumulants of SLK may be derived from Equation 10.2 by differentiating with respect to t and setting t to 0. The next theorem gives the mathematical expressions of the cumulants for a general LK.

Theorem 10.1. *Define*

$$\psi(u) = \frac{d \log \Gamma(u)}{du} = \frac{\Gamma^{(1)}(u)}{\Gamma(u)},$$

and let $\psi^{(n)}(\cdot)$ be the nth derivative of $\psi(\cdot)$ for any positive integer n. Then the nth cumulant of a logistic random variable V with scale parameter s is found to be

$$\kappa_{n,V} = \begin{cases} 0 & \text{if } n \text{ is odd} \\ 2s^n \psi^{(n-1)}(1) & \text{if } n \text{ is even} \end{cases}.$$

For any $n \geq 1$ the value of $\psi^{(n-1)}(1)$ is given by $\psi^{(n-1)}(1) = (-1)^n (n-1)! \zeta(n)$ and $\psi(1) = \Gamma^{(1)}(1) = -0.5772$, where $\zeta(\cdot)$ is the Riemann zeta function. These numbers were tabulated by Abramowitz and Stegun (1972), and the first six values of $\zeta(n)$ *are* $\zeta(1) = \infty$, $\zeta(2) = \pi^2/6$, $\zeta(3) \approx 1.2021$, $\zeta(4) = \pi^4/90$, $\zeta(5) \approx 1.0369$, and $\zeta(6) = \pi^6/945$. Note that $\zeta(n) > 0$ for even $n \geq 2$, so $\kappa_{n,V} > 0$ for even $n \geq 2$.

10.2.2 Uniform Kernel (UK)

Suppose V is a uniform random variable with PDF

$$k(v) = \begin{cases} 1/(2b) & \text{for } -b \leq v \leq b \\ 0 & \text{otherwise} \end{cases},$$

where b is a positive real number, and CDF

$$K(v) = \begin{cases} 0 & \text{for } v < -b \\ (v+b)/2b & \text{for } -b \leq v < b \\ 1 & \text{for } v \geq b \end{cases}.$$

The V has mean 0 and variance $b^2/3$. The *standard uniform* distribution often refers to V with $b = 1/2$; the variance is $\sigma_V^2 = 1/12$. When V is rescaled to have identity variance, the resulting distribution is called *rescaled uniform*. Standard uniform distribution and rescaled uniform distribution will be incorporated in the procedure of continuization; these methods will be denoted as *SUK* and *RUK*, respectively.

Following the previous notation, $\kappa_{n,V}$ is the nth cumulant of V. Kupperman (1952) showed that all odd cumulants vanish and even cumulants are given by

$$\kappa_{n,V} = \frac{(2b)^n B_n}{n} \quad \text{for even number } n,$$

where B_n are Bernoulli numbers. The first 11 Bernoulli numbers are $B_0 = 1$, $B_1 = -1/2$, $B_2 = 1/6$, $B_4 = -1/30$, $B_6 = 1/42$, $B_8 = -1/30$, $B_{10} = 5/66$, and $B_3 = B_5 = B_7 = B_9 = 0$. Note that the even cumulants of UK have no definite sign.

10.3 Continuization With Alternative Kernels

Equation 10.1 illustrates the central idea of kernel smoothing, but $X(h_X)$ can be defined in various ways for different purposes. In test equating, one desirable feature is to preserve moments of the discrete score distribution. Accordingly, in the kernel equating framework $X(h_X)$ is defined to preserve the mean and variance of X by

$$X(h_X) = a_X(X + h_X V) + (1 - a_X)\mu_X, \tag{10.3}$$

where

$$a_X^2 = \frac{\sigma_X^2}{\sigma_X^2 + \sigma_V^2 h_X^2}.$$

The continuous approximation for Y is analogously defined as

$$Y(h_Y) = a_Y(Y + h_Y V) + (1 - a_Y)\mu_Y,$$

where

$$a_Y^2 = \frac{\sigma_Y^2}{\sigma_Y^2 + \sigma_V^2 h_Y^2}.$$

Continuization of X and Y is based on the same formulation with a specific V. We will take X as an example and describe the properties relevant to $X(h_X)$ for different kernels.

Theorems 10.2–10.5 below are generalizations of Theorems 4.1–4.3 in von Davier et al. (2004b) to LK and UK. Theorem 10.2 illustrates a few limiting properties of $X(h_X)$ and a_X^2 as h_X approaches 0 or infinity. Theorems 10.3 and 10.4 define the CDFs and PDFs of $X(h_X)$ in which V is logistically and uniformly distributed, respectively, and Theorem 10.5 shows their forms as h_X approaches 0 or infinity.

Theorem 10.2. *The following statements hold:*

(a) $\lim_{h_X \to 0} a_X = 1$;
(b) $\lim_{h_X \to \infty} a_X = 0$;
(c) $\lim_{h_X \to \infty} h_X a_X = \sigma_X/\sigma_V$;
(d) $\lim_{h_X \to 0} X(h_X) = X$; *and*
(e) $\lim_{h_X \to \infty} X(h_X) = (\sigma_X/\sigma_V)V + \mu_X$.

Theorem 10.3. *Assume that V is logistically distributed with CDF and PDF defined in Section 10.2.1. Then CDF of X(h_X) is given by*

$$F_{h_X}(x;\mathbf{r}) = \sum_i r_i K(R_{iX}(x))$$

with $R_{iX}(x) = (x - a_X x_i - (1 - a_X)\mu_X)/(a_X h_X)$. *The corresponding PDF is*

$$f_{h_X}(x;\mathbf{r}) = \frac{1}{a_X h_X} \sum_i r_i k(R_{iX}(x)).$$

Theorem 10.4. *If V follows a uniform distribution with CDF and PDF given in Section 10.2.2, then the CDF of X(h_X) is*

$$F_{h_X}(x;\mathbf{r}) = \sum_{\substack{i: \\ R_{iX}(x) \geq b}} r_i + \sum_{\substack{i: \\ -b \leq R_{iX}(x) \leq b}} \left\{ r_i \cdot \frac{R_{iX}(x) + b}{2b} \right\}, \tag{10.5}$$

where R_{ix}(x) *is defined in Theorem 10.3. In addition, the PDF is*

$$f_{h_X}(x;\mathbf{r}) = \frac{1}{a_X h_X} \sum_{\substack{i: \\ -b \leq R_{iX}(x) \leq b}} \frac{r_i}{2b}. \tag{10.6}$$

Note that linear interpolation as it is achieved in existing equating practice does not involve rescaling, which leads to a continuous distribution that does not preserve the variance of the discrete score distribution.

Theorem 10.5. *The* $R_{iX}(x)$ *defined in Theorem 10.3 has the following approximate forms when* h_X *approaches 0 and infinity:*

(a) $R_{iX}(x) = \dfrac{x - x_i}{h_X} + o(h_X)$ as $h_X \to 0$, *and*

(b) $R_{iX}(x) = \dfrac{x - \mu_X}{\sigma_X/\sigma_V} - \left(\dfrac{\sigma_X}{\sigma_V h_X}\right) \cdot \left(\dfrac{x - \mu_X}{\sigma_X/\sigma_V}\right) + o\left(\dfrac{\sigma_X}{\sigma_V h_X}\right)$ as $h_X \to \infty$.

10.3.1 Selection of Bandwidth

In the kernel equating framework, the optimal bandwidth minimizes a penalty function comprising two components. One is the least square term

$$\text{PEN}_1(h_X) = \sum_{\mathbf{i}} (\hat{r}_i - f_{h_X}(x_i;\hat{\mathbf{r}}))^2,$$

where $\hat{\mathbf{r}} = \{\hat{r}_i\}_{1 \le i \le I}$ are the fitted score probabilities of $\mathbf{r}$ in the presmoothing step, and $f_{h_X}(x_i; \hat{\mathbf{r}})$ is an estimate of $f_{h_X}(x_i; \mathbf{r})$. The other is a smoothness penalty term that avoids rapid fluctuations in the approximated density,

$$\mathrm{PEN}_2(h_X) = \sum_i A_i(1 - B_i),$$

where

$$A_i = \begin{cases} 1 & \text{if } f_{h_X}^{(1)}(x; \hat{\mathbf{r}}) < 0 \text{ at } x = x_i - 0.25 \\ & 0 \text{ otherwise} \end{cases},$$

$$B_i = \begin{cases} 0 & \text{if } f_{h_X}^{(1)}(x; \hat{\mathbf{r}}) > 0 \text{ at } x = x_i + 0.25 \\ & 1 \text{ otherwise} \end{cases},$$

and $f_{h_X}^{(1)}(x; \hat{\mathbf{r}})$ is the first derivative of $f_{h_X}(x; \hat{\mathbf{r}})$. Choices of h_X that allow a U-shaped $f_{h_X}(x; \hat{\mathbf{r}})$ around the score point x_i would result in a penalty of 1. Combining $\mathrm{PEN}_1(h_X)$ and $\mathrm{PEN}_2(h_X)$ gives the complete penalty function

$$\mathrm{PEN}(h_X) = \mathrm{PEN}_1(h_X) + \mathrm{PEN}_2(h_X), \tag{10.7}$$

which will keep the histogram with fitted score probabilities $\hat{\mathbf{r}}$ and the continuized density $f_{h_X}(x; \hat{\mathbf{r}})$ close to each other at each score point, while preventing $f_{h_X}(x; \hat{\mathbf{r}})$ from having too many 0 derivatives.

For LK, we have

$$f_{h_X}^{(1)}(x; \mathbf{r}) = \frac{1}{s(a_X h_X)^2} \sum_i r_i k(R_{iX}(x))[1 - 2K(R_{iX}(x))].$$

For UK, $f_{h_X}(x; \mathbf{r})$ is piecewise constant and is differentiable at $x = x_i$, $1 \le i \le I$. From Equation 10.6, $f_{h_X}^{(1)}(x; \mathbf{r}) = 0$ for all x satisfying $R_{iX}(x) \neq \pm b$, $1 \le i \le I$. Thus $\mathrm{PEN}_2(h_X) = 0$ with probability 1. The optimal bandwidth for UK should yield $2bh_X$ close to 1, the distance between two consecutive possible scores.

10.3.2 Evaluation

It is common to compare distributions through moments or cumulants. Here we chose to examine cumulants, for each cumulant of a sum of independent random variables is the sum of the corresponding cumulants of the addends. A concise equation can be achieved to describe the relationship between cumulants of the discrete score distribution, kernel function, and the resulting continuous approximation. It allows not only numerical but theoretical comparisons between cumulants of $X(h_X)$ for various kernels.

Theorem 10.6. *Let $\kappa_n(h_X)$ denote the nth cumulant of $X(h_X)$, $\kappa_{n,X}$ denote the nth cumulant of X, and $\kappa_{n,v}$ denote the nth cumulant of V. Then for $n \geq 3$,*

$$\kappa_n(h_X) = (a_X)^n(\kappa_{n,X} + (h_X)^n\kappa_{n,V}). \tag{10.8}$$

Because $a_X \in (0,1)$ and $h_X > 0$, a kernel function with κ_{nv} having the same sign as $\kappa_{n,x}$ leads to a closer approximation in terms of cumulants. Notice that Theorem 4.4 in von Davier et al. (2004b) is a special case of Theorem 10.6 because, for GK, $\kappa_{n,V} = 0$ for any $n \geq 3$.

10.4 Application

The data used for illustration are results from two 20-item mathematics tests given in Chapter 7 of von Davier et al. (2004b). The tests, both number-right scored tests, were administered independently to two samples from a national population of examinees, which yields an equivalent-groups design. The two sample sizes are 1,453 and 1,455, respectively.

The raw data in an equivalent-groups design are often summarized as two sets of univariate frequencies. Figure 10.1 shows the histograms of the observed frequencies. Two univariate log-linear models were fitted independently to each set of frequencies. The moments preserved in the final models were the first two and three for X and Y, respectively. That is, the mean and variance of X and the mean, variance, and skewness of Y were preserved. The model fit was examined through the likelihood ratio test and the Freeman-Tukey residuals; the results showed no evidence of lack of fit. The fitted frequencies for test X and test Y are sketched in Figure 10.1 as well. The $\hat{\mathbf{r}}$, the fitted score probabilities of X, are the ratios between the fitted frequencies and the sample size. The $\hat{\mathbf{s}}$ are attainable by the same means.

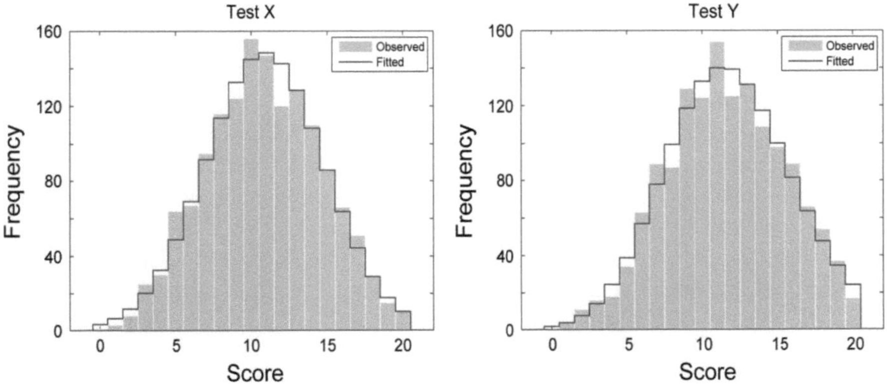

Fig. 10.1 Observed frequencies and fitted frequencies for test X and test Y

Table 10.1 *Optimal Bandwidths for $X(h_X)$ and $Y(h_Y)$*

	Logistic kernel		Uniform kernel		Gaussian kernel
	Standard	Rescaled	Standard	Rescaled	
h_X	0.5117	0.9280	1.0029	0.2895	0.6223
h_Y	0.4462	0.8094	1.0027	0.2895	0.5706
a_X	0.9715	0.9715	0.9971	0.9971	0.9869
a_Y	0.9795	0.9795	0.9973	0.9973	0.9896

The optimal bandwidths using SLK, RLK, SUK, RUK, and GK are listed in Table 10.1. The first finding comes from the comparison between the standard and rescaled versions of LK or UK. Suppose the former has mean 0 and standard deviation σ_1, while the latter has mean 0 and standard deviation σ_2. Then the corresponding optimal bandwidths, h_1 and h_2, for X or Y, satisfy the following equality:

$$\sigma_1 h_1 = \sigma_2 h_2. \tag{10.9}$$

In other words, the scale difference in different versions is adjusted by the selected bandwidths. Different versions of kernel function produce identical continuized score distributions as long as they come from one family of distributions.

The second finding is obtained through the comparison among GK, RLK, and RUK. Their first three moments (i.e., mean, variance, and skewness) are the same, but their major differences in shape can be characterized by the fourth moment or, equivalently, the kurtosis. Among the three, RLK has the largest kurtosis and RUK has the smallest kurtosis (the larger the kurtosis, the heavier the tails). Table 10.1 indicates that the heavier the tails of a kernel function, the larger the optimal bandwidth. Note that kurtosis is a standardized measure, so different versions from the same family of distributions have the same kurtosis. This observation can be generalized to SLK and SUK through Equation 10.9: the heavier the tails of a kernel function, the larger the product of its standard deviation and the optimal bandwidth.

Figure 10.2 displays the $f_{h_X}(x;\hat{\mathbf{r}})$ and the left tail of $F_{h_X}(x;\hat{\mathbf{r}})$ for LK, UK, and GK with optimal bandwidths. The graph in the left panel reveals that the $f_{h_X}(x;\hat{\mathbf{r}})$ for LK and GK are smooth functions and hard to be distinguished. The $f_{h_X}(x;\hat{\mathbf{r}})$ for UK is piecewise constant and appears to outline the histogram of the fitted frequencies for test X in Figure 10.1. The right panel only presents the portion of $F_{h_X}(x;\hat{\mathbf{r}})$ within the range of -1 to 2, for the difference between curves may not be seen easily when graphed against the whole score range. Apparently, the $F_{h_X}(x;\hat{\mathbf{r}})$ for LK has heavier left tail than that for GK, which corresponds to the fact that LK has heavier tails than GK. The use of UK results in a piecewise linear $F_{h_X}(x;\hat{\mathbf{r}})$, which is how linear interpolation functions in the percentile-rank method. Yet, we improved upon the linear interpolation by rescaling it in Equation 10.3 so that its continuous approximation preserves not only the mean but also the variance of the discrete score

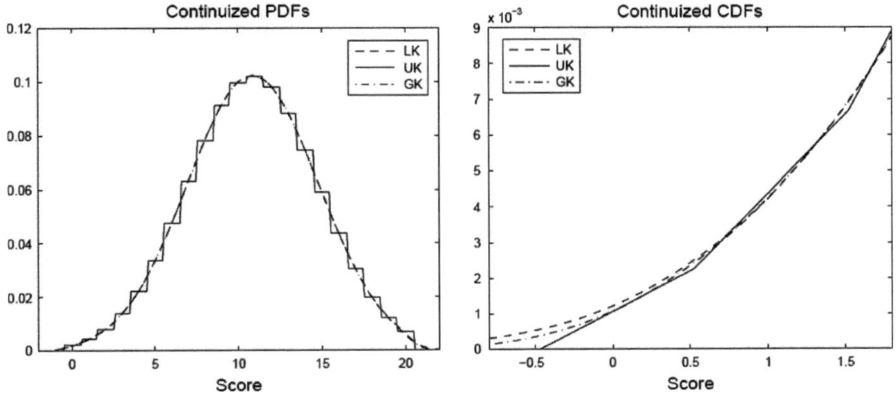

Fig. 10.2 Continuized score distributions of X: probability density functions (PDFs) and left tail of cumulative distribution functions (CDFs)

distribution. It is clear that the distributional characteristics of kernel functions are inherited by the corresponding continuous approximations. Figures for $g_{h_Y}(y;\hat{\mathbf{s}})$ and $G_{h_Y}(y;\hat{\mathbf{s}})$ exhibit the same properties, so they are omitted.

According to Equation 10.8, two phenomena are anticipated in assessing the continuized score distributions. First, the smaller the h_X, the closer the $\kappa_n(h_X)$ to $\kappa_{n,X}$. Second, for a fixed h_X, if $\kappa_{n,X}$ and $\kappa_{n,V}$ have the same sign, the corresponding V will yield a closer continuous approximation in terms of cumulants. Attentions should be paid especially to even cumulants, as the three kernels have 0 odd cumulants. Recall that all even cumulants for LK are positive; the fourth and sixth cumulants for UK are negative and positive, respectively; and the even cumulants for GK of orders higher than three are 0. In this data example, cumulants were calculated numerically and found to coincide with theoretical findings from Equation 10.8. In Table 10.2, the second column shows the cumulants of the fitted, discrete score distributions; the fourth cumulant is negative and the sixth cumulant is positive. Because the comparison of cumulants involves two varying factors, type of kernel and bandwidth, it can be simplified by first examining cumulants for LK, UK, and GK with fixed bandwidths. The three chosen levels of bandwidth were small h_X ($h_X = 0.2895$), moderate h_X ($h_X = 0.6223$), and large h_X ($h_X = 0.9280$). Each h_X is optimal for a certain kernel function, and the cumulants of optimal cases are highlighted in boldface. If we focus on one type of kernel and vary the level of bandwidth, it is evident that the cumulants under small h_X are closest to the corresponding cumulants of the fitted discrete score distributions.

For a fixed h_X, the performance of a kernel function from the viewpoint of how close its $f_{h_X}(x,\hat{\mathbf{r}})$ can approximate the histogram of $\hat{\mathbf{r}}$ has the following orders (from the best to the worst): UK, GK, LK for the fourth cumulant and LK, GK, UK for the sixth cumulant. The discrepancy in the orderings is due to the sign change in $\kappa_{n,X}$ for $n = 4$ and 6. In sum, UK best preserves $\kappa_{n,X}$ for $n \geq 3$ with its optimal

Table 10.2 *Cumulants of $X(h_X)$ With Fixed Bandwidths*

Order	Discrete	LK	UK	GK
		$h_X = 0.2895$		
1	10.82	10.82	**10.82**	10.82
2	14.48	14.48	**14.48**	14.48
3	−3.57	−3.54	**−3.56**	−3.54
4	−63.16	−62.42	**−63.10**	−62.43
5	23.17	22.83	**22.81**	22.83
6	510.69	501.88	**501.86**	501.85
		$h_X = 0.6223$		
1	10.82	10.82	10.82	**10.82**
2	14.48	14.48	14.48	**14.48**
3	−3.57	−3.44	−3.44	**−3.44**
4	−63.16	−59.74	−60.09	**−59.91**
5	23.17	21.70	21.75	**21.71**
6	510.69	472.19	471.72	**471.77**
		$h_X = 0.9280$		
1	10.82	**10.82**	10.82	10.82
2	14.48	**14.48**	14.48	14.48
3	−3.57	**−3.28**	−3.27	−3.28
4	−63.16	**−55.49**	−57.13	−56.27
5	23.17	**20.06**	20.06	20.05
6	510.69	**432.12**	431.89	429.45

Note: Boldface indicates cumulants of a certain kernel function with its optimal bandwidth. LK = logistic kernel; GK = Guassian kernel; UK = uniform kernel

bandwidth. Cumulants of LK with its optimal bandwidth shrink by the most amount since they correspond to the largest bandwidth among the three kernels.

The conversion of scores from test X to test Y is based on the equation $\hat{\mathbf{e}}_Y(x) = G_{h_Y}^{-1}(F_{h_X}(x;\hat{\mathbf{r}});\hat{\mathbf{s}})$ with optimal bandwidths. Similarly, the conversion of scores from test Y to test X is $\hat{e}_X(y) = F_{h_X}^{-1}(G_{h_Y}(y;\hat{\mathbf{s}});\hat{\mathbf{r}})$. They are sample estimates of $e_Y(x)$ and $e_X(x)$ based on $\hat{\mathbf{r}}$ and $\hat{\mathbf{s}}$. In Table 10.3, the equated scores for LK and GK are comparable, except for extreme scores, because their $F_{h_X}(x;\hat{\mathbf{r}})$ and $G_{h_Y}(y;\hat{\mathbf{s}})$ mainly differ at tails. UK tends to provide the most extreme equated scores among the three kernels. In addition, the average difference of equated scores between UK and GK is about twice as large as the average difference between LK and GK for the conversion from test X to test Y. For the inverse conversion, the average difference between UK and GK exceeds three times of the average difference between LK and GK. Overall, the maximal difference between any two kernels is about 0.18 raw-score point.

The sampling variability in $\hat{e}_Y(x)$ or $\hat{e}_X(y)$ is measured by the standard deviation of the asymptotic distribution, or the SEEs. It is known that distributions with heavier tails yield more robust modeling of data with more extreme values, and the same phenomenon is revealed when LK is employed. Figure 10.3 demonstrates that the SEEs for LK and GK do not differ remarkably. There is slightly less variation in the SEEs for LK. However, the SEEs for GK tend to have sharper drops at extreme scores, which are $X = 0$ and 20 and $Y = 0$, 1, and 20 in this example. If the two forms to be equated have more discrepancy in the shape of their score distributions,

Table 10.3 Equated Scores With Optimal Bandwidths

Score	*X* to *Y*			*Y* to *X*		
	LK	UK	GK	LK	UK	GK
0	0.447	0.439	0.394	−0.413	−0.227	−0.322
1	1.573	1.639	1.581	0.486	0.557	0.497
2	2.629	2.678	2.640	1.396	1.429	1.386
3	3.635	3.676	3.644	2.365	2.389	2.356
4	4.625	4.660	4.632	3.367	3.392	3.360
5	5.614	5.643	5.618	4.379	4.405	4.375
6	6.608	6.631	6.610	5.389	5.415	5.387
7	7.612	7.628	7.612	6.392	6.415	6.391
8	8.627	8.636	8.626	7.384	7.403	7.385
9	9.655	9.658	9.653	8.365	8.379	8.366
10	10.696	10.694	10.694	9.333	9.342	9.335
11	11.750	11.745	11.747	10.290	10.295	10.293
12	12.815	12.810	12.813	11.236	11.239	11.239
13	13.888	13.885	13.887	12.174	12.175	12.175
14	14.963	14.964	14.964	13.105	13.105	13.105
15	16.031	16.035	16.034	14.034	14.033	14.033
16	17.072	17.081	17.078	14.971	14.967	14.968
17	18.058	18.073	18.068	15.930	15.920	15.924
18	18.952	18.970	18.961	16.939	16.922	16.929
19	19.734	19.707	19.718	18.058	18.036	18.048
20	20.461	20.278	20.393	19.369	19.399	19.415

Note: LK = logistic kernel; GK = Guassian kernel; UK = uniform kernel

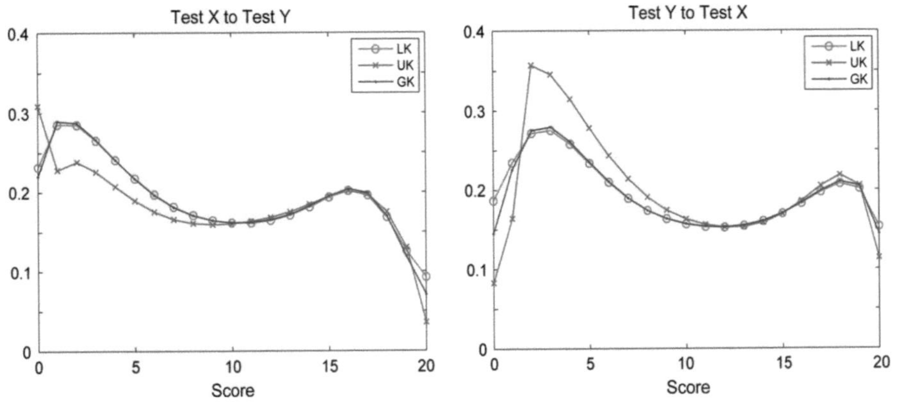

Fig. 10.3 Standard errors of equating (SEEs) for logistic (LK), uniform (UK), and Gaussian (GK) kernels

the equating functions for GK are likely to show sharp humps in the SEEs, but the SEEs for LK will remain less variable. On the other hand, the SEEs for UK do not display the same pattern and have greater variations from one conversion to another.

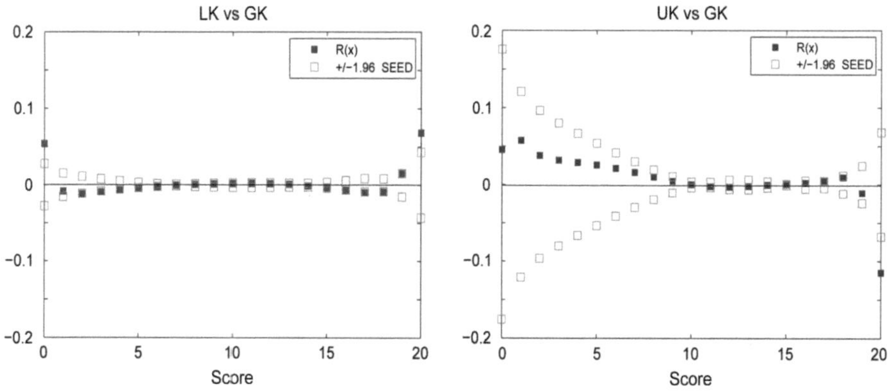

Fig. 10.4 Difference and standard errors of equating difference (SEEDs) between $\hat{e}_Y(x)$ of two kernel functions: logistic (LK) versus Gaussian (GK) and uniform (UK) versus Gaussian (GK)

It is straightforward to compare two estimated equating functions, for example, $\hat{e}_{Y,LK}(x)$ and $\hat{e}_{Y,GK}(x)$ for LK and GK by $R(x) = \hat{e}_{Y,LK}(x) - \hat{e}_{Y,GK}(x)$ with a uncertainty measure, the SEED, to identify the 95% confidence interval for $R(x)$. Analogously, $R(x) = \hat{e}_{Y,UK}(x) - \hat{e}_{Y,GK}(x)$ compares the estimated equating functions for UK and GK. The $R(x)$ for comparisons between LK and GK and between UK and GK are plotted in Figure 10.4, all converting X to Y. Two curves representing ± 1.96 times of the SEEDs are also provided as the upper and lower bounds of the 95% confidence interval. For the comparison between LK and GK, $R(0)$ and $R(20)$ are significantly different at the 0.05 level, but the scale of SEED is less than 0.1 raw-score point, so the difference may still be negligible in practice. Again, the absolute values of $R(x)$ and SEEDs increase as x approaches its boundaries, 0 and 20. The right panel shows that the difference between $\hat{e}_{Y,UK}(x)$ and $\hat{e}_{Y,GK}(x)$ is much larger than that of $\hat{e}_{Y,LK}(x)$ and $\hat{e}_{Y,GK}(x)$ for all score points outside the rage of 9–17. The difference is nonsignificant at the 0.05 level, however, since the corresponding SEEDs are greater in scale.

10.5 Conclusions

Kernel equating is a unified approach for test equating and uses only GK smoothing to continuize the discrete score distributions. This chapter demonstrates the feasibility to incorporate alternative kernels in the five-step process and elaborates on tools for comparisons between various kernels. Equating through LK, UK, or GK has discrepancies in the continuized score distributions (e.g., heavier tails, piecewise continuity, or thinner tails that are inherited from the kernel functions) and hence in any product since the step of continuization. Although these discrepancies do not yield pronounced changes in the equated scores, certain desirable properties in the equating process could be achieved by manipulating the kernels.

Chapter 10 Appendix

10.A.1 Computation of SEE With Alternative Kernels

The equating functions, $e_Y(x)$ and $e_X(y)$, are functions of **r** and **s** through a design function and the composition of $F_{h_X}(x;r)$ and $G_{h_Y}(y;s)$. The asymptotic variances of $\hat{e}_Y(x)$ and $\hat{e}_X(y)$, which are equivalent to the squares of the SEEs, can be derived with the application of delta method given the asymptotic variances of $\hat{\mathbf{r}}$ and $\hat{\mathbf{s}}$. Under the assumption that the bandwidths are fixed constants, for each conversion, the resulting asymptotic variance involves the matrix multiplication of three ingredients: the C-matrix from presmoothing, the Jacobian of the design function, and the Jacobian of the equating function. Changing kernel functions only affects the expression of the third ingredient, whose generalization to LK and UK is depicted in the remainder of this section. Details of the other two ingredients should refer to Chapter 5 of von Davier et al. (2004b).

Let J_{e_Y} denote the Jacobian of $e_Y(x)$ with respect to **r** and **s**. J_{e_Y} is a $1\times(I+J)$ vector in which

$$J_{e_Y}=\left(\frac{\partial e_Y}{\partial \mathbf{r}},\frac{\partial e_Y}{\partial \mathbf{s}}\right)=\left(\frac{\partial e_Y}{\partial r_1},\ldots,\frac{\partial e_Y}{\partial r_I},\frac{\partial e_Y}{\partial s_1},\ldots,\frac{\partial e_Y}{\partial s_J}\right).$$

When the score distributions $F(x)$ and $G(y)$ have been approximated by sufficiently smoothed CDFs, the derivatives of the equating function can be computed,

$$\frac{\partial e_Y}{\partial r_i}=\frac{1}{G^{(1)}}\cdot\frac{\partial F_{h_X}(x;\mathbf{r})}{\partial r_i},\tag{10.A.1}$$

$$\frac{\partial e_Y}{\partial s_j}=-\frac{1}{G^{(1)}}\cdot\frac{\partial G_{h_Y}(e_Y(x);\mathbf{s})}{\partial s_j},\tag{10.A.2}$$

where $G^{(1)}=g_{h_Y}(e_Y(x);\mathbf{s})$. With some calculus, the partial derivative in Equation A.10.1 is found to be

$$\frac{\partial F_{h_X}(x;\mathbf{r})}{\partial r_i}=K(R_{iX}(x))-M_{iX}(x;\mathbf{r})f_{h_X}(x;\mathbf{r}),\tag{10.A.3}$$

where

$$M_{iX}(x,\mathrm{r})=\frac{1}{2}(x-\mu_X)(1-a_X^2)\left(\frac{x_i-\mu_X}{\sigma_X}\right)^2+(1-a_X)x_i,$$

and $K(R_{iX}(x))$ is the CDF of LK or UK evaluated at $R_{iX}(x)$. In general, $K(\cdot)$ can be the CDF of any kernel function. Replacement of X, x, F, and **r** in Equation 10.A.3 by $\mathbf{Y}, y, G$, and **s**, respectively, leads to the partial derivative $\partial G_{h_Y}(y;\mathbf{s})/\partial s_j$ in Equation 10.A.2. An estimate of J_{e_Y} can be achieved given $\mathbf{r}=\hat{\mathbf{r}}$ and $\mathbf{s}=\hat{\mathbf{s}}$. Formulas for the Jacobian of $e_X(y)$ and its estimate are similar in form to those for J_{e_Y}.

Author Note: Any opinions expressed in this chapter are those of the authors and not necessarily of Educational Testing Service.

Chapter 11
A Bayesian Nonparametric Model for Test Equating

George Karabatsos and Stephen G. Walker

11.1 Introduction

In observed score equating, the aim is to infer the *equating* function, $e_Y(X)$, which gives the score on test Y that is equivalent to any chosen score x on test X. Equipercentile equating is based on the premise that test scores x and y are equivalent if and only if $F_X(x) = F_Y(y)$, and therefore assumes that the equating function is defined by:

$$e_Y(x) = F_Y^{-1}(F_X(x)) = y,$$

where (F_X, F_Y) denote the cumulative distribution functions (CDFs) of the scores of test X and test Y. Of course, in order for such equating to be sensible, certain assumptions are required about the tests and the examinee populations. Also, in the practice of test equating, examinee scores on the two tests are collected according to one of the three major types of equating designs, namely, (a) the single-group design, (b) the equivalent-groups design, and (c) the nonequivalent-groups design. The single-group design may be counterbalanced, and either the equivalent-groups or the nonequivalent-groups design may make use of an internal- or external-anchor test. For more details about the aforementioned assumptions and concepts of test equating, see the textbooks by von Davier, Holland, and Thayer (2004b) and Kolen and Brennan (2004).

G. Karabatsos (✉)
College of Education, 1040 W. Harrison St. (MC 147), Chicago, IL 60607-7133, USA
e-mail: georgek@uic.edu

S.G. Walker
Institute of Mathematics, Statistics and Actuarial Science, University of Kent, Canterbury, Kent CT2 7NZ, United Kingdom
e-mail: S.G.Walker@kent.ac.uk

A.A. von Davier (ed.), *Statistical Models for Test Equating, Scaling, and Linking*, Statistics for Social and Behavioral Sciences,
DOI 10.1007/978-0-387-98138-3_11,

If the CDFs F_X and F_Y are discrete distributions, then for virtually any score x on test X, the CDF probability $F_X(x)$ does not coincide with the CDF probability $F_X(y)$ of any possible score y of test Y. Then, the equipercentile equating function is ill-defined. This poses a challenge in equipercentile equating, because in psychometric practice observed test scores are discrete. A solution to this problem is to model (F_X, F_Y) as continuous distributions and treating them as smoothed versions of discrete test score distributions (G_X, G_Y), respectively. This approach is taken by current methods of observed-score equating. In the kernel method of equating (von Davier et al., 2004b), (F_X, F_Y) are each modeled by a mixture of normal densities (the kernels) with mixing weights defined by estimates of (G_X, G_Y), and the number of mixing components (for test X and for test Y) is decided by some model-selection procedure. If the kernels are uniform distributions, then classical equating with the percentile rank method is obtained (Holland & Thayer, 1989; also see Chapter 5 of this book by Lee & von Davier). Also, the classical methods of linear equating and mean equating each provide an approach to equipercentile equating under the assumption that (F_X, F_Y) are distributions with the same shape (Karabatsos & Walker, 2009a). However, in practice, it does not seem reasonable to assume that the (continuized) population distributions of test scores are normal or come from a mixture of specific uniform distributions.

In this chapter we present a Bayesian nonparametric model for test equating, which can be applied to all the major equating designs (see Section 2.4 for details), and we illustrate the model in the analysis of two data sets. This equating model, first introduced by Karabatsos and Walker (2009a), involves the use of a bivariate Bernstein polynomial prior distribution for (F_X, F_Y) that supports the entire space of (random) continuous distributions. In particular, the model specifies (F_X, F_Y) by a mixture of beta densities via a Bernstein polynomial, where (G_X, G_Y) provide mixing weights and are modeled by a bivariate Dirichlet process prior distribution (Walker & Muliere, 2003). Also, the number of mixing components (for test X and for test Y) are modeled as random and assigned a prior distribution. Under Bayes theorem, these priors combine with the data to yield the posterior distribution of (F_X, F_Y) and of the equating function $e_Y(x) = F_Y^{-1}(F_X(x))$. As proven by Diaconis and Ylvisaker (1985), for a sufficiently large number of mixture components, a mixture of beta distributions can approximate arbitrarily well any distribution on a closed interval. For reviews of the many theoretical studies and practical applications of Bayesian nonparametrics, see, for example, Walker, Damien, Laud, and Smith (1999) and Müller and Quintana (2004). Also, see Karabatsos and Walker (2009b) for a review from the psychometric perspective.

The Bayesian nonparametric model for equating provides important advantages over the existing approaches to observed-score equating. In the approach, the Dirichlet process prior distribution can be specified to account for any dependence between (G_X, G_Y), and thus it accounts for any dependence between the continuized test score distributions (F_X, F_Y). This dependence can even be specified for the equivalent-groups design, where the other equating methods assume independence. However, independence is a questionable assumption, especially considering that the two tests to be equated are designed to measure the same construct (e.g., math ability). Moreover, unlike the existing approaches to observed score equating, the Bayesian nonparametric model provides an approach to symmetric equating that always equates scores that fall within the correct range of test scores. Also, using the Bayesian nonparametric model, the posterior distribution of the equating function $e_Y(x) = F_Y^{-1}(F_X(x))$ provides inference of the 95% credible interval of the equated score. Thus, the Bayesian model provides a way to fully account for the uncertainty in the equated scores, for any sample size. In contrast, all the previous approaches to observed-score equating only rely on large-sample approximations to estimate the confidence interval of the equated score.

We present the Bayesian nonparametric equating model in the next section and describe the key concepts of this model, including the Dirichlet process, the bivariate Dirichlet process, the random Bernstein polynomial prior distribution, and the bivariate Bernstein prior distribution. In Section 11.3 we illustrate the Bayesian nonparametric equating model in the analysis of two data sets generated from the equivalent-groups design and the nonequivalent-groups design with internal anchor, respectively. In the first application, we compare the equating results of the Bayesian model against the results obtained by the four other approaches to observed-score equating. We conclude in Section 11.4.

11.2 Bayesian Nonparametric Equating Model

11.2.1 Dirichlet Process Prior

The Dirichlet process prior (Ferguson, 1973) is conveniently described through Sethuraman's (1994) representation, which is based on a countably infinite sampling strategy. So let θ_j, for $j = 1, 2, \ldots$, be independent and identically distributed from a fixed distribution function G_0, and let v_j, for $j = 1, 2, \ldots$, be independent and identically distributed from the Beta $(1, m)$ distribution. Then a random distribution function chosen from a Dirichlet process prior with parameters (m, G_0) can be constructed via

$$G(x) = \sum_{j=1}^{\infty} \omega_j \, 1(\theta_j \leq x),$$

where $\omega_1 = v_1$ and for $j > 1$, $\omega_j = v_j \prod_{l<j} (1 - v_l)$, and $1(\cdot)$ is the indicator function. In other words, realizations of the Dirichlet process can be represented as infinite mixtures of point masses. The locations θ_i of the point masses are a sample from G_0. It is obvious from the above construction that any random distribution G generated from a Dirichlet process prior is discrete with probability 1.

Also, for any value x from a sample space X, the random distribution (CDF) $G(x)$, modeled under the Dirichlet Process prior, has a beta distribution,

$$G(x) \sim \text{Beta}(mG_0(x), m\{1 - G_0(x)\}),$$

with prior mean $\mathrm{E}[G(x)] = G_0(x)$, and prior variance

$$\mathrm{Var}[G(x)] = \frac{G_0(x)[1 - G_0(x)]}{m + 1}.$$

Hence m (the precision parameter) acts as an uncertainty parameter, increasing the variance of G as m becomes small. Given a set of data $\boldsymbol{x}_n = \{x_1, \ldots, x_n\}$ having empirical distribution $\hat{G}(\cdot)$, the posterior distribution of G is also a Dirichlet process, with updated parameters given by $m \to m + n$. The posterior distribution is given by

$$G(x)|\boldsymbol{x}_n \sim \mathrm{Beta}(mG_0(x) + n\hat{G}(x), m[1 - G_0(x)] + n[1 - \hat{G}(x)]),$$

and it has mean $\mathrm{E}[G(x)|\boldsymbol{x}_n] = \frac{mG_0(x)+n\hat{G}(x)}{m+n}$. Thus, the posterior mean is a mixture of the prior guess (G_O) and the data ($\hat{G}$), with the weights of the mixture given by the precision parameter (m) and the sample size (n), respectively.

11.2.2 Random Bernstein Polynomial Prior

As mentioned earlier, the Dirichlet process prior fully supports discrete distributions. Here, a nonparametric prior is described, called the random Bernstein polynomial prior, which gives support to the entire space of continuous distributions and will provide a smooth method for equating test scores. As the name suggests, the random Bernstein polynomial prior distribution depends on the Bernstein polynomial (Lorentz, 1953). For any function G defined on [0,1] (not necessarily a distribution function) such that $G(0) = 0$, the Bernstein polynomial of order p of G is defined by

$$B(x; G, p) = \sum_{k=0}^{p} G\left(\frac{k}{p}\right)\binom{p}{k} x^k (1 - x)^{p-k} \tag{11.1}$$

$$= \sum_{k=1}^{p} \left[G\left(\frac{k}{p}\right) - G\left(\frac{k-1}{p}\right)\right] \mathrm{Beta}(x|k, p - k + 1) \tag{11.2}$$

$$= \sum_{k=1}^{p} w_{k,p} \mathrm{Beta}(x|k, p - k + 1), \tag{11.3}$$

and it has derivative

$$f(x; G, p) = \sum_{k=1}^{p} w_{k,p} \beta(x|k, p - k + 1),$$

where $\beta(\cdot|a,b)$ denotes the density corresponding to the CDF of the beta distribution, Beta(a,b). Also, $w_{k,p} = G(k/p) - G((k-1)/p),\ k = 1,\ldots,p$.

Note that if G is a CDF on [0,1], $B(x;G,p)$ is also a CDF on [0,1], corresponding to probability density function $f(x;\ G,p)$, defined by a mixture of p beta CDFs with mixing weights $(w_{1,p},\ldots,w_{p,p})$. Therefore, if G and p are random, then $B(x;G,p)$ is a random continuous CDF, with corresponding random probability density function $f(x;G,p)$. The random Bernstein-Dirichlet polynomial prior distribution of Petrone (1999) has G as a Dirichlet process with parameters (m,G_0), with p assigned an independent discrete prior distribution $\pi(p)$ defined on $\{1,2,\ldots\}$. Her work extended from the results of Dalal and Hall (1983) and Diaconis and Ylvisaker (1985), who proved that, for sufficiently large p, mixtures of the form given in Equations 11.1–11.3 can approximate any CDF on [0,1], to any arbitrary degree of accuracy. Moreover, as Petrone (1999) has shown, the Bernstein polynomial prior distribution must treat p as random to guarantee that the prior supports the entire space of (Lebesgue-measurable) continuous densities on [0,1]. Suppose that a set of data $x_1,\ldots,x_n \in [0,1]$ are independent and identically distributed samples from a true density, denoted by f_0. Standard arguments of probability theory involving Bayes theorem can be used to show that the data update the Bernstein prior to yield a posterior distribution of the random density f (via the posterior distribution of (G,p)). Walker (2004, Section 6.3) proved the posterior consistency of the random Bernstein model (prior), in the sense that as $n \to \infty$, the posterior distribution of the model converges to a point mass at the true f_0. In fact (Walker, Lijoi, & Prünster, 2007), if the choice of prior distribution $\pi(p)$ satisfies $\pi(p)<\exp(-4p \log p)$, the convergence rate of the posterior matches the convergence rate of the sieve maximum likelihood estimate of f_0.

11.2.3 Dependent Bivariate Model

A model for constructing a bivariate Dirichlet process has been given in Walker and Muliere (2003). The idea is as follows: Take $G_X \sim \Pi(m,\ G_0)$ and then, for some fixed $r \in \{0,1,2,\ldots\}$, take $z_1,\ldots,z_r$ to be independent and identically distributed from G_X. Then take

$$G_Y \sim \Pi(m+r, (mG_0 + r\widehat{F}_r)/(m+r)),$$

where $\hat{F}_r$ is the empirical distribution of $\{z_1,\ldots,z_r\}$. Walker and Muliere (2003) showed that the marginal distribution of G_Y is $\Pi(m,G_0)$. It is possible to have the marginals from different Dirichlet processes. However, it will be assumed that the priors for the two random distributions are the same. It is also easy to show that for any measurable set A, the correlation between $G_X(A)$ and $G_Y(A)$ is given by

$$\text{Corr}(G_X(A), G_Y(A)) = r/(m+r),$$

and hence this provides an interpretation for the prior parameter r.

For modeling continuous test score distributions (F_X, F_Y), it is possible to construct a bivariate random Bernstein polynomial prior distribution on (F_X, F_Y) via the random distributions:

$$F_X(\cdot; G_X, p_X) = \sum_{k=1}^{p_X} \left[G_X\left(\frac{k}{p_X}\right) - G_X\left(\frac{k-1}{p_X}\right) \right] \text{Beta}(\cdot|k, p_X - k + 1),$$

$$F_Y(\cdot; G_Y, p_Y) = \sum_{k=1}^{p_Y} \left[G_Y\left(\frac{k}{p_Y}\right) - G_Y\left(\frac{k-1}{p_Y}\right) \right] \text{Beta}(\cdot|k, p_Y - k + 1).$$

with (G_X, G_Y) coming from the bivariate Dirichlet Process model, and with independent prior distributions $\pi(p_X)$ and $\pi(p_Y)$. Each of these random distributions is defined on (0,1]. However, without loss of generality, it is possible to model observed test scores after transforming each of them into (0,1). For example, if $x_{\min}$ and $x_{\max}$ denote the minimum and maximum possible scores on a test X, each observed test score x can be mapped into (0,1) by the equation $x' = (x - x_{\min} + \varepsilon)/(x_{\max} - x_{\min} + 2\varepsilon)$, where $\varepsilon > 0$ is a very small constant. The scores can be transformed back to their original scale by taking $X = X'(x_{\max} - x_{\min} + 2\varepsilon) + x_{\min} - \varepsilon$.

Given samples of observed scores $\boldsymbol{x}_{n(X)} = \{x_1, \ldots, x_{n(X)}\}$ and $\boldsymbol{y}_{n(Y)} = \{y_1, \ldots, y_{n(Y)}\}$ on the two tests (assumed to be mapped onto a sample space (0,1)), the random bivariate Bernstein polynomial prior combines with these data to define a joint posterior distribution, which we denote by $F_X, F_Y| \boldsymbol{x}_{n(X)}, y_{n(Y)}$. As proven by Walker et al. (2007), posterior consistency of the bivariate model is obtainable when the independent prior distributions $(\pi_X(p_X), \pi_Y(p_Y))$ satisfy $\pi(p_X, p_Y) \propto \exp(-4p_X \log p_X)\exp(-4p_Y \log p_Y)$. Also, this posterior consistency implies consistent estimation of the posterior distribution of the equating function $e_Y(\cdot) = F_{0Y}^{-1}(F_{0X}(\cdot))$, as desired. Karabatsos and Walker (2009b) described a Gibbs sampling algorithm that can be used to infer the posterior distribution F_X, $F_Y| \boldsymbol{x}_{n(X)}, y_{n(Y)}$, which is an extension of Petrone's (1999) Gibbs algorithm. We wrote a MATLAB program to implement the algorithm, and it can be obtained through correspondence with the first author.

At each iteration of this Gibbs algorithm, a current set of $\{p_X, G_X\}$ for test X and $\{p_Y, G_Y\}$ for test Y is available, from which it is possible to construct random distribution functions (F_X, F_Y) and the random equating function

$$e_Y(x) = F_Y^{-1}(F_X(x)) = y.$$

Hence, for each score x on test X, a posterior distribution for the equated score on test Y is available. A (finite-sample) 95% credible ("confidence") interval of an equated score $e_Y(x) = F_Y^{-1}(F_X(x))$ is easily obtained from the samples of posterior distribution $F_X, F_Y| \boldsymbol{x}_{n(X)}, y_{n(Y)}$. A point estimate of an equated score $e_Y(X)$ also can be obtained from this posterior distribution. While one conventional choice of point estimate is given by the posterior mean of $e_Y(X)$, the posterior median point estimate of $e_Y(\cdot)$ has the advantage that it is invariant over monotone transformations. This invariance is important considering that the test scores are transformed into the (0,1) domain and back onto the original scale of the test scores.

11.2.4 Applying the Model to Different Equating Designs

The Bayesian nonparametric equating method presented in Section 11.2.3 readily applies to the equivalent-groups design with no anchor test and applies to the single-group design. However, with minor modifications, this method can be easily extended to an equivalent-groups or nonequivalent-groups design with an anchor test, or to a counterbalanced design.

For an equating design having an anchor test, it is possible to adopt the idea of chained equipercentile equating (Angoff, 1971). In particular, let $\boldsymbol{x}_{n(X)}$ and $\boldsymbol{v}_{n(V_1)}$ denote the set of scores observed from examinee Group 1 who completed test X and an anchor test V, and let $Y_{n(Y)}$ and $\boldsymbol{v}_{n(V_2)}$ denote sets of scores observed from examinee Group 2 who completed test Y and the same anchor test V. Then, under an equating design with anchor test, it is possible to infer the posterior distribution of the random equating functions $e_Y(x) = F_Y^{-1}(F_{V_2}(e_{V_1}(x)))$ and $e_{V_1}(x) = F_{V_1}^{-1}(F_{X_1}(x))$, based on samples from the posterior distributions $F_X, F_{V_1}|x_{n(X)}, v_{n(V_1)}$ and $F_Y, F_{V_2}|y_{n(Y)}, v_{n(V_2)}$, each modeled under a bivariate Bernstein prior.

For a counterbalanced design, it is possible to adopt the ideas from von Davier et al. (2004b, Section 2.3), to combine the information of the two examinee Groups 1 and 2. Specifically, the inference of the posterior distribution of the random equating function $e_Y(x) = F_Y^{-1}(F_X(x))$ is obtained by taking $F_X(\cdot) = \varpi_X F_{X_1}(\cdot) + (1 - \varpi_X)F_{X_2}(\cdot)$ and $F_Y(\cdot) = \varpi_Y F_{Y_1}(\cdot) + (1 - \varpi_Y)F_{Y_2}(\cdot)$, where $(F_{X_1}, F_{X_2}, F_{Y_1}, F_{Y_2})$ are from the posterior distributions $F_{X_1}, F_{Y_2}|x_{n(X_1)}, y_{n(Y_2)}$ and $F_{X_2}, F_{Y_1}|x_{n(X_2)}, y_{n(Y_1)}$ under two bivariate Bernstein models. Also, $0 \leq \varpi_X, \varpi_Y \leq 1$ are chosen weights, and they can be varied to determine how much they change the posterior distribution of $e_Y(\cdot)$.

11.3 Illustrations

The following two subsections illustrate the Bayesian model for the equating of test scores arising from the equivalent-groups design, the counterbalanced design, and the nonequivalent-groups design, respectively. In applying our Bayesian model to each of the three data sets, we assumed the following specification of the prior distributions. In particular, we assumed the bivariate Dirichlet process to have baseline distribution G_0 that equals the Beta(1,1) distribution, and we assumed a relatively noninformative prior by taking $m = 1$ and $r = 4$, reflecting the (rather uncertain) prior belief that the correlation of the scores between two tests is

$0.8 = r/(m+r)$. In particular, the choice of "prior sample size" of $m = 1$ leads to a posterior distribution of F_X, F_Y that is primarily determined by the observed data. Furthermore, up to a constant of proportionality, we specify an independent prior distribution of $\pi(p) \propto \exp(-4p\log p)$ for p_x and for p_y. As discussed in Section 11.2.3, this choice of prior ensures the consistency of the posterior distribution of (F_X, F_Y). Also, for each data set analyzed with the Bayesian model, we implemented the Gibbs sampling algorithm to generate 10,000 samples from the posterior distribution of (F_X, F_Y), including (P_X, P_Y), after discarding the first 2,000 Gibbs samples as burn-in. We found through separate analyses that 10,000 samples had converged to samples from the posterior distribution.

11.3.1 Equivalent-Groups Design

The Bayesian nonparametric equating model is demonstrated in the analysis of a large data set generated from an equivalent-groups design. This data set, obtained from von Davier et al. (2004b, p. 100), consists of 1,453 examinees who completed test *X* and 1,455 examinees completing test *Y* of a national mathematics exam. Each test has 20 items and is scored by number correct. The average score on test *X* is 10.82 (SD = 3.81), and the average score on test *Y* is 11.59 (SD = 3.93), and so the second test is easier than the first. For the Bayesian nonparametric model for equating, the marginal posterior distributions of P_X and of P_Y concentrated on 1 and 2, respectively. Figure 11.1 presents the posterior median estimate of the equating function under the Bayesian equating model.

Figure 11.1 also presents four more estimates of the equating functions, obtained by the kernel, percentile-rank, linear, and mean methods of equating, respectively. We use the kernel estimate that is reported in Chapter 7 of von Davier et al. (2004b). According to the figure, the Bayesian estimate differs substantially from the estimate obtained by the other four methods. This difference suggests that in the

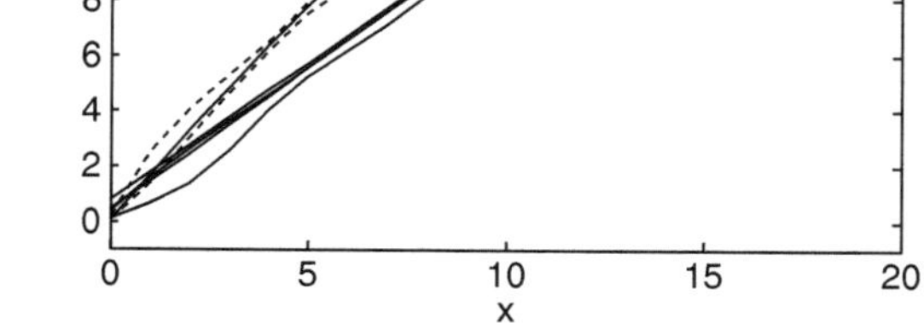

Fig. 11.1 The posterior median estimate of $e_Y(\cdot)$ given by the top solid line, enveloped by the 95% posterior credible interval (dotted lines). The other solid lines give the point-estimates of $e_Y(\cdot)$ obtained via the kernel, percentile-rank (bottom solid line), linear, and mean methods of equating

data, the test score distributions (F_X, F_Y) are correlated. In particular, the Bayesian model accounts for the dependence (correlation) between F_X and F_Y, whereas in the other four methods, they are assumed to be independent (zero correlation) under the equivalent-groups design. However, there must be correlation between the two test forms, given that the two forms were designed to measure the same construct of math ability. Moreover, Figure 11.1 shows that the kernel, linear, and mean equating methods equate some scores on test *X* that fall above the 0–20 range of possible scores on test *Y*. In contrast, the Bayesian nonparametric model equated scores on test *X* with scores that fall inside the range of test *Y*, as it will always do.

11.3.2 Nonequivalent-Groups Design and Chained Equating

In this section we apply the Bayesian nonparametric equating model to analyze a classic data set arising from a nonequivalent-groups design with internal anchor, obtained from Kolen and Brennan (2004). The first group of examinees completed test *X*, and the second group of examinees completed test *Y*, both groups being random samples from different populations. Here, test *X* and test *Y* each have 36 items and is scored by number correct, and both tests have 12 items in common. These 12 common items form an internal anchor test because they contribute to the scoring of test *X* and of test *Y*. While the two examinee groups come from different populations, the anchor test provides a way to link the two groups and the two tests. The anchor test completed by the first examinee group (population) is labeled as V_1 and the anchor test completed by the second examinee group is labeled as V_2, even though both groups completed the same anchor test. The first group of 1,655 examinees had a mean score of 15.82 (SD = 6.53) on test *X*, and a mean score of 5.11 (SD = 2.38) for the anchor test. The second group of examinees had a mean score of 18.67 (SD = 6.88) on test *Y* and a mean score of 5.86 (SD = 2.45) on the anchor test.

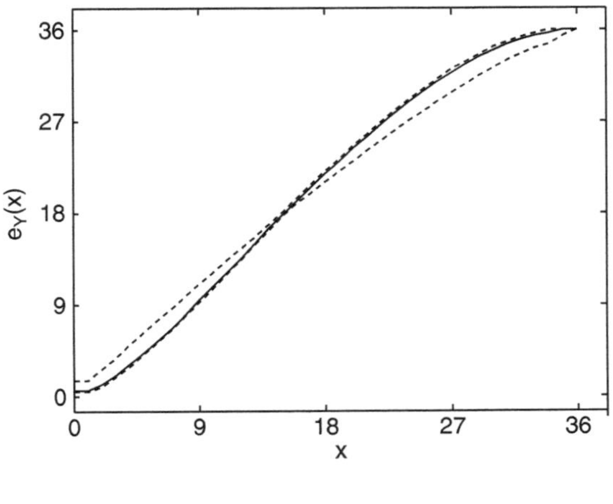

Fig. 11.2 The posterior median estimate of $e_Y(\cdot)$ (solid line), enveloped by the 95% posterior credible interval (dotted lines)

In the analysis of these data from the nonequivalent-groups design, chained equipercentile equating was used with the Bayesian nonparametric model, as described in Section 11.2.4. The marginal posterior distribution of p_{X_1}, p_{V_1}, p_{V_2}, and p_{Y_2} concentrated on values of 6, 1, 3, and 5 respectively. Figure 11.2 presents the posterior median estimate of the equating function estimate, along with the corresponding 95% confidence interval from the posterior distribution.

11.4 Conclusions

This study introduced a Bayesian nonparametric model for test equating. It is defined by a bivariate Bernstein polynomial prior distribution for (F_X, F_Y) that supports the entire space of (random) continuous distributions, with this prior depending on the bivariate Dirichlet process. The Bayesian equating model has important theoretical and practical advantages over all the previous approaches to observed score equating. A key advantage of the Bayesian equating model is that in equivalent-groups designs, it accounts for the realistic situation that the two distributions of test scores (F_X, F_Y) are correlated, instead of independent, as is often assumed in the previous methods of observed score equating. This dependence seems reasonable, considering that in practice, the two tests that are to be equated are designed to measure the same psychological construct (e.g., ability in some math domain). We also note that the Bayesian model provides a method of symmetric equating which yields equated scores within the range of test scores, something which could not be said about the other methods of observed score equating. Finally, through the posterior distribution, the Bayesian model provides a 95% credible interval for the equated score. Thus, unlike previous approaches to observed score equating, the Bayesian model fully accounts for uncertainly in the equating score, for any given sample size.

Chapter 12
Generalized Equating Functions for NEAT Designs

Haiwen H. Chen, Samuel A. Livingston, and Paul W. Holland

12.1 Introduction

The purpose of this chapter is to introduce generalized equating functions for the equating of test scores through an anchor. Depending on the choice of parameter values, the generalized equating function can perform either linear equating or equipercentile equating, either by poststratification on the anchor or by chained linking through the anchor.

The generalized equating functions can represent either linear or equipercentile equating because they are based on the kernel equating procedure (von Davier, Holland, & Thayer, 2004b), which allows the user to choose a bandwidth for converting the discrete distributions of scores into continuous distributions. A large bandwidth causes the equating to be linear; a small bandwidth results in equipercentile equating. In addition, the generalized equating functions translates the choice of assumptions about the test and the anchor—the choice that leads to one or another of the familiar anchor equating methods—into the choice of a value for a new single parameter, called κ. For example, with a large bandwidth, one value of the κ parameter will produce Tucker equating; another value will produce chained linear equating; still another will produce Levine equating (Levine, 1955). Those same three values for κ, used with a small bandwidth, will produce frequency estimation equipercentile equating, chained equipercentile equating, and a nonlinear method analogous to Levine equating. The κ parameter also can take on infinitely many other values, producing a family of equating methods that includes the methods mentioned above as special cases.

H.H. Chen (✉) and S.A. Livingston,
Educational Testing Service, Rosedale Rd, Princeton, New Jersey 08541, USA
e-mail: hchen@ets.org

P.W. Holland
Paul Holland Consulting Corporation, 200 4th Ave South, Apt 100, St Petersburg FL 33701, USA
e-mail: pholland@ets.org

A.A. von Davier (ed.), *Statistical Models for Test Equating, Scaling, and Linking*, Statistics for Social and Behavioral Sciences,
DOI 10.1007/978-0-387-98138-3_12,

Section 12.2 of this chapter presents some of the terminology that will be used. Section 12.3 presents a uniform way to reproduce the three common linear equating methods: (a) the chained linear method, (b) the Tucker method, and (c) the Levine method. Section 12.4 presents the generalized equating function by poststratification on the anchor and shows how it can produce the familiar linear and equipercentile equating methods. Section 12.5 provides an example of the application of the generalized equating function to simulated data derived from an actual data set, varying the value of the κ parameter.

12.2 Terminology

The equating of scores on two different forms of a test is often accomplished on the basis of data collected when the groups of examinees taking the two forms are not of equal ability but are linked by a common "anchor" test taken by both groups. This data collection plan is often referred to as the nonequivalent groups with anchor test (NEAT) design. In this chapter, X and Y will refer to the scores on the two test forms; A will refer to the score on the anchor test. The examinees taking the two forms will be assumed to be sampled from different populations, referred to as P and Q (corresponding to test forms X and Y, respectively).

Several methods have been proposed for equating test scores on the basis of data from a NEAT design. Some of those methods constrain the equating relationship to be of the form $Y=\alpha+\beta X$. Those methods will be referred to as *linear equating* methods. Other methods do not impose this constraint; instead, they estimate the function that transforms the distribution of X into the distribution of Y in some specified population of examinees. Those methods will be referred to as *nonlinear equating* methods. The specified population will be referred to as $\boldsymbol{S}$ and is assumed to be a composite of populations P and Q, represented in the ratio w to $(1 - w)$.

To equate test scores on the basis of data from a NEAT design, it is necessary to assume that some characteristics of the bivariate distributions of test and anchor scores are population invariant—that they are the same in populations P, Q, and S. One common assumption is that the conditional distributions of X and Y, given A, are population invariant. That assumption makes it possible to estimate the distributions of scores X and Y in population S and then use those estimated distributions to equate X to Y. Equating on the basis of this assumption will be referred to as *poststratification equating*. The linear version of poststratification equating is the Braun-Holland method (Braun & Holland, 1982). Other linear equating methods based on similar assumptions include the Tucker method and the Levine method (Kolen & Brennan, 2004, pp. 105–132). The nonlinear version of poststratification equating (described by Angoff, 1971/1984) is commonly known as "frequency estimation" (p. 113) equating.

An alternative set of assumptions is that the symmetric linking relationships of X to A and of Y to A are population invariant. Equating methods based on these assumptions link score X to score A by assuming the linking relationship in population S to be the same as in population P; they then link score A to score Y by assuming the linking relationship in population S to be the same as in population Q. These methods will be referred to as *chained equating*. The linear and nonlinear versions of chained equating are commonly known as *chained linear* and *chained equipercentile equating*.

12.3 A General Form for Tucker, Levine, and Chained Linear Equating

The basic equation for the linear equating of score X to score Y by estimating the means and standard deviations of X and Y in population $\boldsymbol{S}$ is Equation 12.1:

$$y = f(x) = \frac{\sigma_S(Y)}{\sigma_S(X)}[x - \mu_S(X)] + \mu_S(Y). \tag{12.1}$$

The most familiar linear equating methods are Tucker equating, Levine equating, and chained linear equating.

In this section, the equations for the Tucker, Levine, and chained linear equating methods will be derived, with details, in a way that shows clearly how they are similar and how they are different, although many results have been published before in the same or slightly different forms (Kolen & Brennan, 2004; von Davier & Kong, 2005; von Davier, 2008; Kane et al., 2009). There are two types of Levine equating, but they are similar in many important ways. In this chapter, they will be considered as a single method until it becomes necessary to distinguish between them.

12.3.1 Chained Linear Equating

The main assumption of chained linear equating is that the symmetric linear links from score X to score A and from score Y to score A are population invariant. The symmetric linear link from X to A in population P is

$$a = f(x) = \alpha_P + \beta_P \mathrm{x}, \tag{12.2}$$

where a is a value of A and x is a value of X, and

$$\beta_P = \sigma_P(A)/\sigma_P(X). \tag{12.3}$$

$$\alpha_P = \mu_P(A) - \beta_P\mu_P(X), \tag{12.4}$$

Under the assumption that Equation 12.2 is population invariant, the terms in Equations 12.3 and 12.4 have the same values in population $\boldsymbol{P}$ as in population $\boldsymbol{S}$. Hence we have

$$\beta_P = \sigma_S(A)/\sigma_S(X) = \sigma_P(A)/\sigma_P(X); \tag{12.5}$$

$$\mu_S(A) - \beta_P \mu_S(X) = \mu_P(A) - \beta_P \mu_P(X). \tag{12.6}$$

Then Equations 12.5 and 12.6 can be solved for $\mu_S(X)$ and $\sigma_S(X)$. A similar development leads to formulas for $\mu_S(Y)$ and $\sigma_S(Y)$. Using the identity $\mu_S(A) = w\mu_P(A) + (1 - w)\mu_Q(A)$, under the population invariance assumptions of chained linear equating, the means and standard deviations of X and Y in population $\boldsymbol{S}$ are given by Equation 12.7:

$$\begin{aligned}
&(\mathrm{a})\ \mu_S(X) = \mu_P(X) - (1 - w)[\sigma_P(X)/\sigma_P(A)][\mu_P(A) - \mu_Q(A)],\\
&(\mathrm{b})\ \mu_S(Y) = \mu_Q(Y) + w[\sigma_Q(Y)/\sigma_Q(A)][\mu_P(A) - \mu_Q(A)].\\
&(\mathrm{c})\ \sigma_S(X) = \sigma_S(A)[\sigma_P(X)/\sigma_P(A)]\\
&(\mathrm{d})\ \sigma_S(Y) = \sigma_S(A)[\sigma_Q(Y)/\sigma_Q(A)]
\end{aligned} \tag{12.7}$$

Substituting the terms from Equation 12.7 into Equation 12.1, we get the usual form of the equation for chained linear equating:

$$y = f(x) = \mu_Q(Y) + \frac{\sigma_Q(Y)\sigma_P(A)}{\sigma_Q(A)\sigma_P(X)}[x - \mu_P(X)] + \frac{\sigma_Q(Y)}{\sigma_Q(A)}\left[\mu_P(A) - \mu_Q(A)\right]. \tag{12.8}$$

Notice that the weight w cancels out of Equation 12.8. Chained linear equating does not depend on the relative proportions of populations $\boldsymbol{P}$ and $\boldsymbol{Q}$ in population $\boldsymbol{S}$.

12.3.2 Tucker Equating

The main assumption of Tucker equating is that the regressions of X and Y on A (i.e., the best linear predictors of X and Y from A) are population invariant. The best linear predictor of score X from score A in population $\boldsymbol{P}$ can be expressed as

$$x = \mathrm{f}'(a) = \alpha'_P + \beta'_P a, \tag{12.9}$$

where x is a value of X and a is a value of A, and

$$\beta'_P = \rho_P(X, A)[\sigma_P(X)/\sigma_P(A)] \tag{12.10}$$

$$\alpha'_P = \mu_P(X) - \beta'_P \mu_P(A) \tag{12.11}$$

These are the values that minimize $\sum\left(X-\alpha'_P-\beta'_P A\right)^2$ in population P.

The assumption that the best linear predictor is population invariant implies that $\beta'_S=\beta'_P$, so that

$$\rho_S(X,A)[\sigma_S(X)/\sigma_S(A)]=\rho_P(X,A)[\sigma_P(X)/\sigma_P(A)], \tag{12.12}$$

which can be solved for $\sigma_S(X)$. The population invariance assumption also implies that $\alpha'_S=\alpha'_P$, so that

$$\mu_S(X)-\beta'_S\mu_S(A)=\mu_P(X)-\beta'_P\mu_P(A). \tag{12.13}$$

Yet, $\beta'_S=\beta'_P$, and $\mu_S(A)$ can be expressed in terms of the known quantities $\mu_P(A)$, $\mu_Q(A)$, and w. Therefore, Equation 12.13 can be solved for $\mu_S(X)$. A similar development leads to formulas for $\mu_S(Y)$ and $\sigma_S(Y)$.

Therefore, under the assumptions that the best linear predictors of X and Y from A are population invariant, the means and standard deviations of X and Y in population S are given by Equation 12.14:

$$\begin{aligned}
&(\mathrm{a})\mu_S(X)=\mu_P(X)-(1-w)\rho_P(X,A)[\sigma_P(X)/\sigma_P(A)][\mu_P(A)-\mu_Q(A)];\\
&(\mathrm{b})\mu_S(Y)=\mu_Q(Y)+w\rho_Q(Y,A)[\sigma_Q(Y)/\sigma_Q(A)][\mu_P(A)-\mu_Q(A)];\\
&(\mathrm{c})\sigma_S(X)=\sigma_S(A)[\rho_P(X,A)/\rho_S(X,A)][\sigma_P(X)/\sigma_P(A)];\\
&(\mathrm{d})\sigma_S(Y)=\sigma_S(A)[\rho_Q(Y,A)/\rho_S(Y,A)][\sigma_Q(Y)/\sigma_Q(A)].
\end{aligned} \tag{12.14}$$

Substituting the estimated means and standard deviations from Equation 12.14 into Equation 12.1, we get this form of the equation for Tucker equating:

$$\begin{aligned}
y=f(x)=\mu_Q(Y)&+\frac{\rho_Q(Y,A)\rho_S(X,A)\sigma_Q(Y)\sigma_P(A)}{\rho_P(X,A)\rho_S(Y,A)\sigma_Q(A)\sigma_P(X)}[x-\mu_P(X)]\\
&+\frac{\rho_Q(Y,A)\sigma_Q(Y)}{\sigma_Q(A)}[\mu_P(A)-\mu_Q(A)]\\
&+(1-w)\left[1-\frac{\rho_S(X,A)}{\rho_S(Y,A)}\right]\frac{\rho_Q(Y,A)\sigma_Q(Y)}{\sigma_Q(A)}\left[\mu_P(A)-\mu_Q(A)\right].
\end{aligned} \tag{12.15}$$

The weight w does not cancel out of this equation; Tucker equating depends on the relative proportions of populations P and Q in population S. To compare Tucker equating with chained linear equating, we need to remove this dependence, by finding a realistic condition under which the third term of this expression is zero. In a NEAT design, it is not realistic to assume that populations P and Q have equal mean scores on A. However, it may be realistic to assume that the correlations of X with A and of Y with A are equal in population S: $\rho_S(X, A)=\rho_S(Y, A)$. This assumption leads to the equation for a weight-independent version of Tucker equating:

$$y = f(x) = \mu_Q(Y) + \frac{\rho_Q(Y,A)\sigma_Q(Y)\sigma_P(A)}{\rho_P(X,A)\sigma_Q(A)\sigma_P(X)}[x - \mu_P(X)] + \frac{\rho_Q(Y,A)\sigma_Q(Y)}{\sigma_Q(A)}\left[\mu_P(A) - \mu_Q(A)\right]. \tag{12.16}$$

12.3.3 Levine Equating

The Levine equating methods use the notion of true score from classical test theory, which states that any examinee's score on a test can be decomposed into a *true score*, the part that does not vary over repeated testing, and an *error of measurement*, the part that varies:

$$X = T_X + E_X. \tag{12.17}$$

Errors of measurement are assumed to be purely random — uncorrelated with each other and with true scores — and to have a mean of zero. It follows from this assumption that the correlation of X with T_X in a population is the ratio of their standard deviations in that population:

$$\rho_P(X,T_X) = \sigma_P(T_X)/\sigma_P(X) \tag{12.18}$$

One may see that $\rho_P(X,T_X)$ is simply the square root of the reliability of test X in population P.

For equating test scores through an anchor score, it is possible to make assumptions like those of the Tucker method but, instead of applying them to the observed scores and conditional standard deviations, to apply them to the true scores and standard errors of measurement. That approach leads to the Levine method (Kolen & Brennan, 2004).

The main assumptions of the Levine equating methods are that true scores on X and Y are perfectly correlated with true scores on A and that the functions linking true scores on X and Y to true scores on A are population invariant. By definition, the linear link from T_X to T_A on P is

$$\tau_{\mathrm{a}} = f(\tau_x) = a''_P + b''_P\tau_x, \tag{12.19}$$

where τ_a is a value of T_A and τ_x is a value of T_X, and

$$\beta''_P = \sigma_P(T_A)/\sigma_P(T_X) \tag{12.20}$$

$$\alpha''_P = \mu_P(T_A) - \beta''_P\mu_P(T_X) = \mu_P(A) - \beta''_P\mu_P(X) \tag{12.21}$$

Here in Equation 12.21, the assumption that the mean of E_A (the measurement error of A) is 0 is used to replace the mean of T_A (the true score of A) by the mean of A. Similarly, the mean of T_X is replaced by the mean of X.

Using the population invariance assumption,

$$\beta_P'' = \sigma_S(T_A)/\sigma_S(T_X) = \sigma_P(T_A)/\sigma_P(T_X) \tag{12.22}$$

$$\mu_S(A) - \beta_P''\mu_S(X) = \mu_P(A) - \beta_P''\mu_P(X) \tag{12.23}$$

Equations 12.22 and 12.23 can be solved to get formulas for $\mu_S(X)$ and $\sigma_S(X)$. A similar development leads to formulas for $\mu_S(Y)$ and $\sigma_S(Y)$. Under the assumptions that the linear links between the true scores are population invariant, the means and standard deviations of X and Y over S are given by Equation 12.24:

$$\begin{aligned}
&\text{(a) } \mu_S(X) = \mu_P(X) - (1-w)[\sigma_P(T_X)/\sigma_P(T_A)][\mu_P(A) - \mu_Q(A)],\\
&\text{(b) } \mu_S(Y) = \mu_Q(Y) + w[\sigma_Q(T_Y)/\sigma_Q(T_A)][\mu_P(A) - \mu_Q(A)].\\
&\text{(c) } \sigma_S(X) = \sigma_S(T_A)/\rho_S(X,T_X)[\sigma_P(T_X)/\sigma_P(T_A)]\\
&\text{(d) } \sigma_S(Y) = \sigma_S(T_A)/\rho_S(Y,T_Y)[\sigma_Q(T_Y)/\sigma_Q(T_A)]
\end{aligned} \tag{12.24}$$

Here the result given in Equation 12.18 has been used to replace $\sigma_S(T_X)$ with $\sigma_S(X)$ and similarly for $\sigma_S(T_Y)$.

Substituting the estimated means and standard deviations from Equation 12.24 into Equation12.1, we get this form of the equation for Levine observed-score equating:

$$\begin{aligned}
y = f(x) = \mu_Q(Y) &+ \frac{\rho_S(X,T_X)\sigma_Q(T_Y)\sigma_P(T_A)}{\rho_S(Y,T_Y)\sigma_Q(T_A)\sigma_P(T_X)}[x - \mu_P(X)]\\
&+ \frac{\sigma_Q(T_Y)}{\sigma_Q(T_A)}[\mu_P(A) - \mu_Q(A)]\\
&+ (1-w)\left[1 - \frac{\rho_S(X,T_X)}{\rho_S(Y,T_Y)}\right]\frac{\sigma_Q(T_Y)}{\sigma_Q(T_A)}[\mu_P(A) - \mu_Q(A)].
\end{aligned} \tag{12.25}$$

The weight w does not cancel out of this equation; Levine observed-score equating depends on the relative proportions of populations P and Q in population S. To compare Levine observed-score equating with chained linear equating, we need to remove this dependence, by finding a realistic condition under which the third term of this expression is zero. The only likely possibility is that scores X and Y are equally reliable in population S: $\rho_S(X, T_X) = \rho_S(Y, T_Y)$. This assumption leads to a weight-independent version of Levine observed-score equating:

$$
\begin{aligned}
y &= f(x) \\
&= \mu_Q(Y) + \frac{\sigma_Q(T_Y)\sigma_P(T_A)}{\sigma_Q(T_A)\sigma_P(T_X)}[x - \mu_P(X)] + \frac{\sigma_Q(T_Y)}{\sigma_Q(T_A)}[\mu_P(A) - \mu_Q(A)] \qquad (12.26)
\end{aligned}
$$

Equation 12.26 is identical to the equation for Levine true-score equating.

Now the equations for chained linear equating (Equation 12.8), the weight-independent version of Tucker equating (Equation 12.16), and the weight-independent version of Levine equating (Equation 12.26) can be compared. Those three equations can all be written as Equation 12.27:

$$
\begin{aligned}
y = f(x) = \mu_Q(Y) &+ \frac{\varphi_Q(Y,A)\frac{\sigma_Q(Y)}{\sigma_Q(A)}}{\varphi_P(X,A)\frac{\sigma_P(X)}{\sigma_P(A)}}[x - \mu_P(X)] \\
&+ \left[\varphi_Q(Y,A)\frac{\sigma_Q(Y)}{\sigma_Q(A)}\right][\mu_P(A) - \mu_Q(A)]. \qquad (12.27)
\end{aligned}
$$

where $\varphi_P(X, A)$ and $\varphi_Q(Y, A)$ are factors determined by a given equating.

A comparison of this general Equation 12.27 with the equations for the three linear methods shows that

- if $\varphi_P(X, A) = \varphi_Q(Y, A) = 1$, then Equation 12.27 is Equation 12.8, the equation for chained linear equating;
- if $\varphi_P(X, A) = \rho_P(X, A)$ and $\varphi_Q(Y, A) = \rho_Q(Y, A)$, then Equation 12.27 is Equation 12.16, the equation for the weight-independent version of Tucker equating; and
- if $\varphi_P(X, A) = \rho_P(X, TX) / \rho_P(A, TA)$ and $\varphi_Q(Y, A) = \rho_Q(Y, T_Y) / \rho_Q(A, T_A)$, then Equation 12.27 is Equation 12.26, the equation for the weight-independent version of Levine equating.

The quantities $\rho_P(X, A)$ and $\rho_Q(Y,A)$ are necessarily less than 1. The quantities $\rho_P(X,T_X)$ / $\rho_P(A.T_A)$ and $\rho_Q(Y, T_Y)$ / $\rho_Q(A, T_A)$ are nearly always greater than 1. Therefore, the three methods are ordered, with chained linear in between Tucker and Levine. This relationship explains why, in practical equating situations where the three methods produce different results, the results of chained linear equating nearly always are in between those of Tucker equating and Levine equating.

Of course, there are infinitely many possible values for $\varphi_P(X, A)$ and $\varphi_Q(Y, A)$. Each possible set of values for these parameters leads to a different linear equating method.

12.4 A Generalized Equating Function

Equation 12.27 is a general expression for linear equating in a NEAT design. It leads to a family of linear equating methods, including the Tucker, Levine, and chained linear methods and infinitely many others. But is there a corresponding family of nonlinear equating methods?

The kernel equating procedure provides a way to answer this question. Kernel equating is not a single equating method; it is a procedure that leads to many possible equating methods. Two versions of the kernel equating procedure can be used in a NEAT design: One follows the logic of poststratification equating, and the other follows the logic of chained equating. The kernel equating procedure for poststratification equating of X to Y through A involves four steps:

1. Pre-Smoothing (optional): Fit a log-linear model to each of the bivariate test-anchor score distributions (X, A) in population P and (Y, A) in population Q. The output of this step is a pair of discrete bivariate distributions that are smoother (less irregular) than those observed.
2. Estimation: use the poststratification equating assumption to estimate the score distributions of X and Y (still discrete) in population S.
3. Continuization: replace the discrete distributions estimated for population $\boldsymbol{S}$ by continuous distributions.
4. Equating: link each value of X to the value of Y that has the same percentile rank in the continuized distributions of X and Y estimated for population S.

The kernel procedure for chained equating involves two separate linkings. The four steps of the procedure are as follows:

1. Pre-Smoothing (optional): Fit a log-linear model to each of the bivariate test-anchor score distributions (X, A) in population P and (Y, A) in population Q. The output of this step is a pair of discrete bivariate distributions that are smoother (less irregular) than those observed.
2. Estimation: estimate the (marginal) score distributions of X and A (still discrete) in population P and the score distributions of Y and A in population Q, respectively.
3. Continuization: replace the four discrete marginal distributions by continuous distributions.
4. The equating requires two steps: (a) linking of X to A (link each value of X to the value of A that has the same percentile rank in the continuized marginal distributions of X and A) and (b) linking of A to Y (link each value of A determined in Step 4a to the value of Y that has the same percentile rank in the continuized marginal distributions of Y and A).

The continuization step requires the user of the procedure to specify a bandwidth parameter that determines how far the continuized distributions can depart from the discrete distributions. Small values of the bandwidth parameter make the continuized distribution closely match the discrete distribution, so that the kernel equating very closely resembles the usual type of equipercentile equating. Large values of the bandwidth parameter make the continuized distributions closely resemble normal distributions, so that the kernel equating is, for all practical purposes, linear. Therefore, any linear equating method that can be closely reproduced by a kernel equating procedure with a large bandwidth has an analogous nonlinear method: that same kernel equating procedure with a small bandwidth.

To find the nonlinear equating method that corresponds to a given linear equating method, all that is necessary is to find a kernel equating procedure that is essentially equivalent to that linear equating method. The kernel procedure for chained equating has the natural connection between chained equipercentile equating and chained linear, while the kernel procedure for poststratification equating with large bandwidth produces the Braun-Holland equating method. However, it has been shown in Braun & Holland (1982) that with additional assumptions, the Braun-Holland equating becomes the Tucker equating method. This establishment will serve as the cornerstone to build the generalized equating function based on poststratification equating.

What makes it possible to get the Levine equating from the kernel equating procedures is a transformation that can be applied to the pre-smoothed bivariate test-anchor distributions. This transformation is called the mean-preserving linear transformation (MPLT). The MPLT has the effect of changing the standard deviations of the two variables, while leaving the means unchanged. The transformation has two parameters, and the right choice of values for those parameters will change the kernel equating procedure, so that instead of being essentially equivalent to one linear equating method, it becomes essentially equivalent to another linear equating method. The two parameters, denoted here as λ_X and ν_X, function as multipliers for the standard deviations of the two variables. Using X and A represent the test score and anchor score variables before applying the MPLT and X^* and A^* to represent those variables after applying the MPLT,

$$\begin{aligned} &(\mathrm{a})\ \mu(X^*) = \mu(X),\\ &(\mathrm{b})\ \mu(A^*) = \mu(A),\\ &(\mathrm{c})\ \sigma(X^*) = \lambda_X \sigma(X),\\ &(\mathrm{d})\ \sigma(A^*) = \nu_X \sigma(A). \end{aligned} \tag{12.28}$$

If X and A were continuous variables, this change in the standard deviations could be accomplished by simply transforming the variables X and A. However, X and A represent test scores, which are nearly always discrete variables. Transforming X and A would produce a discrete bivariate distribution in which most of the values of each variable would not be possible scores on the test and anchor. Therefore, it is necessary to find a transformation that changes the standard deviations of X and A while keeping the set of possible values unchanged, by redistributing the probabilities. The distribution of X^* and A^* has exactly the same set of possible values as the distribution of X and A. What changes is the probability associated with each pair of values (x, a). (See Brennan & Lee, 2006, and Wang & Brennan, 2007, for details.)

The MPLT can be inserted into the kernel equating procedure by applying it immediately after the pre-smoothing step. The result is a *generalized equating function* with two sets of parameters: a set of four MPLT parameters (λ_X, ν_X, λ_Y and ν_Y) and a set of bandwidth parameters for the continuization step. Poststratification equating has two bandwidth parameters (which generally have the same value);

chained equating has four bandwidth parameters. Because there are two versions of kernel equating, there are two generalized equating functions, generalized post-stratification equating and generalized chained equating.

Although any set of values for the four MPLT parameters will result in an equating function, some sets of values are better than others—more interesting theoretically and more useful practically. The MPLT makes it possible to change one linear equating into another, by expressing the linear equating as a kernel equating procedure with a large bandwidth and by applying the MPLT to the pre-smoothed test-anchor distributions. In particular, it is possible to find a set of MPLT parameters that will transform the kernel equating procedure that replicates Levine equating (Chen & Holland, 2009). In this case, the MPLT parameters are

$$\begin{aligned} \lambda_X &= 1 + \varepsilon_X, \\ v_X &= \lambda_X \rho_P(X,A)\rho_P(A,T_A)/\rho_P(X,T_X), \\ \lambda_Y &= 1 + \varepsilon_Y, \\ v_Y &= \lambda_Y \rho_Q(Y,A)\rho_Q(A,T_A)/\rho_Q(Y,T_Y), \end{aligned} \tag{12.29}$$

where ε_X and ε_Y are, respectively, functions of $\rho_P(X, A)\rho_P(A, T_A)\ /\rho_P(X, T_X)$ and $\rho_Q(Y, A)\rho_Q(A, T_A)\ /\rho_Q(Y, T_Y)$, and the values of both are almost zero.

Then, if the large bandwidth parameter in the continuization step is replaced with a small bandwidth parameter, the result is a kernel equating procedure that produces a nonlinear analogue to Levine equating, called *Levine observed-score equipercentile equating*.

Chen and Holland (2009) generalized this procedure by defining a family of MPLT parameters that depend on a single parameter κ as follows:

$$\begin{aligned} \alpha(\kappa) &= [\rho_P(X,A)\rho_P(A,T_A)/\rho_P(X,T_X)]\kappa; \\ \beta(\kappa) &= [\rho_Q(Y,A)\rho_Q(A,T_A)/\rho_Q(Y,T_Y)]\kappa. \end{aligned} \tag{12.30}$$

$$\lambda_X = 1 + \varepsilon_X(\alpha(\kappa)); v_X = \lambda_X \alpha(\kappa); \lambda_Y = 1 + \varepsilon_Y(\alpha(\kappa)); \quad \text{and} \quad v_Y = \lambda_Y \alpha(\kappa). \tag{12.31}$$

The parameter κ can be any number but preferably should be in the range of [0, 1]. The functions $\varepsilon_X(\,)$ and $\varepsilon_Y(\,)$ have very complicated forms but usually can be ignored when they are evaluated near 1, and $\varepsilon_X(1) = \varepsilon_Y(1) = 0$. This set of MPLT parameters, used in a kernel equating procedure with a small bandwidth, leads to an equipercentile equating associated with κ. Used in the kernel equating procedure for poststratification equating with a large bandwidth, they lead to a linear equating whose weight-independent version is given by Equation 12.27, with $\varphi_Q(Y, A) = \rho_Q(Y, A)^{1-\kappa}(\rho_Q[Y, T_Y]/\rho_Q[A, T_A])^{\kappa}$, and so on. If $\kappa = 0$, then it leads to the Tucker equating; if $\kappa = 1$, then it leads to the Levine equating. Chained linear equating also can be reproduced by an appropriate value for κ, if the correlations of X with A and of Y with A in population S are nearly equal. In that case, we need to determine κ to make both $\varphi_P(X, A) = 1$ and $\varphi_Q(Y, A) = 1$. To make $\varphi_P(X, A) = 1$,

$$\kappa = \frac{\ln \rho_P(X,A)}{\ln \rho_P(X,A) + \ln \rho_P(A,T_A) - \ln \rho_P(X,T_X)} \tag{12.32a}$$

and to make $\varphi_Q(Y, A) = 1$,

$$\kappa = \frac{\ln \rho_Q(Y,A)}{\ln \rho_Q(Y,A) + \ln \rho_Q(A,T_A) - \ln \rho_Q(Y,T_Y)} \tag{12.32b}$$

If the numbers from both Equations 12.32a and 12.32b are nearly equal, their average can be used as the value of κ, so that $\varphi_Q(Y, A) \approx 1$ and $\varphi_P(X, A) \approx 1$, and the equating function will be very nearly equivalent to chained linear equating. However, because it is derived from poststratification equating, it will be weight dependent.

The special case of generalized poststratification equating in which the MPLT parameters are defined as in Equation 12.31 is called κ-PSE. This generalized equating function, with minor adjustments, can approximate all commonly used methods for equating in a NEAT design. Poststratification equating (i.e., frequency-estimation equipercentile equating) is the special form of κ-PSE with $\kappa = 0$ and a small bandwidth. Braun-Holland and Tucker equating is the special form of κ-PSE with $\kappa = 0$ and a large bandwidth. The Levine methods are the special case of κ-PSE with $\kappa = 1$ and a large bandwidth. Chained equipercentile and chained linear equating are the special cases of κ-PSE with the κ value given in Equation12.32- with a small bandwidth for equipercentile equating and a large bandwidth for linear equating. The hybrid Levine method (von Davier, Fournier-Zajac, & Holland 2006b) is similar to the Levine observed-score equipercentile equating we defined in this section, since both have Levine observed-score equating as their linear form under kernel equating. Chen and Holland (2009) showed that the modified post-stratification equating (Wang & Brennan, 2007) for NEAT designs with an external anchor is almost same as the special case of κ-PSE with $\kappa = ½$ and with a small bandwidth. Finally, the chained true-score equipercentile equating developed in Chen and Holland (2008) is the weight-independent version of the Levine observed-score equipercentile equating.

Similarly, we can create a κ-generalized chained equating (κ-CE). The κ-indexed family of λ_X, ν_X, λ_Y, and ν_Y is

$$\lambda_X(\kappa) = \rho_P(X,T_X)^\kappa; \nu_X(\kappa) = \rho_P(A,T_A)^\kappa; \lambda_Y(\kappa) = \rho_Q(Y,T_Y)^\kappa; \quad \text{and} \\ \nu_Y(\kappa) = \rho_Q(A,T_A)^\kappa. \tag{12.33}$$

For $\kappa = 0$ with a small bandwidth, the equating is chained equipercentile; with a large bandwidth, it is chained linear. For $\kappa = 1$ with a small bandwidth, the equating is chained true-score equipercentile equating; with a large bandwidth, it is Levine true-score equating. We can also approximate the poststratification equating and the Tucker equating, but the value of κ will be negative. Notice that κ-CE is weight independent.

12.5 Examples and Discussion

In this section, simulated data based on a data set from an operational testing program is used to demonstrate the generalized equating function, particularly the κ-PSE, illustrating the following specific relationships:

- Tucker equating can be approximated closely by κ-PSE with $\kappa = 0$ and a large kernel equating bandwidth;
- Levine observed-score equating can be approximated closely by κ-PSE with $\kappa = 1$ and a large kernel equating bandwidth;
- Chained equipercentile equating can be approximated closely by κ-PSE with the κ value determined by Equation 12.32and a small kernel equating bandwidth.

The data set contains 2 simulated bivariate distributions, each derived from the same named pre-smoothed distribution described in details in Chapter 10 of A. A. von Davier et al. (2004b). Test *X* and test *Y* each contain 78 items; the external anchor *A* contains 35 items. Table 12.1 shows summary statistics for this simulated data set.

The score distributions in population $\boldsymbol{Q}$ were strongly skewed in a positive direction, on both test form *Y* and the anchor. In population $\boldsymbol{P}$, the distributions of scores on test form *X* was skewed, but less strongly, and in the opposite direction.

The first comparison is between the Tucker equating function with $w = 0.5$ and the κPSE with $\kappa = 0$, $w = 0.5$, and kernel equating bandwidth $=$ 5,400. The difference between these two equating functions is less than 0.02 raw-score points (0.0012 *SD*) at all points of the score scale (see Figure 12.1).

The second comparison is between the Levine observed-score equating function with $w = 0.5$ and the κ PSE with $\kappa = 1$, $w = 0.5$, and kernel equating bandwidth $=$ 5,400. The difference between these two equating functions is less than 0.06 raw-score points (0.0036 *SD*) at all points of the score scale (see Figure 12.1).

Table 12.1 Summary Statistics for the Data Set

Statistic	Sample from population *P*, $n = 10{,}000$		Sample from population *Q*, $n = 10{,}000$	
	Test *X*	Anchor *A*	Test *Y*	Anchor *A*
Mean	39.3	17.1	32.5	14.3
SD	17.2	8.4	16.7	8.2
Correlation	0.88		0.88	
Skewness	−0.11	−0.02	0.23	0.26
Kurtosis	2.24	2.15	2.28	2.25

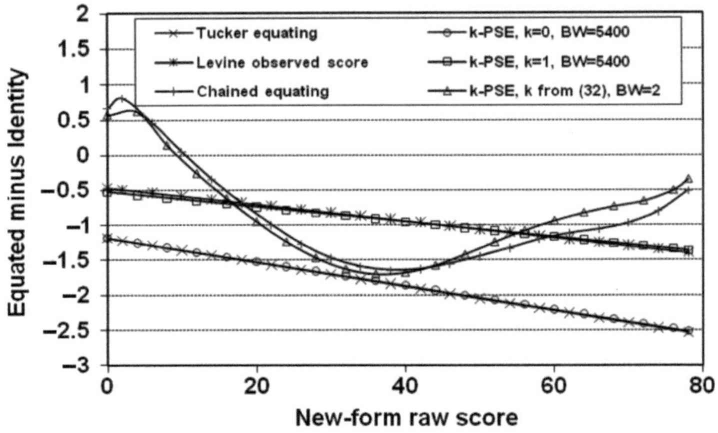

Fig. 12.1 Plots of three equating functions and their counterparts generated by κ-PSE. BW = bandwidth

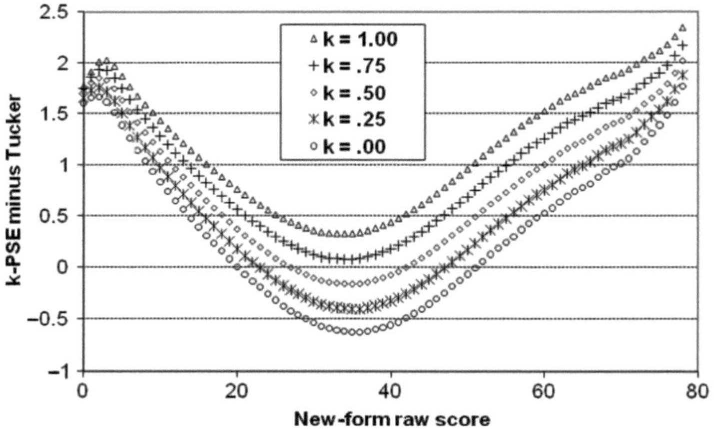

Fig. 12.2 Differences between κ-PSE and Tucker equating, for five values of κ

The third comparison is between the chained equipercentile equating function (produced from kernel equating software with bandwidth = 2) and the κ PSE with κ determined by Equation 12.32 and kernel equating bandwidth = 2. The difference is not as tiny in this comparison as in the previous two comparisons, but still not large; it varies over the score scale from approximately −0.11 to +0.27 raw-score points (−0.007 to +0.016 SD). If both the weight w and the κ were adjusted slightly, the difference would be consistently less than 0.20 raw-score points (0.012 *SD*).

For many years, psychometricians comparing different equating functions computed from the same operational data have observed predictable differences between the Tucker, chained linear, and Levine observed-score equating methods.

When the new-form equating sample scores higher than the reference-form equating sample on the anchor test, the Levine method yields the highest equated scores; the Tucker method yields the lowest. Figure 12.2 shows that similar differences occur with curvilinear κ PSE equating. The plot shows the differences between κ-PSE equating and Tucker equating, for five different values of κ. With $\kappa = 0$ (the lowest curve in the figure), κ-PSE equating corresponds to the usual frequency-estimation method, which is the curvilinear analog to Tucker equating. With $\kappa = 1$ (the highest curve), the κ-PSE equating becomes the curvilinear analog to Levine observed-score equating. As the value of κ increases from 0 to 1, the equated scores become progressively higher.

The kernel equating procedure incorporating the MPLT, with no restrictions on the MPLT parameters λ_X, v_X, λ_Y, and v_X, except that they are all positive, defines a generalized equating function. This generalized equating function provides a framework for creating new equating methods with desired properties. On the other hand, the generalized equating function with κ gives a much better solution for operational work. Each not only pairs the three most familiar linear equatings with its nonlinear counterpart but also expands to a system of equatings indexed with continuous parameters, which the users can choose to get an optimal equating solution based on any criteria they choose.

There are some computation issues. The first is how to compute the true score coefficients defined in Equation 12.18. Currently, we used the formulas in Kolen and Brennan (2004). Interestingly, for NEAT designs using an external anchor, $\alpha(\kappa)$, defined in Equation 12.30 is $\rho_P(A, T_A)^{2\kappa}$; for NEAT designs using an internal anchor, $\alpha(\kappa)$ is $\rho_P(X, A)^{2\kappa}$. These formulas assume that the true scores on the test and the anchor have a perfect linear correlation, which is possible only if the equating relationship is linear. However, even when the relationship is not linear, the correlation of true scores is often close to 1.00 (Chen & Holland, 2008). For most cases, the linear assumption can be used for the computation. More extreme cases are discussed in the Chen and Holland (2008) paper, and the formulas are modified accordingly.

The second issue is how to compute the distribution defined by MPLT (Equation 12.28) on the integers. The distributions of the anchor scores in both samples (from populations $\boldsymbol{P}$ and $\boldsymbol{Q}$) have distributions on the same score points—the possible scores on the anchor. The conditional distributions are computed at these values of the anchor score A. However, the MPLT defined by Equation 12.28 misaligns the anchor scores. Therefore, it is necessary to redistribute the score frequencies at each noninteger value of A to the adjacent integers. The method used by Brennan and Lee (2006) and by Wang and Brennan (2007) produced frequencies of zero at some anchor score points, which distorted the score estimation and made the computation for estimating the standard error of equating impossible. A new method has been created to solve this problem by doing the redistribution in the log-linear pre-smoothing (Chen & Holland, 2010). The implementation of this solution in the pre-smoothing software is currently under development.

12.6 Conclusion

The generalized equating function is built with two basic elements: a base equating—either poststratification equating or chained equating—and the modified kernel equating framework, including the MPLT. If the base equating is poststratification equating, the generalized equating function is called generalized poststratification equating. The generalized poststratification equating is weight dependent; it depends on the relative weights of the two separately sampled examinee populations (***P*** and ***Q***) in the combined population for which the equating function is to be estimated. If the base equating is chained equating, the generalized equating function is called generalized chained equating and is weight independent. In some cases, the generalized poststratification equating is not sensitive to differences in the weights, and in those cases, generalized poststratification equating and generalized chained equating are equivalent. Therefore, generalized poststratification equating can be considered the more general approach.

The κ-equating is a special case of the generalized equating function in which the differences between equating methods are expressed as differences in the value of a parameter, called κ. The κ-equating can unite all the commonly used classical methods for equating in a NEAT design, by reducing the selection of each equating to a choice of a value for κ. By expanding the choice to include other values of κ, the κ-equating can be made to generate a whole family of well-defined equating functions. This modification gives equating practitioners a wide choice of available methods and makes it easy to find the equating method that optimizes some specified criterion.

The approach to equating described in this chapter could lead to at least two types of future development and research. One is the development of criteria for the quality of an equating—criteria for choosing among the many possible values of the MPLT and bandwidth parameters. Another is to expand the family of generalized equating functions, by adapting the generalized equating function to include other existing equating methods (e.g., methods based on pre-smoothing the score distributions using item response theory) or by varying parameters of the generalized equating function to create new equating methods.

Author Note: Any opinions expressed in this chapter are those of the authors and not necessarily of Educational Testing Service.

Chapter 13
Local Observed-Score Equating

Wim J. van der Linden

13.1 Introduction

One of the highlights in the observed-score equating literature is a theorem by Lord in his 1980 monograph, *Applications of Item Response Theory to Practical Testing Problems*. The theorem states that observed scores on two different tests cannot be equated unless the scores are perfectly reliable or the forms are strictly parallel (Lord, 1980, Chapter 13, Theorem 13.3.1). Because the first condition is impossible and equating under the second condition is unnecessary, the theorem is rather sobering.

My research on local equating was deeply motivated by Lord's theorem and its related notion of *equity of equating* introduced in the same chapter to explain the "cannot be equated" part of the theorem. Before discussing the principles of local equating, we therefore review the chapter in which the theorem was introduced.

It is quite instructive to see how cautiously Lord (1980) proceeded in the chapter: He began by introducing the problem of observed-score equating under the ideal condition of no measurement error ("case of infallible measures") and used the equipercentile transformation—one of the historic achievements of observed-score equating research—for this case. His next step was the introduction of measurement error ("case of fallible measures"). For this case he gave his famous theorem to show that the use of the equipercentile transformation either does not hold or is unnecessary. Lord then formulated two alternative methods of equating known as item response theory (IRT) observed-score equating and true-score equating. The former deals only indirectly with measurement error by using a parametric estimate of the observed-score distributions for the two tests rather than sample distributions. The latter ignores measurement error altogether. Interestingly, Lord

W.J. van der Linden
CTB/McGraw-Hill, 20 Ryan Ranch Rd., Monterey, CA 93940, USA
e-mail: wim_vanderlinden@ctb.com

A.A. von Davier (ed.), *Statistical Models for Test Equating, Scaling, and Linking*, Statistics for Social and Behavioral Sciences,
DOI 10.1007/978-0-387-98138-3_13, © Springer Science+Business Media, LLC 2011

appeared unable to express a preference for either of these approximate methods, and the chapter ended entirely open, with an intriguing question that I will discuss below.

It is clear that Lord (1980) was aware of the need of observed-score equating as well as the popularity of the methods practiced in his days. On the other hand, although the presentation of the two approximate methods indicates that he was willing to strike a balance between practice and what psychometric theory allows us to do, the open end of the chapter suggests that he was unable to do so.

Lord's (1980) attitude toward observed-score equating reminds me of a cartoon I once saw, in which one scientist said, "Look at the nice application I have!" and the other responded, "Yes, but does it work in theory?" In a field such as test theory, where numbers do not mean anything unless they can be proven to behave according to a model for their formal properties, our affinity should definitely go to the second scientist.

13.2 Lord's Analysis of Equating

Lord's (1980) treatment of equating is based on the conceptualization of measurement that underlies IRT—the main topic of his monograph. Key in the conceptualization is the observation that responses to test items reflect not only the ability the test measures but also the properties of the items. Equating is an attempt to disentangle these abilities and item properties at the level of the observed scores on different test forms.

I will follow Lord's (1980) notation and use θ to denote the ability parameter. In addition, X and Y denote the number-correct scores on two different tests that measure the same θ, and X and Y denote the tests themselves. For convenience, throughout this chapter, tests X and Y are assumed to have equal length. Because X and Y are dependent both on the abilities of the test takers and the properties of the items, an equating problem exists. Suppose that test Y is the newer form and Y has to be equated back to X. The goal is to find the transformation $x = \varphi(y)$ from Y to the scale of X that guarantees that the transformed scores on test Y are indistinguishable from the scores on test X.

This conceptualization does not restrict the generality of our analysis in any way; it would do so only if a specific response model were assumed and the results depended on the properties of this model. As each of the mainstream response models used in the testing industry involves a different parameterization of the items, in order to maintain generality, we therefore deliberately avoid specifying any item parameters.

Each equating study involves the choice of a sampling design, but the current conceptualization is also neutral with respect to this choice. For any response model with adequate person and item parameters, we can estimate the parameters in the presence of structurally missing responses. Except for a mild requirement of "connectedness" (van der Linden, 2010), equating based on such models, therefore, does not require a specific equating design.

13.2.1 Equating Without Measurement Error

Lord (1980) introduced the equating problem by considering the case of two perfectly reliable scores X and Y ("case of infallible measures"), a condition under which observed scores are fixed quantities and the distinction between observed and true scores disappears. If X and Y are perfectly reliable scores for tests measuring the same θ, each of these three quantities orders any given population of test takers identically. Consequently, the scores on tests X and Y for any test taker always have the same rank in their distributions for the population of choice. This equivalence of rank establishes an immediate equating relation—if an examinee takes one of the forms, we know that he or she always would obtain the score on the other form associated with the same rank in the population.

In more statistical terms, let $F(x)$ be the (cumulative) distribution function of the scores on test X and $G(y)$ the distribution function of the scores on test Y for an arbitrary population of test takers. Both functions are assumed to be monotonic. For convenience, we also will ignore problems due to the discreteness of number-correct scores throughout this chapter. Let y be the quantile in the distribution on test Y for an arbitrary cumulative proportion p of the population; that is,

$$G(y) = p. \tag{13.1}$$

The equivalent score $\varphi(y)$ on test X follows then from

$$F(\varphi(y)) = p. \tag{13.2}$$

Or, making $\varphi(y)$ explicit,

$$\varphi(y) = F^{-1}(G(y)). \tag{13.3}$$

This transformation is the well-known equipercentile transformation in the equating literature. It is typically estimated by sampling the same population twice, administering test forms X and Y to the two samples, estimating the distributions functions of X and Y from the samples, and establishing the relationship by varying p in Equations 13.1 and 13.2 systematically. As the focus of this chapter is not on sampling issues, I do not discuss these issues further.

For perfectly reliable scores, the same transformation from Y to X in Equation 13.3 is obtained for different populations of test takers; that is, use of the equipercentile transformation guarantees population invariance. This invariance is a practical feature, in that it does not seriously restrict equating studies in the choice of their subjects. Also, the choice of population cannot bias the equating in any way: No matter the selection of test takers, the equating errors

$$e_1(x) \equiv \varphi(y) - x \tag{13.4}$$

are always equal to zero for each individual test taker. These two features are documented in the following theorem:

Theorem 1. For perfectly reliable test scores X and Y, the equipercentile transformation $\varphi(y)$ in Equation 6.3 is (a) unbiased and (b) invariant across populations of test takers with distributions that have the full range of X and Y as support.

These attractive properties of population invariance and error-free equating are immediately lost when we move from the ideal world of infallible measurements to the real world of test scores with errors.

13.2.2 Equating With Measurement Error

In the case of fallible measures, test takers no longer have fixed observed scores on test forms X and Y, but their scores vary across replicated administrations of these tests. Statistically, we therefore should view the observed scores x and y for a test taker as realizations of random variables X and Y.

Several things change when scores with measurement error have to be equated. First, it no longer holds that the actually observed scores $X = x$ and $Y = y$ on an administration of the two tests order a given population of test takers identically. Measurement errors distort the ranks of the test takers in the distributions of X and Y for any population; that is, test takers are likely to have a higher rank in one observed-score distribution than dictated by their θS but a lower rank in another. The principle of equivalence of rank of the scores on test forms X and Y, on which the equipercentile transformation in Equation 13.3 was based, is thus violated and the transformation is no longer valid.

Second, the goal of equating is to find the transformation $\varphi(y)$ from Y to the scale of X that guarantees identical scores. But the criterion can never be met for the case of random errors because these errors introduce nonzero components in the definition of equating error $e_1(y)$ in Equation 13.4. In fact, the problem is even more fundamental in that the definition in Equation 13.4 itself is no longer sufficient: Test scores are now to be viewed as random variables, and it is not enough to just evaluate a single realization of them when the interest should be in their full distribution. Lord (1980) was aware of this problem and replaced the criterion in Equation 13.4 for the case of equating with measurement error by the more general criterion of equity, which he defined intuitively as follows: "If an equating of tests X and Y is to be equitable to each applicant, it must be a matter of indifference to applicants at every given ability level θ whether they are to take test X or Y" (p. 195).

Lord's formal definition of equity generalizes Equation 13.4 to the requirement for the *full distributions* of the scores on X and Y given θ and stipulates that

$$f_{\varphi(Y)|\theta} = f_{X|\theta}, \text{ for all } \theta, \tag{13.5}$$

where $f_{\varphi(Y)|\theta}$ and $f_{X|\theta}$ are the probability functions of the transformed scores on test Y and the scores on test X for the chosen population (Lord, 1980, Equation 13.3). This definition of equity is based on a clear concern about fairness of equating: If the two distributions would differ, a test taker might be disadvantaged by taking one test rather than the other. For instance, a high-ability test taker with a larger variance for his or her observed score on test Y than on test X runs a larger risk of not passing a certain cutoff score on the former than the latter.

Thirdly, and lastly, the feature of population invariance of the equipercentile transformation is immediately lost when X and Y have measurement error. This can be shown by deriving their distributions for an arbitrary population with ability distribution $f(\theta)$ as

$$f_X(x) = \int f_{X|\theta}(x) f(\theta) d\theta; \tag{13.6}$$

$$f_Y(y) = \int f_{Y|\theta}(y) f(\theta) d\theta. \tag{13.7}$$

The equipercentile transformation is applied to the marginal distributions $f_X(x)$ and $f_Y(y)$. As test forms X and Y have different items, $f_{X|\theta}(x)$ and $f_{Y|\theta}(y)$ are different. Any change of $f(\theta)$, therefore, has a differential effect on $f_X(x)$ and $f_Y(y)$, and produces a different equating transformation. This is hard to accept for individual test takers who expect their test scores to be adjusted for the differences between the *items* in tests X and Y but actually get a score that depends on the abilities of the *other test takers* who happen to be in the chosen population.

13.2.3 Lord's Theorem

We are now able to discuss Lord's theorem:

Theorem 2. Under realistic conditions, scores X and Y on two tests cannot be equated unless either (i) both scores are perfectly reliable or (ii) the two tests are strictly parallel [in which case $\varphi(y) = y$].

As the equipercentile transformation in Equation 13.3 was derived for the case of perfectly reliable scores, the sufficiency of this condition for equipercentile observed equating is obvious. To prove the sufficiency of the second condition (strictly parallel tests), Lord (1980) used the criterion of equity in Equation 13.5 and showed that the criterion only holds for monotonic transformations $x = \varphi(y)$ when the two tests are item-by-item parallel, in which case $\varphi(y) = y$. I will skip the formal proof and refer interested readers to Lord (1980, Section 13.3).

It is important to observe that Lord's proof shows that the only *monotonic* transformation from Y to X for which equity is possible is the identity transformation when the two tests are strictly parallel. It thus makes no sense to look for any other monotonic transformation than the equipercentile transformation that might result in equitable equating. In fact, the following example makes us even wonder if *any* transformation could ever produce an equitable equating for all test takers: Suppose the test scores that need to be equated are for tests with Guttman items at two different locations $\theta_1 < \theta_2$. All n items in test X are located at θ_1, all n items in test Y at θ_2 For test takers with $\theta < \theta_1$, the distributions of $X|\theta$ and $Y|\theta$ are degenerate distributions at $x = 0$ and $y = 0$, respectively; for test takers with $\theta > \theta_2$, they are degenerate distributions at $x = n$ and $y = n$. Hence, for these two groups of test takers, the two tests automatically produce identically distributed scores. However, for $\theta_1 < \theta < \theta_2$, the distributions of $Y|\theta$ remain at $y = 0$ but those of $X|\theta$ are now at $x = n$. For these test takers, the number-correct scores have to be mapped from 0 on test Y to n on test X. Thus, in order to produce an equitable equating, we have to choose between this extreme transformation (and forget about the test takers below θ_1 and above θ_2) and the identity transformation (and forget about those between θ_1 and θ_2).

13.2.4 Two Approximate Methods

Lord (1980) then offered two approximate methods of equating. One method is IRT true-score equating. Let $i=1, \ldots, n$ denote the items in form X and $j=1,\ldots,n$ those in form Y. Each of the mainstream response models for dichotomously scored items specifies a probability for the correct response as a function of θ. We use $P_i(\theta)$ and $P_j(\theta)$ for the response probabilities on the items in form X and form Y, respectively. The (number-correct) true scores on forms X and Y are given by

$$\xi = \sum_{i=1}^{n} P_i(\theta), \tag{13.8}$$

$$\eta = \sum_{j=1}^{n} P_j(\theta). \tag{13.9}$$

If the item parameters have been estimated from response data with enough precision, the only unknown quantity in Equations 13.8 and 13.9 is θ. (Because the response model is usually not identified, for the item parameters to be on the same scale they have to be estimated simultaneously from response data for an appropriate sampling design.) Variation of the unknown θ creates a relation between ξ and η that represents ξ as a (monotonic) function of η. Ignoring the differences between observed scores X and Y and their true scores ξ and η, IRT true-score equating uses this function to equate Y to X.

The other method is IRT observed-score equating. The method is based on an approximation of Equations 13.6 and 13.7 by

$$\hat{f}_X(x) = N^{-1} \sum_{a=1}^{N} f(x \mid \widehat{\theta}_a), \tag{13.10}$$

$$\hat{f}_Y(y) = N^{-1} \sum_{a=1}^{N} f(y \mid \widehat{\theta}_a), \tag{13.11}$$

where $\hat{\theta}_a$ are the ability estimates for a sample of test takers $a = 1, \ldots, N$. The two estimated marginal distributions of forms X and Y are then used to derive the equipercentile transformation.

13.2.5 An Intriguing Question

Lord (1980) was doubtful about the use of the method of true-score equating: "We do not know an examinee's true score. We can estimate his true score. . . .However, an estimated true score does not have the properties of true scores; an estimated true score, after all, is just another kind of fallible observed score" (Lord, 1980, p. 203). But he also had his doubts about the method of IRT observed-score equating: "Is this better than applying. . .true-score equating. . .to observed scores x and y?".

Lord (1980) then explained the reason for his inability to choose between the two approximate methods: "At present, we have no criterion for evaluating the degree of inadequacy of an imperfect equating. Without such a criterion, the question cannot be answered" (p. 203). The same uncertainty is echoed in the final section of the chapter, which Lord (1980) began by admitting that practical pressures often require that tests be equated at least approximately. He then summarized as follows: "What is really needed is a criterion for evaluating approximate procedures, so as to be able to choose from among them. *If you can't be fair (provide equity) to everyone, what is the best next thing?*" (p. 207).

This final question is intriguing. At the time, Lord already must have worked on his asymptotic standard error of equipercentile equating, which was published 2 years later (Lord, 1982b), so he clearly did not refer to this development. Rather than something that only evaluates the effect of sample size (as a standard error does) but leaves the equating method itself untouched, he wanted a yardstick that would allow him to make a more fundamental comparison between alternative equating methods and to assess which would be closest to equity (provide "*the next best thing*").

13.3 Local Equating

Local equating is an attempt to answer Lord's question. Its basic result is a theorem that identifies an equating that would provide full equity and immediately suggests how to evaluate any actual equating method against this ideal. Also, the theorem involves a twist that forces us to rethink much of our current theory and practice of equating—a process that has led me both to better understanding of the fundamental nature of the observed-score equating problem and a more intuitive appreciation of the idea of local equating. It also suggests new equating methods that better approximate the equity criterion than equipercentile equating. In this section, I review the theorem and provide alternative motivations of local equating. A few new equating methods based on the idea of local equating are discussed in the next section

13.3.1 Main Theorem

The theorem follows directly from the equity criterion in Equation 13.5. Lord (1980) expressed the criterion as an equality of conditional probability functions. Equivalently, it could be expressed as an equality of the conditional distribution functions $F_{\varphi(Y)|\theta}$ for the equated scores on test Y and $F_{X|\theta}$ for the observed score on test X. However, rather than as an equality, we express the criterion as a definition of equating error,

$$e_2(x;\theta) \equiv F_{\varphi(Y)|\theta} - F_{X|\theta}, \tag{13.12}$$

and require all error to be equal to zero for all θ. The transformations $x = \varphi^*(y)$that solve this set of equations are the error-free or true equating transformations.

Thus, it should hold that

$$F_{X|\theta}(x) = F_{\varphi(Y)|\theta}(\varphi(y)), \quad \theta \in R. \tag{13.13}$$

Solving for x by taking the inverse of $F_{X|\theta}$,

$$x = \varphi^*(y;\theta) = F_{X|\theta}^{-1} F_{\varphi(Y)|\theta}(\varphi(y)), \quad \theta \in R. \tag{13.14}$$

However, because $\varphi(\cdot)$ is monotone, $F_{\varphi(Y)|\theta}(\varphi(y)) = F_{Y|\theta}(y)$. Substitution results in

$$\varphi^*(y;\theta) = F_{X|\theta}^{-1}(F_{Y|\theta}(y)), \quad \theta \in R, \tag{13.15}$$

as the family of true equating transformations.

Surprisingly, Equation 13.15 involves the same type of transformation as for the equipercentile equating in Equation 13.3, but it is now applied to each of the conditional distributions of $X|\theta$ and $Y|\theta$ instead of only once to the marginal distributions of X and Y for a population of test takers. The fact that the derivation leads to an entire family of transformations reveals a rather restrictive implicit assumption in Lord's theorem, as well as all of our traditional thinking about equating: namely, that the equating should be based on a single transformation for the entire population of choice. Relaxing the assumption to different transformations for different ability levels opens up a whole new level of possibilities for observed-score equating that is waiting to be explored. The following theorem is offered as an alternative to Lord's (for an extended version, see van der Linden, 2000):

Theorem 3. For the population of test takers P for which test scores X and Y measure the same ability θ, equating with the family of transformations $\varphi^*(y;\theta)$ in Equation 13.15 has the following properties: (i) equity for each $p \in P$; (ii) symmetry in X and Y for each $p \in P$; and (iii) invariance within P.

Proof. (i) For each $p \in P$ there is a corresponding value of θ, and for each θ the transformation in Equation 13.15 matches the conditional distributions of $\varphi^*(Y)$ and X given θ. (ii) The inverse of $F^{-1}_{X|\theta}F_{Y|\theta}(y)$ is $F^{-1}_{Y|\theta}F_{X|\theta}(x)a$, which is Equation 13.15 for the equating from X to Y. (iii) The conditional formulation of Equation 13.15 implies independence from the distribution of θ over P. As a consequence, the family holds for any subpopulation of P.

In addition to equity, the family of transformations thus has the properties of symmetry and population invariance—other criteria identified by Lord (1980, Section 13.5) as essential to equating. The criterion of symmetry is usually motivated by observing that it would be hard to understand why a reversal of the roles of X and Y should lead to a different type of equating. It should—and does—hold for the definition of the true equating transformations in Equation 13.15. When selecting an actual method in an equating study, we sometimes are faced with trade-offs between the three criteria, and it then makes sense to sacrifice some symmetry to get closer to the more desirable property of equity. As we shall see later, the same choice is made for some of the traditional methods of equating.

As for the issue of population invariance, the criterion of equity in Equation 13.5 is defined conditional on θ. Hence, if the criterion holds, it automatically holds for any subpopulation of P as well. But the criterion also implies the definition of the family of transformations in Equation 13.15. It follows that *equity is a sufficient condition for population invariance* within P. This conclusion implies that an effective attempt to get closer to population invariance is approximating equity.

Also, note that the theorem defines the ultimate population P for which the invariance holds as the population of persons for which tests X and Y measure the same θ. We have a clear empirical criterion to evaluate membership of P: the joint fit of the response model in the testing program for the two tests. Besides, although the definition of P excludes arbitrariness, it is nevertheless open in that it not only includes all past or current test takers whose response behavior fit the model but encompasses future test takers for which this can be shown to hold as well. Finally, unlike traditional observed-score equating, the definition of P does not entail any necessity of random sampling of test takers.

The error definition in Equation 13.12 implies the ideal or true equating that provides equity but also offers the "criterion for evaluating approximate procedures" that Lord (1980) wanted so badly: For any arbitrary transformation $\varphi(y)$, the criterion is just the difference between the conditional distribution functions for the equated scores $\varphi(Y)|\theta$ and the scores $X|\theta$ in Equation 13.12. Observe that the difference is a function of x and that we have a different function for each $\theta \in R$. Also, because of its conditioning on θ, the evaluation is population invariant within P—an evaluation of the equated scores $\varphi(Y)$ for any subpopulation of P automatically holds for any other subpopulation.

Alternatively, we can compare any given transformation $\varphi(y)$ directly with the family of true transformations $\varphi^*(y;\theta)$ in Equation 13.15. This comparison leads to the alternative family of error functions:

$$\begin{aligned} e_3(y;\theta) &= \varphi(y) - \varphi^*(y;\theta) \\ &= \varphi(y) - F_{X|\theta}^{-1}(F_{Y|\theta}(y)), \quad \theta \in R. \end{aligned} \tag{13.16}$$

Of course, the results from both evaluations are equivalent: An equating transformation is error free if and only if its equated scores are. A critical difference between Equations 13.12 and 13.16, however, exists with respect to the scale on which they are defined: The error functions in Equation 13.12 are functions of x but those in Equation 13.16 are functions of y. The former are convenient when we have to evaluate an equating from a test Y with a variable composition to a fixed form X, for instance, from an adaptive to a linear test. For a more extensive discussion of these two alternative families of error functions, see van der Linden (2006a, b).

The definition of equating error is only the first step toward a standard statistical evaluation of observed-score equating. For the implementations of local equating discussed later in this chapter, the error functions above will be used to define the *bias* and *mean-square error* functions of an equating, that is, the expectations of the error and squared error over essential random elements in the implementation. These additional steps take the evaluation of equating to the same level as, for instance, the standard evaluation of an estimator of an unknown parameter or a decision rule in statistics.

In principle, we are now ready to look for equating methods that approximate the family in Equation 13.15 as closely as possible and evaluate these methods using these statistical criteria. The challenge, of course, is to find a proxy of the unknown θ that takes us as closely as possible to the true member in the family for each test taker. Before exploring the possibilities, I motivate the idea of local equating from a few alternative points of view.

13.3.2 Alternative Motivations of Local Equating

All of current observed-score equating is based on the use of a single transformation. However, the example at the end of the discussion of Lord's theorem above already hinted at the fact that no transformation whatsoever could ever establish an equitable equating at each ability level for a population of test takers. The following thought experiment illustrates this point again (van der Linden & Wiberg, in press). Suppose a person p with ability level θ_p takes test form Y, and a test specialist is asked to equate his or her observed score y_p to a score on test form X. For the sake of argument, suppose the specialist is given the full observed-score distributions for θ_p on both tests, that is, $F_X(x|\theta_p)$ and $F_Y(y|\theta_p)$. For this single-person population, an obvious choice from a traditional point of view is to use the equipercentile transformation $x = \varphi_p(y) = F^{-1}_{X|\theta_p}(F_{Y|\theta_p}(y))$ to equate the observed score y_p to a score on form X. Now suppose a second person q with another ability level takes the same test, and the same specialist is asked to equate this person's observed score y_q. The specialist, who is also given the distribution functions for q, is then faced with the choice between (a) using a separate equipercentile transformation for q or (b) treating the two test takers as a new population and using the equipercentile transformation for the marginal distributions of it. The first option would only involve establishing another individual transformation $\varphi_q(y)$, analogous to $\varphi_p(y)$. The result would be an equitable, symmetric, and population-invariant equating for both test takers. The second option would require the marginal distribution functions for the population, which is the average of the separate functions for p and q. Letting $F'_X(x)$ and $F'_Y(y)$ denote the two averages, the alternative equating transformation would be $x = \varphi'(y) = F'^{-1}_X(F'_Y(y))$. This second option would miss all three features. In fact, its problem would become even more acute if we kept adding test takers to the population: For each new test taker, the equating transformation would change. Even more embarrassing, the same would happen to the equated scores of all *earlier* test takers.

Clearly, traditional equipercentile equating involves a compromise between the different transformations required for the ability levels of each of the test takers in an assumed population. In doing so, it makes systematic errors for each of them. In more statistical terms, we can conclude that the use of a single equating transformation for different ability levels involves equatings that are structurally biased for each of them. The error function in Equation 13.12 reflects the size of the bias for each individual test taker.

The history of test theory shows an earlier occasion where a similar choice had to be made between a one-size-fits-all approach and one based on individual ability levels—the choice of the standard error of measurement for a test. The classical standard error was a single number for an entire population of test takers derived from the reliability of the test. It was quickly recognized that this error was a compromise between the actual errors at each ability level and was thus always biased. For example, a test that matches an individual test taker's ability level is known to be more informative than one that is much too difficult or too easy—a fact that should be reflected in the standard errors for the individual test takers. The classical standard error is now widely replaced by the conditional standard deviation of the observed score given ability, that is,

$$[Var(X \mid \theta)]^{1/2}. \tag{13.17}$$

The family of true equating transformations $\varphi^*(y;\theta)$ in Equation 13.15 is based on the full conditional distributions of the observed test scores, of which this conditional standard error represents the dispersion.

Interestingly, the family $\varphi^*(y;\theta)$ also can be shown to generalize Lord's first approximate equating method—the true-score equating in Equations 13.8–13.9. The equating following from this set of two equations is usually presented as a table with selected pairs of values of η and ξ used to equate the observed scores on form Y to *X*. It is tempting to think of this format as the representation of a single equating transformation. However, this conclusion would overlook that Equations 13.8–13.9 actually are a system of *parametric* equations, that is, a family of mappings with θ as index. When applied to equate *Y* to *X*, it becomes the family of true equating transformations in Equation 13.15 with its distributions degenerated to their expected values $E(X \mid \theta)$ and $E(Y \mid \theta)$:

$$E(Y|\theta) \to E(X|\theta), \quad \theta \in R. \tag{13.18}$$

Obviously, much is to be gained when we avoid this degeneration and turn to an equating based on the full conditional distributions of *X* and *Y*.

It is also instructive to view Lord's (1980) second approximate method in Equations 13.10–13.11 from the perspective of the family of true equatings in Equation 13.15. This method substitutes ability estimates $\widehat{\theta}_a$ for the test takers in a sample $a = 1, \ldots, N$ into the set of equations for the marginal distributions of *X* and *Y* in Equations 13.6–13.7. However, as already indicated, the factors $f_{X|\theta}(x)$ and $f_{Y|\theta}(y)$ in these equations are for different items, and any change of population $h(\theta)$ (or sample of test takers in this approximate method) has a differential effect on $f_X(x)$ and $f_Y(y)$ and therefore produces a different equipercentile transformation. An effective solution to this problem of population dependency is to just ignore the common second factor $h(\theta)$ in the integrands in Equations 13.6–13.7 and base IRT observed-score equating only on their first factors $f_{X|\theta}(x)$ and $f_{Y|\theta}(y)$ for the estimates $\widehat{\theta}_a$, precisely the choice made in the first local equating method discussed later in this chapter.

On the other hand, the traditional approach to the problem of population dependency has been to identify some special population $h(\theta)$ and use this as a standard for the equating. Two versions of the approach exist. One is based on the idea of a synthetic population to be derived from the two actual populations that take tests X and Y. Braun and Holland (1982, Section 3.3.2), who introduced the notion, defined it as any population with a distribution function equal to a linear combination of the functions for the two separate populations. More formally, if $F_X(\theta)$ and $F_Y(\theta)$ are the distribution functions for the populations who take tests X and Y, the synthetic population has distribution function

$$wF_X(\theta) + (1-w)F_Y(\theta), \tag{13.19}$$

with $0 \leq w \leq 1$ a weight to be specified by the testing program. The definition could be justified by two-stage sampling of the test takers in the equating study from the separate populations for tests X and Y with weights w and 1-w. However, this type of weighted sampling is rarely used in this context. More importantly, equatings are always required only for the scores of the population that takes the new test form, Y, and any nonzero weight w would detract from this goal (van der Linden & Wiberg, in press).

The other approach recognizes this fact and uses the population for Y as the standard. It does so by identifying the critical variables on which the populations for X and Y differ and using them to resample the population for X to match the population for Y. The two matched distributions are then used in the actual equating. For evaluations of this approach with matched samples, see, for instance, Dorans (1990); Dorans, Liu, and Hammond (2008); Liou, Cheng, and Li (2001); and Wright and Dorans (1993).

The use of synthetic or matched populations does not take population dependency away. For each test taker, it still holds that the equated score depends on the abilities of the other test takers in these synthetic or matched populations. Rather than equating X and Y for populations with identical ability distributions, as these two approaches attempt, we should equate them for identical abilities (i.e., condition on ability). Finally, notice that the use of a matched population also implies loss of symmetry of the equating. Except for the case of weight $w = .5$, the same holds for the use of a synthetic population.

At first sight, local equating may seem liable to two different objections, one involving an issue of fairness and the other being more philosophical. The former has to do with the fact that local equating implies different equated scores for the same score $Y = y$ by test takers with different abilities. This different treatment of equal observed scores seems unacceptable. However, the following example shows that actually the opposite holds: Consider the case of two test takers p and q who both have a score of 23 items correct on a 30-item test Y. Traditional equipercentile equating routinely would give both test takers the same equated score, a higher score than 23 if test Y appears to be more difficult than test X and a lower score if it appears to be easier. Now, suppose we are told that p and q have the observed-score distributions in Figure 13.1. As the figure reveals, the score observed for q was in the lower tail of q's distribution. However, p had better luck; p's score was in the upper tail of the distribution. Would it be fair to give the two individuals the same equated score on test X? Or should we adjust their equated scores for measurement error? After all, we do live in a world of fallible measures.

The critical question, of course, is where our knowledge of the abilities and the observed-score distributions of the test takers could come from. The true challenge to local equating lies in the answer to this question, not in any of the conceptual or more formal issues we have dealt with so far. But in fact we often know more than we realize. For instance, in observed-score equating, we generally ignore the information in the response patterns that leads to the observed scores. The example in Figure 13.1 typically arises when two test takers have equal number-correct scores but one fails on some of the easier items and the other on some of the more difficult ones. We immediately return to this important question in the next section.

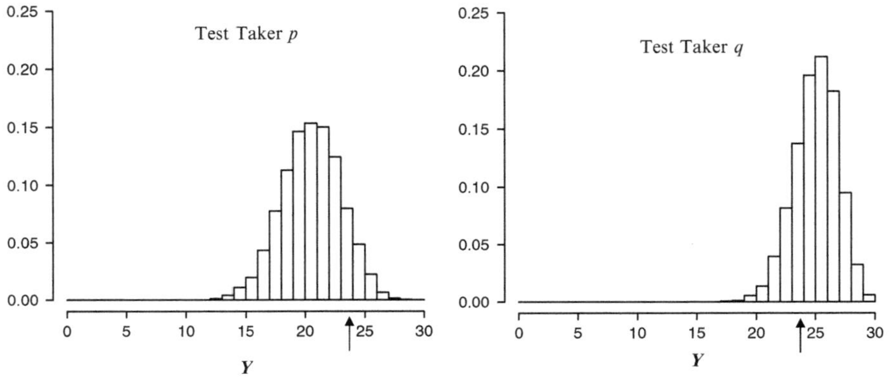

Fig. 13.1 Example of two test takers p and q with different abilities but the same realized observed score $Y = 23$

The more philosophical issue regards the question of how we seriously could propose using different equating transformations for a single measurement instrument. No one would ever consider doing this, for instance, when a tape measure appears to be locally stretched and its (monotonically) distorted measurements need to be equated back to those by a flawless measure. The idea of using different transformations to equate identical measurements on the distorted scale back to the standard scale would seem silly. Why, then, propose this for number-correct score equating in testing? This question is problematic because of its implicit claim of the number-correct score as a measure with the same status as length measured by a tape measure. Number-correct scores are entirely different quantities, though. Unlike length measures, they are not fundamental measures, which always can be reduced to a comparison between the object that is measured and a concatenation of standard objects (e.g., an object on one scale and a set of standard weights on the other). They are also not derived from such measures. (For a classic treatment of fundamental and derived measurement, see Campbell, 1928). More surprisingly, perhaps, although defined as counts of correct responses, number-correct scores are not counting measures, either. They would only be counting measures if all responses were equivalent. But they are not—each of them always is the result of an interaction between a different combination of ability level and item properties.

This last fundamental fact was already noted when I introduced Lord's (1980) notation for observed-score equating in the beginning of this chapter and stated, "Because X and Y are dependent both on the abilities of the test takers and the properties of the items, an equating problem exists." An effective way of disentangling ability and item effects on test scores is to model them at the level of the item-person combinations with separate item and person parameters, as IRT does. Observed-score equating is an attempt to deal with the same problem at the level of test scores in the form of a score transformation. But before applying any transformation to adjust for the differences between the items in different tests, we have to condition on the abilities to get rid of their effects. Monotonic transformations

$x = \varphi(y)$ that adjust simultaneously for item and ability effects on observed test scores on tests X and Y do not exist.

13.4 A Few Local Equating Methods

According to Lord's theorem, observed-score equating is possible only if the scores on forms X and Y are perfectly reliable or strictly parallel. On the other hand, Theorem 3 in this chapter shows that equating under regular conditions is still possible, provided we drop the restriction of a single transformation for all ability levels.

It may seem as if Theorem 3 only replaces one kind of impossible condition (perfect reliability or strictly parallelness) by another (known ability). However, an important difference exists between them. *Post hoc* changes of the reliability and the degree of parallelness of test forms are impossible; when equating the scores on a test form, we cannot go back and make them more reliable or parallel. As a result, Lord's theorem leaves us paralyzed; it offers no hint whatsoever as to what to do when real-world tests have less than perfect reliability or are not parallel. On the other hand, we can always try to approximate the family of true equating transformations in Equation 13.15 using whatever information is available in the test administration or equating study. Clearly, the closer the approximation, the better the equating. In fact, even a rough estimate or a simple classification of the abilities may be better than combining them into an assumed population before conducting the equating.

The name *local equating* is derived from the attempt to get as close as possible to the true equating transformations in Equation 13.15 to perform the equating. The error definitions in Equation 13.12 or Equation 13.16 can be used to evaluate methods based on such attempts in terms of their bias and mean standard error using a computer simulation with response data generated for known abilities under a plausible model.

Now that we know the road to equitable, population-independent equating, and have the tools to evaluate progress along it, we are ready to begin a search for Lord's "next best thing." The local equating methods below are first steps along this road. I only review their basic ideas and show an occasional result from an evaluation. More complete treatments and discussions of available results are found in the references.

13.4.1 Estimating Ability

The first method is a local alternative to the IRT observed-score equating method in Equations 13.10–13.11. It follows the earlier suggestion to obtain population-independent equating by ignoring the common second factor $h(\theta)$ in Equations 13.6–13.7 and basing the equating entirely on their first factors, $f_{X|\theta}(x)$ and $f_{Y|\theta}(y)$.

The main feature of this method is estimation of θ under a response model that fits the testing program, substituting the estimate in the true equating in Equation 13.15. In fact, the procedure is entirely analogous to the use of the conditional standard error of measurement in Equation 13.17, which also involves substitution of a θ estimate when used in operational testing.

For dichotomously scored test items, the conditional distributions of Y and X given θ belong to the generalized binomial family (e.g., Lord, 1980, Section 4.1). Unlike the regular binomial family, its members do not have distribution functions in closed form but are given by the generating function

$$\prod_{i=1}^{n} [Q_i(\theta) + tP_i(\theta)], \tag{13.20}$$

where $P_i(\theta)$ is the success probability on item i for the response model in the testing program and $Q_i(\theta)=1-P_i(\theta)$. Upon multiplication, the coefficients of the factors $t^1, t^2, \ldots$ in the expression are the probabilities of $X = 1, 2, \ldots$. The probabilities are easily calculated for forms X and Y using the well-known recursive procedure in Lord and Wingersky (1984). From these probabilities, we can calculate the family of true equating transformations in Equation 13.15. Thus, the family can be easily calculated for any selection of θs as soon as the items in forms X and Y have been calibrated for the testing program.

The estimates of θ can be point estimates, such as maximum-likelihood estimates assuming known item parameters or Bayesian expected a posterior estimates. But we could also use the full posterior distribution of θ for the test taker's response vector on form X to calculate his or her posterior expectation of the true family in Equation 13.15. However, this alternative is more difficult to calculate and has not shown to lead to any significant improvement over the simple procedures with a point estimate of θ plugged directly into Equation 13.15. More details on this local method are given in van der Linden (2000, 2006a).

The local method of IRT observed-score equating lends itself nicely to observed-score equating problems for test programs based on a response model. Another natural application is the equating of an adaptive test to a reference test released to its test takers for score-reporting purposes. In adaptive testing, θ estimates are immediately available. Surprisingly, this proposed equating of the number-correct scores on an adaptive test is entirely insensitive to the fact that different test takers get different selections of items; the use of the true equating transformations for the test takers' item selections at their θ estimates automatically adjusts both for their ability differences and the selection of the items (van der Linden, 2006b).

Observe that two different summaries of the information in the response patterns on test Y are used: number-correct scores and θ estimates. The latter picks up the information ignored by the former. The earlier example for the two test takers with the same number of items correct on Y in Figure 13.1, used to illustrate that they nevertheless deserved different equated scores, was based precisely on this alternative type of IRT observed-score equating.

For later comparison, it is also interesting to note the different use of the conditional distribution functions in traditional and local IRT observed-score equating. In both versions, θ estimates of the test takers and the conditional distributions of X and Y given these estimates are calculated from Equation 13.20. In the traditional version, the conditional distributions are then averaged over the sample of test takers to get an estimate of the marginal distributions for assumed populations on X and Y, and the equipercentile transformation is calculated for these marginal distributions (e.g., Zeng & Kolen, 1995). In the local version of the method, no averaging takes place, but different equipercentile transformations are calculated directly for the different conditional distributions of X and Y given θ.

Figure 13.2 shows a typical result from a more extensive evaluation of the method of local IRT observed-score equating against traditional equipercentile equating in van der Linden (2006a). The curves in the two plots show the bias functions based on the responses on two 40-item tests X and Y simulated under the three-parameter logistic response model for the simulated values $\theta = -2.0, -1.5, \ldots, 2.0$ (curves more to the left are for lower θ values). The bias functions were the expectations of the error functions in Equation 13.16 across the simulated observed-score distributions on test Y given θ. (The mean standard error functions in this study, which were the expectations of the squares of the same errors, are omitted here because they showed identical patterns of differences.) For the local method, the bias was ignorable. But the bias for the traditional method went up to 4 score points (i.e., 10% of the score range) for some combinations of θs and observed scores. For an increase in test

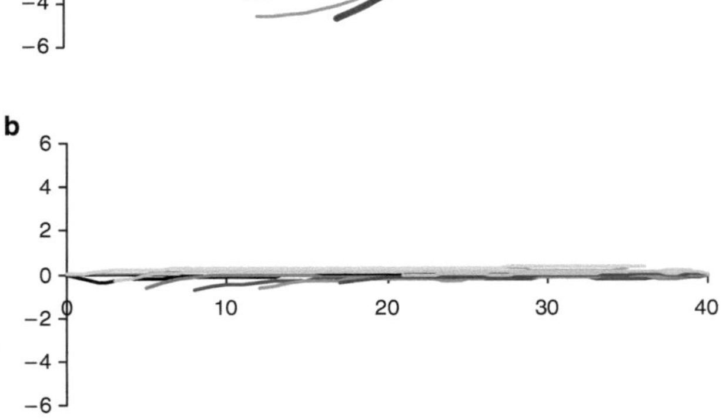

Fig. 13.2 Bias functions for (**a**) traditional equipercentile and (**b**) local item response theory (IRT) observed-score equating for $\theta = -2.0(.5)20$

length, the bias for the traditional method became even worse, but for the local method it vanished because of better estimation of θ. For the same reason, the bias decreased with the discrimination parameters of the items in test Y. Likewise, the local method appeared to be insensitive to differences in item difficulty between tests in X and Y because θ estimates have this property.

13.4.2 Anchor Score as a Proxy of Ability

The traditional methods for observed-score equating for a nonequivalent-groups-and-anchor test (NEAT) design are chain equating and equating with poststratification. The former consist of equipercentile equating from Y to the observed score A on an anchor test A for the population that takes form Y with subsequent equating from A to X for the population that takes form X. The equating transformation from Y to X is the composition of the separate transformations for these two steps. In equating with poststratification, the conditional distributions of X and Y given $A = a$ are used to derive the distributions on forms X and Y for a target population, usually a population that is a synthesis of those that took the two forms as in Equation 13.19, and the actual equating is equipercentile equating of the distributions for this target population (von Davier, Holland, & Thayer, 2004b, Section 2.4.2).

As a local alternative to these traditional methods, it seems natural to use the extra information provided by the anchor test to approximate the true family of equating transformations in Equation 13.15. For simplicity, we assume an anchor test A with score A that is not part of Y ("external anchor"). For an equating with an internal anchor, we just have to add the score on this internal anchor to the equated score derived in this section.

For an anchor test to be usable, A has to be a measure of the same θ as X and Y. Formally, this means a classical true score $\tau_A \equiv E(A)$ that is a monotonic increasing function of the same ability θ as the true scores for X and Y. The exact shape of the function, which in IRT is known as the *test characteristic function*, depends on the items in A as well as the scale chosen for θ. It should thus hold that $\tau_A = g(\theta)$ where g is an (unknown) monotonically increasing function and θ is the same ability as for X and Y.

An important equality follows for the conditional observed-score distributions in the true equating transformations in Equation 13.15. For instance, for the distribution of X given θ it holds that

$$f(x \mid \theta) = f(x \mid g^{-1}(\tau_A)) = f(x \mid \tau_A). \tag{13.21}$$

Similarly, $f(y|\theta) = f(y|\tau_A)$. Thus, whereas θ and the true score on the anchor test are on entirely different scales, the observed-score distributions given these two quantities are always identical.

This fact immediately suggests an alternative to the local method in the preceding section. Instead of using an estimate of θ for each test taker, we could use an estimate of τ_A and, except for estimation error, get the same equating. An obvious estimate of τ_A is the observed score A. The result is a simple approximation of the family of true transformations in Equation 13.15 by

$$\varphi(y;a) = F_{X|a}^{-1}(F_{Y|a}(y)), \quad a = 0, ..., m, \tag{13.22}$$

where m is the length of the anchor test and $F_{X|a}(x)$ and $F_{Y|a}(y)$ are the distribution functions of X and Y given $A = a$. Local equating based on this method is easy to implement; it is just equipercentile equating directly from the conditional distributions of Y to those of X given $A = a$.

It is interesting to compare the use of the different observed-score distributions available in the NEAT design between the two traditional methods and this local method:

1. In chain equating, the equipercentile transformation is derived from four different population distributions, namely, the distributions of X and Y for the populations that take tests X and Y and the distributions of A for the same two populations.
2. In equating with poststratification, the conditional distributions of X and Y given $A = a$ are used to derive the marginal distributions of X and Y for a target population. The equating transformation is applied to these two distributions.
3. The current method of local equating directly uses the conditional distributions of X and Y given $A = a$ to derive the family of equating transformations in Equation 13.22.

The only difference between the previous method of local equating based on maximum likelihood or Bayesian estimation of θ and the use of the anchor test scores $A = a$ as a proxy of θ resides in the estimation or measurement error involved. (I use the term *proxy* instead of *estimate* because, due to scale differences, A is not a good estimate of θ.) These errors have two different consequences. First, for both equatings they lead to a mixing of the conditional distributions in Equation 13.15 that actually should be used. For direct estimation of θ, the mixing is over the distribution of θ given the estimate, $\theta|\widehat{\theta}$. But for Equation 13.22, it is over $\theta \mid A = a$ where $\theta = g^{-1}(\tau_a)$. The former can be expected to be narrower than the latter, which is based on less accurate number-correct scoring. The impact of these mixing distributions, which generally depend on the lengths of X and A as well as the quality of their items, requires further study. But it is undoubtedly less serious than the impact of mixing the conditional distributions on forms X and Y over the entire marginal population distribution $f(\theta)$ in Equations 13.6–13.7, on which the traditional methods are based. Second, in the current local method, the conditional distributions of X and Y given $A = a$ are estimated directly from the sample, whereas in the preceding method they are estimated as the generalized binomial distributions in Equation 13.20. For smaller sample sizes, the former will be less accurate.

Figure 13.3 shows results from the evaluation of the chain-equating, poststratification and local method for a NEAT design in van der Linden and Wiberg

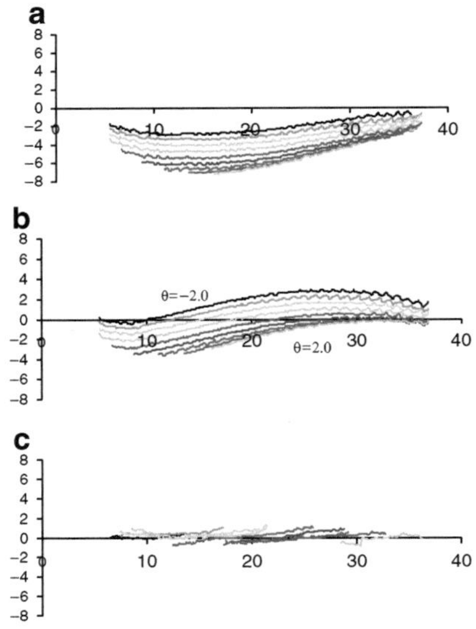

Fig. 13.3 Bias functions for **(a)** chain equating, **(b)** poststratification equating, and **(c)** local equating for the nonequivalent-groups-and-anchor test (NEAT) design for $\theta = -2.0(.5)20$

(in press). The results are for a study with the same setup as for Figure 13.2 but with a 40-item anchor test added to the design. Again, the local method outperformed the two traditional methods. But it had a slightly larger bias than the local method in the preceding section, because of the less favorable mixing of the conditional distributions of X and Y given θ when A is used as a proxy of θ. However, the more accurate the proxy, the narrower the mixing distributions. Hence, as also demonstrated in this study, the bias in the equated scores vanishes with the two main determinants of the reliability of A—the length of the anchor test and the discriminating power of its items. In this respect, the role of the anchor test in the current method is entirely comparable to that of test form Y from which θ is estimated in the preceding method.

For testing programs that are response-model based, Janssen, Magis, San Martin, and Del Pino (2009) presented a version of local equating for the NEAT design with maximum-likelihood estimation of θ from the anchor test instead of the use of A as a proxy for it. The empirical results presented by these authors showed bias functions for this alternative method that are essentially identical to those in Figure 13.2 and better than those in Figure 13.3. Janssen et al. also explained this difference in performance by the fact that maximum-likelihood estimation of θ from A did a better job of approaching the intended conditional distributions of X and Y given θ than the use of number-correct anchor scores.

The study that produced the results in Figure 13.3 did not address the role of sampling error in the estimation of the conditional distributions of X and Y given $A = a$. For small samples, the error will be substantial. A standard approach to small-sample equating for NEAT designs, especially if the main differences between the distributions of the observed scores on forms X and Y are in their first and second moments, is linear equating in the form of Tucker, Levine, or linear chain equating (Kolen & Brennan, 2004, Ch. 4). The use of local methods for linear equating is explored in Wiberg and van der Linden (2009). One of their methods uses the conditional means, $\mu_{X|a}$ and $\mu_{Y|a}$, and standard deviations, $\sigma_{X|a}$ and $\sigma_{Y|a}$, of X and Y given $A = a$ to conduct the equating. The result is the family of transformations

$$x = \varphi(y;a) = \mu_{X|a} + \frac{\sigma_{X|a}}{\sigma_{Y|a}}(y - \mu_{Y|a}), \quad a = 0, ..., m. \tag{13.23}$$

In an empirical evaluation, the method yielded better results than the traditional Tucker, Levine, and linear chain equating methods but also improved on Equation 13.22 because of its reliance only on estimates of the first two moments instead of the full conditional distributions of X and Y given $A = a$.

So far, no explicit smoothing has been applied to any local equating method. The application of smoothing techniques should reduce the impact of sampling error in the estimation of the conditional distributions of X and Y given $A = a$ for the NEAT design to be considerable, especially for the techniques of presmoothing of observed-score distributions proposed in von Davier et al. (2004b, Chapter 3).

13.4.3 $Y = y$ as a Proxy of Ability

The argument for the use of anchor score A as a proxy for θ in the previous section holds equally well for the realized observed score $Y = y$. The score can be assumed to have a true score η that is a function of the same ability θ as the true score on form X; see Equation 13.8–13.9. Again, scale differences between conditioning variables do not matter, and we can just focus on the distributions of X and Y given η instead of θ. As $Y = y$ is an obvious estimate of η, it seems worthwhile exploring the possibilities of local equating based on the conditional distributions of X and Y given $Y = y$ that is, use

$$\varphi(y) = F^{-1}_{X|y}(F_{Y|y}(y)), \quad y = 0, ..., n. \tag{13.24}$$

In an equating study with a single-group design, the distributions of X given $Y = y$ can be estimated directly from the bivariate distribution of X and Y produced by the study. The distributions of Y given y are more difficult to access. In fact, they are only observable for replicated administrations of form Y to the same test takers. However, Wiberg and van der Linden (2009) identified one case for which replications are unnecessary—linear equating conditional on $Y = y$. For this case, the general form of the linear transformation for observed-score equating specifies to

$$x = \varphi(y) = \mu_{X|y} + \frac{\sigma_{X|y}}{\sigma_{Y|y}}(y - \mu_{Y|y}), \quad y = 0, ..., n. \tag{13.25}$$

As classical test theory shows, $\mu_{Y|y} = y$. Hence, the family simplifies to

$$x = \varphi(y) = \mu_{X|y}, \quad y = 0, ..., n. \tag{13.26}$$

For all test takers with score $Y = y$, this local method thus equates the observed scores on Y to their conditional means on X.

In spite of the standard warning against the confusion of equating with regression in the equating literature (e.g., Kolen & Brennan, 2004, Section 2.3), the local linear equating in Equation 13.26 has the same formal structure as the (nonlinear) regression function of Y on X. Actually, however, Equation 13.26 is a family of degenerate mappings with index y, just like the family for IRT true-score equating in Equation 13.18. (In fact, the equating in Equation 13.26 follows directly from Equation 13.18 if we substitute y as proxy for θ.) Although it is thus incorrect to view Equation 13.26 as a direct postulate of the use of the regression function of X on Y for observed-score equating, the formal equivalence between the two is intriguing. Apparently, the fact that we allow for measurement error in X and Y when equating does force us to rethink the relation between equating and regression.

An evaluation of Equation 13.26 showed a favorable bias only for the higher values of y (Wiberg & van der Linden, 2009). Because the responses were simulated under the three-parameter logistic model, the larger bias at the lower values of θ should be interpreted as the effect of guessing for low-ability test takers—a phenomenon known to trouble traditional equipercentile equating as well. This bias problem has to be fixed before practical use of the local method in this section can be recommended.

13.4.4 Proxies Based on Collateral Information

In principle, every variable for which the expected or true scores for the test takers are increasing functions of the θ measured by forms X and Y could be used as a proxy to produce an equating. The best option seems collateral information directly related to the performances by the test takers on X or Y, such as the response times on the items in Y or scores on a earlier related test. However, the use of more general background variables, such as earlier schooling or socioeconomic factors, should be avoided because of the immediate danger of social bias.

Empirical studies with these types of collateral information on θ have not yet been conducted. Of course, different sources of collateral information will yield equatings with different statistical qualities. But the only thing that counts is rigorous evaluation of each of these qualities based on the definitions of equating error in Equations 13.12 and 13.16. These evaluations should help us to identify the best feasible method for an equating problem.

13.5 Concluding Remarks

The role of measurement error has been largely ignored in the equating literature. When I had the opportunity to review two new texts on observed equating that now have become standard references for every specialist and student in this area, I was impressed by their comprehensiveness and technical quality but missed the necessary attention to measurement error. Both reviews ended with the same conclusion: "It is time for test equating to get a firm psychometric footing" (van der Linden, 1997, 2006c).

It is tempting to think of measurement error as "small epsilons to be added to test scores" and to believe that for well-designed tests the only loss involved in ignoring their existence are somewhat less precise equated scores. This chapter shows that this view is incorrect. Equating problems without measurement error are structurally different from problems with error; the score distributions for the former imply single-level modeling; those for the latter hierarchical modeling. Lord's (1980) discussion of observed-score equating for the cases of infallible and fallible measures already revealed some of the differences: Without measurement error equating is automatically equitable and population independent, but with error these features are immediately gone. This chapter has added another difference: Without measurement error the same transformation suffices for any population of test takers, but with error the transformations become ability dependent and we need to look for different transformations for different ability levels.

The statistical consequence of ignoring such structural differences is not "somewhat less precise equated scores" but bias that, under realistic conditions, can become large. This consequence is not unique to equating; it has been well researched and documented in other areas, a prime example being regression with errors in the predictors, which have a long history of study as "errors-in-variables" problems in econometrics.

As the review of the local equating methods above suggests, the main change for equating to allow for measurement error is a shift from equating based on marginal distributions for an assumed population to the conditional distributions given a statistical estimate or a proxy for the ability measured by the tests. In principle, the formal techniques required for distribution estimation, smoothing, and the actual equating, as well as the possible designs for equating studies, remain the same. Thus, in principle, in order to deal with measurement error we do not have to reject a whole history of prolific equating research, only to redirect its application.

Chapter 14
A General Model for IRT Scale Linking and Scale Transformations

Matthias von Davier and Alina A. von Davier

14.1 Introduction

The need for equating arises when two or more tests on the same construct or subject area can yield different scores for the same examinee. The goal of test equating is to allow the scores on different forms of the same tests to be used and interpreted interchangeably. Item response theory (IRT; Hambleton, Swaminathan, & Rogers, 1991; Lord, 1980; Thissen & Wainer, 2001) has provided new ways to approach test equating. Using IRT in the equating process usually also requires some sort of linking procedure to place the IRT parameter estimates on a common scale.

In this chapter we focus on the IRT linking procedures used for data collection designs that involve common items. The data collection designs that use this method are nonequivalent groups with anchor test (NEAT) designs and can have both internal and external anchor tests (see, e.g., Kolen & Brennan, 1995; von Davier, Holland, & Thayer, 2004b).

The NEAT design has two populations of test takers, populations P and Q (P and Q) of test takers and a sample of examinees from each. The sample from P takes test form X, or X.The sample from Q takes test form Y, or Y and both samples take a set of common items, the anchor test V. This design is often used when only one test form can be administered at one test administration because of test security or other practical concerns. The two populations may not be equivalent in that the two samples are not from a common population.

The two test forms X and Y and the anchor V are, in general, not *parallel* test forms, that is, their conditional expectations and error variances for a given examinee will not be identical. More specifically, the anchor test V is usually shorter and less reliable than either X or Y. Angoff (1971/1984) gave advice on

M. von Davier (✉) and A.A. von Davier
Educational Testing Service, Rosedale Rd, Princeton, New Jersey 08541, USA
e-mail: mvondavier@ets.org

A.A. von Davier (ed.), *Statistical Models for Test Equating, Scaling, and Linking*, Statistics for Social and Behavioral Sciences,
DOI 10.1007/978-0-387-98138-3_14,

designing anchor tests. For a comparison of a variety of methods for treating the NEAT design, see Kolen and Brennan (1995); Marco, Petersen, and Stewart (1983b); and Petersen, Marco, and Stewart (1982).

In this chapter we examine the IRT scale transformation and IRT linking methods used in the NEAT design to link X and Y More exactly, we propose a unified approach to the IRT linking methods: mean-sigma and mean-mean, concurrent calibration, fixed-parameters calibration, the Stocking and Lord characteristic-curves approach, and the Haebara characteristic-curves approach (see Kolen & Brennan, 1995, Ch. 6, for a detailed description of these methods). Moreover, we believe that our view of IRT linking can be extended to cover other flavors of IRT scaling and linking procedures.

In our approach, the parameter space is described by all the parameters of the IRT model fitted to the data from both populations in a marginal maximum likelihood framework. Under the usual assumptions for the NEAT design, which are described later, the joint log-likelihood function for this model on the data from both populations can be expressed as the sum of two log-likelihood functions corresponding to each of the two groups of data and parameters.

The main idea in our approach is to view any linking method as a restriction function on the joint parameter space of the instruments to be equated. Once this is understood, rewriting the joint log-likelihood function by including a term for each restriction and an appropriately implemented maximization procedure will accomplish the linking. The maximization is carried out using a vector of Lagrange multipliers (see, e.g., Aitchison & Silvey, 1958; Glas, 1999; von Davier, 2003a).

We will show that the new approach is general enough to cover the usual item response models—the one-parameter logistic (1PL), 2PL, and 3PL models—as well as polytomous, unidimensional IRT models like the generalized partial-credit model.

This new perspective on IRT linking has advantages. First, providing a common framework for all IRT scale linking methods yields a better understanding of the differences between the approaches, which opens paths to more flexible methods of IRT linking. Also, viewing the IRT linking as a restriction function allows us to control the strength of the restriction. For example, the concurrent calibration with fixed item parameters is the most restrictive IRT linking method, as it assumes the equality of all parameters in the anchor test. When such a strong restriction is not appropriate, the proposed method provides alternatives. Moreover, the method provides a family of linking functions that ranges from the most restrictive one, the concurrent calibration with fixed item parameters, to separate calibration (without additional restrictions, i.e., to no linking at all). Finally, the new perspective allows the development of methods to check the IRT linking (such as Lagrange multiplier tests) for appropriateness of different methods. For this, similar principles as developed in Glas (1999, 2006) could be applied to check the invariance of certain parameters or types of parameters.

This chapter, a summarized version of von Davier and von Davier (2007), describes the theoretical framework and derivations of a general approach to IRT linking. It generalizes a linking method implemented and utilized by von Davier

& Yamamoto (2004) to link IRT scales across three student populations. The rest of the chapter is structured as follows. First we introduce our notation and briefly describe the well-known IRT linking methods. Then, we investigate the joint log-likelihood function and the restriction function more formally and for several IRT linking methods. Finally, we discuss the advantages of this perspective on the IRT linking.

14.2 The NEAT Design and IRT Linking

14.2.1 The NEAT Design

The data structure and assumptions needed for the NEAT design are described in von Davier et al. (2004b). Briefly, population *P* yields Sample 1, taking test form X; population *Q* yields Sample 2, taking test form Y. Both samples take anchor test *V*. We denote the matrices of observed item responses to the tests X, V, and Y by *X*, *V* and *Y*. The subscripts *P* and *Q* denote the populations.

The analysis of the NEAT design usually makes the following assumptions:

1. There are two populations of examinees *P* and *Q*, each of which can take one of the tests and the anchor.
2. The two samples are independently and randomly drawn from *P* and *Q*, respectively. In the NEAT design *X* is not observed in population *Q*, and *Y* is not observed in population *P*. To overcome this feature, all linking methods developed for the NEAT design (both observed-score and IRT methods) must make additional assumptions of a type that does not arise in the other linking designs.
3. The tests to be equated, *X* and *Y*, and the anchor *V*, are all unidimensional (i.e., all items measure the same unidimensional construct), carefully constructed tests, in which the local independence assumption holds (Hambleton et al., 1991).

These three assumptions are sufficient for our exposition. We will not impose any constraints on the distributions of *X*, *Y* or *V*, that is, the score distribution will be assumed to be multinomial. Alternatives, such as log-linear models for observed score distributions (Rost & von Davier, 1992, 1995; von Davier, 1994, 2000) and latent skill distributions (Xu & von Davier, 2008) have been discussed and are also used in observed-score equating (von Davier et al., 2004b).

14.2.2 Unidimensional IRT Models

IRT models rely on the assumptions of monotonicity, undimensionality, and local independence (Hambleton et al., 1991). These models express the probability of a response x_{ni} of a given person, n ($n = 1, \ldots, N$), to a given item, i ($i = 1, \ldots, I$), as a function of the person's ability θ_n and a possibly vector valued item parameter, β_i,

$$P_{ni} = P(X = x_{ni}) = f(x_{ni}, \theta_n, \beta_i) \tag{14.1}$$

In the case of the well-known 3PL model (Lord & Novick, 1968), the item parameter is three-dimensional and consists of the slope, the difficulty, and the guessing parameter, $\beta_i^t = (a_i, b_i, c_i)$.The 3PL model, which serves as the standard example of an item response model in this paper, is given by

$$P(x_i = 1|\theta, a_i, b_i, c_i) = c_i + (1 - c_i)\text{logit}^{-1}[a_i(\theta - b_i)], \tag{14.2}$$

with $\text{logit}^{-1}(x) = \exp(x)/(1 + \exp(x))$. However, most results presented here do not depend on the specific choice of the item response model and apply to models for both dichotomous and polytomous data.

14.2.3 IRT Linking

When conducting IRT scale linking in the NEAT design, the parameters of the item response model from different test forms need to be, or need to be brought, on the same IRT scale. IRT models without scale constraints are undetermined: linear transformations of the item, and person parameters do not change the likelihood of observed responses. Therefore, the potentially different scales from separate calibrations can be brought on the same scale in one of the following ways: Assuming that the calibration was carried out separately on the two samples from the two different populations P and Q, two sets of parameter estimates for the anchor test V will be available for examinees in the two groups. These separate parameter estimates of the anchor in the two groups serve as the basis for the scale transformation (mean-mean, mean-sigma methods, or characteristic-curves methods, such as Stocking and Lord or Haebara methods).

As an alternative, the item parameters from X, V (in both populations), and Y can be estimated jointly, coding the items that an examinee did not receive as "not administered," since these outcomes were unobserved and are missing by design. The item parameters are estimated simultaneously, and separate ability distributions are assumed in the two populations, while the parameters of the anchor are assumed to be identical in both populations; this IRT scaling is usually referred to as *concurrent calibration*. Another calibration method is the *fixed-parameters method*. This approach differs from concurrent calibration in that common items whose parameters are known (either from a previous-year calibration or a separate calibration) are anchored or fixed to their known values, often estimates from a previous calibration, during calibration of other forms, or the same common items within a form administered in a different year or in a different population.

By treating the common item parameters as known, they are not estimated, and the item parameters from the unique items are forced onto the same scale as the fixed, common items. This procedure is implemented in IRT calibration using models referred to as multiple-group models with constraints of common items across groups (populations, forms). For more details, see Kolen and Brennan (1995), Stocking and Lord (1983), Haebara (1980), or Hambleton et al. (1991).

14.3 A Lagrangean Approach to IRT Linking

Let the sample size of the group from P that takes (X, V) be denoted by N_P, let the sample size of the group from Q that takes (Y, V) be N_Q and denote $N = N_P + N_Q$. We will use the following notation for the item parameters in the different test forms and populations:

$$\beta_i = \begin{cases} \beta_{X_{Pj}}, & 1 \le i \le J, (1) \\ \beta_{V_{Pl}}, & J+1 \le i \le (J+L), (2) \\ \beta_{V_{Ql}}, & (J+L)+1 \le i \le (J+2L), (3) \\ \beta_{Y_{Qk}}, & (J+2L)+1 \le i \le \mathrm{IP}, \end{cases} \tag{14.3}$$

where $\mathrm{IP} = J + 2L + K$ denotes the total number of items and J, L, and K are the number of the items in the tests X, V, and Y respectively. For example, $\beta_{X_{Pj}}$ denotes the (possible vector-valued) item parameter for item *j* from the set of items from the test X that was taken by the examinees from P. Similarly, $\beta_{V_{Pl}}$ denotes the (possibly vector-valued) item parameter for item *l* from the set of items from the anchor test V that was taken by the examinees from P, and so forth.

The total number of the item parameters (TNIP) is the dimension of the vector of the item parameters times the number of parameters per item. For example, if all items are modeled via the Rasch model, $\mathrm{TNIP} = 1 \times \mathrm{IP}$; for a 2PL model, $\mathrm{TNIP} = 2 \times \mathrm{IP}$; and for the 3PL model, $\mathrm{TNIP} = 3 \times \mathrm{IP}$; For mixtures of item model types in one test, TNIP is the sum of individual item parameter dimensions (1, 2, or 3 for dichotomous items and 2 or more for partial-credit items) over all items.

14.3.1 Separate Calibration

When estimating separately, the item and ability distribution parameters for population P are obtained given data (X, V_P), separately from the item and ability distribution parameters for population Q given data (Y, V_Q). Technically, this can be accomplished by fitting one IRT model to the combined data without assuming that the common items have the same item parameters in both populations.

As mentioned before, the parameter space is described by all the parameters in the IRT model fitted to the data from both populations, in a marginal maximum likelihood framework. Software such as MULTILOG (Thissen, 1991) and PARSCALE (Muraki & Bock, 1991) as well as the more recent *mdltm* (von Davier, 2005) may be used to perform such calibrations.[1]

Let π_P and π_Q denote the parameters used to model the ability distribution. We may think of them as $\pi_{P,Q} = (\mu_{P,Q}, \sigma_{P,Q})$ in the case where we assume normal ability distributions. In somewhat more flexible models, we may assume that the $\pi_{P,Q}$ is a set of multinomial probabilities over quadrature points approximating arbitrary distribution shapes. Hence, the complete parameter space is contained in the (transposed) parameter vector

$$\eta^t = (\beta_{X_P}, \beta_{V_P}, \pi_P, \beta_{Y_Q}, \beta_{V_Q}, \pi_Q), \tag{14.4}$$

Given Assumptions 1 and 2 and the properties of the logit and logarithm functions, we can rewrite the joint log-likelihood function for the IRT model applied to the data from both populations as the sum of the two log-likelihood functions,

$$L(\eta; X, V_P, Y, V_Q) = L(\beta_{X_P}, \beta_{V_P}, \pi_p; X, V_P) + L(\beta_{Y_Q}, \beta_{V_Q}, \pi_Q; Y, V_Q) \tag{14.5}$$

In other words, the two separate models are estimated and the two log-likelihood functions are maximized jointly using marginal maximum likelihood. Now, it is easy to conceive *any* linking function as a restriction function on the parameter space and any linking process as a maximization of Equation 14.5 under the linking restriction. Later we will illustrate in detail how this approach works for each linking method. Next, we illustrate the concurrent calibration method in some detail and then outline how this approach translates to each of the other IRT linking methods: mean-mean, mean-sigma, Stocking and Lord, Haebara, and fixed parameters.

14.3.2 Lagrangean Concurrent Calibration

When estimating concurrently, the item and ability distribution parameters for population P are obtained given data (X, V_P) simultaneously with the item and ability distribution parameters for population Q given data X, V_Q.Technically, two separate ability distributions are estimated and the two log-likelihood

[1]The *mdltm* software is a command line controlled program that runs on various operating systems. Executables can be made available for noncommercial purposes upon request; please contact the first author of this chapter for details.

functions are maximized jointly with certain restrictions on the item parameters, namely

$$\beta_{V_{Pl}} = \beta_{V_{Ql}} \tag{14.6}$$

for $l = 1, \ldots, L$.

Let R denote the L-dimensional restriction function with the components given by

$$R_l(\eta) = k_l(\beta_{V_{Pl}} - \beta_{V_{Ql}}), \tag{14.7}$$

with $k_l = 1$ for active restrictions on item l.

For the 2PL and 3PL, the restrictions may be imposed only on the b parameters and not on the slope and guessing parameters. This can be achieved by first using projections, h, and then imposing the same constraints as before. The projection, say a mapping h would isolate the item difficulty b out of the three-dimensional item parameter in the case of the 3PL, and then apply the restriction function on this parameter only. That is, $b_{Vl} = h(\beta_{Vl})$ to obtain the difficulty, and then use $R_l(\eta) = k_l(h(\beta_{V_{Pl}}) - h(\beta_{V_{Ql}}))$ to impose constraints on the difficulties only.

Hence, the concurrent calibration refers to maximizing Equation 14.5 under the restriction

$$R_l(\eta) = 0. \tag{14.8}$$

This setup, maximizing Equation 14.5 under the restriction Equation 14.8, is used whenever certain item parameters are assumed to be equal across populations, in our case across P and Q.

Given a vector λ of Lagrangean multipliers, the linking process can be viewed as maximizing the modified log-likelihood function

$$\Lambda(\eta,\lambda;X,V_p,Y,V_Q) = L(\beta_{Xp},\beta_{Vp},\pi_P;X,V_P) + L(\beta_{YQ},\beta_{VQ},\pi_Q;Y,V_Q) - \lambda^t R(\eta). \tag{14.9}$$

Note that if we choose $k_l = 0$ for all l the restriction functions, all $R_l(\eta) = k_l(\beta_{V_{Pl}} - \beta_{V_{Ql}})$ vanish. In that case, the β_{V_P} and β_{V_Q} are no longer constrained to be equal; instead of concurrent calibration with equality constraints, maximizing the likelihood simultaneously now yields separate calibrations and allows the item parameters in the anchor test V to differ between P and Q.

The function in Equation 14.9 is then maximized with respect to parameters η and λ.

In concurrent calibration, Equation 14.9 includes a term R_l for each item $l = 1, \ldots, L$ in the anchor test V. This term enables the imposition of equality constraints on the parameters β_{V_P} and β_{V_Q}.

14.3.3 Lagrangean Fixed-Parameters Scale Linkage

In this method, common items whose parameters are known (for example, from a previous administration calibration or a separate calibration) are anchored or fixed to their known estimates, w_l, $l = 1, \ldots L$, during calibration of other forms, or forms with common items in other assessment years or populations. These common item parameters are treated as known and therefore are not estimated; the item parameters from the items that are not common to the forms are forced onto the same scale as the fixed items. This calibration procedure is more restrictive than concurrent calibration.

As before, let now R denote the $2L$-dimensional restriction function with the components given by

$$R(\eta)^t = (R_{Pl}(\eta), R_{Ql}(\eta)). \tag{14.10}$$

where

$$R_{Pl}(\eta) = k_l(\beta_{V_{Pl}} - w_l),$$
$$R_{Ql}(\eta) = k_l(\beta_{V_{Ql}} - w_l), \tag{14.11}$$

and hence the concurrent calibration refers to maximizing Equation 14.9 under the restriction

$$R(\eta) = 0. \tag{14.12}$$

14.3.4 Lagrangean Mean-Mean IRT Scale Linking

If an IRT model fits the data, any linear transformation[2] (with slope A and intercept B) of the θ-scale also fits these data, provided that the item parameters are also transformed (see, e.g., Kolen & Brennan, 1995, pp. 162–167). In the NEAT design, the most straightforward way to transform scales when the parameters were estimated separately is to use the means and standard deviations of the item parameter estimates of the common items for computing the slope and the intercept of the linear transformation. Loyd and Hoover (1980) described the mean-mean method, where the mean of the a-parameter estimates for the common items is used to estimate the slope of the linear transformation. The mean of the b-parameter

---

[2]A more general result holds: All strictly monotone transformations of θ are also permissible. This feature, however, will not be pursued further in this chapter.

estimates of the common items is then used to estimate the intercept of the linear transformation (see Kolen & Brennan, 1995, p. 168).

Lagrange multipliers also may be used to achieve IRT scale linking according to the mean-mean approach. Again, maximizing the modified log-likelihood function Λ given in Equation 14.9 with a different set of restrictions does the trick. For the mean-mean IRT linking, the restriction function is two-dimensional with the components R_a and R_b, $R^t = (R_\mathrm{a}, R_\mathrm{b})$ To match the mean of anchor parameters of population P, define

$$R_a(\eta) = \left(\sum_{l=1}^{L} h_a(\beta_{V_{Ql}}) - A_P \right) \tag{14.13}$$

with a constant term $A_P = \sum h_a(\beta_{V_{Pl}})$, which is not viewed as a function of the β_{VP} (but recomputed at each iteration during maximization) in order to allow unconstrained maximization for P and enforce the mean of β_{VQ} to match this mean in P. As has been explained, h is a projection.

The same is done with the difficulty parameters $b_l = h_b(\beta_l)$:

$$R_b(\eta) = \left(\sum_{l=1}^{L} h_b(\beta_{V_{Ql}}) - B_P \right). \tag{14.14}$$

This new approach to IRT linking includes also a more general approach that handles populations P and Q symmetrically using

$$R_a(\eta) = \left(\sum_{l=1}^{L} h_a(\beta_{V_{Ql}}) - h_a(\beta_{V_{Pl}}) \right) \tag{14.15}$$

with $h_a(\beta_i) = a_i$ and

$$R_b(\eta) = \left(\sum_{l=1}^{L} h_b(\beta_{V_{Ql}}) - h_b(\beta_{V_{Pl}}) \right) \tag{14.16}$$

with $h_b(\beta_i) = b_i$. This avoids the arbitrary choice whether to match P or Q's slope and difficulty means on the anchor test V.

14.3.5 Lagrangean Mean-Var IRT Scale Linking

The mean-var IRT scale linkage (Marco, 1977) obviously can be implemented in the same way, with only a slight difference in the restrictions used. The means and the standard deviations of the b-parameters are used to estimate the slope and the intercept of the linear transformation.

Again, a two-dimensional restriction function with components R_a and R_b is needed. In order to match the mean and variance of the anchor test's difficulty parameter in population P, we define

$$R_a(\eta) = \left(\sum_{l=1}^{L} h_a(\beta_{V_{Ql}}) - B_P \right) \tag{14.17}$$

with a constant term $B_P = \sum h_a(\beta_{V_{Pl}})$, which again is not viewed as a function of the β_{V_P}. The same is done with the squared difficulties, $b_l^2 = h_b^2(\beta_l)$,

$$R_b(\eta) = \left(\sum_{l=1}^{L} h_b^2(\beta_{V_{Ql}}) - B_P^2 \right) \tag{14.18}$$

where $B_P^2 = \sum h_b^2(\beta_{V_{Pl}})$.

As before, a more general approach handles populations P and Q symmetrically using

$$R_a(\eta) = \left(\sum_{l=1}^{L} h_b(\beta_{V_{Ql}}) - \sum_{l=1}^{L} h_b(\beta_{V_{Pl}}) \right) \tag{14.19}$$

with $h_b(\beta_i) = b_i$ and

$$R_b(\eta) = \left(\sum_{l=1}^{L} h_b^2(\beta_{V_{Ql}}) - \sum_{l=1}^{L} h_b^2(\beta_{V_{Pl}}) \right) \tag{14.20}$$

with $h_b^2(\beta_i) = b_i^2$.

14.3.6 Lagrangean Stocking and Lord Scale Linkage

Characteristic-curves transformation methods were proposed (Haebara, 1980; Stocking & Lord, 1983) in order to avoid some issues related to the mean-mean and mean-var approaches. For the mean-mean and mean-var approaches, various combinations of the item parameter estimates produce almost identical item-characteristic curves over the range of ability at which most examinees score.

The Stocking and Lord (1983) IRT scale linkage finds parameters for the linear transformation of item parameters in one population (say, Q) that matches the test characteristic function of the anchor in the reference population (say, P). The Stocking and Lord transformation finds a linear transformation (a slope A and an intercept B) of the item parameters—difficulties and slopes—in one population based on a matching of test characteristic curves. Expressing this in the marginal maximum likelihood framework yields

$$(A,B) = \min\left[\sum_{g=1}^{G} \pi_g^* \left(\sum_{l=1}^{L} (p(\theta_g, \beta_{VPl}) - p(\theta_g, B + A\beta_{VQl}))\right)^2\right], \tag{14.21}$$

where the weights π_g^* of the quadrature points θ_g for $g = 1, \ldots,$ G. are given by

$$\pi_g^* = \frac{n_{Pg}\pi_{Pg} + n_{Qg}\pi_{Qg}}{n_{Pg} + n_{Qg}}. \tag{14.22}$$

We propose using a method employing the same rationale as the Stocking and Lord (1983) approach, namely optimizing the match of the test characteristic curves between the anchors V_P and V_Q. In the proposed framework, the primitive of these functions, which is the criterion to be minimized to match the two test characteristic functions as closely as possible, is defined as

$$R^{SL}(\eta) = \left[\sum_{g=1}^{G} \pi_g^* \left(\sum_{l=1}^{L} (p(\theta_g, \beta_{VPl}) - p(\theta_g, \beta_{VQl}))\right)^2\right]. \tag{14.23}$$

In order to minimize Equation 14.23, we implement the Lagrangean in such a way that

$$\Lambda(\eta, \lambda) = L(X, V_P) + L(Y, V_Q) - \lambda \mathrm{J}_{R^{SL}}(\eta), \tag{14.24}$$

or, more explicitly,

$$\Lambda(\eta, \lambda) = L(X, V_P) + L(Y, V_Q) - \lambda_P^T \mathrm{J}_{P,R^{SL}}(\eta) - \lambda_Q^T \mathrm{J}_{Q,R^{SL}}(\eta). \tag{14.25}$$

The components of interest of the Jacobian $\mathrm{J}_{R^{SL}}(\eta)$ are defined by components for the anchor item parameters in P,

$$\frac{\partial R^{SL}(\eta)}{\partial \beta_{i,P}} = \sum_{g=1}^{G} \pi_g^* \frac{\partial p(\theta_g, \beta_{VPi})}{\partial \beta_{iVP}} 2\left[\sum_{l=1}^{L} (p(\theta_g, \beta_{VPl}) - p(\theta_g, \beta_{VQl}))\right], \tag{14.26}$$

and for the components representing the item parameters in Q we find

$$\frac{\partial R^{SL}(\eta)}{\partial \beta_{i,Q}} = -\sum_{g=1}^{G} \pi_g^* \frac{\partial p(\theta_g, \beta_{VQi})}{\partial \beta_{iVP}} 2\left[\sum_{l=1}^{L} (p(\theta_g, \beta_{VPl}) - p(\theta_g, \beta_{VQl}))\right] \tag{14.27}$$

because of the negative sign of all $\beta_{\bullet,Q}$ terms. Let $W \in \{P, Q\}$ denote that the following exposition applies to both P and Q. The derivatives in the equations above actually represent vector-valued derivatives if $\beta_{i,W}$ is vector valued. For example, we have

$$\frac{\partial R^{SL}(\eta)}{\partial \beta_{i,W}} = \left(\frac{\partial R^{SL}(\eta)}{\partial a_{i,W}}, \frac{\partial R^{SL}(\eta)}{\partial b_{i,W}}, \frac{\partial R^{SL}(\eta)}{\partial c_{i,W}} \right)$$

in the case of the 3PL model, where W stands for either P and Q.

By maximizing Equation 14.19 we will find the transformation of the difficulties and the slopes in one population based on matching test characteristics. Note that in our approach this transformation does not need to be linear (although it will be linear if the model fits the data).

14.3.7 Lagrangean Haebera Scale Linkage

Haebara (1980) expressed the differences between the characteristic curves as the sum of the squared differences between the item characteristic functions for each item over the common items for examinees of a particular ability θ_n. The Haebara method is more restrictive than the Stocking and Lord (1983) method because the restrictions take place at the item level (i.e., for each item), whereas the Stocking and Lord approach poses a global restriction at the test level. The slope and the intercept of the linear transformation can be found by minimizing the expression on the right-hand side of Equation 14.28:

$$(A, B) = \min \left[\sum_{g=1}^{G} \pi_g^* \sum_{l=1}^{L} \left(p(\theta_g, \beta_{VPl}) - p(\theta_g, B + A\beta_{VQl}) \right)^2 \right], \tag{14.28}$$

(see, e.g., Kolen & Brennan, 1995, p. 170).

The algorithm we are proposing is similar to the one described previously for the Stocking and Lord scale linking; the only difference (from the computational point of view) is in the form of the restriction function:

$$R^H(\eta) = \left[\sum_{g=1}^{G} \pi_g^* \sum_{l=1}^{L} \left(p(\theta_g, \beta_{VPl}) - p(\theta_g, \beta_{VQl}) \right)^2 \right] \tag{14.29}$$

As before, in order to minimize Equation 14.29, we implement the Lagrangeans in such a way that

$$\Lambda(\eta, \lambda) = L(X, V_P) + L(Y, V_Q) - \lambda J_{R^H}(\eta), \tag{14.30}$$

or, more explicitly,

$$\Lambda(\eta,\lambda) = L(X,V_P) + L(Y,V_Q) - \lambda_P^T \mathrm{J}_{PR^H}(\eta) - \lambda_Q^T \mathrm{J}_{QR^H}(\eta). \tag{14.31}$$

The components of interest of the Jacobian $\mathrm{J}_{R^H}(\eta)$ are

$$\frac{\partial R^H(\eta)}{\partial \beta_{lP}}, \frac{\partial R^H(\eta)}{\partial \beta_{lQ}}. \tag{14.32}$$

Again, the partial derivatives may be vector valued for each $\beta_{i,P|Q}$, so that the dimension of the restriction is approximately $2L$ times average number of item parameter dimensions, 3 if only the 3PL model is used but maybe higher when generalized partial-credit items or other polytomous item response models are present.

14.4 An Illustration of Concurrent Calibration

The illustration reuses data from a pilot language test that was described in detail by von Davier (2005), where the data were analyzed using diagnostic models as well as IRT models. For the selection of models tested, von Davier (2005) found that the mixed 2PL, generalized partial-credit model fits the data best among the models tested in this study. For illustration of some of the concepts outlined in this chapter, we reproduce only the slopes and difficulties of the dichotomous items, so that the tables of this example will consist of subset items, all with two response categories. Items 11, 25, and 38 were items with a polytomous response format. They were part of the calibration but are not reproduced here in order to keep the tables easy to read and to allow comparisons of constraints based on one slope and one difficulty parameter only.

The data came from different subsamples, each student receiving an identification code number that included information about the testing site. For the example presented here, students were split into two subsamples comprising of identification codes lower than 3,000 and equal to or higher than 3,000. This produced two subsamples that represented similar populations such as the ones observed when data are collected over 2 days of test administration, a common feature of large-scale testing programs. In our example, the data split in such a way produced two subsamples that may differ slightly in average ability, although not expected to demonstrate systematic differences in response rates. The first subsample, from population P, consists of $N_P = 1{,}463$, and the subsample that constitutes population Q consists of $N_Q = 1{,}257$ students. All item calibrations were performed using the *mdltm* software (von Davier, 2005), which incorporates standard ways of constraining the average of item parameters, or the mean and variance of the ability distribution using parameter adjustments in the maximization methods employed, in order to remove the indeterminacy of the IRT scale. More specifically, the estimates of item difficulties and slopes from the current iteration of the maximization procedure are adjusted either to match certain constants or to match the current estimate of the mean and variance of the ability distribution. Then, maximization continues in the following iteration. These steps, or steps equivalent to these, correspond to Equations 14.13 and 14.14 and are necessary to remove the indeterminacy (invariance under linear transformations) of the IRT scale.[3]

For the second calibration in this example, equality constraints across populations were used to link the scales across multiple groups. The equality constraints of item difficulties and slope parameters across two or more populations in a multiple-group IRT model, as shown in the example below, are implemented in *mdltm* in a way that is equivalent to the Lagrangean multiplier approach presented in Section 14.3.3. and 14.3.4.

Table 14.1 shows the item parameter estimates in these two subsamples for a multiple-group, 2PL IRT model with the same set of constraints on the mean of item difficulties and slopes in both populations.

Table 14.2 shows item parameter estimates of a concurrent calibration that sets equality constraints only on a subset of the items, in this example imposing equality of item parameters on the first half, or 19 items. This is, as outlined above, a form of IRT scale linkage that involves setting equality constraints on subsets of items and allowing unique parameters for other items across the groups. If all items were assumed to have the same parameters, this would represent a concurrent calibration with complete equality of all item parameters (see the relevant subsections in Section 14.3).

The ability distributions in the two different calibrations are given in Table 14.3. The constraints on the average difficulty and slope parameters were chosen to match 0.0 for the average difficulty and 1.0 for the average slope. This did not change overall results, because IRT scales are invariant under linear transformations.

Table 14.3 shows that the means and variances of the ability distributions in the two different conditions are comparable. The constraints used in Condition A are weaker than in Condition B. The number of constraints set in Condition B is 41 (19 slopes + 18 dichotomous difficulties + 4 thresholds for the five-category Item 11[4]) and amounts effectively to a reduction of free parameters for the two-group model to be estimated from 170 in Condition A to 129 in Condition B.

The fit of the models estimated in the two conditions is comparable, the log likelihood is $L_a = -56994.954$ (BIC$_a$ = 115334.33) for Condition A and $L_a = -57018.37$ (BIC$_b$=115056.93) for Condition B. Taking the reduction of estimated parameters into account, the smaller Bayesian information criterion

[3]An alternative to procedures relying on these averages is to remove the indeterminacy by setting one item difficulty and the slope of that item to prespecified constants, and fix these values for that item without updating in the maximization.

[4]The polytomous items are not shown in the tables but were part of the data, with mixed item format in both calibrations.

Table 14.1 Multiple Group Calibration in Two Populations, Separately Calibrated

Item	Mean slopes		Mean difficulties	
	Pop. *P*	Pop. *Q*	Pop. *P*	Pop. *Q*
1	0.789	0.867	−0.345	−0.500
2	0.976	0.893	−0.042	0.190
3	1.222	1.503	0.603	0.593
4	1.304	1.405	0.670	0.759
5	0.660	0.770	−0.512	−0.461
6	1.042	1.059	0.710	0.584
7	0.701	0.678	−0.039	−0.113
8	1.672	1.471	0.152	0.351
9	0.373	0.418	0.820	0.749
10	0.830	0.838	−0.804	−0.907
12	1.132	0.872	0.635	0.845
13	2.270	1.787	2.740	2.604
14	0.581	0.530	0.329	0.383
15	1.091	1.243	−0.245	−0.467
16	1.057	0.900	−1.262	−1.052
17	0.751	0.912	−0.919	−1.042
18	1.449	1.670	−1.158	−1.365
19	1.365	1.305	2.021	2.034
20	2.011	1.592	1.937	2.212
21	0.815	0.779	0.328	0.342
22	1.234	1.598	0.850	0.872
23	1.248	1.231	0.329	0.063
24	1.019	1.042	0.301	0.124
26	0.886	0.930	−0.576	−0.550
27	0.979	0.842	−0.494	−0.394
28	0.853	0.930	0.627	0.515
29	0.563	0.609	0.433	0.269
30	1.845	1.768	0.331	0.614
31	0.478	0.530	−0.839	−0.961
32	1.036	1.199	−0.367	−0.468
33	0.628	0.588	0.013	0.307
34	0.645	0.600	0.381	0.606
35	0.914	0.886	−0.590	−0.523
36	0.686	0.904	1.291	0.967
37	0.661	0.504	−0.941	−0.862

(Schwarz, 1978) for Condition B indicates that the model with 19 items constrained to have equal item parameters across groups fits the data relatively better in terms of balancing parsimony and model-data fit.

14.5 Discussion

This chapter presents a new perspective on IRT linking. We introduce a unified approach to IRT linking, emphasizing the similarities between different methods. We show that IRT linking might consist of a family of IRT linking functions, where

Table 14.2 Concurrent Calibration With First 19 Items Constrained to Same Slopes and Difficulties in Both Populations

Item	Slopes		Difficulties	
	Pop. *P*	Pop. *Q*	Pop. *P*	Pop. *Q*
1	0.833	0.833	−0.423	−0.423
2	0.929	0.929	0.075	0.075
3	1.349	1.349	0.588	0.588
4	1.347	1.347	0.711	0.711
5	0.709	0.709	−0.491	−0.491
6	1.059	1.059	0.648	0.648
7	0.694	0.694	−0.073	−0.073
8	1.564	1.564	0.259	0.259
9	0.397	0.397	0.784	0.784
10	0.838	0.838	−0.853	−0.853
12	0.995	0.995	0.750	0.750
13	1.997	1.997	2.669	2.669
14	0.555	0.555	0.359	0.359
15	1.170	1.170	−0.354	−0.354
16	0.979	0.979	−1.153	−1.153
17	0.828	0.828	−0.981	−0.981
18	1.554	1.554	−1.256	−1.256
19	1.338	1.338	2.031	2.031
20	1.993	1.602	1.946	2.206
21	0.821	0.779	0.332	0.338
22	1.241	1.603	0.858	0.865
23	1.256	1.227	0.336	0.058
24	1.023	1.045	0.308	0.118
26	0.894	0.927	−0.574	−0.552
27	0.985	0.843	−0.489	−0.398
28	0.861	0.928	0.631	0.512
29	0.566	0.609	0.436	0.267
30	1.848	1.768	0.343	0.606
31	0.485	0.527	−0.842	−0.961
32	1.046	1.196	−0.365	−0.472
33	0.633	0.588	0.016	0.304
34	0.651	0.601	0.383	0.603
35	0.923	0.884	−0.587	−0.526
36	0.691	0.900	1.295	0.963
37	0.667	0.505	−0.940	−0.865

Table 14.3 Comparison of Mean and Variance Estimates for the Ability Parameter Across the Concurrent Calibration With 19 Items Constrained and the Mean-Mean Linkage Constraining Item Parameters

Population	Mean	Standard deviation
A. Constraints on mean of item difficulties (0.0) and slopes (1.0)		
P	1.041	1.269
Q	0.898	1.369
B. Equality constraints on first 19 items		
P	1.028	1.260
Q	0.904	1.371

restrictions can be turned on or off, according to what the data suggest. Moreover, this new approach allows both generalizations and exactly matching implementations of the existing methods, as the existing IRT linking methods are included as special cases in this new family of IRT linking functions.

We believe that this approach will allow the development of statistical tests (such as Lagrange multiplier tests) for checking the appropriateness of different IRT linking methods (see Glas, 1999, for a similar approach used for investigating nested IRT models). Such a test would allow checking whether lifting certain restrictions will yield a significant improvement in model-data fit, for example in a case where Lagrangean concurrent calibration is used for all anchor items in a vertical linkage and a certain set of items exposes parameter drift over time.

This approach to IRT linking can be easily viewed in a Markov chain Monte Carlo (MCMC) framework, where, by specifying appropriate prior distributions, the estimation of the modified likelihood functions is straightforward. At the same time, the view of any linking function as a restriction function implies a larger flexibility in the linking process: When dealing with vertical linking, this method can incorporate the modeling of growth, possibly expressed as a hierarchical structure of the item parameters in the anchor.

Such a hierarchical structure was proposed by Patz, Yao, Chia, Lewis, and Hoskens (2003), who used the MCMC estimation method. The hierarchical approach Patz et al. proposed is "a more general version of concurrent estimation of the unidimensional IRT model" (p. 40), and their motivation has similarities with ours: to unify the two most commonly used linking methods for vertical equating, the very restrictive concurrent calibration method and separate calibration followed by a test characteristic-curves linking.

If we recast this hierarchical approach of the proficiencies across grades into a hierarchical structure of the (common) item difficulties, a short summary of the Patz et al. (2003) approach (slightly generalized) in our notation is

$$R_l(\eta) = k_l(h(\beta_{V_{Pl}}) - f(h(\beta_{Q_{Pl}}))), \tag{14.33}$$

where $k_l = 1$ for active restrictions on item l, R_l denotes the component l of the restriction function, h is the projection described before, and f is a function of the common item parameters of the old administration (or previous grade). In order to obtain the hierarchical structure at the level of the difficulties of the common items, we consider

$$h(\beta_{V_{Pl}}) = b_{V_{Pl}}.$$

Following the approach of Patz et al. (2003), the relationship between the difficulty of the item parameters across grades can be expressed as a quadratic function,

$$f(h(\beta_{Q_{Pl}})) = f(b_{Q_{Pl}}) = \alpha b_{Q_{Pl}}^2 + \gamma b_{Q_{Pl}} + \delta, \tag{14.34}$$

where α, γ, δ are additional parameters of the model that need to be estimated. Furthermore, the modified likelihood function, with a restriction function described in Equation 14.33, can be maximized using the Lagrange multipliers in the same way as explained for the other linking methods. Note that from a computational point of view, this is only a slight generalization of the restriction functions described for the mean-mean and mean-var linking methods.

Obviously, additional investigations are necessary in order to insure that the model is identified and to insure the convergence of the maximization algorithm. Although here we propose an analytical approach and will try to use an expectation-maximization algorithm, a MCMC estimation method would be straightforward to implement.

Moreover, the approach presented in this paper may easily be extended to multidimensional IRT models, at least for simple-structure, multiscale IRT models (like the one used in the National Assessment of Educational Progress and other large-scale assessments). There is no additional formal work necessary, and the method proposed in this report can be readily applied. Patz et al. (2003) also investigated multidimensional IRT models for vertical linking and used the MCMC estimation method. However, implementing and maximizing modified likelihood functions under such restrictions using analytical methods are of interest for future research.

Longitudinal studies also may benefit from these two approaches: one that assumes a hierarchical structure in the item parameters of the anchor and one that assumes a multidimensionality of the proficiencies (or of the common item difficulties) across school grades. This flexibility also may be a desirable feature in educational large-scale assessments, where in some instances it is necessary to relax the restriction of equality of all item parameters. In conclusion, this new approach is very promising for assessment programs that use IRT linking.

Author Note: Any opinions expressed in this chapter are those of the author and not necessarily of Educational Testing Service.

Chapter 15
Linking With Nonparametric IRT Models

Xueli Xu, Jeff A. Douglas, and Young-Sun Lee

15.1 Introduction

In educational testing, it is a common practice to produce test forms under a nonequivalent groups with anchor test (NEAT) design. In this design, the two test forms share a certain number of common items, while the populations who take the test forms might not be equivalent to each other. Test linking is conducted to establish the equivalency of ability scales from separate item response theory (IRT) calibrations of two test forms. Among existing linking methods, two approaches are related to the study in this paper: IRT model-based linking (Loyd & Hoover, 1980; Marco, 1977; Stocking & Lord, 1983) and equipercentile linking (Kolen & Brennan, 1995; von Davier, Holland, & Thayer, 2004b).

From the viewpoint of IRT models, the necessity of linking is embedded in the models themselves. That is, the linear indeterminancy of ability requires a linear transformation to ensure the equivalency between the two test forms when separately calibrated. If a three-parameter logistic (3PL) model

$$P(\theta; a, b, c) = c + \frac{1 - c}{1 + exp(-a(\theta - b))} \tag{15.1}$$

is used in item calibration, then $P(A\theta + B; a/A, Ab + B, c)$ remains the same value as $P(\theta; a, b, c)$ by an appropriate linear transformation. Thus, the linear transformation is

X. Xu (✉)
Educational Testing Service, Princeton, Rosedale Rd, Princeton, NJ 08541, USA
e-mail: xxu@ets.org

J.A. Douglas
101 Illini Hall, 725 S. Wright St, Champaign, IL 61820, USA
e-mail: jeffdoug@uiuc.edu

Y.-S. Lee
Teachers College, Columbia University, 525 W.120th St, New York, NY 10027, USA
e-mail: yslee@tc.columbia.edu

A.A. von Davier (ed.), *Statistical Models for Test Equating, Scaling, and Linking*, Statistics for Social and Behavioral Sciences,
DOI 10.1007/978-0-387-98138-3_15,

used to maintain the item characteristic curves (ICCs) of common items. However, the linear transformation might not be appropriate if the parametric form is incorrect, or if the difference between ability distributions involves something more than a location and scale change. When assuming that the target score distributions from the two test forms are equivalent when the common-item score is held constant, this issue has been addressed by the equipercentile linking. This method is implemented by transforming raw scores from one test to the scale of raw scores of another test. Obviously, this method is model independent. However, the assumption of equivalence is likely to fail when the two groups differ substantially in ability, age, or other demographic information (Liou, 1998).

An alternative to these two approaches (IRT model-based linking and equipercentile linking) is fitting a more flexible model to the data and conducting linking by using nonparametrically estimated items. Currently, no methods for linking are available when using nonparametrically estimated IRT models. This is a serious practical limitation. These flexible nonparametric models will prove most useful when no single parametric family fits the entire set of ICCs well, and in situations like this, nonparametric methods of linking will be required. Our aim is to make such methods available so that nonparametrically estimated models can be considered to be practical alternatives for operational use.

15.2 Estimating the ICCs Nonparametrically

Methods of nonparametric ICC estimation include kernel smoothing with a selected scale for the latent trait (Douglas, 1997; Ramsay, 1991), isotonic regression (Lee, 2002), monotone splines (Ramsay & Abrahamowicz, 1989), penalized maximum likelihood estimation (Rossi, Wang, & Ramsay, 2002), as well as several others. For the linking methods to be presented later, most of the nonparametric estimation methods will apply. However, due to the need to compute the inverse function of an ICC, monotone methods are preferred. In this paper, we use kernel smoothing to obtain the initial estimates of ICCs and then smooth the estimates once again using a B-spline smoother constrained to be monotone. First we review kernel smoothing and constrained B-spline smoothing.

15.2.1 Kernel Smoothing

Suppose N examinees (i = 1,2,. . ., N) are randomly sampled and take a test of length n (j = 1,2,. . .. n). The kernel smoothed estimate of the ICC of item j, $P_j(\theta)$, is the weighted average of the response vector $\{Y_j\} = \{Y_{1j}, \ldots, Y_{Nj}\}$,

$$P_j(\theta) = \sum_{i=1}^{N} w_i Y_{ij}, \tag{15.2}$$

where the weights w_i of examinee i are defined in a certain way so that they are nonnegative and reach a maximum when $\theta = \theta_i$ and will approach or equal zero as $|\theta - \theta_i|$ increases. In order to keep $P_j(\theta)$ within [0,1], the weights should, at the same time, satisfy two conditions: $w_i \geqslant 0$ and $\sum_i w_i = 1$. Thus, it is preferable to use nonnegative kernel functions and Nadaraya-Watson weights (Nadaraya, 1964; Watson, 1964):

$$w_i = \frac{K(\frac{\theta - \theta_i}{h})}{\sum_i K(\frac{\theta - \theta_i}{h})}, \tag{15.3}$$

where h is a smoothing parameter, θ is a grid point along a desired latent scale, θ_i is the ability of examinee i, and $K(\cdot)$ is a kernel function.

The kernel smoothing estimator of $P_j(\theta)$ is consistent when θ_i can be estimated without error. However, the latent trait values of θ_i are not observable. The Nadaraya-Watson weights still can be used after substituting θ_i for true θ_i. A common and appropriate way to estimate θ_i is to transform the ranked raw scores to the corresponding quantiles of the chosen latent ability distribution, which is usually on a standard uniform U(0,1) scale. This leads to the kernel smoothed estimate

$$P_j(\theta) = \frac{\sum_{i=1}^{N} K(\frac{\theta - \hat{\theta}_i}{h}) Y_{ij}}{\sum_{i=1}^{N} K(\frac{\theta - \hat{\theta}_i}{h})}, \tag{15.4}$$

proposed by Ramsay (1991) and implemented in *TestGraf* (Ramsay, 2001). The consistency of this estimate was proved by Douglas (1997).

In kernel smoothing, the bandwidth h is used to control the balance between the bias and variance of estimation. At this point, there is no theorem on an optimal bandwidth for ICC estimation. However, we can use results from simpler models where the covariate is measured without error as a guideline. For example, Ramsay (1991) suggested that $h = N^{-1/5}$ works well when using a Gaussian kernel.

15.2.2 Constrained B-spline Smoothing

A simple but effective monotone smoothing method using splines was proposed to solve the nonparametric regression problem (He & Shi, 1998). They proposed a method based on the constrained least absolute deviation in the space of B-spline functions. The idea of this method is to characterize the monotonicity by linear constraints as well as to solve the least absolute deviation efficiently via linear programming (He & Shi, 1998). Suppose n pairs of observations (x_i, y_i) are used to estimate the nondecreasing regression curve $g(x)$. The model to be estimated is

$$y_i = g(x_i) + u_i, \quad i = 1, \ldots, n \tag{15.5}$$

where u_i is random error. Assume that $g(x)$ is uniformly continuous and has a second-order derivative. Then the function g and its first-order derivative function g' can be approximated adequately by B-splines and their derivatives. Assuming $x \in [a, b]$, letting the knots t_s be selected as $a = t_1 < t_2, \ldots, < t_{k_n} = b$; He and Shi (1998) chose to use quadratic B-splines with degree of 2. Let $B(x) = (B_1(x), B_2(x), \ldots, B_Q(x))^T$ be the normalized B-splines based on the knots t_s, where $Q = k_n + p$, with $p + 1$ being the order of the B-spline. The estimate of $g(x)$, denoted by $g_n(x) = B(x)^T \hat{\alpha}$ for $\hat{\alpha} \in \mathbf{R}^Q$, is obtained by minimizing

$$\sum_{i=1}^{n} |y_i - B(x_i)^T \alpha|, \tag{15.6}$$

subject to the linear constraint to ensure monotonicity,

$$B'(t_s)^T \alpha > 0 \tag{15.7}$$

where $s = 1, \ldots, k_n$ and is subject to other linear constraints, such as those for the boundary points. Here, $B'(\cdot)$ is a vector of the first derivative functions of $B(\cdot)$. This technique is implemented by an R function *SCOBS* (He & Ng, 1998). The consistency of function estimation and effectiveness of this method have been explored in several papers (He & Shi, 1998; Koenker, Ng, & Portnoy, 1994).

Though this constrained B-spline method cannot be used directly to estimate nonparametric IRT models for binary responses, it can be used as a postsmoother after a nonmonotone method such as kernel smoothing is used to estimate ICCs. In particular, we treat the kernel smoothed estimate $P_j(\theta_m)$ and θ_m as a pair of observations without error, in which θ_m is a grid point on a desired scale.

15.3 Nonparametric IRT Linking

Nonparametrically estimated ICCs provide us not only with more flexible forms to fit the data but also a platform to conduct linking. Two approaches are proposed to conduct linking under nonparametric IRT models. One of them conducts linking on a uniform U(0,1) scale, the other on a normal N(0,1) scale. These two approaches are introduced in the following sections.

15.3.1 Constrained Spline Linking on a U(0,1) Scale

Let η be a point in the sample space of a latent variable and $P(\eta)$ be the probability of giving a correct answer conditional on η. Let F_1 and F_2 be the cumulative distribution functions of two nonequivalent testing populations, with $F_1(\eta) = \theta_1$ and $F_2(\eta) = \theta_2$ being the correspondence in different populations. As mentioned in the introduction to the kernel smoothing method, the nonparametric calibration process implicitly transforms η from its original scale to a U(0,1) scale through the cumulative distribution function. For illustration, Equations 15.8 and 15.9 describe the process of calibration with respect to F_1 and F_2, respectively.

$$P(\eta) = P(F_1^{-1}(\theta_1)) = P_1(\theta_1) \tag{15.8}$$

$$P(\eta) = P(F_2^{-1}(\theta_2)) = P_2(\theta_2). \tag{15.9}$$

Thus, we in fact put the latent variable η on a U(0,1) scale relative to the different groups. This will lead to the "pseudo difference" expressed in ICCs P_1 and P_2. Linking means finding the transformation

$$\theta_2 = F_2 \circ F_1^{-1}(\theta_1) = P_2^{-1} \circ P_1(\theta_1) = g(\theta_1) \tag{15.10}$$

on the U(0,1) scale. Based on the fact that $\hat{P}_1(\theta)$and $\hat{P}_2(\theta)$are consistent estimates of $P_1(\theta)$and $P_2(\theta)$(Douglas, 1997), we can obtain an estimate of the linking function $g(\theta)$ by minimizing the loss function:

$$\int \sum_{j \in common} |\hat{g}(\theta) - \hat{P}_{2j}^{-1} \circ \hat{P}_{1j}(\theta)| d\theta, \tag{15.11}$$

where $P_{1j}(\theta)$ is the estimate of ICC for item j and Group 1, $P_{2j}(\theta)$ for item j and Group 2, and the summation is taken over all the common items in the two test forms. In our application, $\hat{P}_{2j}^{-1} \circ \hat{P}_1 j(\theta)$ is taken as an observation without error. The estimate $\hat{g}(\theta)$ is obtained as the best solution in the span of a family of constrained B-splines. One approximates $\hat{g}(\theta)$ by $\sum_{m=1}^{M} \beta_m B_m(\theta)$, subject to

$$\beta_m B'_m(\theta) > 0,$$

$$g'(\theta) > 0,$$

$$g(0) = 0,$$

$$g(1) = 1,$$

where $B'_m(\cdot)$ and $g'(\cdot)$ are first derivatives of $B_m(\cdot)$ and $g(\cdot)$ defined earlier.

The additional constraints and possible penalty functions make it difficult to derive an explicit standard error of the linking function. However, the bootstrap method can be used to obtain pointwise estimates of the standard error.

15.3.2 Linear Linking on a N(0,1) Scale

It is well known that the linear linking is appropriate for the logistic and the probit IRT models with normally distributed latent traits. Even though the linking function in the nonparametric setting need not be constrained to be linear, linear linking on a N(0,1) scale is still possible when using nonparametrically estimated ICCs. Under a nonparametric IRT framework, we can change the scale of the latent variable if desired. To illustrate this issue, we revisit Equations 15.8 and 15.9 and transform the U(0,1) scale to a N(0,1) scale by inserting the cumulative distribution function of a standard normal random variable, denoted by Φ:

$$P(\eta) = P_1(\theta_1) = P_1(\Phi(\theta_{11})) \tag{15.12}$$

$$P(\eta) = P_2(\theta_2) = P_2(\Phi(\theta_{21})). \tag{15.13}$$

Thus, θ_{11} and θ_{21} are now on a N(0,1) scale. The linear linking is done by finding A and B to minimize the loss function:

$$\int \sum_{j \in (common)} [\theta_i - A\Phi^{-1} \circ P_{2j}{}^{-1} \circ P_{1j} \circ \Phi(\theta_i) - B]^2 d\theta \tag{15.14}$$

where $P_{1j}(\cdot)$ and $P_{2j}(\cdot)$ are the consistent estimates of $P_{1j}(\cdot)$ and $P_{2j}(\cdot)$ for item j in common item set, respectively.

15.4 Simulation Study

15.4.1 Design

In our simulation study, two parallel test forms and four pairs of populations were selected to study the behaviors of the proposed approaches. Each test form contained 30 common items and 10 unique items. The items were characterized by a 2PL model. The parameter a is generated from U(0.75,2.5) and the parameter b is generated from a N(0,1). These two test forms are denoted as form 1 and form 2. The four pairs of populations in this study are:

- N(0,1) vs. N(0.25,1)
- truncated normal N(0,1)I[−2,2] vs. U(−2,2)
- Beta(1,1) vs. Beta(1.5,0.5)
- Beta(1,2) vs. Beta(2,1)

Their corresponding density functions are shown in Figure 15.1.

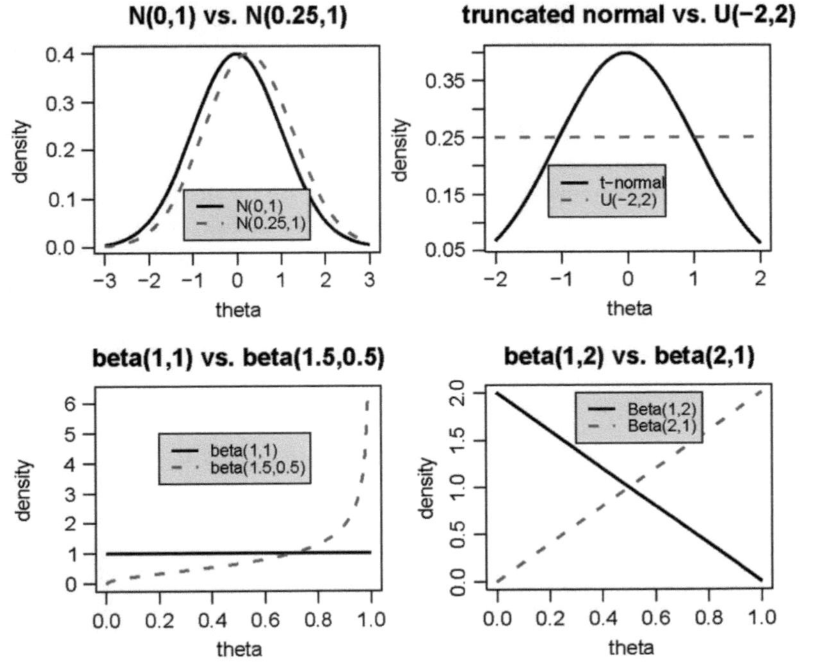

Fig. 15.1 Four pairs of comparison

Figure 15.1 gives us an understanding of how these four pairs of populations compare. In the first pair, both populations have the same shape except for the location. In the second pair, both populations are symmetric about point 0 but have different shapes. For the third pair, one population is symmetric, whereas the other has extreme mass on the high end of the ability scale. In the final pair, both populations have larger mass on the end points of the ability scale, but in different directions. The first pair is an ideal situation for real practice and is more realistic than the other three pairs. These more extreme cases are included to examine how the proposed approaches behave in such situations. If the proposed approaches can work in these extreme situations, then they can be expected to work in less extreme conditions.

Within each pair, the first population is considered the target population; the second one will be linked to the target population. The true linking function in each pair can be derived from the true distribution forms. Suppose F_1 and F_2 are the cumulative distribution functions in each pair. They are on a U(0,1) scale. The true linking function is $F_2^{-1} \circ F_1$, if the first distribution is taken as the target. The true linking function also can be obtained by smoothing techniques such as the constrained splines if its closed form is hard to get. Within each pair, 3,000 examinees are generated from the specified populations respectively and the data are generated according to the 2PL model. Once the responses are generated, these two test forms are calibrated on a U(0,1) scale and a N(0,1) scale for their corresponding populations. The kernel smoothing method is then used to get the initial estimates of the ICCs, with the bandwidth set as 0.20, which is roughly $3000^{-1/5}$. Then *SCOBS* is utilized to make the estimated ICCs monotone and to estimate the linking function $\hat{g}$ when using the constrained spline approach. The maximum number of knots is set at 6, which was recommended by He and Shi (1998). In the linear approach, the linking parameters A and B are estimated from a least squares criterion displayed in Equation 15.14. The entire procedure is repeated 100 times for each pair in order to calculate the linking errors.

Three statistics are used to measure the efficacy of the proposed linking methods. One is the root mean-square error (RMSE) of the linking function along the U(0,1) scale,

$$RMSE = \sqrt{\sum_m \sum_r [g(\theta_m) - \hat{g}_r(\theta_m)]^2 / R / M}, \tag{15.15}$$

where R is the number of replications, M is the number of grid points on θ scale, and m and r are indices for M and R. Here $\hat{g}_r$ is the estimated linking function from the rth repetition, and g is the true linking function. This statistic is used to examine how well the true linking function is recovered by the estimated one. The other is the root mean-square difference (RMSD) of test functions for the anchor items,

$$RMSD = \sqrt{\sum_m \Big(\sum_j P_{2j}(\hat{g}(\theta_m)) - \sum_j P_{1j}(\theta_m)\Big)^2 / M}, \tag{15.16}$$

where j is the index for common items and M has the same meaning as above. This statistic is employed to examine the recovery of the true test characteristic function. The third statistic is called an improvement ratio (IR), which is similar to the statistic used in Kaskowitz and De Ayala (2001).

$$IR = 1 - \frac{F_{equate}}{F_{original}}, \tag{15.17}$$

where

$$F_{equate} = \sum_m \sum_j [P_{2j}(\hat{g}(\theta_m)) - P_{1j}(\theta_m)]^2 / (J * M) \tag{15.18}$$

and

$$F_{original} = \sum_m \sum_j [P_{2j}(\theta_m) - P_{1j}(\theta_m)]^2 / (J * M). \tag{15.19}$$

Here j is the total number of anchor items and M has the same meaning as above. $F_{original}$ represents the largest discrepancy between item response functions on the common set, whereas F_{equate} stands for the discrepancy between item response functions due to linking. This ratio reflects the improvement due to linking.

15.4.2 Results and Discussion

The summary of the results is shown in Tables 15.1–15.3 and Figures 15.2 and 15.3. Table 15.1 presents the RMSE of the estimated linking function. Since the scales of the constrained spline linking and the linear linking are different, the scale of linear linking is transformed to the U(0,1) scale before calculating the RMSE. The label $RMSE_{CS}$ represents the RMSE using the constrained spline linking, whereas $RMSE_L$ represents the RMSE using linear linking. Table 15.1 reveals that linear linking has similar or smaller RMSE in the estimate of the linking function, but all the RMSE

Table 15.1 Root Mean-Square Error (RMSE) Under Two Proposed Approaches Using 3,000 Examinees

	$RMSE_{CS}$	$RMSE_L$
N(0,1) vs. N(0.25,1)	0.0167	0.0134
N(0,1)I[−2,2] vs. U(−2,2)	0.0161	0.0218
Beta(1,1) vs. Beta(1.5,0.5)	0.0267	0.0263
Beta(1,2) vs. Beta(2,1)	0.0229	0.0131
Average	0.0206	0.0187

Note. CS = constrained spline linking; L = linear linking.

Table 15.2 Root Mean-Squared Difference (RMSD) Under Two Proposed Approaches Using 3,000 Examinees

	$RMSD_{CS}$	$RMSD_L$
N(0,1) vs. N(0.25,1)	0.2130	0.2214
N(0,1)I[−2,2] vs. U(−2,2)	0.3363	0.3416
Beta(1,1) vs. Beta(1.5,0.5)	0.3780	0.3760
Beta(1,2) vs. Beta(2,1)	0.3233	0.3186
Average	0.3127	0.3144

Note. CS = constrained spline linking; L = linear linking.

Table 15.3 Improvement Ratio (IR) Under Two Proposed Approaches Using 3,000 Examinees

	IR_{CS}	IR_L
N(0,1) vs. N(0.25,1)	0.868	0.816
N(0,1)I[−2,2] vs. U(−2,2)	0.963	0.903
Beta(1,1) vs. Beta(1.5,0.5)	0.956	0.946
Beta(1,2) vs. Beta(2,1)	0.821	0.808
average	0.902	0.880

Note. CS = constrained spline linking; L = linear linking.

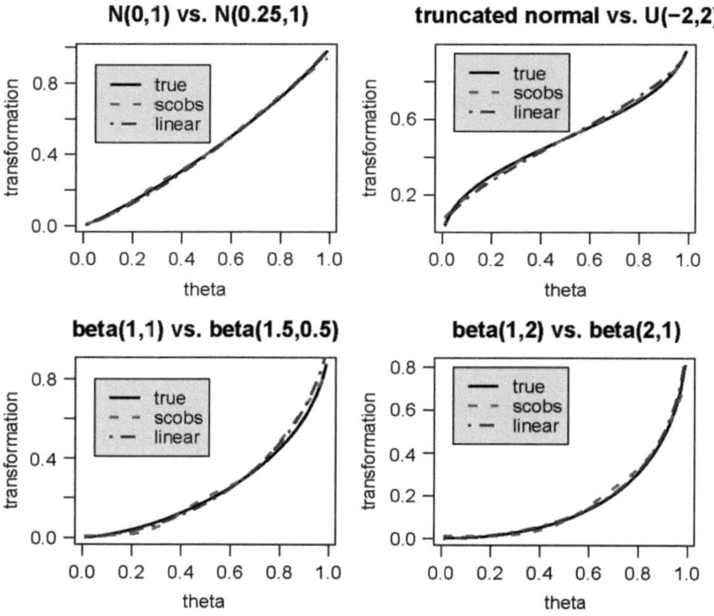

Fig. 15.2 Recovery of true linking functions

are below the nominal level 0.05. Table 15.2 presents the RMSD for the common-item test. The scale of the linear linking is transformed to U(0,1) scale before calculating the RMSD. The label $RMSE_{CS}$ is the RMSD of the test function by constrained spline linking, whereas $RMSE_L$ is the RMSD by linear linking. Notice that the RMSD of the test functions resulted from these two methods are similar to each other. Table 15.3 gives us the IR results for these two proposed linking approaches. Both methods have similar IRs in all cases. Figures 15.2 and 15.3 illustrate the results. Figure 15.2 presents the recovery of the true linking function, and Figure 15.3 presents the recovery of the true test function of the common items. The solid line represents the true function (either a linking function or a test function), and the dashed and the dashed-dotted lines are for the corresponding estimated functions by using the constrained B-spline and the linear methods, respectively. Given the figures are printed in black and white, it is hard to distinguish the lines in some graphs. Specifically, there are three lines in each graph. The solid line represents the true function (either a linking function or a test function), and the dashed and the dashed-dotted lines are for the corresponding estimated functions by using the constrained B-spline and the linear methods, respectively.

The results enable us to say that both proposed methods work well in all four situations in terms of recovering the true linking function. Both methods show similar performances in terms of the RMSD of the estimated test functions and IR. Furthermore, results show that the large population differences in the last two pairs have little impact in recovering the true linking functions but have impact in recovering the true test functions of the common items. When two extremely different populations are linked, it is expected that the test functions of these two

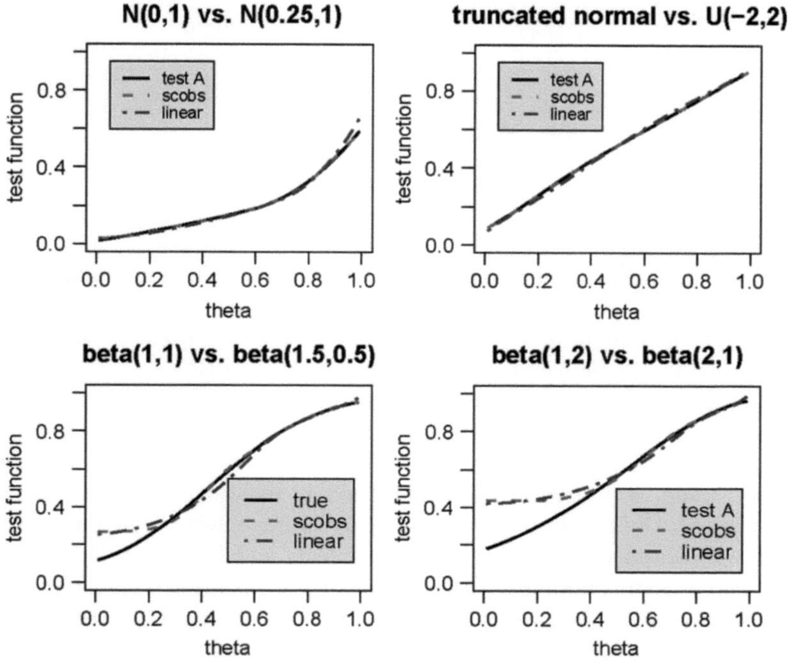

Fig. 15.3 Recovery of true test functions of common items

populations differ on the end points of the ability scale. It turns out that for the last two pairs, the true test functions have a large difference on the lower end of the ability scale. This fact leads to poor recovery of test functions on the lower end of ability, which is displayed in the last two pairs. From the results of the simulation study, we expect that the proposed methods are able to recover the true linking function even when the parametric models do not fit the data or when the testing populations of interest have large discrepancies.

15.5 Real Data Example

A real data example is also used to compare the two proposed methods and the test characteristic curve (TCC; Stocking & Lord, 1983) method. The TCC method is an IRT model-based approach. As described in the introduction, an IRT model-based method is initiated from the linear indeterminancy of ability in IRT functional form:

$$P(\theta; a, b, c) = P(A\theta + B; a/A, Ab + B, c). \tag{15.20}$$

Under the NEAT design, the common items are calibrated separately for each population. According to the TCC method, the slope A and the intercept B are obtained by minimizing the overall squared differences between ICCs for the common items from separate calibrations. The objective function is shown in the equation below, denoted as $SL(\theta)$.

$$SL(\theta) = \int [\sum_{j\in Common} P_j(\theta; a_{1j}, b_{1j}, c_{1j}) - \sum_{j\in Common} P_j(\theta; a_{2j}/A, Ab_{2j} + B, c_{1j})]^2 f_1(\theta)d\theta, \tag{15.21}$$

where $a_{.j}$ is the parameter a of item j for Group 1 or 2. The same indices are for parameter b and c. In this study, the programs BILOG-MG (Zimowski, Muraki, Mislevy, & Bock, 1996) and EQUATE (Baker, 1990) are used to calibrate item parameters and to implement the TCC method, respectively.

The data were taken from the responses to a mathematics placement test administered in 1993 in the University of Wisconsin system. Two forms of 46 multiple-choice-item tests with five alternatives, Form 1 and Form 2, are used in this study. Every 10th item is a pilot item, and all the other items on the test are common items. Omitted responses or not reached items were scored as incorrect. Form 1 was administered to 1,938 male students and Form 2 to 1,716 female students. After some preliminary analysis, one item was deleted from the analysis because its ICC was a decreasing function of the latent ability. It is assumed that the common items should behave similarly across testing populations. Thus SIBTEST (Shealy & Stout, 1993) was used to detect any possible differentially functioning items. In this study, the males were considered as the focal group and the females as the reference group. The critical value was set at $\alpha=0.05$. After this examination, 21 items were left to construct the common-item group. To summarize, each form contained 45 items, with 21 common to both forms.

The empirical raw-score distributions of these two testing samples are shown in Figure 15.4. An empirical transformation function was derived by two steps. Specifically, the first step was to find the empirical raw-score distributions and convert them to a U(0,1) scale and then to find the transformation between these two transformed empirical raw-score distributions. This empirical linking function is shown as the solid line in Figure 15.5. The other estimated linking functions obtained from other methods (represented by the dashed or dashed-dotted lines) are compared to this empirical linking function.

Form 1 and Form 2 were calibrated with male and female groups, respectively. For each group, the items were calibrated parametrically by a 3PL model and nonparametrically on the U(0,1) scale and on the N(0,1) scale, and then transformed back to U(0,1) scale.

After item calibration, constrained spline linking, linear linking, and TCC method linking were used to link the female group to the male group. In the constrained spline approach, we specified the maximum number of knots as 6 and the bandwidth of smoothing as 0.22, which is approximately $1938^{-1/5}$. These methods were compared in terms of (a) the RMSE of the estimated linking functions, taking the empirical linking function as the truth, and (b) linking error, which

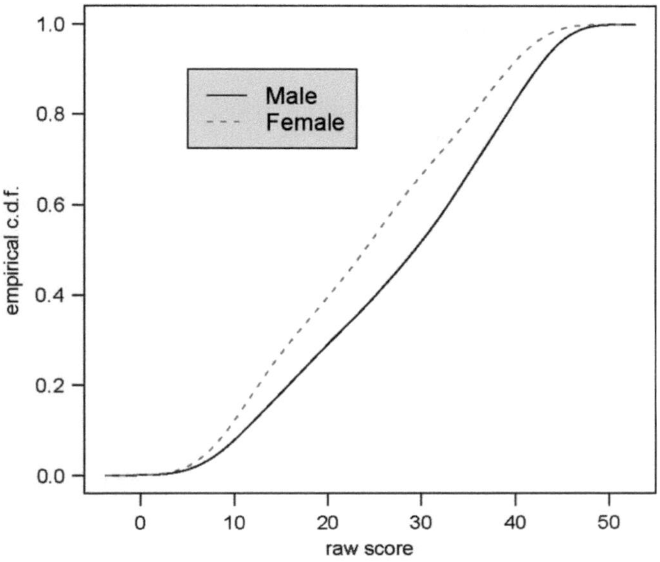

Fig. 15.4 Empirical score distributions for real data

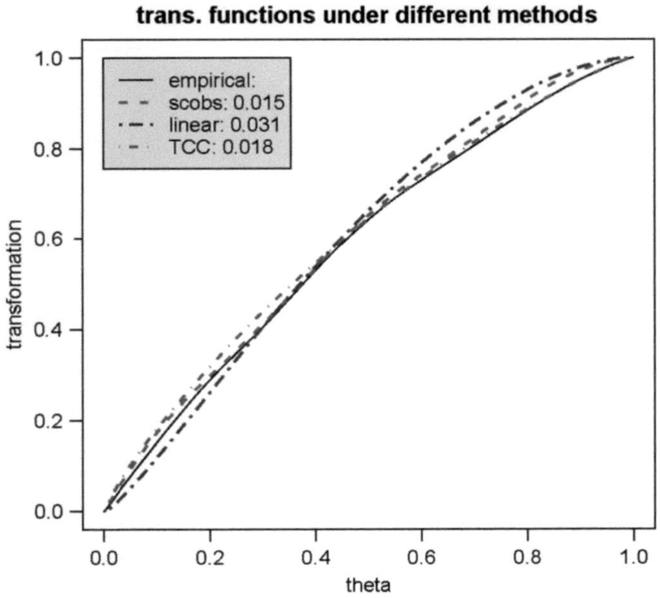

Fig. 15.5 Real data analysis: Transformation functions under different methods

for the constrained spline linking and linear linking is obtained from 100 bootstrap samples. Figure 15.5 depicts how close the estimated linking functions are to the empirical linking function.

The solid line in Figure 15.5 is the empirical relationship between abilities of the male and female groups. The other three curves are the relationship curves after conducting the linking procedures. The legend of the figure gives you the RMSE of these three linking approaches. For example, the RMSE by using constrained spline linking was 0.015, while linear aproach resulted in RMSE 0.031, and the RMSE of the TCC method was 0.018. We noticed that the constrained spline approach had a similar RMSE to the TCC method, whereas the linear approach on N(0,1) scale had a relatively higher RMSE.

Figure 15.6 shows the linking error for the constrained spline linking and linear linking. These linking errors were obtained from the bootstrapping method. On average, the linear approach on the N(0,1) scale had a smaller linking error than the constrained spline approach, though both were within the nominal level.

As for the linking under the TCC method, Table 15.4 summarizes the results. The linking slope is 1.004, and the intercept is -0.3708. For the purpose of comparison, the linking slope obtained from linear linking on the N(0,1) scale was 0.867, and the intercept from this approach was -0.362.

In this real data analysis, we actually employed four different linking methods. The empirical linking function was in fact derived by the equipercentile technique,

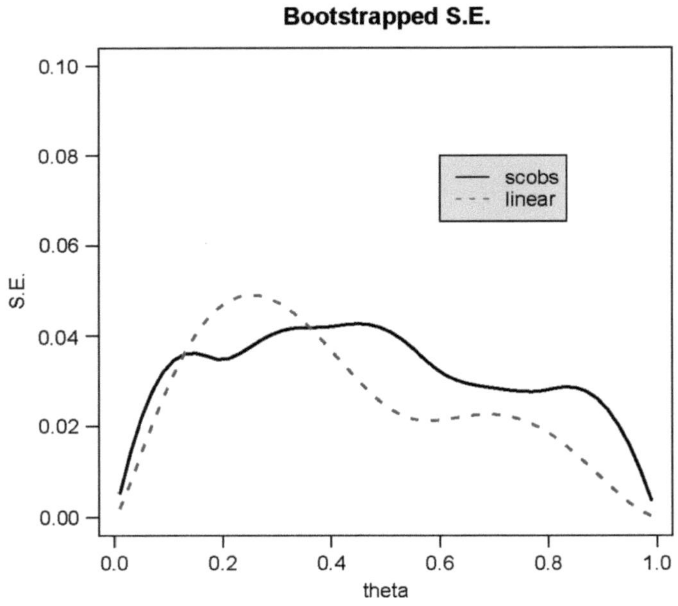

Fig. 15.6 Real data analysis: Bootstrapped *SE*

Table 15.4 Means and Standard Deviations of Item Parameter Estimates and Linking Constants for the Common Items

	Form A			Form B		
	a	b	c	a	b	c
Item *M*	2.284	−0.1316	0.1943	2.2246	0.2218	0.1872
SD	0.6073	0.3246	0.0524	0.6165	0.3205	0.0555
Linking constants	A = 1.0004			B = −0.3696		
Transformed items *M*				2.2236	−0.1477	0.1872
Transformed items *SD*				0.6163	0.3206	0.0555

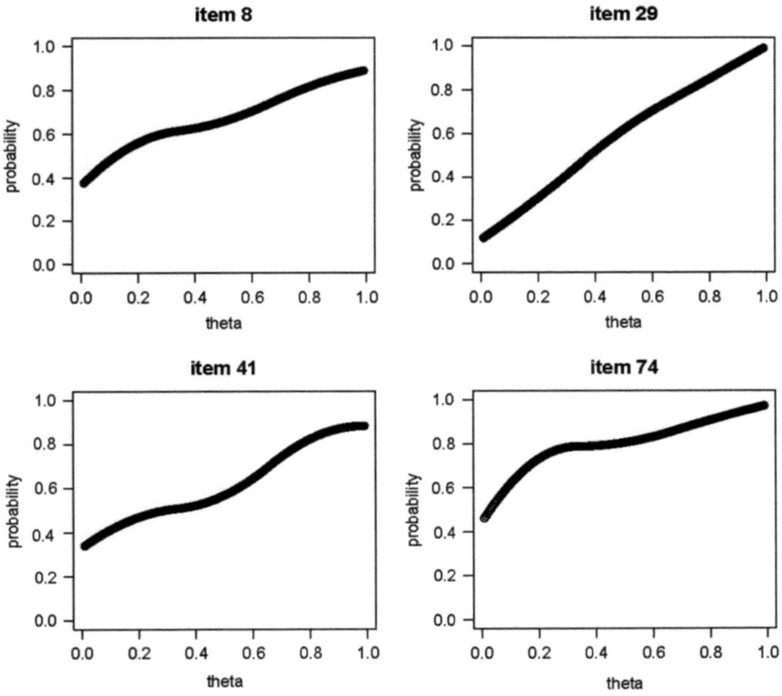

Fig. 15.7 Four nonparametric item characteristic curves

which is a core method in observed score linking. The two proposed methods and the TCC method were compared with the empirical linking function. The results in this study showed that there is not much difference among these four methods, except that the linear linking on the N(0,1) scale is slightly off. This is probably due to the good fit of the parametric model. When the parametric model is appropriate for the data, all methods will converge and show similar results.

15.6 Discussion

It is well admitted that no parametric model for item responses is perfect, even in a large-scale assessment. Figure 15.7 gives us four example items, which are taken from the data of a Psychology 101 exam at McGill University that are featured in the manual of *TestGraf* (Ramsay, 2001). Although these items are often treated as "bad" items relative to the parametric models, we still want to (and have to) include them as a part of data analysis.

Nonparametric IRT models have been developed to fit the data with more flexible functional forms. However, the nonparametric IRT models are not widely used in testing practice. One reason is little knowledge about the applications of this model, such as in linking applications, among other complications. Through the simulation study and the real data analysis, we have shown that both proposed methods are able to recover the true linking functions, even when the nonequivalent populations differ substantially. When a parametric model fits the data well, both of the proposed methods will behave similarly with traditional methods. The results of this study give us hope that we can do real applications with nonparametric IRT models.

Author Note: Any opinions expressed in this chapter are those of the authors and not necessarily of Educational Testing Service.

Part III
Evaluation

Chapter 16
Applications of Asymptotic Expansion in Item Response Theory Linking

Haruhiko Ogasawara

16.1 Introduction

The purpose of this chapter is to have asymptotic expansions of the distributions of the estimators of linking coefficients using item response theory (IRT; see, e.g., Bock & Moustaki, 2007) in the common-item nonequivalent groups design. In IRT linking, usually item parameters are available only as their estimates. Consequently, the parameters in IRT linking, that is, linking coefficients, are subject to sampling variation. So, it is important to see the magnitudes of the estimates considering this variation. One of the typical methods to evaluate their sizes is using the asymptotic standard errors (ASEs) of the estimators of linking coefficients. The ASEs of the coefficient estimators by *the methods using moments of item parameters* (hereafter referred to as *moment methods*; Loyd & Hoover, 1980; Mislevy & Bock, 1990; Marco, 1977; see also Kolen & Brennan, 2004, Ch. 6) were derived by Ogasawara (2000). The corresponding ASEs for the methods using response functions (Haebara, 1980; Stocking & Lord, 1983; see also Kolen & Brennan, 2004, Ch. 6) were obtained by Ogasawara (2001b). The ASEs in equating methods for true and observed scores were obtained by Lord (1982a) and Ogasawara (2001a, 2003), whereas the standard errors by the bootstrap were investigated by Tsai, Hanson, Kolen, and Forsyth (2001; see also Kolen & Brennan, 2004, Ch. 7). The ASEs by kernel equating (see von Davier, Holland, & Thayer, 2004b) were obtained by Liou, Cheng, and Johnson (1997) and von Davier et al. by different methods.

The ASEs can be used with the asymptotic normality of the coefficient estimators based on the central limit theorem. This normality is asymptotically correct and gives reasonable approximations of the actual distributions in many cases, with finite sample sizes encountered in practice. On the other hand, especially in IRT, the

H. Ogasawara
Otaru University of Commerce, 3-5-21, Midori Otaru 047-8501, Japan
e-mail: hogasa@res.otaru-uc.ac.jp

A.A. von Davier (ed.), *Statistical Models for Test Equating, Scaling, and Linking*, Statistics for Social and Behavioral Sciences,
DOI 10.1007/978-0-387-98138-3_16,

speed of convergence to the normal distribution for item parameter estimators seems to be relatively slow with comparison to that for continuous observed variables (e.g., factor loading estimators; see Wirth & Edwards, 2007).

Ogasawara (2009) showed that the actual standard error for the estimator of a difficulty parameter in the two-parameter logistic (2PL) model using Bock and Lieberman's (1970, Table 1) data was as large as 2.00 times the corresponding ASE with $N = 1{,}000$, where N is the sample size. Even when $N = 2{,}000$, the actual standard error was still as large as 1.29 times the corresponding ASE. The slow convergence may be partially explained by limited information available in binary responses.

It is known that the discrepancy between the actual standard errors and the ASEs can be improved by asymptotic expansions beyond the normal approximation. As addressed earlier, the normal approximation uses the normal distribution of a parameter estimator when sample sizes are infinitely large. However, in practice, sample sizes are finite. So, there is some room to improve this approximation. In principle, under some regularity conditions based on asymptotics, the approximation can be improved as much as is desired by successively using higher order terms with respect to powers of sample sizes. This is the method of asymptotic expansion to obtain an approximate distribution of an estimator when it is difficult to determine the exact distribution (see, e.g., Hall, 1992/1997). The results of the next higher order approximation beyond the normal one are given by using the approximations of bias (the difference of the expectation of an estimator and its corresponding true or population value) and the skewness (a measure of the asymmetry of the distribution). The second next higher order results are given by using the approximations of the added term of the higher order variance and the kurtosis of the distribution of the estimator as well as the measures used in the relatively lower order asymptotic expansions (note that the usual normal approximation is seen as an asymptotic expansion using only the first-order ASE).

In IRT, so far the usage of asymptotic expansions has been limited to the level of the asymptotic normality with the usual ASEs. However, in a recent work (Ogasawara, 2009), I obtained the higher order approximations of the distributions of the item parameter estimators. I showed that, for instance, the ratios of 2.00 and 1.29 mentioned above were theoretically predicted by the higher order ASE (HASE) as 1.31 and 1.17, respectively, although the former value 1.31 is still conservative for 2.00.

In IRT linking, the estimators of linking coefficients are functions of item parameter estimators; consequently, the similar slow convergence to asymptotic normality is expected. It will be illustrated that the ratio of the actual standard error to the corresponding ASE can be more than 2 and that using HASE reduces the ratio. This is an example of the practical use of asymptotic expansion.

The organization of this paper is as follows. In Section 16.2, the situation of IRT linking with definitions of some linking coefficients is given. Section 16.3 gives the main results of the asymptotic expansions for the distributions of a coefficient estimator standardized by the population ASE and the corresponding Studentized one. Note that Studentization indicates the standardization by the ASE estimator when the population ASE is unavailable, as is usual in practice. These results will be summarized as Theorems 1 and 2, respectively. In Section 16.4, numerical examples based on data available in the literature are illustrated using simulations for comparison to the corresponding theoretical or asymptotic results. Section 16.5 gives some concluding remarks. The technical details required for the main results are provided in the Appendix.

16.2 Linking Coefficients

In this section, the linking design with the associated unidimensional IRT model is introduced, followed by the definitions of linking coefficients given by the moment methods for illustration. Assume the common-item nonequivalent groups design for linking. The n common (anchor) items can be internal or external to the tests to be linked. If the IRT model fits the data, the item parameters for the common items are expected to be the same up to a linear transformation. Denote the slope and the intercept by coefficients A and B, respectively. Let the number of possibly nonequivalent independent examinee groups be denoted by G, and in many cases $G = 2$. For generality, assume the 3PL model with

$$\Pr(Y_{gj} = 1|\theta_{(g)}, a_{gj}, b_{gj}, c_{gj}) = c_{gj} + \frac{1 - c_{gj}}{1 + \exp\{-Da_{gj}(\theta_{(g)} - b_{gj})\}}, \quad (16.1)$$
$$\theta_{(g)} \sim N(0,1) \quad (g = 1, ..., G; j = 1, ..., n_g)$$

where $Y_{gj} = 1$ indicates that a randomly chosen examinee with the proficiency score $\theta_{(g)}$ in the gth examinee group responds correctly to the jth item in a set of n_g items (including n common ones) whose parameters are jointly estimated. Note that the examinees in the gth group may respond to other items, especially in the case of external common items with separate estimation for the parameters of common and unique (noncommon) items. $Y_{gj} = 0$ indicates a wrong answer in the above case. The same means and variances of $\theta_{(g)}$ over examinee groups are due to the model indeterminacy for the difficulty (b_{gj}) and discrimination (a_{gj}) parameters in the jth item. In Equation 16.1, c_{gj} is the lower asymptote for the guessing probability of the item, and $D = 1.7$ is a conventional constant.

Consider the case of $G = 2$ with the assumption that the scale of $\theta_{(2)}$ is transformed to that of $\theta_{(1)}$ in order to have the same scale by

$$\theta^*_{(2)} = A\theta_{(2)} + B \text{ with } b^*_{2j} = Ab_{2j} + B \text{ and } a^*_{2j} = a_{2j}/A \quad (16.2)$$

(note that c_{2j} s are unchanged). Then,

$$\Pr(Y_{2j} = 1|\theta^*_{(2)}, a^*_{2j}, b^*_{2j}, c_{2j}) = \Pr(Y_{2j} = 1|\theta_{(2)}, a_{2j}, b_{2j}, c_{2j}) \ (j = 1, ..., n_2). \quad (16.3)$$

For illustrative purposes, I deal with the cases of estimating the population coefficients A and B by three moment methods: the mean-sigma (m/s), the mean-mean (m/m), and the mean-geometric mean (m/gm) methods. Let the common items be located in the first n in the n_g items for the gth examinee group. Then,

$$\hat{A}_s \equiv \left(\frac{\sum_{j=1}^{n} \hat{b}_{1j}^2 - n^{-1}\left(\sum_{j=1}^{n} \hat{b}_{1j}\right)^2}{\sum_{j=1}^{n} \hat{b}_{2j}^2 - n^{-1}\left(\sum_{j=1}^{n} \hat{b}_{2j}\right)^2} \right)^{1/2}, \quad \hat{B}_s \equiv n^{-1}\sum_{j=1}^{n} \hat{b}_{1j} - \hat{A}_s n^{-1} \sum_{j=1}^{n} \hat{b}_{2j} \tag{16.4}$$

for the m/s method,

$$\hat{A}_m \equiv \sum_{j=1}^{n} \hat{a}_{2j} \Big/ \sum_{j=1}^{n} \hat{a}_{1j}, \quad \hat{B}_m \equiv n^{-1}\sum_{j=1}^{n} \hat{b}_{1j} - \hat{A}_m n^{-1} \sum_{j=1}^{n} \hat{b}_{2j} \tag{16.5}$$

for the m/m method, and

$$\hat{A}_g \equiv \left(\prod_{j=1}^{n} \hat{a}_{2j}/\hat{a}_{1j} \right)^{1/n}, \quad \hat{B}_g \equiv n^{-1}\sum_{j=1}^{n} \hat{b}_{1j} - \hat{A}_g n^{-1} \sum_{j=1}^{n} \hat{b}_{2j} \tag{16.6}$$

for the m/gm method, where $\hat{a}_{gj}$ and $\hat{b}_{gj}$ $(g = 1, ..., G; j = 1, ..., n)$ are the estimators of a_{gj} and b_{gj}, respectively. The estimators are assumed to be given by marginal maximum likelihood separately in each examinee group:

$$\begin{aligned}
L_g &= \frac{N_g!}{\prod_{k=1}^{K_g} r_{gk}!} \prod_{k=1}^{K_g} \pi_{gk}^{r_{gk}}, \quad K_g = 2^{n_g}, \\
\pi_{gk} &= \int_{-\infty}^{\infty} \left\{ \prod_{j=1}^{n_g} \Psi_{gj}^{X_{gkj}} (1 - \Psi_{gj})^{1-X_{gkj}} \right\} \phi(\theta) d\theta, \\
\Psi_{gj} &= \Psi(\theta, a_{gj}, b_{gj}, c_{gj}) = c_{gj} + \frac{1 - c_{gj}}{1 + \exp\{-Da_{gj}(\theta - b_{gj})\}}, \\
\phi(\theta) &= (1/\sqrt{2}) \exp(-\theta^2/2) \quad (g = 1, ..., G; k = 1, ..., K_g; j = 1, ..., n_g),
\end{aligned} \tag{16.7}$$

where N_g is the number of examinees in the gth group; r_{gk} is the number of examinees showing the kth response pattern in n_g items for the gth group; $X_{gkj} = 1$ and $X_{gkj} = 0$ indicate the success and failure in the jth item of the kth response pattern for the gth group, respectively; and $c_{gj} = c_{g'j}$ $(g,\ g' = 1, ..., G;$ $j = 1, ..., n)$. The integral in Equation 16.7 to have π_{gk} is difficult to obtain algebraically and is approximated by M quadrature points in actual computation:

$$\pi_{gk} \doteq \sum_{m=1}^{M} \left\{ \prod_{j=1}^{n_g} \Psi_{gmj}^{X_{gkj}} (1 - \Psi_{gmj})^{1-X_{gkj}} \right\} W(Q_m) \ (g = 1, ..., G; k = 1, ..., K_g), \tag{16.8}$$

where $\Psi_{gmj} = \Psi(Q_m, a_{gj}, b_{gj}, c_{gj})$, $W(Q_m)$ is the weight at the quadrature point Q_m, and the notation for the parameters, such as a_{gj}, is also used for population parameters for simplicity.

16.3 Asymptotic Expansions for Coefficient Estimators

This section gives main results. First, the asymptotic expansion of the distribution of a linking coefficient estimator standardized by the population ASE is given, which will be summarized as Theorem 1. Second, the corresponding result for the estimator Studentized by the ASE estimator will be shown in Theorem 2. In Theorem 2 a confidence interval will be provided for the population linking coefficient more accurate than that given by the usual normal approximation using only the ASE estimator.

Let

$$\mathrm{E}(\mathbf{p}) = \boldsymbol{\pi}_{\mathrm{T}} = (\boldsymbol{\pi}_{\mathrm{T}(1)}{}', \ldots, \boldsymbol{\pi}_{\mathrm{T(G)}}{}')', \ \boldsymbol{\pi}_{\mathrm{T}(g)} = (\pi_{\mathrm{T}g1}, \ldots, \pi_{\mathrm{T}gK_g})', \\ \mathbf{u} = (\mathbf{u}_{(1)}{}', \ldots, \mathbf{u}_{(G)}{}')' \text{ and } \mathbf{u}_{(g)} = N_g^{1/2}(\mathbf{p}_{(g)} - \boldsymbol{\pi}_{\mathrm{T}(g)}), \tag{16.9}$$

where

$$\mathbf{p} = (\mathbf{p}_{(1)}{}', \ldots, \mathbf{p}_{(G)}{}')', \ \mathbf{p}_{(g)} = (p_{g1}, \ldots, p_{gK_g})'$$

and

$$p_{gk} = r_{gk}/N_g \ (g = 1, \ldots, G; \ k = 1, \ldots, K_g). \tag{16.10}$$

Note that p_{gk} is the sample proportion for the kth response pattern in the gth examinee group. When the IRT model fitted to data is incorrectly specified, the population values for response patterns derived by the model are given by a $(\sum_{g=1}^{G} K_g) \times 1$ vector, say, $\boldsymbol{\pi}_0$ with $\boldsymbol{\pi}_0 \neq \boldsymbol{\pi}_{\mathrm{T}}$. On the other hand, when the model is true, $\boldsymbol{\pi}_0 = \boldsymbol{\pi}_{\mathrm{T}}$.

Let γ be the generic coefficient representing one of $A_m, B_m, \ldots, A_g, B_g$ (note that γ also represents other coefficients given by response function methods, for example, which will be addressed in Section 16.5), and $\hat{\gamma} = \gamma(\hat{\boldsymbol{\alpha}})$, where $\hat{\boldsymbol{\alpha}}$ is a $q \times 1$ vector of item parameter estimators with, for example, $q = 2n$ or $q = 4n$ depending on methods used in Equations 16.4–16.6. We see that $\hat{\boldsymbol{\alpha}} = \boldsymbol{\alpha}(\mathbf{p})$.

For N_g, assume that $\lim_{\substack{N_g \to \infty \\ N_{g}' \to \infty}} N_g/N_{g'} = O(1)$ $(g, g' = 1, \ldots, G)$. Let $\tilde{N}$ be a number satisfying $\lim_{\substack{N_g \to \infty \\ \tilde{N} \to \infty}} N_g/\tilde{N} \stackrel{\sim}{=} \tilde{O}(1) > 0$ $(g = 1, \ldots, G)$, e.g., $\tilde{N} = \sum_{g=1}^{G} N_g/G$, and $\mathbf{N}^a = \mathrm{diag}(N_1^a \mathbf{1}_{K_1}{}', \ldots, N_G^a \mathbf{1}_{K_G}{}')$, where $N_g^a = (N_g)^a$ and $\mathbf{1}_{K_g}$ is the $K_g \times 1$ vector of 1s. Suppose that the Taylor series expansion of $\hat{\gamma}$ about its population value γ_0 holds:

$$\hat{\gamma} = \gamma_0 + \frac{\partial \gamma_0}{\partial \boldsymbol{\pi}_{\mathrm{T}}'}\mathbf{N}^{-\frac{1}{2}}\mathbf{u} + \frac{1}{2}\left\{\left(\frac{\partial}{\partial \boldsymbol{\pi}_{\mathrm{T}}'}\right)^{<2>}\gamma_0\right\}\mathbf{N}^{-\frac{1}{2}<2>}\mathbf{u}^{<2>}$$
$$+\frac{1}{6}\left\{\left(\frac{\partial}{\partial \boldsymbol{\pi}_{\mathrm{T}}'}\right)^{<3>}\gamma_0\right\}\mathbf{N}^{-\frac{1}{2}<3>}\mathbf{u}^{<3>} + O_p(\tilde{N}^{-2}), \tag{16.11}$$

where $\partial\gamma_0/\partial\boldsymbol{\pi}_{\mathrm{T}} \equiv \partial\hat{\gamma}/\partial\mathbf{p}|_{\mathbf{p}=\pi_{\mathrm{T}}}$ for simplicity of notation with other partial derivatives defined similarly, $\mathbf{X}^{<k>} = \mathbf{X}\otimes\cdots\otimes\mathbf{X}$ (k times) is the k-fold Kronecker product, and $\mathbf{N}^{a<k>} = (\mathbf{N}^a)^{<k>}$.

It is known that the asymptotic expansion of the distribution of $\hat{\gamma}$ is determined by the asymptotic cumulants or moments of $\hat{\gamma}$. In Section 16.A.1 of the Appendix, I derive the asymptotic cumulants of $\hat{\gamma}$ up to the fourth order using Equation 16.11. Define $v = \hat{\gamma} - \gamma_0$ with its cumulants

$$\begin{aligned}
\kappa_1(v) &= \mathrm{E}(v) = \zeta_1(v) + O(\tilde{N}^{-2}),\\
\kappa_2(v) &= \mathrm{E}[\{v-\mathrm{E}(v)\}^2] = \zeta_2(v) + \zeta_{\Delta 2}(v) + O(\tilde{N}^{-3}),\\
\kappa_3(v) &= \mathrm{E}[\{v-\mathrm{E}(v)\}^3] = \zeta_3(v) + O(\tilde{N}^{-3}),\\
\kappa_4(v) &= \mathrm{E}[\{v-\mathrm{E}(v)\}^4] - 3\{\kappa_2(v)\}^2 = \zeta_4(v) + O(\tilde{N}^{-4}),
\end{aligned} \tag{16.12}$$

where $\zeta_i(v)$ $(i = 1, ..., 4)$ and $\zeta_{\Delta 2}(v)$ are the asymptotic cumulants of various orders in terms of the powers of $\tilde{N}$ (see Section 16.A.1 of the Appendix). Then, we have one of the main results as follows.

Theorem 1. *Under regularity conditions for validity of asymptotic expansion, the density of* $(\hat{\gamma} - \gamma_0)/\zeta_2^{1/2}$ *at* x *is given by the local Edgeworth expansion*

$$f\left(\frac{\hat{\gamma}-\gamma_0}{\zeta_2^{1/2}} = x\right) = \left[1 + \left\{\frac{\zeta_1 x}{\zeta_2^{1/2}} + \frac{\zeta_3}{6\zeta_2^{3/2}}(x^3 - 3x)\right\}_{\{O(\tilde{N}^{-1/2})\}}\right.$$
$$+\left\{\frac{1}{2}(\zeta_{\Delta 2} + \zeta_1^2)\frac{x^2-1}{\zeta_2} + \left(\frac{\zeta_4}{24} + \frac{\zeta_1\zeta_3}{6}\right)\frac{x^4 - 6x^2 + 3}{\zeta_2^2}\right.$$
$$\left.\left.+\frac{\zeta_3^2(x^6 - 15x^4 + 45x^2 - 15)}{72\zeta_2^3}\right\}_{\{O(\tilde{N}^{-1})\}}\right]\phi(x) + O(\tilde{N}^{-3/2}), \tag{16.13}$$

where for $\phi(\cdot)$ see Equation 16.7; the subscript $\{O(\tilde{N}^a)\}$ denotes for clarity that the subscripted term is of order $O(\tilde{N}^a)$; and $\zeta_i = \zeta_i(v)(i = 1, ..., 4)$ with $\zeta_{\Delta 2} = \zeta_{\Delta 2}(v)$ are given by Equations 16.A.2, 16.A.8, 16.A.9, and 16.A.14 (see Appendix).

Proof. From the standard statistical theory (e.g., Hall, 1992/1997; see also Ogasawara, 2006, 2007b) and from Section 16.A.1 of the Appendix for the asymptotic cumulants of Equation 16.12, we have Equation 16.13. Q.E.D.

Note that Theorem 1 can be used both with and without model misspecification. In order to apply Theorem 1, the partial derivatives of $\hat{\gamma} = \gamma(\mathbf{p})$ with respect to $\mathbf{p}$ up to the third order evaluated at $\mathbf{p} = \boldsymbol{\pi}_{\mathrm{T}}$ are required, which are derived in two steps. The first step is to have the partial derivatives of $\hat{\gamma} = \gamma(\hat{\boldsymbol{\alpha}})$ with respect to $\hat{\boldsymbol{\alpha}}$, which is relatively easy to derive in the cases of the moment methods for linking, since the function $\hat{\gamma} = \gamma(\hat{\boldsymbol{\alpha}})$ is an elementary one (see Equations 16.4–16.6) and will be provided in Section 16.A.2 of the Appendix for completeness. The second step is to derive the partial derivatives of $\hat{\boldsymbol{\alpha}} = \boldsymbol{\alpha}(\mathbf{p})$ with respect to $\mathbf{p}$, which require formulas in implicit functions (see Ogasawara, 2007a, 2007c) and are given by Ogasawara (2009, Appendix) for the 3PL model but not repeated here, as they are involved.

The final results of the required partial derivatives are given by the chain rule

$$\frac{\partial\hat{\gamma}}{\partial p_{gi}} = \frac{\partial\hat{\gamma}}{\partial\hat{\boldsymbol{\alpha}}'}\frac{\partial\hat{\boldsymbol{\alpha}}}{\partial p_{gi}}, \quad \frac{\partial^2\hat{\gamma}}{\partial p_{gi}\partial p_{g'j}} = \frac{\partial\hat{\boldsymbol{\alpha}}'}{\partial p_{gi}}\frac{\partial^2\hat{\gamma}}{\partial\hat{\boldsymbol{\alpha}}\,\partial\hat{\boldsymbol{\alpha}}'}\frac{\partial\hat{\boldsymbol{\alpha}}}{\partial p_{g'j}} + \frac{\partial\hat{\gamma}}{\partial\hat{\boldsymbol{\alpha}}'}\frac{\partial^2\hat{\boldsymbol{\alpha}}}{\partial p_{gi}\partial p_{g'j}},$$

$$\frac{\partial^2\hat{\gamma}}{\partial p_{gi}\partial p_{g'j}\partial p_{g''k}} = \frac{\partial^3\hat{\gamma}}{(\partial\hat{\boldsymbol{\alpha}}')^{<3>}}\frac{\partial\hat{\boldsymbol{\alpha}}}{\partial p_{gi}}\otimes\frac{\partial\hat{\boldsymbol{\alpha}}}{\partial p_{g'j}}\otimes\frac{\partial\hat{\boldsymbol{\alpha}}}{\partial p_{g''k}}$$
$$+\sum_{(gi,g'j,g''k)}^{3}\frac{\partial\hat{\boldsymbol{\alpha}}'}{\partial p_{gi}}\frac{\partial^2\hat{\gamma}}{\partial\hat{\boldsymbol{\alpha}}\,\partial\hat{\boldsymbol{\alpha}}'}\frac{\partial^2\hat{\boldsymbol{\alpha}}}{\partial p_{g'j}\partial p_{g''k}} + \frac{\partial\hat{\gamma}}{\partial\hat{\boldsymbol{\alpha}}'}\frac{\partial^3\hat{\boldsymbol{\alpha}}}{\partial p_{gi}\partial p_{g'j}\partial p_{g''k}}$$
$$(g, g', g'' = 1, ..., G; i = 1, ..., K_g; j = 1, ..., K_{g'}; k = 1, ..., K_{g''}), \tag{16.14}$$

where $\sum_{(\cdot)}^{3}$ denotes the sum of 3 terms having similar patterns with respect to $gi, g'j$ and $g''k$. Note that in Equation 16.14 some of the partial derivatives, such as $\partial^2\hat{\boldsymbol{\alpha}}/\partial p_{gi}\partial p_{g'j}$ when $g \neq g'$, are zero.

In the rest of this section I derive the confidence interval for γ_0. The results are summarized in Theorem 2 below. Note that whereas Theorem 1 gives an improved approximation to the distribution of the coefficient estimators, this approximation cannot directly be used for interval estimation of γ_0 since the population values used in Theorem 1 are usually unavailable in practice. Instead, I focus on the following Studentized coefficient or pivotal statistic for interval estimation of γ_0:

$$t = (\hat{\gamma} - \gamma_o)/\hat{\zeta}_2^{1/2}. \tag{16.15}$$

Assume that the following Taylor series holds:

$$t = \zeta_2^{-1/2}\frac{\partial\gamma_0}{\partial\boldsymbol{\pi}_{\mathrm{T}}'}\mathbf{N}^{-\frac{1}{2}}\mathbf{u} + \frac{1}{2}\zeta_2^{-1/2}\left\{\left(\frac{\partial}{\partial\boldsymbol{\pi}_{\mathrm{T}}'}\right)^{<2>}\gamma_0\right\}\mathbf{N}^{-\frac{1}{2}<2>}\mathbf{u}^{<2>}$$
$$-\frac{1}{2}\zeta_2^{-3/2}\frac{\partial\gamma_0}{\partial\boldsymbol{\pi}_{\mathrm{T}}'}\mathbf{N}^{-\frac{1}{2}}\mathbf{u}\frac{\partial\zeta_2}{\partial\boldsymbol{\pi}_{\mathrm{T}}'}\mathbf{N}^{-\frac{1}{2}}\mathbf{u} + O_p(\tilde{N}^{-1}). \tag{16.16}$$

Then, the first three cumulants of t are given by

$$\kappa_1(t) = \zeta_1{}' + O(\tilde{N}^{-3/2}) \quad (\zeta_1{}' = O(\tilde{N}^{-1/2})),$$
$$\kappa_2(t) = 1 + O(\tilde{N}^{-1}) \quad (\zeta_2{}' = 1), \tag{16.17}$$
$$\kappa_3(t) = \zeta_3{}' + O(\tilde{N}^{-3/2}) \quad (\zeta_3{}' = O(\tilde{N}^{-1/2})).$$

From the standard statistical theory (see the references for Theorem 1) and the asymptotic cumulants given by Equation 16.17 (for $\zeta_1{}'$ and $\zeta_3{}'$ see Section 16.A.3 of the Appendix) using the Cornish-Fisher expansion, we have Theorem 2.

Theorem 2. *The confidence interval for* γ_0 *with asymptotic confidence coefficient* $1-\tilde{\alpha}$ (e.g., $\tilde{\alpha}=0.05$) *accurate up to* $O(\tilde{N}^{-1/2})$, *when the discreteness of the multinomial distribution is neglected, is*

$$\hat{\gamma} + [\pm z_{\tilde{\alpha}/2} - \{\hat{\zeta}_1{}' + (\hat{\zeta}_3{}'/6)(z_{\tilde{\alpha}/2}^2 - 1)\}]\,\hat{\zeta}_2^{1/2}\,, \tag{16.18}$$

where $\int_{-\infty}^{z_{\tilde{\alpha}/2}} \phi(z^*)dz^* = 1-(\tilde{\alpha}/2)$; and $\tilde{N}^{1/2}\hat{\zeta}_i{}'(i=1,3)$ and $\tilde{N}\hat{\zeta}_2$ are consistent estimators of the corresponding asymptotic cumulants independent of $\tilde{N}$.

16.4 Numerical Illustration

In the previous section, the main results of asymptotic expansions were given based on asymptotic theory, which hold when the sample sizes are large. This section gives illustrations of some aspects of the asymptotic expansions in order to show their usefulness with finite sample sizes.

Numerical examples using the two data sets provided by Bock and Lieberman (1970) and reanalyzed by Bock and Aitkin (1981) are shown with simulations. The two data sets consist of binary responses of 5 items selected from the Law School Admission Test (LSAT) by 1,000 examinees. That is, the first data set is comprised of 1,000 $\times$ 5 responses from LSAT Section 6 items, and the second one 1,000 $\times$ 5 responses from LSAT Section 7 items. In a previous study (Ogasawara, 2009), I used these data with the 2PL model, and Bock and his colleagues used the 2P normal ogive or probit model. The 2PL model with $c_j = 0$ in place of the 3PL model in Section 16.2 is used due to the difficulty of estimating item parameters without priors or restrictions on parameters in simulations. Note that the main results in Section 16.3 hold for the 2PL, 3PL, and corresponding probit models with some adaptations.

The population item parameters were given from fitting 2PLM to the two data sets (for selected population values, see Ogasawara, 2009). The 5 items in each data set were regarded as common items for two nonequivalent independent examinee groups ($n = 5$). The second examinee group was constructed such that $\theta_{(2)}^* \sim N(-0.5,\ 1.2^2)$ i.e., $A = 1.2$, $B = -0.5$, while in estimation $\theta_{(g)} \sim N(0,\ 1)$ ($g = 1, 2$) was assumed. That is, on average the ability level of the second group was set to be somewhat lower than the reference group, and the dispersion of ability was larger. This situation was employed considering that the items are relatively easy; the proportions of examinees with all correct responses were 29.8% and 30.8% in the original data sets of LSAT Section 6 and 7, respectively.

For simplicity, no additional items had parameters jointly estimated with those for the 5 common items, which gave $n = n_1 = n_2 = 5$ with $G = 2$. The numbers of examinees in the first and second groups were $N \equiv \tilde{N} = N_1 = N_2 = 1,000$ or $N = 2{,}000$ in simulations. For the number of quadrature points in integration (see Equation 16.7), 15 was used in both simulated and theoretical computation.

Tables 16.1–16.4 show the simulated and asymptotic values (the ratios) of the cumulants of the estimators of the linking coefficients. Simulations were performed by randomly generating item responses without model misspecification. From the generated observations, item parameters were estimated by marginal maximum likelihood followed by estimation of linking coefficients. The number of replications was 10,000 in each condition of the simulations. Some pairs of samples were excluded due to nonconvergence in item parameter estimation. The numbers of the excluded pairs, until regular 10,000 pairs of samples were obtained, are 38 for $N = 1{,}000$ in Tables 16.1 and 16.2 and 1 for $N = 1{,}000$ in Tables 16.3 and 16.4.

The simulated cumulants in Tables 16.1–16.4 were given by k-statistics (unbiased estimators of population cumulants) from 10,000 estimates for each linking coefficient, which were multiplied by appropriate powers of N for ease of comparison to the corresponding asymptotic values independent of N. The ratio HASE/ASE is given by $(\zeta_2 + \zeta_{\Delta 2})^{1/2}/\zeta_2^{1/2}$, which depends on N. The simulated version corresponding to HASE/ASE is SD/ASE, where SD is the square root of the usual unbiased sample variance given from 10,000 estimates for each linking coefficient in simulations.

Table 16.1 Simulated and Asymptotic Cumulants of the Coefficient Estimators for Law School Admission Test Section 6: Dispersion, Bias, and Skewness

	$N^{1/2}\zeta_2^{1/2}$ (dispersion)			$N\zeta_1$ (bias)			$N^{1/2}\zeta_3/\zeta_2^{3/2}$ (skewness)		
	Sim.		Th.	Sim.		Th.	Sim.		Th.
	$N = 1{,}000$	$N = 2{,}000$		$N = 1{,}000$	$N = 2{,}000$		$N = 1{,}000$	$N = 2{,}000$	
A_s	22.5	17.5	10.2	247	208	157	172	787	39
B_s	15.4	12.7	7.1	152	122	91	173	1,110	19
A_m	4.7	4.7	4.6	2	7	5	16	18	16
B_m	12.5	9.5	5.9	−147	−122	−91	−144	−596	−26
A_g	5.4	5.1	4.6	34	34	26	29	31	17
B_g	10.6	8.3	5.6	−108	−89	−65	−148	−624	−21
	$(\zeta_2')^{1/2}$ (dispersion)			$N^{1/2}\zeta_1'$(bias)			$N^{1/2}\zeta_3'$ (skewness)		
A_s	0.84	0.90	1	−0.5	0.5	5.6	−41	−44	−20
B_s	0.77	0.85	1	1.3	2.3	9.1	−27	−27	−4
A_m	0.97	0.99	1	−4.5	−3.7	−2.4	−15	−15	−5
B_m	0.73	0.84	1	−4.2	−5.7	−7.6	23	25	21
A_g	0.94	0.98	1	−0.7	0.5	1.8	−20	−18	−6
B_g	0.80	0.88	1	−2.6	−3.9	−5.7	23	24	15

Note: $N = N_1 = N_2$, Th. = theoretical or asymptotic values, Sim. = simulated values

Table 16.2 Simulated and Asymptotic Cumulants of the Coefficient Estimators for Law School Admission Test Section 6: Kurtosis and Standard Error Ratios

	$N\zeta_4/\zeta_2^2$(kurtosis)			HASE(SD)/ASE for non-Studentized estimators				Population parameters
				$N = 1{,}000$		$N = 2{,}000$		
	Sim.		Th.	Sim.	Th.	Sim.	Th.	
	N =1,000	$N = 2{,}000$						
A_s	61,270	1.7×10^6	4,214	2.21	1.64	1.72	1.36	1.2
B_s	60,939	2.9×10^6	1,333	2.18	1.51	1.79	1.28	−0.5
A_m	610	1,009	905	1.02	1.02	1.02	1.01	1.2
B_m	50,124	1.2×10^6	3,171	2.11	1.56	1.60	1.31	−0.5
A_g	2,832	5,512	1,014	1.17	1.19	1.09	1.10	1.2
B_g	54,327	1.3×10^6	2,192	1.90	1.44	1.50	1.24	−0.5

Note: $N = N_1 = N_2$, Th. = theoretical or asymptotic values, Sim. = simulated values, ASE = asymptotic standard errors = ${\zeta_2}^{1/2}$, HASE = higher order ASE = $(\zeta_2 + \zeta_{\Delta 2})^{1/2}$, SD = standard deviations from simulations

Table 16.3 Simulated and Asymptotic Cumulants of the Coefficient Estimators for Law School Admissions Test Section 7: Dispersion, Bias, and Skewness

	$N^{1/2}\zeta_2^{1/2}$ (dispersion)			$N\zeta_1$ (bias)			$N^{1/2}\zeta_3/\zeta_2^{3/2}$ (skewness)		
	Sim.		Th.	Sim.		Th.	Sim.		Th.
	N=1,000	N=2,000		N=1,000	N=2,000		N=1,000	N=2,000	
A_s	11.0	9.9	9.1	73	66	64	45	38	31
B_s	5.1	4.7	4.5	26	21	20	32	25	19
A_m	3.5	3.4	3.3	2	2	2	11	9	9
B_m	4.3	3.9	3.6	−21	−21	−20	−17	−13	−10
A_g	3.5	3.3	3.3	10	10	9	13	11	10
B_g	3.6	3.3	3.2	−16	−16	−15	−18	−12	−9
	$(\zeta_2')^{1/2}$ (dispersion)			$N^{1/2}\zeta_1{}'$ (bias)			$N^{1/2}\zeta_3{}'$ (skewness)		
A_s	0.98	0.99	1	−3.0	−3.3	−0.4	−29	−29	−14
B_s	0.91	0.95	1	−1.0	−1.6	1.1	−16	−16	−2
A_m	0.97	0.98	1	−2.4	−2.3	−1.2	−8	−10	−1
B_m	0.92	0.96	1	−1.4	−1.8	−2.5	10	10	9
A_g	1.00	1.00	1	−0.8	−0.6	0.7	−10	−11	−2
B_g	0.94	0.97	1	−0.9	−1.4	−2.4	11	10	6

Note: $N = N_1 = N_2$, Th. = theoretical or asymptotic values, Sim. = simulated values

The tables show that on the whole the simulated values are reasonably similar to the corresponding asymptotic values, especially when $N = 2{,}000$. However, some of the simulated standard errors (multiplied by $N^{1/2}$) for $\zeta_2^{1/2}$ are more than 2 times the corresponding asymptotic values with $N = 1{,}000$ (e.g., SD/ASE = 2.21 for A_s in Table 16.2). As mentioned in Section 16.1, this was expected since the similar results were observed for the simulated results for item parameters in LSAT Section 6 (see Ogasawara, 2009) and the linking coefficient estimators are functions of these item parameter estimators. Using HASE, 2.21 was predicted as 1.64 in Table 16.2. In Table 16.4 for LSAT Section 7, the simulated values of SD/ASE are close to the corresponding theoretical ones, where some of the ratios are substantially larger than 1.

Table 16.4 Simulated and Asymptotic Cumulants of the Coefficient Estimators for Law School Admissions Test Section 7: Kurtosis and Standard Error Ratios

	$N\zeta_4/\zeta_2^2$ (kurtosis)			HASE(SD)/ASE for non-Studentized estimators				Population parameters
				$N = 1{,}000$		$N = 2{,}000$		
	Sim.		Th.	Sim.	Th.	Sim.	Th.	
	N=1,000	N=2,000						
A_s	4,588	3,062	3,226	1.21	1.24	1.10	1.13	1.2
B_s	3,417	2,071	1,668	1.14	1.18	1.06	1.09	−0.5
A_m	763	256	299	1.06	1.04	1.01	1.02	1.2
B_m	1,862	1,002	943	1.18	1.19	1.08	1.10	−0.5
A_g	393	382	315	1.06	1.06	1.02	1.03	1.2
B_g	1,615	904	732	1.13	1.15	1.06	1.08	−0.5

Note: $N = N_1 = N_2$, Th. = theoretical or asymptotic values, Sim. = simulated values, ASE = asymptotic standard errors = $\zeta_2^{1/2}$, HASE = higher order ASE = $(\zeta_2 + \zeta_{\Delta 2})^{1/2}$, SD = standard deviations from simulations

It is reassuring to see that the simulated standard errors of Studentized estimators are relatively closer to the corresponding unit asymptotic values than those of the non-Studentized estimators mentioned above (the smallest value is 0.73 for B_m in Table 16.1). The skewnesses of the non-Studentized estimators of coefficient A are all positive, whereas the kurtoses are all positive in Tables 16.2 and 16.4. It is known that among the moment methods, the *m*/*s* method gives unstable results (e.g., Baker & Al-Karni, 1991; Ogasawara, 2000). This is also repeated in Tables 16.1–16.4. In addition, the tables show that the *m*/*s* method gives relatively larger values in other cumulants.

16.5 Some Remarks

In previous sections, the results of the asymptotic expansions of coefficient estimators in IRT linking were shown for the case of the common-item nonequivalent groups design for linking. The numerical illustrations showed that the asymptotic expansions give reasonable approximations to the cumulants of the distributions of the coefficient estimators using the 2PL model.

The number of common or anchor items was 5 in the numerical examples, which was chosen for illustrative purposes to avoid excessively long time for computing. However, the number may be smaller than those used in practice. When the number is increased, more stable results are expected, which was illustrated in a previous study (Ogasawara, 2000, Tables 2 & 4) using $n = 10$ and 15 with the same numbers of unique items whose parameters were jointly estimated with those for the common items.

It is known that the moment methods for linking tend to give less stable results than those using item and test response functions (see Ogasawara, 2001b). Note that the essential results given in this chapter can be applied to the cases of the response function methods when the corresponding partial derivatives of the coefficient estimators with respect to associated item parameters are available. The linking coefficients by the moment methods are elementary functions of item parameters, whereas those by the response function methods are implicit ones. The partial derivatives of the linking coefficients by the response function methods with respect to item parameters concerned can be given straightforwardly (for the first partial derivatives, see Ogasawara, 2001b, Equations 34 & 36) by applying the formulas for the partial derivatives in implicit functions (e.g., Ogasawara, 2007a, c).

Chapter 16 Appendix

16.A.1 Asymptotic Cumulants for Theorem 1

From Equation 16.11, we have

$$\kappa_1(v) = \frac{1}{2}\left\{\left(\frac{\partial}{\partial \boldsymbol{\pi}_{\mathrm{T}}'}\right)^{<2>} \gamma_0\right\}\mathbf{N}^{-\frac{1}{2}<2>}\mathrm{E}(\mathbf{u}^{<2>}) + O(\tilde{N}^{-2}) \tag{16.A.1}$$

where $\mathrm{E}(\mathbf{uu}') = \mathrm{Bdiag}(\boldsymbol{\Omega}_{(1)}, ..., \boldsymbol{\Omega}_{(G)})$; Bdiag $(\cdot)$ denotes a block diagonal matrix with matrices used as arguments being its diagonal blocks; $(\boldsymbol{\Omega}_{(g)})_{ij} = \omega_{gij} = \mathrm{E}(u_{gi}u_{gj})$; $= N_g\mathrm{cov}(p_{gi}, p_{gj}) = \delta_{ij}\pi_{\mathrm{T}gi} - \pi_{\mathrm{T}gi}\pi_{\mathrm{T}gj}$ $(g = 1, ..., G; i, j = 1, ..., K_g)$; $(\cdot)_{ij}$ is the (i, j)th element of a matrix; and δ_{ij} is the Kronecker delta.

From Equation 16.A.1, we have

$$\begin{aligned}\kappa_1(v) &= \sum_{g=1}^{G}\frac{N_g^{-1}}{2}\mathrm{tr}\left(\frac{\partial^2\gamma_0}{\partial \boldsymbol{\pi}_{\mathrm{T}(g)}\,\partial \boldsymbol{\pi}_{\mathrm{T}(g)}'}\boldsymbol{\Omega}_{(g)}\right) + O(\tilde{N}^{-2})\\ &\equiv \zeta_1(v) + O(\tilde{N}^{-2})\end{aligned} \tag{16.A.2}$$

where $\zeta_1(v)$ is the asymptotic bias of v of order $O(\tilde{N}^{-1})$.

For $\kappa_2(v)$, using Equations 16.12 and 16.12,

$$\begin{aligned}\kappa_2(v) =& \sum_{g=1}^{G} N_g^{-1}\frac{\partial\gamma_0}{\partial \boldsymbol{\pi}_{\mathrm{T}(g)}'}\boldsymbol{\Omega}_{(g)}\frac{\partial\gamma_0}{\partial \boldsymbol{\pi}_{\mathrm{T}(g)}} + \left[\frac{\partial\gamma_0}{\partial \boldsymbol{\pi}_{\mathrm{T}}'}\otimes\left\{\left(\frac{\partial}{\partial \boldsymbol{\pi}_{\mathrm{T}}'}\right)^{<2>}\gamma_0\right\}\right]\mathbf{N}^{-\frac{1}{2}<3>}\mathrm{E}(\mathbf{u}^{<3>})\\ &+\mathrm{E}\left\{\frac{1}{4}\left[\left\{\left(\frac{\partial}{\partial \boldsymbol{\pi}_{\mathrm{T}}'}\right)^{<2>}\gamma_0\right\}\mathbf{N}^{-\frac{1}{2}<2>}\mathbf{u}^{<2>}\right]^2\right\}\\ &+\frac{1}{3}\left[\frac{\partial\gamma_0}{\partial \boldsymbol{\pi}_{\mathrm{T}}'}\otimes\left\{\left(\frac{\partial}{\partial \boldsymbol{\pi}_{\mathrm{T}}'}\right)^{<3>}\gamma_0\right\}\right]\mathbf{N}^{-\frac{1}{2}<4>}\mathrm{E}(\mathbf{u}^{<4>}) - \{\kappa_1(v)\}^2 + O(\tilde{N}^{-3})\end{aligned} \tag{16.A.3}$$

The second term on the right-hand side of Equation 16.A.3 is

$$\sum_{g=1}^{G} N_g^{-2} \sum_{i,j,k=1}^{K_g} \frac{\partial \gamma_0}{\partial \pi_{gi}} \frac{\partial^2 \gamma_0}{\partial \pi_{gj} \partial \pi_{gk}} J_g(i,j,k), \tag{16.A.4}$$

where

$$\begin{aligned} J_g(i,j,k) &= N_g^2 \mathrm{E}\{(p_{gi} - \pi_{\mathrm{T}gi})(p_{gj} - \pi_{\mathrm{T}gj})(p_{gk} - \pi_{\mathrm{T}gk})\} \\ &= \delta_{ij}\delta_{ik}(\pi_{\mathrm{T}gi} - 3\pi_{\mathrm{T}gi}^2) - \{\delta_{ij}(1-\delta_{ik})\pi_{\mathrm{T}gi}\pi_{\mathrm{T}gk} + \delta_{ik}(1-\delta_{ij})\pi_{\mathrm{T}gi}\pi_{\mathrm{T}gj} \\ &\quad + \delta_{jk}(1-\delta_{ji})\pi_{\mathrm{T}gj}\pi_{\mathrm{T}gi}\} + 2\pi_{\mathrm{T}gi}\pi_{\mathrm{T}gj}\pi_{\mathrm{T}gk} \ \ (i,j,k = 1,\ldots,K_g) \end{aligned} \tag{16.A.5}$$

(see, e.g., Stuart & Ord, 1994, Equation 7.18). The sum of the third and fifth terms on the right-hand side of Equation 16.A.3 becomes

$$\mathrm{E}\left\{\frac{1}{4}\left[\left\{\left(\frac{\partial}{\partial \boldsymbol{\pi}_{\mathrm{T}}'}\right)^{<2>} \gamma_0\right\} \mathbf{N}^{-\frac{1}{2}<2>} \mathbf{u}^{<2>}\right]^2\right\} - \{\kappa_1(v)\}^2$$

$$\begin{aligned} &= \sum_{g,g'=1}^{G} N_g^{-1} N_{g'}^{-1} \sum_{i,j=1}^{K_g} \sum_{k,l=1}^{K_{g'}} \left(\frac{1}{4} \frac{\partial^2 \gamma_0}{\partial \pi_{\mathrm{T}gi} \partial \pi_{\mathrm{T}gj}} \frac{\partial^2 \gamma_0}{\partial \pi_{\mathrm{T}g'k} \partial \pi_{\mathrm{T}g'l}} \right. \\ &\quad \left. + \frac{1}{4} \frac{\partial^2 \gamma_0}{\partial \pi_{\mathrm{T}gi} \partial \pi_{g'k}} \frac{\partial^2 \gamma_0}{\partial \pi_{\mathrm{T}gj} \partial \pi_{\mathrm{T}g'l}} + \frac{1}{4} \frac{\partial^2 \gamma_0}{\partial \pi_{\mathrm{T}gi} \partial \pi_{\mathrm{T}g'l}} \frac{\partial^2 \gamma_0}{\partial \pi_{\mathrm{T}gj} \partial \pi_{\mathrm{T}g'k}} \right) \\ &\quad \times \omega_{gij}\omega_{g'kl} - \frac{1}{4}\left(\sum_{g=1}^{G} N_g^{-1} \sum_{i,j=1}^{K_g} \frac{\partial^2 \gamma_0}{\partial \pi_{\mathrm{T}gi} \partial \pi_{\mathrm{T}gj}} \omega_{gij} \right)^2 + O(\tilde{N}^{-3}) \end{aligned}$$

$$= \frac{1}{2} \sum_{g,g'=1}^{G} N_g^{-1} N_{g'}^{-1} \sum_{i,j=1}^{K_g} \sum_{k,l=1}^{K_{g'}} \frac{\partial^2 \gamma_0}{\partial \pi_{\mathrm{T}gi} \partial \pi_{\mathrm{T}g'k}} \frac{\partial^2 \gamma_0}{\partial \pi_{\mathrm{T}gj} \partial \pi_{\mathrm{T}g'l}} \omega_{gij}\omega_{g'kl} + O(\tilde{N}^{-3}) \tag{16.A.6}$$

The remaining fourth term on the right-hand side of Equation 16.A.3 is

$$\sum_{g,g'=1}^{G} N_g^{-1} N_{g'}^{-1} \sum_{i,j=1}^{K_g} \sum_{k,l=1}^{K_{g'}} \frac{\partial \gamma_0}{\partial \pi_{\mathrm{T}gi}} \frac{\partial^3 \gamma_0}{\partial \pi_{\mathrm{T}gj} \partial \pi_{\mathrm{T}g'k} \partial \pi_{\mathrm{T}g'l}} \omega_{gij}\omega_{g'kl} + O(\tilde{N}^{-3}) \tag{16.A.7}$$

From Equations 16.A.4–16.A.7, Equation 16.A.3 becomes

$$\kappa_2(v) = \sum_{g=1}^{G} N_g^{-1} \frac{\partial \gamma_0}{\partial \boldsymbol{\pi}_{\mathrm{T}(g)}{}'} \boldsymbol{\Omega}_{(g)} \frac{\partial \gamma_0}{\partial \boldsymbol{\pi}_{\mathrm{T}(g)}} + \sum_{g=1}^{G} N_g^{-2} \sum_{i,j,k=1}^{K_g} \frac{\partial \gamma_0}{\partial \pi_{\mathrm{T}\,gi}} \frac{\partial^2 \gamma_0}{\partial \pi_{\mathrm{T}\,gj} \partial \pi_{\mathrm{T}\,gk}} J_g(i,j,k)$$
$$+ \sum_{g,g'=1}^{G} N_g^{-1} N_{g'}^{-1} \sum_{i,j=1}^{K_g} \sum_{k,l=1}^{K_{g'}} \left(\frac{1}{2} \frac{\partial^2 \gamma_0}{\partial \pi_{\mathrm{T}\,gi} \partial \pi_{\mathrm{T}\,g'k}} \frac{\partial^2 \gamma_0}{\partial \pi_{\mathrm{T}\,gj} \partial \pi_{\mathrm{T}\,g'l}} \right.$$
$$\left. + \frac{\partial \gamma_0}{\partial \pi_{\mathrm{T}\,gi}} \frac{\partial^3 \gamma_0}{\partial \pi_{\mathrm{T}\,gj} \partial \pi_{\mathrm{T}\,g'k} \partial \pi_{\mathrm{T}\,g'l}} \right) \omega_{gij} \omega_{g'kl} + O(\tilde{N}^{-3})$$
$$\equiv \zeta_2(v) + \zeta_{\Delta 2}(v) + O(\tilde{N}^{-3}), \tag{16.A.8}$$

where $\zeta_2(v)$ is the asymptotic variance of v of order $O(\tilde{N}^{-1})$ and $\zeta_{\Delta 2}(v)$ is the added higher order asymptotic variance of v of order $O(\tilde{N}^{-2})$.

Similarly, for $\kappa_3(v)$ we have

$$\kappa_3(v) = \mathrm{E}\left[\left(\frac{\partial \gamma_0}{\partial \boldsymbol{\pi}_{\mathrm{T}}{}'} \mathbf{N}^{-\frac{1}{2}} \mathbf{u} \right)^3 + \frac{3}{2} \left(\frac{\partial \gamma_0}{\partial \boldsymbol{\pi}_{\mathrm{T}}{}'} \mathbf{N}^{-\frac{1}{2}} \mathbf{u} \right)^2 \left\{ \left(\frac{\partial}{\partial \boldsymbol{\pi}_{\mathrm{T}}{}'} \right)^{<2>} \gamma_0 \right\} \mathbf{N}^{-\frac{1}{2}<2>} \mathbf{u}^{<2>} \right.$$
$$\left. -3 \left\{ \left(\frac{\partial \gamma_0}{\partial \boldsymbol{\pi}_{\mathrm{T}}{}'} \mathbf{N}^{-\frac{1}{2}} \mathbf{u} \right)^2 \right\} \kappa_1(v) \right] + O(\tilde{N}^{-3})$$

$$= \sum_{g=1}^{G} N_g^{-2} \sum_{i,j,k=1}^{K_g} \frac{\partial \gamma_0}{\partial \pi_{\mathrm{T}gi}} \frac{\partial \gamma_0}{\partial \pi_{\mathrm{T}gj}} \frac{\partial \gamma_0}{\partial \pi_{\mathrm{T}gk}} J_g(i,j,k) + \frac{3}{2}$$
$$\times \sum_{g,g'=1}^{G} N_g^{-1} N_{g'}^{-1} \sum_{i,j=1}^{K_g} \sum_{k,l=1}^{K_{g'}} \left(\frac{\partial \gamma_0}{\partial \pi_{\mathrm{T}gi}} \frac{\partial \gamma_0}{\partial \pi_{\mathrm{T}gj}} \frac{\partial^2 \gamma_0}{\partial \pi_{\mathrm{T}g'k} \partial \pi_{\mathrm{T}g'l}} + 2 \frac{\partial \gamma_0}{\partial \pi_{\mathrm{T}gi}} \frac{\partial \gamma_0}{\partial \pi_{\mathrm{T}g'k}} \right.$$
$$\left. \times \frac{\partial^2 \gamma_0}{\partial \pi_{\mathrm{T}gj} \partial \pi_{\mathrm{T}g'l}} \right) \omega_{gij} \omega_{g'kl} - \frac{3}{2} \sum_{g,g'=1}^{G} N_g^{-1} N_{g'}^{-1} \sum_{i,j=1}^{K_g} \sum_{k,l=1}^{K_{g'}} \frac{\partial \gamma_0}{\partial \pi_{\mathrm{T}gi}} \frac{\partial \gamma_0}{\partial \pi_{\mathrm{T}gj}}$$
$$\times \frac{\partial^2 \gamma_0}{\partial \pi_{\mathrm{T}g'k} \partial \pi_{\mathrm{T}g'l}} \omega_{gij} \omega_{g'kl} O(\tilde{N}^{-3})$$

$$= \sum_{g=1}^{G} N_g^{-2} \sum_{i,j,k=1}^{K_g} \frac{\partial \gamma_0}{\partial \pi_{\mathrm{T}gi}} \frac{\partial \gamma_0}{\partial \pi_{\mathrm{T}gj}} \frac{\partial \gamma_0}{\partial \pi_{\mathrm{T}gk}} J_g(i,j,k)$$
$$+ 3 \sum_{g,g'=1}^{G} N_g^{-1} N_{g'}^{-1} \frac{\partial \gamma_0}{\partial \boldsymbol{\pi}_{\mathrm{T}(g)}{}'} \boldsymbol{\Omega}_{(g)} \frac{\partial^2 \gamma_0}{\partial \boldsymbol{\pi}_{\mathrm{T}(g)} \partial \boldsymbol{\pi}_{\mathrm{T}(g')}{}'} \boldsymbol{\Omega}_{(g')} \frac{\partial \gamma_0}{\partial \boldsymbol{\pi}_{\mathrm{T}(g')}}$$
$$+ O(\tilde{N}^{-3}) \equiv \zeta_3(v) + O(\tilde{N}^{-3}), \tag{16.A.9}$$

where $\zeta_3(v)$ is the asymptotic third cumulant of v of order $O(\tilde{N}^{-2})$ with $\zeta_3(v)/\{\zeta_2(v)\}^{3/2}$ being the asymptotic skewness of order $O(\tilde{N}^{-1/2})$.

Lastly, for $\kappa_4(v)$, it follows that

$$\begin{aligned}\kappa_4(v) &= \mathrm{E}[\{v-\mathrm{E}(v)\}^4] - 3\{\kappa_2(v)\}^2 \\ &= \mathrm{E}(v^4) - 4\mathrm{E}(v^3)\mathrm{E}(v) - 3\{\mathrm{E}(v^2)\}^2 + 12\mathrm{E}(v^2)\{\mathrm{E}(v)\}^2 - 6\{\mathrm{E}(v)\}^4,\end{aligned} \tag{16.A.10}$$

where from Equation 16.11,

$$\begin{aligned}\mathrm{E}(v^4) = \mathrm{E}\Bigg[&\left(\frac{\partial\gamma_0}{\partial\boldsymbol{\pi}_{\mathrm{T}}{}'}\mathbf{N}^{-\frac{1}{2}}\mathbf{u}\right)^4 + 2\left\{\left(\frac{\partial}{\partial\boldsymbol{\pi}_{\mathrm{T}}{}'}\right)^{<2>}\gamma_0\right\}\mathbf{N}^{-\frac{1}{2}<2>}\mathbf{u}^{<2>}\left(\frac{\partial\gamma_0}{\partial\boldsymbol{\pi}_{\mathrm{T}}{}'}\mathbf{N}^{-\frac{1}{2}}\mathbf{u}\right)^3 \\ &+\frac{3}{2}\left\{\left\{\left(\frac{\partial}{\partial\boldsymbol{\pi}_{\mathrm{T}}{}'}\right)^{<2>}\gamma_0\right\}\mathbf{N}^{-\frac{1}{2}<2>}\mathbf{u}^{<2>}\right\}^2\left(\frac{\partial\gamma_0}{\partial\boldsymbol{\pi}_{\mathrm{T}}{}'}\mathbf{N}^{-\frac{1}{2}}\mathbf{u}\right)^2 \\ &+\frac{2}{3}\left\{\left(\frac{\partial}{\partial\boldsymbol{\pi}_{\mathrm{T}}{}'}\right)^{<3>}\gamma_0\right\}\mathbf{N}^{-\frac{1}{2}<3>}\mathbf{u}^{<3>}\left(\frac{\partial\gamma_0}{\partial\boldsymbol{\pi}_{\mathrm{T}}{}'}\mathbf{N}^{-\frac{1}{2}}\mathbf{u}\right)^3\Bigg] + O(\tilde{N}^{-4})\end{aligned}$$

$$\begin{aligned}&= \sum_{g=1}^{G} N_g^{-3} \sum_{i,j,k,l=1}^{K_g} \frac{\partial\gamma_0}{\partial\pi_{\mathrm{T}gi}}\frac{\partial\gamma_0}{\partial\pi_{\mathrm{T}gj}}\frac{\partial\gamma_0}{\partial\pi_{\mathrm{T}gk}}\frac{\partial\gamma_0}{\partial\pi_{\mathrm{T}gl}} J_g(i,j,k,l) \\ &\quad + 3\sum_{g,g'=1}^{G} N_g^{-1}N_{g'}^{-1}\sum_{i,j=1}^{K_g}\sum_{k,l=1}^{K_{g'}}\frac{\partial\gamma_0}{\partial\pi_{\mathrm{T}gi}}\frac{\partial\gamma_0}{\partial\pi_{\mathrm{T}gj}}\frac{\partial\gamma_0}{\partial\pi_{\mathrm{T}g'k}}\frac{\partial\gamma_0}{\partial\pi_{\mathrm{T}g'l}}\omega_{gij}\omega_{g'kl}\end{aligned}$$

$$+2\sum_{g,g'=1}^{G} N_g^{-1}N_{g'}^{-1}\sum_{i,j=1}^{K_g}\sum_{k,l,m=1}^{K_{g'}}\sum^{10}\frac{\partial^2\gamma_0}{\partial\pi_{\mathrm{T}gi}\partial\pi_{\mathrm{T}gj}}\frac{\partial\gamma_0}{\partial\pi_{\mathrm{T}g'k}}\frac{\partial\gamma_0}{\partial\pi_{\mathrm{T}g'l}}\frac{\partial\gamma_0}{\partial\pi_{\mathrm{T}g'm}}\omega_{gij}J_{g'}(k,l,m)$$

$$+\sum_{\substack{g,g'g'',g^{(3)},\\ g^{(4)}g^{(5)}=1}}^{G}\sum_{i=1}^{K_g}\sum_{j=1}^{K_{g'}}\sum_{k=1}^{K_{g''}}\sum_{l=1}^{K_{g^{(3)}}}\sum_{m=1}^{K_{g^{(4)}}}\sum_{a=1}^{K_{g^{(5)}}}\left(\frac{3}{2}\frac{\partial^2\gamma_0}{\partial\pi_{\mathrm{T}gi}\partial\pi_{\mathrm{T}g'j}}\frac{\partial^2\gamma_0}{\partial\pi_{\mathrm{T}g''k}\partial\pi_{\mathrm{T}g^{(3)}l}}\frac{\partial\gamma_0}{\partial\pi_{\mathrm{T}g^{(4)}m}}\frac{\partial\gamma_0}{\partial\pi_{\mathrm{T}g^{(5)}a}}\right.$$

$$\left.+\frac{2}{3}\frac{\partial^3\gamma_0}{\partial\pi_{\mathrm{T}gi}\partial\pi_{\mathrm{T}g'j}\partial\pi_{\mathrm{T}g''k}}\frac{\partial^2\gamma_0}{\partial\pi_{\mathrm{T}g^{(3)}l}}\frac{\partial\gamma_0}{\partial\pi_{\mathrm{T}g^{(4)}m}}\frac{\partial\gamma_0}{\partial\pi_{\mathrm{T}g^{(5)}a}}\right)$$

$$\times\sum^{15}\delta_{gg'}\delta_{g''g^{(3)}}\delta_{g^{(4)}g^{(5)}}N_g^{-1}N_{g''}^{-1}N_{g^{(4)}}^{-1}\omega_{gij}\omega_{g''kl}\omega_{g^{(4)}ma} + O(\tilde{N}^{-4}); \tag{16.A.11}$$

$J_g(i,j,k,l)$ is the N_g^3 times the multivariate fourth cumulant of p_{gi}, p_{gj}, p_{gk} and p_{gl}, that is,

$$
\begin{aligned}
&N_g^3\kappa(p_{gi},p_{gi},p_{gi},p_{gi}) = \pi_{\mathrm{T}gi}(1-\pi_{\mathrm{T}gi})\{1-6\pi_{\mathrm{T}gi}(1-\pi_{\mathrm{T}gi})\},\\
&N_g^3\kappa(p_{gi},p_{gi},p_{gi},p_{gj}) = -\pi_{\mathrm{T}gi}\pi_{\mathrm{T}gj}\{1-6\pi_{\mathrm{T}gi}(1-\pi_{\mathrm{T}gi})\},\\
&N_g^3\kappa(p_{gi},p_{gi},p_{gj},p_{gj}) = -\pi_{\mathrm{T}gi}\pi_{\mathrm{T}gj}\{(1-2\pi_{\mathrm{T}gi})(1-2\pi_{\mathrm{T}gj})+2\pi_{\mathrm{T}g\,i}\pi_{\mathrm{T}gj}\},\\
&N_g^3\kappa(p_{gi},p_{gi},p_{gj},p_{gk}) = 2\pi_{\mathrm{T}gi}\pi_{\mathrm{T}gj}\pi_{\mathrm{T}gk}(1-3\pi_{\mathrm{T}gi}),\\
&N_g^3\kappa(p_{gi},p_{gj},p_{gk},p_{gl}) = -6\pi_{\mathrm{T}gi}\pi_{\mathrm{T}gj}\pi_{\mathrm{T}gk}\pi_{\mathrm{T}gl}\\
&(g=1,\ldots,G;\ i,j,k,l=1,\ldots,K_g;\ i\neq j, i\neq k, i\neq l, j\neq k, j\neq l, k\neq l)
\end{aligned}
\tag{16.A.12}
$$

(see, e.g., Stuart & Ord, 1994, Equation 7.18); and $\overset{h}{\Sigma}$ is the sum of h terms with similar patterns.

The sum of the remaining terms other than $\mathrm{E}(v^4)$ on the right-hand side of Equation 16.A.10 is given by

$$
\begin{aligned}
&-4\mathrm{E}(v^3)\mathrm{E}(v)-3\{\mathrm{E}(v^2)\}^2+12\mathrm{E}(v^2)\{\mathrm{E}(v)\}^2-6\{\mathrm{E}(v)\}^4\\
&=-4\{\kappa_3(v)+3\kappa_2(v)\kappa_1(v)\}\kappa_1(v)-3[\kappa_2(v)+\{\kappa_1(v)\}^2]^2\\
&\quad+12\kappa_2(v)\{\kappa_1(v)\}^2+O(\tilde{N}^{-4})\\
&=-3\{\zeta_2(v)\}^2-4\zeta_1(v)\zeta_3(v)-6\zeta_2(v)\zeta_{\Delta 2}(v)-6\zeta_2(v)\{\zeta_1(v)\}^2+O(\tilde{N}^{-4}).
\end{aligned}
\tag{16.A.13}
$$

From Equations 16.A.11 and 16.A.13, Equation 16.A.10 becomes

$$
\begin{aligned}
\kappa_4(v)=&\sum_{g=1}^{G}N_g^{-3}\sum_{i,j,k,l=1}^{K_g}\frac{\partial\gamma_0}{\partial\pi_{\mathrm{T}gi}}\frac{\partial\gamma_0}{\partial\pi_{\mathrm{T}gj}}\frac{\partial\gamma_0}{\partial\pi_{\mathrm{T}gk}}\frac{\partial\gamma_0}{\partial\pi_{\mathrm{T}gl}}J_g(i,j,k,l)\\
&+2\sum_{g,g'=1}^{G}N_g^{-1}N_{g'}^{-1}\sum_{i,j=1}^{K_g}\sum_{k,l,m=1}^{K_{g'}}\sum^{10}\frac{\partial^2\gamma_0}{\partial\pi_{\mathrm{T}gi}\partial\pi_{\mathrm{T}gj}}\frac{\partial\gamma_0}{\partial\pi_{\mathrm{T}g'k}}\frac{\partial\gamma_0}{\partial\pi_{\mathrm{T}g'l}}\frac{\partial\gamma_0}{\partial\pi_{\mathrm{T}g'm}}\omega_{gij}J_{g'}(k,l,m)\\
&+\sum_{\substack{g,g',g'',g^{(3)},\\ g^{(4)},g^{(5)}=1}}^{G}\sum_{i=1}^{K_g}\sum_{j=1}^{K_{g'}}\sum_{k=1}^{K_{g''}}\sum_{l=1}^{K_{g^{(3)}}}\sum_{m=1}^{K_{g^{(4)}}}\sum_{a=1}^{K_{g^{(5)}}}\left(\frac{3}{2}\frac{\partial^2\gamma_0}{\partial\pi_{\mathrm{T}gi}\partial\pi_{\mathrm{T}g'j}\partial\pi_{\mathrm{T}g''k}}\frac{\partial^2\gamma_0}{\partial\pi_{\mathrm{T}g^{(3)}l}}\frac{\partial\gamma_0}{\partial\pi_{\mathrm{T}g^{(4)}m}}\frac{\partial\gamma_0}{\partial\pi_{\mathrm{T}g^{(5)}a}}\right.\\
&\qquad\left.+\frac{2}{3}\frac{\partial^3\gamma_0}{\partial\pi_{\mathrm{T}gi}\partial\pi_{\mathrm{T}g'j}\partial\pi_{\mathrm{T}g''k}}\frac{\partial^2\gamma_0}{\partial\pi_{\mathrm{T}g^{(3)}l}}\frac{\partial\gamma_0}{\partial\pi_{\mathrm{T}g^{(4)}m}}\frac{\partial\gamma_0}{\partial\pi_{\mathrm{T}g^{(5)}a}}\right)\\
&\qquad\times\sum^{15}\delta_{gg'}\delta_{g''g^{(3)}}\delta_{g^{(4)}g^{(5)}}N_g^{-1}N_{g''}^{-1}N_{g^{(4)}}^{-1}\omega_{gij}\omega_{g''kl}\omega_{g^{(4)}ma}\\
&\qquad-4\zeta_1(v)\zeta_3(v)-6\zeta_2(v)\zeta_{\Delta 2}(v)-6\zeta_2(v)\{\zeta_1(v)\}^2+O(\tilde{N}^{-4})\\
&\qquad\equiv\zeta_4(v)+O(\tilde{N}^{-4}),
\end{aligned}
\tag{16.A.14}
$$

where $\zeta_4(v)$ is the asymptotic fourth cumulant of v of order $O(\tilde{N}^{-3})$ with $\zeta_4(v)/\{\zeta_2(v)\}^2$ being the asymptotic kurtosis of order $O(\tilde{N}^{-1})$.

16.A.2 Nonzero Partial Derivatives

In the following, subscripts j, k, $l = 1, \ldots, n$.

16.A.2.1 The m/s Method

Define $\sigma_{bg} = \left\{\sum_{i=1}^n b_{gi}^2 - n^{-1}\left(\sum_{i=1}^n b_{gi}\right)^2\right\}^{1/2}$ $(g = 1, 2)$ (note that σ_{bg} is a scaled SD) and $\bar{b}_{g\cdot} = n^{-1}\sum_{i=1}^n b_{gi}$ $(g = 1, 2)$. Then,

$$\frac{\partial A_s}{\partial b_{1j}} = (b_{1j} - \bar{b}_{1\cdot})\sigma_{b1}^{-2}A_s, \quad \frac{\partial A_s}{\partial b_{2j}} = -(b_{2j} - \bar{b}_{2\cdot})\sigma_{b2}^{-2}A_s,$$

$$\frac{\partial B_s}{\partial b_{1j}} = n^{-1} - \bar{b}_{2\cdot}\frac{\partial A_s}{\partial b_{1j}}, \quad \frac{\partial B_s}{\partial b_{2j}} = -n^{-1}A_s - \bar{b}_{2\cdot}\frac{\partial A_s}{\partial b_{2j}},$$

$$\frac{\partial^2 A_s}{\partial b_{1j}\partial b_{1k}} = \{(\delta_{jk} - n^{-1})\sigma_{b1}^{-2} - 2(b_{1j} - \bar{b}_{1\cdot})(b_{1k} - \bar{b}_{1\cdot})\sigma_{b1}^{-4}\}A_s + (b_{1j} - \bar{b}_{1\cdot})\sigma_{b1}^{-2}\frac{\partial A_s}{\partial b_{1k}},$$

$$\frac{\partial^2 A_s}{\partial b_{1j}\partial b_{2k}} = (b_{1j} - \bar{b}_{1\cdot})\sigma_{b1}^{-2}\frac{\partial A_s}{\partial b_{2k}},$$

$$\frac{\partial^2 A_s}{\partial b_{2j}\partial b_{2k}} = \{-(\delta_{jk} - n^{-1})\sigma_{b2}^{-2} + 2(b_{2j} - \bar{b}_{2\cdot})(b_{2k} - \bar{b}_{2\cdot})\sigma_{b2}^{-4}\}A_s - (b_{2j} - \bar{b}_{2\cdot})\sigma_{b2}^{-2}\frac{\partial A_s}{\partial b_{2k}},$$

$$\frac{\partial^2 B_s}{\partial b_{1j}\partial b_{1k}} = -\bar{b}_{2\cdot}\frac{\partial^2 A_s}{\partial b_{1j}\partial b_{1k}}, \quad \frac{\partial^2 B_s}{\partial b_{1j}\partial b_{2k}} = -n^{-1}\frac{\partial A_s}{\partial b_{1j}} - \bar{b}_{2\cdot}\frac{\partial^2 A_s}{\partial b_{1j}\partial b_{2k}},$$
$$\frac{\partial^2 B_s}{\partial b_{2j}\partial b_{2k}} = -n^{-1}\frac{\partial A_s}{\partial b_{2j}} - n^{-1}\frac{\partial A_s}{\partial b_{2k}} - \bar{b}_{2\cdot}\frac{\partial^2 A_s}{\partial b_{2j}\partial b_{2k}},$$

$$\begin{aligned}\frac{\partial^3 A_s}{\partial b_{1j}\partial b_{1k}\partial b_{1l}} = &\left\{-2\sum_{(j,k,l)}^{3}(\delta_{jk} - n^{-1})(b_{1l} - \bar{b}_{1\cdot})\sigma_{b1}^{-4} + 8(b_{1j} - \bar{b}_{1\cdot})(b_{1k} - \bar{b}_{1\cdot})\right.\\ &\left.\times (b_{1l} - \bar{b}_{1\cdot})\sigma_{b1}^{-6}\right\}A_s + \{(\delta_{jk} - n^{-1})\sigma_{b1}^{-2} - 2(b_{1j} - \bar{b}_{1\cdot})\\ &\times (b_{1k} - \bar{b}_{1\cdot})\sigma_{b1}^{-4}\}\partial A_s/\partial b_{1l} + \{(\delta_{jl} - n^{-1})\sigma_{b1}^{-2} - 2(b_{1j} - \bar{b}_{1\cdot})\\ &\times (b_{1l} - \bar{b}_{1\cdot})\sigma_{b1}^{-4}\}\partial A_s/\partial b_{1k} + (b_{1j} - \bar{b}_{1\cdot})\sigma_{b1}^{-2}\partial^2 A_s/\partial b_{1k}\partial b_{1l},\end{aligned}$$

$$\frac{\partial^3 A_s}{\partial b_{1j}\partial b_{1k}\partial b_{2l}} = \{(\delta_{jk} - n^{-1})\sigma_{b1}^{-2} - 2(b_{1j} - \bar{b}_{1\cdot})(b_{1k} - \bar{b}_{1\cdot})\sigma_{b1}^{-4}\}\partial A_s/\partial b_{2l}$$
$$+ (b_{1j} - \bar{b}_{1\cdot})\sigma_{b1}^{-2}\partial^2 A_s/\partial b_{1k}\partial b_{2l},$$

$$\frac{\partial^3 A_s}{\partial b_{1j}\partial b_{2k}\partial b_{2l}} = (b_{1j} - \bar{b}_{1\cdot})\sigma_{b1}^{-2}\partial^2 A_s/\partial b_{2k}\partial b_{2l},$$

$$\frac{\partial^3 A_s}{\partial b_{2j}\partial b_{2k}\partial b_{2l}} = \left\{2\sum_{(j,k,l)}^{3}(\delta_{jk} - n^{-1})(b_{2l} - \bar{b}_{2\cdot})\sigma_{b2}^{-4} - 8(b_{2j} - \bar{b}_{2\cdot})(b_{2k} - \bar{b}_{2\cdot})\right.$$
$$\left.\times (b_{2l} - \bar{b}_{2\cdot})\sigma_{b2}^{-6}\right\}A_s + \{-(\delta_{jk} - n^{-1})\sigma_{b2}^{-2} + 2(b_{2j} - \bar{b}_{2\cdot})$$
$$\times (b_{2k} - \bar{b}_{2\cdot})\sigma_{b2}^{-4}\}\partial A_s/\partial b_{2l} + \{-(\delta_{jl} - n^{-1})\sigma_{b2}^{-2} + 2(b_{2j} - \bar{b}_{2\cdot})$$
$$\times (b_{2l} - \bar{b}_{2\cdot})\sigma_{b2}^{-4}\}\partial A_s/\partial b_{2k} - (b_{2j} - \bar{b}_{2\cdot})\sigma_{b2}^{-2}\partial^2 A_s/\partial b_{2k}\partial b_{2l},$$

$$\frac{\partial^3 B_s}{\partial b_{1j}\partial b_{1k}\partial b_{1l}} = -\bar{b}_{2\cdot}\frac{\partial^3 A_s}{\partial b_{1j}\partial b_{1k}\partial b_{1l}},$$

$$\frac{\partial^3 B_s}{\partial b_{1j}\partial b_{1k}\partial b_{2l}} = -n^{-1}\frac{\partial^2 A_s}{\partial b_{1j}\partial b_{1k}} - \bar{b}_{2\cdot}\frac{\partial^3 A_s}{\partial b_{1j}\partial b_{1k}\partial b_{2l}},$$

$$\frac{\partial^3 B_s}{\partial b_{1j}\partial b_{2k}\partial b_{2l}} = -n^{-1}\frac{\partial^2 A_s}{\partial b_{1j}\partial b_{2k}} - n^{-1}\frac{\partial^2 A_s}{\partial b_{1j}\partial b_{2l}} - \bar{b}_{2\cdot}\frac{\partial^3 A_s}{\partial b_{1j}\partial b_{2k}\partial b_{2l}},$$

$$\frac{\partial^3 B_s}{\partial b_{2j}\partial b_{2k}\partial b_{2l}} = -n^{-1}\frac{\partial^2 A_s}{\partial b_{2j}\partial b_{2k}} - n^{-1}\frac{\partial^2 A_s}{\partial b_{2j}\partial b_{2l}} - n^{-1}\frac{\partial^2 A_s}{\partial b_{2k}\partial b_{2l}} - \bar{b}_{2\cdot}\frac{\partial^3 A_s}{\partial b_{2j}\partial b_{2k}\partial b_{2l}},$$

16.A.2.2 The m/m Method

Define $a_{g\cdot} = \sum_{i=1}^{n} a_{gi}\ (g = 1, 2)$. Then,

$$\frac{\partial A_m}{\partial(a_{1j}, a_{2j})'} = \begin{pmatrix} -a_{1\cdot}^{-2}a_{2\cdot} \\ a_{1\cdot}^{-1} \end{pmatrix}, \quad \frac{\partial B_m}{\partial(a_{1j}, a_{2j})'} = \begin{pmatrix} a_{1\cdot}^{-2}a_{2\cdot}\bar{b}_{2\cdot} \\ -a_{1\cdot}^{-1}\bar{b}_{2\cdot} \end{pmatrix},$$

$$\frac{\partial B_m}{\partial(b_{1j}, b_{2j})'} = \begin{pmatrix} n^{-1} \\ -n^{-1}a_{1\cdot}^{-1}a_{2\cdot} \end{pmatrix},$$

$$\frac{\partial^2 A_m}{\partial a_{1j}\partial(a_{1k}, a_{2k})'} = \begin{pmatrix} 2a_{1\cdot}^{-3}a_{2\cdot} \\ -a_{1\cdot}^{-2} \end{pmatrix}, \quad \frac{\partial^2 B_m}{\partial a_{1j}\partial(a_{1k}, a_{2k})'} = \begin{pmatrix} -2a_{1\cdot}^{-3}a_{2\cdot}\bar{b}_{2\cdot} \\ a_{1\cdot}^{-2}\bar{b}_{2\cdot} \end{pmatrix},$$

$$\frac{\partial^2 B_m}{\partial(a_{1j}, a_{2j})'\partial b_{2k}} = \begin{pmatrix} n^{-1}a_{1\cdot}^{-2}a_{2\cdot} \\ -n^{-1}a_{1\cdot}^{-1} \end{pmatrix},$$

$$\frac{\partial^3 A_m}{\partial a_{1j}\partial a_{1k}\partial a_{1l}} = -6a_{1\cdot}^{-4}a_{2\cdot}, \frac{\partial^3 A_m}{\partial a_{1j}\partial a_{1k}\partial a_{2l}} = 2a_{1}^{-3}, \frac{\partial^3 B_m}{\partial a_{1j}\partial a_{1k}\partial a_{1l}} = 6a_{1}^{-4}a_{2\cdot}\bar{b}_{2\cdot},$$
$$\frac{\partial^3 B_m}{\partial a_{1j}\partial a_{1k}\partial a_{2l}} = -2a_{1\cdot}^{-3}\bar{b}_{2\cdot}, \frac{\partial^3 B_m}{\partial a_{1j}\partial a_{1k}\partial b_{2l}} = -2n^{-1}a_{1\cdot}^{-3}a_{2\cdot}, \frac{\partial^3 B_m}{\partial a_{1j}\partial a_{2k}\partial b_{2l}} = n^{-1}a_{1\cdot}^{-2}.$$

16.A.2.3 The m/gm Method

$$\frac{\partial A_g}{\partial (a_{1j}, a_{2j})'} = \begin{pmatrix} -n^{-1}a_{1j}^{-1}A_g \\ n^{-1}a_{2j}^{-1}A_g \end{pmatrix},$$
$$\frac{\partial B_g}{\partial (a_{1j}, a_{2j})} = -\frac{\partial A_g}{\partial (a_{1j}, a_{2j})}\bar{b}_{2\cdot},$$
$$\frac{\partial B_g}{\partial (b_{1j}, b_{2j})'} = \begin{pmatrix} n^{-1} \\ -n^{-1}A_g \end{pmatrix},$$
$$\frac{\partial^2 A_g}{\partial a_{1j}\partial a_{1k}} = n^{-1}\delta_{jk}a_{1j}^{-2}A_g - n^{-1}a_{1j}^{-1}\frac{\partial A_g}{\partial a_{1k}}, \quad \frac{\partial^2 A_g}{\partial a_{1j}\partial a_{2k}} = -n^{-1}a_{1j}^{-1}\frac{\partial A_g}{\partial a_{2k}},$$
$$\frac{\partial^2 A_g}{\partial a_{2j}\partial a_{2k}} = -n^{-1}\delta_{jk}a_{2j}^{-2}A_g + n^{-1}a_{2j}^{-1}\frac{\partial A_g}{\partial a_{2k}}, \frac{\partial^2 B_g}{\partial a_{1j}\partial a_{1k}} = -\frac{\partial^2 A_g}{\partial a_{1j}\partial a_{1k}}\bar{b}_{2\cdot},$$
$$\frac{\partial^2 B_g}{\partial a_{1j}\partial a_{2k}} = -\frac{\partial^2 A_g}{\partial a_{1j}\partial a_{2k}}\bar{b}_{2\cdot}, \quad \frac{\partial^2 B_g}{\partial a_{1j}\partial b_{2k}} = -n^{-1}\frac{\partial A_g}{\partial a_{1j}},$$
$$\frac{\partial^2 B_g}{\partial a_{2j}\partial a_{2k}} = -\frac{\partial^2 A_g}{\partial a_{2j}\partial a_{2k}}\bar{b}_{2\cdot}, \frac{\partial^2 B_g}{\partial a_{2j}\partial b_{2k}} = -n^{-1}\frac{\partial A_g}{\partial a_{2j}},$$
$$\frac{\partial^3 A_g}{\partial a_{1j}\partial a_{1k}\partial a_{1l}} = -2n^{-1}\delta_{jk}\delta_{jl}a_{1j}^{-3}A_g + n^{-1}\delta_{jk}a_{1j}^{-2}\frac{\partial A_g}{\partial a_{1l}}$$
$$+ n^{-1}\delta_{jl}a_{1j}^{-2}\frac{\partial A_g}{\partial a_{1k}} - n^{-1}a_{1j}^{-1}\frac{\partial^2 A_g}{\partial a_{1k}\partial a_{1l}},$$
$$\frac{\partial^3 A_g}{\partial a_{1j}\partial a_{1k}\partial a_{2l}} = n^{-1}\delta_{jk}a_{1j}^{-2}\frac{\partial A_g}{\partial a_{2l}} - n^{-1}a_{1j}^{-1}\frac{\partial^2 A_g}{\partial a_{1k}\partial a_{2l}},$$
$$\frac{\partial^3 A_g}{\partial a_{1j}\partial a_{2k}\partial a_{2l}} = -n^{-1}a_{1j}^{-1}\frac{\partial^2 A_g}{\partial a_{2k}\partial a_{2l}},$$
$$\frac{\partial^3 A_g}{\partial a_{2j}\partial a_{2k}\partial a_{2l}} = 2n^{-1}\delta_{jk}\delta_{jl}a_{2j}^{-3}A_g - n^{-1}\delta_{jk}a_{2j}^{-2}\frac{\partial A_g}{\partial a_{2l}}$$
$$- n^{-1}\delta_{jl}a_{2j}^{-2}\frac{\partial A_g}{\partial a_{2k}} + n^{-1}a_{2j}^{-1}\frac{\partial^2 A_g}{\partial a_{2k}\partial a_{2l}},$$
$$\frac{\partial^3 B_g}{\partial a_{1j}\partial a_{1k}\partial a_{1l}} = -\frac{\partial^3 A_g}{\partial a_{1j}\partial a_{1k}\partial a_{1l}}\bar{b}_{2\cdot}, \frac{\partial^3 B_g}{\partial a_{1j}\partial a_{1k}\partial a_{2l}} = -\frac{\partial^3 A_g}{\partial a_{1j}\partial a_{1k}\partial a_{2l}}\bar{b}_{2\cdot},$$

$$\frac{\partial^3 B_g}{\partial a_{1j}\partial a_{1k}\partial b_{2l}} = -n^{-1}\frac{\partial^2 A_g}{\partial a_{1j}\partial a_{1k}}, \quad \frac{\partial^3 B_g}{\partial a_{1j}\partial a_{2k}\partial a_{2l}} = -\frac{\partial^3 A_g}{\partial a_{1j}\partial a_{2k}\partial a_{2l}}\bar{b}_{2\cdot},$$
$$\frac{\partial^3 B_g}{\partial a_{1j}\partial a_{2k}\partial b_{2l}} = -n^{-1}\frac{\partial^2 A_g}{\partial a_{1j}\partial a_{2k}}, \quad \frac{\partial^3 B_g}{\partial a_{2j}\partial a_{2k}\partial a_{2l}} = -\frac{\partial^3 A_g}{\partial a_{2j}\partial a_{2k}\partial a_{2l}}\bar{b}_{2\cdot},$$
$$\frac{\partial^3 B_g}{\partial a_{2j}\partial a_{2k}\partial b_{2l}} = -n^{-1}\frac{\partial^2 A_g}{\partial a_{2j}\partial a_{2k}}.$$

16.A.3 Asymptotic Cumulants for Theorem 2

From Equations 16.16 and 16.17, we have

$$\zeta_1{}' = \zeta_2^{-1/2}\zeta_1 - \frac{1}{2}\zeta_2^{-3/2}\sum_{g=1}^{G}\frac{\partial\gamma_0}{\partial\boldsymbol{\pi}_{\mathrm{T}(g)}{}'}\boldsymbol{\Omega}_{(g)}\frac{\partial\zeta_2}{\partial\boldsymbol{\pi}_{\mathrm{T}(g)}},$$
$$\zeta_3{}' = \mathrm{E}[\{t-\mathrm{E}(t)\}^3] + O(\tilde{N}^{-3/2}) = \zeta_2^{-3/2}\zeta_3 - 3\zeta_2^{-3/2}\sum_{g=1}^{G}\frac{\partial\gamma_0}{\partial\boldsymbol{\pi}_{\mathrm{T}(g)}{}'}\boldsymbol{\Omega}_{(g)}\frac{\partial\zeta_2}{\partial\boldsymbol{\pi}_{\mathrm{T}(g)}} \tag{16.A.15}$$

(see also Ogasawara, 2007b), where

$$\frac{\partial\zeta_2}{\partial\pi_{\mathrm{T}gk}} = 2N_g^{-1}\frac{\partial^2\gamma_0}{\partial\pi_{\mathrm{T}gk}\partial\boldsymbol{\pi}_{\mathrm{T}(g)}{}'}\boldsymbol{\Omega}_{(g)}\frac{\partial\gamma_0}{\partial\boldsymbol{\pi}_{\mathrm{T}(g)}} + N_g^{-1}\frac{\partial\gamma_0}{\partial\boldsymbol{\pi}_{\mathrm{T}(g)}{}'}\frac{\partial\boldsymbol{\Omega}_{(g)}}{\partial\pi_{\mathrm{T}gk}}\frac{\partial\gamma_0}{\partial\boldsymbol{\pi}_{\mathrm{T}(g)}},$$
$$\frac{\partial\boldsymbol{\Omega}_{(g)}}{\partial\pi_{\mathrm{T}gk}} = \mathrm{E}_{(g)kk} - \mathbf{e}_{(g)k}\boldsymbol{\pi}_{\mathrm{T}(g)}{}' - \boldsymbol{\pi}_{\mathrm{T}(g)}\mathbf{e}_{(g)k}{}' \quad (g=1,\ldots,G; k=1,\ldots,K_g), \tag{16.A.16}$$

where $\mathrm{E}_{(g)kk}$ is the $K_g \times K_g$ matrix whose (k, k)th element is 1 with others 0; and $\mathbf{e}_{(g)k}$ is the k-th column of the $K_g \times K_g$ identity matrix.

Author Note: The author is indebted to the editor for this work. Without her invitation, this work may not have been carried out. This work was partially supported by Grant-in-Aid for Scientific Research from the Japanese Ministry of Education, Culture, Sports, Science and Technology No.2500249.

Chapter 17
Evaluating the Missing Data Assumptions of the Chain and Poststratification Equating Methods

Sandip Sinharay, Paul W. Holland, and Alina A. von Davier

17.1 Introduction

The nonequivalent groups with anchor test (NEAT) design, also known as the *common-item, nonequivalent groups design* (Kolen & Brennan, 2004), is used for equating several operational tests. Two types of observed-score equating methods often used with the NEAT design are chain equating (CE) and poststratification equating (PSE). Here, we consider their nonlinear versions, that is, the frequency-estimation equipercentile method for PSE and the chained equipercentile methods for CE (see Kolen & Brennan, 2004).

Von Davier, Holland, and Thayer (2004b) showed that both the CE and PSE methods are examples of observed-score equating methods under different assumptions about the missing data in the NEAT design. These assumptions cannot be directly evaluated using the data that are usually available under a NEAT design. Here, we examine some *predictions* of these different assumptions for the distribution of the missing data and compare them to observed data that arise in a special study.

In practical situations, the PSE and CE methods tend to produce different results when the two nonequivalent groups of examinees differ substantially on the anchor test. However, given that both methods rely on assumptions about missing data, it is difficult to conclude which of the two is more appropriate in a given situation. The CE and PSE methods were compared from several perspectives in von Davier, Holland, and Thayer (2003, 2004a, b) and von Davier (2003b). These studies showed that both the PSE and CE methods appear to be similar in their standard errors of equating and in their degrees of population invariance. Thus, those two considerations do not lead to a clear choice between the methods.

S. Sinharay (✉) and A.A. von Davier
Educational Testing Service, Rosedale Rd, Princeton, New Jersey 08541, USA
e-mail: ssinharay@ets.org

P.W. Holland
Paul Holland Consulting Corporation, 200 4th Ave South, Apt 100, St Petersburg FL 33701, USA
e-mail: pholland@ets.org

A.A. von Davier (ed.), *Statistical Models for Test Equating, Scaling, and Linking*, Statistics for Social and Behavioral Sciences,
DOI 10.1007/978-0-387-98138-3_17,

A series of empirical and simulation studies compared CE and PSE with respect to their equating bias and variability. The usual approach in these research works was to design a study where a true or criterion equating is available and to investigate the closeness of the different methods to the criterion equating. Examples of studies that compared the CE and PSE methods using pseudotest data are Livingston, Dorans, and Wright (1990); Wright and Dorans (1993); von Davier et al. (2006); and Ricker and von Davier (2007). Wang, Brennan, and Kolen (2006) compared the CE and PSE methods using an item response theory (IRT) simulation, and Sinharay and Holland (2007) used both pseudotest data and an IRT simulation. All of these studies found that the CE methods tend to show less bias and about the same variability as the corresponding PSE methods when the two groups have large differences. Thus, it is increasingly clear that CE methods may be preferable to PSE methods when the groups differ widely on the anchor test.

Livingston et al. (1990) offered an explanation of the larger bias for PSE. They argued that stratifying on observed scores is a fallible approximation to stratifying on true scores, and this fallibility results in undercorrection of the group differences that increases as the anchor-score difference between the groups increases. However, Wright and Dorans (1993) showed that when the two groups are selected in a manner that closely approximates the missing data assumptions of PSE, the PSE methods are less biased than CE methods (regardless of how different the groups are on the anchor test). Moreover, the difference in bias found for PSE in the IRT simulation study of Wang et al. (2006) and Sinharay and Holland (2007) could be because data simulated from an IRT model cannot satisfy the assumptions of PSE.

The approaches employed in the above-mentioned studies are direct and simple in conception, but they do not allow for any detail in the explanation of why one method is closer to the criterion than the others. For the NEAT design this is especially problematic because both PSE and CE make different assumptions about missing data. It is natural to ask how adequate these different assumptions are.

The present study uses the data described in von Davier et al. (2006), where, in addition to having a natural criterion equating, data are also available that are the missing data of the NEAT design in practice. The presence of these otherwise missing data allows us to evaluate the underlying missing-data assumptions of CE and PSE. The agreement of CE and PSE with the criterion equating for these data has been reported in von Davier et al. (2006) and Ricker and von Davier (2007). In those studies, equipercentile functions of both PSE and CE were very close to the criterion equipercentile function, but the CE results were slightly closer. This chapter, a summarized version of Holland, Sinharay, von Davier, and Han (2008), describes how the satisfaction of the missing-data assumptions of CE and PSE reflect these findings about the equating functions.

17.2 Notation and Basic Ideas

In the NEAT design, two operational tests, X and Y, are given to two different samples of examinees from different test populations (denoted here by P and Q). In addition, an anchor test A is given to both samples. Test X is observed on P but not Q, and Y is observed on Q but not P; data for X in Q and Y in P are always missing in a NEAT design. The task is to equate the scores of X to those of Y on a target population, T, to be described in more detail below. Both external and internal anchor tests are considered in this study.

The *target population T* for the NEAT design is the *synthetic population* based on P and Q (Braun & Holland, 1982), in which P and Q are given weights that indicate their degree of influence on T. Following Braun and Holland (1982), T is denoted by

$$T = wP + (1 - w)Q, \quad 0 \leq w \leq 1. \tag{17.1}$$

The *total population*, often denoted by $P + Q$, that is obtained by pooling the samples from P and Q, is the synthetic population for which w in Equation 17.1 is proportional to the sample size from P, that is, $w = N_P/(N_P + N_Q)$, where N_P and N_Q denote the sample sizes from P and Q.

In our discussion, we will let F, G and H denote the *cumulative distribution functions* (CDFs) of X, Y and A, respectively, and will further specify the populations on which these CDFs are determined by the subscripts P, Q, and T. For example, $F_P(x)$ denotes the proportion of examines in P for which X is less than or equal to the value x, that is, $F_P(x) = \text{Prob}\{X \leq x \mid P\}$.

We take the position that to justify an equating method as an observed-score equating method requires showing that the method is equivalent to an *equipercentile equating function* defined on the target population, that is, for some choices of $F_T(x)$ and $G_T(y)$,

$$\text{Equi}_{XY;T}(x) = G_T{}^{-1}(F_T(x)). \tag{17.2}$$

17.3 Equating Methods for the NEAT Design

A basic requirement for developing an observed-score equating method for the NEAT design is to make sufficiently strong and not directly testable missing-data assumptions that allow $F_T(x)$ and $G_T(y)$ to be estimated in order to apply Equation 17.2. The assumptions of CE and PSE, formalized in von Davier et al. (2004a), are the following:

- *CE assumptions.* The equipercentile function computed in P for linking X to A is the same as that for linking X to A in T for any choice of $T = wP + (1 - w)Q$. An analogous assumption holds for the links from A to Y in Q and in T.
- *PSE assumptions.* The conditional distribution of X given A in P is the same as the conditional distribution of X given A in T for any choice of $T = wP + (1 - w)$ Q. An analogous assumption holds for Y given A in Q and in T.

The PSE assumptions imply missing data assumptions that are conditional on the anchor test. The CE assumptions require some manipulation to see their implication for the missing data, which we do in the next section. There is no simple connection between these two sets of assumptions. Researchers von Davier et al. (2004b) gave an example where the means of A in P and Q differed by about a third of a standard deviation and the two methods produced results that are reliably different enough to have practical consequences. In such an example it is impossible for both sets of assumptions to be simultaneously satisfied—one or both sets must be violated.

17.4 The Predictions of PSE and CE for the Missing Data

The assumptions of both PSE and CE can be used to specify the distributions of X in Q and Y in P that would be observed if they were available in the NEAT design. The approach taken in this paper is to formulate these as predictions and then to evaluate these predictions using data from a special pseudotest study, described later, where the usually missing data are present.

17.4.1 The PSE Predictions

The PSE assumptions are supposed to hold for any choice of $T = wP + (1 - w)Q$, so that in particular they hold for $T = Q$. Thus, the PSE assumptions imply that the conditional distribution of X given A in Q may be expressed as

$$\text{Prob}\{X = x_j|A = a_l, Q\} = \text{Prob}\{X = x_j|A = a_l, P\}. \tag{17.3}$$

Hence, under the PSE assumptions, the marginal distribution of X in Q, $f_{jQ} = \text{Prob}\{X = x_j \mid Q\}$, is given by

$$\begin{aligned} f_{jQ} &= \sum_j \text{Prob}\{X = x_j|Q\} = \sum_j \text{Prob}\{X = x_j|A = a_l, Q\}h_{lQ} \\ &= \text{P}\{X = x_j|A = a_l, P\}h_{lQ}, \end{aligned} \tag{17.4}$$

where $h_{lQ} = \text{Prob}\{A = a_l \mid Q\}$ is the marginal distribution of A in Q. Thus, Equation 17.4 is the PSE prediction of f_{jQ}. Similar predictions for the marginal distribution of Y in P follow from the PSE assumption for the conditional distribution of Y given A in P.

To implement the PSE predictions we first used polynomial log-linear models (Holland & Thayer, 2000) to presmooth the bivariate distribution of (X, A) obtained from P and the bivariate distribution of (Y, A) from Q. The same form of polynomial log-linear model was used for presmoothing the bivariate score distributions of each pseudotest and anchor test. The chosen bivariate model fit five marginal moments for each score variable plus four cross-product moments of the form xa, xa^2, x^2a and x^2a^2. We denote these presmoothed bivariate probabilities as

$$p_{jl} = \text{Prob}\{X = x_j, A = a_l|P\} \text{ and } q_{kl} = \text{Prob}\{Y = y_k, A = a_l|Q\}. \tag{17.5}$$

Second, using these bivariate probabilities, we formed the marginal distributions of A in P and Q, that is, $h_{lP} = \text{Prob}\{A = a_l \mid P\} = \sum_j p_{jl}$ and $h_{lQ} = \text{Prob}\{A = a_l \mid Q\} = \sum_k q_{kl}$.

Third, we computed the conditional probability, $\text{Prob}\{X = x_j \mid A = a_l, P\}$, as the ratio p_{jl}/h_{lP}[1]. Fourth, we used these estimated conditional probabilities and assumption (Equation 17.3) to obtain the predicted score probabilities for X in Q via Equation 17.4, that is,

$$f_{jQ} = \sum_l (p_{jl}/h_{lP}) h_{lQ}.$$

Similarly, the predicted score probabilities for Y in Q are given by $g_{kP} = \sum_l (q_{kl}/h_{lQ}) h_{lP}$.

We denote the observed frequencies of X in Q by n_{jQ} and those of Y in P by n_{kP}. In a real NEAT design, neither of these two sets of frequencies is available, but in the special pseudotest data set that we will use, they are. They satisfy $\sum_j n_{jQ} = N_Q$, and $\sum_k n_{kP} = N_P$. To evaluate the PSE assumptions, we propose to compare in several ways the *predicted frequencies*, $\{N_Q f_{jQ}\}$ and $\{N_P g_{kP}\}$, to the observed frequencies, $\{n_{jQ}\}$ and $\{n_{kP}\}$, from the pseudodata set.

17.4.2 The CE Predictions

The CE assumptions do not directly concern discrete score distributions. Assuming that all distributions have been continuized, von Davier et al. (2004b) formalized the CE assumption for X and A as

$$H^{-1}{}_T(F_T(x)) = H^{-1}{}_P(F_P(x)) \text{ for any } T = wP + (1-w)Q. \tag{17.6}$$

From the definition of inverse functions, Equation 17.6 is equivalent to defining the CDF, $F_T(x)$, by

$$F_T(x) = H_T\left(H^{-1}{}_P(F_P(x))\right), \text{ for any } T = wP + (1-w)Q. \tag{17.7}$$

Thus, Equation 17.7 shows that CE makes very specific assumptions about the form of the continuized CDF of X for any T. In a similar manner, the CE assumption that the equipercentile function linking A to Y is the same for any T is equivalent to defining the inverse CDF, $G^{-1}{}_T(u)$, by

$$G^{-1}{}_T(u) = G^{-1}{}_Q\left(H_Q\left(H^{-1}{}_T(u)\right)\right), \text{ for any } T = wP + (1-w)Q. \tag{17.8}$$

[1]Note that because of the use of presmoothing, all values of h_{lP} are positive.

Equations 17.7 and 17.8 may be combined to form the equipercentile function linking X to Y on any $T = wP + (1 - w)Q$ as

$$G^{-1}{}_T(F_T(x)) = G^{-1}{}_Q\big(H_Q\big(H^{-1}{}_T\big(H_T\big(H^{-1}{}_P(F_P(x))\big)\big)\big)\big)$$
$$= G^{-1}{}_Q\big(H_Q\big(H^{-1}{}_P(F_P(x))\big)\big). \tag{17.9}$$

The right-hand side of Equation 17.9 is the usual formula for the chained equipercentile function, whereas the left-hand side is the definition of the equipercentile function, $\text{Equi}_{\mathbf{XY};T}(x)$, in Equation 17.2. Thus, under the CE assumptions given above, the usual formula for the chained equipercentile function is an equipercentile function on *any* synthetic population, T. The usual justification of CE is informal—a plausible composition of two links, X to A and A to Y. However, Equation 17.9 shows that the CE assumptions result in an actual observed-score equating method, in the sense of Equation 17.2.

If we now take $T = Q$ in Equation 17.7, then for the continuized CDF, the CE assumptions imply that

$$F_Q(x) = H_Q\big(H^{-1}{}_P(F_P(x))\big). \tag{17.10}$$

Similarly, taking $T = P$ in Equation 17.8 and inverting the relationship, the CE assumptions imply that

$$G_P(y) = H_P\big(H^{-1}{}_Q(\text{G}_Q(\text{y}))\big). \tag{17.11}$$

Thus, Equations 17.10 and 17.11 show that the predictions of CE for X in Q and for Y in P are for the continuized CDFs of these distributions rather than for the discrete score distributions themselves. Next, we describe the steps involved in obtaining CE predictions for the discrete score distributions from CE predictions for the continuized CDFs.

We started the computations with the presmoothed discrete bivariate distributions, p_{jl} and q_{kl}, from Equation 17.5 that were also used for the PSE predictions. The presmoothed marginal score probabilities of X in P, A in P, A in Q and Y in Q are obtained by row and column summation of these bivariate distributions and are denoted, respectively, by f_{jP}, h_{lP}, h_{lQ}, and g_{kQ}, in parallel with the notation used earlier.

Then, we continuized these score probabilities to get the continuous CDFs $F_P(x)$, $H_P(a)$, $H_Q(a)$, and $G_Q(y)$. We used the linear interpolation method (Kolen & Brennan, 2004) for continuization.

Then, we used Equations 17.10 and 17.11 to obtain the CE *predicted continuized CDFs* of X in Q and Y in P. We needed to discretize the continuous CDFs in Equations 17.10 and 17.11 to obtain predictions comparable to those of PSE for the discrete distributions. We used an intuitive and simple method for discretizing the continuous CDF $F_Q(x)$. The problem is to associate probabilities from $F_Q(x)$ with the discrete scores on X, denoted by x_j, for $j = 1$ to J. To do this is it is natural to evaluate $F_Q(x)$ at values on either side of each x_j and subtract them. We used the half-way points, $x_j^* = (x_j + x_{j+1})/2$, for $j = 1$ to $J - 1$. Note that for equally spaced integer scores, the half-way points are the corresponding half integers from $x_1 + ½$ to $x_J - ½$. At the ends we use plus or minus infinity as necessary. Thus, a discrete probability, r_{jQ}, for $X = x_j$ in Q is given by

$$\begin{aligned} r_{jQ} &= F_Q\left(x_j^*\right) - F_Q\left(x_{j-1}^*\right), \text{ for } j = 2, 3, \ldots, J - 1, \\ r_{JQ} &= 1 - F_Q\left(x_{J-1}^*\right), \text{ and } r_{1Q} = F_Q(x_1^*). \end{aligned} \tag{17.12}$$

The $\{r_{jQ}\}$ computed above are discrete probabilities that sum to 1.0.

The method of discretization in Equation 17.12 works for any continuous CDF and is of possible independent interest. See Holland, Sinharay, von Davier, and Han (2008) for more on this issue.

The $\{r_{jQ}\}$ in Equation 17.12 are the CE-predicted score probabilities for X in Q. In the same way, using analogous notation, the continuous CDF of Y in P, $G_P(y)$, may be discretized to obtain predicted score probabilities for Y in P given by

$$\begin{aligned} s_{kP} &= G_P(y_k^*) - G_P\left(y_{k-1}^*\right), \text{ for } k = 2, 3, \ldots, K - 1, \\ s_{KP} &= 1 - G_P\left(y_{K-1}^*\right), \text{ and } s_{1P} = G_P(y_1^*). \end{aligned} \tag{17.13}$$

We used the values of $\{N_Q\, r_{jQ}\}$ as the CE predictions of the X-in-Q frequencies, $\{n_{jQ}\}$, just as $\{N_Q\, f_{jQ}\}$ are the PSE predictions of these frequencies. In a similar way, we used $N_P\, s_{kP}$ as the CE predictions of the Y-in-P frequencies, $\{n_{kP}\}$. We are now able to put the CE and PSE assumptions on an equal footing for our comparisons.

17.4.3 Comparing the Predicted Frequencies With the Data

We used three different approaches to compare the observed and predicted frequencies. First, we graphed the observed and predicted frequencies together to get an overall view of how well the predictions track the observed frequencies. To focus attention on the differences between the observed and predicted frequencies, we also graph their Freeman-Tukey (FT) residuals (Holland & Thayer, 2000). The FT residuals have the form

$$\sqrt{n_i} + \sqrt{n_i + 1} - \sqrt{4m_i + 1}, \tag{17.14}$$

where n_i denotes the observed frequencies and m_i the predicted frequencies for either CE or PSE. If the observed frequencies only show random variation around the predictions, the FT residuals will show no pattern and lie in the range expected for approximate normal deviates, that is, within ± 3 (Mosteller & Youtz, 1961).

Second, we used three standard goodness-of-fit measures to get a more summarized assessment of the agreement between the observed and predicted frequencies: (a) likelihood ratio chi-square, (b) Pearson chi-square, and (c) sum of squared FT residuals (Holland & Thayer, 2000). Equations 17.15–17.17 define these measures:

$$\text{Pearson } \chi^2 \text{ statistic, } \chi^2 = \sum_i \frac{(n_i - m_i)^2}{m_i}, \tag{17.15}$$

$$\text{likelihood ratio } \chi^2 \text{ statistic, } G^2 = 2\sum_i n_i \log(n_i/m_i), \tag{17.16}$$

$$\text{and the FT } \chi^2 \text{ statistic, } \chi^2_{FT} = \sum_i \left(\sqrt{n_i} + \sqrt{n_i + 1} - \sqrt{4m_i + 1}\right)^2. \tag{17.17}$$

These three measures are often used as summary indices to assess the overall closeness of fitted frequencies to observed frequencies in discrete distributions of scores.

Third, for an alternative summary look at the predictions, we compared the first two moments—mean and standard deviation—of the predicted and observed frequencies and used the percent relative difference between the predicted and observed moments as a way to quantify the relative accuracy of the predictions.

17.5 Study Details

17.5.1 The Data Set

The original data were from one form of a licensing test for prospective teachers. The form included 120 multiple-choice items, about equally divided among four content areas: language arts, mathematics, social studies, and science. Ordinarily, the single total score from different forms of this test was equated through a NEAT design with an internal anchor test. The form of the test used here was administered twice, and the two examinee populations played the role of populations P and Q in our analysis.

The mean total scores (number right) of the examinees taking the test at these two administrations differed by approximately one fourth of a standard deviation, as can be seen from the second column of Table 17.1.

17.5.2 Construction of the Pseudotests

We used these data to construct two pseudotests, X and Y, as well as three different anchor pseudotests, $A1$, $A2$, and $A3$, of different lengths. A pseudotest consists of a subset of the test items from the original 120-item test, and the score on the pseudotest for an examinee is found from the responses of that examinee to the items in the pseudotest. The pseudotests, X and Y, each contained 44 items, 11 items from each of the four content areas. Tests X and Y having no items in common, were made parallel in content, but test X was constructed to be much easier than test Y.

17.5.3 The External Anchor Test Cases

To create data sets with external anchor tests, a basic set of 24 items (six from each content area) was selected to be representative of the original test and to serve as the largest external anchor, $A1$. This anchor had no items in common with either X or Y. The two other anchor tests, $A2$ and $A3$, were formed by deleting four and eight items, respectively, from $A1$ in such a way that $A2$ was a 20-item subset of $A1$, and $A3$ was a 16-item subset of $A2$. Furthermore, to maintain parallelism in content, test $A2$ had five items from each content area, whereas $A3$ had four. The mean percent correct of the anchor tests approximately equaled that for the original test. The structure of the various pseudotests is given in von Davier et al. (2006).

Table 17.1 also gives the numbers, means, standard deviations, alpha reliabilities, and average proportion correct for the scores on X, Y, $A1$, $A2$, and $A3$ and for the two sums $X1 = X + A1$ and $Y1 = Y + A1$ (that play a role for the internal anchor cases discussed shortly) for the examinees in P, Q and the combined group. X was considerably easier than Y (the average percentage correct on X ranged from 80–83% whereas on Y the range was 60–64%). The mean score on X for the combined group was 127% of a standard deviation larger than the mean score on Y. In addition, all three anchor tests showed differences of approximately a quarter of a standard deviation between P and Q. The reliabilities of the three anchor tests behaved as expected, with $A1$ being the most reliable and $A3$ the least reliable. However, the range of these reliabilities was modest—from.68 to.75 on the combined group.

The pseudotest data were designed to lead to a difficult equating problem for which CE and PSE were expected to give different answers. This was done in order to provide a sharp comparison between these methods in a nonlinear equating situation. The large difference in difficulty between X and Y made the equating problem nonlinear. The difference in the test performance of P and Q was intentionally chosen to be as large as possible; this difference insured that CE and PSE would give different results.

17.5.4 The Internal Anchor Test Cases

To create data sets that had internal anchor tests, we formed $X1 = X + A1$ and $Y1 = Y + A1$. Then, we paired $X1$ and $Y1$ with $A1$, $A2$, or $A3$ as the three internal anchor test cases. Because $A2$ was a subset of $A1$ and $A3$ was a subset of $A2$, each of the

Table 17.1 Means, (Standard Deviations), [Alpha Reliabilities], and Average Proportions Correct for the Scores on the Total and Pseudotests on P, Q, and the Combined Group, P + Q

Pop.	Total (120 items)	X (44 items)	Y (44 items)	$A1$ (24 items)	$A2$ (20 items)	$A3$ (16 items)	$X1 = X + A1$	$Y1 = Y + A1$
P ($n = 6{,}168$)	82.3 (16.0)	35.1 (5.7)	26.6 (6.7)	16.0 (4.2)	13.7 (3.6)	10.8 (3.0)	51.2 (9.3)	42.6 (10.3)
		[.81] .80	[.81] .60	[.75] .67	[.71] .69	[.68] .68	[.88] .75	[.88] .63
Q ($n = 4{,}237$)	86.2 (14.2)	36.4 (4.8)	28.0 (6.3)	17.0 (3.9)	14.5 (3.3)	11.5 (2.8)	53.4 (8.0)	45.0 (9.6)
		[.77] .83	[.79] .64	[.73] .71	[.69] .73	[.66] .72	[.85] .79	[.87] .66
$P + Q$ ($N = 10{,}405$)		35.6 (5.4)	27.2 (6.6)	16.4 (4.1)	14.0 (3.5)	11.1 (3.0)	52.1 (8.9)	43.6 (10.1)
		[.80] .81	[.80] .62	[.75] .68	[.71] .70	[.68] .69	[.87] .77	[.87] .64

three anchor tests was internal to the total scores, $X1$ and $Y1$. This approach allowed us to keep the total tests of the same size ($44 + 24 = 68$ items) as we varied the lengths (and therefore the reliabilities) of the anchor tests.

17.5.5 Mimicking the NEAT Design

Because all the examinees in P and Q took all 120 items on the original test, all of the examinees in P and Q also had scores for X, Y, $X1$, and $Y1$ as well as for each of the three anchor tests, $A1$, $A2$, and $A3$. In order to mimic the structure of the NEAT design, we pretended that scores for X or $X1$ were not available for the examinees in the test administration designated as Q and that scores for Y or $Y1$ were not available for the examinees in P. However, because all scores were, in fact, available for the pseudo-test data, they allowed us to compare the frequencies predicted by the CE and PSE assumptions with the actual frequencies in the data.

17.6 Results

Holland et al. (2008) evaluated for these data the CE and PSE assumptions directly. They found that neither the CE nor the PSE assumptions are exactly correct, but neither is terribly wrong either. They concluded that it is impossible to determine which assumption is violated the most.

This section compares the predictions made by CE and PSE with the observed data for X or $X1$ in Q and for Y or $Y1$ in P. The comparisons are divided into three parts, as described below.

17.6.1 Comparisons of the Observed and Predicted Frequencies

Figure 17.1 shows the observed and predicted frequencies for CE and PSE for X and $X1$ in Q and for Y and $Y1$ in P, for the case of the longest anchor test, $A1$. (All of the graphs for the shorter anchor tests look very similar and are omitted.) The solid lines connect the observed frequencies.

It is evident that the predicted distributions for CE and PSE are very similar and depart from the observed frequencies by similar amounts and in similar directions. In general, the agreement between the observed and predicted frequencies is quite good, indicating that both CE and PSE make predictions that are reasonably close to the data. To look at the differences in more detail, we used the FT residuals that are graphed in Figure 17.2.

Figure 17.2 shows that the patterns of the FT residuals for CE and PSE are very similar and appear fairly random, well within the expected range for well-fitting predictions. However, the residuals for CE often are smaller than those for PSE. This is clearest in the middle range of scores in the top row of plots in Figure 17.2.

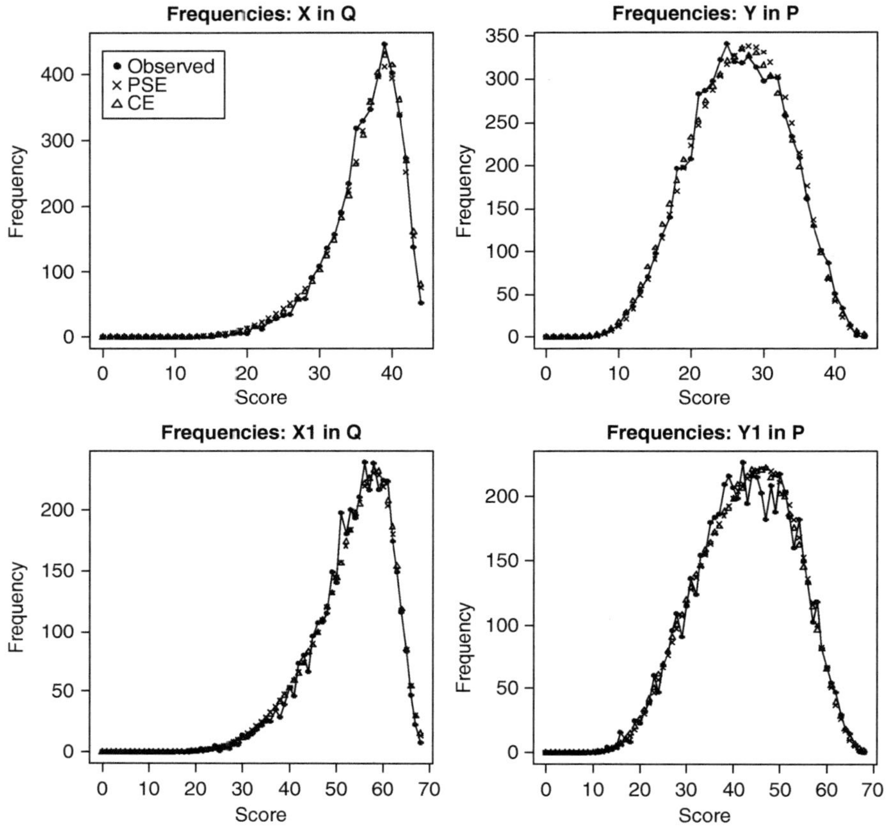

Fig. 17.1 Frequencies for X in Q and Y in P for external anchor test $A1$ (top row) and for $X1$ in Q and $Y1$ in P for internal anchor test $A1$ (bottom row)

In summary, both CE and PSE track the data fairly well and both sets of predictions appear to be somewhat more similar to each other than they are to the observed data.

17.6.2 Comparisons of the Goodness-of-Fit Measures

Table 17.2 gives the values for χ^2, G^2, and χ^2_{FT}, defined earlier, for all the cases in the study. 17.2 shows, just like Figure 17.2, that the predictions of CE are somewhat closer to the observed frequencies than the PSE predictions. In all cases, all of the goodness-of-fit measures are smaller for CE than for PSE. Thus, while the CE and PSE predictions are very similar, as seen in Figure 17.1, those of CE are, on average, slightly closer to the observed frequencies.

In addition, there is a consistent tendency for the goodness-of-fit measures for PSE to get smaller as the length of the anchor test increases. Thus, the length (and

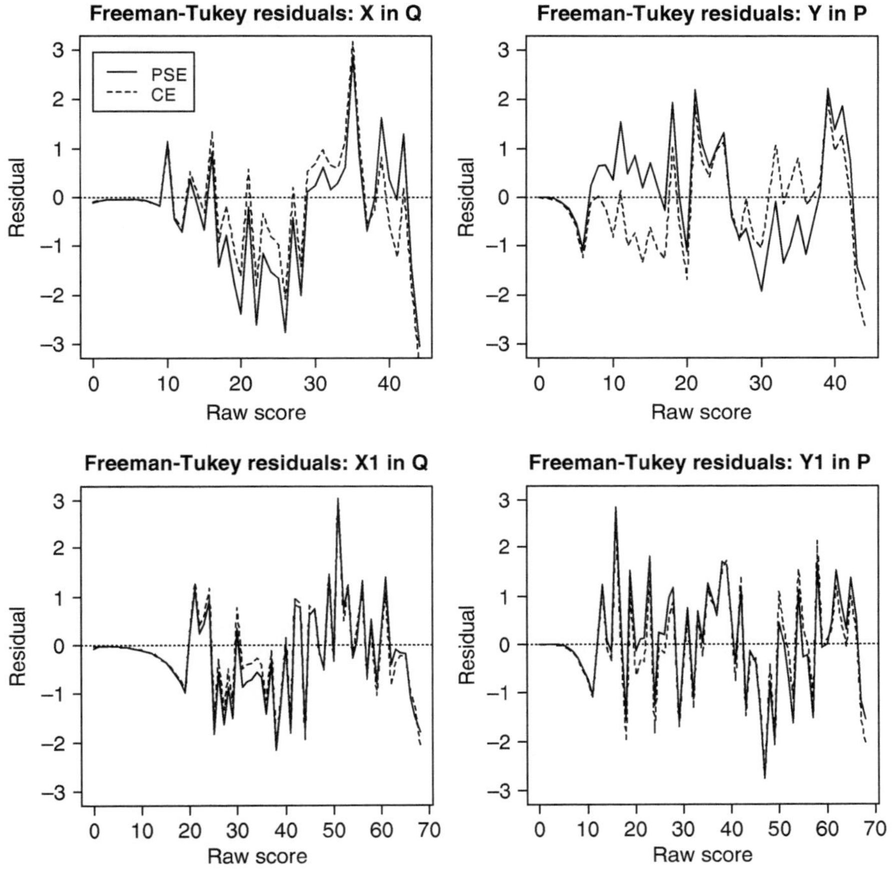

Fig. 17.2 Freeman-Tukey residuals for X in Q and Y in P for external anchor test $A1$ (top row) and for $X1$ in Q and $Y1$ in P for internal anchor test $A1$ (bottom row)

the reliability) of the anchor test has a distinct and measurable effect on improving the predictions of PSE. The predictions for CE do not show this trend for the external anchor test cases, but they do show it for the internal anchor test cases.

17.6.3 Comparisons of the Moments

Our final comparison of the predictions for CE and PSE concerns those of the mean and standard deviation of the observed frequency distributions. The values of these moments are given in Table 17.3. The table also shows the percent relative differences between the observed and predicted moments. The percent relative difference is the predicted moment minus the observed moment divided by the absolute value of the

Table 17.2 *The Three Goodness-of-Fit Measures for Chained Equating (CE) and Poststratification Equating (PSE)*

External anchor cases				Internal anchor cases			
Tests and anchors	χ^2	G^2	χ^2_{FT}	Tests and anchors	χ^2	G^2	χ^2_{FT}
X, *A*1: *Q*				*X*1, *A*1: *Q*			
PSE	63.9	68.5	66.3	PSE	55.4	60.6	56.0
CE	55.5	55.1	52.1	CE-L	50.3	53.7	49.1
X, *A*2				*X*1, *A*2			
PSE	72.0	77.6	76.0	PSE	67.4	73.8	69.4
CE	65.1	65.3	62.9	CE-L	67.2	71.4	66.9
X, *A*3				*X*1, *A*3			
PSE	78.0	86.7	85.1	PSE	74.0	82.9	77.7
CE	60.7	64.0	60.4	CE-L	69.1	75.2	69.4
Y, *A*1: *P*				*Y*1, *A*1: *P*			
PSE	49.3	51.4	49.9	PSE	76.6	75.9	72.3
CE	37.0	40.9	39.2	CE-L	71.2	72.5	69.2
Y, *A*2				*Y*1, *A*2			
PSE	58.7	59.8	58.0	PSE	89.4	87.1	83.5
CE	48.0	50.0	47.4	CE-L	82.6	82.7	79.4
Y, *A*3				*Y*1, *A*3			
PSE	68.3	68.9	67.4	PSE	103.5	97.4	93.7
CE	44.6	46.1	45.0	CE-L	92.8	88.1	85.0

Note. *A*1 is the longest anchor test, *A*3 is the shortest. Shaded cells indicate cases for which PSE has smaller goodness-of-fit values than CE

observed moment times 100. Thus, positive values indicate overprediction, and negative values indicate underprediction.

In almost every case in Table 17.3, in terms of the absolute value of the percent relative difference, the CE predictions are closer than the PSE predictions to the observed data. The predictions of the means are accurate for both methods; the means have the consistently smallest percent relative differences in Table 17.3, but the differences for the CE predictions are always smaller. For the standard deviations, the percent relative differences are generally a little larger than for the means, but again, those for CE are always smaller.

As seen earlier for the goodness-of-fit measures, there is a consistent tendency for the accuracy of the PSE predictions of the means and standard deviations to increase as the length of the anchor test increases. The CE predictions for the mean and standard deviation for the internal anchor test show the same consistent improvement as the length of the anchor test increases.

17.7 Conclusions and Discussion

This study investigated the assumptions that underlie the two most common observed-score equating methods for the NEAT design—CE and PSE. In the usual operational settings, these assumptions are untestable and cannot be evaluated. In this study we

Table 17.3 Observed and Predicted Moments and Percent Relative Differences for External and Internal Anchor-Test Cases

External anchor cases					Internal anchor cases				
Observed & predicted	*M*	*M* % rel. dif.	SD	*SD* % rel. dif.	Observed & predicted	*M*	*M* % rel. dif.	*SD*	*SD* % rel. dif.
X,A1:Q					*X1,A1:Q*				
Obs	36.38		4.77		Obs	53.38		8.04	
PSE	36.16	−0.6	5.15	7.9	PSE	53.17	−0.4	8.47	5.3
CE	36.43	0.1	4.98	4.4	CE	53.31	−0.1	8.35	3.8
X,A2					*X1,A2*				
Obs	36.38		4.77		Obs	53.38		8.04	
PSE	36.13	−0.7	5.19	8.8	PSE	53.11	−0.5	8.57	6.5
CE	36.41	0.1	5.03	5.5	CE	53.29	−0.2	8.44	4.9
X,A3					*X1,A3*				
Obs	36.38		4.77		Obs	53.38		8.04	
PSE	36.04	−0.9	5.26	10.2	PSE	52.94	−0.8	8.67	7.8
CE	36.33	−0.1	5.09	6.7	CE	53.16	−0.4	8.52	5.9
Y,A1:P					*Y1,A1:P*				
Obs	26.59		6.68		Obs	42.62		10.31	
PSE	26.79	0.8	6.56	−1.7	PSE	42.82	0.5	10.17	−1.3
CE	26.44	−0.6	6.72	0.6	CE	42.62	0.0	10.26	−0.4
Y,A2					*Y1,A2*				
Obs	26.59		6.68		Obs	42.62		10.31	
PSE	26.82	0.9	6.52	−2.3	PSE	42.89	0.6	10.18	−2.2
CE	26.45	−0.5	6.64	−0.5	CE	42.64	0.0	10.16	−1.4
Y,A3					*Y1,A3*				
Obs	26.59		6.68		Obs	42.62		10.31	
PSE	26.91	1.2	6.49	−2.8	PSE	43.08	1.1	10.00	−3.0
CE	26.55	−0.2	6.62	−0.9	CE	42.80	0.4	10.11	−1.9

Note. *A1* is the longest anchor test, *A3* is the shortest. Obs = observed; PSE = poststratification equating; CE = chained equating; M = Mean used a special data set that allowed us to evaluate the predictions that result from the two sets of missing data assumptions.

The special study was designed as a stringent test of CE versus PSE in that the mean on the anchor tests was specifically selected to be very different. The tests to be equated, *X* and *Y*, were constructed to be very different in difficulty so nonlinear functions would be necessary for the equatings. The tests were not unusual in terms of their reliabilities for the numbers of items in them, and they were constructed to mimic the multitopic content coverage of the original test. We found that CE and PSE were similar in terms of how well the predicted distributions approximated the observed distributions, with the CE-based predictions being slightly closer to the observed distributions than those of PSE.

So how general are these results? First of all, our results follow an ever-increasing set of findings that slightly favor CE over PSE methods in real test situations, and we do not expect that to change with further research. Second, we tried to find a case where real data would show a big difference between CE and PSE, which did not happen. Thus, we suggest that it will take a more extreme equating situation to find bigger differences between CE and PSE methods. Sinharay and Holland (in press) further discuss this issue.

Where do we stand on CE versus PSE? It is fair to say that for many years the psychometric basis for CE was cloudy. It appears to use two equatings of unequally reliable tests and then chain them together for the final result. Such a procedure might inherit some problems because of the unequal reliability issues of each link. Kolen and Brennan (2004, p. 146) referred to CE as having "theoretical shortcomings" for this reason. We have attempted to discover what these problems might be but currently regard such efforts as pointless. The theoretical basis of CE is exactly like that of PSE and consists of sets of assumptions about the missing data in the NEAT design that, in turn, allow CE to be interpreted as an observed-score equipercentile equating function for the NEAT design. Moreover, there is accumulating evidence that the assumptions of CE are reasonable and likely to be useful in a variety of circumstances (see, for example, Sinharay & Holland, 2010, in press). We show that although CE and PSE make nearly the same predictions in an equating situation that was designed to make them differ, those of CE are consistently, if only slightly, more accurate than those of PSE. Further research is surely needed to help distinguish situations where one of these methods is to be preferred. Yet, CE is a clear competitor to PSE and the other observed-score equating methods for the NEAT design. In our opinion, CE has no obvious theoretical shortcomings.

Author Note: Any opinions expressed in this chapter are those of the authors and not necessarily of Educational Testing Service.

Chapter 18
Robustness of IRT Observed-Score Equating

C.A.W. Glas and Anton A. Béguin

18.1 Introduction

One of the most important aspects of equating, scaling, and linking is whether the models used are appropriate. In this chapter, some heuristic methods and a more formal model test for the evaluation of the robustness of the procedures used for equating, scaling, and linking are presented. The methods are outlined in the framework of item response theory (IRT) observed score (OS) equating of number-correct (NC) scores (Kolen & Brennan, 1995; Zeng & Kolen, 1995). The methods for the evaluation of IRT-OS-NC equating will be demonstrated using concurrent estimation of the parameters of the one-parameter logistic (1PL) model and the three-parameter logistic (3PL) model. In this procedure the parameters are estimated on a common scale by using all available data simultaneously. The data used are from the national school-leaving examinations at the end of secondary education in the Netherlands. To put the presentation into perspective, the application will be presented first.

18.2 Equating of School-Leaving Examinations

Although much attention is given to producing equivalent school-leaving examinations for secondary education from year to year, research has shown (see the Inspectorate of Secondary Education in the Netherlands, 1992) that the difficulty of examinations and the level of proficiency of the examinees can still fluctuate significantly over time. Therefore, the following equating procedure was developed for setting the cut-off scores of the examinations. For all examinations participating

C.A.W. Glas (✉) and A.A. Béguin
University of Twente, P.O. Box 217, 7500, AE Enschede, Netherlands
e-mail: C.A.W.Glas@gw.utwente.nl

A.A. von Davier (ed.), *Statistical Models for Test Equating, Scaling, and Linking*, Statistics for Social and Behavioral Sciences,
DOI 10.1007/978-0-387-98138-3_18,

in the procedure, the committee for the examinations in secondary education chose a reference examination where the quality and the difficulty of the items were such that the cut-off score presented a suitable reference point. The cut-off scores of new examinations are equated to this reference point. One of the main difficulties of equating new examinations is the problem of secrecy: Examinations cannot be made public until they are administered. Another problem is that the examinations have no overlapping items. These problems are overcome by collecting additional data to create a link between the data from the two examinations. These additional data are collected in so-called *linking groups* which are sampled from another stream of secondary education. These linking groups respond to items from the old and the new examination directly after the new examination has been administered.

Figure 18.1 displays the data collection design for equating the 1992 English language comprehension examinations at the higher general secondary education (HAVO) level to the analogous 1998 examination. The figure is a symbolic representation of an item administration design in form of a persons-by-items matrix; the shaded areas represent a combination of persons and items were data are available, and the blank areas are unobserved.

Both examinations consisted of 50 dichotomously scored items. So the total number of items in the design was 100. Further, it can be seen that the design contains five linking groups and the design is such that the linking groups cover all items of the two examinations. Every linking group responded to a test with a test length between 18 and 22 items, and every item in the design was presented to exactly one of the linking groups.

Based on the data of the two examinations, one could directly apply equipercentile equating using the two OS distributions of the two examinations. This, however, would be based on the assumption that either the ability level of the two examinations populations (i.e., the 1992 and the 1998 population) or the difficulty level of the two examinations (i.e., the 1992 examination and the 1998 examination) had not changed. In practice, this assumption may not be tenable. The purpose of the linking groups is to collect additional information that makes it possible to estimate differences in ability levels and differences in difficulty levels using

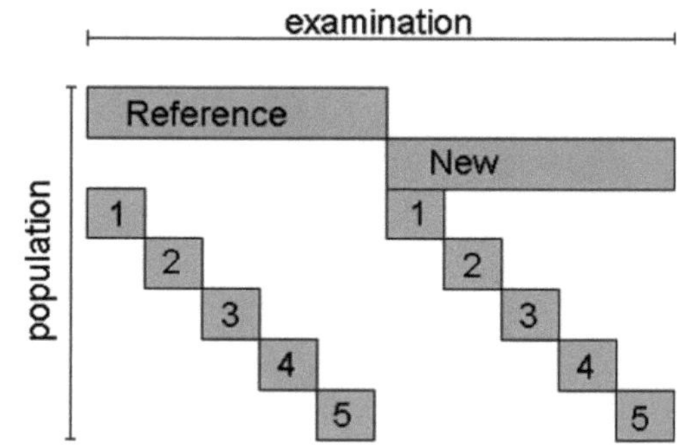

Fig. 18.1 Item administration design for equating examinations. The area labeled "Reference" pertains to the 1992 examination; the area labeled "New" pertains to the 1998 examination

concurrent marginal maximum likelihood (MML) estimation of an IRT model. This procedure will be outlined in detail below.

In concurrent MML estimation, the item and population parameters are estimated concurrently on a common scale. So, contrary to procedures where separate sets of parameters are estimated for different groups of respondents that are subsequently linked to a common scale, in concurrent estimation the model has only one set of item parameter estimates to describe all response data. That is, it is assumed that each item has the same difficulty parameters in each of the groups in which the item was administered (see, for instance, von Davier & von Davier, 2004). Although simulation studies (Hanson & Béguin, 2002; Kim & Cohen, 2002) have shown that concurrent calibration leads to better parameter recovery, Kolen and Brennan (1995) argued that separate calibration is preferred because it gives a check on the unidimentionality of the model. In the present chapter, examples of testing the model using concurrent MML estimates are given.

Using IRT creates some freedom in designing the data collection. For instance, the proficiency level of the linking groups and the examination populations need not be exactly the same; in the MML estimation procedure outlined below, every group in the design has its own ability distribution. On the other hand, the assumption underlying the procedure is that the responses of the linking groups fit the same IRT model as the responses of the examination groups. For instance, if the linking groups do not seriously respond to the items administered, equating the two examinations via these linking groups would be threatened. Therefore, much attention is given to the procedure for collecting the data of the linking groups; in fact, the tests are presented to these students as school tests with consequences for their final appraisal. One of the procedures for testing model fit proposed below will focus on the quality of the responses of the linking groups.

18.3 IRT Models

In this chapter, only examinations with dichotomously scored items are discussed. Consider an equating design with I items and N persons. Let item administration variable d_{in} be defined as

$$d_{ni} = \begin{cases} 1 \text{ if item } i, \text{ is presented to person } n, \\ 0 \text{ otherwise,} \end{cases} \tag{18.1}$$

for $i = 1, \ldots, I$ and $n = 1, \ldots, N$, and let the response of person n to the item i be represented by an stochastic variable X_{ni}, with realization x_{ni}. If $d_{ni} = 1$, x_{ni} is defined by

$$x_{ni} = \begin{cases} 1 & \text{if the response of person } n \text{to item } i \text{ is correct,} \\ 0 & \text{otherwise} \end{cases} \tag{18.2}$$

If $d_{ni} = 0$, then x_{ni} is equal to an arbitrary constant

Two approaches to modeling the responses are used: the 1PL model (Rasch, 1960) and the 3PL model (Birnbaum, 1968; Lord, 1980). In the 1PL model, the probability of a correct response of person n on item i is given by

$$P(X_{ni} = 1|\theta_n, \beta_i) = \frac{\exp(\theta_n - \beta_i)}{1 + \exp(\theta_n - \beta_i)}, \tag{18.3}$$

where β_i is the item parameter of item i. A computational advantage of this model is that the respondent's NC score is a minimal sufficient statistic for the ability parameter. The alternative model, the 3PL model, is a more general model, where for each item two additional item parameters are introduced. First, the ability parameter θ is multiplied by an item parameter α_i, which is commonly referred to as the discrimination parameter. Second, the model is extended with a guessing parameter γ_i which allows for describing guessing behavior. In this model, the probability of a correct response of person n on item i, is

$$P(X_{ni} = 1|\theta_n, \alpha_i, \beta_i, \gamma_i) = \psi_i(\theta_n) = \gamma_i + (1 - \gamma_i)\frac{\exp(\alpha_i\theta_n - \beta_i)}{1 + \exp(\alpha_i\theta_n - \beta_i)}. \tag{18.4}$$

Note that if $\gamma_i = 0$ and $\alpha_i = 1$, $\psi_i(\theta_n)$ specializes to the response probability in the 1PL model.

The advantage of the 3PL over the 1PL model is that guessing of responses can be taken into account. The examinations used here as an example contain multiple-choice items so the 3PL model may fit better than the 1PL model. An advantage of the 1PL model over the 3PL model is that with small sample sizes it may result in more stable parameter estimates (Lord, 1983).

To estimate the item parameters, a multiple-group MML estimation procedure is used. Let the elements of the vector of item parameters, ξ, be defined as $\xi_i = (\beta_i)$ for the 1PL model and as $\xi_i = (\alpha_i, \beta_i, \gamma_i)$ for the 3PL model. The probability of observing response pattern $\mathbf{X}_n$, conditional on the item administration vector $\mathbf{d}_n$, is given by

$$p(\mathbf{x}_n \, \mathbf{d}_n, \theta_n, \boldsymbol{\xi}) = \prod_{i=1}^{I} \left(\psi_i(\theta_n)^{x_{ni}}(1 - \psi_i(\theta_n))^{1-x_{ni}}\right)^{d_{ni}} \tag{18.5}$$

with $\psi_i(\theta_n)$ as defined in 18.4. Notice that through d_{ni}, the probability, $p(\mathbf{x}_n|\mathbf{d}_n, \theta_n, \boldsymbol{\xi})$ only depends on the parameters of the items actually administered to person n. The likelihood in Equation 18.5 implies the usual assumption of local independence; that is, it is assumed that the responses are independent given θ_n. Further, throughout this chapter we will make the assumption of independence between respondents and ignorable missing data. The latter holds because the design vectors $\mathbf{d}_n$ are fixed.

Table 18.1 Cumulative Percentages of the Reference (1992) and New (1998) Population on the Reference and New Examination

Score	Reference population		New population	
	Reference exam	New exam	Reference exam	New exam
25	19.8	14.5	12.1	15.7
26	23.6	17.5	14.7	18.7
27	28.0	20.7	17.8	22.0
28	31.8	24.5	21.2	25.7
29	35.9	28.6	25.1	29.7
30	41.0	33.1	29.4	34.0
31	45.6	37.9	34.0	38.6
32	50.4	43.0	39.0	43.4
Mean	32.3	33.2	33.9	33.2
SD	7.5	7.0	6.8	7.3
SE (Mean)		0.41		0.39
SE (*SD*)		0.13		0.10

In the concurrent MML estimation procedure, it will be assumed that every group in the design is sampled from a specific ability distribution. So, for instance, the data in the design in Figure 18.1 are evaluated using seven ability distributions; that is, one distribution for the examinees administered the reference examinations, one for the examinees administered the new examination, and five were for the linking groups. Let the ability parameters of the respondents of group b have a normal distribution with density $g(\theta|\mu_b, \sigma_b)$. More specifically, the ability parameter of a random respondent n has a normal distribution with density $g(\theta_n|\mu_{b(n)}, \sigma_{b(n)})$, where $b(n)$ denotes the population to which person n belongs. The probability of observing response pattern $\boldsymbol{x}_n$, given $\boldsymbol{d}_n$, as a function of the item and population parameters is

$$p(\boldsymbol{x}_n|\boldsymbol{d}_n, \boldsymbol{\xi}, \mu_{\boldsymbol{b(n)}}, \sigma_{\boldsymbol{b(n)}}) = \int \boldsymbol{p}(\boldsymbol{x}_n|\boldsymbol{d}_n, \theta_n, \boldsymbol{\xi})\boldsymbol{g}(\theta_{\boldsymbol{n}}|\mu_{\boldsymbol{b(n)}}, \sigma_{\boldsymbol{b(n)}})\boldsymbol{d}\theta_n \;, \tag{18.6}$$

where $p(\mathbf{x}_n|\mathbf{d}_n, \theta_n, \boldsymbol{\xi})$ is defined in Equation 18.5. MML estimation boils down to maximizing the log-likelihood

$$L(\boldsymbol{\xi}, \boldsymbol{\mu}, \boldsymbol{\sigma}) = \sum_n \log p(\mathbf{x}_n|\mathbf{d}_n, \boldsymbol{\xi}, \mu_{b(n)}, \sigma_{b(n)}), \tag{18.7}$$

with respect to all item parameters $\boldsymbol{\xi}$ and all population parameters $\boldsymbol{\mu}$ and $\boldsymbol{\sigma}$.

All item and population parameters can be concurrently estimated on a common scale using readily available software, for instance with BILOG-MG (Zimowski, Muraki, Mislevy, & Bock, 1996). Béguin (2000) and Béguin and Glas (2001) presented an alternative Bayesian approach to estimation of IRT models in the framework of IRT-OS-NC equating, but that approach is beyond the scope of this chapter.

18.4 IRT-OS-NC Equating

Once the parameters of the IRT model have been estimated, the next step is equipercentile equating carried out as if respondents of one population had taken both examinations. Consider the example in Table 18.1. The example was computed using the data of the 1992 and 1998 English language comprehension examinations at HAVO level introduced above. The second and fourth column of Table 18.1 display the cumulative relative frequencies for the reference and new examination as observed in 1992 and 1998, respectively. These two cumulative distributions were based on the actual OS distributions obtained from the two examinations. These distributions are displayed in Figure 18.2. Figure 18.2 also contains estimates of two score distributions that were not observed: the score distribution on the 1992 examination if it had been administered to the 1998 population and the score distribution on the 1998 examination if it had been administered to the 1992 population. The estimates of these two distributions are based on the concurrent MML estimates of the item and population parameters. These two estimated score distributions were used to compute the cumulative distributions in the third and fifth column of Table 18.1. The estimation method will be discussed in the next section. Essentially, the distribution of the reference population (1992) on the new (1998) examination is computed using the parameters of the items of the 1998 examination and the population parameters of the 1992 population.

The third column of Table 18.1 contains a part of the cumulative score distribution of the reference population on the new examination. This cumulative score distribution is displayed in Figure 18.2b, together with a confidence interval and the observed cumulative distribution produced by the reference sample. The computation of confidence intervals will be returned to below. The cut-off score for the new examination is set in such a way that the expected percentage of respondents

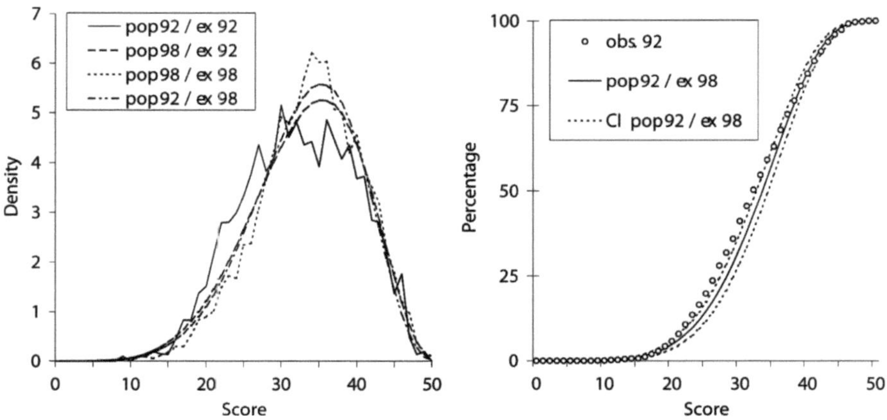

Fig. 18.2 Observed and expected score distributions

failing the new examination in the reference population is approximately equal to the percentage of examinees in the reference population failing the reference examination. In the example in Table 18.1, the cut-off score of the reference examination was 27; as a result, 28.0% failed the examination. The new cut-off score was set to 29, because at this cut-off score the percentage of the reference population failing the new examination was approximately equal to 28.0, which is the percentage failing the reference examination. Obviously, the new examination was easier. This is also reflected in the mean score of the two examinations displayed at the bottom of Table 18.1. The old and the new cut-off scores are marked by a straight line under the percentages. It can be seen that 25.1% of students in the new population failed the new examination, suggesting that the new population is more proficient than the reference population. This is also reflected in the mean scores of the two populations.

The procedure has two interesting aspects. First, the score distributions on the reference examination for the reference population can be obtained in two different ways: It can be computed directly from the data, as done above, or it can be estimated based on the IRT model. Analogously, the score distribution on the new examination for the new population also can be obtained in two different ways: using the actual examination data with the associated score distribution and using an estimate of this score distribution under an IRT model. The expected score distribution estimated under an IRT model will be referred to as *expected score distribution*, whereas the distribution determined directly from the data will be referred to as *OS distribution*. The difference between the observed and expected frequencies can be the basis for a Pearson-type test statistic for testing the model fit in either the reference-examination data set or the new-examination data set (see Glas & Verhelst, 1989, the R_0-statistic). In the example of equating examinations English HAVO, Figure 18.3 contains only expected-score distributions, whereas Figure 18.2 contains OS distributions for the reference population on the

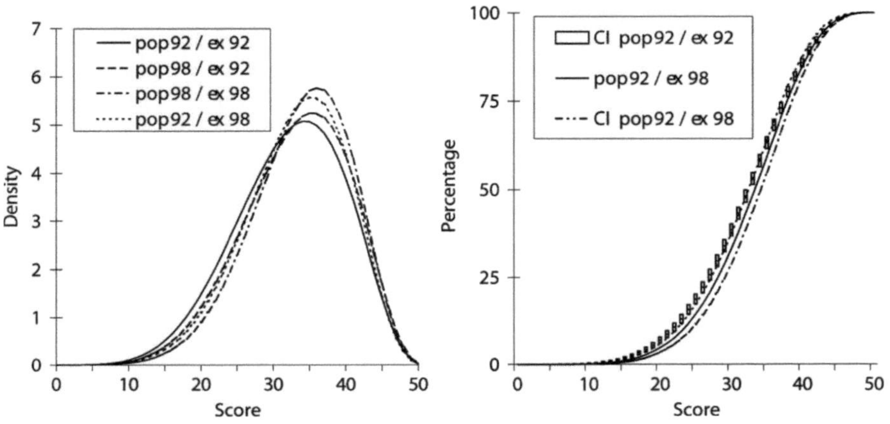

Fig. 18.3 Expected score distributions

reference examination and for the new population on the new examination. Consequently, equating could be performed in two different ways, based on the curves of Figure 18.3 or on the curves of Figure 18.2.

Second, the cut-off scores of the two examinations could be equated based on the score distributions of the new population or based on the score distributions of the reference population. If the IRT model fits, a choice between these possibilities should not influence the outcome of the equating procedure. This provides a basis for the evaluation of the appropriateness of the procedure, which we return to below, together with a comparison of the results obtained using the 1PL and 3PL models.

18.5 Some Computational Aspects of IRT-OS-NC Equating

After the parameters of the IRT model have been estimated on a common scale, the estimates of the frequency distributions are computed as follows. Label the populations in the design displayed in Figure 18.1 as $b = new, reference, 1,...,5$. In this design, every population is associated with a specific design vector, d_b, that indicates which items were administered to the sample of examinees from population b. Let d_{ref} and d_{new} be the design vector of the examinees from the reference and new examination, respectively. The probability of obtaining a score r on the reference examination for the examinees in population b (b = *new*, reference, 1,...,5) is denoted by $p(r;\ ref,\ b)$ Given the IRT item and population parameters, this probability is given by

$$p(r; ref, b) = \sum_{\{\mathbf{x}|r,\mathbf{d}_{ref}\}} \int p(\mathbf{x}|\mathbf{d}_{ref}, \theta, \boldsymbol{\xi}) g(\theta|\mu_b, \sigma_b) d\theta, \qquad (18.8)$$

where $\{\mathbf{x}|r, \mathbf{d}_{ref}\}$ stands for the set of all possible response patterns on the reference examination resulting in a score r and $p(\mathbf{x}|\mathbf{d}_{ref}, \theta, \xi)$ is the probability of a response pattern on the reference examination given θ computed as defined in Equation 18.5. In the same manner, one can compute the probability of students in population b ($b = new, reference, 1, \ldots, 5$) obtaining a score r on the new examination using

$$p(r; new, b) = \sum_{\{\mathbf{x}|r,\mathbf{d}_{new}\}} \int p(\mathbf{x}|\mathbf{d}_{new}, \theta, \boldsymbol{\xi}) g(\theta|\mu_b, \sigma_b) d\theta\ , \qquad (18.9)$$

where $\{\mathbf{x}|r, \mathbf{d}_{new}\}$ stands for the set of all possible response patterns on the new examination resulting in a score r.

Computation of the distributions defined by Equations 18.8 and 18.9 involves summing over the set of all possible response patterns $\mathbf{x}$ on some examination resulting in a score r, $\{\mathbf{x}|r, \mathbf{d}\}$, where $\mathbf{d}$ is a design vector. For a given proficiency θ the score distribution is a compound binomial distribution (Kolen & Brennan,

1995). A recursion formula (Lord & Wingersky, 1984) can be used to compute the score distribution of respondents of a given ability. Define $f_k(r|\theta_i)$ as the probability of a NC score r over the first k items, given the ability θ. Define $f_1(r=0|\theta)=(1-p_1)$ as the probability of earning a score of 0 on the first item and $f_1(r=1|\theta)=p_1$ as the probability of earning a score 1 on the first item. For $k>1$, the recursion formula is given by

$$f_k(r|\theta) = \begin{cases} f_{k-1}(r|\theta)(1-p_k) & \text{if } r=0, \\ f_{k-1}(r|\theta)(1-p_k)+f_{k-1}(r-1|\theta)p_k & \text{if } 0<r<k, \\ f_{k-1}(r-1|\theta)p_k & \text{if } r=k. \end{cases} \tag{18.10}$$

The expected score distribution for a population can be obtained from Equations 18.8 and 18.9 by changing the order of summation and integration. The integration over a normal distribution can be evaluated using Gauss-Hermite quadrature (Abramowitz & Stegun, 1972). In the examples presented in this chapter, 180 quadrature points were used for every one of the seven ability distributions (new, reference and linking groups 1, ..., 5) involved. At each of the quadrature points the result of the summation is obtained using the recursion formula shown in Equation 18.10.

18.6 Evaluation of the Results of the Equating Procedure

The cut-off scores of six examinations in language comprehension administered in 1998 were equated to the cut-off scores of reference examinations administered in 1992. The subjects of the examinations are listed under the heading "Subject" in Table 18.2. The examinations were administered at two levels: subjects labeled "D" in Table 18.2 were at the intermediate general secondary education level (MAVO-D-level), and subjects labeled "H" were at HAVO level. All examinations consisted of 50 dichotomous items. All designs were as depicted in Figure 18.1.

In this section, it is investigated whether the 1PL and 3PL models produced similar results. Two other aspects of the procedure will be compared. First, two

Table 18.2 Data Overview

Subject	Reference exam			New exam			Link
	N_{Ref}	Mean	*SD*	N_{New}	Mean	*SD*	N_{link}
English D	1,693	35.16	6.92	4,000	34.42	7.47	1,101
English H	2,039	32.32	7.45	4,000	33.89	6.76	673
German D	2,021	34.00	6.28	4,000	29.72	6.45	803
German H	2,129	34.51	5.59	4,000	32.19	6.57	327
French D	2,097	32.28	7.23	4,000	30.13	7.06	750
French H	2,144	35.72	6.80	4,000	31.48	6.69	454

Note: Mean = mean observed frequency distribution; SD = standard deviation observed frequency distribution versions of the equating procedure are compared, one version where all relevant distributions are expected score distributions, and one version where the available OS distributions are used, that is, the score distribution observed in 1992 and the score distribution observed in 1998. Second, results obtained using either the reference or the new population as the basis for equating the examinations are compared.

In Table 18.3, the results of the equating procedure are given for the version of the procedure where only expected score distributions are used. These score distributions were obtained for the reference population and for the new population. In Table 18.3, equivalent scores on the new examinations are presented for

Table 18.3 Results of the Equating Procedure With Expected Score Distributions

Subject	$r^{(b)}$	ϕ_R^1	ϕ_R^3	ϕ_{RR}^{13}	ϕ_N^1	ϕ_N^3	Δ_{NN}^{13}	Δ_{RN}^{11}	Δ_{RN}^{33}
German D	25	23	23	0	23	23	0	0	0
	30	28	27	1	28	27	1	0	0
	31	29	28	1	29	28	1	0	0
	35	33	32	1	33	32	1	0	0
	40	39	37	2	39	37	2	0	0
German H	25	26	25	1	26	25	1	0	0
	30	31	30	1	31	30	1	0	0
	35	36	36	0	36	36	0	0	0
	40	41	41	0	41	41	0	0	0
English D	25	23	25	−2	23	25	−2	0	0
	28	26	27	−1	26	28	−2	0	−1
	30	29	29	0	29	30	−1	0	−1
	35	34	35	−1	34	35	−1	0	0
	40	40	40	0	40	40	0	0	0
English H	25	26	26	0	26	26	0	0	0
	27	28	28	0	28	28	0	0	0
	30	31	31	0	31	31	0	0	0
	35	36	36	0	36	36	0	0	0
	40	40	40	0	40	40	0	0	0
French D	**25**	27	27	0	27	27	0	0	0
	30	32	32	0	32	32	0	0	0
	35	37	37	0	37	37	0	0	0
	40	41	42	−1	41	42	−1	0	0
French H	25	23	23	0	23	23	0	0	0
	30	28	28	0	28	28	0	0	0
	35	34	33	1	34	33	1	0	0
	40	39	38	1	39	38	1	0	0
Abs. sum				14			16	0	2

r: number-correct score (boldface: cut-off score)
ϕ_R^1: equated scores using 1PLM and Reference population
ϕ_R^3: equated scores using 3PLM and Reference population
ϕ_N^1: equated scores using 1PLM and New population
ϕ_N^3: equated scores using 3PLM and New population
Δ_{RR}^{13} : difference $\phi_R^1 - \phi_R^3$; Δ_{NN}^{13} : difference $\phi_N^1 - \phi_N^3$
Δ_{RN}^{11} : difference $\phi_R^1 - \phi_N^1$; Δ_{RN}^{33} : difference $\phi_R^3 - \phi_N^3$

a number of different score points on the reference examination. The score points listed in Table 18.3 are the actual cut-off score and the score points, r=25,30,35,40 on the reference examination. In Table 18.3, the results pertaining to the actual cut-off scores are printed in boldface characters. The results obtained using score distributions based on the reference population are listed in Columns 3–5, and the results obtained using score distributions based on the new population are listed in Columns 6– 8. The scores on the new examination associated with the scores of the reference examination computed using the 1PL model are given in Column 3. For instance, a score of 25 on the reference examination Reading Comprehension in German at MAVO-D level is equated to a score of 23 on the new examination, and a score of 30 on the reference examination is equated to a score of 28 on the new examination. In the Column 4, the scores obtained under the 3PL model are given. For this case, a score of 30 on the reference examination is equated to a score of 27 on the new one. Notice that for a score of 30 the results for the 1PL and the 3PL models differ by 1 score point. Column 5 contains the difference between the new scores obtained via the 1PL and 3PL models. For convenience, the sum of the absolute values of these differences is given at the bottom line of the table. So, for the 27 scores equated here, the absolute difference in equated score points computed using the 1PL and the 3PL models equals 14 score points, and the absolute difference between equated scores is never more than 2 points. The three following columns contain information comparable to the three previous ones, but the scores on the new examination were computed using score distributions for the new population. Notice that the results obtained using the reference and the new population are much alike. This is corroborated in the two last columns that contain the differences in results obtained using score distributions based on either the reference or new population. The column labeled "Δ_{RN}^{11}" shows the differences for the 1PL model and column labeled "Δ_{RN}^{33}" shows the differences for the 3PL model.

Two conclusions can be drawn from Table 18.3. First, the 1PL and 3PL models produce quite similar results. On average there was less than 1 score point difference, with differences never larger than 2 score points. The second conclusion is that using either the reference or new population for determining the difference between the examination made little difference. The bottom of Table 18.3 shows that the sum of the absolute values of the differences are 0 and 2 score points.

As already mentioned, the procedure can be carried out in two manners: one where all relevant score distributions are estimated using the IRT model and one where the available OS distributions of the two examinations are used. The above results used the former approach. Results of application of the second approach are given in Table 18.4.

The format of Table 18.4 is the same as the format of Table 18.3. The indices in Tables 18.3 and 18.4 (explained at the bottom of the two tables) are defined exactly the same, only they are computed using two alternative methods. In Table 18.3 expected score distributions are used, and in Table 18.4 the available OS distributions on the examination are used. The latter approach produced results that were far less satisfactory. For the 1PL model, the summed differences between using the reference and the new population, Δ_{RN}^{11}, rose from 0 to 11 score points. For the

Table 18.4 Results of the Equating Procedure With Observed Score Distributions

	$r^{(b)}$	ϕ_R^1	ϕ_R^3	ϕ_{RR}^{13}	ϕ_N^1	ϕ_N^3	Δ_{NN}^{13}	Δ_{RN}^{11}	Δ_{RN}^{13}
German D	25	23	23	0	23	22	1	0	1
	30	28	27	1	28	27	1	0	0
	31	29	28	1	29	28	1	0	0
	35	33	32	1	33	32	1	0	0
	40	39	36	3	39	37	2	0	−1
German H	25	25	25	0	26	24	2	−1	1
	30	31	30	1	31	30	1	0	0
	35	36	36	0	36	36	0	0	0
	40	41	41	0	42	41	1	−1	0
English D	25	23	25	−2	23	24	−1	0	1
	28	27	28	−1	27	27	0	0	1
	30	29	30	−1	28	29	−1	1	1
	35	34	35	−1	34	35	−1	0	0
	40	40	39	1	39	40	−1	1	−1
English H	25	27	27	0	27	26	1	0	1
	27	29	29	0	28	28	0	1	1
	30	32	31	1	31	31	0	1	0
	35	36	35	1	35	35	0	1	0
	40	40	40	0	40	40	0	0	0
French D	**25**	27	28	−1	27	27	0	0	1
	30	33	33	0	31	33	−2	2	0
	35	37	37	0	37	37	0	0	0
	40	41	41	0	42	42	0	−1	−1
French H	25	23	23	0	23	22	1	0	1
	30	28	28	0	28	27	1	0	1
	35	34	33	1	33	32	1	1	1
	40	39	38	1	39	38	1	0	0
Abs. sum				18			21	11	14

r: number-correct score (boldface: cut-off score)
ϕ_R^1: equated scores using 1PLM and Reference population
ϕ_R^3: equated scores using 3PLM and Reference population
ϕ_N^1: equated scores using 1PLM and New population
ϕ_N^3: equated scores using 3PLM and New population
Δ_{RR}^{13}: difference $\phi_R^1 - \phi_R^3$; Δ_{NN}^{13} difference $\phi_N^1 - \phi_N^3$
Δ_{RN}^{13}: difference $\phi_R^1 - \phi_N^1$; Δ_{RN}^{3} difference $\phi_R^3 - \phi_N^3$

3PL model, this difference, Δ_{RN}^{33}, rose from 2 to 14 points. In other words, the requirement of an equating function that is invariant over populations (Petersen, Kolen, & Hoover, 1989) is better met when using frequencies that are all based on the IRT model. An explanation for this outcome is that results of equipercentile equating are vulnerable to fluctuations due to sampling error in the OS distributions. To overcome this problem it is common practice to use smoothing techniques to reduce the fluctuation in the score distributions. The expected score distribution computed using IRT models can be considered as a smoothed score distribution. Therefore, IRT equating using only expected score distributions reduces fluctuations in the results of equating and, consequently, improves the invariance of equating over populations.

18.7 Confidence Intervals for Score Distributions

When a practitioner must set a cut-off score on an examination that is equivalent to the cut-off on some reference examination, the first question that comes to mind is about the reliability of the equating function. In the example in Table 18.1, a cut-off score of 27 on the reference examination is equated with a cut-off score 29 on the new examination upon observing that the observed 28.0% in the second column is closest to the 28.7% in the third column. To what extent are these percentages reliable? In Table 18.5, 90% confidence intervals are given for the estimated percentages on which equating is based. Their computation will be explained below. Consider the information on the English reading comprehension examination, which was also used for producing Table 18.1. In the boldface row labeled "English H," information is given on the results of the reference population taking the reference examination. This row contains the observed percentage of students

Table 18.5 90% Confidence Intervals for Cumulative Percentages

Subject	Score	Observed %	Lower bound	%	Upper bound	Observed-Expected	Z
German D	**31**	**33.1**	**31.6**	**33.0**	**34.4**	**0.0**	**0.06**
	28		24.2	27.9	31.5		
	29		29.1	32.7	36.4		
	30		34.4	37.9	41.5		
German H	**30**	**23.4**	**22.0**	**23.4**	**24.8**	**0.0**	**0.04**
	30		14.8	18.4	21.9		
	31		19.3	22.7	26.1		
	32		24.4	27.6	30.7		
English D	**28**	**18.1**	**16.3**	**17.5**	**18.6**	**0.6**	**0.84**
	25		11.1	13.6	16.1		
	26		13.5	16.1	18.7		
	27		16.2	19.0	21.7		
English H	**27**	**28.0**	**24.4**	**25.7**	**27.0**	**0.3**	**2.92**
	27		17.0	20.7	24.4		
	28		20.7	24.5	28.3		
	29		24.7	28.6	32.4		
French D	**25**	**18.8**	**17.5**	**18.6**	**19.7**	**0.2**	**0.29**
	26		11.8	14.7	17.6		
	27		14.7	17.8	20.9		
	28		18.0	21.2	24.4		
French H	**30**	**22.4**	**20.6**	**21.8**	**23.0**	**0.6**	**0.84**
	27		13.1	17.5	22.0		
	28		16.0	20.7	25.3		
	29		19.4	24.2	29.0		

Note: Obs. % = observed cumulative percentage; Expected % = expected cumulative percentage under the one-parameter-logistic model. Lower and upper bounds are of 90% confidence interval of expected %. Z: normalized difference Observed – Expected scoring 27 points or less, the cumulative percentage under the 1PL model, the lower and upper bound of the 90% confidence interval for this percentage, and the difference and normalized difference between the observed cumulative percentage and the cumulative percentage under the 1PL model. The normalized difference was computed by dividing the difference by its standard error. This normalized difference can be seen as a very crude measure of model fit. Together with the plots of the frequency distributions given in Figures 18.1 and 18.2, these differences give a first indication of how well the model applied.

Continuing the example labeled "English H" in Table 18.5, in the three rows under the boldface row, for three scores the estimates of the cumulative percentages for the reference population on the new examination and their confidence intervals are given. These three scores are chosen in such a way that the middle score is the new cut-off score if equating is performed using only expected score distributions. The other two scores can be considered as possible alternative cut-off scores. For instance, in the "English H" example in Table 18.5, the observed cumulative percentage 28% is located within the confidence band related to score 29, while it is near the upper confidence bound related to score 28. If the observed percentage of the cut-off score is replaced by an expected percentage, the confidence band of this estimate, which is given in the boldface row, also comes into play.

But the basic question essentially remains the same: Are the estimates precise enough to justify equating an old cut-off score to a unique new cut-off score? Or are the random fluctuations such that several new cut-off scores are plausible? Summarizing the results of Table 18.5, the exams German D and German H each has only one plausible cut-off score of 29 and 31, respectively. Notice that the cumulative percentages of 33.0% and 23.4% are well outside the confidence bands of the scores directly above and below the chosen cut-off score. For the exams French D, English D, and English H, two cut-off scores could be considered plausible. For the exams in English it also made a difference whether equating was performed using only expected score distributions or using available OS distributions. Finally, for the examination French H, the confidence interval of Score 27, 28 and 29 contained the percentage 21.8. So using the cumulative percentage of examinees under the cut-off score on the reference examination estimated under the IRT model, all three scores could be considered plausible values for the cut-off score in the new examination.

18.8 Computation of Confidence Intervals for Score Distributions

In this section, the parametric and nonparametric bootstrap method (Efron, 1979, 1982; Efron & Tibshirani, 1993) will be introduced as a method for computing confidence intervals of the expected score distributions. The nonparametric bootstrap proceeds by resampling with replacement from the data. The sample size is the same as the size of the original sample, and the probability of an element being sampled is the same for all response patterns in the original sample. By estimating the parameters of the IRT model on every sample, the standard error of the estimator of the computed score distribution can be evaluated. In the parametric bootstrap, new values for the parameters are drawn based on the parameter estimates and estimated inverse information matrix. Using these repeated draws, the score distributions can be computed and their standard errors can be evaluated by assessing the variance over repeated draws.

Results of application of both bootstrap procedures are presented for the data from the English language proficiency examination on HAVO level in 1992 and 1998. These data were also used for producing the Figures 18.2 and 18.3 and Table 18.1. The confidence intervals presented in the two figures and the standard

Table 18.6 Confidence Intervals Using Bootstrap Procedures, English HAVO 1998, Population 1992

r	Nonparametric, 400 replications				Parametric, 400 replications			
	P_r	Cum.	$SE(P_r)$	SE(Cum.)	$E(P_r)$	Cum.	$SE(P_r)$	SE(Cum)
5	0.003	0.01	0.001	0.001	0.004	0.01	0.001	0.002
10	0.054	0.13	0.010	0.026	0.057	0.14	0.013	0.036
15	0.318	1.06	0.041	0.157	0.329	1.10	0.053	0.206
20	1.085	4.68	0.097	0.519	1.106	4.82	0.119	0.658
25	2.566	14.27	0.147	1.151	2.590	14.52	0.172	1.410
30	4.463	32.79	0.130	1.817	4.469	33.12	0.148	2.157
35	5.594	59.14	0.086	1.980	5.571	59.41	0.114	2.292
40	4.439	84.73	0.213	1.254	4.405	84.84	0.248	1.433
45	1.460	98.13	0.156	0.258	1.450	98.14	0.178	0.296
50	0.019	100.00	0.004	0.000	0.020	100.00	0.005	0.000
	Mean	33.25	*SD*	6.98	Mean	33.20	*SD*	7.01
	SE	0.35	*SE*	0.10	*SE*	0.41	*SE*	0.13

Note: *r* = number-correct score; P = estimated percentage; Cum. = cumulative percentage

Table 18.7 Confidence Intervals Using Bootstrap Procedures English HAVO 1998, Population 1998

r	Nonparametric, 400 replications				Parametric, 400 replications			
	P_r	Cum.	$SE(P_r)$	SE(Cum.)	$E(P_r)$	Cum.	$SE(P_r)$	SE(Cum)
5	0.002	0.00	0.000	0.001	0.002	0.00	0.000	0.001
10	0.038	0.09	0.004	0.011	0.038	0.09	0.004	0.012
15	0.244	0.78	0.015	0.062	0.244	0.78	0.018	0.070
20	0.901	3.73	0.030	0.183	0.901	3.73	0.038	0.218
25	2.288	12.07	0.037	0.345	2.290	12.08	0.049	0.437
30	4.257	29.33	0.050	0.465	4.261	29.35	0.052	0.616
35	5.702	55.51	0.063	0.526	5.705	55.55	0.065	0.651
40	4.839	82.63	0.054	0.447	4.835	82.67	0.070	0.481
45	1.707	97.76	0.065	0.130	1.700	97.77	0.067	0.130
50	0.024	100.00	0.003	0.000	0.024	100.00	0.003	0.000
	Mean	33.90	*SD*	6.84	Mean	33.90	*SD*	6.83
	SE	0.09	*SE*	0.07	*SE*	0.11	*SE*	0.07

Note: *r* = number-correct score; P = estimated percentage; Cum. = cumulative percentage errors reported in the two bottom lines of Table 18.1 were computed using a parametric bootstrap procedure with 400 replications. Table 18.6 shows results for the parametric and nonparametric bootstrap estimate of the score distribution of the 1992 population on the 1998 examination using the 1PL model. Table 18.7 shows the results for the 1998 population on the 1998 examination using the 1PL model. For brevity, only the results for every fifth score point are presented. In the two bottom lines of the tables, the mean, the standard deviation, and their standard errors are given.

The standard errors in Table 18.7 are much smaller than the standard errors in Table 18.6. So, the computed standard errors dropped markedly when the score distribution was estimated on the test the candidates actually took. For instance, the standard error of the mean using the nonparametric bootstrap was 0.09, markedly smaller than 0.35, the standard error of for the mean on the test not taken by the candidates. The same results held for the estimated score distributions. For instance, the standard error of the estimate of the percentage of candidates with score 25 dropped from.147 to .037. This effect can also be seen in the two bottom lines of Table 18.1. For instance, for the reference population, the standard error of the mean was.16 for the reference examination and .38 for the new examination. This difference, of course, was as expected, since the data provide more information on the examination 1998 for population 1998 than for population 1992. Furthermore, the estimated standard error of the nonparametric bootstrap is a bit smaller than the estimate using the parametric bootstrap. This result is as expected since the parametric bootstrap accounts for an additional source of variance, that is, the uncertainty about the parameters. Therefore, in this context, the parametric bootstrap is preferred over the nonparametric bootstrap. A disadvantage of the parametric bootstrap is that it cannot be applied in problems where the number of parameters is such that the inverse of the information matrix cannot be precisely computed. An example is the 3PL model in the above design. With two examinations of 50 items each and seven population parameter distributions, the number of parameters is 312. In such cases, the nonparametric bootstrap is the only feasible alternative.

18.9 A Wald Test for IRT-OS-NC Equating

In this last section, a procedure for evaluating model fit in the framework of IRT-OS-NC equating will be discussed. Of course, there are many possible sources of model violations, and many test statistics have been proposed for evaluating model fit, which are quite relevant in the present context (see Andersen, 1973; Glas, 1988, 1999; Glas & Verhelst, 1989, 1995; Molenaar, 1983; and Orlando & Thissen, 2000). Besides the model violations covered by these statistics, in the present application one specific violation deserves special attention: the question whether the data from the linking groups are suited for equating the examinations. Therefore, the focus of the present section will be on the stability of the estimated score distributions if different linking groups are used. The idea is to cross-validate the procedure using independent replications sampled from the original data. This is accomplished by partitioning the data of both examinations into G data sets, that is, into G subsamples. To every one of these data sets, the data of one or more linking groups are added, but in such a way that the data sets will have no linking groups in common. Summing up, each data set consists of a sample from the data of both the examinations and of one or more linking groups. In this way, the equating procedure can be carried out in G independent samples. The stability of the procedure will be evaluated in two ways: (a) by computing equivalent scores as was done above and evaluating whether the two equating functions produce similar results and (b) by performing a Wald test. The Wald test will be explained first.

Glas and Verhelst (1995) pointed out that in the framework of IRT, the Wald test (Wald, 1943) can be used for testing whether some IRT model holds in meaningful subsamples of the complete sample of respondents. In this section, the Wald test will be used to evaluate the null hypothesis that the expected score distributions on which the equating procedure is based are constant over subsamples against the alternative that they are not. Let the parameters of the IRT model for the g-th subsample be denoted λ_g, $g \in \{1, 2, \ldots, G\}$. Define a vector $\mathbf{f}(\lambda)$ with elements P_r, where P_r is the probability of obtaining a score r such as defined in Equations 18.8 and 18.9. In the example below, this will be the expected score distribution on the reference examination. Because of the restriction $\sum_r P_r = 1$, at least one proportion P_r is deleted. Let $\mathbf{f}(\lambda_\mathbf{g})$ be a distribution computed using the data of subsample g. Further, let λ_g and λ_g be the parameter estimates in two subsamples g and g, respectively. We will test the null hypothesis that the two score distributions are identical, that is,

$$\mathbf{h} = \mathbf{f}(\lambda_g) - \mathbf{f}(\lambda_{g'}) = 0. \tag{18.11}$$

The difference $\mathbf{h}$ is estimated using independent samples of examination candidates and different and independent linking groups. Since the responses of the two subsamples are independent, the Wald test statistic is given by the quadratic form

$$W = \mathbf{h}'[\Sigma_g + \Sigma_{g'}]^{-1}\mathbf{h}, \tag{18.12}$$

where Σ_g and Σ_g are the covariance matrices of $\mathbf{f}(\lambda_g)$ and $\mathbf{f}(\lambda_g)$, respectively. W is asymptotically chi-square distributed with degrees of freedom equal to the number of elements of $\mathbf{h}$ (Wald, 1943). For shorter tests, W can be evaluated using MML estimates and the covariance matrices can be explicitly computed. For longer tests and models with many parameters, such as the 3PL model, both the covariance matrices and the value of the test statistic W can be estimated using the nonparametric bootstrap method described above. This approach was followed in the present example.

Some results of the test are given in Table 18.8. The tests pertain to estimated score distributions on the reference examination. To test the stability of the score distribution, the samples of respondents of the examinations were divided into four

Table 18.8 Results of the Wald Test for Stability of Estimated Score Distributions, by Population Subsample

Subject	Reference		New	
	1 vs 2	3 vs 4	1 vs 2	3 vs 4
German D	97.9**	12.0	202.3**	180.0**
German H	156.5**	16.8	8.1	232.7**
English D	24.6	8.9	460.1**	19.5
English H	52.9**	8.1	239.8**	4.1
French D	120.3**	100.4**	547.6**	158.2**
French H	4.5	15.6	21.7	10.8

**p <0.01

subsamples of approximately equal sample size. Next, four data sets were assembled, each consisting of the data of one linking group, the data of one of the four subsamples from the reference examination, and the data of one of the four subsamples from the new examination. The design for these four new data sets is similar to the design depicted in Figure 18.1, except that in the prevailing case only one linking group is present. In this way four data sets were constructed, for each data set the item and population parameters of the 3PL model were estimated, all relevant distributions were estimated by computing their expected values, and the equating procedure was conducted. Finally, four Wald statistics were computed.

Consider Table 18.8. The first column concerns the hypothesis that there is no difference between the estimated distributions of the reference population on the reference examination in the setup where the first linking group provided the link and the setup where this link was forged by the second linking group. The next column pertains to a similar hypothesis concerning the third and fourth linking group. The last two columns contain the result for a similar hypothesis concerning the estimated distributions of the new population on the reference examination. For all six examination topics, the score distribution considered ranged from 21 to 40, that is, 20 of the 50 possible score points were considered. In Table 18.8, the Wald tests with a significance probability less than.01 are marked with a double asterisk. It can be seen that model fit is not overwhelmingly good: 12 out of 24 tests are significant at the.01 level. However, there seem to be differences between the various topics; for instance, French at HAVO-level seems to fit quite well. This was corroborated further by a procedure were equivalent scores were computed for a partition of the data into five different subsamples, each one with its own linking group.

Consider Table 18.9. For six topics four scores on the reference test were considered. For each of the five subsamples, these four scores were equated to scores on the new examination via the reference population. The columns labeled "L1" to "L5" show the resulting scores on the new test. These new scores seem to fluctuate quite a bit, but it must be kept in mind that every one of these scores was computed using only a fifth of the original sample size, so the precision has suffered considerably. The column labeled "Total" displays the sum of the absolute differences between all pairs of new scores. Since there are five new scores for every original score, there are 10 such pairs. So, for instance, the mean absolute difference

Table 18.9 Stability of Equating Functions in Subsamples

Topic	r(b)	L1	L2	L3	L4	L5	Total	Expected	p
German D	20	16	23	21	15	14	48	15.5	0.00
	25	20	28	27	21	19	50	14.5	0.00
	30	26	32	32	27	24	44	13.1	0.00
	35	31	37	37	33	29	44	11.4	0.00
German H	20	16	19	17	21	17	24	15.2	0.10
	25	22	24	22	26	22	20	12.4	0.15
	30	27	29	27	31	28	20	10.3	0.05
	35	33	34	32	36	33	18	9.5	0.10
English D	20	20	26	18	19	20	34	14.1	0.00
	25	24	31	23	24	25	34	12.5	0.00
	30	29	35	28	29	30	30	10.3	0.00
	35	34	39	33	34	34	24	8.8	0.00
English H	20	21	26	19	18	23	40	12.8	0.00
	25	26	31	24	23	28	40	12.0	0.00
	30	31	36	29	28	32	38	10.0	0.00
	35	36	40	34	33	37	34	9.2	0.00
French D	20	18	13	19	16	23	46	13.2	0.00
	25	24	18	24	20	27	44	13.7	0.00
	30	29	22	29	25	32	48	13.4	0.00
	35	35	28	34	29	36	44	12.7	0.00
French H	20	21	20	18	18	19	16	16.0	0.55
	25	26	25	23	24	24	14	15.4	0.75
	30	31	30	29	29	29	10	12.8	0.85
	35	36	35	34	34	34	10	10.7	0.70

between the new scores associated with the original score 20 on the D-level examination in German is 4.8 score points.

An interesting question in this context is how this result must be interpreted given the small sample sizes in the subsamples. To shed some light on this question, the following procedure was followed. For every examination, new data sets were generated using the parameter estimates obtained on the original complete data sets, that is, the data sets described in Table 18.2. These new generated data sets conformed the null hypothesis of the 3PL model. Next, for every data set, the procedure of equating the two examinations via the reference population in the five subsamples was conducted. For every examination this procedure was replicated 100 times. In this manner, the distribution of the sum of the absolute differences of new scores under the null hypothesis that the 3PL model (with true parameters as estimated) holds could be approximated, and the approximated significance probability of the realization using the real data could be determined. The mean sum of absolute differences over the 100 replications and the significance probability of the real data realization are given in the last two columns of Table 18.9. The overall model fit is not very good, however. Also, here French at HAVO-level stands out as well fitting, and German at HAVO-level shows acceptable model fit.

18.10 Conclusions

In this chapter, we proposed some heuristic methods and a more formal model test for the evaluation of the robustness of IRT-OS-NC equating, and we showed the feasibility of the methods in a practical situation using an application in a real examination situation. In the application, the differences between the results obtained using the 1PL and the 3PL models were not very striking. Overall model fit was not very satisfactory; only one of the examination topics fitted well, and a second topic fitted acceptably. The case presented here was further analyzed by Béguin (2000) and by Béguin and Glas (2001) using multidimensional IRT models (Bock, Gibbons, & Muraki, 1988) and a Bayesian approach to estimation. However, the methods presented in this chapter easily can be adapted to an MML framework for multidimensional IRT models; the main difference is replacing the normal ability distribution $g(\theta|\mu_b, \sigma_b)$ with a multivariate normal distribution $g(\theta|\mu_b, \Sigma_b)$.

Chapter 19
Hypothesis Testing of Equating Differences in the Kernel Equating Framework

Frank Rijmen, Yanxuan Qu, and Alina A. von Davier

19.1 Introduction

Test equating methods are used to produce scores that are interchangeable across different test forms (Kolen & Brennan, 2004). In practice, often more than one equating method is applied to the data stemming from a particular test administration. If differences in estimated equating functions are observed, the question arises as to whether these differences reflect real differences in the underlying "true" equating functions or merely reflect sampling error. That is, are observed differences in equating functions statistically significant?

By dividing the squared estimated equating difference at a given score point by the square of its asymptotic standard error, a Wald test (Wald, 1943) is obtained to test for the statistical significance of the equating difference. Carrying out a Wald test at a particular score point is tantamount to the decision rule that was proposed by von Davier, Holland, and Thayer (2004b), who used twice the standard error of the equating difference as a critical value for determining whether there is a difference between two equation functions at a given score point (using 1.96 times the standard error would be formally equivalent to carrying out a Wald test at a type I error rate of .05).

Typically, one will be interested in whether one equating function results in different equated scores than another equation function over a range of score points (e.g., a range of potential cut points in a licensure examination). The procedure proposed by von Davier et al. (2004b), being equivalent with carrying out a Wald test at each individual score point with a type I error rate of α, suffers from the multiple testing problem. That is, by carrying out multiple tests at a specific level of significance α, one test for each score point of interest, the actual type I error rate is higher than α. Because the tests are not independent, correcting the significance

F. Rijmen (✉), Y. Qu, and A.A. von Davier
Educational Testing Service, Rosedale Rd., Princeton, New Jersey 08541, USA
e-mail: frijmen@ets.org

A.A. von Davier (ed.), *Statistical Models for Test Equating, Scaling, and Linking*, Statistics for Social and Behavioral Sciences,
DOI 10.1007/978-0-387-98138-3_19,

level of the individual test by dividing α by the number of tests carried out (the Bonferroni method of adjustment) will be overly conservative.

In this study, we generalize the expressions for the standard error of an equated score and for the standard error of the equating difference at an individual score point to expressions for the variance-covariance matrix of the set of equated scores, and for the variance-covariance matrix of the differences between equating functions over the whole range of score points. The latter matrix can be used to construct a multivariate Wald test for a set of linear functions of differences between equated scores.

The multivariate Wald test offers two main advantages. First, the test can be used as an omnibus test due to its multivariate nature. This way, a set of hypotheses can be tested simultaneously at a type I error rate of α, thus alleviating the multiple testing problem. For example, the Wald test allows for testing the joint hypothesis that there are no differences between two equating functions over a certain range of score points. Second, one can test for a larger variety of hypotheses because each hypothesis is specified as a *linear function* of differences between equating functions. For example, one can test whether, over a certain range of interest, one equating function results in a higher average equated score than another function.

The expressions are derived within the general framework of the kernel method of test equating (von Davier et al., 2004b). In the next section, the kernel method of equating is introduced, together with some notational conventions. Subsequently, we derive the asymptotic variance-covariance matrix for the set of equated scores and for the set of differences between equated scores. The derivation is very similar to the derivation of the asymptotic standard errors presented in von Davier et al. (2004b). In a fourth section, we explain how Wald tests can be constructed based on the expression for the asymptotic variance-covariance matrix of differences in equated scores. The use of this Wald test is illustrated with a dataset from a professional licensure examination.

19.2 The Kernel Method of Equating

The kernel method of equating is a general procedure to equate one test form to another. The kernel method of equating can be described in five steps. The interested reader is referred to von Davier et al. (2004b). Throughout, we adopt the convention that the form to be equated is denoted by Y, and the base form is denoted by X. X and Y also denote the random variables for the score on the respective forms. Without loss of generality, we assume that possible scores on both X and Y range from 1 to J. The following is a brief description of each of the five steps of kernel equating.

1. In a first step, a statistical model for the observed test scores is constructed. Depending on the design, the score distributions of X and Y are modeled separately (equivalent-groups design), their bivariate distribution is modeled (single-group

design, counterbalanced design), or the bivariate distributions of X and an anchor test Z, and of Y and Z are modeled (nonequivalent groups with anchor test design). The score distribution being discrete, a typical choice is to model the score distributions with a log-linear model, but other choices could be made.
The structural part of the statistical model specifies a functional relation between the model parameters and the probabilities of the score distribution. Collecting all these probabilities in a vector $\mathbf{p}$ and all model parameters in a vector $\boldsymbol{\theta}$,

$$\mathbf{p} = g(\boldsymbol{\theta}). \tag{19.1}$$

That is, the statistical model is a vector-valued function, where each component specifies the probability of a score (or combination of scores when bivariate score distributions are modeled) as a function of the parameters $\boldsymbol{\theta}$ of the statistical model.

2. Second, the probabilities of the scores of X and Y in the target population are expressed as a function of the probabilities obtained in Step 1. The function is called the design function (*DF*) because its form is determined by the test equating design,

$$\mathbf{r} = DF(\mathbf{p}), \tag{19.2}$$

where $\mathbf{r}$ consists of two subvectors $\mathbf{r}_X$ and $\mathbf{r}_Y$, denoting the score probabilities of X and Y, respectively.

3. Since X and Y are discrete variables, their cumulative distributions F_X and F_Y are piecewise constant functions. In this step, the continuous random variables X_c and Y_c are defined so that their distribution functions F_{sX} and F_{sY} are smooth continuous approximations of F_X and F_Y, respectively. Several smoothing methods are available. The kernel method of equating is named from the use of Gaussian kernel smoothing techniques. The motivation for this smoothing step is that piecewise constant functions are not invertible. However, invertible functions are needed for computing the equipercentile equating function, as given in Equation 19.3. Von Davier et al. (2004b) described how linear and percentile rank equating functions can be mimicked by controlling the smoothness of the functions through a particular choice of the "bandwidth" of a Gaussian kernel. Given a choice for the bandwidth, F_{sX} and F_{sY} functionally depend on $\mathbf{r}$ only. More specifically, F_{sX} and F_{sY} are weighted sums of J Gaussian cumulative distribution functions, where the weights are the score probabilities collected in $\mathbf{r}_X$ and $\mathbf{r}_Y$, respectively (for technical details, see A.A. von Davier et al., 2004b, Chapters 3 & 4).
4. The previous three steps were preparatory steps for the equating step. Here, each possible score on Y is equated to a comparable score on X through the equipercentile equating function,

$$e_X^*(y) = F_{sX}^{-1}(F_{sY}(y)) \tag{19.3}$$

Even though F_{sX} and F_{sY} are functions with a continuous domain, they are only evaluated at the discrete points $y = 1, \ldots, J$, and $F_{sY}(y)$, respectively.

5. Calculating the standard error of equating is the final step. The next section is devoted to this step.

Steps 1–4 are described in a very general way. They will be instantiated differently depending on the equating design, the choice of a statistical model, the desired degree of smoothing, and so forth. Using this quite general framework offers the advantage of demonstrating what is common to many equating methods. At its very general level, the kernel equating method can be described as a vector-valued function with J components, where each component maps score j, $j = 1, \ldots, J$, on Y onto its equated score on X, and where each component is a function of the parameters of the statistical model for the score distribution. Furthermore, this function is a composition of functions itself, reflecting Steps 1–4 of the kernel equating method described above. Let **eq** denote the vector-valued function that describes Steps 1–4,

$$\mathbf{eq} = \begin{pmatrix} eq_1(\boldsymbol{\theta}) \\ \vdots \\ eq_j(\boldsymbol{\theta}) \\ \vdots \\ eq_J(\boldsymbol{\theta}) \end{pmatrix}. \tag{19.4}$$

Each component j of **eq** can be written as a composition of the functions described in Steps 1–4:

$$eq_j = e_X^j \circ DF \circ g, \tag{19.5}$$

Hence, starting with model parameters $\boldsymbol{\theta}$, the score probabilities $\mathbf{r}$ of X and Y are obtained by applying the design function DF to $\mathbf{p} = g(\boldsymbol{\theta})$. The score probabilities provide the weights for the smoothed cumulative distribution functions F_{sX} and F_{sY}, so that e_X^j is a function that maps $\mathbf{r}$ on the equated score on X of the jth score on Y. Note that there are J e_X^j functions, one for each score Y. Furthermore, e_X^* in Equation 19.3 is a function that maps y onto its equated score on X, whereas e_X^j maps $\mathbf{r}$ on the equated score on X.

19.3 The Standard Error of Equating

Population equating functions are estimated from a sample and therefore subject to sampling variability. The standard error is a measure of the variability of the estimated quantities. Von Davier et al. (2004b) described how the standard errors of equated scores can be obtained using the delta method. Without going into the mathematical details (which can be found in, e.g., Lehmann, 1999), the delta method is based on the property that, if a vector of parameter estimates $\hat{\boldsymbol{\beta}}$ is (asymptotically) normally distributed with variance matrix $\hat{\mathbf{I}}$, a vector-valued continuously differentiable function f of $\hat{\boldsymbol{\beta}}$ is asymptotically normally distributed as well, and its variance is obtained by pre- and postmultiplying $\hat{\mathbf{I}}$ with the Jacobian matrix $\mathbf{J}_f$ of the function evaluated at the parameter estimates,

$$\mathrm{COV}(f(\hat{\boldsymbol{\beta}})) = \mathbf{J}_f(\hat{\boldsymbol{\beta}})\Sigma(\mathbf{J}_f(\hat{\boldsymbol{\beta}}))^t \tag{19.6}$$

The delta method is based on a first-order Taylor approximation of f in $\hat{\boldsymbol{\beta}}$, and therefore, for a finite sample size, the asymptotic approximation will be less accurate the more nonlinear f is in the neighborhood of $\hat{\boldsymbol{\beta}}$. The rank of the covariance matrix $\mathrm{COV}(f(\hat{\boldsymbol{\beta}}))$ is at most the minimum of the ranks of $\hat{\mathbf{I}}$ and $\mathbf{J}_f$. Hence, a necessary condition to ensure that the distribution of $f(\hat{\boldsymbol{\beta}})$ is a proper distribution is that the dimensionality of $f(\hat{\boldsymbol{\beta}})$ is not larger than the dimensionality of $\hat{\boldsymbol{\beta}}$.

Applied to the kernel method of equating, the parameters of the statistical model for the score distributions, $\boldsymbol{\theta}$, play the role of $\boldsymbol{\beta}$ in Equation 19.6, and the equation function eq the role of function f. Hence,

$$\mathrm{COV}(\mathbf{eq}(\hat{\boldsymbol{\theta}})) = \mathbf{J}_{eq}(\hat{\boldsymbol{\theta}})\Sigma(\mathbf{J}_{eq}(\hat{\boldsymbol{\theta}}))^t \tag{19.7}$$

Since eq is a composition of functions, its Jacobian may be computed as the product of their Jacobians (the chain rule of differentiation):

$$\begin{aligned}\mathbf{J}_{eq} &= \frac{\partial\, eq(\boldsymbol{\theta})}{\partial\boldsymbol{\theta}}\\ &= \frac{\partial\, e_X(\mathbf{r})}{\partial\mathbf{r}}\frac{\partial DF(\mathbf{p})}{\partial\mathbf{p}}\frac{\partial g(\boldsymbol{\theta})}{\partial\boldsymbol{\theta}}\\ &= \mathbf{J}_e\mathbf{J}_{DF}\mathbf{J}_g\end{aligned} \tag{19.8}$$

Holland and Thayer (1987) gave expressions for $\mathbf{J}_g$ when the score distributions are modeled with log-linear models, and von Davier et al. (2004b) presented $\mathbf{J}_{DF}$ for the different equating designs. Von Davier et al. also gave the row vector of derivatives $\left(\frac{\partial e_X^j}{\partial\mathbf{r}}\right)^t$, which forms the jth row of $\mathbf{J}_e$ in Equation 19.8.

The rank of the variance matrix $\mathrm{COV}(\mathbf{eq}(\hat{\boldsymbol{\theta}}))$ is at most the minimum of the ranks of $\mathbf{J}_e$, $\mathbf{J}_{DF}$ and $\mathbf{J}_g$. Hence, unless a completely saturated log-linear model is used during presmoothing, $\mathrm{COV}(\mathbf{eq}(\hat{\boldsymbol{\theta}}))$ will not be of full rank, and the multivariate distribution of $\mathbf{eq}(\hat{\boldsymbol{\theta}})$ is degenerate. However, Equation 19.7 is still useful, since the asymptotic distributions of single equated scores and pairs, triples, and so forth of equated scores are simply obtained by selecting the corresponding entries in $\mathrm{COV}(\mathbf{eq}(\hat{\boldsymbol{\theta}}))$.

Von Davier et al. (2004b) also presented expressions for the standard error of the difference between two equating functions evaluated in the same score of Y. Using Equations 19.5 and 19.7, their result is easily generalized to the variance-covariance matrix of the vector of differences between two equating functions. In particular, let the same log-linear model be used for both equating functions. Having the same design function by definition, the equating difference function mapping each score of Y into the difference of equated scores is a vector-valued function with as the jth component

$$\Delta_{\mathbf{eq}}^{j} = \left(e_{1X}^{j} - e_{2X}^{j}\right) \circ DF \circ g, \tag{19.9}$$

The asymptotic variance matrix is obtained as

$$\mathrm{COV}\left(\Delta_{\mathbf{eq}}\left(\hat{\boldsymbol{\theta}}\right)\right) = \mathbf{J}_{\Delta_{eq}}\left(\hat{\boldsymbol{\theta}}\right)\Sigma\left(\mathbf{J}_{\Delta_{eq}}\left(\hat{\boldsymbol{\theta}}\right)\right)^{t}, \tag{19.10}$$

where

$$\begin{aligned} \mathbf{J}_{\Delta_{eq}} &= \frac{\partial\,\Delta_{\mathbf{eq}}(\boldsymbol{\theta})}{\partial\boldsymbol{\theta}} \\ &= \frac{\partial\,(e_{1X} - e_{2X})(\mathbf{r})}{\partial\mathbf{r}}\,\frac{\partial DF(\mathbf{R})}{\partial\mathbf{R}}\,\frac{\partial g(\boldsymbol{\theta})}{\partial\boldsymbol{\theta}} \\ &= (\mathbf{J}_{e_1} - \mathbf{J}_{e_2})\mathbf{J}_{DF}\mathbf{J}_{g} \end{aligned} \tag{19.11}$$

19.4 Wald Tests to Assess the Difference Between Equating Functions

In this section, we present a generalization of the Wald test presented in von Davier et al. (2004b), which tests for the difference between two equating functions at individual score points. Von Davier et al. divided the equating difference at a given score point by its asymptotic standard error. This statistic is asymptotically standard normally distributed under the null hypothesis that there is no difference between the two equating functions. This is a specific instantiation of the Wald test.

In its general form, the Wald statistic to test a set of linear hypotheses $\mathbf{L}\boldsymbol{\beta} = \mathbf{0}$, where each row of $\mathbf{L}$ represents a linear hypothesis on $\boldsymbol{\beta}$, has the following form:

$$w = \left(\mathbf{L}\hat{\boldsymbol{\beta}}\right)'\left(\mathbf{L}\,\mathrm{COV}\left(\hat{\boldsymbol{\beta}}\right)\mathbf{L}'\right)^{-1}\mathbf{L}\hat{\boldsymbol{\beta}}. \tag{19.12}$$

If $\hat{\boldsymbol{\beta}}$ is asymptotically normally distributed, w is asymptotically chi-squared distributed with as degrees of freedom the number of rows of $\mathbf{L}$.

In the context of testing for a difference between two equating methods, $\Delta_{eq}(\hat{\boldsymbol{\theta}})$ fulfills the role of $\hat{\boldsymbol{\beta}}$, and its covariance matrix is given in Equations 19.10 and 19.11. Hence,

$$w_{\Delta_{eq}} = (\mathbf{L}\boldsymbol{\Delta}_{\mathbf{eq}}(\hat{\boldsymbol{\theta}}))'(\mathbf{L}\,\mathrm{COV}(\boldsymbol{\Delta}_{\mathbf{eq}}(\hat{\boldsymbol{\theta}}))\mathbf{L}')^{-1}\mathbf{L}\boldsymbol{\Delta}_{\mathbf{eq}}(\hat{\boldsymbol{\theta}})\ldots \tag{19.13}$$

Even though $\mathrm{COV}(\boldsymbol{\Delta}_{\mathbf{eq}}(\hat{\boldsymbol{\theta}}))$ is in general not of full rank, as explained above, a valid test statistic can be obtained as long as $\mathbf{L}\,\mathrm{COV}(\boldsymbol{\Delta}_{\mathbf{eq}}(\hat{\boldsymbol{\theta}}))\mathbf{L}'$ is of full rank. In general, if the number of linear hypotheses tested is low, this will be the case, because each linear hypothesis represents a row in $\mathbf{L}$, and the number of rows in $\mathbf{L}$ equals the size of $\mathbf{L}\,\mathrm{COV}(\boldsymbol{\Delta}_{\mathbf{eq}}(\hat{\boldsymbol{\theta}}))\mathbf{L}'$.

Three immediate choices for $\mathbf{L}$ come to mind. First, if $\mathbf{L}$ is a vector of zeros except for element j, which equals 1, the test developed by von Davier et al. (2004b) for testing for the equating difference at a single score point is obtained. Second, one can test the joint hypothesis that the equating difference is different from zero at a subset of score points. The number of hypotheses that can be tested simultaneously equals the rank of $\mathrm{COV}(\boldsymbol{\Delta}_{\mathbf{eq}}(\hat{\boldsymbol{\theta}}))$ and hence is bounded from above by the number of parameters of the log-linear model. Third, if interest lies only in an average difference on a certain range of scores, this is accomplished by letting $\mathbf{L}$ be a vector with its jth element equal to one if the equating difference at score j is of interest, and zero otherwise.

19.5 Application

The use of the multivariate Wald test is illustrated with data stemming from two forms of a professional licensure test. The data were collected under an equivalent-groups design. The descriptive statistics for both forms are provided in Table 19.1. The test scores ranged from 0 to 40. Cut points for passing the licensure examination ranged from 24 to 32 on the base form. The results in this section are based on a random sample of 1,000 examinees for each form.

Using Akaike's (1974) information criterion as a selection criterion, log-linear models with 6 and 6 moments were selected, for Test Forms X and Y (*X* and *Y*), respectively. Two equating functions were computed. In the first equating function, equipercentile equating, the bandwidths of the Gaussian kernels (used during the continuization step of the kernel method of equating) were automatically chosen by minimizing the sum of the first and second penalty function presented in von Davier et al. (2004b, Equation 4.30, $K = 1$). The optimal bandwidth values

Table 19.1 Descriptive Statistics for the Raw Scores of Forms X and Y

Form	*N*	Mean	*SD*	Min.	Max.	Skew	Kurtosis	Reliability
X	5,407	29.40	7.17	6.00	40.00	−0.68	−0.23	0.88
Y	5,389	30.69	7.24	4.00	40.00	−0.91	0.09	0.90

were 0.54 and 0.53, for form X and form Y, respectively. For the second equating function (linear equating), the bandwidths were set to a large value, 100 times the standard deviation of the scores for each form, in order to mimic the linear equating function. The difference between the equipercentile (with optimal bandwidth) and linear equating function is plotted in Figure 19.1, together with the 95% confidence bands (and 99.4% confidence bands, see below). Since the possible cut points range from 24 to 32, special interest lies in whether the two equating functions are significantly different from each other in that range. For scorepoints 26–32, zero is outside the 95% confidence interval, suggesting that the two equating functions result in a significantly different equated score for those score points.

Because one is testing nine hypotheses, the overall type I error is much higher than 0.05. Applying the Bonferroni correction for multiple testing (Abdi, 2007), the two equating functions are declared significantly different at a score point when zero falls outside the 99.4% (100 – 5/9) confidence interval. In this case, the difference is no longer significant at score points 26 and 27.

As can be seen in Figure 19.1, the difference between the equipercentile and the linear equating function is a smooth function. Hence, testing for a difference between the two equating functions at scorepoint j is likely not independent of the test at scorepoint $j + 1$. Consequently, the Bonferroni correction for multiple testing is too conservative.

Fisher's (1960) protected least significance difference test offers a procedure to control the overall type I error rate while being less conservative than the

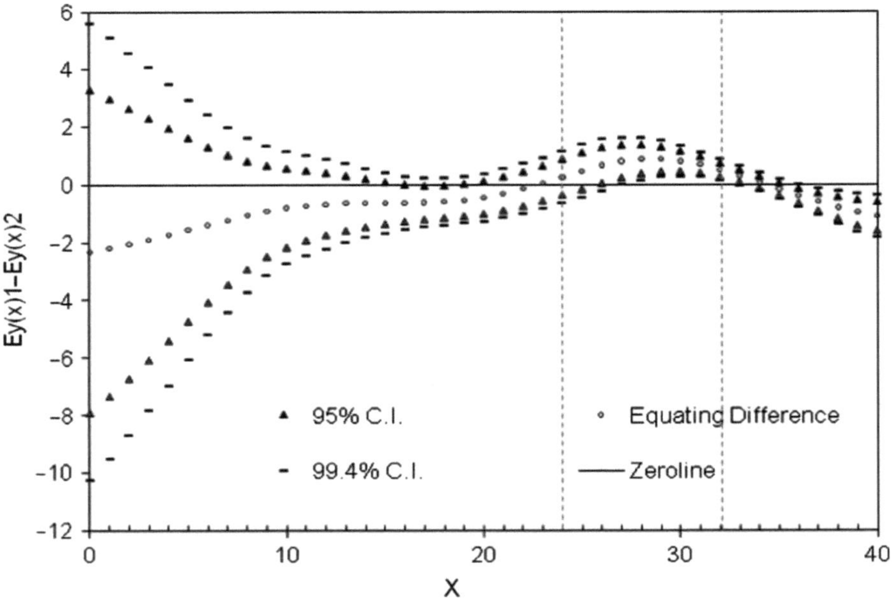

Fig. 19.1 Equating differences and their confidence intervals

Bonferroni correction. In this context, first an omnibus test is carried out at a specific α level that tests the null hypothesis that there is no difference between the two equating functions at any of the nine score points within the range of interest. Only if the omnibus test rejects the null hypothesis, an individual test at the same α level as the omnibus test is carried out for each score point.

The omnibus test was performed using the multivariate Wald test. **L** consisted of nine rows, one for each score point in the range from 24 to 32, where in each row j all entries were set to zero, except entry $23 + j$. The Wald statistic was 7,146.81, $df = 9, p < .001$. Hence, the two equation functions were not the same in the range 24 to 32. Carrying out the second step of Fisher's protected least significant difference test at $\alpha = 0.05$ revealed significant differences for scores 26 to 32. Note that Fisher's protected least squares difference test does not allow for claiming significant differences outside the range from 24 to 32 when zero falls outside the 95% confidence interval. The reason is that those score points were not included in the omnibus test and thus were not "protected" against an inflated type I error rate due to multiple testing.

As a second illustration of the use of the Wald test, we tested whether the equipercentile equating function resulted in higher equated scores on average over the score range from 24 to 32. This hypothesis was tested by defining **L** to be a vector with its jth element equal to one if $24 \leq j \leq 32$, and zero otherwise. The Wald statistic amounted to 7.61, $df = 1$, $p < .001$. On average, the curvilinear equating function resulted in higher equated scores. This means that, on average over all potential cut points, more examinees would pass the test if form Y was equated to form X with a curvilinear equation function than if when a linear equating function were used.

19.6 Discussion

In this paper, we presented the general expressions for the variance-covariance matrix of the differences in equated scores stemming from different equating functions. The derivations were presented within the overall framework of the kernel method of equating (von Davier et al., 2004b). This matrix can be used to construct a multivariate Wald test for a set of linear functions of differences between equated scores.

The multivariate Wald test is general and versatile in its use, as was illustrated with data stemming from a professional licensure exam. A first use is to specify a multivariate omnibus test as a first step in Fisher's protected least significance difference test. The use of the omnibus test protects for an inflated type I error rate due to multiple testing, in that no individual tests are carried out if the omnibus test does not reject the null hypothesis.

In the example, an omnibus test was specified to test for the difference between two equating functions over the range of potential cut scores of the test. The result indicated that the curvilinear equating function did not result in the same equated scores as the linear equating function overall. The tests for differences at the individual score points that were carried out as the second stage of Fisher's least significant difference test indicated that the two equating functions resulted in different equated scores at cut scores 26 to 32.

Fisher's protected least significant difference test is a very old procedure, and many other procedures exist (Carmer & Swanson, 1973; Kuehl, 2000). Insofar these procedures incorporate the use of an omnibus test, the multivariate Wald test will be a part of these procedures as well.

Second, the Wald test can be used to test any hypothesis on a linear combination of differences between equating functions. In the application, this use was illustrated by constructing a test for the average difference between the curvilinear and the linear equating function over the range of potential cut scores. The result indicated that, on average, the curvilinear equating function resulted in higher equated scores than the linear equating function.

The Wald test has many other useful applications. For example, when a test is used to classify examinees in more than two proficiency levels, more than one cut point has to be specified. An omnibus Wald test could be used to test whether two equating functions are different at any of the cut points. In addition, one could test whether one equating function consistently leads to more examinees in higher proficiency levels.

The data of the application were collected using an equivalent-groups design, and subsequently we compared the linear with the equipercentile equating function. However, the expressions for the variance-covariance matrix of the set of equated scores and for the variance-covariance matrix of the differences between equating functions were presented within the general framework of kernel equating. Therefore, multivariate Wald tests can be constructed straightforwardly to assess differences between equating functions other than the linear and equipercentile function, and for data collection designs other than the equivalent-groups design. For example, it may be of interest to use multivariate Wald tests to assess the differences between chain equating and poststratification methods in a nonequivalent groups with anchor test design.

The fact that the difference between two equating functions is statistically significant is only one part of the story. For large samples, even a small difference may reach statistical significance. In order to judge the practical significance between two equating functions, Dorans and Feigenbaum (1994) introduced the difference that matters, the difference that would result in a different score after rounding. A difference between two equating functions is judged to be practically significant whenever it exceeds the difference that matters.

Author Note: The authors would like to thank Tim Moses for sharing SAS macros to carry out kernel equating and to compute the standard error of the equating difference at a given score point. The results reported in this paper were obtained through an adaptation of Tim's SAS macros. Any opinions expressed in this chapter are those of the authors and not necessarily of Educational Testing Service.

Chapter 20
Applying Time-Series Analysis to Detect Scale Drift

Deping Li, Shuhong Li, and Alina A. von Davier

20.1 Introduction

This chapter focuses on applying the method of regression with autoregressive moving-average (ARMA) errors to monitor equated scores over time. This method can provide a whole picture of equated scores without the use of any additional equating designs. Depending on how a test is scored (e.g., scored by number correct, formula scored, item response theory [IRT] scored), the raw score of an examinee on a test will look different. In order to aid the interpretability of the scores provided to test users and test takers, the raw scores are transformed to scale scores. The scale scores are the reported scores received by test users and therefore are the most visible and important part of an assessment. Typically, scaling is established by mapping raw scores from a single test form to scale scores. Establishing the scale for reporting scores is a process that is both statistically and policy based, and it should support the purpose of the assessment. The reporting scale should (a) have an established mean and variance, (b) allow for a good representation of easier or more difficult subsequent test forms, (c) avoid (misleading) comparisons with different and already established assessments, and (d) incorporate score precision (such as reflecting a special relationship of the standard error of measurement across the score points, or deciding about the number of score scale points). It is common to talk about equating and scaling as a two-step process. In practice, the scaling of the scores from a new test form is accomplished as follows: Raw scores on the new test form are equated back to the raw scores of the previous (old) form for which the scaling has been established.

The reported scores provide information regarding pass-fail decisions and policy decisions and facilitate comparisons across individuals and institutions. Score scales could be criterion referenced, so that reported scores are associated with

D. Li (✉), S. Li, and A.A. von Davier
Educational Testing Service, Rosedale Rd., Princeton, New Jersey 08541, USA
e-mail: dli@ets.org

A.A. von Davier (ed.), *Statistical Models for Test Equating, Scaling, and Linking*, Statistics for Social and Behavioral Sciences,
DOI 10.1007/978-0-387-98138-3_20,

levels of achievement on content domains. Score scale also could be norm referenced, so that reported scores are associated with specific percentiles in the populations taking the test. In order for a test to be fair towards test takers who take different forms, maintaining the same meaning of score scales over time is critical for educational testing programs.

Equating methods are used to maintain the meaning of scale scores as new forms are developed, but equating involves various sources of errors (Kolen & Brennan, 2004). Equating errors can accumulate and lead to problems for comparing equated scores across forms (e.g., Livingston, 2004), or even worse, can lead to *scale drift*. Scale drift makes a scale no longer a relevant basis for interpreting test results.

In the past, it was common to investigate potential scale drift for a standardized program, and scale drift was usually corrected or avoided by a carefully designed braiding plan for equating. However, for some programs, an equating braiding plan is not feasible because of security concerns.

Several methods have been put forward for evaluating scale drift. For example, in some studies, scale drift was evaluated through the differences between equated scores and certain criteria using *equating in a circle* (Petersen, Cook, & Stocking, 1983) and *direct/indirect* equating methods (Kao, Kim, & Hatrak, 2005; Morrison & Fitzpatrick, 1992). However, the traditional techniques available to psychometricians have been developed for tests with only a small number of administrations per year; therefore, they are not appropriate to catch changes in a complex flow of equated scores. Similar challenges arise in computerized adaptive testing and in conventional linear testing with very large numbers of distinct forms. Moreover, these classical approaches for detecting scale drift require additional equating designs and form reuses, which are usually costly, insecure, and infeasible for some testing programs. As a result, there is a strong need to seek appropriate methodologies to detect changes in the reported scores in particular for some testing programs that have a large number of administrations in a year.

The outline of this chapter is as follows. After a brief introduction on the scaling procedures and the traditional methods for investigating issues of scale drift, the quality assurance tools in educational assessments and the regression models with ARMA errors are discussed. A simulation study is then presented, followed by the discussion of the results and conclusions as well as recommendations from the simulation study using regression with ARMA errors.

20.2 Traditional Approaches to Assessing Scale Drift

Ideally, the approach to monitoring equated scores and assessing potential scale drift problems is to have a well-planned equating design, in which a reference form (old form) is readministered to an equivalent group and re-equated back to the base form (Kolen & Brennan, 2004). If the conversion from directly equating the reference form to the base form and the conversion from equating the reference form back to the base form through some intervening forms agree with each other, the equating results in question are considered consistent. However, this approach requires finding equivalent groups for equating and readministration of a reference form. Repeating an old form as an intact form or an intact part of a form may not be allowed by some testing programs because of test security concerns or the difficulty of interpreting scores on the old form, due to the evolution of curriculum and content.

Morrison and Fitzpatrick (1992) suggested evaluating equating and scale stability by comparing the results from a *direct equating* and an *indirect equating* function. A direct equating function, which served as the criterion, was obtained from equating new forms directly back to base forms; an indirect equating function was obtained from equating new forms back to base forms through some intermediate forms. The differences between these two functions indicated whether equated scores were aberrant and whether potential scale drift existed. To make a circular chain of equatings was another widely used approach of assessing equating and scale stability. In this approach, a base form, which had previously been put on scale, was equated to itself through some intervening forms. Any discrepancy between the conversion from a circular chain of equatings and the conversion from the base form to itself (identity) were attributed to potential scale drift (e.g., Petersen et al., 1983). These traditional approaches require additional equating designs—a direct equating and a circular equating—and also require form reuses. Additionally, the results may not necessarily be consistent when different numbers of intermediate forms are involved into the evaluation.

20.3 Quality Assurance Tools in Educational Assessment

Regression with ARMA errors is in fact a time-series analysis method that views a sequence of equated scores or other test results in educational assessments as a random process. Methods of statistical process control, which have been widespread in industrial settings for quality assurance of mass production, were applied to the field of educational measurement in the last decades. Van Krimpen-Stoop and Meijer (2001) employed cumulative sum (CUSUM) control charts to develop a person-fit index in a computer-adaptive testing environment. Armstrong and Shi (2009) further developed model-free CUSUM methods to detect person-fit problems. Meijer (2009) explored the statistical process control techniques to ensure quality in a measurement process for rating performance items in operational assessments. Veerkamp and Glas (2000) used CUSUM charts to detect drifts in item parameter estimates in a computer-adaptive testing environment. The motivation of the present study was to explore how time-series methods can be used further as a device to monitor reported scores and detect potential scale drift problems.

The time-series methods employ all available results of unrounded raw-to-scale conversions on each test form. Therefore, they can provide a holistic picture on how score conversions change over time. Note that the methods are applied to a sequence of raw-to-scale score conversions for a given raw score point. For a test form, there are $r = 0, 1, 2, R$ raw score points. Correspondingly, there are R sequences of raw-to-scale score conversions. Raw-to-scale conversions vary at different raw score points and vary across forms as well. For a given raw score point, the degree to which raw-to-scale conversions vary often indicates the equating and scale stability. The larger the variability of score conversions, the less stable the equating results. The range of score conversions depicts the largest change in raw-to-scale conversions across forms.

The variability of score conversions is closely associated with test form constructions, test taker demographics, and the quality of equating. In an extreme case in which forms are strictly parallel, no equating is needed, and therefore, no variability exists among score conversions at any raw score point. On the other hand, if equating were free of errors, the variability of raw-to-scale conversions for a given raw score could be entirely explained by the actual differences in form difficulty because "*equating adjusts for differences in form difficulty, not for differences in content*" (Kolen & Brennan, 2004, p. 3). In this situation, score conversions were considered free of error accumulation. However, equating is never perfect. Measurement errors, sampling errors, systematic errors, errors from rounding, and errors resulting from a failure to meet equating assumptions can accumulate to affect equating and scale stability. Moreover, as pointed by Kolen and Brennan,

> even though test developers attempt to construct test forms that are as similar as possible to one another in content and statistical specifications, the forms typically differ somewhat in difficulty. Equating is intended to adjust for these difficulty differences, allowing the forms to be used interchangeably. (p. 3)

Therefore, the variability of score conversions will reflect both the differences in form difficulty and the cumulative effects of various sources of errors.

Regression with errors that satisfies an ARMA model is hardly a new topic, although it has not yet been used widely to study score conversions. Box and Jenkins (1970) have developed a systematic class of ARMA models to handle time-correlated data for modeling and forecasting, and the ARMA models are an important parametric family of a stationary time-series, in which joint probability distributions do not change when shifted in time. More details on these models can be found from Box and Jenkins (1970); Box, Jenkins, and Reinsel (1994); Shumway and Stoffer (2006); Brockwell and Davis (2002); and Chatfield (2003).

If a time series appears to have trend and seasonal components, it may be necessary to apply a preliminary transformation to the series. Fitting an ARMA model to a series of equated scores $X_1, X_2, \ldots, X_T$ (across forms) for a given raw score point r ($r = 0, 1, 2, \ldots, R$) assumes the series are generated by a stationary time series. There are several ways in which the trend and seasonality can be removed, some involving estimating the components and subtracting them from the data, and others depending on differencing the data, replacing the original series X_t by $U_t = X_t - X_{t-d}$ for some positive integer d. Whichever method is used, the aim is to produce a stationary series (e.g., Brockwell & Davis, 2002, p. 23).

Typically, in time-series modeling the knowledge of the underlying mechanism generating the data is limited, and the choice of a suitable class of models is usually data driven (Brockwell & Davis, 2002, pp. 97–98). For a series of score conversions at a given raw score point, the basic measures of the autocorrelation function (ACF) and partial autocorrelation function (PACF) using the graphical representation may be used to suggest a model for the series (see the Appendix for more discussions on ACF and PACF). An effective application of the Box and Jenkins's models requires at least a moderately long series. Chatfield (2003) recommended at least 50 observations (i.e., in our case, administrations), whereas many others have recommended at least 100 observations.

Since equated scores across forms naturally form a time-correlated series, it is not appropriate to analyze them using the standard linear regression method, in which the errors are assumed to be independent and identically distributed. The autocorrelation may arise from the dependency of the equating function on a new form and a previous form. For example, in the chained equating design, if the traditional equipercentile method is used for equating, then the equating function depends on the score distributions for the new form and the previous form—so do the equated scores at any given raw score point. Similarly, if the IRT true-score equating method is used, the equating function relies on the test characteristic curve on the new form and the test characteristic curve on the previous form. Note that equating functions are not established for each form independently; they depend on both the new forms and the previous reference forms. Therefore, a series of equated scores at a raw score point is not observed independently and is inappropriate for the regular regression analysis.

Let a simple regression with ARMA errors be fitted to a series of equated scores X_t for $1 \leq t \leq T$ for T administrations, with form difficulty $f(t)$ as an explanatory variable. That is equivalently written as

$$X_t = \beta_0 + \beta_1 f(t) + W_t. \tag{20.1}$$

The form difficulty $f(t)$ in Equation 20.1 is the major explanatory variable for predicting equated scores, because equating adjusts differences in form difficulty, which can be the average difficulty parameters of items in a form.[1] In Equation 20.1, W_t is an error sequence for $1 \leq t \leq T$; β_0 is the intercept; and β_1 is the effect of form difficulty on changes in the equated scores, X_t. If W_t is a random error for all t, or if W_t is white noise—$W_t \sim WN(0\,\sigma^2)$—Equation 20.1 becomes the ordinary regression, and β_0, β_1, and σ^2 can be obtained through the least-squares estimation method. However, in equating contexts, where forms are linked or chained from each other, the error sequence W_t may be time correlated, and it is more appropriate to fit a suitable ARMA (p, q) model. For example, if W_t in Equation 20.1 could follow an AR(1)

[1] Item parameter estimates need to be transformed onto the same IRT scale so that the average form difficulty *can* be compared from one test form to another.

model for every t (i.e., an autoregressive process with order $p = 1$, $q = 0$), then W_t can be written as

$$\mathrm{W_t} - \psi\ W_{t-1} = Z_t,\ |\psi|<1,\ \mathrm{Z_t} \sim WN(0, \sigma^2). \tag{20.2}$$

Or if W_t could follow a MA(2) (i.e., a moving-average process with order ($p = 0$, $q = 2$) process for every t, then

$$W_t = Z_t + \eta_1\ Z_{t-1} + \eta_2\ Z_{t-2},\ Z_t \sim WN(0, \sigma^2). \tag{20.3}$$

Regardless of what ARMA (p, q) models can fit W_t, it is necessary to test whether or not W_t is random for all t (see below). If autocorrelations exist in the error sequence W_t, it is often more appropriate to assume that the errors W_t are observations of a zero-mean stationary process.

Two procedures are often employed to test whether autocorrelations exist in errors W_t. One is the Durbin-Watson test (e.g., Chatfield, 2003, p. 69; Montgomery, Peck & Vining, 2001) and the other is the Ljung-Box test (Ljung & Box, 1978). The null hypothesis for the Durbin-Watson test is that autocorrelation is 0 at a lag of 1. Rejecting the test suggests that autocorrelations exist in W_t and that W_t may not be random, for all t, $1 \le t \le T$. The null hypothesis for the Ljung-Box test is that the residuals are independent. Rejecting the test suggests W_t may not be independent.

The above discussions on a simple regression can be extended to a more general form of regression with ARMA (p, q) errors, in which Equation 20.1 becomes

$$X_\mathrm{t} = \mathbf{y}'_\mathrm{t}\boldsymbol{\beta} + W_t, t = 1, \ldots, T, \tag{20.4}$$

where $\boldsymbol{y}_t = (y_{t1}, \ldots, y_{tk})$ consists of a vector of explanatory variables at time t, and β is a vector of their effects $\boldsymbol{\beta} = (\beta_1, \ldots, \beta_k)$. The error sequence W_t in Equation 20.4 satisfies a more general ARMA(p, q) process if

$$\psi(B)W_t = \eta(B)Z_t, Z_t \sim WN(0, \sigma^2), \tag{20.5}$$

where $\psi(B)$ and $\eta(B)$ stand for the autoregressive operator and moving-average operator, respectively. The autoregressive operator $\psi(B)$ is defined to be $\psi(B) = 1 - \psi_1 B - \psi_2 B^2 - \cdots - \psi_p B^\mathrm{p}$ and the moving-average operator $\eta(B)$ is defined to be $\eta(B) = 1 - \eta_1\ B^2 - \cdots - \eta_q B^q$, where B is a backward shift operator.[2] For special cases, the model is said to be an autoregressive process AR(p) of order p if $\eta(B) \equiv 1$ (see AR(1) in Equation 20.2). The model is said to be a moving-average process MA (q) of order q if $\psi(B) \equiv 1$ (see MA(2) in Equation 20.3).

Model parameters in Equations 20.4 and 20.5 include regression coefficients $\boldsymbol{\beta} = (\beta_0, \beta_1, \ldots, \beta_k)$, the ARMA model parameters $(\psi_1, \ldots, \psi_p)$ and $(\eta_1, \ldots, \eta_q)$, and the residual variance σ^2. Generalized least-squares estimates for the regression

[2]The backward shift operator is defined as $BX_t = X_{t\text{-}1}$, $B^j\ (X_t) = X_{t\text{-}j}$ for $j \ge 1$.

effects $\boldsymbol{\beta}$ and maximum likelihood estimates of the ARMA model parameters $(\psi_1, \ldots, \psi_p)$ and $(\eta_1, \ldots, \eta_q)$, as well as σ^2 can be obtained simultaneously through an extension of an iterative scheme proposed by Cochrane and Orcutt in 1949 (as cited in Brockwell & Davis, 2002, pp. 210–219; also see Cochrane & Orcutt, 1987).

When regression with ARMA errors is applied to a series of equated scores, three indicators can be used to monitor the equated scores over time: (a) the effect for form difficulty, (b) the effect for form order, and (c) the residual variance. Since form difficulty $f(t)$, as is shown in Equation 20.1, is one major explanatory variable to explain the variability in equated scores, it is hypothesized that the effect for form difficulty would be significant. In addition, the order of the form administration may have implications on changes in equated scores due to accumulation of errors. In theory, the form order should not have a large effect on the equated scores. However, due to accumulation of errors in a longer chain, a greater amount of errors may be involved in equated results. If the effect of the form order is significant, equated scores would increase or decrease according to the form order even conditional on the same value of form difficulty, which is an indicator of problems in the linking and equating results. Besides, the residual standard deviation σ (or the variance of the deviation of the regression function and data observations) that depicts the variation in equated scores after accounting for differences in form difficulty would be quite small when compared to the standard error of measurement and the standard deviation of the sequence of equated scores. A large amount of residual variance implies a large amount of variability in equated scores that are due to errors. For successful equating, at least 80% of the variability in equated scores corresponding to middle score levels is due to the differences in form difficulties.

20.4 Simulation Design

A simulation study was carried out to illustrate how the method of regression with ARMA errors can be used to monitor score conversions over time. Two specific scenarios were considered in the simulation study. In the first scenario (equivalent groups), we hypothesized that the equating results and the underlying scale would be stable over time because the test forms were taken by equivalent groups of simulees. In the second scenario (nonequivalent groups), we hypothesized that the equating results would have a large variability across forms and might involve more errors because the population ability differences were intentionally simulated to be too large for observing stable equating results. We expected to see that the form difficulty would predict the equated scores. We also expected the amount of variability after accounting for form difficulty to be smaller for the samples that were similar in ability (equivalent groups) than for the samples that were largely different in the case of nonequivalent groups.

For the purpose of the study, 100 test forms were simulated using an anchor test design, with each form consisting of 50 unique items and 30 common items that did not contribute to test scores. Each anchor of 30 common items linked only two

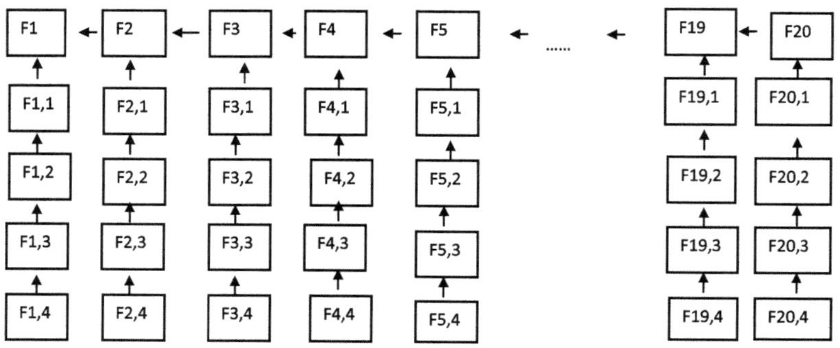

Fig. 20.1 Data collection design used for the simulation study

adjacent forms and did not overlap with any other anchor of 30 common items that linked another pair of adjacent forms. The forms were not linked in a single chain; instead, the forms were linked together with 20 strands (i.e., a strand starting with a form from F1 to F20; see Figure 20.1), each involving five forms. The first form of each strand (e.g., F3, F4, . . . , F20) did not link directly to the base form (i.e., F1). These forms created another chain of 20 forms (i.e., F1 to F20).[3] The graphic presentation of the equating design is given in Figure 20.1.

The 100 test forms in the simulation study were generated for 100 groups of simulees. The item responses were simulated using a two-parameter logistic IRT model (e.g., Hambleton & Swaminathan, 1985; Lord, 1980). All items in a form were dichotomous. One group responding to a form involved a sample of 5,000 simulees, who were generated from a standard normal distribution (i.e., equivalent groups). All forms were calibrated separately, and the item parameters were transformed onto the same metric using the Stocking and Lord (1983) method. To create a scale for further analysis, the first form on the first strand was treated as the base form (F1) with a score range between 0 and 50, and scores on the other forms were eventually equated to the base form scale using the IRT true-score method. An unrounded conversion function of raw-to-equated-raw scores was obtained on each form (except the base form). These conversion functions for raw-to-equated-raw scores formed a series of equated scores at any fixed raw-score point, and the time-series method was employed to analyze these series of equated scores at different raw-score points. The forms were simulated to differ in difficulty.

The study was then repeated with samples from nonequivalent groups of simulees. Specifically, the 100 test forms were given to 100 groups of simulees (each group having 5,000 simulees), which were simulated from normal distributions with the same standard deviation but different means (from a uniform distribution

[3]Note that this equating design is used to collect data for the analysis in the simulation study. It is used only for illustrative purpose. The effects of equating design on equating and scale stability are not the focus of this chapter.

within an interval between −.20 and .20). Under conditions in which population ability difference is large, linking and equating would involve a large amount of errors; therefore, a series of equated scores at a given raw score point would have larger variability. The study for nonequivalent groups was used to evaluate whether the time-series method had adequate power to detect problems in equated scores due to large differences in population ability.

In the case of nonequivalent groups, in addition to form difficulty, form order also might also affect the equating results due to error accumulation. If a new form was directly equated to the base form, the order was 1; if a form was equated back to the base form through 4 intervening forms, then the order was 5. The maximum order in the simulation was 23. The longer a chain, the more errors might accumulate within equating results. If the effect of the form order was significant, it was more likely to obtain aberrant equating results. In this sense, the method could provide a statistical device in terms of the effect of the form order to detect any atypical results in equated scores.

20.5 Results

The unrounded equating functions for raw-to-equated-raw scores from the 100 test forms constitute a series of equated scores at any given raw scores. Figure 20.2 displays the series of equated scores across the 100 test forms from equivalent

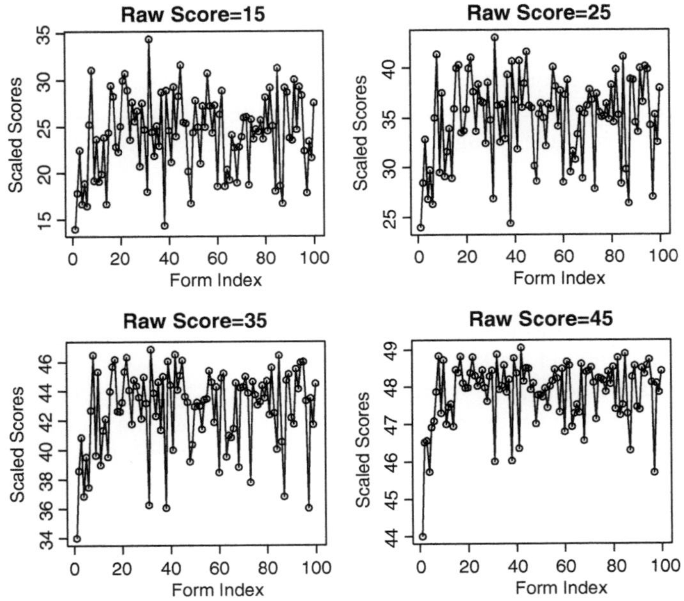

Fig. 20.2 Four examples of series of equated scores (equivalent groups)

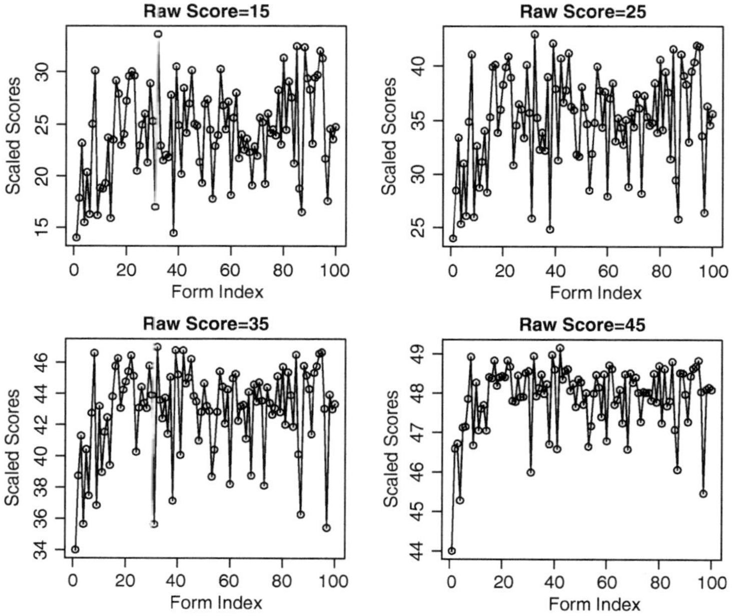

Fig. 20.3 Four examples of series of equated scores (nonequivalent groups)

groups when the raw score was 15, 25, 35, and 45, respectively. Figure 20.3 displays the series of equated scores across the 100 test forms from nonequivalent groups when the raw score was 15, 25, 35, and 45, respectively. The figures provide a whole picture of the changes in equated scores over time, from which one can identify when equated scores appeared to be outliers, when equated score increase or decrease, and how the changes in equated scores were different for different raw score points.

Tables 20.1 and 20.2 summarize the equating functions for the raw-to-equated-raw scores for all test forms at various raw score points and their correlations with form difficulty (denote Corr1 and Corr2. Corr1 represents the correlation between the equated scores corresponding to given a raw score and the average item difficulty; Corr2 is the correlation between the equated scores and the mean of the average item scores) in the simulation study. The equated scores for a given raw-score point varied across test forms, and the variability appeared to be greater for the middle scores than for the extreme scores. For example, the standard deviations for the series of equated scores corresponding to raw score $r = 19$ were greater than 4, and the range for the series was about 20. However, the standard deviations for the series corresponding to raw scores r ($r < 3$ or $r > 33$) appeared to be less than 3 (see Table 20.1). The correlations between series of equated scores and form difficulty were also stronger for the series corresponding to the middle raw-score levels than the extremes (Tables 20.1 and 20.2), and the correlations for series of equated scores from equivalent groups were greater than the counterparts from

Table 20.1 Descriptive Statistics for Score Conversions Over 100 Forms (Equivalent Groups)

Raw score	Mean	*SD*	Min	Median	Max	Range	Corr1	Corr2
1	1.52	0.83	0.34	1.31	3.92	3.57	.53	−0.50
3	5.79	2.51	2.00	5.08	13.89	11.89	.75	−0.72
5	10.35	3.29	4.46	9.86	19.35	14.89	.85	−0.83
7	14.21	3.59	6.73	14.28	23.56	16.83	.90	−0.88
9	17.44	3.81	9.04	17.57	27.18	18.14	.93	−0.91
11	20.29	4.03	11.32	20.42	30.34	19.02	.94	−0.93
13	22.90	4.22	13.39	23.20	33.11	19.72	.95	−0.94
15	25.33	4.37	15.33	25.71	35.53	20.20	.95	−0.95
17	27.63	4.47	17.25	28.13	37.65	20.39	.96	−0.96
19	29.81	4.50	19.20	30.43	39.49	20.29	.96	−0.96
21	31.89	4.47	21.20	32.43	41.07	19.86	.96	−0.96
23	33.86	4.38	23.30	34.49	42.41	19.11	.96	−0.96
25	35.72	4.22	25.49	36.56	43.55	18.06	.96	−0.96
27	37.48	3.99	27.76	38.44	44.51	16.75	.95	−0.96
29	39.12	3.71	30.11	40.00	45.32	15.22	.94	−0.95
31	40.65	3.37	32.49	41.40	46.02	13.52	.94	−0.94
33	42.07	2.98	34.88	42.73	46.60	11.71	.93	−0.93
35	43.36	2.57	36.99	43.97	47.11	10.11	.91	−0.92
37	44.55	2.15	38.94	45.12	47.56	8.62	.90	−0.91
39	45.62	1.74	40.91	46.02	48.01	7.10	.88	−0.89
41	46.58	1.36	42.87	46.87	48.47	5.60	.86	−0.86
43	47.44	1.01	44.78	47.69	48.87	4.09	.83	−0.83
45	48.23	0.70	46.34	48.44	49.24	2.89	.79	−0.78
47	48.96	0.43	47.52	49.07	49.56	2.03	.72	−0.70
49	49.67	0.17	48.86	49.71	49.89	1.03	.46	−0.44

Note: Corr1 = the correlation between the equated scores at each raw score point and the average form difficulty; Corr2 = the correlation between the equated scores and the average p values (p value means the proportion of number correct for each item). The results for the even scores are similar to the results for the odd scores and they are available from the authors. The means of the equated scores at many score points (Column 2) are much greater than the corresponding raw score point because the average item difficulty for the base form happened to be much smaller than the subsequent forms.

nonequivalent groups. The form-to-form difference in difficulty is larger in this study than those observed in typical operational practice in order to clearly investigate the effect of the form difficulty on score conversions. In addition, the average item difficulty for the base form happened to be much easier than the subsequent forms. As a result, the means of the equated scores were much greater than the corresponding raw scores (Tables 20.1 and 20.2). The results corresponding to the extreme scores were slightly different from the results corresponding to the middle raw-score levels (e.g., smaller correlations and standard deviations), and the differences may be closely related to the ceiling effects for IRT true-score equating functions at extremes because the minimum and maximum equated scores (or true scores) are constrained within [0, 50], regardless of the differences in form difficulties.

Figures 20.4 and 20.5 display the plots of the equated scores and form difficulty at four different raw scores (r = 15, 25, 35, 45) for equivalent groups and

Table 20.2 Descriptive Statistics for Score Conversions Over 100 Forms (Nonequivalent Groups)

Raw scores	Mean	SD	Min	Median	Max	Range	Corr1	Corr2
1	1.55	0.90	0.29	1.28	4.97	4.68	0.49	−0.47
3	5.89	2.58	1.56	5.40	13.73	12.17	0.70	−0.67
5	10.50	3.38	3.86	10.03	19.25	15.39	0.79	−0.76
7	14.33	3.71	6.65	14.11	23.12	16.47	0.82	−0.78
9	17.53	3.96	9.04	17.46	26.26	17.22	0.84	−0.79
11	20.36	4.20	11.32	20.26	29.41	18.09	0.85	−0.81
13	22.95	4.41	13.44	22.83	32.32	18.88	0.86	−0.81
15	25.38	4.58	15.46	25.50	34.90	19.44	0.87	−0.82
17	27.68	4.68	17.46	27.73	37.16	19.70	0.87	−0.83
19	29.88	4.73	19.47	29.84	39.15	19.68	0.88	−0.83
21	31.97	4.70	21.55	32.09	40.86	19.31	0.88	−0.84
23	33.95	4.60	23.73	34.22	42.32	18.59	0.88	−0.84
25	35.83	4.43	26.00	36.24	43.54	17.54	0.88	−0.84
27	37.60	4.19	28.35	38.19	44.56	16.22	0.87	−0.84
29	39.26	3.89	30.38	39.86	45.42	15.04	0.87	−0.83
31	40.80	3.53	32.45	41.36	46.13	13.68	0.86	−0.82
33	42.21	3.13	34.49	42.78	46.73	12.24	0.85	−0.81
35	43.50	2.70	36.41	43.98	47.23	10.82	0.83	−0.80
37	44.67	2.25	38.41	45.12	47.71	9.31	0.82	−0.78
39	45.73	1.81	40.45	46.10	48.21	7.76	0.80	−0.76
41	46.67	1.40	42.50	46.97	48.63	6.13	0.78	−0.74
43	47.50	1.04	44.51	47.73	48.99	4.49	0.75	−0.70
45	48.26	0.72	45.97	48.43	49.32	3.35	0.72	−0.66
47	48.97	0.44	47.30	49.08	49.61	2.31	0.64	−0.58
49	49.67	0.18	48.78	49.71	49.88	1.10	0.42	−0.35

Note: Corr1 = the correlation between the equated scores at each raw score point and the average form difficulty; Corr2 = the correlation between the equated scores and the mean p values (p value means the proportion of number correct for each item). The results for the even scores are similar to the results for the odd scores and are available from the authors. The means of the equated scores at many score points (Column 2) are much greater than the corresponding raw score points because the average item difficulty for the base form happened to be much smaller than the subsequent forms.

nonequivalent groups, respectively. One can see whether the score conversions are consistent or inconsistent with the average item difficulties. Both figures show that the equated scores and the average form difficulty are strongly correlated, but stronger correlations appear for equivalent groups in Figure 20.4 than for nonequivalent groups in Figure 20.5. Intuitively, one may think of using the standard linear regression analysis for these data.

The results for parameter estimates from a simple regression analysis between the equated scores and the average item difficulties for equivalent and nonequivalent groups are presented in Tables 20.3 and 20.4, respectively. Note that the slopes $\hat{\beta}_1$ for form difficulty were all significant ($p < .000$ in column 9). The R-squares in the simple regression models corresponding to the middle score levels are about 90% and 80% for the equivalent groups and nonequivalent groups, respectively, suggesting about 90% variability in the equated scores are due to the form difficulties for the equivalent groups, and about 80% for the nonequivalent groups.

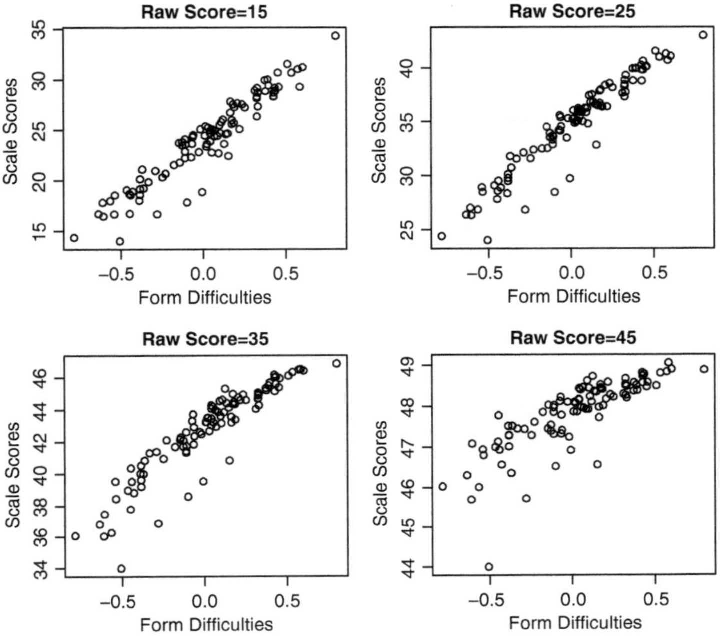

Fig. 20.4 Equated scores from equivalent groups

In order to check whether the simple regression model as given in Equation 20.1 adequately described the data. (i.e., to check whether the errors were correlated), the Durbin-Watson test (e.g., Chatfield, 2003, p. 69; Montgomery et al., 2001) and the Ljung-Box test (Ljung & Box, 1978) were employed to test the residuals (or deviations of the observations from the regression function) of the simple regression model (see columns 10 and 11 in Tables 20.3 and 20.4). The Durbin-Watson tests were significant for models on the series of equated scores corresponding to raw scores greater than 9 for equivalent groups (Table 20.3), implying the autocorrelations do exist at most series of equated scores at many raw score levels. The Durbin-Watson tests were significant for series of equated scores at every score level for nonequivalent groups (Table 20.4). Similar results from the Ljung-Box test (Ljung & Box, 1978), also at a lag of 1 (last two columns in Tables 20.3 and 20.4) confirmed the results from the Durbin-Watson test. These two tests provided some consistent evidence that the residuals were not random or independent and that the simple regression model was inadequate.

Based on the results from the regular regression analysis (Tables 20.3 and 20.4), a correction of autocorrelations using ARMA models was suggested. Before fitting a suitable ARMA model to the residuals, differencing was applied to remove the trend in order to obtain a stationary series. Thus, the original series X_t were replaced with the differenced data $U_t = X_t - X_{t-2}$ and a moving-average process with order $q = 2$ (i.e., MA(2); see Equation 20.3) was fitted to the stationary residuals

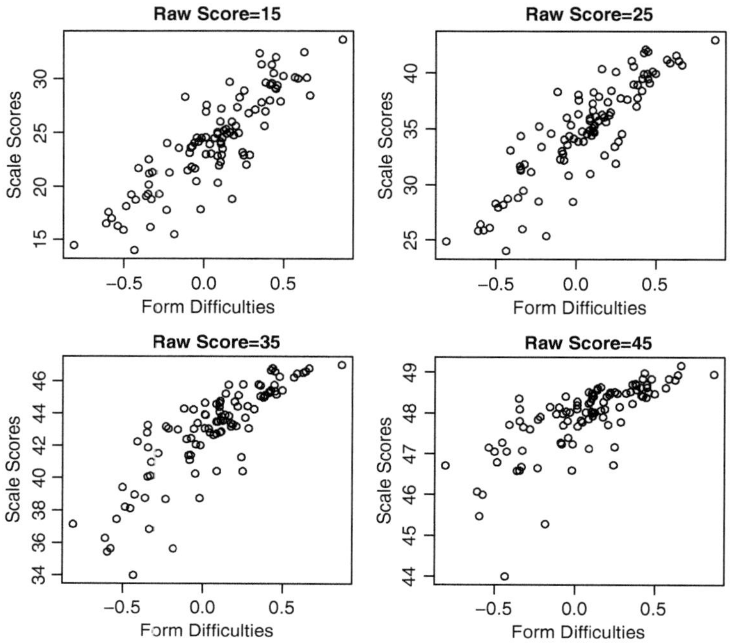

Fig. 20.5 Equated scores from nonequivalent groups

$N_t = W_t - W_{t-2}$ for $t = 3, 4, \ldots, T$. Table 20.5 presents the results of fitting a simple regression with an MA(2) model to the differenced data from equivalent groups.[4] Again at each raw score level, the slopes for form difficulty $\hat{\beta}_1$ were significant (see columns 6 and 7 of Table 20.5), as is expected. The standard errors of the slopes $SE(\hat{\beta}_1)$ became smaller in the new model. Most of the standard deviations of the residuals $\hat{\sigma}$ were even less than those in the simple regression model (column 6 in Table 20.3). Comparing the total variability of the equated scores (column 3 in Table 20.1) and the standard error of measurement (on overage 2.5 for each form), one notices that the residual standard deviation σ's were quite small, which is also expected in the example for equivalent groups. The Ljung-Box test (at a lag of 1) of randomness for the residuals (last two columns in Table 20.5) was not significant, implying that the residuals were random and the new model was appropriate and adequate. In short, the results from the example of equivalent groups (Table 20.5) appeared to be what are expected: Although long chains of equatings with 100 test forms were involved, the equating results were stable because the samples were equivalent groups. As a result, the equating results were consistent across forms. The results from the models for the series of equated scores corresponding to extreme scores were slightly different from the results for the series corresponding

[4]Except the models for lower score levels since a simple regression model appeared to be adequate.

Table 20.3 Results for Simple Regression Models and for the Durbin-Watson and Ljung-Box Tests (Equivalent Groups)

Raw score	$\hat{\beta}_0$	SE($\hat{\beta}_0$)	$\hat{\beta}_1$	SE($\hat{\beta}_1$)	$\hat{\sigma}$	R^2	*t*-value	*p*	*DW*	*p*	χ^2_{Box}	*p*
1	1.49	.07	1.34	.22	0.71	.28	6.23	.000	1.63	.031	3.18	.075
3	5.67	.17	5.71	.51	1.67	.56	11.2	.000	1.80	.162	0.84	.358
5	10.17	.17	8.53	.52	1.72	.73	16.31	.000	1.80	.153	1.00	.317
7	14.00	.16	9.82	.47	1.55	.82	20.8	.000	1.73	.085	1.62	.203
9	17.22	.14	10.71	.44	1.44	.86	24.33	.000	1.60	.021	3.26	.071
11	20.05	.14	11.48	.42	1.39	.88	27.12	.000	1.46	.003	5.58	.018
13	22.65	.13	12.15	.41	1.35	.90	29.58	.000	1.34	.000	8.52	.004
15	25.07	.13	12.66	.40	1.31	.91	31.62	.000	1.21	.000	12.07	.001
17	27.36	.13	12.97	.39	1.29	.92	33.09	.000	1.10	.000	16.03	.000
19	29.54	.13	13.09	.39	1.27	.92	33.88	.000	1.00	.000	19.97	.000
21	31.62	.13	13.01	.38	1.26	.92	33.94	.000	0.92	.000	23.13	.000
23	33.59	.13	12.72	.38	1.25	.92	33.25	.000	0.88	.000	24.87	.000
25	35.47	.13	12.21	.38	1.25	.91	31.95	.000	0.87	.000	25.21	.000
27	37.24	.13	11.50	.38	1.25	.90	30.20	.000	0.88	.000	24.33	.000
29	38.90	.12	10.60	.38	1.23	.89	28.23	.000	0.90	.000	22.68	.000
31	40.46	.12	9.55	.36	1.20	.88	26.20	.000	0.93	.000	20.75	.000
33	41.89	.11	8.37	.35	1.14	.86	24.19	.000	0.96	.000	18.65	.000
35	43.22	.11	7.13	.32	1.05	.83	22.26	.000	0.99	.000	16.50	.000
37	44.43	.09	5.87	.29	0.94	.81	20.39	.000	1.01	.000	14.38	.000
39	45.52	.08	4.65	.25	0.82	.78	18.52	.000	1.04	.000	12.35	.000
41	46.5	.07	3.53	.21	0.70	.74	16.66	.000	1.05	.000	10.73	.001
43	47.39	.06	2.54	.17	0.56	.69	14.78	.000	1.06	.000	9.93	.002
45	48.19	.04	1.68	.13	0.43	.63	12.79	.000	1.07	.000	9.77	.002
47	48.94	.03	0.92	.09	0.30	.51	10.14	.000	1.15	.000	8.88	.003
49	49.67	.02	0.24	.05	0.15	.22	5.20	.000	1.33	.000	7.12	.008

Note: R^2 = the estimate of the multiple R square. *t*-values are used in testing the hypothesis $\beta_1 = 0$, where β_1 is the slope of form difficulty. *DW* values are used for the Durbin-Watson test at a lag of 1. The null hypothesis is the autocorrelation is 0 at a lag of 1. χ^2_{Box} is the chi-squared value using Ljung-Box test at a lag of 1. The results for the even scores are similar to the results for the odd scores and are available from the authors.

to the middle raw-score levels, and again the differences may be closely related to the ceiling effects for IRT true-score equating functions at extremes, which would lead to less accurate results as those from the middle scores.

The regression with MA(2) errors was applied to the differenced data for the case of nonequivalent groups, and the administration order[5] was added to interpret the variability of equated scores. Comparing the results of this new model (Table 20.6) to the results from the simple regression model (Table 20.4) for nonequivalent groups, one observes that the effects for the form difficulty $\hat{\beta}_1$ were significant for series of equated scores at all raw score levels, which is not different from our expectation. Their standard errors *SE* ($\hat{\beta}_1$), however, were much smaller than their counterparts from the regular regression analysis (Table 20.4). It is worth noting that the slopes for the administration order, $\hat{\beta}_2$ (column 4 in Table 20.6), appeared to

[5]The administration order in this simulation study was not the same as the form order. However, in general, the greater the administration order, the greater the form order.

Table 20.4 Results for Simple Regression Models and for the Durbin-Watson and Ljung-Box Tests (Nonequivalent Groups)

Raw score	$\hat{\beta}_0$	SE($\hat{\beta}_0$)	$\hat{\beta}_1$	SE($\hat{\beta}_1$)	$\hat{\sigma}$	R^2	t-value	p	DW	p	χ^2_{Box}	p
1	1.47	.08	1.32	.24	0.79	.24	5.53	.000	1.40	.001	8.53	.003
3	5.57	.19	5.47	.56	1.85	.49	9.77	.000	1.43	.002	7.58	.006
5	10.03	.21	8.09	.63	2.07	.63	12.89	.000	1.31	.000	11.32	.001
7	13.79	.21	9.22	.64	2.11	.68	14.41	.000	1.20	.000	15.23	.000
9	16.95	.22	10.05	.65	2.15	.71	15.44	.000	1.13	.000	17.48	.000
11	19.73	.22	10.80	.67	2.20	.73	16.19	.000	1.10	.000	18.54	.000
13	22.28	.23	11.46	.68	2.25	.74	16.80	.000	1.08	.000	19.21	.000
15	24.68	.23	11.98	.69	2.28	.75	17.31	.000	1.06	.000	20.11	.000
17	26.96	.23	12.33	.70	2.30	.76	17.71	.000	1.04	.000	21.24	.000
19	29.15	.23	12.50	.69	2.29	.77	18.03	.000	1.00	.000	22.60	.000
21	31.24	.23	12.46	.68	2.26	.77	18.21	.000	0.98	.000	23.86	.000
23	33.24	.22	12.20	.67	2.21	.77	18.23	.000	0.95	.000	24.75	.000
25	35.15	.22	11.73	.65	2.14	.77	18.07	.000	0.94	.000	25.06	.000
27	36.96	.21	11.04	.62	2.06	.76	17.72	.000	0.94	.000	24.66	.000
29	38.67	.20	10.17	.59	1.95	.75	17.18	.000	0.95	.000	23.53	.000
31	40.26	.19	9.13	.55	1.83	.74	16.50	.000	0.98	.000	21.76	.000
33	41.75	.17	7.99	.51	1.68	.72	15.72	.000	1.01	.000	19.70	.000
35	43.11	.15	6.77	.45	1.50	.69	14.91	.000	1.04	.000	17.53	.000
37	44.35	.13	5.55	.39	1.30	.67	14.08	.000	1.07	.000	15.43	.000
39	45.47	.11	4.37	.33	1.09	.64	13.22	.000	1.08	.000	13.59	.000
41	46.47	.09	3.30	.27	0.88	.61	12.32	.000	1.09	.000	12.12	.000
43	47.37	.07	2.35	.21	0.68	.57	11.32	.000	1.09	.000	11.25	.001
45	48.17	.05	1.54	.15	0.50	.51	10.14	.000	1.10	.000	10.60	.001
47	48.92	.03	0.85	.10	0.33	.42	8.35	.000	1.17	.000	9.26	.002
49	49.66	.02	0.23	.05	0.16	.18	4.60	.000	1.33	.000	7.39	.007

Note: (1) R^2 represents the estimate of the multiple R square. (2) t-values are used in testing the hypothesis $\beta_1 = 0$, where β_1 is the slope of form difficulty. (3) DW values are used for the Durbin-Watson test. The null hypothesis is the autocorrelation is 0 at a lag of 1. (4) $\chi^2{}_{Box}$ is the Chi-squared value using the Ljung-Box test at a lag of 1. (5) The results for the even scores are similar to the results for the odd scores and are available from the authors.

be significant in particular for models of the series of equated scores at the upper score levels ($r \geq 37$), implying that equated scores would increase over time, probably due to accumulation of errors. For example, the series of equated scores corresponding to a raw score $r = 37$ would increase .22 score points when one form was administered even conditionally on the same value of the form difficulty. The equated scores would increase more than 1 score point were five forms added for an example like this. The equated scores would increase less for models for the series of equated scores at raw scores greater than 37 due to the ceiling effects.

The residual standard deviation $\hat{\sigma}s$ appeared to be a bit large for the case of nonequivalent groups (Table 20.6), with many $\hat{\sigma}s$ greater than the standard error of measurement (on average 2.5 in the simulation study). More than 20% of the variability in the equated scores corresponding to the middle score levels was due to random errors or accumulation of errors. As expected, large $\hat{\sigma}$ values suggest that a large amount of errors has accumulated and that equating and the underlying scale

Table 20.5 Parameter Estimates for Regression With Autoregressive Moving-Average Errors (Equivalent Groups)

Raw score	$\hat{\beta}_1$	SE($\hat{\beta}_1$)	*t*-value	$\hat{\sigma}$	$\hat{\eta}_1$	$\hat{\eta}_2$	χ^2_{Box}	*p*
11	10.99	.36	30.56	1.61	.22	−.69	.10	.75
13	11.63	.33	34.74	1.50	.26	−.66	.28	.60
15	12.12	.31	38.82	1.41	.31	−.62	.56	.45
17	12.44	.29	42.55	1.33	.35	−.58	.82	.36
19	12.58	.28	45.63	1.26	.38	−.55	.99	.32
21	12.53	.26	47.55	1.21	.41	−.53	1.01	.31
23	12.27	.26	47.73	1.19	.41	−.51	.90	.34
25	11.79	.25	46.23	1.18	.41	−.51	.76	.38
27	11.12	.26	47.38	1.18	.40	−.51	.64	.42
29	10.25	.26	39.85	1.18	.39	−.51	.56	.45
31	9.23	.25	31.20	1.17	.38	−.52	.53	.47
33	8.09	.25	32.72	1.13	.37	−.53	.52	.47
35	6.89	.23	29.62	1.06	.63	−.53	.53	.47
37	5.67	.21	26.87	0.96	.35	−.53	.51	.48
39	4.48	.18	24.31	0.84	.35	−.52	.48	.49
41	3.39	.15	21.89	0.71	.35	−.51	.44	.51
43	2.43	.12	19.43	0.57	.35	−.50	.44	.51
45	1.59	.10	16.54	0.44	.34	−.50	.48	.49
47	0.86	.07	11.97	0.32	.38	−.62	.29	.59
49	0.20	.04	5.13	0.18	.28	−.72	.01	.92

Note: Prob (> |t|) =. 000 for all results. $\hat{\beta}_1$ is the slope for form difficulty. $\hat{\eta}_1$ and $\hat{\eta}_2$ are the model parameters in the moving-average process. χ^2_{Box} is the chi-squared value using Ljung-Box test at a lag of 1. The results for the even scores are similar to the results for the odd scores and are available from the authors.

may not be stable. However, the Ljung-Box test (at a lag of 1) of randomness of errors (last two columns in Table 20.6) were not significant ($p < .01$), suggesting that the residuals were random (or independent) and the time-series model was appropriate and adequate.

Population differences in ability may explain for the problem of a large amount of residual variance in the case of nonequivalent groups. Kolen and Brennan (2004) pointed out, "*Mean group differences of around .3 or more standard deviation unit can result in substantial differences among methods, and differences larger than .5 standard deviation unit can be especially troublesome*" (p. 286). In the simulation study, the mean group difference was about .4 standard deviation units for the case of nonequivalent groups, which was considered troublesome. Therefore, the effects of examinee population differences were reflected in the equating results from nonequivalent groups (Table 20.6). Compared to the results from the same equating method for the same test forms from equivalent groups, the results from nonequivalent groups (in Table 20.6) involved much larger errors. Although the slopes for the form difficulty were still significant, the corresponding residual standard deviations were much larger than the counterparts for equivalent groups (Table 20.5) and were even greater than the standard error of measurement (on average 2.5 in the simulation study) at many score points. Moreover, the effects for the administration order were also significant for the series of equated scores at some raw score points,

Table 20.6 Parameter Estimates for Regression With Autoregressive Moving-Average Errors (Nonequivalent Groups)

Raw score	$\hat{\beta}_1$	SE($\hat{\beta}_1$)	$\hat{\beta}_2$	SE($\hat{\beta}_2$)	$\hat{\sigma}$	$\hat{\eta}_1$	$\hat{\eta}_2$	χ^2_{Box}	p
1	1.31*	.20	−.08	.05	0.91	.28	−.72	0.21	.65
3	5.40*	.48	−.26	.12	2.18	.28	−.72	0.04	.83
5	7.83*	.54	−.22	.13	2.44	.26	−.74	1.21	.27
7	8.90*	.54	−.10	.12	2.46	.23	−.77	2.15	.14
9	9.71*	.54	−.01	.12	2.48	.20	−.79	2.84	.09
11	10.45*	.56	.06	.12	2.55	.18	−.81	3.54	.06
13	11.11*	.58	.11	.12	2.63	.17	−.83	4.17	.04
15	11.61*	.59	.14	.12	2.68	.17	−.83	4.76	.03
17	11.95*	.59	.16	.13	2.69	.18	−.82	5.21	.02
19	12.09*	.58	.18	.13	2.65	.21	−.79	5.50	.02
21	12.04*	.57	.20	.13	2.57	.25	−.75	5.61	.02
23	11.80*	.54	.22	.13	2.47	.30	−.70	5.54	.02
25	11.35*	.52	.24	.13	2.36	.33	−.67	5.32	.02
27	10.70*	.49	.25	.13	2.24	.35	−.65	4.98	.03
29	9.85*	.46	.26	.12	2.12	.36	−.64	4.53	.03
31	8.85*	.43	.26	.11	1.99	.35	−.65	4.01	.05
33	7.73*	.40	.26	.10	1.84	.35	−.65	3.48	.06
35	6.54*	.36	.24	.09	1.65	.34	−.66	2.93	.09
37	5.35*	.31	.22*	.08	1.43	.34	−.66	2.39	.12
39	4.19*	.26	.19*	.07	1.17	.30	−.60	1.87	.17
41	3.14*	.20	.16*	.05	0.92	.30	−.57	1.34	.25
43	2.23*	.15	.12*	.04	0.70	.31	.54	0.88	.35
45	1.45*	.11	.09*	.03	0.51	.30	−.53	0.55	.46
47	0.78*	.08	.06*	.02	0.35	.27	−.55	0.27	.61
49	0.19*	.04	.02	.01	0.19	.28	−.72	0.02	.89

Note: $\hat{\beta}_1$ is the slope for the average form difficulty; $\hat{\beta}_2$ is the slope for the form order. $\hat{\eta}_1$ and $\hat{\eta}_2$ are the model parameters in the moving-average process. χ^2 is the chi-squared value using Ljung-Box test at a lag of 1. The results for the even scores are similar to the results for the odd scores and are available from the authors.
*p <.01

showing that equated scores would increase as new forms were administered. This increase would be indicative of potential issues.

20.6 Discussion

In this paper, the regression with ARMA errors borrowed from time-series analysis field was applied to a test with a large number of distinct forms. Specifically, the method was described and a simulation study was carried out to illustrate how to apply these models in monitoring the stability of the equated scores and how to evaluate the effectiveness of the models to inform choosing among them.

The findings from the two scenarios considered in the simulation study seemed to suggest that form difficulty would effectively explain changes in equated scores over time because the results from the hypothesis testing for the effects of form difficulty were significant. The results from the simulation study also showed that the method of regression with ARMA errors was more appropriate than the regular regression analysis for time-correlated series from equating functions. Based on the results, the time-series method effectively identified which series of equated scores had potential problems for equating through the analysis of the variability in the equated scores.

Equating can lead to variable equated scores due to errors, but it does not necessarily yield scale drift. The time-series method does not directly measure scale drift, and it does not exactly measure or even identify scale drift in the same sense as traditional approaches do. Instead, it shows whether a large amount of variability in equated scores is due to differences in form difficulty or due to errors. If equating is successful, a large amount of variability in equated scores is due to differences in form difficulties. The variability due to form difficulty differences can be effectively controlled by form constructions, anchor selections, and better choice of equating methods, but the variability due to errors may be more difficult to explain and control. Therefore, the results from the time-series method can give testing programs important information on assessing the quality of equating results as a whole. Furthermore, time-series plots of equated scores can also identify which test form at which score level show inconsistent results with the rest of the test forms (i.e., the outlier test forms).

Finally, the focus of this chapter is to introduce the time-series method for monitoring the stability of a series of equating results. For illustrative purpose, the simulation study only addresses how a suitable ARMA model can be considered for time-correlated series of equated scores and how psychometricians can employ this method to monitor equating and scale stability over time. Though this is beyond the scope of this chapter, it is necessary to conduct further research to compare the differences of results in various ARMA models to identify better models to describe the data. Moreover, it is sometimes not feasible to have a moderately long sequence of equating results, which is required for reliable parameter estimation for the time-series method. As a consequence, the method is limited by the need for many administrations for this method to work (at least 50), which is a challenge for many educational assessment instruments that have only several administrations per year. In practice, it is not uncommon to have a large number of administrations (or test forms) if the IRT methods are used for linking and equating. Therefore, the time-series method may be considered as one potential alternative approach for monitoring equated scores and detecting potential scale drift when the IRT methods are used for linking and equating.

Chapter 20 Appendix

20.A.1 Basic Terms for Times-Series Analysis

The terms ACF and PACF are fundamental for time-series analysis. Here we give the basic definitions for these terms. For more detailed discussion, see Brockwell and Davis (2002), Shumway and Stoffer (2006), and Chatfield (2003).

20.A.2 Autocorrelation Function (ACF)

Autocorrelation is a measure of the linear relationship between two separate instances of the same random variable, as distinct from correlation, which refers to the linear relationship between two distinct random variables. As with correlation, the possible values lie between -1 and 1 inclusive, with unrelated instances having a theoretical autocorrelation of 0. In time-series analysis, autocorrelation often measures the extent of the linear relation between values at time points that are a fixed interval (the lag) apart.

When the autocorrelation is used to detect nonrandomness, it is usually the first (or lag 1) autocorrelation that is of interest. When the autocorrelation is used to suggest an appropriate time-series model, the autocorrelation is usually plotted for many lags.

20.A.3 Partial Autocorrelation Function (PACF)

PACF at lag h is the autocorrelation between X_t and X_{t-h} that is not accounted for by lags 1 through h $-$ 1. The values of PACF also vary between -1 and 1, with the value near -1 or 1 indicating stronger correlation. The PACF removes the effect of shorter lag autocorrelation from the correlation estimate for longer lags. Sample ACFs and PACFs can be estimated from data observations $x_1, x_2, \ldots, x_T$.

A partial correlation is the amount of correlation between a variable and a lag of itself that is not explained by correlations at all lower order lags. A sample ACF may suggest which of the many possible stationary time-series models is a suitable candidate for representing the dependency among the series. For example, the sample ACF that is close to zero for all nonzero lags suggests that an appropriate model for the data might be a model of independent and identically distributed noise. Every stationary process with mean zero and autocorrelations vanishing at lags greater than q can be represented as a moving-average process of order q. The PACF of a causal AR(p) process is 0 for lags larger than p.

Author Note: Any opinions expressed in this chapter are those of the authors and not necessarily of Educational Testing Service.

References

Abdi, H. (2007). Bonferroni and Sidak corrections for multiple comparisons. In N. J. Salkind (Ed.), *Encyclopedia of measurement and statistics* (pp. 103–107). Thousand Oaks, CA: Sage.

Abramowitz, M., & Stegun, I. A. (1965). *Handbook of mathematical functions*. New York, NY: Dover.

Abramowitz, M., & Stegun, I. A. (Eds.). (1972). *Handbook of mathematical functions with formulas, graphs, and mathematical tables*. New York, NY: Dover.

Achenbach, T. M., & Rescorla, L. A. (2001). *Manual for the ASEBA school-age forms and profiles*. Burlington, VT: University of Vermont.

ACT. (2001). *EXPLORE technical manual*. Iowa City, IA: Author.

Aitchison, J., & Silvey, S. D. (1958). Maximum likelihood estimation of parameters subject to restraints. *Annals of Mathematical Statistics*, *29*, 813–828.

Akaike, H. (1974). A new look at the statistical model identification. *IEEE Transactions on Automatic Control*, *19*, 716–723.

Allen, N. L., Carlson, J. E., & Zelenak, C. A. (1999). *The NAEP 1996 technical report*. Washington, DC: National Center for Education Statistics.

Andersen, E. B. (1973). A goodness of for test for the Rasch model. *Psychometrika*, *38*, 123–140.

Angoff, W. H. (1971). Scales, norms and equivalent scores. In R. L. Thorndike (Ed.), *Educational measurement* (2nd ed., pp. 508–600). Washington DC: American Council on Education.

Armstrong, R. D., & Shi, M. (2009). Model-free CUSUM methods for person fit. *Journal of Educational Measurement*, *46*(4), 408–428.

Baker, F. B. (1990). *EQUATE: Computer program for linking two metrics in item response theory*. Madison: University of Wisconsin, Laboratory of Experimental Design.

Baker, F. B., & Al-Karni, A. (1991). A comparison of two procedures for computing IRT equating coefficients. *Journal of Educational Measurement*, *28*, 147–162.

Balakrishnan, N. (1992). *Handbook of the logistic distribution*. New York, NY: Marcel Dekker.

Ban, J.-C., & Lee, W.-C. (2007). *Defining a score scale in relation to measurement error for mixed format tests* (CASMA Research Report Number 24). Iowa City, IA: Center for Advanced Studies in Measurement and Assessment.

Bayley, N. (1933). *The California first-year mental scale*. Berkeley, CA: University of California Press.

Béguin, A. A. (2000). *Robustness of equating high-stakes tests* (Doctoral thesis). University of Twente, Enschede.

Béguin, A. A., & Glas, C. A. W. (2001). MCMC estimation and some fit analysis of multidimensional IRT models. *Psychometrika*, *66*, 541–562.

Birnbaum, A. (1968). Some latent trait models. In F. M. Lord & M. R. Novick (Eds.), *Statistical theories of mental test scores* (pp. 397–479). Reading, MA: Addison-Wesley.

Bishop, Y. M. M., Fienberg, S. E., & Holland, P. W. (1975). *Discrete multivariate analysis: theory and practice*. Cambridge, MA: MIT Press.

Bock, R. D., & Aitkin, M. (1981). Marginal maximum likelihood estimation of item parameters: Application of an EM algorithm. *Psychometrika, 46*, 443–459.

Bock, R. D., Gibbons, R. D., & Muraki, E. (1988). Full-information factor analysis. *Applied Psychological Measurement, 12*, 261–280.

Bock, R. D., & Lieberman, M. (1970). Fitting a response model for *n* dichotomously scored items. *Psychometrika, 35*, 179–197.

Bock, R. D., & Moustaki, I. (2007). Item response theory in a general framework. In C. R. Rao & S. Sinharay (Eds.), *Handbook of statistics, Vol. 26. Psychometrics* (pp. 469–513). New York, NY: Elsevier.

Bock, R. D., Thissen, D., & Zimowski, M. F. (1997). IRT estimation of domain scores. *Journal of Educational Measurement, 34*(3), 197–211.

Box, G. E. P., & Draper, N. R. (1987). *Empirical model-building and response surfaces*. New York, NY: Wiley.

Box, G. E. P., & Jenkins, G. M. (1970). *Time-series analysis, forecasting, and control*. Oakland, CA: Holden-Day.

Box, G. E. P., Jenkins, G. M., & Reinsel, G. C. (1994). *Time-series analysis, forecasting and control* (3rd ed.). Englewood Cliffs, NJ: Prentice Hall.

Bozdogan, H. (1987). Model selection and Akaike's information criterion (AIC): the general theory and its analytical extensions. *Psychometrika, 52*(3), 345–370.

Bradlow, E. T., Wainer, H., & Wang, X. (1999). A Bayesian random effects model for testlets. *Psychometrika, 64*, 153–168.

Bradway, K. P. (1944). IQ constancy on the Revised Stanford-Binet from the preschool to the junior high school level. *Journal of Genetic Psychology, 65*, 197–217.

Bradway, K. P. (1945a). An experimental study of factors associated with Stanford-Binet IQ changes from preschool to the junior high school. *Journal of Genetic Psychology, 66*, 107–128.

Bradway, K. P. (1945b). Predictive value of the Stanford-Binet preschool items. *Journal of Educational Psychology, 36*, 1–16.

Braun, H. I., & Holland, P. W. (1982). Observed score test equating: A mathematical analysis of some ETS equating procedures. In P. W. Holland & D. B. Rubin (Eds.). *Test equating* (pp. 9–49). New York, NY: Academic Press.

Brennan, R. L. (1992). The context of context effects. *Applied Measurement in Education, 5*, 225–264.

Brennan, R. L. (2007). Tests in transition: Synthesis and discussion. In N. J. Dorans, M. Pommerich, & P.W. Holland, (Eds.), *Linking and aligning scores and scales* (pp. 161–175). New York, NY: Springer-Verlag.

Brennan, R. L., & Lee, W. (2006). *Correcting for bias in single-administration decision consistency indexes* (CASMA Research Report No. 18). Iowa City: University of Iowa, Center for Advanced Studies in Measurement and Assessment.

Brockwell, P. J., & Davis, R. A. (2002). *Introduction to time-series and forecasting* (2nd ed.). New York, NY: Springer-Verlag.

Campbell, N. R. (1928). *An account of the principles of measurement and calculation*. London, England: Longmans, Green & Co.

Carmer, S. G., & Swanson, M. R. (1973). An evaluation of ten pairwise multiple comparison procedures by Monte Carlo methods. *Journal of the American Statistical Association, 68*, 66–74.

Chatfield, C. (2003). *The analysis of time-series: An introduction* (6th ed.). London, England: Chapman and Hall.

Chen, H., & Holland, P. W. (2008). *Construction of chained true score equipercentile equatings under the KE framework and their relationship to Levine true score equating*. (ETS Research Rept. RR-09-24). Princeton, NJ: ETS.

Chen, H., & Holland, P. W. (2009). *The construction of Levine observed score equipercentile equating under kernel equating framework*. Paper presented at the annual meeting of the National Council of Measurement in Education, San Diego.

Chen, H., & Holland, P. W. (2010). *Fit log-linear model with a linear transformation on the discrete distribution*. Manuscript in preparation.

Chen, H., Yan, D., Han, N., & von Davier, A. (2006). *LOGLIN/KE user guide: Version 2.1*. Princeton, NJ: ETS.

Cochran, D., & Orcutt, G. H. (1987). Applications of least square regression to relationships containing autocorrelated errors. *Journal of American Statistical Association, 44*, 32–61.

Conceptual framework. (n.d.). Retrieved from Wikipedia: http://en.wikipedia.org/wiki/

Cook, L. L. (2007). Practical problems in equating test scores: A practitioner's perspective. In N. J. Dorans, M. Pommerich, & P. W. Holland (Eds.), *Linking and aligning scores and scales* (pp. 73–88). New York, NY: Springer-Verlag.

Cudeck, R. (2000). An estimate of the covariance between two variables which are not jointly observed. *Psychometrika, 65*, 539–546.

Dalal, S., & Hall, W. (1983). Approximating priors by mixtures of natural conjugate priors. *Journal fo the Royal Statistical Society, Series B, 45*, 278–286.

Diaconis, P., & Ylvisaker, D. (1985). Conjugate priors for exponential families. *Annals of Statistics, 7*, 269–281.

Divgi, D. R. (1987). *A stable curvilinear alternative to linear equating* (Report CRC 571). Alexandria, VA: Center for Naval Analyses.

Dorans, N. J. (2008, December). *Holland's advice for the fourth generation of test theory: Blood tests can be contests*. Invited paper presented at Holland's Festschrift: A Conference in Honor of Paul W. Holland, Princeton, NJ.

Dorans, N. J. (Ed.). (1990). Selecting samples for equating: To match or not to match [Special issue]. *Applied Measurement in Education, 3*, 1–113.

Dorans, N. J. (2002). Recentering and realigning the SAT score distributions: How and why. *Journal of Educational Measurement, 39*(1), 59–84.

Dorans, N. J. (2007). Linking scores from multiple health outcome instruments. *Quality of Life Research, 16*, 85–94. 116

Dorans, N. J., & Feigenbaum, M. D. (1994). Equating issues engendered by changes to the SAT and PSAT/NMSQT®. In I. M. Lawrence, N.J. Dorans, M. D. Feigenbaum, N. J. Feryok, & N. K. Wright (Eds.), *Technical issues related to the introduction of the new SAT and PSAT/NMSQT* (ETS Research Memorandum RM-94-10). Princeton, NJ: ETS.

Dorans, N. J., & Holland, P. W. (2000). Population invariance and the equatability of tests: Basic theory and the linear case. *Journal of Educational Measurement, 37*, 281–306.

Dorans, N. J., & Liu, J. (2009). *Score equity assessment: Development of a prototype analysis using SAT mathematics test data across several administrations* (ETS Research Rept. RR-09-08). Princeton, NJ: ETS.

Dorans, N. J., Liu, J., & Hammond, S. (2008). Anchor test type and population invariance: An exploration across subpopulations and test administrations. *Applied Psychological Measurement, 32*, 81–97.

Dorans, N. J., Pommerich, M., & Holland, P.W. (Eds.). (2007). *Linking and aligning scores and scales*. New York, NY: Springer-Verlag.

Douglas, J. (1997). Joint consistency of nonparametric item characteristic curve and ability estimation. *Psychometrika, 62*, 7–28.

Drasgow, F., Luecht, R. M., & Bennett, R. E. (2006). Technology and testing. In R. L. Brennan (Ed.), *Educational measurement* (4th ed., pp. 471–515). Westport, CT: American Council on Education and Praeger.

Ebel, R. L. (1962). Content standard test scores. *Educational and Psychological Measurement, 22*(1), 15–25.

Edwards, M. C., & Wirth, R. J. (2009). Measurement and the study of change. *Research in Human Development, 2–3*, 74–96.

Efron, B. (1979). Bootstrap methods: Another look at the jackknife. *Annals of Statistics, 7*, 1–26.

Efron, B. (1982). *The jackknife, the bootstrap and other resampling plans*. Philadelphia, PA: Society for Industrial and Applied Mathematics.

Efron, B., & Morris, C. (1977). Stein's paradox in statistics. *Scientific American, 236*, 119–127.

Efron, B., & Tibshirani, R. J. (1993). *An introduction to the bootstrap*. New York, NY: Chapman & Hall.

Embretson, S. E. (1996). The new rules of measurement. *Psychological Assessment, 8*, 341–349.

Embretson, S. E., & Reise, S. P. (2000). *Item response theory for psychologists*. Hillsdale, NJ: Erlbaum.

Fairbank, B. A. (1987). The use of presmoothing and postsmoothing to increase the precision of equipercentile equating. *Applied Psychological Measurement, 11*, 245–262.

Ferguson, T. (1973). A Bayesian analysis of some nonparametric problems. *Annals of Statistics, 1*, 209–230.

Feuer, M. J., Holland, P. W., Green, B. F., Bertenthal, M. W., & Hemphill, F.C. (Eds.). (1999). *Uncommon measures: Equivalence and linkage among educational tests* (Report of the Committee on Equivalency and Linkage of Educational Tests, National Research Council). Washington DC: National Academy Press.

Fisher, R. A. (1960). *The design of experiments* (7th ed.). New York, NY: Hafner.

Flanagan, J. C. (1951). Units, scores, and norms. In E. F. Lindquist (Ed.), *Educational measurement* (pp. 695–763). Washington DC: American Council on Education.

Freeman, M. F., & Tukey, J. W. (1950). Transformations related to the angular and square root. *Annals of Mathematical Statistics, 21*(4), 607–611.

Gibbons, R. D., & Hedeker, D. (1992). Full-information item bi-factor analysis. *Psychometrika, 57*, 423–436.

Gilula, Z., & Haberman, S. J. (2000). Density approximation by summary statistics: An information-theoretic approach. *Scandinavian Journal of Statistics, 27*, 521–534.

Glas, C. A. W. (1988). The RM and multi-stage testing. *Journal of Educational Statistics, 13*, 45–52.

Glas, C. A. W. (1999). Modification indices for the 2-pl and the nominal response model. *Psychometrika, 64*, 273–294.

Glas, C. A. W. (2006). Testing generalized Rasch models. In M. von Davier & C. H. Carstensen (Eds.), *Multivariate and mixture distribution Rasch models* (pp. 37–46). New York, NY: Springer-Verlag.

Glas, C. A. W., & Verhelst, N. D. (1989). Extensions of the partial credit model. *Psychometrika, 54*, 635–659.

Glas, C. A. W., & Verhelst, N. D. (1995). Testing the Rasch model. In G. H. Fischer & I. W. Molenaar (Eds.), *Rasch models: Foundations, recent developments and applications* (pp. 69–96). New York, NY: Springer-Verlag.

Grimm, K. J. (n.d.). *Kevin J. Grimm: Script downloads*. Available from the University of California–Davis website: http://psychology.ucdavis.edu/labs/Grimm/personal/downloads.html

Haberman, S., Guo, H., Liu, J., & Dorans, N. J. (2008). *Trend analysis in seasonal time series models. Consistency of SAT® reasoning score conversions* (ETS Research Rept. RR-08-67). Princeton, NJ: ETS.

Haebara, T. (1980). Equating logistic ability scales by a weighted least squares method. *Japanese Psychological Research, 22*, 144–149.

Hall, P. (1997). *The bootstrap and Edgeworth expansion*. New York, NY: Springer-Verlag. (Corrected printing of 1992 ed.).

Hambleton, R. K., & Pitoniak, M. J. (2006) Setting performance standards. In R. L. Brennan (Ed.), *Educational measurement* (4th ed., pp. 433–470). Westport, CT: American Council on Education and Praeger.

Hambleton, R. K., & Swaminathan, H. (1985). *Item response theory: Practices and applications*. Boston, MA: Kluwer Academic.

Hambleton, R. K., Swaminathan, H., & Rogers, H. J. (1991). *Fundamentals of item response theory*. Newbury Park, CA: Sage.

Hanson, B. A., & Béguin, A. A. (2002). Obtaining a common scale for item response theory item parameters using separate versus concurrent estimation in the common-item equating design. *Applied Psychological measurement, 26*, 3–24.

Harris, D. J. (2007). Practical issues in vertical scaling. In N. J. Dorans, M. Pommerich, & P. W. Holland (Eds.), *Linking and aligning scores and scales* (pp. 233–251). New York, NY: Springer-Verlag.

Harris, D. J., & Gao, X. (2003, April). A conceptual synthesis of context effect. In *Context effects: Implications for pretesting and CBT*. Symposium conducted at the meeting of the American Educational Research Association, Chicago, IL.

He, X., & Ng, P. (1998). *SCOBS: Qualitatively constrained smoothing via linear programming*. Unpublished sofware manual.

He, X., & Shi, P. (1998). Monotone B-splines smoothing. *Journal of the American Statistical Association, 93*, 643–650.

Holland, P. W. (1994). Measurements or contests? Comments on Zwick, Bond and Allen/Donoghue. In *Proceedings of the Social Statistics Section of the American Statistical Association* (pp. 27–29). Alexandria, VA: American Statistical Association.

Holland, P. W. (2007). A framework and history for score linking. In N. J. Dorans, M. Pommerich, & P. W. Holland (Eds.), *Linking and aligning scores and scales* (pp. 5–30). New York, NY: Springer-Verlag.

Holland, P. W., & Dorans, N. J. (2006). Linking and equating. In R. L. Brennan (Ed.), *Educational measurement* (4th ed., pp. 189–220). Westport, CT: Praeger.

Holland, P. W., & Hoskens, M. (2003). Classical test theory as a first-order item response theory: Application to true-score prediction from a possibly nonparallel test. *Psychometrika, 68*, 123–149.

Holland, P. W., King, B. F., & Thayer, D. T. (1989). *The standard error of equating for the kernel method of equating score distributions* (ETS Tech. Rept. No. TR-89-83). Princeton, NJ: ETS.

Holland, P. W., & Rubin, D. B. (Eds.). (1982). *Test equating*. New York, NY: Academic Press.

Holland, P. W., Sinharay, S., von Davier, A. A., & Han, N. (2008). An approach to evaluating the missing data assumptions of the chain and post-stratification equating methods for the NEAT design. *Journal of Educational Measurement, 45*, 17–43.

Holland, P. W., & Strawderman, W. (1989). *The symmetric average of equating functions*. Unpublished manuscript.

Holland, P. W., & Thayer, D. T. (1987). *Notes on the use of log-linear models for fitting discrete probability distributions* (ETS Research Rept. RR-87-31). Princeton, NJ: ETS.

Holland, P. W., & Thayer, D. T. (1989). *The kernel method of equating score distributions* (ETS Research Rept. RR-89-07). Princeton, NJ: ETS.

Holland, P. W., & Thayer, D. T. (2000). Univariate and bivariate loglinear models for discrete test score distributions. *Journal of Educational and Behavioral Statistics, 25*, 133–183.

Holland, P. W., & Wainer, H. (1993). *Differential item functioning*. Hillsdale, NJ: Erlbaum.

Horn, J. L., & McArdle, J. J. (1992). A practical guide to measurement invariance in aging research. *Experimental Aging Research, 18*, 117–144.

Horn, J. L., McArdle, J. J., & Mason, R. (1983). When is invariance not invariant: A practical scientist's view of the ethereal concept of factorial invariance. *The Southern Psychologist, 1*, 179–188.

Jaffa, A. S. (1934). The California Preschool Mental Scale, Form A. Berkeley, CA: University of California Press.

Inspectorate of Secondary Education in the Netherlands. (1992). *Examens op Punten Getoetst Evaluation of Examinations*. Gravenhage, The Netherlands: Inspectie van het Voortgezet Onderwijs.

Iowa Tests of Educational Development. (1958). *Manual for the school administrator* (Rev. ed.). Iowa City: State University of Iowa.

Janssen, R., Magis, D., San Martin, E., & Del Pino, G. (2009, April). *Local equating in the NEAT design*. Paper presented at the meeting of the National Council on Measurement in Education, San Diego, CA.

Kane, M. T., Mroch, A. A., Suh, Y., & Ripkey, D. R. (2009). Linear equating for the NEAT design: Parameter substitution models and chained linear relationship models. *Measurement: Interdisciplinary Research & Perspective*, 7(3&4), 125– 146.

Kao, C. W., Kim, S., & Hatrak, N. (2005, October). *Scale drift study for a large-scale English proficiency test*. Paper presented at the meeting of the Northeastern Educational Research Association, Kerhonkson, NY.

Karabatsos, G., & Walker, S. (2009a). A Bayesian nonparametric approach to test equating. *Psychometrika*, *74*(2), 211–232.

Karabatsos, G., & Walker, S. (2009b). Coherent psychometric modeling with Bayesian nonparametrics. *British Journal of Mathematical and Statistical Psychology*, *62*(1), 1–20.

Kaskowitz, G. S., & De Ayala, R. J. (2001). The effect of error in item parameter estimates on the test response function method of linking. *Applied Psychological Measurement*, *25*(1), 39–52.

Kendall, M. G., & Stuart, A. (1977). *The advanced theory of statistics* (4th ed.). New York, NY: Macmillan.

Kim, S., & Cohen, A. S. (2002). A comparison of linking and concurrent calibration under the graded response model, *Applied Psychological measurement*, *26*, 25–41.

Kim, S., & Livingston, S. A. (2010). *Comparisons among small sample equating methods in a common-item design*. Manuscript submitted for publication.

Kim, S., & Livingston, S. (2009). *Methods of linking with small samples in a common-item design: An empirical comparison* (ETS Research Rept. RR-09-38). Princeton, NJ: ETS.

Kim, S., Livingston, S. A., & Lewis, C. (2008). *Investigating the effectiveness of collateral information on small-sample equating* (ETS Research Rept. RR-08-52). Princeton, NJ: ETS.

Kim, S., Livingston, S. A., & Lewis, C. (2009). *Evaluating sources of collateral information on small-sample equating* (ETS Research Rept. RR-09-14). Princeton, NJ: ETS.

Kim, S., & von Davier, A. A. (2006, April). Equating with small samples in non-equivalent-groups anchor test design. In *Recent advances in score equating*. Symposium conducted at the meeting of the National Council for Measurement in Education, San Francisco, CA.

Kim, S., von Davier, A. A., & Haberman, S. (2008). Small sample equating using a synthetic linking function. *Journal of Educational Measurement*, *45*, 325–342.

Koenker, R., Ng, P., & Portnoy, S. (1994). Quantile smoothing splines. *Biometrika*, *81*, 673–680.

Kolen, M. J. (1988). Defining score scales in relation to measurement error. *Journal of Educational Measurement*, *25*(2), 97–110.

Kolen, M. J. (2004). Linking assessments: Concept and history. *Applied Psychological Measurement*, *28*, 219–226.

Kolen, M. J. (2006). Scaling and norming. In R. L. Brennan (Ed.), *Educational measurement* (4th ed., pp. 155–186). Westport, CT: Praeger.

Kolen, M. J. (2007). Data collection designs and linking procedures. In N. J. Dorans, M. Pommerich, & P. W. Holland (Eds.), *Linking and aligning scores and scales* (pp. 31–55). New York, NY: Springer-Verlag.

Kolen, M. J., & Brennan, R. J. (1995). *Test equating: methods and practices*. New York, NY: Springer-Verlag.

Kolen, M. J., & Brennan R. L. (2004). *Test equating, scaling, and linking: Method and practice* (2nd ed.). New York, NY: Springer-Verlag.

Kolen, M. J., Hanson, B. A., & Brennan, R. L. (1992). Conditional standard errors of measurement for scale scores. *Journal of Educational Measurement*, *29*(4), 285–307.

Kolen, M. J., & Jarjoura, D. (1987). Analytic smoothing for equipercentile equating under the common item nonequivalent populations design. *Psychometrika*, *52*, 43–59.

Kolen, M. J., Zeng, L., & Hanson, B. A. (1996). Conditional standard errors of measurement for scale scores using IRT. *Journal of Educational Measurement*, *33*(2), 129–140.

Koretz, D., Barron, S., Mitchell, K., & Stecher, B. M. (1999). *Perceived effects of the Kentucky Instructional Results Information System (KIRIS)*. Santa Monica, CA: Rand Corporation.

Koretz, D. M., Bertenthal, M. W., & Green, B. F. (Eds.). (1999). *Embedding questions: The pursuit of a common measure in uncommon tests* (Report of the Committee on Embedding Common Test Items in State and District Assessments, National Research Council). Washington DC: National Academy Press.

Kuehl, R. O. (2000). *Design of experiments: Statistical principles of research design and analysis* (2nd ed.). Duxbury, MA: Thomson Learning.

Kupperman, M. (1952). On exact grouping correlations to moments and cumulants. *Biometrika, 39*, 429–434.

Leary, L. F., & Dorans, N. J. (1985). Implications for altering the context in which test items appear: An historical perspective on an immediate concern. *Review of Educational Research, 55*, 387–413.

Lee, Y.-H., & von Davier, A. A. (2008). *Comparing alternative kernels for the kernel method of test equating: Gaussian, logistic and uniform kernels* (ETS Research Rept. RR-08-12). Princeton, NJ: ETS.

Lee, Y.-S. (2002). *Applications of isotonic regression in item response theory* (Unpublished doctoral dissertation). University of Wisconsin, Madison.

Lehmann, E.L. (1999). *Elements of large-sample theory*. New York, NY: Springer-Verlag.

Levine, R. (1955). *Equating the score scales of alternative forms administered to samples of different ability* (ETS Research Bulletin RB-55-23). Princeton, NJ: ETS.

Liang, L., Dorans, N. J., & Sinharay, S. (2009). *First language of examinees and its relationship to equating* (ETS Research Rept. RR-09-05). Princeton, NJ: ETS.

Liou, M. (1998). Establishing score comparability in heterogeneous populations. *Statistica Sinica, 8*, 669–690.

Liou, M., Cheng, P. E., & Johnson, E. G. (1997). Standard errors of the kernel equating methods under the common-item design. *Applied Psychological Measurement, 21*, 349–369.

Liou, M., Cheng, P. E., & Li, M.-Y. (2001). Estimating comparable scores using surrogate variables. *Applied Psychological Measurement, 25*, 197–207.

Livingston, S. A. (1993). Small-sample equating with log-linear smoothing. *Journal of Educational Measurement, 30*, 23–29.

Livingston, S. A. (2004). *Equating test scores (without IRT)*. Princeton, NJ: ETS.

Livingston, S. A., Dorans, N. J., & Wright, N. K. (1990). What combination of sampling and equating methods works best? *Applied Measurement in Education, 3*, 73–95.

Livingston, S. A., & Kim, S. (2008). *Small-sample equating by the circle-arc method* (ETS Research Rept. RR-08-39). Princeton, NJ: ETS.

Livingston, S. A., & Kim, S. (2009). The circle-arc method for equating in small samples. *Journal of Educational Measurement, 46*, 330–343.

Livingston, S. A., & Kim, S. (2010). *An empirical comparison of methods for equating with randomly equivalent groups of 50 to 400 test takers* (ETS Research Rept. RR-10-05). Princeton, NJ: ETS.

Livingston, S. A., & Kim, S. (in press). Random-groups equating with samples of 50 to 400 test takers. *Journal of Educational Measurement*.

Livingston, S. A., & Lewis, C. (2009). *Small-sample equating with prior information* (ETS Research Rept. RR-09-25). Princeton, NJ: ETS.

Ljung, G., & Box, G. (1978). On a measure of lack of fit in time-series models. *Biometrika, 65*, 297–303.

Lord, F. M. (1950). *Notes on comparable scales for test scores* (ETS Research Bulletin RB-50-48). Princeton, NJ: ETS.

Lord, F. M. (1955a). Equating test scores—A maximum likelihood solution. *Psychometrika, 20*, 193–200.

Lord, F. M. (1955b). Estimation of parameters from incomplete data. *Journal of the American Statistical Association, 50*, 870–876.

Lord, F. M. (1980). *Applications of item response theory to practical testing problems*. Hillsdale, NJ: Erlbaum.

Lord, F. M. (1982a). Standard error of an equating by item response theory. *Applied Psychological Measurement, 6*, 463–472.

Lord, F. M. (1982b). The standard error of equipercentile equating. *Journal of Educational Statistics, 7*, 165–174.

Lord, F. M. (1983). *Small N justifies Rasch model*. In D. J. Weiss (Ed.), *New horizons in testing* (pp. 51–61). New York, NY: Academic Press.

Lord, F. M., & Novick, M. R. (1968). *Statistical theories of mental test scores*. Reading, MA: Addison Wesley.

Lord, F. M., & Wingersky, M. S. (1984). Comparison of IRT true-score and equipercentile observed-score "equatings." *Applied Psychological Measurement, 8*, 452–461.

Lorentz, G. (1953). *Bernstein polynomials*. Toronto, Ontario, Canada: University of Toronto Press.

Loyd, B. H., & Hoover, H. D. (1980). Vertical equating using the Rasch model. *Journal of Educational Measurement, 17*, 179–193.

Marco, G. L. (1977). Item characteristic curve solutions to three intractable testing problems. *Journal of Educational Measurement, 14*, 139–160.

Marco, G. L., Petersen, N. S., & Stewart, E. E. (1983a). *A large-scale evaluation of linear and curvilinear score equating models, Volumes I and II* (ETS Research Memorandum RM-83-02). Princeton, NJ: ETS.

Marco, G. L., Petersen, N. S., & Stewart, E. E. (1983b). A test of the adequacy of curvilinear score equating models. In D. J. Weiss (Ed.), *New horizons in testing* (pp. 147–176). New York, NY: Academic Press.

Masters, G. N. (1982). A Rasch model for partial credit scoring. *Psychometrika, 47*, 149–174.

McArdle, J. J. (2007). Five steps in the structural factor analysis of longitudinal data. In R. Cudeck & R. MacCallum (Eds.), *Factor analysis at 100 years* (pp. 99–130). Mahwah, NJ: Erlbaum.

McArdle, J. J. (1994). Structural factor analysis experiments with incomplete data. *Multivariate Behavioral Research, 29*, 409–454.

McArdle, J. J., & Cattell, R. B. (1994). Structural equation models of factorial invariance in parallel proportional profiles and oblique confactor problems. *Multivariate Behavioral Research, 29*, 63–113.

McArdle, J. J., Ferrer-Caja, E., Hamagami, F., & Woodcock, R. W. (2002). Comparative longitudinal structural analyses of the growth and decline of multiple intellectual abilities over the life span. *Developmental Psychology, 38*, 115–142.

McArdle, J. J., Grimm, K. J., Hamagami, F., Bowles, R., & Meredith, W. (2009). Modeling life-span growth curves of cognition using longitudinal data with multiple samples and changing scales of measurement. *Psychological Methods, 14*, 126–149.

McArdle, J. J., Hamagami, F., Meredith, W., & Bradway, K. P. (2000). Modeling the dynamic hypotheses of Gf-Gc theory using longitudinal life-span data. *Learning and Individual Differences, 12*, 53–79.

McCall, W. A. (1939). *Measurement: A revision of how to measure in education*. New York, NY: Macmillan.

Mislevy, R. J., & Bock, R. D. (1990). *BILOG 3. Item analysis and test scoring with binary logistic models*. Mooresville, IN: Scientific Software.

Molenaar, I. W. (1983). Some improved diagnostics for failure in the Rasch model. *Psychometrika, 48*, 49–72.

Montgomery, D. C., Peck, E. A., & Vining, G. G. (2001). *Introduction to linear regression analysis* (3rd ed.). New York, NY: John Wiley & Sons.

Morris, C. N. (1982). On the foundations of test equating. In P. W. Holland & D. B. Rubin (Eds.), *Test equating* (pp. 9–49). New York, NY: Academic Press.

Morrison, C. A., & Fitzpatrick, S. J. (1992). *Direct and indirect equating: A comparison of four methods using the Rasch model* (Report No. RB-91-3). Austin: University of Texas, Measurement and Evaluation Center.

Moses, T., & Holland, P. W. (2008). *The influence of strategies for selecting loglinear smoothing models on equating functions* (ETS Research Rept. RR-08-25). Princeton, NJ: ETS.

Moses, T., & Kim, S. (2007). *Reliability and the nonequivalent groups with anchor test design* (ETS Research Rept. RR-07-16). Princeton, NJ: ETS.

Mosteller, F., & Youtz, C. (1961). Tables of the Freeman-Tukey transformations for the binomial and Poisson distributions. *Biometrika, 48*, 433–440.

Müller, P., & Quintana, F. (2004). Nonparametric Bayesian data analysis. *Statistical Science, 19*, 95–110.

Muraki, E. (1993) Information functions of the generalized partial credit model. *Applied Psychological Measurement, 14*(4), 351–363.

Muraki, E. (1992) A generalized partial credit model: Application of an EM algorithm. *Applied Psychological Measurement, 16*, 159–176.

Muraki, E., & Bock, R. D. (1991). *PARSCALE: Parametric scaling of rating data.* Chicago, IL: Scientific Software International.

Nadaraya, E. A. (1964). On estimating regression. *Theory of Probability and its Applications, 9*, 141–142.

Ogasawara, H. (2000). Asymptotic standard errors of IRT equating coefficients using moments. *Economic Review, Otaru University of Commerce, 51*(1), 1–23.

Ogasawara, H. (2001a). Item response theory true score equatings and their standard errors. *Journal of Educational and Behavioral Statistics, 26*, 31–50.

Ogasawara, H. (2001b). Standard errors of item response theory equating/linking by response function methods. *Applied Psychological Measurement, 25*, 53–67.

Ogasawara, H. (2003). Asymptotic standard errors of IRT observed-score equating methods. *Psychometrika, 68*, 193–211.

Ogasawara, H. (2006). Asymptotic expansion of the sample correlation coefficient under nonnormality. *Computational Statistics and Data Analysis, 50*, 891–910.

Ogasawara, H. (2007a). Asymptotic expansions of the distributions of the estimators in canonical correlation analysis under nonnormality. *Journal of Multivariate Analysis, 98*, 1726–1750.

Ogasawara, H. (2007b). Asymptotic expansion of the distributions of the estimators in factor analysis under nonnormality. *British Journal of Mathematical and Statistical Psychology, 60*, 395–420.

Ogasawara, H. (2007c). Higher-order estimation error in structural equation modeling. *Economic Review, Otaru University of Commerce, 57*(4), 131–160.

Ogasawara, H. (2009). Asymptotic cumulants of the parameter estimators in item response theory. *Computational Statistics, 24*, 313–331.

Orlando, M., & Thissen, D. (2000). Likelihood-based item-fit indices for dichotomous item response theory models. *Applied Psychological Measurement, 24*, 50–64.

Patz, R. J., & Yao, L. (2007). Methods and models for vertical scaling. In N. J. Dorans, M. Pommerich, & P. W. Holland (Eds.), *Linking and aligning scores and scales* (pp. 253–272). New York, NY: Springer-Verlag.

Patz, R., Yao, L., Chia, M., Lewis, D., & Hoskens, M. (2003, April). *Hierarchical and multidimensional models for vertical scaling.* Paper presented at the meeting of the National Council on Measurement in Education, Chicago, IL.

Peterson, N. S. (2007). Equating: Best practices and challenges to best practices. In N. J. Dorans, M. Pommerich, & P. W. Holland (Eds.), *Linking and aligning scores and scales* (pp. 59–72). New York, NY: Springer-Verlag.

Petersen, N. S., Cook, L. L., & Stocking, M. L. (1983). IRT versus conventional equating methods: A comparative study of scale stability. *Journal of Educational Statistics, 8*(2), 137–156.

Petersen, N. S., Kolen, M. J., & Hoover, H. D. (1989). Scaling, norming and equating. In R. L. Linn (Ed.), *Educational measurement* (3rd ed., pp. 221–262). New York, NY: American Council on Education and Macmillan.

Petersen, N. S., Marco, G. L., & Stewart, E. E. (1982). A test of the adequacy of linear score equating models. In P. W. Holland & D. B. Rubin (Eds.), *Test equating* (pp. 71–135). New York, NY: Academic Press.

Petrone, S. (1999). Random Bernstein polynomials. *Scandinavian Journal of Statistics, 26*, 373–393.

Pommerich, M., & Dorans, N. J. (Eds.). (2004). Concordance [Special issue]. *Applied Psychological Measurement, 28*(4).

Pommerich, M., Nicewander, W. A., & Hanson, B. A. (1999). Estimating average domain scores. *Journal of Educational Measurement, 36*(3), 199–216.

Puhan, G., Moses, T. P., Grant, M. C., & McHale, F. (2009). Small-sample equating using a single-group nearly equivalent test (SiGNET) design. *Journal of Educational Measurement, 46*, 344–362.

Ramsay, J. O. (1991). Kernel smoothing approaches to nonparametric item characteristic curve estimation. *Psychometrika, 56*, 611–630.

Ramsay, J. O. (2001). *TestGraf98. A program for the graphical analysis of multiple choice test and questionnaire data*. Retrieved from http://www.psych.mcgill.ca/faculty/ramsay/TestGraf.html

Ramsay, J. O., & Abrahamowicz, M. (1989). Binomial regression with monotone splines: A psychometric application. *Journal of the American Statistical Association, 84*, 906–915.

Rao, C. R. (1973). *Linear statistical inference and its applications* (2nd ed.). New York, NY: Wiley.

Rasch, G. (1960). *Probabilistic models for some intelligence and attainment tests.* Chicago, IL: University of Chicago Press.

Ricker, K., & von Davier, A. A. (2007). *The impact of anchor test length on equating results in a non-equivalent group design* (ETS Research Rept. RR-07-44). Princeton, NJ: ETS.

Rijmen, F. (2009a, July). *A hierarchical factor IRT model for items that are clustered at multiple levels.* Paper presented at the International Meeting of the Psychometric Society, Cambridge, UK.

Rijmen, F. (2009b). *Three multidimensional models for testlet based tests: Formal relations and an empirical comparison* (ETS Research Rept. No. RR-09-37). Princeton, NJ: ETS.

Rock, D. A. (1982). Equating using confirmatory factor analysis. In P. W. Holland & D. B. Rubin (Eds.), *Test equating* (pp. 247–258). New York, NY: Academic Press.

Rodriguez, M. C. (2003). Construct equivalence of multiple-choice and constructed-response items: A random effects synthesis of correlations. *Journal of Educational Measurement, 40*(2), 163–184.

Rosa, K., Swygert, K. A., Nelson, L., & Thissen, D. (2001). Item response theory applied to combinations of multiple-choice and constructed-response items—Scale scores for patterns of summed scores. In D. Thissen & H. Wainer (Eds.), *Test scoring* (pp. 253–292). Mahwah, NJ: Erlbaum.

Rosenbaum, P. R. (1995). *Observational studies.* New York, NY: Springer-Verlag.

Rossi, N., Wang, X., & Ramsay, J. O. (2002). Nonparametric item response function estimates with the EM algorithm. *Journal of Educational and Behavioral Statistics, 27*, 291–317.

Rost, J., & von Davier, M. (1992). MIRA – A PC program for the mixed Rasch model [User manual]. Kiel, Germany: IPN.

Rost, J., & von Davier, M. (1995). Mixture distribution Rasch models. In G. H. Fischer & I. W. Molenaar (Eds.), *Rasch models—Foundations, recent developments and applications* (pp. 257–268). New York, NY: Springer-Verlag.

Rubin, D. (1982). Discussion of "Observed-score test equating: A mathematical analysis of some ETS equating procedures." In P. W. Holland & D. B. Rubin (Eds.), *Test equating* (pp. 51–54). New York, NY: Academic Press.

Samejima, F. (1969). Estimation of latent ability using a response pattern of graded scores. *Psychometrika Monograph Supplement, 34*(4, Pt. 2), 100–114.

Schwarz, G. (1978). Estimating the dimensions of a model. *Annals of Statistics, 6*, 461–464.

Sethuraman, J. (1994). A constructive definition of Dirichlet priors. *Statistica Sinica, 4*, 639–650.

Shealy, R., & Stout, W. F. (1993). A model-based standardization approach that separates true bias/DIF from group ability differences and detects test bias/DTF as well as item bias/DIF. *Psychometrika, 58*, 159–194.

Shumway, R. H., & Stoffer, D. S. (2006). *Time-series analysis and its applications with R examples* (2nd ed.). New York, NY: Springer-Verlag.

Sinharay, S., & Holland, P. W. (2007). Is it necessary to make anchor tests mini-versions of the tests being equated or can some restrictions be relaxed? *Journal of Educational Measurement, 44*, 249–275.

Sinharay, S., & Holland, P. W. (2010a). The missing data assumptions of the NEAT design and their implications for test equating. *Psychometrika*, 75, 309–327.

Sinharay, S., & Holland, P. W. (2010b). A new approach to comparing several equating methods in the context of the NEAT design. *Journal of Educational Measurement*, 47(3), 261–285.

Sinharay, S., & Holland, P. W. (in press). A fair comparison of three nonlinear equating methods in applications of the NEAT design. *Journal of Educational Measurement*.

Skaggs, G. (2005). Accuracy of random groups equating with very small samples. *Journal of Educational Measurement, 42*, 309–330.

Stocking, M. L., & Lord, F. M. (1983). Developing a common metric in item response theory. *Applied Psychological Measurement, 7*, 201–210.

Stuart, A., & Ord, K. (1994). *Kendall's advanced theory of statistics: Distribution theory* (6th ed., Vol. 1). London, England: Arnold.

Terman, L. M. (1916). *The measurement of intelligence: An explanation of and a complete guide for the use of the Stanford revision and extension of the Binet-Simon Intelligence Scale*. Cambridge, MA: The Riverside Press.

Terman, L. M., & Merrill, M. A. (1937). *Measuring intelligence: A guide to the administration of the new Revised Stanford-Binet tests of intelligence*. Cambridge, MA: The Riverside Press.

Terman, L. M., & Merrill, M. A. (1960). *Stanford-Binet Intelligence Scale: Manual for the third revision Form L-M*. Cambridge, MA: The Riverside Press.

Thissen, D. (1991). *Multilog user's guide: Multiple, categorization analysis and test scoring using item response theory*. Chicago, IL: Scientific Software International.

Thissen, D., Nelson, L., & Swygert, K. A. (2001). Item response theory applied to combinations of multiple-choice and constructed-response items—Approximation methods for scale scores. In D. Thissen & H. Wainer (Eds.), *Test scoring* (pp. 293–341). Mahwah, NJ: Erlbaum.

Thissen, D., & Orlando, M. (2001). Item response theory for items scored in two categories. In D. Thissen & H. Wainer (Eds.), *Test scoring* (pp. 73–140). Mahwah, NJ: Erlbaum.

Thissen, D., Pommerich, M., Billeaud, K., & Williams, V. S. L. (1995). Item response theory for scores on tests including polytomous items with ordered responses. *Applied Psychological Measurement, 19*(1), 39–49.

Thissen, D., & Steinberg, L. (1986). A taxonomy of item response models. *Psychometrika, 51*, 567–577.

Thissen, D., & Wainer, H. (Eds.). (2001). *Test scoring*. Mahwah, NJ: Erlbaum.

Thisted, R. A. (1988). *Elements of statistical computing: Numerical computation*. New York, NY: Champman & Hall/CRC.

Tong, Y., & Kolen, M. J. (2005). Assessing equating results on different equating criteria. *Applied Psychological Measurement, 29*(6), 418–432.

Tong, Y., & Kolen, M. J. (2007). Comparisons of methodologies and results in vertical scaling for educational achievement tests. *Applied Measurement in Education, 20*(2), 227–253.

Tsai, T.-H., Hanson, B. A., Kolen, M. J., & Forsyth, R. A. (2001). A comparison of bootstrap standard errors of IRT equating methods for the common-item nonequivalent groups design. *Applied Measurement in Education, 14*, 17–30.

Tukey, J. W. (1963). Mathematics 596—An introduction to the frequency analysis of time series. In D. R. Brillinger (Ed.), *The collected works of John W. Tukey, Volume I: Time series, 1949–1964*. London, England: Chapman & Hall.

van der Linden, W. J. (1997). [Review of the book *Test equating: Methods and practices* by M. J. Kolen & R. L Brennan]. *Psychometrika, 62*, 287–290.

van der Linden, W. J. (2000). A test-theoretic approach to observed-score equating. *Psychometrika, 65*, 437–456.

van der Linden, W. J. (2005). *Linear models for optimal test design*. New York, NY: Springer-Verlag.
van der Linden, W. J. (2006a). Equating error in observed-score equating. *Applied Psychological Measurement*, *30*, 355–378.
van der Linden, W. J. (2006b). Equating an adaptive test to a linear test. *Applied Psychological Measurement*, *30*, 493–508.
van der Linden, W. J. (2006c). [Review of the book *The kernel method of test equating* by A. A. von Davier, P. W. Holland & D. T. Thayer]. *Journal of Educational Measurement*, *43*, 291–294.
van der Linden, W. J. (2010). Linking response-time parameters onto a common scale. *Journal of Educational Measurement*, *47*, 92–114.
van der Linden, W. J., & Hambleton, R. K. (Eds.). (1997). *Handbook of modern item response theory*. New York, NY: Springer-Verlag.
van der Linden, W. J., & Wiberg, M. (in press). Local observed score equating with anchor test designs. *Applied Psychological Measurement*, *34*.
Van Krimpen-Stoop, E. M. L. A., & Meijer, R. R. (2001). CUSUM-based person-fit statistics for adaptive testing. *Journal of Educational and Behavioral Statistics*, *26*, 199–217.
Veerkamp, W. J. J., & Glas, C. A.W. (2000). Detection of known items in adaptive testing with a statistical quality control method. *Journal of Educational and Behavioral Statistics*, *25*, 373–389.
von Davier, A. A. (2003a). *Large sample tests for comparing regression coefficients in models with normally distributed variables* (ETS Research Rept. RR-03-19). Princeton, NJ: ETS.
von Davier, A. A. (2003b). *Notes on linear equating methods for the non-equivalent groups design* (ETS Research Rept. RR-03-24). Princeton, NJ: ETS.
von Davier, A. A. (2007). Potential solutions to practical equating issues. In N. J. Dorans, M. Pommerich, & P. W. Holland (Eds.), *Linking and aligning scores and scales* (pp. 89–106). New York, NY: Springer-Verlag.
von Davier, A. A. (2008). New results on the linear equating methods for the non-equivalent-group design. *Journal of Educational and Behavioral Statistics*, 33, 186–203.
von Davier, A. A. (in press). An observed-score equating framework. In N. J. Dorans & S. Sinharay (Eds.), *A conference in honor of Paul W. Holland*. New York, NY: Springer-Verlag.
von Davier, A. A., Fournier-Zajac, S., & Holland, P. W. (2006, April). *An equipercentile version of the Levine linear observed-score equating function using the methods of kernel equating*. Paper presented at the meeting of the National Council of Measurement in Education, San Francisco, CA.
von Davier, A. A., Fournier-Zajac, S., & Holland, P. W. (2007). *An equipercentile version of the Levine linear observed-score equating function using the methods of kernel equating* (ETS Research Rept. RR-07-14). Princeton, NJ: ETS.
von Davier, A. A., Holland, P. W., Livingston, S. A., Casabianca, J., Grant, M. C., & Martin, K. (2006). *An evaluation of the kernel equating method: A special study with pseudo-tests constructed from real test data* (ETS Research Rept. RR-06-02). Princeton, NJ: ETS.
von Davier, A. A., Holland, P. W., & Thayer, D. T. (2003). Population invariance and chain versus poststratification methods for equating and test linking. In N. Dorans (Ed.), *Population invariance of score linking: Theory and applications to Advanced Placement Program® Examinations* (ETS Research Rept. RR-03-27). Princeton, NJ: ETS.
von Davier, A. A., Holland, P. W., & Thayer, D. T. (2004a). The chain and poststratification methods for observed-score equating: Their relationship to population invariance. *Journal of Educational Measurement*, *41*, 15–32.
von Davier, A. A., Holland, P. W., & Thayer, D. T. (2004b). *The kernel method of test equating*. New York, NY: Springer-Verlag.
von Davier, A. A., & Kong, N. (2005). A unified approach to linear equating for the nonequivalent group design. *Journal of Educational and Behavioral Statistics*, 30, 313–342.
von Davier, M. (1994). WINMIRA—A program for analyses with the Rasch model, with the latent class analysis and with the mixed Rasch model [Computer software]. Kiel, Germany: IPN Software, Institute for Science Education.

von Davier, M. (2000). WINMIRA 2001. A Windows program for analyses with the Rasch model, with the latent class analysis and with the mixed Rasch model [Computer software]. St. Paul, MN: Assessment Systems Corporation.

von Davier, M. (2005). *A general diagnostic model applied to language testing data* (ETS Research Rept. RR-05-16). Princeton, NJ: ETS.

von Davier, M., & von Davier, A. A. (2004). *Unified approach to IRT scale linking and scale transformations* (ETS Research Rept. RR-04-09). Princeton, NJ: ETS.

von Davier, M., & von Davier, A.A. (2007). A unified approach to IRT scale linking and scale transformation. *Methodology, European Journal of Research Methods for the Behavioral and Social Sciences, 3*(3), 115–124.

von Davier, M., & Yamamoto, K. (2004). Partially observed mixtures of IRT models: An extension of the generalized partial credit model. *Applied Psychological Measurement 28*(6), 389–406.

Wainer, H., & Thissen, D. (1993). Combining multiple-choice and constructed-response test scores: Toward a Marxist theory of test construction. *Applied Measurement in Education, 6*(2), 103–118.

Wald, A. (1943). Tests of statistical hypotheses concerning several parameters when the number of observations is large. *Transactions of the American Mathematical Society, 54*, 426–482.

Walker, S. (2004). New approaches to Bayesian consistency. *Annals of Statistics, 32*, 2028–2043.

Walker, S., Damien, P., Laud, P., & Smith, A. (1999). Bayesian nonparametric inference for random distributions and related functions. *Journal of the Royal Statistical Society, Series B, 61*, 485–527.

Walker, S., Lijoi, A., & Prünster, I. (2007). On rates of convergence for posterior distributions in infinite-dimensional models. *Annals of Statistics, 35*, 738–746.

Walker, S., & Muliere, P. (2003). A bivariate Dirichlet process. *Statistics and Probability Letters, 64*, 1–7.

Wang, T. (2008). The continuized log-linear method: An alternative to the kernel method of continuization in test equating. *Applied Psychological Measurement, 32*, 527–542.

Wang, T., & Brennan, R. L. (2007, April). *A modified frequency estimation equating method for the common-item non-equivalent groups design.* Paper presented at the meeting of the National Council of Measurement in Education, Chicago, IL.

Wang, T., Kolen, M. J., & Harris, D. J. (2000). Psychometric properties of scale scores and performance levels for performance assessments using polytomous IRT. *Journal of Educational Measurement, 37*(2), 141–162.

Wang, T., Lee, W., Brennan, R. J., & Kolen, M. J. (2006, April). *A comparison of the frequency estimation and chained equipercentile methods under the common-item non-equivalent groups design.* Paper presented at the meeting of the National Council on Measurement in Education, San Francisco, CA.

Wasserman, L. (2006). *All of nonparametric statistics*. New York, NY: Springer-Verlag.

Watson, G. S. (1964). Smooth regression analysis. *Sankhya Series A, 26*, 359–372.

Wechsler, D. (1955). *Manual for the Wechsler Adult Intelligence Scale*. New York, NY: The Psychological Corporation.

Wechsler, D. (1981). *Wechsler Adult Intelligence Scale-Revised manual.* San Antonio, TX: The Psychological Corporation.

Wechsler, D. (1946). *Wechsler-Bellevue Intelligence Scale: Form I. Manual for administering and scoring the test.* New York, NY: The Psychological Corporation.

Wiberg, M., & van der Linden, W. J. (2009). *Local linear observed-score equating.* Manuscript submitted for publication.

Wirth, R. J., & Edwards, M. C. (2007). Item factor analysis: Current approaches and future directions. *Psychological Methods, 12*, 58–79.

Wright, N. K., & Dorans, N. J. (1993). *Using the selection variable for matching or equating* (ETS Research Rept. RR-93-04). Princeton, NJ: ETS.

Xu, X.; & von Davier, M. (2008). Comparing multiple-group multinomial loglinear models for multidimensional skill distributions in the general diagnostic model (ETS Research Rept. RR-08-35). Princeton, NJ: ETS.

Yen, W. M. (1984). Obtaining maximum likelihood trait estimates from number-correct scores for the three-parameter logistic model. *Journal of Educational Measurement*, *21*, 93–111.

Yen, W. M. (1986). The choice of scale for educational measurement: An IRT perspective. *Journal of Educational Measurement*, *23*(4), 299–325.

Yen, W. M. (2007). Vertical scaling and no child left behind. In N. J. Dorans, M. Pommerich, & P. W. Holland (Eds.), *Linking and aligning scores and scales* (pp. 273–283). New York, NY: Springer-Verlag.

Yen, W. M., & Fitzpatrick, A. R. (2006). Item response theory. In R. L. Brennan (Ed.), *Educational measurement* (4th ed., pp. 111–153). Westport, CT: Praeger.

Zeng, L., & Kolen, M. J. (1995). An alternative approach for IRT observed-score equating of number-correct scores. *Applied Psychological Measurement*, *19*, 231–240.

Zimowski, M. F., Muraki, E., Mislevy, R. J., & Bock, R. D. (1996). *BILOG-MG: Multiple-group IRT analysis and test maintenance for binary items* [Computer software]. Chicago, IL: Scientific Software International.

Zwick, R., Senturk, D., Wang, J., & Loomis, S. C. (2001). An investigation of alternative methods for item mapping in the National Assessment of Educational Progress. *Educational Measurement: Issues and Practice*, *20*(2), 15–25.

Index

MIX
Papier aus verantwortungsvollen Quellen
Paper from responsible sources
FSC® C105338

If you have any concerns about our products,
you can contact us on
ProductSafety@springernature.com

In case Publisher is established outside the EU,
the EU authorized representative is:
Springer Nature Customer Service Center GmbH
Europaplatz 3, 69115 Heidelberg, Germany

Printed by Libri Plureos GmbH
in Hamburg, Germany